# Fully Human and Fully Alive

*JDV Philosophy Series - 12*

# Fully Human and Fully Alive

## Essays on Being Human Today in Honour of Dr Cyril Desbruslais SJ

*Editor:*
**Kuruvilla Pandikattu SJ**

Jnana-Deepa Vidyapeeth

&

Christian World Imprints

First Published in 2020 by

**Jnana-Deepa Vidyapeeth**
Ramwadi, Nagar Road, **Pune-411014**
jdvoffice@jdv.edu.in
www.jdv.edu.in
Phone: +91 20 41036111

&

**Christian World Imprints**
*Christian Publishing & Books from India*
C-3, Shop No. 14, Ground Floor
Wazirpur Industrial Area, **Delhi-110052**
cwidelhi2017@gmail.com
www.ChristianWorldImprints.com
Phone: +91 11 41526079

ISBN: 978-93-5148-416-5

"Published with the help of the Institute of Missiology – Germany"

**About the Cover:** Desbruslais stands in front of Greek sculpture known as the Laocoön Group, or Laocoön and His Sons. Trojan priest Laocoön and his two sons Antiphas and Thymbraeus being killed by giant snakes sent by gods for attempting to expose the ruse of the Trojan Horse. Standing some 8 feet in height, this famous statue was sculpted by Hagesander, Athenodoros and Polydorus between 42-20 BCE.



Printed in India.

# CONTENTS

# JDV PHILOSOPHY SERIES - 12

Since 1893 Jnana-Deepa Vidyapeeth has been pioneering philosophy discussion and debate inspired by prominent personalities like Richard De Smet, Jean de Marneffe, Salvino Azzopardi, Cyril Desbruslais, Noel Sheth, John Vattanky, etc. It has been in the forefront of promoting Indian philosophy and making philosophical thinking relevant for contemporary times. In its effort to reach out to like-minded scholars, JDV Philosophy Series has been visualized as a catalyst for interdisciplinary thinking and contemporary exploration on social issues fostering holistic liberation, integral development and creative engagement.

## JDV Philosophy Series

1. Salvino Azzopardi: ***Epistemology and Phenomenology of Religions*** (2018)
2. Kuruvilla Pandikattu & Thomas Karimundackal (eds): ***Melodies from the Flute***: For Prof Noel Sheth SJ (2018)
3. Kurien Kunnumpuram: ***Freedom and Joy*** (2018)
4. Cyril Desbruslais SJ: ***Postmodernity: An Indian Christian Philosophical Appraisal*** (2019)
5. Cyril Desbruslais SJ: ***Metaphysics: Philosophy of Be-ing for Today*** (2019)
6. John Peter Vallabadoss: ***Indian Thinkers: Modern and Contemporary Period*** (2019)
7. Thomas Karimundackal & Kuruvilla Pandikattu (eds): ***Logic and Love***: For Prof John Vattanky SJ (2019)
8. Fabian Jose UMI: ***Relevance of Thomas Merton's Spirituality for the Consecrated Life in India*** (2019)
9. Kuruvilla Pandikattu & PT Mathew (eds): ***Committed to the Church and the Country***: For Prof Kurien Kunnumpuam SJ (2019)
10. Cyril Desbruslais SJ: ***The Philosophy of God*** (2019)
11. Thomas Karimundackal & Kuruvilla Pandikattu: ***Fully Spiritual, Fully Human:*** For Dr Stephen Chundanthadam SJ (2020)
12. Kuruvilla Pandikattu: ***Fully Human and Fully Alive:*** For Dr Cyril Desbruslais SJ (2020)

# FOREWORD

Cyril Desbruslais is a man of many parts. However, unlike the curate's egg, he is excellent in every part. First and foremost, Cyril is a Jesuit and priest. He is also a philosopher (not only teaching it as a subject but doing it as a way of life), a playwright and director, spiritual guide, retreat director and preacher, youth animator, and a wonderful human being.

Perhaps the best way to characterise Cyril is to see him as someone who accompanies and communicates with each at his/her own level. This marvellous capacity to accompany is best seen in his dealings with youth. He founded his youth club in 1972 and nearly 50 years later continues to accompany the group (adolescents who joined in 1972 passed into adulthood, parenthood and continue to be members, often accompanied by their progeny!) However, Pune city youth were not the only beneficiaries of Cyril's skills at accompaniment. Numerous Jesuits and others who studied at JDV will testify to how graciously and competently Cyril accompanied them as spiritual and/or academic guide, an accompaniment especially needed for those doing philosophical studies when they are exposed to a bewildering array of diverse thinking and positions that are sometimes diametrically opposed to their religious beliefs. To do this not through slogans or by exhortations to pray, as if prayer were a panacea, but through challenging one to think personally and honestly and to relate this to one's experience demands patience and insight. This is what Cyril manifested and which made him so successful as a guide.

Equally astonishing for me is that for decades Cyril Desbruslais celebrated the Sunday Eucharist at St. Xavier's Church Pune, at the same time, drawing the same large crowd, Sunday after Sunday. Imagine having to preach to much the same congregation on the same scripture texts for 40 years and more! This demands a creativity that few of us possess. Cyril's homilies were always challenging, even radical to many. They were rooted in a solid grasp of Sacred Scripture, thorough knowledge and commitment to the teaching and perspectives of Vatican Council II and emerged from deep reflection on the Word of God. This, in tandem with Cyril's passion, personal conviction and fine articulation ensured that people never missed participating in the Sunday

Eucharist with Cyril as celebrant, unless they just could not. I recall Fr. George Soares-Prabhu, a biblical scholar of international repute and an outstanding lecturer once confessing that he was jealous of Cyril. Cyril, he said, listens to a lecture I have painstakingly prepared, assimilates it and then reels it off to a wide variety of audiences, adapting it to each, with an unction, and in a language that makes deep thought readily accessible.

Cyril's reputation as a playwright and director is well established by the list of his productions. My own memory, however, takes me back to the academic year 1966-67 when we were both philosophy students in De Nobili College, Pune. Cyril directed Bernard Shaw's "St Joan", and I, was designated his co-director, euphemistically! The performance was such a success that, by popular demand, it was staged again at Gulati Hall, St. Vincent's School, Pune. I believe this launched Cyril's career as a director for prior to that we were not permitted to stage our De Nobili College productions outside Jnana-Deepa Vidyapeeth (then called the Pontifical Athenaeum), Pune, campus. Since that heady venture into a "secular" environment and public, a second or third presentation of our dramas at Gulati Hall became routine.

The themes in the volume of articles to felicitate Cyril Desbruslais on his 80th birthday celebrate Cyril's primary philosophical concerns. In this he was influenced greatly by French intellectuals like Gabriel Marcel whose exploration of life as mystery and the metaphysics of hope he found fascinating and the *L'Action* of Maurice Blondel with its insistence on the necessity of the human condition to act and its analysis of the relation of immanence and transcendence. The insights of these great French thinkers find an echo in much that Cyril taught. Existentialist thinkers were his lodestars but British analytic philosophy left Cyril cold, and logic curdled his artistic soul. Like these two French philosophers whose thought was deeply religious and Christian, Cyril, while respecting the uniqueness of philosophical thought and its own specific method, was at pains to show how the social issues he treated found their best response in values that Jesus lived, preached and died for.

I am grateful to Fr. Kuruvilla Pandikattu for initiating and accompanying this project in honour of Cyril Desbruslais to a successful conclusion. He choice of themes reflects his intimate acquaintance with Cyril, as student and colleague in the Philosophy Faculty of JDV. His choice of topics is built, as he notes, around a saying of Irenaeus that was very dear to Cyril: the glory of God is humans fully alive. Cyril's special contribution to promoting a more humane society was to invite those searching for meaning to personal reflection and accompany and guide them in this process lest they be distracted by the many voices that can lead one astray. Cyril strove and still strives to do this through the many *avatars* he adopts to enter the lives of people. As we honour Cyril on his birthday for the person he is and his role in shaping the lives of so many, we pray that we may be inspired to contribute in whatever way we can to make the world more just and humane.

**Rev Dr Lisbert D'Soua SJ**
Jesuit Regional Assistant for South Asia, Rome
Former Vice-Chancellor, Jnana-Deepa Vidyapeeth, Pune

# MESSAGES

## God's Abundant Blessings for Cyril

The book is indeed a modest but fitting tribute to Fr. Cyril Desbruslais, S.J., on his 80th birthday. He was a friend, philosopher and guide to innumerable young people in Pune. He was also an effective teacher and an inspiration to hundreds of philosophy students who passed through the portals of Jnana Deepa Vidyapeeth, Pune, during the 35 years he taught there. He had a passion for philosophy, especially a Philosophy of Liberation. In addition to authoring several books, he was also a good playwright and his annual plays in Pune drew crowds. May he experience God's abundant blessings as he carries on the mission entrusted to him.

**Rev Fr Arturo Sosa SJ**
Superior General of the Society of Jesus

## Intelligently Holy

There are moments in our life-journey, when life and journey are passionately intertwined. Journeying is living; living becomes journey. Perhaps not many among us know that Cyril with his sister was literally thrown out into the streets of Calcutta at a very young age. In a way Cyril's journey of life was coloured by the noise, bustle, despair and refuge of the then Calcutta streets! Perhaps that event so shaped Cyril that, in spite of it or because of it, he turned out to be an incorrigible optimist, relentless thinker and incisive critic. He was nurtured by 'audacious faith' in the Lord that shaped intelligent 'holiness' of life. That made him a much sought-after friend of numerous students of Pune city, and the ever-available mentor of so many Jesuit scholastics of De Nobili.

That audacious faith and intelligent holiness did not leave him even though he is somewhat physically weakened. Audacious faith makes Cyril a daring person because like his Master he saw the goodness of his Father all over. Rather than being hemmed in by certain type of rationality, Cyril was led by 'faith' that opened up vast horizon before him and he coined a liberating pedagogy out of everything. The audacity of goodness can't be confined. His was an intelligent holiness, asking us to throw the stone if we are sinless, articulating a new logic of seeking after the lost and embracing the returnee without questions.

'Learned and holy' are mutually compatible in Cyril; 'faithful and critical' are attributes that go together in his thinking. Cyril journeyed/cycled to live in the hearts of his students and lived to be available to the seekers of all variety. Eighty years are perhaps too short to become fully holy; eighty years are long enough to be audacious.

We rejoice with Cyril for 'Life and Journey' – for audacious fidelity and for intelligent holiness – that connected the city of Pune to the quiet of DNC. Let us be believing and let us be journeying, knowing that the tomb remains empty and that He is perennially on his way to Galilee; perhaps that is all what matters for Cyril.

**Rt Rev George Pattery SJ**

The author is Jesuit President of South Asia (POSA) and Vice-Chancellor, Jnana-Deepa Vidyapeeth

## A Prophet for the Poor

I wish to congratulate Cyril Desbruslais for all that he has contributed as a teacher, researcher in Philosophy. He had also a special love for the youth and that is why his Search in Service and Unity (SSU) has been so successful for so many years. He had also a special place for the poor and the marginalized. He was passionately committed to Second Vatican Council, 32 General Congregation which opened the Church and Society of Jesus to the world and to those in the periphery. Fr Pedro Arrupe, a Jesuit priest committed to Christ and a visionary and prophet for the poor, was his role model. As he is celebrating 80 years of his joyous, passionate and compassionate life, may he be beacon of hope for the many young people of today!

**Rt Rev Andrew Fernandes SJ**

Provincial, Poona Jesuit Province

## Forever in Youthful Spirit, Fr Cyril Desbruslais

Fr. Cyril has touched the lives of thousands of people from all walks of life. Even as he closes 80, to us he remains forever young. He was the quintessential Calcuttan who chose to live the bulk of his Jesuit life elsewhere. He was first and foremost a solid Jesuit, an example to the younger men whom he nurtured, taught, and inspired. He was a profound intellectual, well versed in his subject, a born teacher, articulate and comprehensive. He was a thinker, phenomenal pastor, author, in short, a great human being. He will be remembered by generations of Jesuits and young people as their mentor and guide, a formator with deep personal concern for those under his charge, one who had a deep respect for individual freedom and yet inculcated a sense of responsibility. Yes, even his occasional irreverence was an intrinsic part of his charm. I wish him many more years of dedicated, loving service to Christ and his people, especially the youth closest to his heart.

**Rev Fr Raphael Joseph Hyde SJ**
Provincial, Calcutta Jesuit Province

## Mentor, Philosopher, Teacher

On his 80th birthday, I offer my sincere congratulations and gratitude to Fr. Cyril Desbruslais, SJ and wish him many happy returns of the day. Fr. Cyril comes across to me as a prayerful person who is committed to his ministry beyond his likes and dislikes. His decisions related to his ministries were always the fruits of his profound discernment based on his affective experiences of God and affective experiences of the world. His convictions have deep roots in the compassion of God and in his conscience. He is a great thinker, philosopher and teacher whose teaching always has a blend of God's compassionate love and a depth of knowledge existing in the world. His passion and commitment to the wellbeing of the youth from all walks of life are beyond imagination.

Keeping all good works and commitments of Fr. Cyril in mind, his students and admirers have put together their affective experiences of him in a book form, expressing their appreciation, gratitude and love to their *Guru* Fr. Cyril. It is a noble gesture on their part. I appreciate them for their kind gesture. My heartiest congratulations to Jnana-Deepa Vidyapeeth (JDV) for releasing a book on Fr. Cyril Desbruslais, SJ, as a token of their gratitude for his committed services to JDV. This book will treasure memories of many of Fr. Cyril. It will continue inspiring thousands and thousands. May God bless Fr. Cyril with good health and good life!

**Rev Fr Bhausaheb Sansare SJ**
Former Provincial, Poona Jesuit Province and Rector, Papal Seminary, Pune

## Reminding Me of Pope Francis

At the very outset, I offer my heartiest congratulations to my friend and colleague at Jnana-Deepa Vidyapeeth Fr Cyril Desbruslais as he enters into his eightieth year. His has been a distinguished, rich and resourceful priestly ministry. As Professor he was arguably the most popular and sought-after member on our campus. He has been a multi-talented and multi-tasking person. He was concurrently involved in extra-curricular priestly activities. The youth in Pune would interact with him. His immensely successful academic career was further embellished with creativity, imagination and dynamism. Some of Pope Francis' bold and fresh initiatives and linguistic expressions remind me of the ways of Fr. Cyril Desbruslais.

**Rt Rev Bishop Thomas Dabre**
Bishop of Poona and Former Professor. Jnana Deepa Vidyapeeth. Pune

## A Friend of the Youth

Cyril Desbruslais is very knowledgeable and a very brilliant professor for what he knew and what he shared with his students. He was very close to the youth. Every Sunday evening he used cycle to St. Xavier's Church and celebrate the Eucharist for them. He moved with them and understood them. They too understood him. The recent illness has put a break, but not dampened his enthusiasm and passion. Truly he was an efficient professor and creative philosopher, whom students and colleagues liked immensely.

**Rt Rev Bishop (Emeritus) Valerian D'Souza**
Diocese of Poona

## A Philosopher of Liberation

I had the privilege of knowing and interacting with Dr Cyril Desbruslais for more than forty years. I am happy to say that he is a committed visionary, a constant seeker and an untiring guide. As a visionary, he has motivated many people with his vision for a just and liberative society. As a seeker, he has been always keen to know more and more and share that knowledge with hundreds of his students. As a guide, he has been accompanying, encouraging and empowering thousands of young men and women. He has been passionately committed to the church and the nation. He has been one of the most inspiring professors Jnana-Deepa Vidyapeeth. Truly he is a philosopher of liberation, who has helped many to free themselves and live more human lives. I have been personally transformed by him. More than that JDV has been challenged and changed by his vision, search and guidance. I wish Cyril Desbruslais continued good health and fulfilling life.

**Rev Fr Selva Rathinam SJ**
President, Jnana-Deepa Vidyapeeth

## Man of the Magis

It is my pleasure to pen a few lines on the occasion when Cyril Desbruslais will be turning 80 years "young"! I have purposely chosen the word "young" instead of old because even at this age, and even after suffering a serious stroke, he maintains an irrepressible, creative, youthful, inquisitive and energetic spirit. He is a sort of 'youth charmer'; the young cling to his words, ideas and dynamic spirit and in turn they themselves are liberated and transformed and become keen observers of our society, the injustices and the plight of the people at the periphery. The energy that is generated as a result is given creative expressions through art, music, plays, involvement with the marginalised and other forms of liberative praxis. All during his teaching career, Cyril has been a member of De Nobili community. His influence on the scholastics and the staff has been remarkable. When some of the alumni of DNC come back for a visit after several years, the one person they inquire about is Cyril and some of the wonderful things they had done together, often out of step with the normal way of doing things! This was Cyril's way of teaching them the "the Ignatian Magis", the quintessence of Jesuit Vocation. May God give Cyril good health and a long life to continue to inspire the young to make a difference in the Church and the society!

**Rev Fr Edward Mudavassery SJ**
Rector, De Nobili College, Pune-411014, Maharashtra

## A Genuine Inspiration for the Youth

Cyril Desbruslais is a person of great talents. In spite of the recent sickness and speech impedments, he has been working fullday. His ability to get along with young people is remarkable, despite age. He is able to talk to them, sometimes with the aid of translation. He arranges a couple of meetings and seminars with them on a regular basis. He is readily available to them to sort our difficulties. Truly, he is an inspiration to hem and he has changed the course of their lives many times, by giving them a sense of direction and meaning. Though they come from different communities, there is no discrimination among the students of SSU. He is an asset to our community and I am very proud of him. May he contrinue to contribute to the well-being of all, especially of the students.

**Rev Fr Kennett Mesquite SJ**
Rector, St. Vincent's School, Camp, Pune

## Remembering Cyril Desbruslais, Teacher, Mentor and Friend

I heartily congratulate and deeply appreciate the magnificent gesture and initiative of Dr. Kuruvilla Pandikattu for bringing out a Festschrift in honour of our Professor and friend, Fr. Cyril Desbruslais, on the occasion of his 80th birthday. Our dearest and best Teacher Cyril deserves it more than we can commend.

This volume consists of 36 articles. The thirty eight eminent contributors bring together essays which represent the breadth of Cyril's personal and professional vocations and interests. The contributions are organized in five categories which reflect upon Cyril's own life, passion and copious work in the field of philosophy, Liberation, Education, Social Commitment, Multi-pluralism, Fuller Living, Teaching, Mentorship, Dramatics, Mission among the youth and so on.

"Philosophy," of course, is the subject Cyril taught for thirty-five years at Jnana-Deepa Vidyapeeth, Pune. Some of his colleagues, all scholars of renown, who have contributed to the epic span Cyril's entire teaching career. All rank themselves among his closest friends.

The editor warrants a special note. Dr. Kuruvilla Pandikattu is Professor and the Dean of Philosophy at JDV, Pune. He is a prolific writer in the field of philosophy, Religion and Science. This festschrift is the outcome of his effective coordination and faithful expression of his admiration of Cyril.

"A Good Teacher Is Like a Candle that Consumes Itself While Lighting the Way for Others." This Italian proverb is apt for Cyril, an outstanding teacher of philosophy, mentor and friend of many Jesuit and non-Jesuit students of Philosophy at Jnana-Deepa Vidyapeeth (JDV), Pune and an inspiration to the youth of Pune City. He was such an inspiring teacher that his students – religious and secular, loved and respected him immensely and recall him with reverential adoration.

While I was a student of philosophy for two years between July 1982 and June 1984, and particularly as a member of the JDV Students' Council, I came to associate closely with young and charismatic Cyril. We worked together for the seminar on "Relevance of Christianity in India Today" and later published the proceedings in the form of a book. I greatly admired the plethora of his knowledge and clarity of mind, and his transparent readiness to share his wisdom with others. I sought his advice on many occasion for discussions, debates and for contributing papers to journals.

A couple of months ago Shashi Tharoor, a Xaverian MP from Thiruvananthapuram constituency and a former Central Minister had visited St. Xavier's University, Kolkata; during our conversation, he spoke very highly of Cyril Desbruslais who had a year of regency(1970-71) at St. Xavier's Collegiate School, Calcutta. I quote Tharoor:

"I still remember what it felt like to come to St. Xavier's School, Calcutta for the first time, as a rather nervous young boy, not yet in his teens. St. Xavier's Calcutta was unquestionably in my day the best school in the city, particularly in terms of its intellectual rigour. The excellence of the institution was derived from the high quality of the teaching staff, especially the Jesuits themselves. St Xavier's is an exemplar of what makes Jesuit education so worthwhile".

"A number of the Jesuit priests at these schools were very well trained themselves. I remember a young Jesuit Father Cyril Desbruslais, who actually took us through an epistemological argument for the existence of God, which certainly impressed my fourteen-year-old imagination no end because I was just beginning to flirt with the idea of atheism".

"When you discover rationality, your religion doesn't seem so impressive anymore, and when you discover the limitations of rationality it all comes back, but in between I had this very rational, structured philosophical argument from a Jesuit priest who lectured us teenagers on the proof for divinity, citing Kant and Thomas Aquinas in the process. And that was very striking".

"We were absolutely free to express our beliefs. Elsewhere, you learn to answer the questions. At St. Xavier's, you learn to question the answers and later I went on to question the questions, too". St Xavier's inspired secularism. An education there gives you the pan-India outlook, the well-rounded education, the eclectic social interests, the questioning spirit, the humanitarian regard for the wellbeing of others that are all the vital ingredients of the Xaverian ethos".

Like his favourite Jesuit Philosopher, Teilhard de Chardin, Cyril combines religion with scientific philosophy. He believes that 'science provides the best and most warranted knowledge of the natural and social world, and that such knowledge is the only sound basis for moral decision and social and political reform'. Cyril has often argued for the unity of knowledge. Science and philosophy constitute a fruitful and necessary partnership in his exposition.

Teachers, Researchers and Students of philosophy, social science and scholars of liberal education will discover the wisdom of this approach and will gain insight into the utility of multi-disciplinary scholarship.

This volume celebrates the spirit and work of a Maestro – as a fellow Jesuit and a student of Cyril, I am honoured and blessed that Cyril is receiving such a beatific and philosophical present on his 80th birthday. Long live Cyril and his liberating ideas.

**Rev Dr J. Felix Raj SJ**
Vice-Chancellor of St. Xavier's University,
Kolkata and a former student of Cyril

# EDITORIAL

Dr Cyril Desbruslais SJ has done yeomen service to thousands of youths and students of Jnana-Deepa Vidyapeeth and Pune. He was an inspiring teacher, effective mentor and practical philosopher. Through his lectures and plays, he has shaped the destiny of many young men and women.

To honour him on his 80th birthday (DoB: 21 December 1940), some of his friends and colleagues are bringing out this volume. It hopes to highlight his main vision and articulate his insight on life.

He has been fond of quoting repeatedly St Irenaeus of Lyons, "The glory of God is humans fully alive." Throughout his career, he has struggled to bring out the liberative dimension of every ideology, vision and system. He has also tried to make us more human and humane.

One of his most inspiring courses and books is *Philosophy of Liberation*,[1] for which he has taken insights from Theology of Liberation. Through other courses, like "Hunger and Violence," "Philosophy of Technology," "Postmodernity,"[2] "Existentialism," and "Ethics," he has striven to radiate a vision of human beings who are freedom from shackles of poverty, injustice and ignorance.

## 1. List of Themes Close to His Heart

His life ambition has been to enable and empower the youth and thus make their lives more meaningful and liberative. To honour this great philosopher-playwright, some of his colleagues and admirers have come together to reflect on the contribution Cyril Desbruslais (populary known by his friends and students just "Cyril") has made to philosophyin general and understanding of human person in particular. They requested to make their contribution in the following sub-themes, which lie close to the heart of Cyril Desbruslais:

---

1 Desbruslais, Cyril. *The Philosophy of Liberation: Revisiting Genuine Religious Experiences with Special Reference to Christianity*. New Delhi: Christian World Imprints, 2016.

2 This has also been published as a book. Desbruslais, Cyril. *Postmodernity: An Indian Christian Philosophical Appraisal*. New Delhi: Christian World Imprints 2019.

- Evolving a theory of Liberation in the Indian context
- Fully human, fully alive
- Irenaeus approach to the mystery of evil
- "Idols must die, so that symbols might live." Humans as *animal symbolicum.*
- Freeing God from the Popular idols
- Learning from the masters of suspicions
- Ethics as a way of life
- Are we really free? Reflections from the Indian context?
- Living and dying: Making most of the tensions of daily life
- Towards a liberative understanding of Marxism, Christianity, etc.
- Teilhard de Chardin's liberative understanding of evolution
- "Life is not a problem to be solved, but a mystery to be lived."
- "He who has found a WHY to live for can cope with any HOW." (Human beings as meaning making animals)
- The right for rites: Need for rituals for embodied human beings
- Priests as prophets: A liberative understanding of priesthood
- Do we need institutional religions?
- Embodied, enabled and empowered: Human beings who are fully alive
- "Every understanding is self-understanding."
- "Theology is anthropology."
- "The most practical thing is a good theory."
- Jesus as a liberator
- Towards a liberative understanding of Gita, Communist Manifesto, etc.
- Humans as myth-making animals (our contemporary collective myths)
- Technological progress and moral regress
- "Evolution become conscious of itself."
- Possibility of life *before* and after death
- Christianity as "Platonism for the masses"
- Resurrection of the BODY: The uniqueness of Christianity
- Need and significance of proofs for God's existence?
- Believing in and believing that.
- A spirituality for contemporary youth
- Pope Francis: The prophet for today
- Pedagogy of the oppressed
- Topics of their own choice, that will vibe with Cyril's basic contribution

The writers were also encouraged to express their appreciation for his contribution to theatre as a playwright. The 36 articles collected in this volume are efforts by his colleagues, friends and admirers to express our gratitude to the tremendous and creative work he has done. They were many more writers who were willing to contribute, but I had to discourage them, since we wanted the volume to see the light of day on December 21, 2019.

As such this books want to evoke the meaning, message and vision of Cyril Desbruslais. As a person, he has been remarkably forthwright and articulate in his view for a more humane and liberative understanding of God and of human beings. As a philosopher, he was amazingly critical of the structure and ideology that dehumanise us. As a playwright, he was been extraordinarily creative in inspiring the young minds to love the world and experience the fullness of life, which definitely includes the experience of the Divine.

## 2. Structure of the Book

This book seeks to understand Cyril's passionate search for truth and life, by focussing on the main aspects of his own thinking and living.

### a. Seeking Holistic Liberation

Keeping in mind Desbruslais' passion for philosophy, the articles are divided into five parts. The first part deals with his philosophy of liberation. Drawing from liberation theology and convinced that India needs a philosophy (not theology) of liberation, he has been advocating a philosophy that humanises, empowers and liberates. He could trace the liberating and dehumanising potential in every attempt at philosophising, thinking and being. So his advocacy for a philosophy that enables and inspires everyone, especially the disadvantaged and the marginalised.

We begin this section with an article by Errol Fernandes SJ, Vice Principal (Commerce), St. Xavier's College, Mumbai, who explores Jesus also brought about liberation from social and structural sin. This liberation was in order to free those who encountered him to love as they are loved. The next article by Thomas Karimundackal SJ, Scriptural Studies, Jnana-Deepa Vidyapeeth, Pune, focuses on the hermeneutic study of Jesus' visit to Nazareth, his home town, from the perspective of liberation. Next, Patricia Santos RJM, Faculty of Theology, Jnana-Deepa Vidyapeeth, Pune integrates and builds on some of the varied aspects of flourishing as reflected in the different disciplines of philosophy, psychology, education, anthropology, ecology and spirituality from a feminist theological perspective in order to present a synthesized theological understanding of flourishing as fullness of life for all.

The succeeding article of Anil Thomas CM, Department of Systematic Theology, Jnana-Deepa Vidyapeeth, Pune, studies the change that Vatican II has brought about in the perception of liberating mission and how this new understanding of mission has been at the heart of many documents of Vatican II as well as the teachings of all post-conciliar Popes.

Next Lawrence S. Fernandes SJ, Principal, Sacred Heart College, Satya Nilayam, Chennai argues that education is and can be a source of empowerment and liberation taking the cases of Mahatma Gandhi and B.R. Ambedkar. This is followed by Dolichan Kollareth SJ, Dept of Social Sciences, Jnana-Deepa Vidyapeeth, Pune, who advocates from a liberation psychology, inspired by Ignacio Martín-Baró SJ, for whom , the ultimate purpose of the discipline of psychology should be the liberation of the oppressed people. Next Sathya Balan SJ, Jnana-Deepa Vidyapeeth, Pune explores Heidegger's invitation to think deeply and radically to be freed from the clutches of practical and calculative thinking in our hyperactive society to emancipatory meditative thinking.

The last article in this section is by Joby Tharamangalam OP, Research Scholar, Jnana-Deepa Vidyapeeth, Pune, who attempts to discern the liberating face of God in the midst of our temptation to make GODs in our own image.

### b. Socially Committed

The second Part dwells on his social concerns. Fascinated by Second Vatican Council of the Church and by 32nd General Congregation of the Society of Jesus, he has been an ardent advocate for the cause of the poor and the exploited. He has stood for a Church that stands for and with the weak, as did Fr Pedro Arrupe in the 1980s and Pope Francis today. Together with his colleagues, George Soares-Prabhu and Francis D'Sa, he has been in the forefront in Jnana-Deepa Vidyapeeth's attempt to change the society structurally.

The first article by Roy J. Pereira, SJ, St Xavier's College, Mumbai, interprets the parable of the Good Samaritan, from the perspective of the youth, to whom Desbruslais has dedicated his whole life. Next, Educationist and Biodiversity Conservator, Hector Andrade, provides hope for the ecological crisis that we are all facing. In the subsequent article, S. Stephen Jayard, Professor of Science, Jnana-Deepa Vidyapeeth, Pune, India outlines a "seasoned" spiritualty for today's youth. Job Kozhamthadam SJ, Director, Indian Institute of Science and Religion, New Delhi, investigates the significant role that science plays in the modern India, which helps in the emergence of a new world-view. This is followed by the plea of Kuruvilla Pandikattu, Dean, Faculty of Philosophy, JDV, Pune, to understand and appreciate the mystery of evil in our highly complex world.

The next article by researcher and publisher Joji Valli shows that relationship and responsibility are hallmarks of human existence because life is a gift and a one-time opportunity, in the context of corporate social responsibility. VM Jose SJ, Moral and Pastoral Theology, Jnana-Deepa Vidyapeeth, Pune, deliberates on the life of physically challenged people, enabling them to live happy and fulfilled lives. The last two articles takes up specific problems which Desbruslais would be very much involved in. That of feminine entry into the Ayyappa temple by Sacaria Joseph, St. Xavier's College, Kolkata and Anuradha Mazumder, Prafulla Chandra College, Kolkata. James Ponniah, University of Chennai deals with the question of refugees and religion.

## c. Open to Difference and Dissent

The third Part invites us to respect difference and affirm dissent in view of fostering freedom, pluralism and diversity. Recognising that India is a land of plurality (of religions, cultures, languages, etc.) Desbruslais has been keen to foster a liberal mentality of openness, courage and conviction. Such a search will unsettle the settled and naturally create trouble and tension. So this section represents the convinced and committed rebel that Cyril is. He is a prophet who would courageously criticise the structural sins of the society and stand for the rights of the poor and those who are different.

In the first article, Gnana Patrick, Department of Christian Studies, University of Madras argues that religious pluralism cannot be grasped deeply in a-historical manner; it needs, on the other hand, a context-specific exploration in order to make meaningful statements upon it. The next one by M.X. Gnanadhas, Research Scholar, University of Innsbruck, Austria, identifies and analyses the varieties of epistemic injustice, which are prevalent all over the world especially in the arena of gender and race. Next, Paul Thelakat, Chief Editor, *Light of Truth*, Ernakulam ruminates on the meaning of human lives provided by religions and on the role of images and temples as possible scandals.

In a similar vein, Victor Ferrao, Dean of Studies, Rachol Seminary, Goa reflects on spectres of Hinduism from postmodern perspectives. Three young and promising scholars, Suchetana Banerjee, Gayatri Mendanha and Ananya Dutta, from the Symbiosis School for Liberal Arts, explore William Blake's symbolic use of language to seek answers to questions of ultimate concern through the deliberate subversion of text in lyrical poetry. Similarly, Sacaria Joseph, St. Xavier's College, Kolkata, points out the difficulties to relate Salman Rushdie's *The Satanic Verses* with freedom of speech and expression. The final article in this secton is on ambiguity in philosopher Jean-Paul Sartre's understanding of "bad faith" or *"mauvaise foi"*.

## d. Towards Fuller Living

The fourth Part invites the reads to experience fuller living both personally and socially. Desbruslais has been pleading for fuller life, which recognises the brokenness and vulnerabilities of ordinary human beings. Still he is able to recognise the potential that each one of us is capable of individually and collectively. So the invitation to affirm life in its abundance and seek joy in everything and everyone.

This section begins with an article by Libin Joseph CST, Pontificia Università della Santa Croce, Rome. Basing himself on Martin Seligman and William James, he argues that teleological perspective is a guiding map for a meaningful life and that 'the meaning of life' consists in responding optimistically and creatively to the struggles of life with purposes. Another young and enthusiastic research scholar from Jnana-Deepa Vidyapeeth meditates on a quote which Desbruslais, borrowing from Gabriel Marcel, is fond of: "Life is not a problem to be solved, but a mystery to be lived." A former college of Desbruslais, Subhash Anand, Professor (Emeritus), Jnana-Deepa Vidyapeeth, Pune, explores the symbolic connection between symbols and rights and their significant role in religions. This is followed by an article on human dignity by J. Charles Davis, Humboldt Research Fellow, Albert-Ludwigs University of Freiburg, Germany. He locates the human dignity in the human body, moving away from our rational capacities.

Next, Nishant A Irudayadason, Professor of Ethics at JDV, Pune, relates discourse ethics with ethics of liberation, by creative interpretation of Karl-Otto Apel and Enrique Dussel. This is followed by another article on the role of human beings in the universe. Isaac Parackal OIC, Professor of Metaphyscis, JDV, is inspired by A.R Peacocke and explores our ecological relationship to the universe. The final article by Ginish Cheruparambil, Christ University (Deemed), Lavasa, Maharashtra studies Social Progress Index (SPI) as alternative to Gross Domestic Product (GDP) and Human Development Index (HDI), a topic significant to appreciate collective human progress and liberation.

### e. The Concluding Articles

The final Part focusses on the message, philosophy and person of Desbruslais. Here we study the unique contribution to Desbruslais to the society at large and the Indian Church in particular.

Rajan J. Barrett, Maharaja Sayajirao University of Baroda Vadodara, Gujarat, traces the development of Cyril Desbruslais S.J. as a playwright who has a predilection for a German theatre practitioner and playwright Bertolt Brecht. It also looks at what I term as 'Minority Theatre' because it works for a minority community. G. Lazar SVD, Director, SANSKRUTI, Hyderabad, investigates Desbruslais' approach to virtues and values and shows that Desbruslais holds on to the basic goodness of human beings, in spite of our failures and vulnerabilities. Then V. Y. Dasappan SJ, Principal, St. Xavier's College, Thumba, Thiruvananthapuram, encounters Desbruslais as a "Philosopher with Angel's Wings." He traces the Jesuit vision of art and theatre through the lens of Desbruslais' plays. In this spirit, Babu Joseph Karakombil SVD, Director, Satprachar Press, Indore, M.P investigates the "Life-World" (*Lebenswelt*) of Cyril Desbruslais. The final article by Cedric Prakash, a Jesuit social activit from Gujarat and an ardent admirer of Desbruslais. He sees the life and message of Cyril as being fully young and alive, by being with the young, challenging and inspiring them.

As already mentioned, Cyril Desbruslais has been repeatedly fond of quoting St. Irenaeus of Lyons (c 120-200), "the glory of God is man fully alive," [3] we have taken this quote to sum up Desbruslais' philosophical life and horizon. In all his work, he has been trying to deepen the human beings dignity, freedom and nobility so that we can be truly in touch with God. We can truly glorify God by becoming genuinely ourselves more and more. By reaching out to others, loving them deeply and embracing and empowering them, we become more human and give glory to God. This explains title of this volume, Fully Human and Fully Alive.

## 3. Words of Gratitude

The editor would like the thank the three communities; Dr Cyril Desbruslais has been closely associated with: Papal Seminary community along with Fr. Bhausaheb Sansare SJ, Rector and Fr Vincent Crasta SJ, administrator, where the editor spent more than twenty three years. Jnana-Deepa Vidyapeeth, along with Fr Selva Rathinam SJ, President and Fr Jose Thayil SJ, Registrar, where Dr Desbruslais has been academically involved for more than forty years; and De Nobili College Community, along with Fr Edward Mudavassery SJ, Rector and Fr Jacob Kulangara SJ, Administrator. It is these communities that gave Desbruslais to proper ambience to live and flourish! We are also grateful to the Rector, Fr Kenneth Misquita, St Vincent's Community, Pune and the Jesuit Provinces of Pune and Calcutta and the Provincials Fr Andrew Fernandes SJ and Fr Raphael Hyde SJ, where Desbruslais feels totally at home.

May this volume be a modest contribution, inspired by Dr Cyril Desbruslais SJ, to foster a shared and collective life of love, joy, peace and freedom! May we be inspired by his life to enable and empower the weak and to dedicate ourselves fully to remove the tears from the faces of the marginalised and to contribute to the physical, emotional and spiritual well-being of all, especially the youth, for whom Desbruslais has a special devotion.

**The Editor**

---

3 "*Gloria enim Dei vivens homo, vita autem hominis visio Dei.*" This Latin quote may be correctly translated as "For/truly the glory of God is a living man; and the life of man consists in beholding God" and not simply as "the glory of God man fully alive" thereby promoting the cult of self-fulfilment. The quote actually speaks about the fulfilment of human beings in beatific vision of God, namely in Christ (cf. Eph 3:18- 19). Paulraj Mariapushpam, "Love of Neighbour as Axis of Pauline Ethis: A Brief Study of Gal 5:13-14 and Rom 13:8-10," Kuruvilla Pandikattu and Thomas Karimundackal (eds) *Committed to the Church and the Country,* New Delhi: Christian World Imprints, 2019, p. 388.

PART ONE

---

# SEEKING LIBERATION

1

# Jesus the Liberator: Fostering the Love that Frees

**Errol Fernandes SJ**

*Vice Principal (Commerce), St. Xavier's College, Mumbai*

**Abstract:** To describe Jesus as Liberator might seem redundant since the name Jesus means "God saves". Yet, there is the danger of understanding liberation in a narrow and restricted way. Such an understanding sees liberation as merely individual and spiritual. However, the fact is that Jesus was not merely individual saviour and liberator. The liberation he proclaimed and acted out through his life, mission, death and resurrection was a universal and holistic liberation.

This liberation consisted of a move away from a constricted image of God as one who had only to be placated, obeyed and feared to a revelation of God as one who loved unconditionally. It was also a revelation of a God who loved first. Besides this, Jesus also brought about liberation from social and structural sin. This liberation was in order to free those who encountered him to love as they are loved.

**Keywords:** Liberator, Jesus as Liberator, Sin, Structural Sin, Grace, Merit

In their attempt to understand, describe and relate to the person of Jesus of Nazareth, Christians over the centuries have used many titles.[1] As we know,

1 Synonyms for the term 'Liberator' are Saviour, Messiah, Freer, Emancipator, Deliverer, and some of these will be used interchangeably. In this article I have restricted myself to Jesus as portrayed in the Gospels and other New Testament writings.

the Gospels and characters in the Gospels use a variety of titles to describe, understand and relate to the person of Jesus. In their Infancy narratives, Matthew (1:18-2:23) and Luke (1:26-38; 2:1-20) state that the name Jesus is given to the child by the angel, and not chosen by the parents (Mt 1:21; Lk 1:31). As a matter of fact, the mother and foster father have no choice in this regard (Lk 2:21). The name Jesus was chosen by God through the angel. When the angel Gabriel appears to Mary in the Gospel of Luke, it is he who directs her to name the child Jesus (Lk 1:31). At the time of the naming of the child, Luke reminds us that the child was given the name Jesus which was the name the angel had given him before he was conceived in the womb (Lk 2:21).This is reiterated by Matthew in his infancy narrative when he states that in a dream Joseph was told not only to take the pregnant Mary as his wife (Mt 1:20) but also that he must name the child Jesus (Mt 1:21).The name chosen anticipates the future career of Jesus and reveals that God has taken the initiative to do more than provide humanity with merely a prophet.

Matthew gives us the etymology of the name Jesus, "for he will save his people from their sins" (Mt 1:21), and through this indicates that through the incarnation, God has acted to redeem the whole of humanity. Matthew also adds the interpretation of the name "Emmanuel" (God is with us - Mt 1:23) to underline the fact that salvation comes from God who acts in and through Jesus conceived by the Holy Spirit.[2] Matthew then goes on to tell us why the child will be named Jesus and explains that the name means "Saviour from sin" (Mt 1:21).

This salvation from sin was shown by Jesus in his ministry. This included reaching out to the poorest of the poor, the marginalized, the downtrodden, and those considered the scum of society (Mk 2:15-17). Jesus lived out the meaning of his name through the miracles he worked, the parables he told and through his teaching. Through them, he announced emphatically that God was a God who loved unconditionally and wanted all to be saved (Jn 3:17; see also 2 Cor 5:19). However, since God was a just God, God's justice would be shown in God making an option for the poor.

To describe Jesus as Liberator, therefore, seems redundant. Yet, because there is the danger of understanding salvation from sins only as personal salvation, I intend to show in this article that Jesus is much more than this. The liberation that Jesus proclaimed and brought through his life, mission, death and resurrection was a wholistic liberation.

## 1. Liberation from a Constricted Image of God

In his initial proclamation in both Mark (1:14-15) and Matthew (4:17) which was his first public act in these Gospels after his Baptism, Jesus makes explicit

2 Garland David E, *Reading Matthew: A Literary and Theological Commentary on the First Gospel*, (Macon, Georgia: Smyth & Helwys, 2001).

that the core of his Mission is the Kingdom of God/Heaven with all that it entails.[3] The proclamation of Jesus in Mark is *"The time is fulfilled, and the kingdom of God has come near; repent, and believe in the good news.'* (Mk 1:15) and is the opposite of that of John the Baptiser. John proclaimed a baptism of repentance for the forgiveness of sins (Mk 1:4). This means that for John, repentance of sins was a condition for the coming of the kingdom.[4] In the case of Jesus, however, the coming of the kingdom was the Indicative and the repentance that followed was the Imperative. In other words, repentance was not a condition for, but a consequence of the coming of the kingdom. The call to repentance was BECAUSE the kingdom had come. It was not a call to bring about the kingdom. This was because the kingdom was given as a free gift from God. That this is so is made explicit when Mark tells us in the previous verse that Jesus came into Galilee proclaiming *"the good news of God",* (Mk 1:14) which here shows him as a herald of good tidings. Jesus is portrayed here as the messenger from God bringing the good news which belongs to God and which is also the news about who God is.

This proclamation was radical and revolutionary and it set Jesus apart from all other Rabbis and teachers. It also set him and his proclamation in stark contrast with John the Baptiser who also came preaching (Mk 1:7). Whereas John proclaimed a repentance-baptism, Jesus demonstrates that he is indeed the "Greater One" by proclaiming as the one promised by Isaiah (Isa 52:7; 61:1), the good news of or from God. It demonstrated that the God whom Jesus proclaimed was a God who loved unconditionally (Jn 3:16) and wanted to gather all people to himself (Jn 12:32). The radicalness of this proclamation and its being acted out by Jesus is more than evident in the reaction of John the Baptist who heard in prison about all that Jesus was saying and doing (Mt 11:2; Lk 7:18). John had proclaimed the coming Son of Man as one who would come with a winnowing fork in his hand and who would clear the threshing floor and burn the chaff (Mt 3:11-12)[5]. By this John meant that the one who would come after him would separate sinners from the righteous. He would reject the

---

3 For a fairly comprehensive explanation of the Kingdom of God see *The Collected Writings of George M Soares-Prabhu S.J.*, Jnana-Deepa Vidyapeeth, Pune, 2001) pp 223 244; The Kingdom has been defined variously as "Gods rule" or as a situation in which justice, freedom and love prevail or where God will reveal himself to be king.

4 Matthew describes the baptism by John differently from Mark. In Matthew, John's baptism is a call to repentance and not a baptism of repentance. John also asserts in 3:11 that he baptizes on the basis of repentance. In Matthew John has no authority to forgive sins as Jesus has. For a fuller explanation on the meaning of John's baptism see Garland, David E, (n. 2 above).

5 See John P Meier, "John the Baptist in Matthew's Gospel," JBL 99 (1980) pp 383-405. See also Luz, Ulrich, A Commentary on Matthew 8-20, pp 132-134, who also gives a history of Interpretation of the 'doubt' of John the Baptist and the various interpretations of that 'doubt'.

sinners and accept the righteous. However, Jesus was revealing himself not only as one who would not burn the chaff and so not reject sinners but also as one who would gather it along with the wheat. The chaff, which here must be interpreted as those who were accused of not keeping the law, were friends of Jesus[6]. This unusual way of proceeding possibly confused John the Baptist who had to seek clarification from Jesus through his disciples.[7] The response of Jesus to the disciples of John was typical of who Jesus is. While in Matthew the disciples of John are told that they must believe the words of Jesus who narrates what has happened (11:4), in Luke, the disciples of John witness that "Jesus had just then cured many people of diseases, plagues, and evil spirits, and had given sight to many who were blind."(7:21).The explanation of Jesus in both the Gospels is the same. The invalids who are cured of their ailments are the blind, lame, lepers, deaf. The dead are also raised to life. The fact that both Matthew and Luke have ended their lists with the statement "and the poor have good news brought to them." (Mt 11:5; Lk 7:22) might seem anticlimactic after mention of the raising of the dead. However, when we realise the "poor" denotes those who are completely dependent on God for help, it results in a summary of all those mentioned on the list, including the dead.[8] Also, that good news was being brought to the poor was the clearest sign of Jesus being the one who was to come. This was because it was unthinkable that the poor who were despised and trampled upon should be invited into the Kingdom.[9]

Very clearly then Jesus' portrayal of God was radically different from the image of God prevalent at that time. While all other rabbis and teachers including John the Baptist would reveal a God who would reward for righteousness and punish for wrong doing, the God Jesus proclaimed was forgiving, accepting and unconditional love. (1 Jn 4:10).This God could be addressed as Father (Mt 6:9; Lk 11:2) and with whom therefore one could have an intimate and personal relationship.

---

6 See especially Mk 2:17 where Jesus states the purpose of his coming into the world. It is to call sinners. While here, Matthew (9:13) has retained Mark, Luke (5:32) possibly found it too extreme and so thought it necessary to add the words "to repentance". That Mark (and Matthew) have not added a reason why sinners are called highlights the radicality of the message of Jesus.

7 See also Plummer, Alfred A., *A Critical and Exegetical Commentary on the Gospel According to St. Luke,* p 201. Here, Plummer summarises the discussion on the meaning of the question of John, "Are you the one who is to come or are we to wait for another?" (Lk 7:19). See also Fitzmyer, Joseph, Gospel According to Luke I-IX: Introduction, Translation and Notes p. 665.

8 Garland, David E, (n.2 above) p 126.

9 Plummer, Alfred A. (n. 7 above) p 203.

## 2. Liberation from Social and Structural Sin

This image of a loving God is evident even in the initial proclamation of Jesus in Luke (4:18-19). However, because God loves all equally, he would love the poor more than he loves the rich.[10] This love of God is manifested in the removal of fetters and all that binds. Thus the focus of the proclamation here is redemption from all that binds. Though it is evident from Lk 4:23 (…."Do here also in your home town the things that we have heard you did at Capernaum") that Jesus ministered in Capernaum BEFORE coming to his hometown, Luke consciously makes this episode the first one in the ministry of Jesus. A possible reason for this is that he wants this to be that incident which will influence the entire ministry of Jesus.[11]

The reading in Lk 4:18-19, is from Isa 61:1-2a and 58:6. Luke omits "to bind up the broken hearted" from Isa 61:1 and adds, from Isa 58:6, "to set at liberty those who are oppressed". The threefold repetition of the pronoun "me" is an indication that this passage describes the ministry of Jesus rather than that of Isaiah. It is also important to note that Jesus, in Luke, does not go on to read the second part of Isa 61:2 "and the day of vengeance of our God." Jesus' proclamation from Isaiah here, impinges directly on the major dimensions of social and political life: the use of wealth and power, the exclusion of the weak and disadvantaged from full participation in the community, and the use of violence sometimes lethal to protect the unjust status quo. It was a call not merely to the individual but communal repentance. It is a critique of the injustices of the prevailing order and a call to the order that God intended.[12]

The anointing of Jesus by the Spirit here possibly refers to his baptism (Lk 3:22) where the voice from heaven invited him to be son and servant and is here to be understood as a prophetic anointing. The anointing is with a mandate to "bring good news" to the poor" (Lk 4:18).

Significantly, therefore, Jesus' work will be good news to the poor. The "poor" figure more prominently in Jesus' teachings in Luke than in any other Gospel (see 14:13, 21; 16.20, 22; 18:22; 21:3). More than in the other Synoptics, the Lucan Jesus reveals God not only as a God of and for the poor, but also as a God who challenges the rich to introspect and not make idols out of their riches.[13] In the New Testament, the poor are understood in mostly

---

10 Mk 2:17; 10:23-24; 12:43-44; Lk 6.20,24; 16:25-26.

11 Fitzmyer, Joseph (n 7 above) p. 525.

12 See S Barry, The year of jubilee: A hermeneutic for social and moral transformation in South Africa. http://www.scielo.org.za/pdf/ids/v45n4/08.pdf. Accessed on October 3, 2019.

13 It is only in the Gospel of Luke that Jesus pronounces exclusively a beatitude on the poor (Lk 6:20) unlike Matthew whose Jesus announces a beatitude on the "poor in spirit" (Mt 5:3). Corresponding to the beatitude on the poor, it is only in Luke that there is a woe to the rich (Lk 6:24).

a literal way.[14] In most instances, the word "poor" is used of a person who is impoverished and thus who lacks even the basic necessities of life like food clothing and shelter. However, these would also include the illiterate, the socially outcast, the differently-abled and those possessed. These poor are victims of both individual callousness (Lk 12:14-21; 16:19-31)[15] and unjust structures (Lk 5:12-14, 33-39; 6:1-11; 11:37-54)[16].

---

Luke alone has the parable of the rich fool (Lk 12:16-20). The rich man is referred to as a "Fool" because he has allowed his riches to take the place of God and has identified himself with the fools in Prov 14:1 who say in their hearts that there is no God. Luke alone has the Parable of the rich man and Lazarus (Lk 16:19-31) where the rich man is *seemingly* oblivious to the presence of Lazarus. This is evident when we read that while in Hades he needs help, he even knows Lazarus' name.

In contrast to the rich ruler who could not follow Jesus because he let his riches come in the way of that following (18:23), Luke shows the effect of renunciation when he also tells the story of Zacchaeus' encounter with Jesus (19:1-10).

14 For a more detailed explanation on the meaning of the word "Poor" in both the Old and New Testaments, see *The Collected Writings of George M Soares Prabhu S.J., Volume V* (Jnana-Deepa Vidyapeeth 2001), pp 89-93 who ends the section by stating that there is a growing consensus among scholars to regard the poor as a sociological category.

15 Individual callousness is seen in the parable of the rich fool who thinks only of himself (Lk 12:17-19) as well as in the Rich man in the parable of the rich man and Lazarus (Lk 16:19-31).

16 The Old Testament stated a number of restrictions for those who had leprosy. These were excluded from the community, and had to live often outside of towns (Ex 4:6; Num 5:2-3; 12:10-12; Deut 24:8; 2 Kgs 5:27; 7:3-9). In the healing of the leper, Jesus reaches out and touches the leper (Lk 5:13) in a deliberate attempt to reach out physically to the "excluded one". It is also possibly an attempt to show that law of love supersedes ceremonial law. This seems more evident in Mk 1:41 where the more difficult reading is that Jesus was "moved with anger" possibly at the manner in which lepers were treated.

In defence of his disciples who were accused of eating and drinking and not fasting (Lk 5:33), Jesus points out that fasting is an expression of sorrow which is out of place at a wedding banquet and when the bridegroom is present. In other words, the law is not supreme.

In the first (Lk 6:1-6) of the two Sabbath controversies which maybe be regarded as Pronouncement stories the pronouncement is that "The Son of Man is lord of the Sabbath", which here refers to Jesus having "superiority over regulations in scripture" Fitzmyer, Joseph, (n. 7 above) p 609. In the second story it is not clear how the man's life is saved, when only his "right hand was withered" (Lk 6:6) However, it explains yet again that love takes precedence over law.

When invited to dine with a Pharisee (Lk 11:37), Jesus is able to read the thoughts of the Pharisee who is surprised that Jesus did not wash before the meal (Lk 11:38). It is in this context that Jesus pronounces woes against the Pharisees and Scribes. These include three against each group. The first woe to the Pharisees (Lk 11:42) is about the focus on minute details while not focussing on what is really important, namely justice and the love of God. The second woe berates them for their focus on self and self-importance and self-righteousness (Lk 11:43). The third woe (LK 11:44) is castigates them for appearing to

## 3. Jesus' Challenge to the Social and Structural Sins

The challenge of Jesus to the social and structural sins of his time can be seen on two levels.

The first of these is his challenge on the individual level. This is issued in his a) Teaching and b) Miracles The challenge on the structural level is seen in what may be termed as 'Carefrontation'

### 3.1. Challenge on the Individual Level

#### a. Teaching

Immediately after overcoming temptation (Mk 1:12; Mt 4:1-11), and beginning with the first proclamation (Mk 1:14-15; Mt 4:17), Jesus elucidates what his ministry will be. It will primarily be a ministry where openness is imperative. This is why the main method that Jesus chose to teach was parables. In their Parable Discourses (Mk 4:1-34; Mt 13:1-53), both Mark and Matthew state that there was a parabolic character to all of Jesus' public teaching (Mk 4:33-34; Mt 13:31-32). This means that Jesus' way of teaching was dialogical. It did not supply the lesson, it involved the listener and invited the listener to supply the lesson. It did not force a particular point of view or ridicule a different point of view. It challenged the listener to look at life itself in a different way. [17]

A parable which gives an overarching view of the stand of Jesus is termed variously as the Beelzebul and God's spirit and the Beelzebul controversy.[18] In response to the allegation that Jesus was casting out demons by the power of Beelzebul (Mk 3:22; Mt 11:24; Lk 11:15), Jesus tells a parable. In it he portrays himself as the stronger man who overpowers the strong man (Satan) and takes away his armour (Lk 11:22). The explanation of Jesus here, elucidates what he has come to do and what his mission is. It is the destruction of the kingdom of Satan by establishing a kingdom of justice, peace and love. It is in this context that the Parables of the rich fool (Lk 12:13-21) and the rich man and Lazarus (Lk 16:19-31) must be read. The Parable of the rich fool is prefaced by the words, "'Take care! Be on your guard against all kinds of greed; for one's life does not consist in the abundance of possessions.'" (Lk 12:15). Greed here stands for the desire to have more than is needed. It may also mean the desire to keep accumulating and possibly even at the cost of someone else not having

---

be what they are not. The scribes or lawyers are then berated for burdening people with external laws (Lk 11:46). The second woe (Lk 11:47-48) criticises them for approving violent actions against God's prophets. The third woe (Lk 11:52) criticises them for being selfish and self-centred.

17 *The Collected Writings* (n.14 above) pp 141-152.

18 Fitzmyer, (n. 7 above) p 916; see also Luz, Ulrich, *Matthew 1-7, A Commentary on Matthew 1-7*, (Fortress Press, Minneapolis, 2007) p. 197.

enough. It leads to being possessed by one's possessions and of worshipping wealth and not God (Mt 6:24).

The parable of the rich man and Lazarus is addressed to those who "were lovers of money" (Lk 16:14)[19]. It is a parable that is found only in the Gospel of Luke. It is also the only parable in which a character in the story is given a name. It is surely not a coincidence that the name of the poor man is Lazarus, a name which means "God helps". This is what happens indeed. However, the rich man has to bear the consequences of his 'non-action' and/or obliviousness to the plight of Lazarus. The reason for his lack of awareness is that he is too caught up in himself. This is evident because when he is in Hades, he recognises Lazarus and even knows his name. However, even here he wants Lazarus to be his errand boy and cater to his wants. When this is not possible, he pleads to let Lazarus carry a message to his brothers from him. To be sure, the errand now is not for him personally but for the members of his family. Nevertheless, it is still an errand that he wants carried out on his behalf. The request is not carried out and the parable ends with a note of solemn warning.[20]

## b. Miracles

The miracles of Jesus of Jesus were not an appendix to his ministry but an integral part of it. Matthew shows this in his Gospel when he brackets the Words of Jesus as proclaimed in the Sermon on the Mount (5:1-7:29) and the Deeds of Jesus in his "Miracle cycle" (8:1-9:34) with two summary statements (4:23 and 9:35). The three categories: teaching, proclaiming and curing appear in both summaries which are very similar.[21] In his response to the disciples of John who come to him with the question about whether he is indeed the Messiah (Mt 11:2), the Matthean Jesus responds with an allusion to passages in Isaiah which describe God's saving activity (Isa 29:18; 35:5-6). By ending his response with the words "and the poor have good news brought to them" after the list of healings of the blind, lame, lepers, the deaf and the raising of the dead, the Matthean Jesus shows clearly that there was no separation between the healings and the preaching and teaching. They were parts of one composite whole. One could even say that the good news that was being preached to the poor was that they were being made whole.[22]

---

19 *Ibid.*, 1125.

20 For a fuller explanation of the parable see I Howard Marshall, *The New International Greek Testament Commentary: The Gospel of Luke* (Paternoster Press, Grand Rapids, Michigan, 1978) pp. 632- 638, see also Fitzmyer (n. 7 above) pp. 1124-1134.

21 See, Grant R. Osborne, *Matthew/ZECNT,* (Zondervan, 2010) pp. 154, 364. France, R.T, *Matthew: An Introduction and Commentary*/TNTC, (Inter-Varsity Press, England, 1985) p. 109, 178.

22 France (n. 21 above) p. 195; Luz (n. 18 above) p. 133; Shelly Bruce, *The Collegeville Bible Commentary* (The Liturgical Press, Collegeville Minnesota, 1989) p 878; Osborne

Some of the miracles that Jesus performed were to reach out to the one in need.[23] However, the larger majority of miracles were performed with a view to communicate an important theological message not so much to the one being healed but to the witnesses of the miracle and especially the objectors. Thus, when Jesus heals the Man with the withered arm in the synagogue and on the Sabbath (Mk 3:1-6; Mt 12:9-14; Lk 6:6-11) the message is that the need of a human person takes precedence over the law. There are instances when the law may be transgressed and this is one of them.

This is also the case with the healing of the crippled woman on the Sabbath (Lk 13:10-17) which is exclusive to Luke. In his response to both the leader of the synagogue who raises the objection to healing on the Sabbath (Lk 13:14) and to others who also oppose that healing, Jesus responds logically and theologically. The logical response is seen when Jesus states that an ox or donkey is 'released' on the Sabbath so that they might drink water (Lk 13:15). The theological response is seen when Jesus prioritises the woman's healing even over the Sabbath.

In the context of the "cleansing of the temple" (Mt 21:12-13), Matthew states that Jesus healed the blind and the crippled who came to him in the temple (Mt 21:14). It seems that this insertion is deliberate because it is through these healings that Jesus also demonstrates what true worship means. This is worship in the truest sense of the word and is worship that is pleasing to God.[24]

## 3.2 Challenge on the Structural Level

## "Carefrontation"

To be sure, Jesus was not aware of the socio-economic structures of his time as we are today, [25] yet there is little doubt that he opposed legalism and casuistry.[26] It must also be noted that Jesus did not oppose for the sake of opposition and thus

(n. 21 above) p 414 shows how for every kind of invalid (blind, lame, leper, deaf, dead) mentioned by Jesus, there is an actual healing within Matthew's Gospel. Accordingly the healing of the blind is narrated in Mt 9:27-31; the lame in 9:1-8; the cleansing of the leper in 8:1-4; the healing of the deaf in 9:32-34 and the raising of the dead in 9:18-19, 23-26.

23 Mk 1:29-31 and parallels which narrates the healing of Simon's Mother-in-law; the summary of healings in Mk 1:32-34 and parallels.

24 Osborne (n. 21 above) p 763; France (n. 21 above) p 305; contra Luz (n. 18 above) p 12 who is of the opinion that 2 Sam 5:8 which restricts the blind and lame from coming into the Temple was never used in Judaism to regulate entry into the Temple. However, he considers it important that Jesus healed them in the temple and in doing so offered a sign that the gathering of the people of God had begun.

25 Carefrontation is defined as confrontation done in a loving manner https://en.wiktionary.org/wiki/carefrontation.

26 See G M. Soares-Prabhu, "Class in the Bible: The Biblical Poor as a Social Class?" *Vidyajyoti* 49 (1985) pp 322-346.

his approach was not one of confrontation but 'carefrontation'. He challenged his adversaries to see the folly of their ways. Thus when he 'carefronts' the scribes and Pharisees (Mt 23:13-33; Lk 11:37-52) it is with the intention that the crowds and his disciples (so Matthew) and the Pharisees, represented by the one who invited Jesus to dine (so Luke) will rise from concentration on the petty and insignificant to what was really important. The carefrontation in Luke concentrates largely on the fact that the externals have been made more important than the attitude of the heart.[27] Thus in his challenge to them Jesus invites then to get rid of greed and wickedness which lie within (Lk 11:39). These do not allow a person to be truly selfless. The call to "give for alms those things that are within" (Lk 11:41) is a call to magnanimity from within. Benevolence is an attitude more than an action. Three woes are pronounced against the scribes or lawyers. These have burdened people with the external observance of the law more than teaching an internal disposition (Lk 11:46). This burdening is seen in the scene where Jesus denounces the scribes again (Lk 20:45-47) and in the scene that follows (Lk 21:1-4). At the end of his denouncement of the scribes here, Jesus accuses them of devouring widows' houses (Lk 20:47). In the scene that follows, Jesus laments that a widow had to also put money in the treasury. She has been taught and encouraged by the religious leaders to donate as she does. Jesus thus condemns the whole value system that motivates her action. Jesus' words here are not words of praise for the widow's offering but words of lament at her plight.[28] They have also approved of their ancestors deeds who rejected the prophets (Lk 11:48).[29]The scribes are also accused of having interpreted the scriptures falsely and considered others as incapable of understanding them. Because of their false interpretation, they have not had an encounter with God and have prevented others from having this experience because of their pride.[30]

The woes in Matthew (23:13-33) are seven in number and the carefrontation here is even stronger than in Luke. In Matthew, both the scribes and Pharisees are accused in the first woe (23:13) of closing the door to the experience of God to others because of their own small-mindedness. The second woe (23:15) deals with the same subject matter but goes even further. Here the allegation is even more pronounced. Those whom they covert begin to imitate them in observing the letter of the law. In their doing so, they become even more fundamentalist than the ones who converted them. The three woes that follow (23:16-26) rebuke them for their minute concentration on what is of little or no consequence and their (conveniently?) overlooking what really

---

27 See Plummer Alfred (n. 7 above) pp. 309-315.

28 Fitzmyer (n. 7 above) X-XXIV p. 1320.

29 I Howard Marshall (n. 20 above) pp. 501-507.

30 See Plummer (n. 7 above) p. 314.

matters. The sixth woe (23:27-28) sharpens the contrast between the internal and external while the seventh reprimands them for their approval of their ancestors' lawlessness (23:29-31)[31]. It is not within the scope of this paper to discuss the historicity of these texts. The fact, however, is that it stands in the Gospels as canonical and we must contend with that. It may, therefore, be prudent and balanced to say that Jesus was carefronting not the persons but the narrow and restricting attitudes. These were carefronted especially when they resulted in injustice or harm to others.

In all the Sabbath controversies in the Gospels (Mt12:1-8 and parallels; 12:9-14 and parallels see also Jn 5:16-47), Jesus is shown as challenging the interpretation of the Sabbath. He intends that those who oppose him understand that the structure of the Sabbath was created as an aid. It ought not to become a hindrance which it does if one regards it as an end in itself which his opponents often did.

## 4. Liberation for Freedom and Love

When the Matthean Jesus states in his Inaugural Sermon (Mt 5:1-7:29) that he has come not to abolish but to fulfil the law (Mt 5:17) he means that while iotas and strokes of the law (Mt 5:18) have their place, they must be interpreted in the light of the love command (Mt 22:37-40). In Matthew unlike in Mark (Mk 12:31), the second command is "like" the first. Matthew thus highlights the importance of the second by means of "like". The love of neighbour is cited from Lev 19:18 and the context there (Lev 19:11-18) refers to neighbour as those who are "socially weak or an opponent in a court of law"[32] It is also in this context that the commands not to steal, deal falsely, lie, swear, defraud, rob, curse, render an unjust judgement, slander and hate (Lev 19:11-17) are given. Coming as it does at the end of these commands, it explains what love of neighbour means. In Matthew, 'neighbour' is expanded to include everybody. That this is so is clear from the sixth antithesis about love of one's enemy (Mt 5:43-48) and also from the Golden rule 'In everything do to others as you would have them do to you; for this is the law and the prophets.' (Mt 7:12)[33] Also when answering the rich young man (Mt 19:16-19) about the commandments, Jesus adds to the five commandments of the Decalogue (Ex 20:1-17) the command to love one's neighbour (Mt 19:19). This means that for the Matthean Jesus neighbour was a broad term that went beyond the narrow confines of tribe. Thus the core message of the kingdom was freedom from legalism and freedom for love.

---

31 For a detailed explanation of the woes see Luz (n. 18 above) Matthew 21-28, pp 111-137

32 *Ibid.*, p. 83

33 *Ibid*, p. 83.

This love because it is genuine and tangible (Jn 3:16) is a love which frees one for love. This freedom is both on the individual and societal level. On the individual level it is born out of a deep realisation of the unconditional love of God manifested in Jesus (1 Jn 4:10). This love frees us from the weight of the external law and challenges us instead to internalise the commands (Mt 5:21-48). It dares us to deny self (Mk 8:34) and to be detached from possessions (Mk 10:21) by stating that riches have a way of coming in the way of love of God and neighbour (MK 1:23-24; Lk 12:20; 16:31). This denial of self is not easy because many of us prefer to think that we can earn or merit God's love. We lay so much stress on self and our achievement that we behave like the elder son who protests that because he has been faithful and kept the commandments even to the letter of the law, he must now be given his rightful and 'earned' inheritance (Lk 15:25-32). This is also visible in modern times when in the New Revised Missal the end of the Eucharist Prayer II reads "Have mercy on us all, we pray, that with the Blessed Virgin Mary, Mother of God, with the blessed Apostles, and all the Saints who have pleased you throughout the ages, we may *merit* to be coheirs to eternal life, and may praise and glorify you through your son Jesus Christ.[34] It is not easy to accept that we have been *graced* and can merit nothing. This is one possible reason why Jesus found it so difficult to convey his message of love to those who depended on their own merit.

## Concluding Remarks

Even as it calls us to individual commitments to love it also invites us to do away with the structures that prevent such love. We live in a world in which the rich are getting richer and the poor poorer. A January 2017 study by Oxfam shows that just eight men own the same wealth as the poorest half of the world. It also quotes the President of the United States who said in September 2016 that we live in a world where 1% of humanity controls as much wealth as the bottom 99%. He went on to conclude that such an economy could never be stable.[35] There are many reasons for this inequality and we will need another paper to discuss these. Here, it is enough to say that the situation today is not

34 "Liturgy Office | Roman Missal." n.d. Accessed December 5, 2019.

35 Oxfarm Briefing Paper, "An Econmy for the 99%," https://www-cdn.oxfam.org/s3fs-public/file_attachments/bp-economy-for-99-percent-160117-en.pdf. Accessed December 5, 2019. It also states that since 2015 the richest 1% has earned more wealth that the rest of the planet. Over the next 20 years, 500 people will hand over \$2.1 trillion to their heirs – a sum larger than the Gross Domestic Product (GDP) of India which is a country of 1.3 billion people. The incomes of the poorest 10% of people increased by less than \$3 a year between 1988 and 2011, while the incomes of the richest 1% increased 182 times as much. In Vietnam, the country's richest person earns more in a day than the poorest person earns in 10 years.

very different from the time of Jesus. This is why his message which calls for a change of structures is still relevant today. Any structure which propagates and perpetuates the difference between the rich and the poor must be brought down (Lk 1:52-53) in favour of one which aims at lessening the difference.

Jesus did not provide a blue-print for such a society. However, his orientation provides us with enough matter to continue his work of making the Kingdom that he inaugurated and proclaimed a reality in our times. It is a kingdom where God will show himself to be king. The fast that is pleasing to the Lord and one which he chooses is "to share your bread with the hungry, and bring the homeless poor into your house; when you see the naked, to cover them, and not to hide yourself from your own kin?" (Isa 58:7). It is when this is done that "the Lord will answer; and say, Here I am." (Isa 58:9). This will be a move toward the vision of John in Revelation who sees the new heaven and the new earth for the former things have passed away (Rev 21:1-5).

2

# Jesus as Liberator: A Hermeneutical Reading of Lk 4:16-30

**Thomas Karimundackal SJ**
*Scriptural Studies, Jnana-Deepa Vidyapeeth, Pune*

**Abstract:** The Lucan story of Jesus' visit to Nazareth (Lk 4:16-30) is both *kerygmatic* and programmatic for its message and location in the gospel. Luke has deliberately put this story at the beginning of the public ministry of Jesus to encapsulate the entire ministry of Jesus and people's reaction to it. The narrative illustrates the liberative ministry of Jesus as a fulfillment of the OT prophecies (cf. Isa 61:1-2a; cf. 42:7; 58:6). It presents Jesus as the promised "anointed one", the sole liberator of humanity. The words of Lk 4:18-21 powerfully demonstrates Jesus' ministry of preaching, healing, and liberating the poor, blind, and oppressed. The narrative shows that in Jesus new hope abounds, and he leads people to liberation and transformation. This paper makes an attempt to understand the literary context of Lk 4:16-30, its sources, structure, and theological meaning.

**Keywords:** "Anointed one," Liberative, Kerygmatic, Programmatic, Poor, Blind, Captive, Oppressed

The Biblical passage Lk 4:16-30 is a programmatic passage in the gospel of Luke both for its location and for the message. It is at times referred to as the frontispiece or as the curtain-raiser. This pericope is foreshadowed in the prophesy of Simeon (Lk 2:34), and in a certain sense the entire ministry that follows (Lk 4:14- 9:50). The narrative emphasizes that the liberative ministry of Jesus is the fulfilment of the OT prophecies (cf. Isa 61:1-2a; cf. 42:7; 58:6). The narrative as it stands definitely has a programmatic character: the first part (Lk 4:16-22a) stresses the success dimension and the second part (Lk 4:22b-30) the failure dimension of Jesus' mission. The rejection of him by the people of his own hometown is a symbol of his eventual rejection by the Jewish nation. By its placement at the beginning of the Gospel, Luke makes Jesus' pronouncement on this occasion weighty and as a liberative paradigm for his ministry.

I am indeed happy to offer some reflection on this biblical passage (Lk 4:16-30), a passage that I have heard very often from Cyril Desbruslais in the class. He was so passionate with the mission mandate of Jesus in Lk 4:16-30, and challenged the students to embrace the liberative dimension of Jesus' mission manifesto in their future ministries. The Image of "Jesus as Liberator," that he had inculcated in our minds remains still fresh in my memory.

In this paper I make an attempt to understand the literary context of Lk 4:16-30, its sources, structure, and theological meaning with a special focus on the liberative character of Jesus' mission revealed in the text.

## 1. The Literary Context of Lk 4:16-30

### a. The Immediate Context

We find this programmatic text within a greater context of Jesus' Galilean ministry (Lk 4:14- 9:50). The section's basic theological question is who is Jesus? Who can do such works and teach with such power (cf. Lk 4:32)? Lk 4:16-30 initiates answers to these questions raised in Lk 4:14- 9:50. In quoting Isaiah (Isa 61:1-2), Jesus is presented as consciously aware of the influence of the Spirit upon him (cf. Lk 4:18), and the fulfilment of this very Old Testament prophecy (Lk 4:21). What Isaiah announced to the people of his day is now being announced to the poor, the prisoners, the blind, and the downtrodden of Jesus' day (cf. Lk 4:18-19). What was announced in a prophetic way to the exiles returning to Jerusalem by the prophet has now been turned by Luke into a prediction, the fulfilment of which is found in the person, words, and deeds of Jesus. But his own people fail to realize it and reject him (cf. Lk 4:28-29). When he finally slips away (cf. Lk 4:30), he becomes a 'liberator' to the gentiles, gentiles among the Jews of Galilee (cf. 4:31-44).

The pericope begins with the assertion that Jesus came to his hometown and went to the synagogue, as was his custom on the Sabbath (cf. Lk 4:16). Therefore, synagogal gatherings and Sabbath observance of the Jews gives us an understanding of the immediate context of the text.[1] The preceding pericope

1 Following procedure is normally followed for the prayer in the synagogue: "recitation of the Shema (Deut. 6:4-9), prayers (including some set prayers like the *Tephillah* and the *Shemoneh Esreh* [Eighteen Benedictions]), a reading from the Law, a reading from the

4:14-15 introduces and summarizes the nature of Jesus' ministry. Jesus is presented as the teacher filled with the power of the Spirit (Lk 4:14), and his teachings are appreciated by everyone (Lk 4:14). Although some news about his miracles has been circulated in Galilee, it is his teaching in the synagogue on a Sabbath draw most of Luke's attention (Lk 4:15).

## b. The Remote Context

Lk 4:16-30 would remind the Lukan audience, whether Jew or gentile, of the conflict they face with Jews who feel threatened by the Christian movement. In particular, the angry reaction to Jesus' statements about the widow and Naaman may partially parallel the effect of gentiles in the Church (whether of low or high status) on Jewish critics of the Lukan communities. The scene of Jesus in Nazareth would urge all Christian believers to recognize the importance of carrying Jesus' benefits beyond the 'in-group.'

The emphasis on good news for the poor (cf. Lk 4:18) stands in tension with the strong tendency in ancient Mediterranean society to regard the elite as those rightly favoured by gods and humans. The Lukan audience might need repeated reminders of Jesus' orientation toward the poor and other people in need. This passage may also intend to awake the disciple's faith and the subsequent teaching to them about discipleship, especially about rejection and suffering. For Luke, faith is understood as God's doing, and what matters is not the intellectual appropriation of some (*kerygmatic* or theological-historical) principles in which God can be captured, but a life in which God bears self-witness.

The synagogue as a centre of Jesus' activity parallels the church's activity around the synagogue or temple (Acts 3-4; 13). Christianity did not attempt immediately to isolate itself from Judaism. Rather, it saw itself as the natural fulfilment of Judaism's hope. Christianity conflicted with Judaism not because the new movement consciously tried to isolate itself from the nation, but because it was forced out. This rejection is evident in Acts, but the seeds are sown in the rejection of Jesus so carefully detailed in Luke 9-13 and 22-23. For Luke, the new community is broad in its extension of blessing because

---

Prophets, instruction on the passages, and a benediction. The Hebrew Scripture would be read in a standing position in one to three verse units. Then the text was translated into Aramaic, the local language, an oral procedure that often involved targumic renderings of the text. The Torah was always read, and often a reading from the Prophets followed. After the reading came an invitation for someone to instruct the audience. Based on the texts already read or on new texts, this instruction could be done by any qualified male in the audience, provided ten males were present," Darrell L. Bock, *Luke: 1:1-9:50,* (BECNT; Downers Grove, Inter Varsity Press, 1994), 403.

Jesus preached that it to be so (cf. Lk 4:16-30; 5:30-32; 19: 10; 24:44-47) and God directed that it to be so (cf. Acts 10:34-43; 15:1-21; 22:6-11; 26:15-20).[2]

The succeeding pericope (4:31-44) directs our attention to this remote context by presenting Jesus' successful preaching in Capernaum. The section begins with the healing of a demon-possessed man (v31-37), followed by the healing of peter's mother-in-law (v38-39) and a series of healings in the evening involving a variety of miracles (v40-41), and describing the nature of his mission (v42-44). The beneficiaries of Jesus ministry are the crowd including the man with unclean spirit, Simon's mother in law, various diseased persons with unclean spirits etc. So what Jesus has announced in Lk 4:18-19 is actualized in Lk 4:31-34. Lk 4:31-34 could almost be entitled 'a day in the Life of Jesus,' beginning with a synagogue service, moving from there to a home, the coming of the sick at sunset, and departure the next morning.

### c. Significance of the Context

Luke says nothing of the object of Jesus' teaching or proclamation in Lk 4:16-30. In fact, the narrative does not explicitly say that Jesus even read the passage from the Scripture. It only says that Jesus "unrolled the scroll" and "saw" the place where the relevant passage stood. All what Jesus says is the brief sentence regarding the prophet's words finding fulfilment. This reluctance of the evangelist to elaborate the discourse of Jesus is puzzling especially because everything that happens on the occasion is recorded in minute detail. Probably, it is done with a deliberate design. The implication is that Jesus' ministry is taking off then and there. Given the content of the citation of Isaiah (cf. Isa 61:1-2a; cf. 42:7; 58:6), Jesus' declaration "today this scripture has been fulfilled in your hearing" has the effect of identifying himself as the anointed bearer of the good news and defining his mission in terms of Isaiah's prophetic words. Both these elements are important aspects of the ministry of Jesus as Luke presents it.

## 2. The Sources of the Pericope

A synoptic reading of Lk 4:16-30 reveals its connections with Mark (Mk 6:1-6a) and Matthew (Matt 13:53-58).[3] Like Mark and Matthew, Luke contains a synagogue message, a question about heritage, a reference to a prophet without honour, and the comment about rejection in unbelief. But the picture is more complex than this. In the Markan and Matthean accounts, the sequence has

2 The situation of the Christian community of Luke is that of a typical Hellenistic city of the oriental part of the Roman Empire of the second generation, around 80 A.D., 50 years after the death of Jesus, represented by two classes: The elite, the rich and non-elite, the poor. So naturally, there were problems over table fellowship, gentile inclusion etc.

3 Following discussion is an adapted version of Bock's discussion of sources and historicity of Lk 4:16-30 in Bock, *Luke,* 394-395.

eight parts 1) entry into the synagogue; 2) astonishment at Jesus' teaching; 3) source of Jesus' wisdom questioned; 4) Jesus' kinship questioned; 5) the offense that some took at Jesus; 6) a prophet's lack of honour; 7) Jesus' stoppage of works there; 8) and Jesus' marvelling at their unbelief. In contrast, the Lucan account has thirteen elements, including three overlaps with the synoptic parallels (nos. 1, 7, and 9): 1) entry into the synagogue on the Sabbath (Lk 4:16; Matt. 13:54; Mk 6:2); 2) Jesus' standing to read Isaiah; 3) citation of the passage; 4) closing of the book; 5) Jesus' declaration that fulfilment has come today; 6) the crowd's speaking well of Jesus' gracious words; 7) Jesus' relationship to Joseph questioned (Lk 4:22; Matt 13:55-56; Mk 6:3); 8) the proverb that a physician should heal himself and do great works; 9) a prophet's lack of honour (Luke 4:24; Matt. 13:57; Mark 6:4); 10) the Elijah-Elisha parallel; 11) the crowd's filling with anger; 12) the crowd's desire to throw Jesus over a cliff; 13) Jesus' passing through the crowd.

For many scholars the present narrative is due to Lucan redaction of Mk 6:1-6, perhaps with the aid of some material drawn from tradition. However there are different positions regarding the source of the pericope.[4]

1. Scholars like Godet,[5] Lane,[6] Carson[7] argue that two distinct events are present. In addition, they argue that the summary of Jesus' ministry in 4:15 is background for the reference to the Capernaum miracles in 4:23. Without the summary, this allusion to Capernaum is a problem, since no event has yet occurred there.[8]
2. Many attribute the additions simply to Luke's hand for his own theological purposes.[9]

---

4 Following arguments have been taken from Bock, *Luke,* 396-397.

5 Cf. Godet, F., *A Commentary on the Gospel of St. Luke*. 2 vol. trans. E. W. Shalders and M. D. Cusin, (Edinburgh: Clark 1875), 240-241.

6 Lane, W.L., *The Gospel according to Mark* (NICNT; Grand Rapids: Eerdmans., 1974), 201 n.2.

7 Carson, D.A., "Matthew," in The Expositor's Bible Commentary, F. E. Gaebelein (ed.), (Grand Rapids: Zondervan).

8 Bock, *Luke*, 394.

9 "Often this position suggests that Luke's additions are only theological, not historical, since the Gentile theme alluded to in the Elijah-Elisha reference is not a major theme in the other Gospels. But such a capricious treatment of material is not in character for Luke, as Marshall shows. In addition, the Gentile theme is present in Gospel tradition and is a part of Jesus' teaching (Luke 20:9-19; Matt. 15:21-28; 21:33-46; Mark 7:24-30; 12:1-12). The presence of this theme in various sources reflects the possibility of multiple attestations and suggests its authenticity." Bock, *Luke,* 396. See Bultmann, R., *The History of the Synoptic Tradition*, trans. by J.Marsh, (New York: Harper & Row/Oxford: Blackwell, 1963) 31-32.

3. Luce[10] suggests that Luke combined two distinct events into a single event.
4. Some scholars like Schramm[11] argue that Luke has used an additional non-Markan source with material from Mark 6:9. Schramm shows that Mark cannot be the source for Luke 4:24, which on the surface looks like the strongest point of contact with Mark. Mark's direct influence on the account is less than clear in light of such considerations. This may suggest that Luke, instead of using Mark, has independent information.
5. Luke knows Mark 6, but chooses to use another source for this event. Marshall notes that the event is historically plausible and should not be challenged because of the presence of these additional features in Luke.[12] This approach to the problem is the most satisfying, since it recognizes Luke's research and summarizing hand in the material, while explaining how the parallels between the accounts can exist. It explains how the accounts can run so similarly without having much verbal overlap. If this is the correct view, Luke chose to follow his other source because of its detail.

The variety of suggestions offered above shows that there is no simple solution to determine the source of the narrative.

## a. Influence of the OT on Lk 4:16-30

### i. The book of Isaiah

The OT background of the Pericope is evident in Isa 61. This Servant Song-like passage describes the prophet's role in terms used of the Servant of Isaiah, especially in 42:1-4 and 49:1-11.[22] The figure of Isa 61 brings a message of God's deliverance to exiles. The deliverance imagery parallels the description of the Jubilee year (Lev 25:8-17), when debts were cancelled and slaves were freed every fiftieth year. The words of Isaiah relate closely to the Lucan portrait of Jesus and provide an interpretation of his ministry. In short, Isaiah 61:1-2 is presented by Jesus as a statement of his own commission from God.

10 Luce, H. K., *The Gospel according to St. Luke*, (Cambridge: Cambridge University Press, 1933), 121.

11 Schramm, T., *Der Markus-Stoff bei Lukas: Eine literarkritische und redaktionsgeschichtliche Untersuchung*, (Cambridge: Cambridge University Press, 1971), 37.

12 Marshal, I. H., The Gospel of Luke: A Commentary on the Greek Text, (Grand Rapids: Eerdmans, 1978), 179.

### ii. The Book of Kings

Jesus, who takes the role of prophet during his ministry, is governed by the purpose of God and the precedent of scriptural prophets. Therefore, his ministry will focus not on the in-group but on the excluded. The way the scriptural prophets behaved is indicated by two incidents, one involving Elijah, the other Elisha (cf. 1 Kings 17:1-24; 2 Kings 5:1-19). In both cases the brief story-summaries emphasize that there were many in Israel who might have benefited from the wonder-working prophet, yet it was actually a gentile who received the benefit. These incidents show that the work of a prophet is not guided and limited by in-group loyalties. Moreover, these cases provide scriptural precedent for the gentile mission in Acts. In one sense, they are out of place, for Jesus himself will seldom minister to gentiles. Yet the rejection Jesus will experience in Nazareth will be experienced by his witnesses in Acts, leading them to turn from Jews to gentiles (Acts 13:44-47; 18:5 7; 28:24-28; cf. also 22;17-22). It is possible that the widow and Naaman had further significance for the Lukan audience. The widow was a very poor woman; Naaman was the commander of the Syrian king's army, a wealthy man of high rank. Although both are gentiles, they could represent the social, economic, and gender diversity of the Lukan communities. Elijah and Elisha will serve as models of Jesus' healing ministry later in Luke.[13]

## b. Palestinian Coloration

Luke's Nazareth synagogue scene contains the earliest extant report of a synagogue service. Jesus is sometimes thought to be presented here as Messiah. In the OT *masiah*, "anointed one," is perhaps used of prophets in Ps 105:15 and 1 Chr 16:22. However, the idea of prophets as anointed servants of Yahweh does emerge in later pre-Christian Palestinian Judaism, e.g. in Qumran literature. Moreover, the "herald" (*mebassér*) of good news in Isa 52:7 appears in 11QMelch 18 precisely as one "anointed with the Spirit." The Melchizedek text from Qumran Cave 11 gives the use of Isa 61:1; 52:7 and Lev 25:9-13 providing an interesting Palestinian background to this distinctive Lucan story. Whether the "anointing" of Jesus is to be understood of the "prophetic" sort or the "heraldic" sort, it gives a nuance to his anointing which is not that of the political, kingly sort. This, too, makes it intelligible why Jesus is compared to Elijah and Elisha in the verses toward the end of the episode.

## c. Influence of the LXX

One of the characteristics of Luke is to resort to the style and the vocabulary of the LXX, so that his text has a 'veterotestamentary' coloration.[14] Jesus'

13 Tannehill, R. C. *Luke* (ANTC; Abington Press, Nashevelle 1996), 94.

14 Bovon, F., *Il vangelo di Luca,* 26.

citation (vv.18-21) comes from Isa 61:1-2 and, probably, from Isa 58:6. In its textual form, the citation is very close to the LXX in omitting repeated references to the divine name and in rendering a difficult Masoretic Text phrase as "sight to the blind."[15] The more significant differences with the LXX are as follows:

- In Luke 4:19, Luke uses the synonymous κερυξαι ("to preach") in place of the LXX's καλεσαι ("to call"). Luke's term, which suits his picture of Jesus' preaching ministry, was used traditionally to describe his work.[16]
- Luke omits the phrase "heal the broken hearted" (Isa 61:1). This change involves a text-critical problem, but the evidence is strong for the line's omission.
- If there is no Targumic reading of Isa 61 here, then there is a probable insertion of Isa 58. The linkage that creates the association of these texts could emerge from various terms: αφεσιν and αφεσει are parallel in the Greek texts (both terms mean forgiveness and differ only in case); *shalah* to send, appears in both passages; and *razon* 'acceptable' appears in Isa 61:2 and Isa 58:5. These Hebrew links make it possible that a traditional source is present. There is also the parallel Sabbath-Jubilee-year imagery in both Isaiah texts, a conceptual link to the Jubilee theme of Luke 4. In addition, Judaism linked Isa. 58 and Isa. 61.
- Luke's omission of the line in Isa 61:2 where God's vengeance appears is not so much a textual issue, but as a literary-theological one. It reflects a choice about how much of the passage to cite and why. The omission is theologically significant in that Jesus characterizes the current time as one primarily of release, and not of judgment, though he does have a warning later (Lk 4:24-27).[17]

## 3. Structure of the Passage

Finding a reasonable structure becomes a difficult task because of the presence of different motifs in the passage. Bock suggests a chiastic structure within this account.[18] In this view, the centre of the account is found within the citation:

15 Bock, *Luke*, 106-07

16 Bock, *Luke*, 316-17

17 Bock, *Luke*, 404-05

18 Bock, *Luke*,399.

the synagogue (4:16b)
standing (4:16c)
receiving the Scripture (4:17a)
opening the Scripture (4:17b)
preaching the good news (4:18c)
proclaiming release to the captive (4:18d)
giving sight to the blind (4:18e)
setting free the oppressed (4:18f)
proclaiming acceptable year of the Lord (4: 19a)
closing the Scripture (4:20a)
returning the Scripture (4:20b)
sitting (4:20c
the synagogue (4:20d)

The quotation in vv.18-19 can be seen again framed by a chiasm formed by the verbs ἀνέστη, ἐπεδόθη, ἀνοίξας ("stood up," "was handed," "unrolled" vv.16-17) and πτύξας, ἀποδούς, ἐκάθισεν ("rolled up," "handed," "sat down" v.20). The quotation itself is structured by the thrice-repeated "me" (ἐμε, με, με) and by the resolution of "to evangelize the poor" into parallel infinitive clauses. The juxtaposition of ἀπεστάλην, "I was sent," and εὐαγγελίσασθαι, "to preach good news," in 4:43 suggests that εὐαγγελίσασθαι πτωχοῖς, "to evangelize the poor," in 4:18c should be linked with ἀπέσταλκέν με, "he has sent me," (4:18d) rather than with ἔχρισέν με, "he anointed me" (4:18b).

As Bock notes "the broad outline of the chiasm is possible, though there are breaks at points. However it is better to speak of two cycles of presentation and rejection:"[19] cycle 1 is the speech and the crowd's doubt (4:18-22), and cycle 2 is the proverb with its following warning and the crowd's anger (4:23-29. The crowd's hostility grows in the account. The two cycles are bracketed by an introduction (4;16-17) and a conclusion (4:30), both of which may be Lucan narrative summaries.

Setting of the Scripture reading (4:16-17)
Cycle 1: Scripture reading and its exposition (4:18-21)
Cycle 1 response: the initial questioning of the crowd (4:22)
Cycle 2: a proverb and a historical picture of their rejection (4:23-27)
Cycle 2 response: the crowd's anger and hostile desire (4:28-29)
Jesus' departure (4:30)

19 Bock, *Luke*, 399.

## a. The Unity and Coherence of the Pericope

As we see from the structure, the sequence of sentences is not smooth. Part of the difficulty is because of the lack of clear logic in the development of the story from its first part to the second. It is fairly clear that two episodes have been fused together. The first one describing a successful visit of Jesus to Nazareth and it is contained in vv.16-22a. The second episode narrated an experience of rejection and it is found in vv.22b- 30.[20] As the episode now stands, there is a progressive build-up of popular reaction, but it takes place with conflicting reactions.

Verses 20-22 record the first reaction, a pleasant surprise at Jesus' gracious and learned words. We can see two parallel climaxes evidenced in vv.16-21: the first one brought about by the Isaiah's citation in vv.18-19 and the second by Jesus declaration in v.21b. The following figures bring it out:

1. He came to Nazaret → he went to the synagogue → he stood up to read → the scroll was given to him → he unrolled the scroll and saw (vv.18-19).
2. He rolled up the scroll → gave it back → sat down → all eyes in the synagogue → and he began to say to them → Jesus' pronouncement of the prophetic fulfilment (vv. 20-21).

However, immediately v.23 puts on Jesus' lips the first proverb, and his comment about the people's expectation.[21] They seem to reflect a context of sign-seeking that is really foreign to the foregoing verses. Verse 24 contains the second proverb and formulates a still more hostile reaction of non-acceptance or incredulity. But vv. 25-27 move the story into a still further dimension to the OT prophets and lack a strong connection with vv. 23-24. The ultimate reaction to Jesus takes the form of hostile, even diabolic, rejection, as he is led out of the town (v.29).[22] Therefore we can see that the passage from the first to the second part of the episode is not all smooth. The reason for the change in the attitude of the audience is not adequately explained. However, it should be noted that there is an essential continuity between what the former part established and what results from Jesus' words reported in the second.

## 4. Theological Meaning of the Text

The synagogue scene is recounted entirely with reference to Jesus' role, and a sense of his initiative dominates the narrative. Jesus is presented as reader of

---

20 Some authors even say that three separate stories are combined here (4:16-22a; 22b-24; 25-30).

21 The proverb and comment are introduced without apparent motivation and undoubtedly stem from an independent context or source.

22 Fitzmyer, A. J., *The Gospel According to Luke* vol. I., 528.

the synagogue lesson from the Prophets (vv.16-20) and as preacher for the day (vv.20-21). The centrality of the pericope is that the prophetic text now finds its fulfillment in him. His anointing signals appointment and empowering to be Isaiah's prophetic figure who heralds and brings salvation. The salvation in view is represented with Jubilee imagery, but is no call for an implementation of Jubilee legislation.

As a charismatic figure, Jesus speaks words with the power of God's grace (v.22). This grace guarantees a dramatic impact. Jesus' listeners testify to their experience of the presence of the Spirit in Jesus' words, and so to Jesus, by their involuntary amazement and thus head the ranks of impressed unbelievers whom Luke brings forward as witnesses for the claims of Christian faith (cf. Acts 4:13-16; 6:15). However, they are determined not to be drawn in, so at once they find grounds for objection: "Isn't this fellow Joseph's son?" At this point (v.23) Jesus takes matters out of their hands. Here, he plucks the words from his respondents' mouths by announcing to them what they were about to say. By means of a traditional proverb they intended to play off Jesus' claim to offer the glories of salvation against his own modest state (cf. 23:35). Jesus meets proverb with proverb (v.24). He responds as one who has been clearly rejected and interprets his rejection as a prophet's fate: it is the lot of the prophet to be rejected by those to whom he is sent (cf. 6:23; 11:47, 48-50; 13:33-34; 20:9-19; Acts 7:52; 28:25).

The conversation moves a stage further with the introduction of scenes from the ministry of the prophets Elijah and Elisha (vv.25-27). Here were instances of prophetic ministry from which the Israelites had not benefited: the many needy widows and lepers in Israel remained without help. So too the people of Nazareth will not benefit since they have chosen by their unbelief to be outsiders to what God is presently doing (cf. Acts 7:51). Labeled as those who reject God's prophets and identified as outsiders to what God is now doing, the people respond in murderous rage (v.28). They hustle him out of the city in order to send him to his death (v. 29). However, Jesus' hour has not yet come (cf. 22:3 and 53), so he escapes from their midst and continues on the way laid out for him in the divine pattern (v.30).[23]

### a. Jesus as the Messiah: the Anointed One

Jesus is presented as "the anointed One" with a message of good news. He is "the anointed One" to the poor, captive, and blind. Anointed with the Spirit, Jesus is the Messiah, the king of Israel, yet his immediate function is not royal but prophetic. The anointing of the Spirit here may refer to Jesus' baptism in

23 Nolland, J., *Luke 1:1-9:20* vol. 35A, (WBC, Dallas 1989), 202-03.

3:22 (cf. Acts 10:38) and the divine commissioning for Jesus' ministry.[24] Jesus' baptism was an anointing (ἔχρισέν με, "anointed me"). This anointing was not just a prophetic anointing (4:24) but a messianic one as well (3:22; Acts 4:26–27; 10:38),[25] for Jesus is the bringer, not just the herald, of salvation.[26] It is his anointing that makes Jesus "Messiah," and in being presented as Messiah, Jesus is presented as David's successor, Israel's long-awaited king. However, his statement, along with what follows, shows that he is both an anointed one and a prophetic figure (Lk 4:4-18-21). The Messiah - "the Anointed One" - is a direct derivative of the Hebrew word (*masih*) used in this passage. Luke would later record, "God anointed Jesus of Nazareth with the Holy Spirit and power, and he went around doing good and healing all who were under the power of the devil, because God was with him" (Acts 10:38).

## b. Liberation to the Poor

Bringing good news to the poor is considered as the prime motif of the anointed one in the episode (cf. Lk 4:18). Theologically the good news is brought to the poor in Spirit yet in Luke the "poor" means first of all those at the bottom of the economic scale, who may lack even the basics for survival. In the Gospel Luke pays special attention to Jesus' dealing with the poor and his teachings about poverty and wealth. The poor or rejected are mentioned in several instances (1:46-55; 4:18; 6:20-23; 7:22; 10:21-22; 14:13, 21-24; 16:19-31; 21:1-4). Therefore, "the poor" has a role in the mission manifesto of Jesus.[27]

In the *Magnificat* Mary praises God because "he has put down the mighty from their thrones, and exalted those of low degree; he has filled the hungry with good things, and the rich he has sent empty away" (1:52f). The shepherds

24 Anointing was a rite performed by a representative of God, usually involving oil poured on the head of an individual who was set apart for divine use (cf. 1Sam 10:1; 16:13; 1 Kgs 1:39; 2Kgs 9:6; Exod 29:7etc). The anointing conferred divine empowerment to accomplish the assignment.

25 Tannehill has argued that Jesus' anointing which refers back to the baptism 3:22 is royal, not simply prophetic, cf. Robert C. Tannehill, The Narrative Unity of Luke–Acts: A Literary Interpretation: Vo 1: The Gospel According to Luke, Foundations and Facets, (Philadelphia: Fortress, 1986), 58-59, 62-63. However, Fitzmyer holds that it is merely prophetic, Fitzmyer, J.A., *The Gospel According to Luke*, 2 vol, (Garden City: Doubleday, 1981-85), 529-30).

26 Although only Jesus was said by Luke to have been anointed by the Spirit (cf. Acts 4:26; 10:38), this term is also used for a model for Spirit-filled teachers and healers in Acts, cf. Robert H. Stein, vol. 24, *Luke* (Nashville: Broadman & Holman Publishers, 2001), 156.

27 Following explanation of the concept of poor in Luke is taken from Karimundackal, T., "Breaking the Barriers: The Challenge of the Church in India", in: *With Gratitude and Trust: Serving the Church and the Nation*, K. Pandikattu, S. Vazhapilly, and P. Lankapalli, (eds.), Papal Semianry, Pune 2019, 42-44.

to whom the angels came to announce the good news (2:8ff.) are from a poor class. Mary offers the offering of the poor for her purification (2:24; cf. Lev 12:8). Jesus' announces at Nazareth that at the center of his ministry is preaching "good news to the poor" (4:18). When he begins teaching, looking at his audience he says "blessed are you poor" (6:20). When he is asked to give his credentials of his identity, he tells the emissaries of John that "the poor have good news preached to them" (7:22). On a few occasions he commands his followers to help the poor (4:18; 12:33; 14:13). He praises the poor widow for her faith in God (21:1-4). On two instances Jesus calls on the would-be disciples to renounce or sell their possessions (12:33; 18:22; cf. 14:33). He exhorts his disciples to give to those in need (12:32-34) and to those who give banquets to invite "the poor, the crippled, the lame, the blind", rather than their rich friends (14:13).

Jesus pointed out the dangers of wealth and the impossibility of serving both God and money (16:13): "woe" to the rich (6:24-25); the parable of the rich fool (12:16-21); the parable of the unjust steward (16:1-13); the parable of the rich man and Lazarus (16:19-31); the rich young man (18:18-30). The rich are strongly warned in the "woes" of 6:24-26. According to Luke, as the rich have already received their comfort, they will be hungry, and they will mourn and weep (6:24-26). The rich fool builds large barns in view of the future, but God calls him to quick judgment (12:16-21). The parable of the unjust steward (16:1-13) leads Jesus to say that "no one can serve both God and wealth" (16:13). Luke alone tells the parable of the poor Lazarus and the rich man (16:19-31), a story that illustrates Jesus' special concern for those with few possessions. The rich young man refuses to sell what he has in order to follow Jesus, and consequently his attachment to the riches becomes a stumbling block to follow the Lord (18:18-30). The rich young man's attitude towards his possessions leads Jesus to say that "it is easier for a camel to go through the eye of a needle than for a rich man to enter the kingdom of heaven" (18:25). There are also warnings for the rich in the stories of Zacchaeus (19:1-10), and of the widow's mite (21:1-4). The point of all these stories is that there is a proper use of wealth. It is to be used to help the poor.

There is no teaching in the Gospel of Luke which is repeated more often than Jesus' blessings on the poor and his warnings to the rich. Luke is interested in the rich (19:2; 23:50), but he champions the poor because they needed a friend (1:53; 2:7, 8, 24; 4:18; 6:20, 21; 7:22; 14:13, 22; 16:20, 23). In short, Jesus concerns himself with the interests of the poor (1:53; 6:30; 14:11-13, 21; 16:19ff.), and preaching good news to them is characteristic of his ministry (4:18; 7:22).

## c. Liberation to the Captives

Jesus is sent to proclaim release for the prisoners. The term ἄφεσις translated "release" is more often in Luke translated "forgiveness,"[28] and indeed in its three other occurrences in Luke (1:77; 3:3; 24:47; cf. Acts 2:38; 5:31; 10:43; 13:38; 26:18),[29] it specifically means the forgiveness of sins, i.e., "release from sins". "Remembering that forgiveness implies restoration to or entry into the community, this mission of "release" would have important spiritual and social ramifications (cf. 5:27–32; 7:36–50)."[30] Forgiveness of sins is an important part of Jesus" ministry, and at the end of Luke, Jesus' followers are instructed to proclaim forgiveness of sins in his name (24:47).

The term ἄφεσις can be also used to mean 'release from captivity.' This is certainly its meaning in the context of Isaiah 61 and 58 and seems to be the dominant intent of Luke 4:18. Luke's view of Jesus' mission, as set forth in 4:18-19, to include preaching, physical healing, and exorcism.[31] It is also clear that the "release" made available through Jesus' ministry is set in opposition to the binding power of Satan (cf. 13:10-17 and Acts 10:38). We know that the healing in Jesus' healing ministry signifies not only physical healing but also signifies wholeness, freedom from both diabolic and social restrictions.[32]

## d. Liberation to the Blind

The "anointed one" was sent to proclaim recovery of sight to the blind (Lk 4:18). "Recovery of sight to the blind" refers at least to the literal healing of the blind which Jesus accomplished (18:35-43; cf. 7:21-22). It may also refer to the "seeing" which comes to those who are in darkness or are otherwise spiritually blind (1:78-79; 2:30-32; 3:6; 6:39; Acts 9:8-18; 13:47; 22:11-13; 26:17-18).[33] "It is also presented as a metaphor for receiving revelation and experiencing salvation and inclusion in God's family (cf. 1:78-79; 2:9, 29-

28 Mark C. Black, *Luke,* (Joplin, Mo.: College Press Pub., 1996), Lk 4:16.

29 See the further use of ἀφίημι-Luke 5:20, 21, 23, 24; 7:47 (2x), 48, 49; 11:4 (2x); 12:10; 17:3, 4; 23:34; Acts 8:22.

30 Joel B. Green, *The Gospel of Luke* (Grand Rapids, MI: Wm. B. Eerdmans Publishing Co., 1997), 211.

31 Esler, Philip F., *Community and Gospel in Luke-Acts: The Social and Political Motivations of Lucan Theology*, (Cambridge: CUP, 1987), 181-82 believes that "release" must be taken literally, so that the holding of thousands of Jewish slaves following the Roman conquest of 70 C.E. provides the *Sitz im Leben* for this mandate. But Luke does not develop this meaning anywhere in Luke-Acts.

32 Allison A. Trites and William J. Larkin, *The Gospel of Luke and Acts* (Carol Stream, IL: Tyndale House Publishers, 2006), 81.

33 Robert H. Stein, *Luke* (NAC; Nashville: Broadman & Holman Publishers, 2001), 156. The latter example is especially interesting because of the close parallels: sent-Luke 4:18

32; 3:6).[34] Jesus' words in Lk 4:18, then, work at two levels simultaneously: he will heal the blind, but that also pictures the coming of light to those in darkness (1:78-79). For example, "the healing of the blind man in 18:35-43 also pictures what Jesus does for Zacchaeus in 19:1-10."[35] The fact that Jesus physically healed the blind is an essential part of Jesus' testimony to John that he is "the coming One" (Lk 7:21-22). In his healing ministry, "Jesus cured many who had diseases, sicknesses and evil spirits, and gave sight to many who were blind" (7:21). Zechariah spoke of the Savior's ministry of recovery of sight for the blind when he said, "the rising sun will come to us from heaven to shine on those living in darkness and in the shadow of death, to guide our feet" (1:78). In short, Jesus would fulfill this ministry in both the physical and spiritual arena.

### e. Liberation to the Oppressed

The "anointed one" was also sent to let the oppressed go free (Lk 4:18). The 'oppressed' is a generic category, covering all those who are beaten down by sin, demons, sickness, circumstances, and other people.[36] The term τεθραυσμένους (*tethrausmenous*) literally means 'the broken ones', which figuratively means 'the oppressed,' 'the down-trodden,' socially and religiously. Luke pays unique attention to these 'broken ones' of the society in his gospel, namely gentiles (4:25-27; 7:9-10; 7:11-17), Samaritans (9:51-56; 10:30-37; 17:11-19), tax collectors (5:27-32; 7:34; 18:9-14; 19:1-10), lepers (5:12-16; 17:11-19), shepherds (2:8-20), men with unclean spirits (4:31-37; 8:26-39;9:37-43), the physically challenged (5:17-26; 6:6-11;13:10-17;14:1-6). In 15:1 Luke clearly tells his readers that 'the tax collectors and sinners were all drawing near to hear' Jesus. This is not an isolated incident, for Luke mentions many instances where Jesus goes against the traditional socio-religious barriers and embraces them with a liberative human touch.

In 5:27-32 Jesus purposefully welcomes a group of Israel's outcasts to his community, namely tax collectors, a group which has already been mentioned in 3:12-13 and will be seen again in 7:29, 34; 15:1; 18:10-14; 19:1-10. This episode also mentions Jesus eating with "sinners," an undefined group which Luke mentions some ten times in his Gospel (5:27-32; 7:28, 30, 34, 36-50; 15:1-2; 19:7). Luke tells us of Zacchaeus who was dismissed by the bystanders as 'a sinner' (19:7). To these we may add the people whose diseases rendered them "untouchable and outcasts". Jesus constantly ministers to and even

---

and Acts 26:17; sight-Luke 4:18 and Acts 26:18; release/forgiveness-Luke 4:18 and Acts 26:18. Cf. also Isa 42:7; 49:6; 58:8, 10.

34 Green, *Luke*, 211.

35 Bock, *Luke*, 403.

36 Black, *Luke*, Lk 4:16.

touches these “untouchable and outcasts”, whom others avoid at almost all costs, namely lepers (5:13), the dead (7:14), and people with various diseases (8:44-47). In the same way Luke recounts the story of the sinful woman who wept over Jesus’ feet and anointed them and of whom Jesus said that her many sins were forgiven (7:37-50).

In short, the “captives” and the “broken ones” (αἰχμαλώτοις, τεθραυσμένους) include both those who are in physical bondage, e.g., to sickness or demon possession, or in spiritual bondage to sin and death. The Good News is that now in Jesus all of creation has been freed from the bondage of its fallenness.[37] Therefore, Jesus’ statement that he liberates the oppressed makes it clear that he brings liberation to the suffering humanity.

## f. The Year of the Release and the Year of the Lord’s Favour

The anointed one was also sent to proclaim the year of the release and the year of Lord’s favour (Lk 4:19). “The year of the Lord’s favour refers to the opportune time in which Jesus’ listeners were privileged to live, the time of salvation for which the prophets longed.”[38] Here we have allusion to the jubilee year, which occurred every fifty years, the year of cancellation of debts in Lev 25:8-17. In the Jubilee year slaves were liberated, debts were forgiven, people returned to their homes and stopped all sowing and reaping. The people were to live in peace, plenty, and freedom (cf. Lev 25:8-17). The theme of jubilee is most evident in 4:18-19 by the repeated use of “release” (cf., e.g., “the year of release” - Lev 25:10) and the phrase, “the year of the Lord’s favour,” borrowed from Isa 61:2.[39] Jesus here builds on the picture of Isaiah’s ministry, and in fulfilling Isaiah’s prophecy Jesus was fulfilling the blessings of the year of jubilee, declaring it to be the year of the Lord’s favour.[40] In short, Lk 4:18-19 announces the eschatological epoch of liberation, the time of God’s gracious visitation, by presenting Jesus himself as its anointed herald.

## g. Liberation is “Here and Now”

Jesus declares that the time for liberation envisaged in Isa 61 is now. The adverb σεμερον (*semeron*) is scarcely to be understood in the generic sense of “nowadays” but as “today.” Given its emphatic position at the head of the clause (v.21b), it marks an important point in Lucan historical perspective. It is a key term in Luke’s theology and stresses that the opportunity for salvation

37 Arthur A. Just, *Luke 1:1-9:50* (St. Louis, MO: Concordia Pub. House, 1996), 193.

38 Mark C. Black, *Luke*, Lk 4:16.

39 It is now widely recognized that Isaiah 58 and 61 develop jubilary themes, describing the coming redemption from exile and captivity in the eschatological language of jubilary release.

40 Ken Heer, *Luke: A Commentary for Bible Students* (Indianapolis, IN: Wesleyan Publishing House, 2007), 78.

is this very moment. Luke uses repeatedly in his Gospel to make this point clear (cf. 2:11; 5:26; 12:28; 13:32-33; 19:5, 9; 22:34, 61; 23:43). According to Conzelmann, it stands in contrast to the Pauline declaration, "now is the acceptable time" (2 Cor 6:2), by which the Apostle identifies his own period as the *eschaton*[41] because Luke "sees salvation as a thing of the past," as something brought about in the Period of Jesus, the centre of time. However, the idea of current fulfilment in Acts 1:6 and 3:18 shows that the period associated with the church is a part of this "today".[42] Moreover, "it's recurrence in many passages also makes the point that the "today" is not so much a "now and only now" affair, as much as it is a timeless "now," a reference to the immediate present, when fulfilment is available and a life-changing decision can be made."[43] In short, the 'today' of Jesus is still addressed to all readers of the Gospel and assures them that the era of salvation is present.

## Conclusion

The Lucan story of Jesus' visit to Nazerath (Lk 4:16-30) has a definitive programmatic character as it sets the tone of Jesus' mission and ministry in the Gospel. Luke has deliberately put this story at the beginning of the public ministry of Jesus to encapsulate the entire ministry of Jesus and people's reaction to it. While the fulfilment-story stresses the success of his teaching under the guidance of the Spirit, the rejection story symbolizes the opposition that his ministry will evoke among his own.[44]

Luke's concern to stress the liberative dimension of Jesus' ministry is seen clearly in his use of Isaiah's texts (61:1-2a; cf. 42:7; 58:6). The words of Isaiah relate closely to the Lucan portrait of Jesus and provide an interpretation of his ministry. Isaiah 61:1-2 is presented by Jesus as a statement of his own commission from God. It is Luke's way of announcing that Jesus is the "anointed one" and God's sole instrument of liberation for all human beings (Acts 4:12). Isaiah's prediction primarily regarded the liberation of Israel from Babylonian captivity, but Jesus' proclamation of liberation is both spiritual and historical.

The words of Lk 4:18-21 speak powerfully of Jesus' ministry of preaching, healing, and liberating the poor, blind, and oppressed. It makes five points clear to the reader: (1) Jesus is anointed with the Spirit. In order to liberate the humanity from all sorts of bondages, the *Messiah* was to be "anointed" with

41 Conzelmann, H., *The theology of St. Luke*, trans. by G. Buswell (New York: Harper and row, 1960), 36-37. What Conzelmann means is that the term σεμερον limits the time of fulfilment to Jesus' earthly ministry.

42 Cf. Fitzmayer, J.A, *The Gospel According to Luke*, 533-534.

43 Bock, *Luke*, 412.

44 Fitzmyer, *The Gospel According to Luke*, 529.

the Holy Spirit and thereby empowered to carry out his divinely appointed role (4:18; cf. Acts 4:27; 10:38); (2) Jesus is the prophet of fulfilment who declares good news to the poor; (3) Jesus is the *Messiah* who brings release to the captives and oppressed, and sight to the blind, as well as the one who proclaims it; (4) This is the beginning of the fulfilment of God's promise, and Jesus is the source of that fulfilment, and (5) Through his reading, Jesus was announcing the coming of the messianic age, "the time of the Lord's favour." In short, Lk 4:16-30 is both *kerygmatic* and programmatic. Lk 4:16-30 presents Jesus as the promised "anointed one", the sole liberator of humanity. Jesus' life and ministry bring God's promises to completion, just as he has inaugurated them. In Jesus new hope abounds, and he leads people to liberation and transformation.

3

# Human Flourishing: Towards Fullness of Life for All Persons and the Entire Ecosystem

**Patricia Santos RJM**
*Faculty of Theology, Jnana-Deepa Vidyapeeth, Pune 411014*

**Abstract:** Human flourishing is gathering increased interest across disciplines. It is also being explored from different angles within each discipline by scholars who highlight or focus on a specific aspect of flourishing. From a theological outlook, flourishing as wholeness or fullness of life if a gift from God as well as a task to be accomplished. This article integrates and builds on some of the varied aspects of flourishing as reflected in the different disciplines of philosophy, psychology, education, anthropology, ecology and spirituality from a feminist theological perspective in order to present a synthesized theological understanding of flourishing as fullness of life for all persons and the entire ecosystem. An integral view of flourishing must take into consideration the context, experiences and the interconnections within and between the self, others, God and all of creation.

**Keywords:** Human Flourishing, Ecosystem, Virtuous life, Eudaimonism, Agapeic Love

The word 'flourish' comes from the Latin *florire* or *florēre*, the Anglo-French *flurir* or *florir*, and Middle English *florisshen,* which simply means to bloom or flower.[1] When referring to plants and animals it infers a growth that is

1 Cf. Frank R Abate, "Flourishing," *The Oxford Desk Dictionary and Thesaurus American Edition* (Oxford: Oxford University Press, 1997); Jonathan Crowther Oxford,

expanding, increasing and luxuriant; whereas for humans the references are for thriving and prospering. Other overtones of the word include prosperity, wealth, happiness, success, creativity, production, progress, height of development, excelling, well-being, healthy growth and being in one's prime.[2] While there is some association between these different senses of the term, there are also subtle differences. Hence, the implication of flourishing may vary depending on which connotation is chosen and highlighted. Since flourishing involves living one's life in the best way possible, it requires favourable and enabling internal and external conditions. In order to offer an integral, interconnected and inclusive perspective of flourishing that befits all persons and all creation, I integrate some of the different aspects of flourishing across the disciplines of philosophy, positive psychology, sociology, education, sociology, theology and spirituality.

## 1. Flourishing as a Well-Lived Virtuous Life

There is a renewed interest in human flourishing in the field of philosophy and ethics with contemporary moral and social philosophers reflecting back on the Aristotelian notion of *eudaimonia* or the well-lived life culminating in virtuous activity or good action.[3] Aristotle's account of *eudaimonia* focused on the teleological fulfilment of human nature through rational agency and the cultivation of virtue, which was not for the individual alone but for the good of the society.[4] However, women and slaves were excluded as they were not seen to be capable of rationality. Mary Grey, ecofeminist liberation theologian, acknowledging the philosophical roots of flourishing in Aristotle's *eudaimonia,* sees the need for flourishing to be lifted "out of Aristotle's context", which identified it mainly with rationality, so that it can have significance for all people and the earth.[5]

Douglas Rasmussen, a neo-Aristotelian ethicist, considering the connection between human flourishing and human nature, sees flourishing or human good as "objective, inclusive, individualized, agent-relative, self-

---

"Flourishing," *Oxford Advanced Learners Dictionary of Current English* (Oxford: Oxford University Press, 1995).

2 Cf. Abate, "Flourishing," 296; Oxford, "Flourishing," 450; J. A Simpson and E.S.C, "Flourishing," *The Oxford English Dictionary* (Clarendon Press, 1989), 1087–88.

3 Cf. Rosalind Hursthouse, "Virtue Ethics," *The Stanford Encyclopedia of Philosophy*, 2013, accessed January 26, 2017, http://plato.stanford.edu/archives/fall2013/entries/ethics-virtue/; Ellen Frankel Paul, Fred D. Miller, and Jeffrey Paul, eds., "Introduction," in *Human Flourishing* (New York, NY: Cambridge University Press, 1999), vii–xiv.

4 Cf. "Aristotle's Ethics," *Stanford Encyclopedia of Philosophy*, accessed April 10, 2018, https://plato.stanford.edu/entries/aristotle-ethics/.

5 Mary C. Grey, "The Shape of the Human Home - A Response to Professor T. Gorringe," *Political Theology* 2, no. 1 (2000): 95–103.

directed and social".[6] Rasmussen upholds human flourishing as "a self-directed activity" that involves actualizing one's potentialities through one's own efforts.[7] Flourishing is perceived as universal yet highly personal by Rasmussen, who in continuation with Aristotle stresses the necessity of theoretical and practical wisdom in exercising agency to achieve wholeness. This is because while all human nature has a capacity for flourishing, each person needs to exercise moral virtue, rational agency and practical wisdom to live a meaningful life and reach perfection or excellence.[8] When striving towards perfection, Rasmussen does not discount concern for others, community and culture, but he considers human choice and human good as unique and totally personal. This view of human flourishing seems quite limited and individualistic with its emphasis on self-direction, rational agency, virtuous activity, personal striving, human effort and self-fulfilment. In defending his position against individualism, Rasmussen highlights the role of practical wisdom in human flourishing, which requires personal discernment in making moral choices for each action depending on every situation.[9] Proper exercise of practical wisdom allows humans to manage their life intelligently, utilizing and enjoying the necessary goods and virtues in a humanly fitting manner.[10] This attention to discernment, choice and pursuit of self-perfection upholds the rational aspects of the individual person but does not consider the social, emotional and spiritual requirements necessary for human flourishing.

Doris Kieser, associate professor of theology and ethics, tracing the history and moral theory of flourishing, incorporates and revises some of the views of Rasmussen on flourishing as self-directed virtuous activity.[11] Though Rasmussen stresses practical wisdom as essential for virtuous living, Kieser thinks that for practical wisdom to be realized fully, a person requires "communal living, maturity, personal integrity, intelligence, and self-awareness".[12] The emphasis for Rasmussen is on individual responsibility and agency, whereas for Kieser flourishing is relational and integrated, involving the individual and community, and dependent on universal and particular experiences of humans.[13] Kieser considers flourishing in relation to people's

---

6 Rasmussen, "Human Flourishing and the Appeal to Human Nature," 3.

7 *Ibid.*, 10.

8 Cf. *Ibid.*, 42.

9 Cf. *Ibid.*, 16–17.

10 Cf. *Ibid.*, 17.

11 Cf. Doris Kieser, *Catholic Sexual Theology and Adolescent Girls: Embodied Flourishing* (Ontario: Wilfrid Laurier University Press, 2015).

12 *Ibid.*, 12.

13 *Ibid.*, 11.

actual everyday lives within their particular context and community.[14] Kieser also brings in a spiritual component to flourishing as virtuous activity, wherein exercising and striving towards virtuous actions is geared towards union with the divine, where the fullness of human flourishing is one's union with God.[15] God is thus the "ultimate good" and virtuous activity is "seeking to do the good that is God's will".[16]

In her regard of flourishing as union with God, Kieser affirms the view of Thomas Aquinas (1225-1274), who adapted to some extent Aristotle's *eudaimonism*. For Aquinas, the telos to which all humans aspire, consists in "beatitude" which is mystical union with God leading to the ultimate good or perfection.[17] A virtuous life alone cannot lead to beatitude. For Aquinas, along with virtuous activity humans need God's grace to attain complete happiness.[18] Aquinas therefore connects virtues with the gifts and fruits of the Spirit. The problem with Aquinas arises, however, because he sees virtue as the power of the soul, which is seen as separate from the body.[19] Kieser makes no such distinction between body and soul. For Kieser, God is to be known and loved "as embodied persons - soul in flesh, flesh in soul".[20] Flourishing is not just a desired end or goal for the soul to be united with God, but an ongoing "journey into and with the heart of God".[21] The body with all its sensory experiences is the medium through which the mind can reason and discern the movements of the Spirit. Thus, physical, emotional, sexual and spiritual needs must be considered for flourishing.[22] Kieser's primary concern in exploring flourishing is in the context of sexual flourishing of adolescent girls. Her research focusses on universal virtues, values and moral behaviour in sexuality, which affect the embodied sexual flourishing of girls. Her reflections remain within the realm of natural law and are mainly confined to taking the experiences and contexts of adolescent girls into consideration for sexual flourishing. Nevertheless, Kieser offers a significant contribution to thriving and flourishing, by including the physical, intellectual, emotional, social, ethical, and spiritual requirements

14 *Ibid.*, 13.

15 Cf. *Ibid.*, 14.

16 *Ibid.*, 14.

17 *Ibid.*, 13, 24, 25, 26.

18 Cf. Thomas Aquinas, *Summa Theologica (Complete and Unabridged)*, trans. Fathers of the English Dominican Province (Claremont, CA: Coyote Canyon Press, 2010), 12, 35, 49, 55.

19 Aquinas, sec. I–II, QQ.55.

20 Kieser, *Catholic Sexual Theology and Adolescent Girls*, 14.

21 *Ibid.*, 22.

22 Cf. *Ibid.*, 2.

for flourishing. These involve fulfilment of one's basic needs for survival, freedom, dignity, relationships, self-esteem, knowledge and meaning in life.[23]

Although flourishing as virtuous activity has been upheld by Rasmussen and Kieser, there are other scholars such as Nicholas Wolterstorff and George Terzis who have certain reservations with this virtue-based view and offer a critique to the *eudaimonist* virtue ethics.[24] Nicholas Wolterstorff, Professor Emeritus of philosophical theology, finds *eudaimonist virtue ethics* to be very narrow and limited. From the different philosophical understandings of flourishing, Wolterstorff observes three ways of perceiving a good life.[25] The view of a good life from the utilitarian tradition is one that is "experientially satisfying", or one that is good for the individual person.[26] A good life in the *eudaimonist* tradition is the life well-lived wherein a person makes a deliberate choice on the basis of what he/she thinks will allow for living one's life well. This life is oriented towards agency and virtuous activity, whereby the excellence of one's life is the yardstick and not the good or excellence of others. Wolterstorff, judging both these views as inadequate from a Christian perspective of love and justice, considers a third way of a flourishing life which is one that is "both lived well and goes well".[27]

A life that is lived well and goes well, for Wolterstorff, is one in which a person has inherent rights based on one's worth as a human person and hence deserves to be treated well. Thus, flourishing is not only about living a virtuous life but having the right to being respected and treated with dignity by others. Wolterstorff's reflections thus move from individual agency to social relationships defending justice based on rights as prescriptive for good relations between oneself and others.[28] Love and justice, for Wolterstorff, involve caring about the well-being of oneself and others, honouring the rights of all people and treating everyone with due respect on the basis of their worth.[29] This view of flourishing takes into account human worth as stemming first from

23 *Ibid.*, 9–10.

24 Cf. Nicholas Wolterstorff, "God's Power and Human Flourishing," The God and Human Flourishing Program (New Haven, CT: Yale Center for Faith and Culture at Yale Divinity School), accessed April 15, 2018, https://faith.yale.edu/sites/default/files/nicholas_wolterstorff_-_gods_power_and_human_flourishing_0_0.pdf.; George N. Terzis, "Human Flourishing: A Psychological Critique of Virtue Ethics," *American Philosophical Quarterly* 31, no. 4 (1994): 333–42.

25 Cf. Nicholas Wolterstorff, *Justice. Rights and Wrongs* (Princeton, NJ: Princeton University Press, 2008), 145; See also Wolterstorff, "God's Power and Human Flourishing."

26 Wolterstorff, *Justice*, 145.

27 *Ibid.*, 145.

28 Cf. *Ibid.*, 4, 263.

29 Nicholas Wolterstorff, *Justice in Love*, Emory University Studies in Law and Religion (Grand Rapids, MI and Cambridge: William. B. Eerdmans, 2011), 101.

God's love and not any human capacity or function which then makes one accountable to show love, care and respect for oneself, others and God.

Another critical assessment of the *eudaimonistic* perspective of flourishing is offered by George Terzis, for whom the virtue ethics view of flourishing does not consider an individual's "actual motivational capacities" in pursuing a life suited to one's unique personality.[30] In order to live well and flourish, self-awareness and self-understanding are crucial for humans to discover and develop their core traits.[31] To build on one's strengths in the light of one's core traits, it is necessary to evaluate which traits are basic to one's nature. Terzis thus favours a "trait-relative" view of flourishing using a psychological framework by which the character traits a person needs to flourish must be in accordance with one's central traits.[32] Thus, flourishing for Terzis, does not consist only in a successful life but a successful way of life specifically motivated in accordance with one's unique core traits.[33] While Terzis makes a shift from general virtues to specific traits, the focus is still very much only on the individual. The positive contribution made by Terzis is the necessity of self-awareness and self-understanding for flourishing, which is also considered important for Kieser.

In considering flourishing as a well-lived life of virtuous activity, the exercise or practice of virtues is essential to live a good life. The insights of Wolterstorff and Kieser offer a wider scope of flourishing from a preoccupation with individual virtuous living for a better life in the future, to living a good life in the present in relation to oneself, others and God.

## 2. Flourishing as Optimal Well-being

Optimal well-being is the key focus of positive psychology, which integrates virtues, character strengths and traits in considering psychological and social development. Positive psychology tried to shift the focus from mental illness, pathology and disease to positivity, wholeness and capacity building. While strengths and virtues were considered important for happiness by ancient philosophies and religions, it was Martin Seligman, who initiated the positive psychology network in 1999.[34] Seligman opined that much of one's thinking

30 Terzis, "Human Flourishing," 333.

31 Cf. ibid., 336–37.

32 *Ibid.*, 340.

33 *Ibid.*, 340.

34 Martin Seligman is the director of the Positive Psychology Centre at the University of Pennsylvania and founder of positive psychology. Cf. Shane J. Lopez and C. R. Snyder, *The Oxford Handbook of Positive Psychology (New York: Oxford University Press, 2011), 7–8.*

revolved around the wrong or negative, rather than on what is right, leading to unnecessary anxiety and stress.[35]

What matters, for Seligman, is to increase one's strengths and create positive conditions, rather than worry about reducing one's misery or analysing what is going wrong. This does not mean that Seligman discounts negative circumstances and traumatic events. On the contrary, for Seligman, well-being and flourishing can be reached even in adversity through education and training in becoming more resilient, optimistic and empowered. In countering negativity Seligman emphasizes the need to cultivate and reinforce strengths and virtues rather than try to get rid of the obstacles. In the case of negative emotions, Seligman advocates acquiring knowledge on how to function well in the midst of distress, rather than only minimizing the negative emotion or removing the disabling conditions.[36] Human flourishing, according to Seligman, requires the development of five interconnected elements under the mnemonic *PERMA* – positive emotion, engagement, relationships, meaning and accomplishment.[37] Seligman developed a number of exercises to build the positive and to become aware of one's blessings and gifts.[38] However, these exercises do not offer ways to deal with distress and know how to flourish in adversity. The contribution of Maureen Gaffney on how to achieve well-being when facing adversity, complements this lacuna in Seligman's approach.[39]

For Gaffney, flourishing is neither just about building positive virtues, strengths, traits, emotions and relationships, nor wiping away all the negativity and problems from one's life. Flourishing involves finding "the right balance between the positive and negative" in one's thoughts, emotions, behaviours and relationships, in order to overcome challenges and transform setbacks.[40] The right ratio between the positive and negative, identified by Gaffney, is 5:1, because the negative emotions and reactions are more powerful and have a much greater impact on the flourishing of humans.[41] It is a known fact that one mistake or negative remark is sufficient to wipe out all the good done by persons. In families, communities as well as in organizations, lack of support accompanied by hurtful or discouraging remarks affects one's wellbeing, and

35 Cf. Seligman, *Flourish*, 33.

36 Cf. *Ibid.*, 51.

37 Cf. *Ibid.*, 16–24.

38 For instance, the "Kindness Exercise"; "The Gratitude Visit"; "What-Went-Well Exercise (Also called 'Three Blessings')"; "Signature Strengths Exercise". Cf. *Ibid*, 20, 30, 33, 38.

39 Cf. Maureen Gaffney, *Flourishing: How to Achieve a Deeper Sense of Well-Being, Meaning and Purpose – Even When Facing Adversity*, Kindle ed. (Dublin: Penguin, 2011).

40 *Ibid.*, x, xi.

41 Cf. *Ibid.*, 25, 43.

therefore it is necessary to build the positive five times more than the negative.[42] The threshold of flourishing as 5:1 is significant for Gaffney, since normal functioning requires a minimum ratio of 3:1.[43] Anyone having a positive-negative ratio below 3:1 is said to be languishing. Nonetheless, Gaffney thinks that too much positivity can also be problematic, and hence the threshold ratio of positivity to negativity arrived at through empirically tested studies is "between 3:1 and 11:1".[44] Acknowledging Aristotle's perception of flourishing as the teleologically oriented life of excellence, Gaffney sees flourishing as an intrinsic capacity to live currently in the best way possible. Each person, for Gaffney, exhibits "three related but quite distinct 'selves' or modes of being in the world" – the usual ordinary "good but not great self", the "best self" and the "worst self".[45] Humans keep fluctuating daily between these three modes. The main sign of a flourishing life, for Gaffney, is being for most amount of time at one's best self. However, it is difficult to ascertain what being at one's best self really implies and if this is the same for all persons in all contexts.

Gaffney considers four elements essential for the flourishing of any individual – owning and facing challenge; connectivity within and around; autonomy as sufficient control to make significant choices; and using one's special or valued competencies – all of which need to be exercised in combination and proper balance.[46] The deciding factors to determine if one is flourishing require a right combination and proper balance of the four elements. Thus, the more people take responsibility for their lives and choose to live out their roles in freedom to the best of their ability, the more they will be able to deal with the challenges that beset them, which will consequently lead to their flourishing. In the second part of her book on Flourishing, Gaffney outlines ten strategies which focus on nurturing a flourishing life by building one's positivity, resilience, capacity for happiness, meaning and engagement, as well as understanding oneself and setting goals. [47] These tools can help to understand oneself and to be in control of one's thoughts and feelings; but they place the full responsibility of flourishing on the individual person without considering relationships and the community.

Flourishing as virtuous activity required more of rational agency in practicing the virtues whereas Seligman's and Gaffney's views on wellbeing and flourishing call for awareness and acceptance of feelings and emotions along with the right motivation and appropriate interpretation of one's thoughts,

---

42 Cf. *Ibid.*, 77.

43 Cf. *Ibid.*, 24–43.

44 *Ibid.*, 39–41.

45 *Ibid.*, 3–4.

46 Cf. *Ibid.*, 6.

47 Cf. *Ibid.*

feelings and actions. While Seligman's theory of well-being is descriptive based on empirical findings, Gaffney's work goes deeper into understanding the power of the positive and negative; reflecting on how people think, feel and behave; and evaluating how one can work towards finding the right balance between the positive and negative. Although psychological, intellectual and emotional aspects of flourishing have been considered in this approach of optimal well-being, there is a further need to include the social and spiritual dimensions for the integral development of all persons.

## 3. Flourishing as Creating Just Opportunities for Human Functioning

The insights of Martha Nussbaum, feminist philosopher and professor of law and ethics, on flourishing move beyond an emphasis on individual striving towards well-being to the necessity of considering the opportunities available to persons in order for them to develop and flourish.[48] What is of prime importance for Nussbaum, is ensuring that all persons, especially women and other marginalized persons, have the basic capabilities or opportunities to function fully as humans. The choices that they then make towards achieving their well-being depends on each individual. Thus, Nussbaum's concern is with providing universal norms to uphold and protect human rights, leaving freedom for humans to make their own choices.[49] Nussbaum finds value in some of Aristotle's political and ethical thoughts and his views on *eudaimonia* as virtuous self-directed action, which she recognizes as one of the earliest significant sources for the *Human Development* or *Capability Approach*, initiated by Indian economist Amartya Sen and further developed by her.[50] The concepts of justice and freedom assume priority in Nussbaum's approach. Nussbaum's work also incorporates some of the aspects found lacking in the *eudaimonist* virtue ethics such as motivation, emotions, self-understanding and religion. Although Nussbaum considers religion as an important value for people to find ultimate meaning in life, she includes it with the "capabilities of the senses, imagination, and thought", and with "affiliation", as religion does not need to be separately protected by public policy. [51] Thus, religion and spirituality do not have a unique place in the capabilities enlisted by Nussbaum, even though she acknowledges the value of religious traditions as significant sources for defending human rights and ushering social transformation.

---

48 Cf. Martha C. Nussbaum, *Creating Capabilities: The Human Development Approach* (Cambridge, MA and London: Harvard University Press, 2011).

49 Cf. Martha C. Nussbaum, *Women and Human Development: The Capabilities Approach* (New York, NY - Cambridge: Cambridge University Press, 2001), 106.

50 Cf. Nussbaum, *Creating Capabilities*, 17-20, 23.

51 Nussbaum, *Women and Human Development*, 179.

Concerning Seligman's views on authentic happiness and flourishing, Nussbaum acknowledges that some of his insights concerning a positive meaningful life of activity, are in keeping with the principle of Aristotle's *eudaimonist* virtue ethics, which aim towards living an active virtuous life of excellence.[52] At the same time, Nussbaum finds Seligman's claim that positive emotions are necessary for flourishing to be misleading.[53] Emotions, for Nussbaum, are neither good nor bad in themselves since they are "conceptually interconnected" and depend on the evaluation of their worth and the beliefs that accompany them.[54] For example, one expresses grief at the death of a loved one, or one could have righteous anger for an injustice or punishment meted out to an innocent person. These are appropriate emotions for Nussbaum, but positive emotions arising out of negative or selfish activities cannot be good in themselves. Nussbaum questions whether privileged persons enjoying a luxurious life can be said to be happy.[55] Hence, while all positive emotions may not necessarily be valuable or virtuous; there could be some negative emotions that have value in themselves if they are appropriate for a good cause. Nussbaum's *Capabilities Approach* (CA), thus, to some extent, builds on the views of flourishing as virtuous activity and optimal well-being, though she is more concerned with public policy to create opportunities for people to flourish.

Nussbaum is convinced that the *Capabilities Approach* could serve well to respond to the inequalities, deprivation and problems of human life universally, since most of the central concerns, issues and problems are applicable to all people even if they differ in value according to each context. Capabilities for Nussbaum are "not just abilities residing inside a person but also the freedoms or opportunities created by a combination of personal abilities and the political, social, and economic environment".[56] In the development of the capabilities, Nussbaum sees the importance of the concept of threshold, which is the "basic social minimum" for each capability, that is required for a person to live a decent human life and that should be made available for all citizens by their governments.[57]

For Nussbaum, flourishing is the basic ability to live fully with dignity and freedom. Although her approach is based on Aristotle's concept of

52 Cf. Martha C. Nussbaum, "Who Is the Happy Warrior? Philosophy Poses Questions to Psychology," *Journal of Legal Studies* 37, no. S2 (2008): S88-92; Cf. Seligman, *Authentic Happiness*.

53 Cf. *Ibid*., "Who Is the Happy Warrior?"

54 *Ibid*., S94.

55 *Ibid*., S98.

56 Nussbaum, *Creating Capabilities*, 20.

57 Nussbaum, *Women and Human Development*, 12, 75.

*eudaimonia,* it does not imply living to the best of one's ability or striving towards a life of excellence, as required by Aristotelian virtue ethics. The emphasis for Nussbaum is on the necessary opportunities created for humans to live well, and the freedom they can have to choose what they value or consider best to live well.

Merridy Wilson-Strydom and Melanie Walker, applied some of Nussbaum's central capabilities to the field of higher education to promote greater social and moral consciousness and well-being among university students.[58] Their main concern was to observe whether "students are flourishing within educational environments", and in what way "education enables flourishing in other aspects of life".[59] From among the ten capabilities enlisted by Nussbaum, Wilson-Strydom and Walker consider "Practical Reason" and "Affiliation" to be most important for students.[60] They also observe a difference in the approaches of positive psychology and the Capabilities Approach (CA) concerning well-being. The emphasis in positive psychology is on individual wellbeing, whereas with the CA, agentic choices are made on the basis of moral judgements and social relationships for the well-being of the individual as well as for the protection of institutions that can nurture morality and relationships.[61]

When evaluating the flourishing of students, one cannot assess it on the basis of academic achievement alone. One must take into consideration the opportunities provided for affiliation and practical reasoning, as well as look at the social structures of race, class and gender, which either limit or enable a student to flourish.[62] Thus, for Wilson-Strydom and Walker, flourishing can be attained by providing opportunities to students for human development, for the formation of moral and social consciousness and for exercising agency.[63]

A positive point in Nussbaum's approach is that it aims at respecting "each person's struggle for flourishing" and treats "each person as an end and as a source of agency and worth in her own right".[64] Nussbaum sees the importance of leaving space for individual choices, considering the socio-

58 Cf. Merridy Wilson-Strydom and Melanie Walker, "A Capabilities-Friendly Conceptualization of Flourishing in and through Education," *Journal of Moral Education* 44, no. 3 (2015): 310–24. Merridy Wilson-Strydom is associate professor of Higher Education Studies and Melanie Walker is the Director of the Centre for Research on Higher Education and Development.

59 *Ibid.*, 311

60 *Ibid.*, 312.

61 Cf. *Ibid.*, 312, 313.

62 Cf. *Ibid.*, 315.

63 Agency for Wilson-Strydom and Walker is "about having opportunities and choices as well as the autonomy to be able to make one's own decisions." See *Ibid.*, 314.

64 Nussbaum, *Women and Human Development*, 69–70.

cultural and historical context, needs, capacities, obstacles and values of people. For Nussbaum, what matters is the freedom that all persons must have to make choices, without forcing them to act in a particular way, since the context determines one's desires and choices.

## 4. Flourishing as an Inherent Potential

In the above three views of flourishing that I have identified, namely that of a well-lived life of virtuous activity, well-being and optimal living, and creating just opportunities, flourishing can be perceived as an activity or something that must be achieved. When reading the work of Sandra Levy-Achtemeier, American psychologist, theologian and episcopal priest, I discovered a significant dimension of flourishing as an inherent potential that all persons possess to grow and flourish. This inborn potential considers humans as recipients of "God's grace-filled Spirit".[65] Influenced by the spirituality of Teilhard de Chardin, Levy-Achtemeier considers the ability of humans to flourish a definitive possibility, with the assurance of God's active presence and grace in persons and in the world. Levy-Achtemeier acknowledges the importance of developing one's strengths and abilities through education and practice, but it is ultimately God who draws humans toward excellence and self-transcendence, and who is fully involved in their flourishing.[66] The initiative to flourish as well as the grace to bring it to fruition is from God, but I firmly believe that this requires an accountability from humans to cooperate with God's grace and collaborate with other creatures on the earth. Flourishing is thus a God-given gift as well as a responsibility requiring faithfulness and some effort from humans.

Since Levy-Achtemeier thinks that the potential to flourish is from God, she is more concerned with understanding human nature and what enables or prevents people from living a flourishing life in receptivity and cooperation with God's grace. For Levy-Achtemeier, persons are created in the image of God and have the power to transcend themselves and engage with others and God.[67] The question then that arises for Levy-Achtemeier is, if all persons are endowed with God's grace and have an innate potential to flourish, why is it that only some flourish and others do not. She posits that people can languish and things can turn out negative and evil because of the human choice to "shut off the Divine call", resulting in the destruction of oneself and society.[68] One's potential for flourishing can thus be thwarted and hampered because of evil

65 Sandra M. Levy-Achtemeier, *Flourishing Life: Now and in the Time to Come*, Kindle ed. (Eugene, OR: Wipf and Stock, 2012), nn. 235, 1446.

66 Cf. Levy-Achtemeier, *Flourishing Life*, nn. 205–214.

67 Cf. *Ibid.*, n. 133.

68 *Ibid.*, nn. 237–238.

inclinations and frailty within humans and also because of destructive forces all around. Thus, Levy-Achtemeier sees the impact of the context and culture, and the support that people receive from their family, communities, social and religious institutions as crucial to grow and live fully.[69] Flourishing, since it is a God-given potential, is not for oneself alone; rather it is meant for all persons and hence requires responsible living to continue the mission of establishing the reign of God here on earth. The ultimate flourishing for Levy-Achtemeier is not only in this life, but also a future possibility in the resurrected life obtained by Jesus' triumph over death.[70]

Levy-Achtemeier's focus on flourishing as an inherent potential is expressed slightly differently in the work of feminist theologian Serene Jones, who is concerned with the flourishing of women.[71] For Jones, the universal theological assertion that "God wills the flourishing of all persons, including women", is an "already/not-yet" vision.[72] This vision accepts that flourishing is a present reality as well as a future hope in which all pain and oppression will be wiped away. Nevertheless, the realization of the flourishing of women, as Jones sees it, is not just a universal given claim requiring human cooperation. It requires theoretical and theological reflection on the beliefs, assumptions, norms and constructions that contribute to the "oppression and the ultimate flourishing of women".[73] Jones thus recognizes the need for systemic and structural changes to establish right relations and ensure the flourishing of all persons. I agree with Jones' eschatological vision of flourishing, which is not a passive waiting in hope and expectation. Rather, the vision of a renewed humanity challenges people to deal seriously with one's choices, decisions and actions, here and now, in a way that all can experience fullness of life. Women are not only victims of oppression, but "active agents and ever-engaged protagonists" for flourishing.[74] It is necessary for women and others to work together to bring about systemic and structural changes that will enable the flourishing of all persons.

## 5. Flourishing as the Fruit of Spirituality and Right Relationships

Most of the studies on flourishing do not consider spirituality directly in relation to flourishing. This was observed by the psychologists Maureen Miner, Martin Dowson and Stuart Devenish, when studying the contribution

---

69 Cf. *Ibid.*, nn. 355–366.

70 Cf. *Ibid.*, n. 2139

71 Cf. Serene Jones, *Feminist Theory and Christian Theology: Cartographies of Grace*, Guides to Theological Inquiry (Minneapolis, MN: Augsburg Fortress, 2000).

72 *Ibid.*, 108.

73 *Ibid.*, 4.

74 *Ibid.*, 6.

and significance of spirituality, particularly Christian spirituality, to human flourishing.[75] Miner and Dowson's main concern was to observe if and how Christian spirituality contributes to human flourishing, in contrast to the view of flourishing propagated by the media and popular culture. They make a distinction between a happy successful life of pleasure, and a *flourishing* life which is purposeful, hopeful and well-integrated.[76] They see spirituality as a necessary but not sufficient condition for flourishing, since other dimensions also need to be considered along with spirituality.[77] In looking at maturity in relation to flourishing and spirituality, Miner and Dowson recognize the main dimensions of human functioning as physical or biological, psychological (including the emotional and intellectual dimensions), social and spiritual.[78] The psychological, psychosocial and psychospiritual dimensions at intrapersonal, inter-personal and transpersonal levels need to be connected and integrated for true flourishing of persons. [79]

The emphasis on spirituality as a significant dimension of human life is also considered by Daniel Sulmasy, American medical ethicist, who proposed a "Biopsychosocial-Spiritual Model" for the palliative care of patients.[80] This model expands the previous 'biopsychosocial model' to include spiritual needs, which become significantly more important at the end of one's life.[81] In researching the religious and spiritual needs of dying patients, Sulmasy emphasized that the spiritual aspects need to be considered along with the "bio-medical, psychosocial, and ethical aspects" for meaning and wholeness in life.[82] The importance of spirituality for flourishing, is also highlighted by Ursula King, for whom, "spirituality is no longer a luxury of life, of mere interest to religious minorities or mystics, but it now appears as an absolute imperative for human sanity and survival".[83] Spirituality can creatively

---

75 Cf. Maureen Miner, Martin Dowson, and Stuart Devenish, eds., *Beyond Well-Being: Spirituality and Human Flourishing* (Charlotte, NC: Information Age, 2012).

76 Cf. Maureen Miner, Martin Dowson, and Stuart Devenish, eds., "Foreword," in *Beyond Well-Being: Spirituality and Human Flourishing*, vii.

77 Cf. Martin Dowson and Maureen Miner, "Towards a Theory of Personal Maturity: Links to Spirituality and Human Flourishing," in *Beyond Well-Being: Spirituality and Human Flourishing*, 127–49.

78 Cf. *Ibid.*, 129.

79 *Ibid.*, 135, 139.

80 Cf. Daniel P. Sulmasy, "A Biopsychosocial-Spiritual Model for the Care of Patients at the End of Life," *The Gerontologist* 42, no. Special Issue III (2002): 24–33.

81 Cf. Daniel P. Sulmasy, "Spiritual Issues in the Care of Dying Patients ' . . . It's Okay Between Me and God,'" *JAMA* 296, no. 11 (2006): 1385–92.

82 *Ibid.*, 1386.

83 Ursula King, The Search for Spirituality: Our Global Quest for a Spiritual Life (London - Norwich: Canterbury Press, 2009), 56.

energize persons, in religious and secular matters, to work towards creating a better world for all.[84] Besides seeing spirituality as essential for flourishing, King also thinks that human flourishing must be seen as an integral dimension of one's spirituality.

Flourishing, though an inherent potential and the fruit of spirituality, is not for individual well-being alone; it is always in relationship to others and to the whole of creation. This is affirmed by Levy-Achtemcier who sees humans as interdependent, relational and communal. For Kieser, human flourishing is the outcome of a right relationship with God embodied in one's "relationship with others, with self, and with creation."[85] The responsibility for the well-being of all creation is endorsed by Mary Grey, who sees flourishing as an ecological life-giving concept for all people and creatures of the earth.[86] She incorporates the well-being of the earth along with biological, social, psychological and spiritual well-being.

Grey discounts the societal conception of flourishing that promotes the accumulation of wealth and the pursuit of pleasure through addiction to drugs, alcohol, money and sex.[87] Grey presses the need to rediscover the rhythms of nature and honour the sacredness of life. This view of flourishing opens connections between persons, communities, creatures, and the environment, in relation to needs, rights and desires that are interwoven at every stage. It is not only connecting and relating that is important for flourishing but also the kind of connections and relationships that one establishes. It is for this reason, that Grey considers establishing right relationships in society and with all of creation as the vision of feminist liberation theology.[88] In contrast to patriarchal power which is dominating, disconnecting and disordered, the vision of flourishing heralds love, compassion, justice and reconciliation which unite all people and the earth.[89] Thus, while flourishing can be considered the fruit of authentic spirituality, it is important to recognize the essential connection between flourishing and spirituality, which involves right relationships with oneself, others, God, and the earth.

---

84 Cf. *Ibid.*, 54.

85 Kieser, *Catholic Sexual Theology and Adolescent Girls*, 2, 15.

86 Cf. Mary C. Grey, "Survive or Thrive? A Theology of Flourishing for the Next Millennium," *Studies: An Irish Quarterly Review* 88, no. 352 (1999): 402; Cf. Mary C. Grey, "It All Began with Miriam. Feminist Theology's Journey from Liberation to Reconciliation," *Feminist Theology* 20, no. 3 (2012): 228.

87 Cf. Grey, "Survive or Thrive?," 404.

88 Cf. Grey, "It All Began with Miriam," 228.

89 *Ibid.*, 228–29.

## 6. Flourishing as Wholeness or Fullness of Life

From a feminist theological perspective, flourishing can be seen as wholeness or fullness of life offered by Jesus as recorded in John 10:10 ("I came that they may have life and have it abundantly"). This was affirmed by St. Irenaeus in his profound statement – 'The glory of God is [hu]man fully alive.' The quest for wholeness and fullness of life has been shared by many humanists, and feminist and liberation theologians although the focus, means, methods and strategies differ. Taking women's lived experiences as the starting point of theological reflection, feminist theologians are interested in the flourishing and well-being of all persons especially women and girls as well as in the flourishing of all creation. Susan Miller, feminist New Testament professor, reflecting on John 10:10 observes that the material imagery and symbols used by Jesus in the Johannine accounts reveal a connection with the earth and earth creatures.[90] Hence the gift of abundant life is not for individuals alone but for the natural world as well.[91] Flourishing from an ecological reading must be seen as the renewal and restoration of relationships with humans, God and the earth.[92] Connections at all levels are significant for flourishing and fullness of life. Thus, according to Miller, an eco-spiritual outlook on John 10:10 rightly emphasises the interconnectedness of all life and the flourishing of the entire earth community.

While Miller looks at flourishing from a Johannine ecological reading, Jonathan Pennington, New Testament scholar, locates flourishing and wholeness in the Matthean Sermon on the Mount (Matthew 5-7).[93] The vision of flourishing as exemplified in the exhortations of the Sermon on the Mount are meant for personal, social and structural transformation.[94] This implies that true flourishing, which is a Trinitarian experience of communion with God through Jesus by the Spirit, can be experienced through faithful discipleship following in the footsteps of Jesus.[95] Flourishing, for Pennington, from a faith perspective, is living in accordance with the life and teaching of Jesus Christ.[96] Human flourishing is associated with blessedness, wholeness,

---

90 Cf. Susan Miller, "'I Came That They May Have Life, and Have It Abundantly' (John 10:10): An Ecological Reading of John's Gospel," *The Expository Times* 124, no. 2 (2012): 71.

91 *Ibid.*, 68, 69.

92 *Ibid.*, 71.

93 Cf. Jonathan T. Pennington, *The Sermon on the Mount and Human Flourishing: A Theological Commentary* (Grand Rapids, MI: Baker, 2017).

94 Cf. *Ibid.*, 15.

95 Cf. *Ibid.*, 14–15.

96 *Ibid.*, 289.

peace, prosperity, security, fertility and fullness of life, which, according to Pennington, come from a covenantal relationship with God.[97]

This covenantal relationship is to be lived in relation to oneself, others and all creation. The biblical understanding of wholeness concerns life in the present as well as for the future. God will restore fullness of life at the end of time, but this must also be brought about in this life through good interpersonal relationships, and healthy functioning of all systems and structures.[98] Pennington therefore sees the biblical vision of flourishing as eschatological but also for the present life in the midst of one's suffering and concerns. Flourishing is for the individual yet also other-centred and communal; and is oriented towards a universal mission of the restoration of wholeness for the entire creation.[99] Mary Grey sees the ecological links of flourishing, as life-giving for persons and all creatures, not only in the Bible but also in the sacred texts of all faiths.[100] For Grey, "all the major religions, indigenous and tribal traditions, and new forms of religion emerging from ecofeminism and from the recovery of forgotten traditions, contain dimensions of life-giving processes", which relate with flourishing.[101]

Flourishing as wholeness or fullness of life thus offers an integral view of flourishing incorporating aspects of all the diverse approaches to flourishing. Stephen Pope, Professor of theology, when reflecting on flourishing in relation to Christ notes that there are diverse views among Christians with regard to human flourishing. Some see flourishing as the fruit of unconditional love, exemplified by Jesus Christ, which reaches out to others in compassion and service. Others see the Cross, self-sacrifice and suffering endured by Christ as the true way to flourishing. Pope considers the key Christian concepts of love and suffering from two diverse perspectives - *dialectical* and *humanistic*.[102] The dialectical view of Christianity emphasizes *agapic* or self-denying love whereas the humanistic perspective stresses the human capacity for empathy, compassion and mutuality.[103] While these two Christian views are distinct, Pope finds them converging on Christian theological principles. Rather than discard some of the ideals, values and theological formulations of Christianity, or opt

97 Cf. *Ibid.*, 14, 43.

98 *Ibid.*, 72.

99 Cf. *Ibid.*, 296–97.

100 Cf. Grey, "Survive or Thrive?," 402–3.

101 *Ibid.*, 404.

102 Cf. Stephen J. Pope, "Jesus Christ and Human Flourishing: An Incarnational Perspective," The God and Human Flourishing Program (New Haven, CT: Yale Center for Faith and Culture at Yale Divinity School), accessed April 15, 2018, https://faith.yale.edu/sites/default/files/pope_christ_and_flourishing.pdf.

103 *Ibid.*, 2.

for an either-or approach, Pope recommends an "incarnational integrationist position" for transformation and wholeness. To clarify his incarnational integrationist position, Pope situates it in the context of three Christian standpoints, that of "the verticalist, the horizontalist, and the integrationist". [104]

The *verticalist* position, held by some Christians and theologians, regards flourishing as eschatological, equating it with eternal life and salvation.[105] From this perception, Christ is seen exclusively as the only Saviour of the world, who took human flesh to save souls. The soul is also considered more important than the body from this position. Salvation only through Christ excludes people of other faiths from being saved. The exclusivist Christian position, for Pope, finds no value in the views of positive psychology and the capabilities approach since they do not consider salvation for flourishing.[106] The *horizontalist* position is more "liberal" in looking at flourishing as love for persons and striving for freedom from oppression.[107] For Pope, those who hold this perception regard Christ as a prophetic leader, like other religious leaders, who came to bring liberation to the captives, the poor and the oppressed. Liberal minded people can accept all views of flourishing that suggest ethical living and working for justice and liberation. The third *integrationist* position attempts to combine the views of the first, which enforce exclusivist positions of Christian theology, and the second humanist position of compassion, freedom and justice. The *integrationist* position considers Christ's offer of fullness of life as God's grace given freely to all persons so that all humans can flourish and grow in relationship with God and others.[108] For Pope, human flourishing from the incarnational integrationist position views flourishing as material, spiritual, social, moral, historical and eternal, and can be witnessed in love of God and neighbour.[109] While acknowledging the eschatological view of flourishing as eternal life, this position accepts the incarnational vision of temporal flourishing in this present life.[110] It understands the necessity of human effort for flourishing but also recognizes the importance of God's grace for transformation and wholeness. Thus, flourishing or fullness of life, for Pope is not exercised in a "separate sphere called the 'sacred' but in and through every part of our daily lives", which involve "right relationships to God, one another, oneself, and all of creation".[111] When using Christ as the

104 *Ibid.*, 16.

105 Cf. *Ibid.*

106 Cf. *Ibid.*

107 *Ibid.*

108 Cf. *Ibid.*, 17.

109 *Ibid.*, 17, 22.

110 Cf. *Ibid.*, 17.

111 *Ibid.*, 19, 23.

standard for flourishing, it is important to also engage with other perspectives that are genuinely concerned with the well-being of humans and the earth.

## Concluding Remarks

Integrating the positive aspects of the different perspectives on flourishing as well as revising or reframing some of the limitations can offer an integral inclusive incarnational approach to flourishing. The emphasis in flourishing as a well-lived life of virtuous activity and as equated with well-being and optimal living, is on individual and personal well-being. In creating just opportunities for people to flourish, importance is given to ensuring conducive social and political structures for personal and social well-being. The communitarian and relational dimension in flourishing is accentuated in the view of flourishing as the fruit of right relationships and spirituality. This outlook, while taking into consideration emotional, intellectual, psychological and spiritual well-being of individuals, stresses right and just relationships with persons, God and the earth. These perspectives of flourishing are end or goal-directed, involving a process of effort and determination, physically, emotionally, intellectually, psychologically and spiritually, towards flourishing as the final outcome. Flourishing as an inherent potential, underscores the innate God-given ability to all persons to flourish irrespective of one's class, caste, culture, religion, gender, race and ethnicity.

The perception of flourishing as wholeness or fullness of life takes all the aspects of flourishing into consideration to offer a critical constructive response for the flourishing of all persons and the earth. Flourishing is considered as a gift and grace offered by the Lord to all persons in the present, as well as a future hope and goal to be reached through personal and communitarian efforts. It also takes into account the experiences of the poor and marginalized, in advocating for just socio-cultural, political and economic structures to ensure their flourishing. All these diverse aspects of flourishing taken together offer an integral understanding of human flourishing that favours the flourishing of all persons, inclusive of those on the margins, with respecting the rhythm and requirements of the entire ecosystem. They herald an urgent theological consciousness among people, so as to think through and challenge the beliefs, myths, narratives, symbols and rhetoric preserved by the dominant cultures and traditions to maintain and perpetuate the oppression and dehumanization of the weakest and poorest. The concrete realization of fullness of life for all persons and the ecosystem requires sensitivity to each context, culture and needs, as well as connectedness and collaboration with people of all faiths for the well-being of all creation.

4

# Missionary by Its Very Nature: Baptised and Sent to Liberate

**Anil Thomas CM**

*Department of Systematic Theology, Jnana-Deepa Vidyapeeth, Pune*

**Abstract:** The article looks at the change that Vatican II has brought about in the perception of mission and how this new understanding of mission has been at the heart of many documents of Vatican II as well as the teachings of all post-conciliar Popes. It explores the way Pope Francis interprets this concept of mission in the present context giving it concrete expression. The article indicates that People of God in their baptismal commitment constantly reach out to everyone in need with the same love and mercy of God. Baptised and sent on the mission the Church is a missionary by her very nature.

**Keywords:** Mission, Church as missionary, Second Vatican Council, Pope Francis

In the past, to be precise, before the Second Vatican Council (1962-65), mission was often understood and explained primarily from the perspective of the mission command of Jesus "Go, therefore, and make disciples of all nations; baptise them in the name of the Father and of the Son and of the Holy Spirit, and teach them to observe all the commands I gave you. And look, I am with you always, yes, to the end of time" (Mt 28:19). Mission was essentially seen as a response in obedience to a command of Christ. Missionary commitment came to be regarded as an entrusted duty, especially to some people engaged in full-time missionary activity. The mission command was, therefore, considered to be the foundation of the missionary commitment. As a result of this understanding, the territorial concept of mission predominantly prevailed the Church's evangelising activity. A command is not given for its own sake and so is not an end in itself. The Second Vatican Council without diminishing or minimising the importance of the mission command, and without making an iota of difference to it, placed the mission of the Church on a more solid, broader, theological and trinitarian foundation. The council fathers of Vatican II realised that not only the mission command of Christ but also his entire life and mission on earth go back to God's will for the salvation of the entire human race. The Church is sent forth to participate in and continue this same mission of God's love made manifest in Jesus Christ and continued through the actions of the Holy Spirit.[1]

## 1. Ad Gentes

The Second Vatican Council in its famous decree on the Church's Missionary Activity (*Ad Gentes of AG*) categorically states, "The Church on earth is by its very nature missionary since, according to the plan of the Father, it has its origin in the mission of the Son and the Holy Spirit according to the will of the Father" (AG 2). This indeed was substantially a radical statement in the sense that it greatly influenced the way the post-conciliar Church understood and explained what it means to be a member of the Church and more specifically what it means to be a missionary. Mission is a participation in the life of the Trinity and this participation begins in and through one's baptism. Thus, the Church, which Vatican II defined as the "People of God" (LG 9-17), is missionary by its very nature. In *Ad Gentes* for the first time in her long history, the Church teaches that the Church's mission (and her missionary nature) is rooted in the mission of God. Mission springs from the very nature of God who is love. This teaching has two essential implications from the perspective of practical evangelisation. The first is that all the disciples of Christ are called to be missionaries by participating in the very life of God in and through baptism. The second is that this divine mission (divine life) entrusted to the Church in general and to every Christian in particular reaches out to all, especially those who are poor or in need. "The Church, sent by Christ to reveal and communicate the love of God to all men and all peoples, is aware that for her a tremendous missionary work still remains to be done" (AG 10).

1 I believe that Dr Cyril Desbruslais had such a mission and he communicated this mission to the youth with zeal and joy. So this article is written in his honour, for whom his life was a mission.

## 2. Lumen Gentium

Vatican II proposes many meaningful definitions of the Church. It is interesting to note that the first definition of the Church given by the Council in its dogmatic constitution on the Church, *Lumen Gentium (LG)* states "the Church, in Christ, is in the nature of a sacrament - a sign and instrument, that is, of communion with God and unity among all men..." (LG 1). It is true that after the Council this definition of Church exposed by the Council, unfortunately, did not attract the attention it deserved from the theologians. However, from the point of view of mission and mission theology, this understanding of Church as the sacrament, sign and instrument of communion with God and unity among human beings is of enormous significance. The Church is sent forth to bring human beings to God (communion with God) and to bring human beings to one another. Indeed this is her identity, her mission and the primary purpose of her existence. A Christian's deepest identity emerges from this fundamental definition of the Church set forth in *Lumen Gentium*. The entire second chapter of *Lumen Gentium* dealing with the Church as the People of God too manifests her missionary nature and commitment to the whole human race because all humanity is related to the Church in various ways (LG 12-16).

## 3. Sacrosanctum Concilium

In fact, the very first document of Vatican II *Sacrosanctum Concilium*, *SC*, the constitution on sacred liturgy in its very opening paragraph makes explicit reference to this missionary nature of the Church and of all her sons and daughters. It states that the Council intends to "foster whatever can promote union among all who believe in Christ; to strengthen whatever can help to call all mankind into the Church's fold" (SC 1). It goes on to substantiate this missionary task of the people of God. Through the reform of the liturgy, according to *Sacrosanctum Concilium,* "the faithful are enabled to express in their lives and manifest to others the mystery of Christ and the real nature of the true Church... increase their power to preach Christ and thus show forth the Church, a sign lifted up among the nations, to those outside, a sign under which the scattered children of God may be gathered together..." (SC 2). *Sacrosanctum Concilium* also makes an explicit reference to the universal salvific will of God in the context of the Church's mission to preach the Gospel to every creature (SC 5; 1 Tim. 2:4). Thus the constitution on sacred liturgy observes "just as Christ was sent by the Father so also he sent the apostles, filled with the Holy Spirit. This he did so that they might preach the Gospel to every creature and proclaim that the Son of God by his death and resurrection had freed us from the power of Satan..." (SC 6).

## 4. Dei Verbum

The dogmatic constitution on divine revelation *Dei Verbum (DV)* also makes both explicit and implicit references to the missionary nature of the Church and her duty to foster human beings' communion with God and unity among themselves. *Dei Verbum* states that it is the Church's duty to proclaim the Word of God with reverence and faith. "That which we have seen and heard we proclaim also to you, so that you may have fellowship with us; and our fellowship is with the Father and with his Son Jesus Christ" (DV 1). This vocation to proclaim the Gospel to all people is undertaken seriously by the Church because she "wants the whole world to hear the summons to salvation, so that through hearing it may believe, through belief it may hope, through hope it may come to love" (DV 1). In preaching the Gospel the Church is to communicate the gifts of God to the entire humanity.

## 5. Gaudium et Spes

Second Vatican Council's famous pastoral constitution on the Church in the modern world *Gaudium et Spes (GS)* is a document that substantiates the Church's missionary nature and her missionary commitment to the entire world. The Church is not for herself but for others. She reaches out to one and all in her resolve to remain faithful to the missionary character. Thus, *Gaudium et Spes* declares "The joy and hope, the grief and anguish of the men of our time, especially of those who are poor or afflicted in any way, are the joy and hope, the grief and anguish of the followers of Christ as well. Nothing that is genuinely human fails to find an echo in their hearts" (GS 1). The Church is depicted as a community of disciples of Christ moving forward to the kingdom of the Father and bears a "message of salvation intended for all men" because of which "Christians cherish a feeling of deep solidarity with the human race" (GS 1). The Council, having deeply studied the mystery of the Church (missionary by her very nature) is interested not only in the sons and daughters of the Church but the whole of humanity as well (GS 2). Today the human race is troubled and perplexed due to various reasons. With solidarity and respectful affection for the whole humanity, the Church desires to enter into dialogue with them. She "offers to cooperate unreservedly with mankind in fostering a sense of brotherhood to correspond to this destiny of theirs" (GS 3).

All the four constitutions of Vatican II demonstrate and underline, at the very beginning itself, the missionary nature of the Church and her missionary commitment to the entire human race. This is also very true of many other documents of Vatican II like *Nostra Aetate* and *Dignitatis Humanae*. After Vatican II all the four Popes have deliberately carried forward this conciliar emphasis on the missionary nature of the People of God and the Church's missionary commitment to humanity as a whole.

## 6. Pope Paul VI

Pope Paul VI in his Apostolic Exhortation *Evangelii Nuntiandi* (*EN,* Evangelisation in the Modern World) reiterated this nature of the Church and the people of God. He pointed out that the Church's mission is to follow Christ the missionary (the greatest evangeliser). "We wish to confirm once more that the task of evangelising all people constitutes the essential mission of the Church" (EN 14). Mission is the reason for her existence. "Evangelising is, in fact, the grace and vocation proper to the Church, her deepest identity. She exists in order to evangelise" (EN 14). *Evangelii Nuntiandi* taught that to be a missionary (evangeliser) means to bear witness to God's love for the whole human race, "to bear witness that in his Son, God has loved the world" (EN 26). In the encyclical *Ecclesiam Suam (ES)*, which Pope Paul VI wrote during the Council, he compared the Church to a mother. "The Church was founded by Jesus Christ to be the loving mother of the whole human family and minister to its salvation" (ES 1). Thus, in his first encyclical the Holy Father points out that the Church has the mission to reach out to all human beings like a mother.

## 7. Pope John Paul II

Pope John Paul II wrote his significant encyclical *Redemtoris Missio* (*RM,* Mission of the Redeemer) precisely to emphasise the missionary responsibility of the whole people of God. John Paul II said, "From the beginning of my Pontificate I have chosen to travel to the ends of the earth in order to show this missionary concern" (RM 1). In his opinion, the teaching of *Ad Gentes* that the Church is missionary by her very nature would imply that the Church is on mission always and everywhere. Therefore, further developing this teaching of *Ad Gentes* Pope John Paul II explains in *Redemptoris Missio* that the Church is always and everywhere on the mission. Looking at today's world from the view point of mission and evangelisation Pope John Paul II distinguished three mission situations. First, there is mission to peoples, groups and socio-cultural contexts in which Christ and his Gospel are not known. This is mission *ad gentes*. Then there is another mission situation where there are Christian communities with adequate and solid ecclesial structures. They are fervent in their faith, Christian living and bear witness to the Gospel in their daily life. They also have a commitment to the universal mission of the Church. In these communities also the Church is engaged in the mission activity and it is called pastoral care. Thirdly, there is an intermediate situation where the entire groups of the baptised have lost a living sense of the faith and often no longer consider themselves members of the Church. In these places the Church engages in the mission of new evangelisation or re-evangelisation (RM 33).

Pope John Paul II reminded every Christian that with the Second Vatican Council "there is a new awareness that missionary activity is a matter for all

Christians, for all dioceses and parishes, Church institutions and associations" (RM 2). Substantiating this view further, he said, "The need for all the faithful to share in this responsibility (mission) is not merely a matter of making the apostolate more effective; it is a right and duty based on their baptismal dignity whereby the faithful participate…in the threefold mission of Christ as Priest, Prophet and King" (RM71).

## 8. Pope Benedict XVI

Pope Benedict XVI in his first encyclical *Deus Caritas Est* (*DCE,* God is Love) stated that Church in her mission does essentially three tasks. The Church worships God, she takes care of the poor and finally, she teaches, preaches and evangelises. They are so intimately related that the Church cannot do one without the other two. Pope Benedict XVI stated that the love of God and love of neighbour are intimately and profoundly interconnected (DCE 1). Jesus united the love of God and love of the neighbour into one single precept. The Church's mission is to love God and love one another and in that process, Christians become witnesses, missionaries and evangelisers. God is love (1 Jn 4:8), Jesus Christ is the incarnate love of God and the Church is a continuation of this love of God made manifest in Jesus Christ. "Love of neighbour, grounded in the love of God, is first and foremost a responsibility for each individual member of the faithful, but it is also a responsibility for the entire ecclesial community at every level: from the local community to the particular Church and to the universal Church in its entirety. As a community, the Church must practise love" (DCE 20).

## 9. Pope Francis

Pope Francis in his Apostolic Exhortation *Evangelii Gaudium (EG)* has reminded the whole Church of the great missionary commitment and responsibility. Reiterating the views of Pope John Paul II, Pope Francis said, "there must be no lessening of the impetus to preach the Gospel to those who are far from Christ because this is the first task of the Church… missionary outreach is paradigmatic for all the Church's activity" (EG 15). He has, again and again, demonstrated what does it mean to be a missionary by nature. "In all the baptised, from first to last, the sanctifying power of the Spirit is at work, impelling us to evangelisation" (EG 119). In his opinion, all Christians are missionary disciples of Jesus. "In virtue of their baptism, all the members of the People of God have become missionary disciples (cf. Mt 28: 19). All the baptised, whatever their position in the Church or their level of instruction in the faith are agents of evangelisation, and it would be insufficient to envisage a plan of evangelisation to be carried out by professionals while the rest of the faithful would simply be passive recipients. The new evangelisation calls for personal involvement on the part of each of the baptised. Every Christian is challenged, here and now, to be actively engaged in evangelisation" (EG 120). From the magisterium of Pope Francis it becomes all the more clearer that it is baptism that makes us missionaries.

We are all meant to have the divine life in us and having that divine life within us through our incorporation into Christ in baptism makes us holy. In this way Christians are set apart to participate in the divine otherness. Divine life or holiness is primarily a matter of love. It is in our love that we are set apart from the world. In the evening of our life we will be judged on this love (Mt 25:31-46). The legitimate question is; what precisely is this love? In the simplest explanation, love can be understood as willing the good of the other as the other is. Love makes us children of God who loves saint and sinner in the same way, who wills the good of good people and bad people alike (cf. Mt 5:45). Like our God we are also meant to reach out to others without measuring our love and without expecting anything in return. Jesus asks "If you love only those who love you, what reward will you have? Even the tax collectors do the same. If you greet only your brothers, what is unusual about that? Even the pagans do the same. So be perfect just as your heavenly Father is perfect" (Mt 5:46-48). Thus, having the divine life in us, we are meant to love God and others in a radical way. This is an important implication of the conciliar teaching that we are missionaries by our very nature.

To be a Christian is to be a missionary and to be a missionary means to be caught up in the very life of God, the Trinity. In the sacred scripture, we encounter God as one who invites us to share his life and glory (AG 2) and reaches out to everyone especially the "poor" with his saving presence and unconditional love (Lk 4:18-19). Pope Francis said to a gathering of the members of the religious orders and charitable groups inspired by St. Vincent de Paul, "Love of God always translates into an active love of the poor, leading Christians to get up and go out to anyone in need. One who loves does not sit in an armchair and watch, awaiting the coming of a better world, but he gets up and goes with enthusiasm and simplicity"[2] This missionary outreach is "paradigmatic for all the Church's activity" (EG 15). Thus, the Holy Father invites all Christians to be "permanently in a state of mission" (EG 25).

Pope Francis envisions a Church that goes out with a renewed missionary commitment. The Church is sent by Christ to reveal and to communicate the love of God to all human beings. It invites us to have a sense of duty towards the mission. In his message for the World Mission Day 2019 once again Pope Francis spoke about the importance of renewing the Church's missionary

2 Cindy Wooden, "St. Vincent de Paul inspired people to pray and reach out, pope says," Oct 16, 2017, https://cruxnow.com/vatican/2017/10/16/st-vincent-de-paul-inspired-people-pray-reach-pope-says/ Accessed on 10 October 2019.

commitment.[3] It is an invitation "to rediscover the missionary dimension of our faith in Jesus Christ, a faith graciously bestowed on us in baptism."[4] In baptism, we are born to a new life and are invited to share this new life of love with those around us. The Church of Christ is on a mission in the world and mission is an integral part of our identity as Christians. "Each of us is a mission to the world, for each of us is the fruit of God's love."[5]

## Conclusion

In line with *Ad Gentes, Lumen Gentium* and other Magisterial teachings, Pope Francis reiterates that the Church is not for herself. As a sign of unity and salvation, it needs to reach out to the world. The Church as the community of the missionary disciples of Christ, is sent out to share the love of God with everyone. We can say that the Church does not have a mission but the Church is a mission (cf. EN 14-15; EG 120). In this sense, the whole purpose of the Church's existence is to call all human beings to the encounter with Christ so that everyone can see and experience the mercy of Christ. Reflecting upon this missionary character of the Church Pope Francis said that she is "like a field-hospital that must care for the sick."[6] In the same way the Holy Father asks the priests to bring this healing power of God's grace and mercy to everyone in need and "to stay close to the marginalised and to be shepherds living with the smell of the sheep."[7] Christians who do not go out of themselves do not live their missionary vocation faithfully. The People of God in their baptismal commitment constantly reach out to everyone in need with the same love and mercy of God. Baptised and sent on the mission the Church is a missionary by her very nature.

---

3 Pope Francis, *Baptized and Sent: The Church of Christ on Mission in the World. Message for the World Mission Day 2019*. (Mumbai: Better Yourself Books, 2019).

4 *Ibid.*

5 *Ibid.*

6 Pope Francis' message during the General Audience on 28 August 2019. https://www.vaticannews.va/en/pope/news/2019-08/pope-francis-general-audience-church-cares-for-sick.html. Accessed on 14 October 2019.

7 Pope Francis' message on 28 March 1913 during the Chrism Mass in St. Peter's Basilica. https://www.thecatholictelegraph.com/pope-francis-priests-should-be-shepherds-living-with-the-smell-of-the-sheep/13439.

5

# Education for Change: *Sarvodaya* to *Antyodaya*

**Lawrence S. Fernandes SJ**
*Principal, Sacred Heart College, Satya Nilayam, Chennai 600041*

**Abstract:** Education is and can be a source of empowerment. Mahatma Gandhi and B.R. Ambedkar not only were born in two different communities in India, but also had different ideologies regarding the ways and means for the wellbeing and development of Indians, specially those who belonged to the lowest rung in the society. Gandhiji who promoted basic education aimed at the economic and cultural empowerment of all people, whereas Ambedkar viewed education as a tool to uplift the marginalised, the underprivileged and depressed classes in the society. Education for a long time has been in the hands of the affluent and the elite, depriving the people in the lower strata from its benefits. The need for education today is to be a tool that not only liberates the weaker sections, especially Dalits, from ignorance and injustice but also becomes an instrument that strengthens their resolve to face the challenges that life and society places before them in a creative and confident manner.

**Keywords:** Education, Sarvodaya, Empowerment, Pedagogy, Liberation. Consciousness, humanisation

## Introduction

Learning is an ongoing process and education, be it formal, informal, or non-formal – aims at building the society and empowering persons. Education has within it the power to craft the mind, build people, and mould a new generation and thus reflects the assumptions of society. Education is a tool that has within it the capacity to empower the individual and this in turn ushers a social change. Therefore, education brings in about a critical consciousness which in turn helps to transform society. Dr Cyril Desbrulais who has been an educationist, has always tried to impart education to empower the subaltern and always aimed that education is to be liberative force... To him, who has been one of my inspiration with deep reverence I express my tribute through this essay on education that has to be reaching to the least and the last.

When we view education from the perspective of people, we also see it as an ethical enterprise. Education is not merely a way of being, it is also a way, art of becoming. Therefore, education has to be the highest task of human culture.[1] Both Gandhiji and Paulo Friere had known this well that prompted them to make education a source of empowerment.

Mahatma Gandhi, the Father of our nation, through his many writings and Paulo Freire, a Brazilian educator and philosopher in his The *Pedagogy of the Oppressed* and other works brought forth the need to build, reform and transform society through education of the marginalised, oppressed and the weaker sections. Mahatma Gandhi's aim for *sarvodaya* which literally means, 'universal upliftment', aimed at making education informal in nature, rural-centred, craft-based and self-sustaining. It was to prepare Indians to develop a wholesome personality and to improve the quality of life. Paulo Freire through his work brought out the need to provide the world's poor and oppressed with educational experiences that make it possible for them to have better control over their livelihood.

Hence this is an attempt at the 're-reading' of Mahatma Gandhi and Paulo Freire in today's context. This attempt is essential given the global context of the Indian educational system and the growing gap between the rich and the poor. Education to foster social change has to reassert the primacy of human beings, especially of the weaker sections, which ensure empowerment of the underprivileged. Social change is not an option but an essential requirement of every educator. Hence a critical analysis of education in the present context and from the perspective of these two significant thinkers is a positive step in this direction.

## 1. Education as Power

Education today has to be a positive force in building peaceful communities in a fast-changing world. The question is: how does one look at the whole arena of education, the different approaches towards it, and the methodology employed

1 Ramin Jahanbegloo, Teaching Peace to Humanity, *The Hindu*, January 6, 2017, https://www.thehindu.com/opinion/op-ed/Teaching-peace-to-humanity/article16994008.ece accessed on 25 November, 2019.

for imparting education to the masses. The approach towards education would decide the content matter, the methodology and outcome of the process of education. The postmodern scenario of our society calls for a new methodology, new approach; and a totally new outlook towards the students, the teachers, the subject matter, and the society at large. Education has undergone rapid change though the basic framework of the British-imparted style of education still continues to exist in many parts of India.

Education is power.[2] The history of our nation shows that certain sections of the society were barred from learning, from reading sacred scriptures, from attending schools and from participating in intellectual debates and discussions. Education remained for long a tool in the hands of the elite who, at times, used it to suppress the weaker sections. Even today education, at times, becomes a prey to the elements and forces of certain groups that have vested interests thus failing to serve the national interest or the interests of the poor. Commercialization and politicization of education are the symptoms that reveal the role of vested interests in the field of education. Therefore, it is important to think of education as an organism promoting not only *sarvodaya*;- which means 'well being of all', – a concept made popular by Mahatma Gandhi; but also aims at *antyoday*a – well being of the least, lost and the marginalised in the society. Education is not and cannot be neutral. It needs to have a focus and direction in life. Right to education is a human right. The Right of Children to Free and Compulsory Education Act came into force from April 1, 2010. Accordingly, every child in the age group of 6 to 14 years are to be provided free and compulsory education in an appropriate classroom in the vicinity of his/her neighbourhood. (RTE Act, 2009). This is certainly a milestone in the history of education in India. But 'how much of this act remains a mere documentation than an action plan for people's wellbeing' is a question worth pondering.

## 2. Clarification of Terms

*Sarvodaya*: is a term which means 'universal upliftment' coined by Mahatma Gandhi, who borrowed this concept from Ruskin's *Unto the Last*. The well being of the individual is contained in the well being of all people. Therefore no one section can claim priority or importance over the other. The aim of education must seek the welfare of all people and not of any particular section of society.

*Antyodaya* would literally mean ' rise of the last.[3] *Antyodaya* signifies the focus on the bottom stratum of the society. It does not merely focus on the weak, poor or the marginalised, rather it looks at the lowest rung in the society

2 Theodore Brameld, *Education as Power,* Fawcett publications, New York, 1965. P. 1

3 D.D. Narula, Jyoti Kiran, *Antyodaya:Rise of the Last*, Bangcock, UNESCO, 1989, p. ii

and aims at the upliftment of the poorest of the poor, lowliest and the most marginalised sections of the society.

## 3. Highlights of the Gandhian Concept of Education

Education was one of the areas close to the heart of Mahatma Gandhi. Gandhiji believed that education is a pivotal activity on which not only the social, but also the moral, political and economical progress of society ultimately depends on.[4] Gandhiji always aimed at the total well being of the person, and did not focus on only one area of life. The ideology was that education must draw out and stimulate the spiritual, intellectual and physical faculties of children.[5]

Character building is an important aspect of Gandhiji's scheme of education. He would not compromise his values of non-violence and truth and would speak of formation of character as an important aim of all education. Education is for the building up of character. Therefore, truth and non-violence has to be integral part of any education that aims for character building of the pupils.

For Gandhiji education has to foster all-round development of an individual. For him, mere literacy is no education. He said, – By education, I mean an all round drawing out of the best in child and man – body, mind and spirit. Literacy is not the end of education nor even the beginning. It is one of the means whereby man and woman can be educated. Literacy itself is no education."[6] For this Gandhi advocated not merely literacy but total education that would look into all the spheres of human growth. Education is to go beyond caste-class distinctions and for this he advocated 'Basic Education' which would take care of the total well being – physical, mental, spiritual and emotional. The human being is one therefore all dichotomies in the sphere of education have to be avoided.

Gandhiji who advocated Basic Education, speaking of its aims and objectives said, – "Basic education will provide a healthy and moral basis of relationship between the city and the village and thus go a long way towards eradicating some of the worst evils of the present social insecurity and the poisoned relationship between the classes. It will check the progressive decay of our villages and lay the foundation of a just social order in which there is no unnatural division between the "haves" and the "have-nots" and everybody is assured of a living wage and the right to freedom. And all this would be accomplished without the horrors of bloody class war or a colossal capital expenditure such as would be involved in the mechanization of a vast

4 M.S. Patel, *The Educational Philosophy of Mahatma Gandhi,* Navjivan Publishing House, Ahmedabad.1953. p.10.

5 Mahatma Gandhi, *Harijjan,* 11th September, 1937.

6 Mahatma Gandhi, *Harijan,* July 31, 1937

continent like India. Nor would it entail a helpless dependence on foreign imported machinery or technical skill. Lastly, by obviating the necessity for highly specialized talent, it would place the destiny of the masses, as it were, in their own hands."[7]

Gandhiji was conscious that Western type of education has created only labourers for the British government and, therefore, his concept of Basic Education, has to suit India's socio-economic and cultural scenario and is to cater to the needs of Indian masses. Therefore, mere literacy which would create clerks for British offices was not Gandhiji liking. So he aimed at education that would not only take care of imparting knowledge about how to live but also inculcate skills for a decent livelihood. So learning a craft that would provide vocation was an integral part of Gandhiji's scheme of education,

Education is not only for life but also for livelihood. Therefore, learning a craft as part of our educational system was art for Gandhiji. It must be taught in a scientific manner so as to the child interested in such a study. "I would, therefore, begin the child's education by teaching it a useful handicraft and enabling it to produce from the moment it begins its training… I hold that the highest development of the mind and the soul is possible under such a system of education. Only every handicraft has to be taught not merely mechanically as is done today, but scientifically i.e. the child should know the why and the wherefore of every process."[8]

Gandhiji's belief that a vocation should have economic value and that there is nothing baneful in it is also the view supported by educationist John Dewey who said, "to charge that the various activities of gardening, weaving, construction in wood, manipulations of metals, cooking, etc., which carry over these fundamental human concerns into school resources, have a merely bread and butter value is to miss their point. If the mass of humankind has usually found in its industrial occupations nothing but evils which had to be endured for the sake of maintaining existence, the fault is not in the occupations, but in the conditions under which they are carried on. The continually increasing importance of economic factors in contemporary life makes it the more needed that education should reveal their scientific content and their social value."[9]

Yet another feature of Gandhiji's educational philosophy is the self-supporting aspect of the craft chosen as a means of education. Gandhiji believes that the handicraft should, besides developing the personality of the child, make education self-supporting. The craft chosen should be so learnt that its produce should have economic value. The self-supporting aspect of

---

7 Mahatma Gandhi, *Harijan,* October 9, 1937.

8 Mahatma Gandhi, Harijan, October, 30, 1937.

9 John Dewey, *Democracy and Education,* New York, Mac Millan Publishers, p.234-235.

education can be viewed in two ways, namely, education that will help one to be self-supporting, in later life and education which in itself is self-supporting.

In short, Gandhiji's *sarvodaya* scheme of education had the following tenets. Compulsory education for all boys and girls between the ages of 7 and 14 years and it is to be imparted through some craft or productive work and this work scheme should be self-supporting while the mother tongue should be the medium of instruction.

The final result of education is liberation. For Gandhiji, education is something that truly liberates human beings from all bonds and oppressive structures. Besides, character-building Gandhiji made *sa vidya ya vimuktaye* (education is that which liberates) one of the most important aims of education. It has been the motto of the Gujarat Vidyapith founded by Gandhiji in 1920.[10] Thus Gandhiji established a framework of education which is people friendly in general and poor friendly in particular.

## 4. Highlights of Paulo Freire's View on Education

Paulo Freire, a Brazilian educator, philosopher, and influential theorist of critical pedagogy is best known for his influential work 'Pedagogy of the Oppressed'. He spoke and wrote extensively on the liberative potential in education. Freire who reflected on the Brazilian scenario advocated a principle of education for liberation, education for justice, and education for all.

The work of Paulo Freire within a short while gripped the attention of people and countries beyond Brazil and awakened to the new reality of educating the oppressed who would, in turn, get off their shackles and experience freedom. It began as a struggle for national development but later it aimed at a new awareness among people who would examine the social situation in which they find themselves and take an initiative in order to transform these oppressive structures by active participation in the struggle for justice and thus empower them against the dehumanising forces and powers.

The vocation of every human being is to be fully human: yet, this vocation is thwarted, distorted, and destroyed by dehumanising forces who through injustice, violence and force, take away what is human. Freire was very conscious of the dehumanising forces that operate in society. Therefore humanisation of an individual and the entire society seemed to be the main task at hand for him. He would say, 'Dehumanisation distorts both the oppressor and the oppressed. Therefore the historical task is the liberation of both oppressor and the oppressed. There is fear of freedom for the oppressed.'

Any pedagogy in order to be of value has to be a humanising and liberative pedagogy. In the pedagogy one can trace two distinct stages. In the first, the oppressed unveil the world of oppression and through the praxis commit themselves to its transformation. In the second stage, in which the

10 Mahatma Gandhi, *Harijan,* March, 10, 1946.

reality of oppression has already been transformed this pedagogy ceases to belong to the oppressed and becomes the pedagogy of all men in the process of permanent liberation. In both stages, it is always through action in-depth action that the culture of domination is culturally confronted. In the first stage this confrontation occurs through the change in the way the oppressed perceive the world of oppression, in the second stage, this happens through the expulsion of the myths created and developed in the old order, which like specters haunt the new structure emerging from the revolutionary transformation.[11]

The pedagogy is for the oppressed and not for the oppressor because the oppressor would never feel the need nor is he aware of the call of the oppressive elements caused by him seeking its eradication. Oppressor being in an advantaged position would prefer to keep the status quo. So it becomes the task of the oppressed to become aware of their dehumanizing situation through critical consciousness which would lead them to usher in freedom and liberation.

Friere's method has two distinct features: In the first, the individual becomes conscious of both his oppressed reality and the decisions the oppressors impose; the second refers to the initiative of the oppressed to fight and emancipate themselves from the oppressors. This would naturally arouse resistance from the oppressors and would require courage to withhold any move that tries to break or suppress the moment, and this can only be done by the self-awareness of their own status and that of the oppressor.

In his work Friere strongly criticized the 'banking' system in the education which treats the student as an empty vessel that needs to be filled by the teacher. A lot of importance is given to lecture and memorisation with little importance given to reflection of what is being memorised. This will only make people passive and submissive to oppressive roles.[12] It will bring in loss of interest in life and liberation. Therefore a change of pedagogy is important to counter this trend. The authentic approach must enable people to become conscious of their situation with a desire to change it.

Freire was very particular that the present context is what really matters. Therefore the starting point of the programme content of education or political action or anything must be in the present context, the existential, the concrete situation that in truth depicts the reality of people here and now. Therefore all the discussion on education must be context-based. Many a time our content of education, methodology and curriculum are disconnected from life. They are archaic, away from the here and now, "centred on words emptied of reality they are meant to represent, lacking in concrete activity could never develop a critical consciousness. Indeed, its own naïve dependence on high sounding

11 Paulo Freire, *Pedagogy of the Oppressed,* p.31.

12 *Ibid.* p. 45ff.

phrases, reliance on rote, and tendency toward abstractness actually intensified our naivete."[13]

He said the education our situation demanded would enable men to discuss courageously the problems of their context – and to intervene in that context; it would warn men of the dangers of the time and offer them the confidence and the strength to confront those dangers instead of surrendering their sense of self through submission to the decisions of others. By predisposing men to reevaluate constantly, to analyse – "findings"– to adopt scientific methods and processes, and to perceive themselves in dialectical relationship with their social reality, that education could help men to assume an increasingly critical attitude toward the world and so to transform it.[14]

Change in educational system has to be ushered in through a political movement in which people are conscientised and made aware of the oppressive forces that are prevalent in the society, their deprivation and the oppressive structures that are prevalent would be manifested through this process of conscientisation which would reveal their socio-cultural deprivation. Thus he believed that mere educational changes will not transform society, and any change in education or in society is possible through a political movement: a movement of the masses.

He was wary of technological developments, for he believed that the technology in fact was helping the oppressors than the oppressed. Many times technology was used against the oppressed. When a human person is prevented, disabled and made incapable of expressing himself, it was violence. Poverty itself is violence. This reality cannot be changed by our consciousness. It can be changed only through political, revolutionary action.[15]

He firmly believed that schools do not shape society nor they have the power to do so. It is transformative political action alone that can bring about social transformation. He has borrowed a great deal from Marxian principles that emphasized economic determinism. Though he does not specifically use the word superstructure and infrastructure Freire states that education is at the service of the rich and the powerful oppressors. Only liberation would liberate the oppressor too. Hence, a pedagogy of the oppressed when put in force will enable true liberation and humanisation of both the oppressed and the oppressor.

---

13 Paulo Freire, *Education for Critical Consciousness,* Shed and Ward, London, 1974. p.37.

14 *Ibid.*, p.34

15 See Paulo Friere, *Education for Liberation,* Ecumenical Christian Centre Publications, Bangalore, 1983. p. 24.

## 5. The Present Educational Scenario

Gandhiji and Paulo Freire were concerned that education to be of any value must respond to the challenges and questions raised contextually.[16] Hence, it is important to contextualise the educational scenario today in the light of globalisation and postmodernist settings. With the prevalence of market economy influencing and at times guiding and governing educational curriculum and policies the plight of the poor and the marginalised has been one of deprivation and oppression. Some of the salient features of modern education would include among other things – greater advantage for students from the city, with the easy availability of technical and media education and information opposed to the rural poor who at times struggle due to lack of basic facilities like electricity in their villages. So, in such scenario technical skills seem important and are easily accessible for the rich and the wealthy. In such a situation, traditional knowledge and skills get replaced or displaced by a higher degree of learning and skills. These are in dire contrast to the principle of equality and nation-building.

There is a greater demand in the current scenario for the students to think critically about information, solve problems, communicate and collaborate, create new products and processes, and adapt to change and this will place them in a better footing than others.

Today's education calls for a number of skills, to name a few: automation, caused by computerisation in many workplaces, and skills in communication and problem solving, and also human skills. As there is a corporate change due to technology, globalisation and such competitive forces, companies have radically restructured how the work gets done. Many companies have flat organizational structures with less hierarchy, and workers experience greater autonomy and personal responsibility. Students are expected to able to use what they learn in school to understand critical information, and so there is a need to apply learning to real life situation.

There is also a need for broader competencies: students who are able to solve new problems and think critically with strong interpersonal skills for communication and collaboration, creativity and intellectual flexibility and also self-sufficiency including the ability to learn new things when necessary. This is needed for times when there are less predictability and less stability.

---

16 For this section see Mohit Chakravarti, *Education in the 21st century,* Kalpaz Publications, Delhi, 2007, Digumarti Bhaskar Rao, *Education for the 21st century,* Discovery Publishing House, New Delhi, 2010, http://www.centerforpubliceducation.org/Learn-About/gm-node/270.aspx, See also http://www.centerforpubliceducation.org/Learn-About/21st-Centuryhttp://www.jongus.se/The%20Challenges%20of%20Globalization%20in%20 Education.pdf and http://www.nesta.org.uk/library/documents/Meeting-the-challenge-v6. pdf

The current scenario promotes competition among the urban rich and rural poor students and in this rat race the loser is the poor who is weak socially, economically and not in the position to face these tough challenges of the society he gets thrown out of the system and this may, at times lead to frustration and loss of hope in life.

In the mechanized society with limited job opportunities, it becomes the 'survival of the fittest', which would naturally throw the poor out of the race in the society. Hence there is a need to empower the weak, strengthen the rural-based children and youth by providing opportunities, fostering critical consciousness and at times even challenging and questioning the current oppressive global culture in order to create a more humane culture that would give space and opportunities for the weaker sections to progress enabling them not only by providing opportunities for livelihood but creating conditions for living a dignified human life.

## 6. A Movement towards Antyodaya

It will be a too simplistic generalisation to attribute the concept of Sarvodaya to Mahatma Gandhiji and a*ntyodaya* to Paulo Freire. Both these thinkers in their writings have spelt out the well being, upliftment and empowerment of weaker sections.

Gandhiji desired that all children under the age of 14 are to be educated without any restriction. The Right to Education which is now a human right aims towards fulfilling the dream of Gandhiji. The weaker and subaltern sections are not to be deprived of the educational opportunity. Education, in itself should not be understood as merely primary education, but as Gandhiji suggested, education not just for living but also for a decent livelihood.

Freire who was aware of the societal structures controlling the education system in Brazil called for a change. Given the globalized context, one can see the market forces guiding and governing the choice of subjects, curriculum, exam patterns today to a great extent. It is the industry and job market which indirectly holds a sway on the educational institutions today. As a result there are few takers for the humanities like Sociology, Anthropology, History, Philosophy etc. while there are increases in sections for commerce, MBA, BCA, Visual communication, Media and related areas of study. It is important that the society that seeks to uphold values does not get swept away by market forces. This calls for a critical consciousness that would free education from market forces.

The overall goal of education is a 'living' and not merely for earning a livelihood. As education is for life, there is a need for upholding a value-based life, formation of character, rebuilding society, challenging oppressive structures and developing a critical consciousness. In such society the weak, poor and the subaltern sections will have a voice and a place to assert their identity and seek justice, or else they will be swept away by the oppressive market forces. As Freire stated it is humanisation that is to be the main aim of education and not mechanisation nor marketisation.

Growing in critical consciousness would enable the subalterns to face the onslaught of oppressive and exploitative structure of the society. Freire clearly noted that it is those people who are conscious and vigilant that could face the onslaught of the oppressive forces collectively Though he was influenced by Marxian ideology, he established the need to unite and face the oppressive onslaught on education in the globalised world.

The competitive mode of education brought in by the technological growth, and the use of English as medium of instruction has in fact deprived many rural youths to enter into competitive urban educational institutions; which, in turn ,brings in not only low self esteem in an individual but provides less opportunity in rising up the ladder of economic progress. Education in the mother tongue though has its advantages, has made many incapable to face competition as many of the technical, computer-savvy job centres deem English so essential.

While merit is given importance in government-managed institutions, the competitive structure puts the rich and the powerful in a better position than the others. It is important that the government and other supportive structures provide means and measure to empower the weak with tools of knowledge and communication that would enable them to face the onslaught of the rich and powerful who would sweep off the educational and employment opportunities in the society today.

As Paulo Freire indicated the students of the lower rung of society too must be equipped with similar skills and possibilities that the rich, urban youth are exposed too. In a dialogue with Ira Shor, Paulo Friere expressed the need to study the standard usage and technical skills because of the political realities facing the teachers and the students who live in a non-egalitarian society. What we need to invent are liberatory methods which develop student command of correct usage and of job skills while encouraging them to respect their own idioms and to criticize the very nature of the unequal job-market.[17]

Education for social transformation is the key principle in Gandhi and Friere. Social transformation is an ongoing process and there is continuous critique of the society through the medium of education. Given the current scenario it is unlikely that the oppressive forces are open to the critique. The educational system must challenge any attempt to domesticate the masses and direct education by determining the curriculum, syllabus and other academic activities. Social transformation would also mean a critical consciousness

17 Paulo Freire and Ira Shor, *A Pedagogy for Liberation,* Macmillan, London, p.72.

of the existing reality, which would enable the student to question, critique, challenge the existing structures in order to build and transform the society.

In his work *A Pedagogy for Liberation*, Paulo Friere chalks out different dimensions of liberative education which would in turn help in transforming the society and herald *antyodaya*. Education today needs to go beyond classrooms to the homes and communities that we live in. The 'banking system' which Friere criticised as dehumanising, to some extent continues even today which in turn makes the students only 'receivers' without providing them the opportunity to share their wealth of knowledge.

## Conclusion

Mahatma Gandhi and Paulo Freire still continue to inspire the field of education through their creative writings and speeches. These thinkers who had a preferential option towards the poor and oppressed not only sought education for all masses but sought special attention for the marginalised sections that are deprived of educational opportunity. Though the context of the thinkers and world scenario has changed much since these thinkers expressed their view on education, their guidelines still find an echo and meaning in our world today where education continue to reel under the domination of oppressive forces who many a time make students only receivers and fail to bring about the element of justice for the weaker sections. This is not to paint a completely negative picture of education. There is a continuous rethinking on education at the government level in particular and at the level of society in general which would eventually and hopefully would free education from the shackles of market forces and give it its due place in our society by empowering the weak, the poor, and the marginalized.

## Bibliography

Bell, Brenda, Gaventa John and Peters John, *We Make The Road by Walking, Conversations on Education and Social Change, Myles Horton and Paulo Freire.* Temple University Press, Philadelphia, 1990.

Brameld, Theodore. *Education as Power.* Fawcett Publications, New York, 1965.

Clarke, F. *Education and Social Change.* The Sheldon Press, London, 1940.

Chakravarti, Mohit. *Education in the 21st Century.* Kalpaz Publications, Delhi, 2007.

Freire Paul. *Education for Liberation.* Ecumenical Christian Centre Publication, Bangalore, 1983.

_________ *Pedagogy of the Oppressed.* Tranlated Myra Bergman Ramos, Penguin Books, Australia, 1972.

_________ *Education for Critical Consciousness.* Sheed and Ward, London, 1974.

_________ and Shor Ira. *A Pedagogy for Liberation.* Macmillan Publications, London, 1987.

Gandhi, M.K., *The Story of My Experiments With Truth.* Penguin Books, Delhi, 2007.

Kappen Mercy. *Gandhi and Social Action Today.* Sterling Publishers, New Delhi, 1990.

Kaushik, Vijjaya Kumari, Sharma S.R. (Ed.). *Education and Social Change.* Anmol Publications Pvt. Lt., New Delhi, 2004.

Mathias, T.A. (ed.) *Education and Social Concern.* Jesuit Educational Association of India, Delhi, 1968.

Mathur, Vishwanath Sahai. *Gandhiji as an Educationist.* Metropolitan Book Co., Delhi, 1951.

Palmer, Joy. ed. *Fifty Thinkers on Education, from Confucius to Dewey.* Routledge Publications, London, 2010.

Patel, M.S. *The Educational Philosophy of Mahatma Gandhi.* Navajivan Publishing House, Ahmadabad, 1953.

Prasad, Mahadeva. *Social Philosophy of Mahatma Gandhi.* Vishwavidyalaya Prakashan, Gorakhpur, 1958.

Pellegrino, James and Hilton Margaret. ed. Education for Life and Work: Developing Transferable Knowledge and Skills in the 21$^{ST}$ Century, National Academies Press, Washington, 2012.

Rao, Digumarti Bhaskara. *Education for the 21$^{st}$ Century,* Discovery Publishing House, New Delhi, 2001.

Shrimali, K.L. *A Search for values in Indian Education.* Vikas Publications, Delhi, 1971.

## Websites Consulted:

http://www.centerforpubliceducation.org/Learn-About/gm-node/270.aspx,

http://www.centerforpubliceducation.org/Learn-About/21st-Century

http://www.jongus.se/The%20Challenges%20of%20Globalization%20in%20 Education.pdf

http://www.nesta.org.uk/library/documents/Meeting-the-challenge-v6.pdf

http://www.infed.org/thinkers/et gand.htm

http://www.gandhifoundation.net/about%20gandhi1.htm

http://www.infed.org/thinkers/et-freir.htm

6

# Liberation Psychology of Martín-Baró and its Relevance

**Dolichan Kollareth SJ**

*Dept of Social Sciences, Jnana-Deepa Vidyapeeth, Pune*

**Abstract:** Ignacio Martín-Baró SJ, along the line of liberation theology, advocated for liberation psychology. For him, the ultimate purpose of the discipline of psychology should be the liberation of the oppressed people. He is critical of the mainstream psychology for its individual orientation and for a powerful few utilizing it as an instrument of oppression. Instead, liberation psychology is to uncover the ideologies that maintain and perpetuate exploitation. Martín-Baró advocates methodological eclecticism and objects political neutrality. The researcher ought to have a clear option for the poor. However, he attempts to strike a balance when warning against political commitment biasing the researcher's commitment to social reality. Liberation psychology calls for a psychology that is context relevant, sensitive to the social nature of the human being, and far from narrow positivist research strategies.

**Keywords:** Psychology, Liberation, Social orientation, Methodological eclecticism, Value neutrality, Deideologization, Oppressed majority

Mainstream psychology was developed in Britain and North America. The practice of psychology as a discipline outside these countries are often imitations of mainstream psychology. Nevertheless, there were attempts to originate more context sensitive psychological theories and practice. One such attempt is the liberation psychology originated by Ignacio Martín-Baró SJ in El Salvador, South America. This article will identify the main characteristics of liberation psychology and will explore its implications for the development of psychology as a discipline.

Ignacio Martín-Baró was born in Spain in 1942. He was a social psychologist, philosopher, and a Jesuit priest. He entered the Society of Jesus in in 1959 and was sent to El Salvador, where he studied psychology. He did his doctorate in social psychology from the University of Chicago. After his doctorate, he returned to the midst of the violent civil war in El Salvador. Despite death threats, Martín Baró pursued a brilliant teaching and research career at the Central American University (UCA). Finally, in 1989, Salvadoran army soldiers came for the Jesuits in the University campus. Martín Baró was among the six Jesuits and two others who were killed by the army.

In a letter that Martín-Baró wrote a few months before his murder, he refers to the repeated attacks that the UCA Jesuits faced: "we have moved forward and will continue to move forward. These attacks confirm that our activities at the university, which we have conducted peacefully, are challenging our oppressors at their very core."[1] Since 1976 the paramilitary groups had set off bombs in the UCA library, print shop, and computer center, and in 1980 the Jesuit residence was machine-gunned and later raided four times, dynamited twice and bombed once again in 1983. All of these attacks took place before November 1989 when the military, after having failed to silence the Jesuits, killed them.[2]

## 1. Characteristics of Liberation Psychology

Martín-Baró developed liberation psychology in response to the problems within mainstream empirical psychology. Psychological knowledge seemed far away from people's pressing problems. The discipline heavily relied on certain sections of the population for their studies. That is, for psychological studies, experimenters regularly gathered their sample of participants from the undergraduate student populations the Western Universities. However, it claimed universal valid knowledge applicable to anyone anywhere in the world. It relied on certain restricted methods such as game-like methods of experimental social psychology. Finally, much of the mainstream psychology production remained within the academic community at a highly theoretical level, practically irrelevant to the profound social problems.

1 B. Jiménez-Domínguez, "Ignacio Martín-Baró's social psychology of liberation: Situated knowledge and critical commitment against objectivism" in *Psychology of Liberation*, Edited by M. Montero and C.C. Sonn (New York: Springer, 2009), 46.

2 Jiménez-Domínguez, "Ignacio Martín-Baró's social psychology"

To overcome the limitations of mainstream psychology, Martín-Baró proposed liberation psychology, rooted in the South American context. Following are some of its key features.

### *a. Option for the Oppressed Majorities*

An essential focus of liberation psychology is serving the needs of the oppressed majorities. On its commitment to the poor, liberation psychology remains close to liberation theology. Both makes a preferential option for the poor. According to Duque, the theology of liberation is contextual theology.[3] It arises from the common reflections of the poor communities with regard to their faith and experience of God. Theology of liberation stands outside the official theological institutions. Thus for Martín-Baró' liberation psychology also has to take a stance outside the institution of mainstream psychology and opt for the liberation of the poor.

Social liberation should be the focus of psychology because the social structures that keep the poor people oppressed. He reinterpreted some of the traditional theories from the point of view of the poor. For example, Martín-Baró redefined traditional categories of social psychology such as prosocial behavior with a critical and a historical sense, proposing instead typologies more consistent with the daily experience of the poor in El Salvador.[4] From a socio-historical perspective, he distinguished three kinds of prosocial actions: acts of cooperation, acts of solidarity, and acts of altruism. Acts of solidarity contribute to social unity and give priority to the common rather than individual good. Acts of solidarity contribute to the development of just structures through the support of the weak. Acts of altruism contribute to the sustenance of society by solving difficult problems.

### *b. Social Orientation*

Liberation psychology places an emphasis on social orientation. The major critique of liberation psychology is that the mainstream psychology promotes individualism. It needs to be really social. Psychology, in general, has often put social and economic factors beyond its disciplinary boundary, preferring instead to look to intrapsychic explanations.[5] However, human beings develop and become who and what they are through the process of interacting in a socially organized and defined world. Definitely, humans are animals with

---

3 Jiménez-Domínguez, "Ignacio Martín-Baró's social psychology"

4 M. Burton and C. Kagan, "Towards a really social psychology: Liberation psychology beyond Latin America." In *Psychology of liberation*, Edited by M. Montero and C.C. Sonn (New York: Springer, 2009) pp. 51-72.

5 Burton and Kagan. "Towards a really social psychology"

brains but constantly formed from our interactions with multiple environments.[6] Therefore, psychology needs to look beyond the individual. Psychologists need to understand how society is structured and how its dynamics influence the human being.

The societal orientation that Martín-Baró' advocates is also historical.[7] Psychology needs to have a sense of how things got to be the way they are, and how this history is ever present in the subjectivity of the people. Similarly, the recognition of the conflictive nature of society and the omnipresence of power is two fundamental features of this societal orientation of psychology. There is hierarchy and distinct social interests that give rise to conflict. Power is to be understood not just on an interpersonal basis but in terms of its organization in society. Conflict and power have both economic and ideological dimensions, and the latter could be analyzed using psychology. Psychology should aim beyond individual liberation. It should also concern itself with breaking the chains of social oppression.

### *c. Deideologization*

For Martín-Baró yet another objective of liberation psychology is to examine the ideological component of human behavior.[8] For liberation psychology, individual behavior is not neutral, but originates from an ideological context. Thus, what is required is deideologization--demonstrate how elites enable an oppressive social system, by upholding and promoting beliefs and assumptions that favor status quo.[9] However, for Martín-Baró, to be truly emancipatory, psychology must be first liberated from its own ideological chains.[10] This assumes that the mainstream psychology itself is adopted in serving the interests of the ruling power.

Martín-Baró highlighted Freire's concept of the process of conscientization.[11] Conscientization leads to transforming the human person through changing his or her understanding of reality. It requires an active process

---

6 M. Burton and C. Kagan, "The verbal community and the societal construction of consciousness" in *Behavior and Social Issues* (1994), 87–96.

7 I. Martín-Baró, "From dirty war to psychological war: The case of El Salvador" in *Flight, Exile and Return: Mental Health and the Refugee* by A. Aron and S. Corne (Eds.) (San Francisco: CHRICA, 1988).

8 I. Martín-Baró, "The lazy Latino: The ideological nature of Latin American fatalism" in *Writings for a Liberation Psychology* by A. Aron and S. Corne (Eds.) (Cambridge: Harvard University Press, 1996a).

9 Martín-Baró, "The lazy Latino"

10 I. Martín-Baró, "Public opinion research as a de-ideologizing instrument" in *Writings for a Liberation Psychology* by A. Aron and S. Corne (Eds.) (Cambridge: Harvard University Press, 1996b).

11 Martín-Baró, "Public opinion research"

of dialogue that leads to an understanding of the mechanisms of oppression and dehumanization. This opens up new possibilities for action where new knowledge of the surrounding reality leads to new self-understanding about the roots of what people are at present and what they could become. Martín-Baró stressed that ultimately the liberation of the people would imply the liberation of the oppressors too.[12]

### *d. Methodological Eclecticism*

Liberation psychology is open to the use of methods that stem from diverse paradigms.[13] The pressing social problems require a methodological eclecticism. Traditional techniques (e.g. surveys, use of official statistics, content analyses) are combined with new approaches (e.g. social representations, use of interviews and testimonies, collaborative photography, textual analysis and drama).

There is an emphasis on participatory action research.[14] Relatedly, the method demands the commitment to and engagement with the oppressed, an antidote to academic isolation. Martín-Baró used opinion polls as a tool that could contribute to the formation of a new collective identity for the poor.[15] Thus, research itself became social involvement and a process that identified the knowledge of the poor. This knowledge was not to be used for formulating isolated theories, instead for provoking constructive interventions in the society.[16]

Among others, one reason that provoked the army was the University Institute of Public Opinion (IUDOP). The military regime was keen on using the media for winning the hearts and minds of the people through spreading news that they wanted. Those in power constructed the news and other information. When the UCA created the IUDOP, it became a channel for Salvadorans to express what they felt without partisan filters or interference. In this way, the public opinion polls that the government had used to maintain the established order were refashioned into a tool to thwart official discourse, its lies and deceptions. Ignacio Martín-Baró saw the public opinion poll as a powerful tool in the confrontation of ideologies.[17]

---

12 Martín-Baró, "Public opinion research"

13 P. Reason and H. Bradbury, *Handbook of Action Research: Participative Inquiry and Practice.* (London: Sage), 2001.

14 M. Montero, "Psychosocial community work as an alternative mode of political action" in *Community Work and Family* (1998).

15 I. Martín-Baró, "Toward a liberation psychology" in *Writings for a Liberation Psychology* by A. Aron and S. Corne (Eds.) (Cambridge: Harvard University Press, 1996c).

16 Martín-Baró, "Toward a liberation psychology"

17 Martín-Baró, "Public opinion research"

### e. Objection to Value Neutrality

Martín-Baró objected value neutrality.[18] Instead, liberation psychology should be committed to oppressed people. The researcher takes a situated standpoint on the side of the oppressed. Value neutrality serves only the interests of the ruling ideology. Social psychologists must abandon the notion of objectivity, but rather explore the subjective experience of the poor and marginalized. Thus, objectivity is redefined as a matter of ethics, a commitment to the liberation of the poor.

Martín-Baró, however, did not favour an uncritical commitment: There has to be an identification with the oppressed and at the same time necessary distance to examine with critical eyes the proposals emerging from their own praxis. Thus, there has to be a combining of the logic of action with the logic of research. In other words, liberation psychology must recognize the importance of combining both the knowledge of academia and the people in popular praxis and struggles. He did distinguish between political activism and his own commitment to social reality as an academic. For him, scientist political neutrality was ethically unacceptable. Yet he also warned against political commitment biasing social psychologist's objectivity.[19]

## 2. Relevance of Liberation Psychology

Martín-Baró was committed to his research by situating psychology in his social context. He attempted to understand and develop psychology as a social science committed to the poor. He used empirical tools at his disposal at that moment to unmask the repressive character of the government and to challenge the lies of the State through opinion polling. This was the real reason for his assassination by an elite force of the Salvadoran Army. Martín-Baró challenges us to own up a psychology that is relevant to real social contexts and problems without dictating or homogenizing the ways of doing psychology in different contexts.

Further, I wish to situate Martín-Baró's liberation psychology in the context of the different paradigms in psychology. Here I use Danziger's "Constructing the subject" that traces the history of psychological methods from the nineteenth century to the currently favorite model.[20] He begins by tracing three competing models of investigation in psychology: the Leipzig model, the clinical model, and the anthropometric model. Each of these models had its social context, characteristic structuring of the experimental situation, and specific knowledge goals. The Leipzig model from Germany originated in a

---

18 Martín-Baró, "Toward a liberation psychology".

19 Martín-Baró, "Toward a liberation psychology".

20 K. Danziger, *Constructing the Subject: Historical Origins of Psychological Research.* (Cambridge: Cambridge University Press), 1994.

University context, its experimental situation was characterized by the fluidity of experimenter-subject division, and its knowledge goal was to understand the processes of the human mind. The clinical model from France originated in a medical context, its experimental situation was characterized by doctor-patient interaction, and its knowledge goal was the treatment of the patients. The anthropometric model from England had schools as its most favourite context, its experimental situation consisted of the test-administrator-subject interactions, and its knowledge goal was the creation of aggregate data to aid administrative practices in various social institutions.

From the "alternative rival conceptions" of psychological investigation, the anthropometric model became predominant in the interwar period. Danziger lists a number of reasons for this narrowing of the investigative practices. Predominant among them is the practical aspirations of psychology that was typified in the way psychology was practiced in U.S. Psychology that increasingly occupied a space in schools, military and industries needed large data in a short time to aid administrative decisions. Therefore, the aggregate of data (modeled after the social survey) was preferred to time-consuming experimental and clinical investigations. Any skepticism of the 'scientificity' of the aggregate data was overcome by a number of strategies. The experimentation, modeled after the classroom experiments, provided them with an aura of being scientific. Assigning an individual a space in an aggregate went hand in hand with the propaganda that the measured characteristics (intelligence, personality) were expressions of innate biology. Therefore, studying the laws of behaviour (biological and similar to physical laws) was necessary and sufficient to understand individual behavior. Besides, research reports stripped individuals of all their identities "to create the illusion of empiricism."[21]

Danziger, unhappy with the narrowing of the investigative practices, concludes with a hope to recover the lost continents of psychological realities for a more liberating praxis of psychology. "The worldly success of modern psychology was built on a narrow social basis. That entailed a very considerable narrowing of epistemic access to the variety of psychological realities. Critical analysis can give us some insight into the nature of that narrowing. Further insight depends on some knowledge of that which has been excluded – in other words, the knowledge that has emerged in different social contexts. The receptivity of the discipline to such knowledge, however, would seem to be tied to changes in its social and cultural commitments."[22]

21 Danziger, *Constructing the Subject,* 100.

22 Danziger, *Constructing the Subject,* 197.

## Conclusion

Danziger's critical analysis of the history of psychology shows the narrowing of the investigative practices in the discipline. From alternative and competing models of approaching human reality, psychology came to be relied heavily on positivist research strategies aiming for successful applicability in schools, military, and industry. Instead, Danziger calls for regaining the multiple models for approaching human reality for a more liberating praxis of psychology. Martín-Baró's proposal for a liberation psychology exemplifies each of Danziger's analyses. Martín-Baró sees mainstream psychology as a tool of oppression and instead calls for psychology aiding the liberation of the oppressed majorities. He is critical of the overreliance on experimental methods and instead calls for methodological eclecticism. The challenge of liberation psychology for psychology as a discipline is to explore its various possibilities by relocating the subject in social, cultural, and historical context.

## References

Burton, M., & Kagan, C. (1994). "The verbal community and the societal construction of consciousness." *Behavior and Social Issues*, 4, 87–96.

Burton, M., & Kagan, C. (2009)."Towards a really social psychology: Liberation psychology beyond Latin America." In *Psychology of liberation*, Edited by M. Montero and C.C. Sonn. New York: Springer.

Danziger, Kurt. (1994). *Constructing the Subject: Historical Origins of Psychological Research*. Cambridge: Cambridge University Press.

Fals Borda, O. & Rahman, M. A. (1991). *Action and Knowledge: Breaking the monopoly of power with participatory action-research*. London: Intermediate Technology Publications.

Jiménez-Domínguez, Bernardo (2009) "Ignacio Martín-Baró's social psychology of liberation: Situated knowledge and critical commitment against objectivism." In *Psychology of Liberation*, Edited by M. Montero and C.C. Sonn. New York: Springer.

Martín-Baró, I. (1988). "From dirty war to psychological war: The case of El Salvador." In A. Aron & S. Corne (Eds.), *Flight, Exile and Return: Mental Health and the Refugee*. San Francisco: CHRICA.

Martín-Baró, I. (1996a). "The Lazy Latino: The ideological nature of Latin American fatalism." In A. Aron & S. Corne (Eds.), *Writings for a Liberation Psychology*. Cambridge: Harvard University Press.

Martín-Baró, I. (1996b). "Public opinion research as a de-ideologizing instrument." In A. Aron & S. Corne (Eds.), *Writings for a Liberation Psychology*. Cambridge: Harvard University Press.

Martín-Baró, I. (1996c). "Toward a liberation psychology." In A. Aron & S. Corne (Eds.), *Writings for a Liberation Psychology*. Cambridge: Harvard University Press.

Montero, M. (1998). "Psychosocial community work as an alternative mode of political action." *Community Work and Family*,1(1), 65–78.

Reason, P., & Bradbury, H. (Eds.) (2001). *Handbook of Action Research: Participative Inquiry and Practice*. London: Sage.

7

# Meditative Thinking and Poetic Dwelling: Invitation of Heidegger for Contemporary Society

**Sathya Balan SJ**
*Jnana-Deepa Vidyapeeth, Pune*

**Abstract:** This paper is aimed to bring the analysis of one of the influential thinkers, Martin Heidegger, on the plight of the contemporary humans as they have become thought-poor in our age of science and technology. He sharply pointed out, "*The most thought-provoking thing in our thought-provoking time is that we are still not thinking.*" In this context, he contrasts the essential differences between calculative thinking and meditative thinking as well as the sources of these two types of thinking. The former is the manifestation of traditional metaphysics as a consequence of forgetting the primordial question of being, whereas the latter emerges from humans' unique relation to the fact of being (ek-static openness). The meditative thinking demands an inner disposition to listen to the disclosure of being which could be related to Dr. Cyril Desbruslais' vision of life 'fully human and fully alive'. Heidegger is urging us to think deeply and radically to be freed from the clutches of practical and calculative thinking in our hyperactive society to emancipatory meditative thinking.

**Keywords**: Alienation, calculative thinking, Ek-sistence, Meditative thinking, Flight from thinking, Poetic dwelling, Releasement.

One of the best Experiences I've had since coming to Pune is meeting Dr. Cyril Desbruslais (popularly known as Cyril as he prefers to be called).

My admiration for him began in 2011 when I was a young student at De Nobili College (DNC), pursuing a bachelor's degree in Philosophy. My first impression of Cyril was sheer admiration for the kind of person he was. What struck me was his complete and dedicated commitment to various apostolates. At that time, Cyril was the Director (Superior) of the Students of Philosophy at DNC. His approach was radically different: He genuinely inspired us to seek conviction in our Jesuit vocation and get involved with our ministries by using all our talents and creativity. At Jnana-Deepa Vidyapeeth (JDV), he conducted a number of courses for which I was most fortunate to attend. The enrichment I experienced will no doubt last me a lifetime! His clarity of thought and his ability to articulate them made him one of the most popular and beloved professors on the campus!

Among the various courses Cyril was offering at JDV, "Philosophy of Liberation" stands out as one of my favourite subjects. It revealed his intellectual depth, highlighting his radical and critical dimensions about life and reality. He brings out his liberative vision of life more creatively and effectively in the subjects he taught at JDV and other places or through his Annual Plays with the SSU! In his room at DNC, there hung on the wall an upside down quote which read, "But we've always done it this way**".** This accurately sums up the kind of person he is, one who can think otherwise in bringing about a change in the hearts and minds of people to grow into 'fully human and fully alive'. Cyril has truly been a source of inspiration for all who encountered him, the biggest beneficiaries being the Students of JDV and the Youth of SSU.

I admire Cyril immensely for his multi-tasking abilities; I have witnessed from close quarters his remarkable availability for various engagements throughout the year, be it academic commitments at JDV and other places, his availability for the students of DNC for varied tasks, SSU youth ministry activities including its time-consuming annual SSU play, the weekly bible classes in the city, to name some of them. Besides, he always found time for reading books and novels (a compulsive reader as once he told me about his reading habit). Moreover, I found him always on time for everything (most often waiting for people because of his rigid punctuality). Once I quizzed him about his mantra for time management, he casually replied "There is a time for everything and everything in its time". Of course, he had time for everything and he did everything amazingly well in his own unique way.

What I also admire about Cyril is that despite his age and physical challenge, he is able to effectively lead a very busy life and makes it all look very easy! In the midst of various hectic activities throughout the year, he is amazingly well-organised. I heard people saying that he is gifted with many such remarkable qualities. However, what strikes me most is his rootedness in spirituality. All his apostolic commitments flow form here like a running stream. Cyril has the unique ability to be available for all his commitments and yet remain deeply rooted in life. It is not possible to be deeply committed, unless you are genuinely connected to your inner core. I consider this singular quality as something special of Cyril and he does it so effortlessly.

This attitude of being in touch with oneself in the midst of various activities poses a challenge for contemporary society. People lose their focus and get carried away from their busy life schedule and as a consequence get disconnected from their true selves. In this regard, I present in this paper, *Meditative Thinking and Poetic Dwelling*, which investigates the reasons behind the plight of contemporary humans and spells out the conception of meditative thinking after the philosophy of Martin Heidegger.

Martin Heidegger, the German Philosopher, is considered as one of the major forces of the 20th century of European thought. His was a strange, but a very important and significant, concern in philosophical search. This rare and strange preoccupation makes him a real heuristic thinker who thought out-side the box and paved the way to question the fact of being. Traditional western philosophy, spanning nearly 2,500 years, was concerned about beings (the noun aspect) but had forgotten to question the verb being itself. What was forgotten in more than two millennia has affected humanity and this has resulted in a state of thoughtlessness. Thus it has become a central preoccupation for Heidegger to address it. To turn to the act of being makes him in a way an anti-tradionalist, i.e. he turned away from the traditional concerns, methods, concepts and their underlying assumptions. And what he discovered from his up-side down approach was a ground-breaking work and he left an indelible legacy behind. Few heuristic thinkers, such as Heidegger, who have created such a radical disturbance in the history of philosophy!

It has been my long-cherished desire to study what such a heuristic philosopher like Heidegger has to say about our thinking itself. His famous memorial address, on October 30, 1955, in honour of 175 birthday of the German Composer and a native of his region, Conradin Kreutzer, entitled '*Discourse on Thinking*'[1] is a disclosure in this regard. It deeply reflects his concern for the essence of human thinking and, in particular his call for meditative thinking. Also, his '*Letter on Humanism*'[2] is a classic which delves deeply and elaborates in detail the essence of human thinking. Based principally on these sources, this paper explores the poverty of thinking of contemporary humans because of the onslaught of the traditional metaphysics.

1 Martin Heidegger, *Discourse on Thinking*, trans. Anderson & Freund (New York: Harper Torchbooks, 1966).

2 Martin Heidegger, "Letter on Humanism," trans. Frank A. Capuzzi in William McNeill (ed.), *Pathmarks* (Cambridge: Cambridge University Press, 1998).

## 1. Calculative Thinking of Contemporary Humans and the Alienation

While addressing the gathering in honour of Conradin Kreutzer, Heidegger, at the outset, begins his memorial address with a question that challenges his audience; he finds fault with the way the celebration is organised, reducing such a memorial to the mere playing and singing some of the works of the composer, Conradin Kreutzer; because that is the way memorial celebrations are organised everywhere. Heidegger finds much discomfort with such a prevalent culture that people are not urged to think deeply enough and they end up being just too practical, choosing an easy way out. Taking a cue from there, he digs deeper into the core issue with this generation who are thought-poor and thought-less. Thoughtlessness, as he writes, is an uncanny visitor who comes and goes everywhere in today's world.[3]

Heidegger gives a critical analysis for the root cause for this kind of human *flight from thinking*[4], as thinking has become merely practical and calculative. Thinking has become just an instrument of education as a classroom matter and a cultural concern. As a result, language also has become a mere means of objectification. This kind of representational thinking, to objectify unconditionally everything, is the result, as Heidegger points out, of the traditional metaphysics; because this kind of thinking does not permit us to go deeper into the fact of being of the beings. Right from the time of pre-Socrates, the philosophers have failed to account this ontological ground of being. Philosophy as metaphysics had forgotten its primary task, and as a result thinking about being and the truth of being is forgotten in and through metaphysics. And this long tradition of metaphysics was obsessed by contemporary humans so badly that the act of very thinking and language has become mere servants of communication.

As a result, this threatened the very essence of humanity; because for Heidegger, the human person at the core of his being has the capacity to think. He details at length this unique position of human person which distinguishes from other beings. The human person is the only being which is concerned about his being and that makes a human as a unique and special way of being in the world. But from the time of Aristotle, human beings are conceived as being only rational animals. After Immanuel Kant, the human being is seen as a rational and autonomous being. But the human person is much more than that, not just a being among other beings. Heidegger points out that giving attributes to humans such as spirit, mind, soul etc. is the manner of traditional metaphysics. As a matter of fact, the question of being itself suppressed in this way, along with its ontological difference between being

3 *Ibid.*, p. 45.

4 *Ibid.*

and beings; and it has been fixed by other metaphysical interpretations. As a result, what is nearer than the nearest for the humans, i.e. the truth of being, is pushed away to farther than the farthest.[5] Sadly, this kind of metaphysical thinking has entrapped human person to conceive oneself just another being among beings.

Now what sets off human person from other beings is his ek-sistence which is his unique openness to the self-showing or disclosure of being. Heidegger describes this state of being-in-the-world as only proper to the human person. And most importantly, the proper way of human thinking arises from this unique relation to being. That is the essence of human thinking as Heidegger writes, "*Only from that claim "has" he found that wherein his essence dwells. Only from this dwelling does he "have" "language" as the home that preserves the ecstatic for his essence. Such standing in the clearing of being I call the ek-sistence of human beings. This way of being is proper only to the human being.*"[6] In the ek-static openness, being discloses itself, and its truth is appropriated by the human being by listening to it. For Heidegger, it is thinking which brings the essence of humans into relation with being and it is precisely the poetic language which maintains this relation with being.[7] Humans living ecstatically amidst the truth of being become the core argument for Heidegger's understanding of humanism.

Moreover, this ek-sistence should not be confused with the traditional metaphysical notion of existence. Heidegger explains in detail, in his *Letter on Humanism*, that ek-sistence is fundamentally contrasted to existence of the traditional metaphysics as he writes, '*The ecstatic essence of human being consists in ek-sistence which is different from metaphysically conceived existentia.*'[8] Traditionally, existence is the realisation of something that is as it appears in its Idea. This kind of traditional metaphysical determinations 'existence and essence' has dominated the entire Western Philosophy for a long time. Medieval Philosophy considered existence as actuality. Kant termed it as actuality in the sense of objectivity of the experience. For Hegel, it is the self-knowing Idea of absolute subjectivity and Nietzsche termed it as the eternal recurrence of the same. But Heidegger's insight of ek-sistence is totally different from this kind of traditional metaphysical determinations. The ek-static dwelling of humans is the humanism that realises the proper dignity

5 Letter on Humanism, p. 253.

6 *Ibid.*, p. 247.

7 James Luchte, "Heidegger's 'Letter on Humanism'- A Reading," https://www.academia.edu/6049524/Heideggers_Letter_on_Humanism_A_Reading, p. 8.

8 Letter on Humanism, p. 248.

of the human person: "*It is a humanism that thinks the humanity of the human being from nearness to being.*"[9]

But the calculative thinking reduces the capacity of human person to just mere mechanical and less creative in their endeavours. The point in case for Heidegger is that calculative thinking never stops, as if machines do, and never collects itself (loss of reflective thinking) just racing from one prospect to the next.[10] It is here that Heidegger makes a crucial observation that science and technology adds more to the growing thoughtlessness of contemporary man, taking humans away from their unique ek-static dwelling. Though we are living in the age of Science and technology with its tremendous success in many fields, we have as consequence ended up being slaves to technology; as a result, we behave like machines and we lose touch with ourselves, our depth of being. Losing touch with the core of our being, that which determines us humans, is the key issue of this crisis of thoughtlessness which dehumanises the contemporary human person.

As a matter of fact, this state of flight from thinking of contemporary humans has resulted in a state of homelessness – being away from the core of one's being: "*Homelessness so understood consists in the abandonment of beings by being. Homelessness is the symptom of oblivion of being. Because of it the truth of being remains unthought*."[11] This state of brokenness is dehumanising as the alienation touches the very essence that constitutes that what is human itself. It is the challenge of contemporary humans to resonate with Heidegger's thoughts if our thinking does not account deeply the truth of being. The saddest part is that contemporary humans are not even aware of this state of alienation as they are conditioned by the technical interpretation of thinking. Here at this plight of contemporary humans, Heidegger proposes an alternative way of thinking that paves the way back to the truth of being.

## 2. Meditative Thinking and Poetic Dwelling

How can we relate to Science and technology without losing our inner and real core? What type of thinking is needed to realise human's worth and his true potential? It is the awakening of the meditative thinking that Heidegger proposes as the alternative to the mechanical calculative thinking. Essentially, man is thinking, that is, a meditative being.[12] He quotes a poem from Johann Peter Hebel to describe the state of meditative thinking: "*We are plants which-whether we like to admit it to ourselves or not- must with our roots rise out of*

9 *Ibid.*, p. 261.

10 *Ibid.*, p. 46.

11 *Ibid.*, p. 258.

12 *Ibid.*, p. 47.

*the earth in order to bloom in the ether and to bear fruit.*"[13] The image of the plant in the poem emphasises the rootedness, being in touch with the core of its being. Unlike calculative thinking, meditative thinking permits us to stay rooted always in our human ek-static essence and branch out to bear much fruit in our endeavours. Meditative thinking is all about this rootedness in '*our life-giving homeland*'[14] of human uniqueness.

Our relation to the world and to technology needs to stem from this rootedness of our thinking. It is to be noted that Heidegger is not against science and technology itself but he is concerned about our relation to them. We should not be encircled by the forces of technology. Then we lose touch with ourselves and that disturb our meditative thinking. To remedy such a dangerous position of being carried away from our meditative thinking, Heidegger proposes that our relation to technology be proper and balanced. He wants that our relation to technology to become wonderfully simple and relaxed, which does not affect our inner and real core.[15]

In this context, he uses a technical term '*releasement toward things and openness to the mystery*'[16] which, to put it in simple terms, is an inner disposition to listen to the voice of being. It is in a way a step-back approach to muse over being, "*The stance of man seems almost a devotional passivity which will be completely open to the voice of being.*"[17] But at this passive openness to being, being discloses itself more and more what was hidden. Calculative thinking does not give us this inner disposition, but meditative thinking allows us this balanced state of relating to the technology. Heidegger emphasises that his proposed stance of releasement toward things and openness to the mystery does not befall us accidentally but only through persistent and courageous thinking.[18]

In the same line of thinking of meditative thinking, Heidegger quotes Aristotle's *Poetics*[19] to clarify that poetic composition is truer than explorations of being, because the former is claimed by being, guided by being, and its task is to bring being into language.[20] He invites humans to be poetic dwellers who meditate being. In the same vein of thought, Heidegger gives another instance that Aristotle reports from the life of Heraclitus, the Greek philosopher. Some

13 *Ibid.*

14 Discourse on Thinking, p. 48.

15 *Ibid.*, p. 54.

16 *Ibid.*

17 Richard E. Palmer, *Hermeneutics. Interpretation Theory in Schleiermacher, Dilthey, Heidegger and Gadamer*. (Evanston: Northwestern University Press, 1969) p. 149.

18 Discourse on thinking, p. 56.

19 Letter on Humanism, p. 275.

20 James Luchte, "Heidegger's 'Letter on Humanism'- A Reading," p. 21.

strangers wanted to pay a visit to Heraclitus, but upon their arrival, they were surprised to see that Heraclitus was warming himself at a stove. To their wonderment, Heraclitus invites them to come in with the following words, "*For here too the gods are present.*"[21] The significance of the instance is that the strangers thought that a great philosopher must be busy doing something great. But Heraclitus taught them that we need to muse over the ordinary and common activities of our life. Meditative thinking gifts us with such an inner disposition to be present intensively to the familiar everydayness of our life, and listen to the voice of being of the ordinary instances.

## Conclusion

'*Discourse on thinking*' of Heidegger is one of his deep concerns for contemporary humans. The seriousness of his concern is summed up in his words, "*The most thought-provoking thing in our thought-provoking time is that we are still not thinking.*" It is at this background of his deep observation of contemporary humans that he wants us not to lose our essential nature by the onslaught of science and technology. It is very true that his genuine concern is much more relevant today than when he made the discourse about 65 years ago in 1955. Today technology is enjoying unprecedented success in its history, and its success is going to be increasingly on the rise; the danger of being swayed by its almost omnipresent presence in every sphere of human endeavours must serve as a wake-up call for everyone not to lose their rootedness of thinking.

Having said this, it has to be reemphasised that Heidegger is not against the technological advancements, but rather he is concerned about our relation to science and technology. He would like to have the relation as that of simplicity and relaxedness but at the same time what is near, as Heidegger warns us, for this is always the longest and the hardest for humans.[22] Only persistent deeper thinking could bring us to the awareness of our thoughtlessness and the danger it presents to contemporary humans.

The seriousness of Heidegger's concern is that humans are to be rooted in their essence where meditative thinking is an integral part of their nature. Failing to be in touch with this inner and real core of our nature makes us to be in the state of alienation and homelessness. Calculative thinking is the product of the brokenness to be in touch with our inner core of human essence at the expense of our meditative thinking. The former makes the humans thought-poor whereas the latter gifts us the inner disposition to listen to the disclosure of being. The lifestyle of the contemporary generation is too busy and hyperactive; it becomes a huge challenge to have that sense of pondering and wondering at

21 Letter on Humanism, p. 270.

22 Discourse on thinking, p. 53.

reality. "*Discourse on thinking*" is aimed at inviting contemporary humans to contemplate the mystery of being. It is dwelling at this mystery of being that gives new ground and foundation for creativity for producing lasting works to strike new roots.[23]

23 *Ibid.*, p. 57.

8

# 'Our Beloved GODs': The Hindrance to the Genuine One

**Joby Tharamangalam OP**

*Research Scholar, Jnana-Deepa Vidyapeeth, Pune*

**Abstract:** There is an urgency to reflect whether the GODs we love and serve leave us impoverished or give us life.[1] We are overfed by innumerous images of God today. Some of these GODs defend inhuman and exploiting approaches instead of liberating the vulnerable. These disfigured faces of God are laid upon us when we are helpless, or we buy them when we want to hide. Since these masks of god possess exploiting capacity, and dehumanise their worshippers they have no place in the kingdom of justice and freedom. All these GODs bring along some essential qualities to our own person and society. Their ultimate evil lies in the fact that they feed on the poor, the unemployed, the helpless, the disappointed, the abused. In a world of victims, it is imperative to know in which GOD one is led to believe!

**Keywords:** Oppressive God, Liberative God, Created gods, Idolatry, God-business

Seeing a poor man eating some puffed rice, someone supplied for him four sacks of it, just because 'the poor man liked it.' In similar like-ability we too perform many things of/for God. There is an urgency to reflect whether the

1 GOD that we fabricate is always a SUPER-GOD. This article is based on Cyril Desbruslais' idea of a liberative God, instead of oppressive gods, which he has been advocating all through his life.

GODs we love and serve leave us impoverished or give us life. We are overfed by innumerous images of God today. Some of these GODs defend inhuman and exploiting approaches instead of liberating the vulnerable. These disfigured faces of God are laid upon us when we are helpless, or we buy them when we want to hide. Such GODs are the greatest obstacle in our search for God. This paper intends to show the burdening effect of these puffed GODs, and invites for rejection of these self-centred models that just treat our feelings.

## 1. In GOD's Image We Create Our Self and History

What we prefer to imagine about God is not an image of God alone, it is a revelation of our own commitment and activity in our personal and social existence. So, the way we imagine 'God,' also indicates the values it symbolises in our lives and shapes our character.[2] We may have conceptualised convenient images of God since we also search for our own self. We can find justifications for our GOD-concepts just as how we want our disguised interior self to be treated. What we find here is a second-hand GODs framed from favoured feelings, and from imaginative inputs shaped by books, films, or advices. Their characters are according to the conclusions we draw from providences, rewards and punishments, and the perspectives received from our experiences. Since God is the source of life and existence, the image that facilitates us with life would be truer to the reality of God. Those images that intimidate us, and keep us feeble or in fear are fake.

## 2. God Feeding on Sin

Society stresses on the accumulation of cultural symbols and rules of social behaviour. While this emphasis promotes formal correctness and adherence to systems, personally convincing and critically reflective approaches are subordinated. 'GOD' functions as a controlling symbol to keep the norms of the society intact. GOD in their imagination would be a massively magnified picture of someone who upholds moral prejudices and judgements in minute details. We need only to see how this loyalty/obedience benefit the authorities or society in order to understand its manipulative power. Promotion of guilt is an easy tool for keeping the people obedient to the system. People 'learn' to envision their faith, morality and mode of living within the system. Promotion of guilt is an easy tool for keeping the people obedient to the system.

Sin is thought to be the failure to observe laws. The misconceived link between sin and suffering has been misused as a fertile field for exploitation.[3] An insecure and suspicious person might falsely imagine one's protectiveness

---

2 Juan Segundo, *Our Idea of God,* Vol. 3 of *A Theology for Artisans of a New Humanity*. 5 Vols. trans. John Drury, (New York: Orbis Books, 1979), 90.

3 Albert Nolan, *Jesus Before Christianity: Twenty-fifth Anniversary Edition*, (New York: Orbis Books, 2002), 32.

as purity and holiness. A guilty-'righteous' person can project suspicion and disapproval onto others blaming, shaming and frightening oneself and others.[4] They reach a no-escape situation as these persons justify and intensify these feelings.

The feeling of guilt also holds two fears within: being unworthy of oneself (shame), and losing the love of the other. These fears lead to narcissism or perfectionism consequently affirming an image of a destructive GOD who does not allow his subjects any of their desires, and is content with their life of misery.[5] Those who have the manipulative power emerges as the exemplary righteous. Reparatory devotions and morality become components within a system of retribution and payment whereby 'others' can desire for righteousness.

### a. God and the Loathsome World

The contempt of the world, body and sexuality are constructed within several thoughts – the Judaic concern with ritual purity, the rejection of the body by neoplatonic pessimism, and the mistrust of worldly attachments common to stoicism and the Book of Wisdom.[6]

If we could see the signs of God being active in natural, cultural and social changes, we could avoid thoughts such as, "since GOD is in enmity with the world which is evil, we must live in this world as though we just happened to be here. The world we live in is a realm of Satan." Envisioning a supernatural world in such a way is a form of escape that makes it all the more difficult to solve our problems.[7] We find our inability to appreciate the world due to our constant encounter with miseries and challenges, and we attribute that loathsome attitude to God. We are pleased to consider evil and suffering as the work of evil and the effect of sin, but seldom acknowledge the reality of an exploited humanity, nor do we ask ourselves what is our responsibility for such a world.[8] The neotraditionalist blend of seeing medieval 'ascetic' symbols as forms of pure spirituality, is either a spiritually justified escape mechanism amidst the complexities of life, or a search to find comfortable identity providers. From a false assumption that GOD who does not like the

---

4 John Bertram Phillips, *Your God is Too Small,* (1956; Reprint, London: Wyvern Books, 1960), 54.

5 Jean Delumeau, *Sin and Fear: The Emergence of a Western Guilt Culture 13th-18th Centuries,* trans., Eric Nicholson (New York: St. Martin's Press, 1990), 300.

6 Delumeau, *Sin and Fear*, 446.

7 Nolan, *Jesus Before Christianity,* 11.

8 Jon Sobrino, *The Principle of Mercy: Taking the Crucified People from the Cross*, (New York: Orbis Books, 1994), 5.

world would be pleased to see the avoidance of all joys 'for his glory,' we make masochist self-righteous self for ourselves and a sadist GOD.[9]

## b. Humanity Condemned to Punishment and Reparations

Guilt conscience of an 'unworthy self' compels for reparations either for one's own fault or for the fault of others, because it holds a vision of the world which is always under punishment. A melancholic attitude becomes appreciated cultural trend within religion. A number of scrupulous frequent examinations of conscience becomes the guiding pattern of life, not in sincerity, but out of fear and to be safe from punishment. One becomes more cautious of a profane and decaying universe and submits to ever-increasing mortifications. It is a collective guilt conscience formed as deviance of a Christianity that focuses its message on the evocation of sin and which narrows its aim to the fight against sinning.[10] There are many salesmen of fake-crosses who say that we must pain ourselves for the love of Christ. They are the modern-day money-changers of the temple. Sacrifices demanded and interpreted to be 'sacrifice and commitment for the Lord,' are often unjustly channelled for someone's ulterior benefits. Guilt is the GOD they serve, and shame is the relation they have with GOD.

Like a child who takes advantage of a sympathetic mother, we frame a GOD who becomes very lenient and loving if we inflict pains on ourselves through severe fasting and afflicting pious practices. Through the Spirit, God gives us the strength to involve in history and keep God's love alive in the world. God does not want us to hide behind as a fearful or irresponsible child, instead enables us to face conflicts and improve our strength.

Devotions emphasising on reparations have emerged in a historical context when humanity faced atrocities. Christian asceticism is mistaken for indifference or repulsion from the life issues in the world as though God does not appreciate that we have any joy. Being a grace, liberation cannot represent an inhuman apathy towards life, as it is often presented. True asceticism is a quest for deeper truth and authenticity in one's development as a person, in order to achieve an interior calmness undisturbed by emotional extremities.[11]

It is fear and false-humility that drive many to 'say' that everything is by the grace of God. GOD who feels bad if we don't use flattery is a God of adulators. It is a GOD like a king in his Darbar who is pleased with music, dance and offerings of his choice. Servants of this GOD involve more and more in

9 True faith involves our conviction that God is good to humanity and the world. The power of faith is the power of goodness and truth, which is the power of God. See Nolan, *Jesus Before Christianity,* 39.

10 Delumeau, *Sin and Fear*, 297.

11 Juan Segundo, *Grace and Human Condition,* Vol. 2 of *A Theology for Artisans of a New Humanity*. 5 Vols. trans. John Drury, (New York: Orbis Books, 1968), 49

rituals and piety expecting to please God. Testimonies become advertisements and limit God to be a GOD of the rich and who can spend.

GOD is imagined as a child who is happy when it is given chocolate or when someone entertains it. GOD is happy when pleased, and otherwise can be easily offended. Those who possess such an approach neither use their critical faculties, nor speak the plain truth, nor behave 'naturally' for fear of sinning against this sentimental GOD. Such people's actions, and even their thoughts are led by a false sentimentality which they call as 'loving God.' Forced to be in a sentimental care, they have never been free to love.[12] Yet society often acknowledges this 'saintliness,' because it is never challenged by these saints. They are very nice outside, but inside they suffer because they cannot be themselves.

## c. Super-Perfect GOD and Imperfect Followers

GOD is imagined after a monarch sitting on his throne as an omniscient and intolerant judge with the book of all human acts. We are all at fault (guilt), and deserve vengeance (fear), and unable to look up to God and others (shame). The image of the 'god of one hundred per cent,' and his demand on us to be without faults keep us condemned to be always in an imaginary ideal. The more it is considered as God's demand, the more guilty and miserable people become. What was meant to be a life of perfect freedom has become an anxious slavery.[13] Some take this GOD to justify their own revengeful attitudes towards others.

## d. God's Costly Laundry

To remedy these imperfections GOD appears as a laundry man. It can be either at the cost of sacrifices, prayers, and rituals, or it can be 'free' forgiveness of debts but bound to innumerable obligations. The story of redemption and atonement is dramatized as a monarch offended by the failings of his ungrateful and rebellious subjects, would take vengeance. The act of redemption "is not automutilation as payment of an insolvent debt. It does not seek to pay a debt at all; rather it affirms that there is no debt to pay."[14] Jesus the saviour-deity becomes a mere object of religious cultic worship. If Jesus is given due importance, it necessarily demands serious modification of the picture of GOD

12 God is a loving presence, but this love is not sentimentality. It is a responsible belonging, a mutual giving and receiving of one another. There is fidelity ie an intention of permanence in relationship. There is fulfilment within which there are both union of love, and pain of one's inability to enter completely into the deepest thought, intentions, aspirations, desires, pain and failures of the other. Love is creative, enabling the lover rise to one's potentiality. See Norman Pittenger, *Picturing God*, (London: SCM Press, 1982), 77, 78.

13 Phillips, *Your God is Too Small*, 28.

14 Delumeau, *Sin and Fear*, 300.

as dictator and moral governor. Cultic image of a bleeding saviour is over-projected to the effect that it further accuses us of sins than reminding us of the redemption and life of grace.

### e. God of the Righteous Hypocrites

Many behave 'nice' because 'someone is watching' them. It is a conscience shaped after guilt, shame, and the fear of punishment. The root of their hidden 'sin' or 'rebelliousness' could be their own responses to persons in authority in their early years.[15] Their behaviour may be appreciated for 'reverence and piety' because it supports not only one's own hiding, but also the hypocritical and irresponsible stand of the society in the name of fake loyalty and obedience. Unfortunately, these emerge as exemplar within religious systems and become influential contributors in conscientization of others. It is reinforced by retributive theology and ethics that demands perfection, and grants approval and recognition. Gradually it becomes the cultural trend, and 'others' are damned ungodly.

### f. GOD of the Holy People

Some tend to take the mind of God into their custody. These isolated groups, as a 'privileged class' believe that their values and patterns of life are the true ways of God, and only they follow them correctly. They are characterised by attitudes of 'separatedness' from others, rather than as a creative responsibility toward others. Since they are 'special,' they are more perfect, real, authentic, and holier than others, and go on creating and discovering 'our GOD,' 'our traditions and customs' etc. They find their false GOD in the manipulation of isolated texts of Scripture.

Faith is set on some calculative beliefs that provide conceptual clarity avoiding all risks of reflection. They fail to accept that what they emphasise are some religious, social or political ideology or culture as if that is the way of God. Their fear to think or imagine outside the box, they call zeal for truth. Those who follow it gradually abandon faith, or begin to use it politically as a pressure group.[16] We can see it in gathering, numbers, prayer protests, faith rallies etc with an appeal of faith. We can understand their political or economic interest in their rigorous demands to adhere to a special scheme of faith emphasising on clear differences from others.

### g. God of the Exemplar

In defence of these ideologies, some assume the role of hero prophets. They make GOD jump through their rings confining God to their definitions. The

15 Phillips, *Your God is Too Small*, 15, 17.

16 Segundo, *Our Idea of God,* 79.

rigid attitudes and arrogant defence of beliefs also function as a convert neurosis defending one's 'distancing from an earlier system of belief.' Religion becomes a new personal or professional identity and can lead to religious fanaticism. Abandoning their profession and responsibilities receives magnified interpretation as 'great sacrifice.' Innocents who see them as 'ideal heroes' follow them and do everything in the name of faith, and the heroes do their new business. Sometimes these GODs seem to be in a hurry looking for an immediate result. These promoters urge themselves and their followers with tension and anxiety. They usually pin their practices to something of the past, and consequently shape a GOD in love with things of the past, understands and likes archaic language or the oldest available form of modern languages.[17]

This GOD is always in danger, attacked by enemies, and in need of protection. God who presupposes a necessary enemy, and who cease to exist if no one is there to believe is not God at all. The crisis felt is about the tension of changing the familiar images, structures, and practices.

Encountering the real face of God would make us struggle to rise to life. Our falsified and inauthentic ways of dealing with our society are allied to our distorted images of God.[18] Here we can see the exploitative power of the fake faces of GOD. We defend our own egotism devising countless ways to keep God far away. People do make use of the church and the faithful promoting these fake images while overlooking human liberty by forcing certain performances as the ways of authentic faith.[19]

## h. GOD on the Cheap Paths

'This statue' will give 'this special favour,' 'this prayer' will work miracles, and 'Hail Mary's without breaking,' 'write Bible verses for thousands of times,' 'light a candle online,' or 'offer flower emoticons, show distortions of 'devotions.' Something that was misinterpreted and idolised in recent times is 'First commandment' whose 'devotion' has resulted in isolating the faithful, and looking others with suspect. Similarly, 'special powers' are attached to certain Scripture verses that are expected to produce their 'magical' effects. Some have unknowingly become faithful devotees of the hero prophets and spiritual leaders.

When devotions emphasise heavily on the 'miraculous objects, prayers, and practices' they potentially become superstitions.[20] Often the emphasis on particular devotions happens at the manipulation of fear, insecurity, uncertainty, and results in personal subjugation or economic gain. Devotions are not a

17 Phillips, *Your God is Too Small*, 22.

18 Segundo, *Our Idea of God,* 7, 8.

19 Segundo, *Grace and Human Condition,* 52.

20 *Catechism of the Catholic Church* §2111.

magical process but based on the trust in God's living presence. Devotions devoid of this can turn out to be opium, a self-consolation onto which we gradually become dependent (even on retreats and some retreat centres).

Within devotional system, for some, the matters of the evil and the ways to have protection has become the primary concern of life. Unknown insecurities triggered by popular preachers make a peaceful stay at home or a comfortable travel nearly impossible. They find the presence and the influence of devils everywhere around them. They are 'happy' to have devil because he becomes a cause-answer for all their troubles, and saves them from serious introspection into social and personal responsibilities. Fear and suspect is the service they do, and devil is their GOD though they always attempt to chase him.

## 3. GOD Business or Competitive Business

Business and market transactions have become a familiar model in religious thought and image of God. GODs are operating on zones and behaviour patterns of non-liberty that all of us have.[21] These GODs are effective actors in religious-secular and intra-religious competitions at different levels of society. They want to possess the power to interpret, define and instruct the values and morality, authority over the rules of coexistence, and the monopoly for solving problems. Competition arises because the goods offered by religious and secular suppliers today often satisfy the same needs of customers whether they are served with proper provisions or not.[22] We can also see GOD marketized and sold. Remember the advertiser telling to buy 'our product,' and we bought what they said to be the best. At the end, we are left with bags of sparkling wrappers.

### a. Business Man-Banker

We are welcomed well in a bank if we are to deposit, but there are conditions to get a loan. God will reward with more blessings (interest) if we invest more with the number of prayers, etc (investments). Similarly, God will bless (pay the wages) if we 'work.' 'These prayers, these number of times, for these purposes ...' is quantification and materialising of faith.[23] Relationship with God is not a business; blessings are not a reward, but it is gratuitous.[24] It gives an image of a God whom we can condition by our doings, praying or paying.

21 Segundo, *Grace and Human Condition,* 51.

22 Jörg Stolz and Judith Könemann, "A Theory of Religious-Secular Competition," in *(Un) Believing in Modern Society: Religion, Spiritulaity, and Religious-Secular Competition,* ed. Jörg Stolz, and others, (London: Routledge, 2016), 19, 25, 26.

23 Segundo, *Grace and Human Condition,* 53.

24 Right attitude of praying or giving is as a sign of our gratitude and sincere openness before god. It is not to be thought that blessing is conditional as God blesses more as we pray or

God is shaped in the tendency to bring Christian life and its effectiveness in terms of money and number. God who blesses according to the money given is not a god at all.

## b. God Who Runs Pyramid Schemes

GOD guaranteeing some sure blessings for sharing pictures or prayers to 1,00,000s functions like chain money, chain letters, pyramid schemes. 'The prayer' or 'the act of sharing' itself appears to be easy techniques with magical effects; a way of using God. We can expect only 'cheap graces' from a GOD who is pleased with the number of 'Likes,' 'Shares' and 'type Amen' categories, and offer deliverance, healing, and relief of debts in online packages.

## c. Robot Programmer

God is seen as a manager or a Puppeteer GOD who controls everything that happens in the world. The subjective unpleasant events, apparently GOD's failures, challenge our views on 'providentialism.' God gives us a world that functions in accord with its proper laws, through human affairs and efforts God leads us to shoulder the task of freeing all its dynamisms for the service of love and the construction of the world.[25] We are not mere puppets or robotic creatures who behave very nice, kind and cheerful within God's control. God does not treat the humankind as a kindergarten where he has to discipline everyone every time. It is our discerning power to recognise what should have been done and what we need to do.[26]

## d. Problem Solver Sale

Nowadays many are experts not only creating and selling GODs but also playing a GOD. They provide problem-solving rituals, beliefs, values, and methods of healing, most of them as 'directly revealed by God.' Some gradually form groups around them, while others maintain personal supplier-client relationship, as participants or customers. These hero figures offer particular services (remedies, massages, predictions for the future) as demands arise. These consumers consume spiritual products, books, TV programmes etc., choosing from the options that give them the greatest 'satisfaction.'[27] They sell

pay more, and does not bless if we do not. According to the goodness of heart we are able to receive God's grace.

25 Segundo, *Our Idea of God,* 44.

26 Cyril Desbruslais, *The Philosophy of God: Faith and Traditions,* Vol. 10,"JDV Philosophy Series," Edited by Kuruvilla Pandikattu, (Pune: Jnana-Deepa Vidyapeeth, 2019.), 17.

27 Jörg Stolz and Thomas Englberger, "Major Churches, Evangelical Churches and Alternative-Spiritual Suppliers," in *(Un)Believing in Modern Society: Religion, Spiritulaity, and Religious-Secular Competition,* ed. Jörg Stolz, and others, (London: Routledge, 2016), 111, 113, 121. See also Jörg Stolz, Thomas Englberger, Michael Krüggeler, Judith

well because these 'services all for the glory of God' gives the best appeal of faith to gather both money and crowd.

This GOD possesses an expertise that no human knowledge and effectiveness has ever reached. Similar to God of the gaps, God who appears as 'the answer' for anything not currently explained by human knowledge. This GOD goes on losing the grasp as human knowledge and expertise increase more and more. God is in one way or the another behind all events. If we cannot wonder except when the so-called laws of nature are broken, then we must be in a sorry state.[28] We are reducing god to a magician.

GOD is a problem-solver who is approached only when there is a problem. A mythical presentation given to the ways that God intervenes in struggles can bring God only as *Deus ex machina,* a GOD arrives at emergency demands. Often our prayers and devotions are in favour of this GOD. GOD is used like paracetamol, kerchief, or an umbrella according to our convenience and forgotten until the next use comes.[29]

We can imagine what happens when these GODs fail. The whole religiosity ends with its sad conclusion: 'God is a Disappointment.'[30] Only a faithful believer can trust in a God who is as helpless as the victims themselves, and know that it is God's way of proclaiming that God loves the victimised of this world.[31] It powerfully contradicts GODs of prosperity gospels. They present the rich already in a blessed a state, the needy are so because of their sins, and have to 'spend' if they are to be 'blessed.' Greed is their God.

## Conclusion: Why We Must Reject 'Our' GODs?

The first cure from idolatry is to acknowledge that the image of God is distorted according to the religious and cultural caves in which we live. It is true that God becomes an empty abstraction without those anthropomorphic images. Our only option is to use them with constant critical evaluation. Idolatry of the highest form is seen when we assume that our picture of God perfectly reflects who God is.[32]

Since these masks of god possess exploiting capacity, and dehumanise their worshippers they have no place in the kingdom of justice and freedom. All these GODs bring along some essential qualities to our own person and

---

Könemann and Mallory Schneuwly Purdie, """The Change in Religiosity, Spirituality and Secularity," *Ibid.*, 179.

28 Nolan, *Jesus Before Christianity,* 41.

29 Desbruslais, *Philosophy of God,* 17.

30 Phillips, *Your God is Too Small*, 47.

31 Sobrino, *The Principle of Mercy,* 9.

32 Robert M. Baird, "Picturing God," in *Journal of Religion and Health,* 28, no. 3 (1989), 234, 235.http://www.jstor.org.library.britishcouncil.org.in:2048/stable/27506026http://www.jstor.org.library.britishcouncil.org.in:2048/stable/27506026

society. Their ultimate evil lies in the fact that they feed on the poor, the unemployed, the helpless, the disappointed, the abused. In a world of victims, it is imperative to know in which GOD one is led to believe.[33] For the sake of the survival of these GODs people are instructed not to think, and believing is encouraged to be an irrational process. Here we have a God who demands a brainless people. Prophets of these GODs are actually saying that they have no answer to the concerns of today. Here these images have come from distorted views of the world, anthropology, holiness and sin. They do matter for someone who sincerely seeks divine life and these fake faces will not suffice.

Who makes us play a puppet? It is our own liberative process to unmask the face of our GOD; then we will find what we have created of ourselves and our society, and why.

33 Sobrino, *The Principle of Mercy,* 9.

PART TWO

# SOCIALLY COMMITTED

9

# Search for Meaning: Youth's Re-Reading of Lk 10, 25-42

**Roy J. J. Pereira SJ**
*St. Xavier's College, Mumbai*

**Abstract**: The key problems of young people are emptiness, lack of interiority, lack of objects of identification, peer group pressure, isolation and alienation. Underlying all this is the search for meaning in life. In order to find meaning in life one has to have a vision. There are many visions on offer like that offered by market forces or the media. We are offering youth a vision of life based on God's dream for humanity as portrayed in the Bible. Or to put it more accurately our understanding of God's vision for God's people. The Love Commandment of Jesus is offered as a paradigm to youth. We feel that the search of our young people finds an echo in the question of the lawyer, "What must I do to inherit eternal life?"

**Keywords**: One-centredeness, Helping, Integration, Human dignity, Self-Image, Purpose.

All the five years that I was at Jnana-Deepa Vidyapeeth (JDV), the Pontifical Athaneum for my Philosophy and then Theology studies, I have worked with Cyril (no Father for him, as he would insist) and his youth group SSU which if I remember right stands for Students in Search of Unity specially when they put up their annual play. During the time I collaborated with Cyril and the youth group on their annual plays, all of which were musicals, given my own gifts in this regard. In 1990, we put up 'Inigo' on the life of St. Ignatius of

Loyola, where I also played the lead role of Ignatius. In 1991 we put up 'Pedro' on the life of Fr Pedro Arrupe, the former General of the Society of Jesus who had passed on earlier that year. When I returned for Theology after regency in 1994 we put up 'Adam and Eve' and in 1996 'Two by two' based on the story of Noah's ark. In all these plays I directed the music and choreography with help from others as well. After leaving JDV, I also helped out with the music of three more plays. "A. T. Thomas" came out in 1999 on the life of the Jesuit (alumnus of St. Xavier's College, Mumbai) who was killed in Northern India for fighting for the rights of the Dalits. In 2000, the play was on the life of Fr. Tom Gaffney, the Jesuit who was killed in Nepal by the drug mafia whilst working with youth afflicted by drug addiction. And in 2001, the musical was on the life of Bishop Oscar Romero.[1]

In a way the joy of working with Cyril and the youth group led to my own lifetime involvement with youth through my teaching at St. Xavier's College, Mumbai as well as being responsible for reviving the AICUF in Maharashtra in 1998. The experience of working with youth for nearly 20 years resulted in the above-mentioned dissertation on youth. The first chapter, "What must I do?" dealt with the Situation of Youth based on a survey that I had done. The second chapter "What is written?" dealt with scriptural exegesis of the text in question: context, analysis and exploring the lines of meaning in the text. And here below is the third chapter, "What do you read there?" a youth's re-reading of Lk 10, 25-42.

## 1. Recapitulation and Moving Forward

We can Lukan text 10:25-42 using various approaches. We can study the world-behind-the-text. Then we can ask: What circumstances prompted the author to write the gospel? What sources were used? What was the geographical location of the author and the ecclesiastical tradition of that location? What was the history of the text's development? These questions are usually associated with the historical-critical method. Here we used Source, Form and Redaction Criticisms. However, meaning is not located behind-the-text. But our understanding of the text is enriched when we immerse ourselves in its history. We then studied the world-in-the-text paying attention to various linguistic and literary relationships within the text as well as to its structure. But meaning does not lie here alone. Ultimately, "meaning results from

1 This article comprises the third chapter of my dissertation for the Masters in Biblical Theology degree which I completed at Vidyajyoti, New Delhil some time ago. The title of the dissertation was "A Youth Re-reading of Luke 10, 25-42. Since Fr. Cyril Desbruslais, S.J. was involved with youth all his life I felt it would be apt to retrieve a chapter of my work for his Festschrift since the themes so resound not only with his work but also his basic philosophy of living life to the fullest

a conversation between the world of the text and the world of the reader, a conversation informed by the world of the author."[2]

The world of the reader is the world of the youth today. Hence the situation of youth and their problems was presented in Chapter One. Certain questions arise from this vision of life. With these hooks (isn't every question a hook?) or with the vision arising from these "spectacles", I studied our pericope not assuming that all the answers to our questions of today are found 'ready-made' in the Bible. Instead, I try to find the questions to which this text was an answer as well as to see what questions the text raises to the youth. This does not mean that we are excluding the meaningfulness that could arise from other symbols in the text. Maybe these questions that arose within the Lukan community will resonate with the questions asked by our youth today. We shall then see whether the answers in the Bible have implications for us today. These are my interpretive aims. It is important to put down interpretive aims because aims dictate method. And thus, one method of hermeneutics is reader response criticism. Thus, in this chapter, we shall try to see what meaning arises from the conversation between the world of the youth and the world of the text. It should be understood that the message or significance of the text, is not something separate. It has been present all through our investigation. In other words, if we are attentive, we can find hermeneutical moments in our exegetical process where an understanding of the text can become also an application of it to life.

The key problems of the young people that we saw in the first chapter are problems of emptiness, lack of interiority, lack of objects of identification, peer group pressure, isolation and alienation. Underlying this is the search for meaning in life. In order to find meaning in one's life one has to have a vision. What sort of vision? There may be many visions one could offer to the youth of today. The market forces are offering them one vision of life. The media is offering another vision of life. We are offering them a vision of life based on God's dream for humanity as painted in the Bible. Or to put it more accurately our understanding of God's vision for God's people. The Love Commandment of Jesus is offered as a paradigm to youth. We feel that the search of our young people finds an echo in the question of the lawyer: What must I do to inherit eternal life?

'Eternal life' should not be understood as referring only to the hereafter. We must avoid an excessive spiritualist and eschatological reading of the New

2 W. Randolf Tate, *Biblical Interpretation: An Integrated Approach* (Massachusetts: Hendrickson Publishers, 1991) xx.

Testament.[3] In Luke in particular the kingdom is not eschatologized.[4] Thus, the reference is to life here as well. That the question refers also to life here on earth is further confirmed by the statement of Jesus in v. 28, "Do this and you will live" meaning that the person who puts the command of love into practice will find meaning in life living a truly human life in joy and contentment. Obviously he couldn't be referring only to life in the hereafter. Confer also, a parallel text where the same question is asked (Lk 18:18). There, Luke has Jesus end this pericope with, "Truly, I say to you, there is no man who has left house…for the sake of the kingdom of God, who will not receive manifold more in this time, and in the age to come eternal life." Hence this question refers to life here and now and thus resonates with the question of our youth today: What must we do to truly "live"? Who can give us our center of gravity? What can we do to prevent ourselves from being flung off the merry-go-round of the rat-race?

**What must I do to inherit eternal life?** We develop this vision from the ensuing narrative.

The lawyer himself gave the answer of "loving God with all our heart, and with all your soul, and with all your strength, and with all your mind and your and neighbor as yourself." But the force of the narrative is in the doing. The Lukan Jesus uses it in verse 29 as well as in verse 37 and in commending Mary for doing the one thing that is necessary. We shall come back to this point later but first we have to see how we understand these commands.

## 2. One-Centredness/Single-Mindedness of Purpose

As we saw in the last chapter the commandment to love God with all your heart, and with all your soul, and with all your strength, and with all your mind is a graphic way of expressing that we are called to love God with the totality of our being – the totality of our personal life. God's claim on us reaches to every area of our experience, to our innermost being (heart); our lives – what gives us our individual identity (soul); our energy, strength, resolve, and resources (might); and our understanding and intellectual capacities (mind). No part of ourselves is to be withheld from God. This is what will be our center of gravity, our anchor, or to come back to the imagery we used, the center pole of the merry-go-round. Nothing, absolutely nothing can take its place. Humanly speaking, we may agree to have God as our center but would like to have some "small" other centers, not permanently "you see," but now and then. This text clearly indicates otherwise. The world offers other centers: money, fame, power, pleasure and so on. Youth are opting for these as we saw

3 Severino Croalto, "Biblical Hermeneutics in the Theology of the Oppressed," in *VJTR* 46 (1982) 62.

4 Croalto, 68.

in the Mc Cann survey. But they are also realizing the effervescent quality of these centers. The text calls them to renounce completely those idols that do not bring life, only at the most a temporary high. They have a place in human living but never at the centre.

## 3. Helping Anyone in Need ... Even One's Enemy

The command of 'love your neighbor' which is exemplified in the story of the Good Samaritan points out that loving neighbor is expressed in action, in helping neighbor out, in doing. Love is not an internal state or feeling or emotion but love, as understood in the Mediterranean culture implies personal attachment. Therefore, the text speaks about having personal attachment for neighbor which naturally would be expressed in helping the neighbor when in need. But lest we get a sense of complacency that we **are** loving to those who live around us, the text refuses to define the limits of neighbor but instead stretches it out to "anyone in need" through the clever use of language, "a certain man." Rather than limiting it to one own's community (Lev 19:18; 29:18) as part of the OT does, he broadens it out to "anyone in need" as we see in our pericope. Here, the listeners are not given any information about this "half-dead" person except that he is in need. Thus, 'neighbor' knows no religious boundary, no ethnic boundary, no caste boundary, no ideological boundary. In fact, he radicalizes the definition of neighbor by asking, "Which of these three, do you think, was a neighbor to the man who fell into the hands of robbers?" Jesus' question concerns the subject of love. Therefore, rather than trying to define the limits of our love, we are called to a limitless showing of mercy.

But the radicalness of the text is seen in encompassing even the enemy [the use of the Samaritan (enemy to the Jewish listeners) in the story] in its understanding of who is neighbor. Jesus upsets the expectations of his listeners when he tells them the story of the "Good Samaritan." His listeners would have been quite comfortable with the fact that the priest and the Levite didn't help the man who fell among robbers, given the anti-clericalism (to use a modern word) present at that time. Or even that they ought not help given that status. When they heard of the third person coming they would have expected it to be a Jewish lay-person. So when Jesus mentions Samaritan he turns their world upside down. While in our pericope love for enemy is symbolized in the use of the 'Samaritan,' in another text (Lk 6:27,35) Jesus mentions specifically the need to love one's enemies because of the fact that our Father is merciful to all (Lk 6:36). In our Christian context it would an RSS man helping out. The youth are thus challenged to set aside the prejudices they have. Christians have the idea that Muslims are dirty, fanatical and fighting with everyone. Muslims feel all Hindus are against them. Hindus believe Christians are of loose morals and pleasure-seeking (stereotyped in Hindi films). Among Christians, Goans have a bias against Mangaloreans, Tamilians against Malayalees, and so on. Caste still plays a great role at various levels though among city-dwellers it surfaces only at the time of marriage. Recently, when some of our youth went to help out after the Gujarat earthquake they came back with stories of how the younger RSS members shared with them their relief materials and medicines.

## 4. Integration

We have seen earlier that there is no dichotomy between the two commandments. They form the two axes of one graph. The y-axis or the vertical dimension and the x-axis or the horizontal dimension. Thus, when we have mercy on the one in need (loving neighbor) we become persons who listen to God's commandments (love God). When we reach out, when we forgive, when we share, when we obey all of these and other commandments of God we are loving neighbor and in the same breath loving God. In loving neighbor we are loving God. In showing concern for the other, we are listening to what God has to tell us. And when we spend time in listening to God, in being with God, we understand what God wants us to do. This in turn guides us to where we are needed. This is an ongoing dialectic. In having mercy on the other we are listening to God and in listening to God we understand who is my neighbor who needs my help.

## 5. Dying to Oneself

Thus the message that we get from the text is that in order to have life, life eternal we need to love God, symbolized in the text as listening to God's prophet, Jesus and in following God's commandments that he gives us which includes having mercy on the one in need, which is the expression of loving neighbor. Having mercy on the other involves in the Samaritan story spending time, money as well as risking one's life because the thieves who robbed the man could certainly be back. The focus that one gives to the other necessarily involves sacrificing time, money and maybe also risking one's life. There is a dying to oneself in small ways and big. At a deeper level the text is trying to convey that it is only in dying to oneself can we really hope to live life fully, to experience eternal life here and now. This theme recurs in Luke. For example in Lk 18:18 in reply to the same question asked now by the ruler, the answer given is keeping the commandments and selling all you have to give to the poor. In the former we see an expression of loving God and in the latter that of loving neighbor. In asking the ruler to sell all he had we see a call to dying to oneself, one's riches, one's security. The next part of the story shows how difficult this is and how riches come in the way of entering the kingdom of God, of receiving manifold more in this time and in the age to come, eternal life. In other texts we have the imagery of the seed needing to die in order to produce abundant fruit.

## 6. Love Yourself?

Just a note about the "as yourself" in "loving neighbor as yourself." The 'as yourself' in "Loving your neighbor as yourself" can be understood rhetorically and this would have been why the author used the language in such a way. We refer to Makujina:

> Study of the relevant scriptural data does not support the interpretation of "You shall love neighbor as yourself" (Lev 19:18; Mt 19:19; 22:39; Mk 12:31,33; Lk 10:27; Rom 13:9; Gal 5:14; Eph 5:28, 33; Jas 2:8) as expressing the modern concept of self-esteem. Rather, the concept of self-love in these texts is inseparably bound up with one's natural disposition for one's own well-being, in both body and soul, and with the self-interest that is necessary for survival and easily prone to over-indulgence.[5]

But when looked at from the psychological lenses of today we see a deeper insight into that symbol. While it is taken for granted then and now that a person loves himself or herself, we learn more and more today that at a deeper level this is not so. We are upset with certain of our physical appearances or with certain mental traits. We are angry with certain behavior patterns up to the extent of hating ourselves. And because we do not love ourselves, we cannot be expected to love others. Thus, we are called to accept ourselves and forgive ourselves; in other words, to love ourselves. When we love ourselves we will begun the first stage in the process of loving others. Thus, we see how when we study a text with the help of other disciplines the surplus of meaning, the hidden beauty of a text flowers forth.

## 7. Walk Your Talk

We are already in the "information age" or the age of knowledge. Knowledge is accessible at one's finger-tips thanks to the internet, television channels, newspapers and books. Today, if you want information on any topic, the internet will throw up literally ten thousands of sites (try google.com). For a single ailment hundreds of remedies are available. To lose weight I can advise you of many methods but I myself will not get down to doing it. A lady when asked whether she lost weight after joining a gym replied, "To lose weight I joined a gym but they expected me to come there everyday." If there is a social problem to be tackled thousands of solutions are proposed but we like to talk about these and discuss them rather than implement them. This situation is not unlike the time of Jesus. As pointed out earlier, Jesus' contribution was not the distilling of the commandments, nor even his putting them together but his

5 J. Makujina "The Second Greatest Commandment and Self-Esteem," *Mast Sem Journ* 8 (2, '97) 211-225.

emphasis on their implementation, on the 'doing' part, "Do this and you will live." His message assumes an urgent relevancy today.

## 8. Choosing Carefully

So central to the vision of the Lukan Jesus is an other-centerdness. This other-centeredness expresses itself differently in the various contexts of a young person's life. In his college or work context, in his family context, in his recreation or games context. Young people are called to reach out to those in need even when they are already busy; to forgive past enmity, to look after the small details, to show commitment. Alienation and isolation is caused by focussing inwards on my needs, my time etc to the exclusion of others. There is no time to listen to the other and no time to listen to God. Or they find themselves busy with many other things when only a few are necessary. The need for choosing correctly is also one of the insights that we get from the pericope, more directly from the Mary-Martha story but also in the Good Samaritan story. P. Ellis puts it as follows: "By saying that Mary has "chosen the better part," he is stressing the necessity of discerning what is actually needed and appropriate in a given situation. The notion of appropriateness is crucial to understanding the idea of service in the gospels."[6] In this story, what is hinted at is not that looking after material needs is less important than being with the Lord (rather "doing" has been stressed as important) but the need for discerning what is appropriate at the given moment. Action versus contemplation is too superficial a reading of our text. Rather, there is an appropriate time for "doing" action (loving neighbor) and an appropriate time for "doing" listening (loving God). "Choosing the better part" is always context specific.

## 9. Respect for Human Dignity above Human Codes of Purity

Respect for human dignity is an important value because we are all created in the image of God (Gen1:26) and we are all children of our Father (Lk 11:2; 6:35-36). From the parable one attitude that comes forth is the respect for human dignity irrespective of the state or condition of the person. This attitude is evident in the Samaritan but not in the priest and Levite. They are not entirely to blame. "All enduring human societies provide their members with ways of making sense out of human living. The purity system is one such system of meaning. Such purity distinctions embody the core values of a society and thereby provide a clarity of meaning, direction of activity and consistency for social behavior. Controversy between Jesus and the Pharisees over such purity norms can be seen throughout the Gospels, often as a result of Jesus' disregard

6 Pamela Ellis, "The better part," *Month* 31 (2, '98) 58-61.

of accepted interpretations of the maps."[7] Jesus rejects such interpretations when they violate the dignity of the human person. For "the Son of Man is lord of the Sabbath" (Lk 6:5). For him, rules, laws and systems are made for the human person and not vice-versa. If they oppress the human person then these systems should be modified or thrown out altogether.[8]

Today we may have thrown purity systems but there are other systems that dehumanize the person. The Gospel challenges us to oppose such systems and fight for the dignity of the human person.

Thus, new patterns of relationships within society are envisaged. This would entail acceptance of persons irrespective of their background, service to those in need (Lk 10:25-37) as part of one's duty without expecting thanks (Lk 17:9-10). Love of neighbor i.e. responding to one in need also involves being on the look out for those who are being cheated (Lk 20:47). Multinational companies who hire and fire at their own free will, without bothering about the person or the family. Sexual harassment at work which violates the dignity of the woman. International banking systems which were started to help people are today responsible for squeezing the poor in developing countries. Thus, the teaching of Jesus needs to interact with culture and customs, attitudes, behavior and societal structures even if these are sanctioned by legal or religious authorities.

## 10. Turning the World Upside Down

In other places in Luke's gospel we see how Jesus exemplifies through his behaviour the turning of the world upside down. He goes into Gentile territory (Lk 8:26 ff), he dines with tax-collectors and upsets rules of purity. He challenges the Jews to invite the socially outcaste to their celebrations (Lk 14:12-14) and preaches about "the last shall be first" (Lk 13:30; See also 22:24 ff) and "those who humble themselves shall be exalted" (Lk 14:11; 18:14). The section on what we call the "beatitudes" also refers to the reversal of values. Thus, like Jesus, we are called to shatter the stereotypes of social boundaries and class division and render void any system of religious quid pro quid. The aim of turning the world upside down is to establish a new world where the values of love, fraternity, service, universality, freedom serve as guiding principles.

7 Malina and Rohrbaugh, 318.

8 The D manuscript (Codex Bezae Cantabrigiensis) for Lk 6:5 reads: On the same day, seeing someone working on the sabbath, Jesus said, "You, if indeed you know what you are doing, you are blessed; but if you do not, you are cursed and a transgressor of the law." Thus, Jesus is not an iconoclast but breaks the law only if it is oppressive to the human person and goes against human dignity.

## 11. Building Their Self-Image

The detailed description of how the Samaritan cares for the man symbolizes the commitment of the Samaritan. His help is not mere tokenism, not some superficial first-aid but an expression of his deep caring and commitment. Luke brings this out through giving us a close-up of the scene wherein the Samaritan administers to the injured man. He is not interested in only administering first aid but takes him to an inn so that he completely recovers. Luke is trying to point out that commitment is an essential ingredient if we want to experience "life" (The human person is made for commitment).

There are other examples in the Gospel of Luke where we see the rebuilding of self-image taking place. For e.g. in the pericope of the man possessed by demons Lk 8: 26-39 and in the story of the Pharisee and the tax-collector Lk 18: 9-14. A vast majority of the youth of today especially those belonging to economically weaker backgrounds suffer from very poor self-images. It could be from negative comments made on them either at school or in the neighbourhood or even just by observing other's doing better than them because of greater opportunities. They may not have the most "up-to-date" clothing or even maybe cannot afford movies and discos. They may not have a car nor own a computer at home. All these 'lacks' have a great effect on their self-image; a subtle effect of humiliation on them. The Good Samaritan is a model of those interested in caring for the total person, in building up the self-image of people.

These ten pointers encapsulate the vision of the text of Lk 10, 25-42 from the point of view of youth today. Incorporating these into one's life could serve to mitigate the problems of emptiness, lack of interiority, lack of objects of identification, peer group pressure, isolation and alienation. These will also serve positively to bring in a sense of meaning to one's life so that one can live life abundantly, a theme so dear to the heart of Cyril Desbruslais. I would like to end this article with a composition of mine which I have used in the play "A. T. Thomas" which attempts to address the plight of the oppressed villagers and give them a sense of hope. The title of this song is, "**Hope, Faith and Love**."

Is there something in your life that's not going right?
Is there something that you'd like to change?
Is there something in your life that makes no sense?
Do you feel like just giving up?

Are there times in your life when you've had enough?
Are there times the clouds seem all black?
Are there days in your life when there seems no way?
Are there nights when life seems a cross?

Hope, Faith and Love's what keeps life moving on
Hope, Faith and Love that's what life's all about
Hope, Faith and Love my friend
Will see us through

Yes there were times in my life too
Days when I had enough
But Hope just kept me going on
Hope in a God who loves

Hope, Faith and Love's what keeps life moving on
Hope, Faith and Love that's what life's all about
Hope, Faith and Love my friend
Will see us through
Hope Faith and Love my friend
In a God who loves.

10

# Climate Change and Worldviews: Hope for Our Children and Grandchildren

**Hector Andrade**
*Educationist and Biodiversity Conservator, Pune*

**Abstract:** Climate change is upon us and people all over the world are searching for answers to the questions: where did we go wrong and how can we turn things around? What we need is a serious interrogation of the worldviews that have consciously and subconsciously influenced our way of proceeding with regards to the earth. This article explores the thoughts and ideas of Lynn White and Martin Heidegger as they analyze the roots of the ecological crisis, and proposes that some of the answers to the health and well-being of the planet as well as our ourselves may lie in the interrogation of traditional ecological knowledge that has helped humanity survive and thrive for thousands of years across the different climatic zones of the earth.

**Keywords**: Climate Change, Ecological Crisis, Historical roots, Worldviews, Traditional Ecological Knowledge, Enframing, Health and wellness, Technology, Science.

## Introduction

We have just come to the end of one of the most unprecedented monsoons in the history of the country, and the areas surrounding the city of Pune received more rainfall than the wettest spot in the world. Climate change is upon us and this leaves us with several questions to ruminate, and issues to act upon. While scientists and politicians squabble over whether or not this change is due to human actions, or whether the change is happening at all, it is the poor farmers who have to bear the brunt of the climate change that one cannot ignore. When the elephants fight, it is the grass that gets hurt the most.

## 1. Interrogating the Historical Roots

As persons fulfilling the function of being philosophers in society, one of the questions that we need to look at closely is whether our existing worldviews have brought us to the brink of an apocalypse. Lynn White in his landmark essay titled, "The Historical Roots of Our Ecologic Crisis"[1] had laid the proximate blame for the ecological crisis on the Industrial Revolution during which the relationship between humans and the earth saw a paradigmatic shift. Armed with hitherto inaccessible physical power, human beings began plundering the earth, and every living and non-living element of the ecosystem was transformed into a resource to be exploited. White, being the professor of history that he was, goes on to explore how the roots of the ecological crisis can be traced way back to the Book of Genesis. God's exhortation to Adam and Eve, to go forth and "have **dominion** over the fish of the sea, and over the fowl of the air, and over every living thing that moveth upon the earth"[2], is seen as the original cause for the anthropocentric worldview which began the normalisation of the exploitation of the earth. He claims that this worldview swept aside the animistic worldview that many tribal societies had and still have in several parts of the world.

There are two saving graces in White's article. The first, is that he acknowledges that the word "dominion" is not the root of the verb to "dominate." To have dominion means to treat the earth as God (Domine) would and within the semantic axis of the Bible would more readily read as us being given the stewardship of the earth, rather than being given the license to rule, exploit, dominate and destroy. The second is that, White, in a brief paragraph, actually puts forth St. Francis of Assisi as the role model and the patron saint for all of us who are fighting to save the earth, and ourselves whose survival is inextricably linked to the earth. The worldview of St. Francis of Assisi challenges the anthropocentric worldview, and instead puts forth a way of seeing each and every element on the planet as essential and thus deserving equal filial respect.

1 White, Lynn Jr., "The Historical Roots of Our Ecological Crisis", *Science*, 10 March 1967, Vol. 155, Issue 3767, pp 1203-1207

2 King James Bible, Gen 1:28.

## 2. Interrogating the Role of Technology

Going deeper into this question a la Hans-Georg Gadamer's Hermeneutic Circle[3], one cannot overlook the huge contribution made by Martin Heidegger. In his very insightful work titled, *The Question Concerning Technology*, (1954), Heidegger interrogates the very essence of technology. The most obvious understanding of technology is its instrumentality, its use by humans as a means to an end. Here technology aids us to bring forth things into existence which is akin to the Greek word "poesis" which meant bringing-forth things from "concealment to unconcealment"[4]. However, Heidegger finds a subtle change in the way "modern" technology brings about this "unconcealment." Rather than a bringing-forth, modern technology reveals by "challenging-forth." In this fashion, Technology changes the essence of everything that it comes in contact with. We no longer see a river as a river but as a potential source of hydro-electric power, we no longer see a tree as a tree but probably as furniture and so on and so forth. Heidegger, arrives at his central idea of "gestell" or enframing, via a discussion on how technology looks at everything as "standing-reserve." No-thing has an essence in-itself, but it only has value in as much as it stands in reserve to the ends of technology.

What is most useful to the current discussion on Climate change and the consequent need for a liberative worldview, is this concept of enframing. Taking his idea forward, one could surmise that most people today wear glasses tinted by technology. We have lost our deeper connections with nature, because we see everything as merely having "use" value in as much as they stand in reserve. We have experienced and are experiencing the greatest dehumanising danger of this worldview when we began seeing human beings merely as standing-reserve, as resources to be exploited. The spectacular loss of millions of human lives, often in unknown trenches, during the second world war was a result of this worldview and perhaps prompted Heidegger to write about the dangers of this technological worldview. However, for Heidegger, the greatest danger is when human beings are prevented by enframing from experiencing what he calls a more "primal truth" that they have no access to, since "bringing-forth" has been replaced by "challenging-forth", "poesis" by forcing out. This perhaps is seen through the various experiments of modern science, the Large Hadron Collider at Cern can be cited as a case in point. Technology now distances us from what he believes is a genuine revealing or the truth.

3 "Hans-Georg Gadamer", *Stanford Encyclopaedia of Philosophy, 2005.*

4 Martin Heidegger, "The Question Concerning Technology," *Basic Writings Ed.* David Farrell Krell (Harper & Row, 1977), 287.

## 3. The Way Out

So what is the way out of this enframing, this trap that we have fallen into? For a solution to this dilemma, Heidegger turns to Art. Art has still remained true to "Poesis." It aids the bringing-forth of reality and reveals the deeper truth. As his guru, Friedrich Nietzsche would say, "We have art so that we may not perish by the truth."[5] Picasso will say, "Art is a lie that tells us the truth."[6] So where are the alternate worldviews that will save us from the dangers of climate change? The answers lie perhaps in our traditional ecological knowledge, which is very often portrayed in the form of stories and folktales, sometimes taking the form of sculpture or paintings, and sometimes dance. In many "enlightened" communities, especially in the west, there is now a conscious turning towards the "old" practices. People are moving away from microwaves and refrigerators to freshly grown food, from melamine and teflon-coated cookware to cast iron and earthen pots, from allopathic medicine to herbal and other alternate/traditional modes of health care. The biggest sufferer of the technological worldview, along with the health of the earth, was the health of human beings. Whereas most indigenous health care traditions understood human health in wholistic terms and hence in several ways inextricably linked to the health of the earth, the modern technological worldview forced a siloed understanding of the ways and means to maintain health and wellness. The rampant use of pesticides, sanitizers and antibiotics, meant the majority of the beneficial insects, as well as microorganisms were eliminated along with the small percentage of harmful ones. No where was this battle fought more vigorously than in the human gut. Modern medicine destroyed the thousands of species of the gut microbiome without even understanding the vital role they play in preserving the delicate balance that defines and maintains human health and wellbeing. The rise of allergies all kinds in our children is a direct result of such narrow understanding of healthcare. Without the use of microscopes, many of the wise women and men belonging to so-called "native", "tribal", "uncivilised", "backward", cultures and traditions, had "seen" that which our naked eyes cannot see. They saw the subtle interconnections that exist between human life and the rest of the cosmos. They understood the unique role that each and every living and non-living element of the ecosystem plays in maintaining the harmony that is the hallmark of a healthy earth. An exploration of the eating habits and food preparations in many of the traditional societies throw up signs of this alternate worldview that understood the meaning of balance and interdependence.

5 Friedrich Nietzsche, *Will to Power*, ed Kauffman, Sec 822.

6 Pablo Picasso, "STATEMENT TO MARIUS DE ZAYAS," 1923, 'Picasso Speaks,' *The Arts, New York, May 1923,* pp. 315-26

Some may retort by saying that there were several shortcomings in the traditional societies as well, especially among those groups that practice/d the slash and burn method of farming (*Des-brulais*!). However, today we discover that several ecosystems are depended on fire and some seeds do not germinate unless they have been exposed to fire. Besides the scale of the slash and burn farming was miniscule compared to the scale of destruction that was wreaked upon the earth post the Industrial Revolution.

## Conclusion

So is there hope that we can turn things around and ensure that we hand over a safe and healthy home for our children and grandchildren? Those trained in the rigours of modern science find it difficult to see beyond the blinkers and silos prescribed by their training when it comes to looking after the health of the planet, which includes our own health and well-being. However, one can argue that populations in several so-called traditional communities survived and multiplied relying exclusively on their indigenous knowledge systems, and the insights that they provided to them about their role in the circle of life. Some of the answers to climate change and the ecological crisis may be found in a serious exploration of the traditional ecological knowledge that has been accumulated across the world. For the scientific mind, this knowledge would fall under the category of "myth". But then maybe we should agree with Claude Levi-Strauss, the father of Anthropology when he says that Science itself is a modern myth.

# 11

# Spirituality: Seasoned or Seasonal? – An Attempt to Make Spirituality Relevant for Today's Youth

**S. Stephen Jayard**
*Jnana-Deepa Vidyapeeth, Pune, India*

**Abstract:** Given the extremely minute fabrications that have gone behind the universe and the innumerable biotic coincidences several scientists tend to think that the universe is not self-explanatory. Though the universe is immense in its size and age yet it is finite; there are more evidences emerging now, to show that the universe had a beginning (Big Bang!) and will have an end; of course there are several proposals to narrate the end of the universe, like Big Crunch theory! As the universe cannot explain its own existence it is not difficult to think of an agent outside of it. Catholic Church is among the many believing communities to take this fact to show that human reason can certainly take us to believe in the existence of God: "The world cannot have its origin and its destination within itself. In everything that exists, there is more than we see. The order, the beauty, and the development of the world point beyond themselves toward God. Every man is receptive to what is true, good and beautiful. He hears within himself the voice of conscience, which urges him to what is good and warns him against what is evil. Anyone who follows this path reasonably finds God." So in this article, the author pleads for an enduring and seasoned spirituality that is relevant for the youth of today.

**Keywords:** Spirituality, Seasoned spirituality, Youth, Religious relevance for today, Science and Spirituality.

Spirituality is a word that is usually not attractive to the modern youth; many of them are indifferent to them and some of them run away, and still others would even argue against the very concept of spirituality, saying that it is not only unnecessary and irrelevant in the modern society but also dangerous to the peace and harmony in society. It is in this context this paper takes up this notion of spirituality for some clarification and suggestions to modern society, especially to our youth today.

First, it begins to clarify the very notion of spirituality, by contrasting it against the idea of religion; spirituality goes beyond the 'confines' of religion; it is not proper to identify spirituality with the idea of religion, though both are not unrelated. Since the modern youth is generally carried away by the contemporary science some efforts are taken to show that science in its real sense is, not only not against spirituality, but in fact it even enriches the notion of spirituality. Thus, in section two, it is shown that modern youth can be very comfortable with the notion of spirituality even in the ethos of science today. In section three, the notions of seasoned and seasonal spirituality are clarified, by showing that seasonal spirituality cannot be genuine spirituality. Finally concluding remarks are made along with some suggestions to make studies of spirituality and meditation as part of the regular curriculum of our education, so that our children get holistic growth and development in life.

## I. Religion and Spirituality: Some Clarifications

Today's young people are often disillusioned with religion due to many factors. The number of conflicts at various levels, the number of wars, the amount of violence and bloodshed – ironically all in the name of religions, that instruct us to love everyone, disturb any thinking person, and especially the modern youth. Many regions seem to have unfortunately forgotten their original charism and vitality; they seem to be more of an institution rather than a way of life; they do not affect the value-systems and convictions. The externals and the rituals dominate over the inner convictions and attitudes of the believers. For instance, as Krishnamurthy points out, "[T]oday religion has almost degraded into a vast fund of apparently meaningless rituals and rites, coupled too often with fundamentalist dogmatic attitudes. And on top of this it has come to be massively used as an alibi for acquiring political power and economic domination and for condoning violence".[1] Religion is identified with its founder(s) and their lives, holy books and worship places, rites and rituals, dogmas and doctrines. But spirituality, though it can have religion as its starting point and an enriching element, goes beyond the 'limits' of religion. Tom Boyd has claimed 'that the current attempt to split spirituality

1 V. Krishnamurthy, *Science and Spirituality: A Vedanta Perception* (Mumbai: Bharatiya VIdya Bhavan, 2002), p.186.

away from religion is an expression of postmodern thinking', yet he contends that 'spirituality and religion, while distinguishable, cannot be separated.'[2]

Samuel Rayan distinguishes three models of spirituality – *distributive spirituality* (some follow a spiritual life and others don't); *alternating model of spirituality* (same people alternate their activities between spiritual and other engagements) and *interpenetrative model of spirituality*; (all are spiritually engaged in all their actions, in such a way that action and contemplation are integrally connected).[3] Spirituality is today seen as the quest for enlightenment, meaning and purpose in life; for instance, according to Elena Lugo: "Spirituality is the pursuit of meaning, of an intimation of purpose and sense of vital connection to one's ultimate environment – the dimension of depth in all of life's endeavours and institutions. In short, a spirituality functions, as a principle of enlightenment, integration and finality without which our self-reflection, self-realization and self-surrender would become superficial, chaotic and aimless."[4] Nowadays, spirituality has been defined more inclusively: "Spirituality has been described as an attempt to grow in sensitivity, to self, to others, to non human creation and to God, or as an exploration into what is involved in becoming human".[5] It is now common to see spirituality as a tool to achieve self-transcendence; it is "that dimension of the human subject in virtue of which the person is capable of self-transcending integration in relation to the Ultimate, whatever this Ultimate is for the person in question. In this sense, every human being has a capacity for spirituality or is a spiritual being."[6] The dichotomy between spiritual and secular realms is getting thinner: "New spiritualties are formulated and practised within a secular context, and these challenge the traditional, homogenized and universal understanding of spirituality in established religions traditions".[7]

---

2 Tom Boyd, "*Is Spirituality Possible without Religion? A Query for the Postmodern Era", in* Ann W. Astell (ed.), *Divine Representations: Postmodernism and Spirituality* (New York and Mahwah, NJ: Paulist Press, 1994), pp. 83-101, p. 83.

3 Samuel Rayan 'The Search for an Asian Spirituality of liberation', in V. Fabella, P. K. H. Lee and D. Kwang sun Suh (eds), *Asian Christian Spirituality: Reclaiming Traditions* (Maryknoll, NY: Orbis Books, 1992), pp. 11-30.

4 Elea Lugo, 'Reflections on Philosophy, spirituality and Mariology' in Astell (ed.), *Divine Representations: Postmodernism and Spirituality* (New York and Mahwah, NJ: Paulist Press, 1994), pp.248-66; p. 252.

5 Tom Boyd, "*Is Spirituality Possible without religion? A Query for the postmodern era", in* Ann W. Astell (ed.), *Divine Representations: Postmodernism and Spirituality*, p. 100.

6 Sandra Schneiders, "Spirituality as an academic discipline", in *Christian Spirituality Bulletin*, 1.2 (Fall 1993), pp. 10-15, p. 11.

7 Ursula King (ed.), *Faith and Praxis in a Postmodern Age* (London: Cassell Wellington House, 1998), p. 11.

Down the centuries various religions and religious ideologies have been upholding various claims about God, Divinity and Spirituality. Given the fact that human beings are not perfect their understanding of God is also not perfect. Every religion and ideology seems to have some lacuna or fallacy in some aspects or the other. In the words of Neale Walsch one can point out a few major fallacies about God and Life, which are responsible for deep crises and wars, killing and violence in our societies: "God needs something; God can fail to get what God needs; God has separated you from God because you have not given God what God needs; ... God needs so badly that God now requires you, from your separated position, to provide it; and God will destroy you if you do not meet God's requirements."[8] These fallacies are so harmful that they affect the convictions and value-systems; when fallacious beliefs come together they even create more harmful beliefs and teachings about the very nature of human beings, the purpose, the origin and their destiny. Such harmful teachings claim that: "Human beings are separate from each other; there is not enough of what human beings need to be happy; to get the stuff of which there is not enough, human beings must compete with each other; and some human beings are better than other human beings."[9]

Walsch looks for refined spirituality which appreciate the efforts and methods of others which try to experience and express the inner drives towards the Divine; it would neither ridicule nor attack the other ways of experiencing and expressing and "This New Spirituality will do more than simply create religious tolerance, however. It will offer a whole new set of basic values around which humanity could choose to organize. [It is] a New way to create and experience its politics, its economics, its religions, its educational systems, and its social constructions of every kind."[10] Further, he looks forward to having a new type of spirituality that would make inter- and intra-religious fights unnecessary, meaningless and impossible; that spirituality would be rooted upon the, what he calls, the Big Idea about One God. The basis for that Bid Idea is nothing but love... love in its genuine sense: "The Big Idea is that We Are All One. The Big Idea is that there is Only One God, and this One God does not care whether you are Catholic or Protestant, Jewish or Muslim, Hindu or Mormon or have no religion at all. The Big Idea is that all we have to do is love each other, and everything else in our world will take care of itself out of our willingness to act in loving ways with each other... The Big Idea is that all the earth's natural resources belong to all the world's people, and this

8 Neale Donald Walsch, *Tomorrow's God – Our Greatest Spiritual Challenge* (London: Hodder and Stoughton Ltd, 2004), p. 111

9 Neale Donald Walsch, p. 390.

10 *Ibid.*

has nothing to do with what land mass that resources is located on, over, or under."[11]

According to Ursula, the concept of spirituality is today used "as transcending the assumptions of specific religious traditions. It has become a general code word for the search of direction, purpose and meaning related to the deepest dimension of human existence. Spirituality is thus no longer exclusively based on an a priori theological standpoint, but is rooted in a search, in experimentation, questioning and exploring".[12] It is seen, "not as an idea or concept but as praxis, is a perennial human concern which entails encounter with self-transcendence."[13] Such a refined understanding of spirituality cannot be inimical to science, and vice versa.

## 2. Science and Spirituality: Mutually Strengthened

Contrary to the much popularized notion that science is against spirituality, today we realize that science not only not against spirituality, it can even be seen as contributor towards it. Several hard core scientists do agree that science, with all its discoveries and explorations, can easily add to a sense of awe and wonder, divinity and spirituality. Science can easily take us to the level of spirituality, which cannot be reduced or identified with religion as such.

In spite of all growth in many fields of science and religion, there are some lacunae in understanding their role and relevance to humanity. Integrated and inter-disciplinary approach is sadly lacking in looking at science and religion. The differences between them are focused so much that the similarities are overlooked or unduly denied. That is why, there are several myths about them; for instance, Krishnamurthy points out three such myths, entertained in India and elsewhere: i) "Science and religion are opposed to each other. They cannot coexist for the same personality; ii) It is the exclusive privilege of Science and Technology to do good to the Society and take care of their well-being. Religious education is a superficial luxury that can be dispensed with and iii) Religion and Spirituality are only two different names for the same game that adults play when they have nothing else to do. Religion is the cause of several

---

11 Neale Donald Walsch, p. 241. As a follower of one particular religion, one may be convinced of the teachings and doctrines of that particular religion, but one need not absolutize them to the extent of claiming superiority over all religions, still worse, going to the irrational extent of eliminating others just because their beliefs are different from one's own; this sort of approach is basically illogical as no one can comprehend God in totality and it goes against the very love (for God, for humans and nature!) that every religion professes.

12 Ursula King "Spirituality in a Postmodern Age – Faith and Praxis in New Contexts", in *Faith and Praxis in a Postmodern Age*, 94-112, p. 96.

13 Ursula King "Spirituality in a Postmodern Age – Faith and Praxis in New Contexts", in *Faith and Praxis in a Postmodern Age*, p. 97.

wars and killings and so Spirituality has no place in the civilized world of Science and Technology". [14]

However, contemporary science gradually discovers umpteen number of biotic coincidences hidden nature. Some of them so extremely fine-tuned and minutely fabricated that one cannot but think of some design, and thereby a designer, behind these fabulous structures. Just to mention a few of the mysterious coincidences in the universe: a) A stronger nuclear strong force (by as little as 2 per cent) would have prevented the formation of protons – yielding a universe without atoms. Decreasing it by five per cent would have given us a universe without stars; b) Gravity is roughly $10^{39}$ times weaker than electromagnetism. If gravity has been $10^{33}$ times weaker than electromagnetism, 'stars would be billion times less massive and would burn a million times faster'; c) The nuclear weak force is $10^{28}$ times stronger than gravity. Had the weak force been slightly weaker, all the hydrogen in the universe would have been turned to helium (making water impossible)[15] d) The very nature of water, so vital to life, is a big mystery – unique among the molecules, water is lighter that its solid than liquid form; ice floats. If it did not, the oceans would freeze from the bottom up and earth would now be covered with solid ice and no life would have survived in the oceans.[16]

The origin and the nature of life seem to be another mystery for science. Is life available only on the earth? So far, no substantial evidence of life as we know on the earth, or in any form for that matter, has been obtained from anywhere in the vast known space. But this does not rule out the possibility of some sort of life in the billions of planets. It is estimated that there could be one hundred billion trillion Earth-like planets in space, and it is inevitable that some sort of life exists there. Edward J. Weiler, Director of NASA, points out that "We know the number of stars in the universe is something like one followed by 23 zeros. Given that number, how arrogant to think our is the only sun with a planet that supports life, and that it's the only solar system with intelligent life".[17]

Whether life is found only on the earth or on some other planets as well, it is still a mystery. Paul Daives[18] wonders about life on the earth: "Most textbooks focus on the chemistry of life: which molecules do what inside the

14 V. Krishnamurthy, *Science and Spirituality – A Vedanta Perception* (Mumbai: Bharatiya VIdya Bhavan, 2002), p. 184.

15 John Leslie, *Universes* (London: Routledge, 1989), pp. 4-5, p. 34.

16 Barrow and Tipler, *The Anthropic Cosmological Principle* (Oxford: OUP, 1988), pp. 143-144.

17 *Washington Post*, 20 July 2008.

18 Paul Davies an internationally acclaimed physicist, cosmologist and astro-biologist at Arizona State University, where he runs the pioneering BEYOND centre for Fundamental Concepts in Science; he has authored more than 20 books, including *The Mind of God,*

cell. Obviously, life is a chemical phenomenon, but its distinctiveness lies not in the chemistry as such. The secret of life comes instead from its informational properties; a living organism is a complex information-processing system."[19] Complexity is said to be a criterion for all known forms of life; even single-celled bacteria is amazingly complex. But even hurricane, galaxy and all the known and the unknown universes are also extremely complex, but are they living? That is why, Francis Crick rightly wonders: "the origin of life appears... to be almost a miracle, so many are the conditions which would have had to be satisfied to get it going."[20]

The very notions of life, origin and destiny of the universe and everything in it including humans, meaning and purpose of human life, the fact of human consciousness, memory, emotions and so on, the nature and functions of human brain – are some of the areas in which science realizes that it has to go beyond itself to make any meaningful investigations. Biologically humans and all other creatures are the same in terms of some fundamental features and functions, but humans totally differ from the aspects of consciousness, and its derivatives like morality, spirituality, and different degrees of commitment and dedication. As Krishnamurthy points out, "Hunger, sleep, insecurity and sex urge are common to man and animals but the understanding of dharma is the extra quality of Man."[21] Several philosophers of science point out that even to justify its very existence, science has to go beyond itself. Thus we are made to realize that 'science alone' is neither possible nor desirable! When we take science in its larger sense it becomes more productive, relevant and vibrant; it gets more human and humane. Science cannot prescribe values. "Science is know-how without know-whether. Science describes what is (or was, or will be), not what ought to be. Scientists, *qua* scientists alone, are not ipso *facto* wise. After science, we still need help deciding what to value; what is right and wrong, good and evil; how to behave as we cope. The end of life still lies in its meaning, the domain of religion and ethics."[22]

Gottfried Wilhelm Leibnitz (1646-1716), the mathematical and philosophical genius, who had invented differential and integral calculus

---

*About Time, How to Build a Time Machine* and *the Godlicoks Enigma.* The asteroid 199920G was officially renamed Paul Davies in his honour.

19 Paul Davies, *The 5th Miracle – The Search for the Origin and Meaning of Life* (New York: Touchstone, 1999), p. 19.

20 Francis Crick, *Life Itself: Its Nature and Origin* (N Y: Simon & Schuster, 1981), p. 88.

21 V. Krishnamurthy, p. 2. By dharma, "it means Righteousness, duty, law; the inner characteristic of a thing without which it cannot be what it is; (also) the path which a man should follow in accordance with his evolutionary nature and Ashrama in life; (also) religion, responsibility, justice"; p. 222.

22 Holmes Rolston III, *Genes, Genesis and God* (Cambridge: Cambridge University Press), 1999, pp. 161-162.

independently of Isaac Newton, argued that God should be the wall that stopped all further questioning; in his *Principles of Nature and Grace*, he declares: "Why does something exist rather than nothing? For 'nothing' is simpler than 'something'. Now this is sufficient reason for the existence of the universe… which has no need of any other reason… must be a necessary being, else we should not have a sufficient reason with which we could stop."[23]

Finally, Krishnamurthy gives an analogy to show that there is no contradiction between science and spirituality. "We need both. The same person has to be a father at one time, a husband at another time, a son in another context, and a subordinate under a boss in a totally different circumstance – these are not contradictions but different presentations of the same personality. So also science and spirituality are different presentations of the same ultimate Truth."[24]

## 3. Signs of Seasoned Spirituality

What I mean by seasonal spatiality is that spirituality which emerges in a person only in a given situation, say, during the time of stress and difficulties; it is like thinking of God only when one becomes sick, one faces some challenges in life or finds oneself in a situation beyond one's control. If one tends to think of God only when one becomes 'old', then that spirituality is seasonal; if one thinks of God only when one gets into some trouble, only when one wants to be delivered from some difficulties, then that spirituality is seasonal; if one experiences the presence of God only during one's visits to some holy shrines or in the charismatic conventions and prayer meetings, then one's spirituality is seasonal.

Spirituality, being an experiential reality, cannot be captured in clear, precise and absolute definitions. However we can think of ten measures to understand the nature and the meaning of, what I call *Seasoned Spirituality*. First let us see what seasoned spirituality is NOT: i) **To be spiritual does not mean** being found always at the places of worship, nor to be found carrying the Sacred Books. For, a goat that is housed in the library will certainly not become intelligent or wise! It is not the place where we are but with what dispositions we are, that matters; ii) **To be spiritual is not merely** in performing the religious rituals all the times. One can perform them very diligently but still can be very far away from God and people. It is not uncommon to see people who attend the Holy Mass in the church (or the *Namaaz* at the mosque or perform *Puja* at the temple) in the morning and during the very day getting bribe to do their duty or exploit innocent people in dealing with them. Their conscience

23 Quoted by: Ann Druyan, (ed.), *Carl Sagan – The Varieties of Scientific Experience* (New York: The Penguin Press, 2006), p. xvi.

24 V. Krishnamurthy, p. 185.

does not prick them, probably because they think they pacify God by offering something to God from the bribery that they receive!; iii) **To be spiritual is not** to be ignorant of facts about life, world, scientific developments, one's self, religion, Sacred Scriptures etc. It is in fact glory to God when one fully uses her / his reasoning power and equips oneself in every aspect; iv) **To be spiritual is not** in hiding under the shield of 'God-will-take-care-of' attitudes. God will, in fact, pity those, for having given them the intelligence which is one of the fundamental distinguishing characteristics of being humans; v) **Genuine spirituality does not depend on** how long we pray, but how deep we pray! It is not in how holy we look, but in how holy we think! It is not in the good certificates given by people, but by God! Yes, the more spirituality is seen outside, perhaps, it is less likely that is found inside.

Let us now see what seasoned spirituality is: vi) **To be spiritual means** to be consciously aware of God's presence, not only in the places of worship but also on the dusty streets of one's locality; it is the ability to see God in the suffering humanity, to see him who longs for consolation, who longs for a ray of hope and meaning in one's life. Yes, it is the ability to see God in all, and all in God; vii) **To be spiritual means** to see God in people, not only in those, whom one loves, which is relatively easier, but also in those whom one does not like, or does not like even to think of them.[25] viii) **To be spiritual implies** being genuinely human and genuine humanness has certainly room for occasional stumbling and unintended mistakes. Yet, one is truly sorry for the sins, and is determined not to repeat them with the strength that comes from God. We need to be practical in having expectations about ourselves; being over-angry for our mistakes, or being scrupulous or pre-occupied about our sins are, in fact, signs of not trusting the forgiving mercy of God; or it may even be the indication of our arrogance that makes us think of ourselves too big to sin! ix) **To be spiritual means** being firm, without being harsh; being principle-oriented, without being arrogant; being compassionate without being compromising and being humble without reducing oneself to nothingness. (Genuine humility means the constant awareness of my dependence on God, others and nature for my very living); x) **To be spiritual means** to be cool, calm and serene even in the midst of the moments of uncertainty and anxiety. Such a person is convinced of doing one's best and leaving the rest to God; she/he never doubts the fact that God always gives the best to those who leave the choice to him; it is easy for such people to drop their ego; dropping one's ego is, in fact, a real challenge, even to a yogi, who has dropped everything else!

25 Loving and liking can be differentiated this way: it is easier to love someone when there are things to like in him/her, but one is called to love someone even when there is nothing 'likable' in him/her; precisely that is what God does with us – even though there is nothing to like in us, he still loves us!

The idea of 'seasoned' spirituality is also related to the notion of 'seasoned' understanding of God. I have elsewhere elaborated the 'seasoned' notion of God, under the title: *"The God I Don't /Can't Believe In"*. True, there are millions in the world who don't believe in God, who deny God's existence, who even just ignore the whole issue, or just humbly accept that they don't know whether there is God. On the other hand billions of believers are convinced of God's existence and they dedicate their lives to religions or spiritual movements. All these, of course, conceive God in their own ways, according to the teachings of their religions or the revelations received by the saintly seers of those traditions. The understanding of God differs from religion to religion, time to time, culture to culture and place to place; there is nothing wrong in that and, in fact, it has to be like that; for it is not humanly possible to confine God, who is infinite, into our limited concepts. If we succeed so, then perhaps God ceases to be God, because by the very definition of God, we all understand, including those who deny God, that God must be infinite in every positive quality, like, truth, love, mercy, forgiveness, compassion, presence, existence, time – in all possible positive aspects God must be infinite. Of course this must not make one think that God can be infinite in having negative aspects as well. For instance, God is infinite in telling lies and having hatred! No, because God being TRUTH cannot violate himself by telling lies, and God being LOVE cannot violate himself by hating anyone and this in no way diminish his omnipotent (all-powerful) nature! Therefore as long as we are limited by space and time, we can never ever have the final and absolute understanding of God, as God is. May be the day when we see God face to face, as most of the religious traditions believe, we will understand God totally.

However, every now and then we need to critically evaluate our understanding of God and our claims about God; if they are oppressive and negative they will do more harm than good. In fact, no religion or no faith is much better than a wrong one! When our concepts of God are wrong and faulty, dehumanizing and enslaving, we end up justifying many wrong ideologies, and even go to the extent of harming and destroying one another! It is a sad, undeniable yet, fact that in today's world violence, massacre and blood-shed are perpetuated and justified in the name of religions, though, paradoxically, no religion advocates it. Many people deny God and religions because of the negative witness borne by the followers of religions. That is why, the need to constantly introspect our convictions, to evaluate our own belief-systems and to critically look at the religious rituals, arises very strongly.

Here I would like to spell out certain ideas and convictions that don't suit the 'real' nature and attributes of God.[26] It is, perhaps, easier to spell out

26 I put the word real within quotes, because we don't know the 'really real' nature of God but given our limited understanding of his infinite love, knowledge and power, we can hold

in what sort of God I don't believe in rather than what sort of God I believe in! *Yes, I shall never believe in the God or the God who does not deserve my faith and surrender is:*

The God who is heartless not to answer the painful cries of an honest man / woman in agony…

The God who enjoys seeing his own people in pain and delights in their sufferings, which cannot be explained with sufficient and convincing reasons…

The God who makes himself so dreadful that people hesitate to approach him and to have an enslaving and oppressing allegiance to him …

The God who reserves a set of sins as too big for him to forgive, when the sinners approach him with sincere repentance, genuine remorse and deep resolutions of not committing them again…

The God who makes certain people suffer from cancer or sterility or impotency and is happy about it…

The God who abandons those who, in spite of their sincere and eager search, have not known him…

The God who does not take initiative to meet even those who, for some reasons or the other, have abandoned him… like a loving mother reaches out to her child, who in a moment anger shouts at her, "go away, I don't want you, I don't love you'…

The God who does not make everything and every person that he touches, new and fresh creation…

The God who does not create everyone with a specific purpose and goal in his / her life…

The God who does not get 'melted' in the cries of the child for food and in the tears of its mother who is incapable of feeding that child…

The God who will be happy with someone who goes through his / her life without making even a single person happy and giving them hope and meaning in their lives…

The God who destroys nature, which is his own creation, and the God who delights in those who disfigure and deform the environment...

The God who would not incarnate himself into the world to love and participate in the daily joys and struggles of humans…

The God who does not delight in the discoveries and inventions of humans, who achieve them by legitimately and wisely using their intelligence and reasoning power…

The God who cannot be the bedrock of all my hopes…

The God who causes some accidents, even fatal ones, just to teach others some strong lessons…

---

certain claims with sufficient confidence!

The God who does not bring under his justice those who deliberately exploit others, violate their human dignity and live a selfish and meaningless life…

The God who does not fill with his grace and presence, those whom he touches…

The God who does not get drenched himself in the painful tears of those who have lost their loved ones and culture, language and land, due to the mindless warfare and inhuman exploitation…

The God who hesitates to create human beings with the gift of 'freedom', in spite of the dangerous possibility of denying him with the wrong use of the very freedom given by him...

The God who does not delight and strengthen those who toil for human rights and dignity, who risk their lives to establish harmonious and egalitarian society…

The God who does not light a ray of hope and give a sense of meaning to those who sincerely turn to him…

Yes, I can't believe in such God… I don't want to believe in such God… and such God does not deserve my surrender and worship… because, my God is a *God with a DIFFERENCE!*[27]

## Concluding Remarks with Some Suggestions

Given the extremely minute fabrications that have gone behind the universe and the innumerable biotic coincidences several scientists tend to think that the universe is not self-explanatory. Though the universe is immense in its size and age yet it is finite; there are more evidences emerging now, to show that the universe had a beginning (Big Bang!) and will have an end; of course there are several proposals to narrate the end of the universe, like Big Crunch theory! As the universe cannot explain its own existence it is not difficult to think of an agent outside of it. Catholic Church is among the many believing communities to take this fact to show that human reason can certainly take us to believe in the existence of God: "The world cannot have its origin and its destination within itself. In everything that exists, there is more than we see. The order, the beauty, and the development of the world point beyond themselves toward God. Every man is receptive to what is true, good and beautiful. He hears within himself the voice of conscience, which urges him

---

27 S. Stephen Jayard, *A Book That Cannot Be Titled* (Christian World Imprints, New Delhi), pp.111-113. Some ideas for this reflection I owe to Juan Arias' book, *The God I Don't Believe In*, 1973. One may look at my book for more reflections on God, Faith and Spirituality.

to what is good and warns him against what is evil. Anyone who follows this path reasonably finds God".[28]

Among the traditional arguments proposed to prove God's existence, the one put forward by John Henry Newman (1801-1890) is known as the 'Moral Argument for God's Existence'. We feel good when we do good, and we feel bad when we do wrong; he is wondering about the origin or the cause of the good / bad feeling. There is a natural drive within us to reach out to those in suffering or pain; we spontaneously express sympathy / empathy with those in struggles or dangers. Why do we have the feeling of moral responsibility over our actions? That is why, he is convinced that "If… we feel responsibility, are ashamed, are frightened, at transgressing the voice of conscience, this implies that there is one to whom we are responsible, before whom we are ashamed, and whose claims upon us we fear."[29]

In spite of enormous growth and scientific achievements among the rich nations there are millions who find no meaning in their lives; having lost it they don't find life worth the while in spite of huge possessions and big positions. The material riches don't satisfy the inner longing of the human spirit; in a way, there are poor everywhere, both in the poor countries and the rich as well – either economically poor or emotionally poor. One may have everything to make one's life comfortable and enjoyable but may not have the basic thing that makes life meaningful. That is why, St. Teresa of Kolkatta, a modern saint who can certainly inspire the modern youth, is convinced: "There is hunger for ordinary bread, but there is also hunger for love, kindness, and mutual respect – and that is the great poverty from which people today suffer so much".[30] Thinking along the same lines, she explains how the lack of real love makes human lives a tragedy and drudgery. Lack of love leads humanity to emptiness, both individually and collectively. That is the reason why St. Teresa abhors this type of 'sickness' of all others sicknesses: "Tuberculosis and cancer are not the most terrible sicknesses. I think that a much more terrible sickness is to be unwanted and unloved"[31]

Today what the youth needs is intellectual clarity and spiritual experience. Often they get only instructions and orders about do's and don't's in their traditional religions. Their parents, elders and the religious authorities make sure that they follow certain rules and regulations that give them the clear identity of belonging to certain religious or believing community. The modern youngsters, exposed to more of rational approaches by the contemporary

28 *Youth Catechism of the Catholic Church*; trans from German, Michael J. Miller (Bangalore: Asian Trading Corporation, California: Ignatius Press, 2010, pp.5-6.

29 *Youth Catechism of the Catholic Church*, p. 171.

30 *Youth Catechism of the Catholic Church*, p.282.

31 *Youth Catechism of the Catholic Church*, p.203.

science around, look for rational basis for their beliefs and faith-claims but the followers of the traditional religions are often unaware of such rational explanations for their faith and therefore they are not able to convince most of the youth about the need and relevance of following a religion. So what the modern youth need today is intellectual clarity of what they are asked to believe. Of course, though purely rational and logical approach to religion, or even to life in general, is neither possible nor desirable.

Today's youth need to be taught that only rational or scientific approach is neither desirable nor possible in every aspect of our life. There are lots of grey areas where reason and logic seem to be insufficient to explain everything. We need to stop at certain brute facts and have to accept as they are; for instance, no one can give the rational justification to the inductive reasoning, which uses the assumption that 'the future will resemble the past' – this can never have complete logical justification; to justify this principle one has to assume the very principle of inductive reasoning, that since it has worked in the past it will work in future as well! Further, for virtues and moral principles one cannot have pure scientific basis. As Einstein points out, "You are right in speaking of the moral foundations of science, but you cannot turn around and speak of the scientific foundations of morality."[32]

Nevertheless, some rational basis and clarity is very essential so that one is not misled by superstitions and illogical practices in the name of their religion. So the religious leaders, parents and elders are bound to help our youngsters to have intellectual clarity about what they believe and without this they cannot be rooted in what they believe. If at all they want to have conviction of certain principles and ideals they need to know them with clarity and this can lead them to spiritual convictions. Perhaps some suggestions and guidelines such as given below can be thought of.

It is high time that our education system became holistic. It must involve dimensions of spirituality in the syllabus of the students from the early stages. There must be elaborate plans "to incorporate the habits of spirituality, like introspection, meditation, analysis of human behaviour through study of Biography and Religion – in the curriculum from as early a level as possible".[33] It is unfortunate that our education focuses only upon the rational aspects of our human existence, but obviously there are many more aspects to our existence in addition to rationality. Krishnamurthy argues that humanity is educated only half, in the sense only science is taught and spirituality is ignored. We can progress holistically only with the integration of science and spirituality,

---

32 See: https://www.goodreads.com/quotes/449844-you-are-right-in-speaking-of-the-moral-foundations-of. Accessed on 28 Nov, 2019

33 V. Krishnamurthy, *Science and Spirituality – A Vedanta Perception* (Mumbai: Bharatiya Vidya Bhavan, 2002), p. 179.

because only science and technology cannot give the real and meaningful progress of humanity. We may be successful in conquering the space out there, but not the 'inner' space; "it may be possible because of science and technology to talk across the vast emptiness of space but it is important to know and decide what to talk".[34]

Fortunately, today some schools in India and abroad include yoga classes as part of their curriculum. They need to be taken more seriously by both the students and the management. It is often sees as mere physical exercise-techniques. Along with it, the young minds need to be trained in various techniques of meditation as well, which will draw out the spiritual powers from them. "Meditation, being the higher and better use of the enormous spiritual force lying hidden in us, should be included as a compulsory part of a curriculum for value education right from the school level" and this will enable them to be familiar with the Absolute and the Supreme Wisdom: "just as the scientific pursuit of Truth consists of the sole reliance on rationality, the spiritual pursuit of Truth relies on the omnipresence of the Absolute in our own consciousness in everything that we do or think."[35]

Krishnamurthy proposes a nine-point master plan for value education to be symbolically embedded in the educational system: "i) Human qualities of sympathy, compassion, kindliness and brotherhood must be inculcated into the minds of young children for the sake of family, nation and the world; ii) Biographies of great men and women of the world to be taught at every level of the education, according to their age and background – scholars, saints, innovators, leaders, reformers, religious heads, social workers, scientists, devotees of the Lord, writers, poets, thinkers, philosophers, perfomers of the arts, managers, administrators, entrepreneurs, and professionals; iii) Awareness of the disasters of the ecology and the urgent need for protecting the planet must be given to the students; for that they need to learn that the whole planet is one living entity; iv) They must be encouraged reading books and classics; v) As early as the age of 5, the practice of silent prayer must be a daily routine irrespective of the religious denomination or religion; they need to be taught God-experience; vi) From the age of 7, they need to be taught the habit of sitting for an introspection and meditation; vii) From the age of 11, regular lessons on meditation should form part of the curriculum; viii) From the age of 15, the basic elements of genuine spirituality must be taught to them; to teach them objectively the commonness of spirituality in all religions; they must be motivated in comparative religion… If religion is totally left to the individual private affair, the students will be left out without the means of understanding any culture beyond a limited subset of their own and ix) They should be taught

34 V. Krishnamurthy, p. 180.

35 V. Krishnamurthy, p.197.

history, not as history of the different countries but as history of humanity; peace is not just the absence of war, but mutual understanding and respectful attitude towards the rights of the others".[36]

The absence of such spirituality in the modern society has created violence and hatred, vacuum and meaninglessness in life; being bogged down with the materialistic approaches and short-cut gains, there is a lack of transcendent horizon; no depth dimension, no degrees of interiority; a sense of soul is lost, sense of the spiritual nature and destiny of the human being is dwindling. There is now an effort to see spirituality as an academic discipline; many universities have it as their regular course; many encyclopaedias include this topic and volumes are written every year.[37]

This seasoned spirituality would keep us virtuous, and therefore we can be free from anxiety; wise and therefore we can be free from perplexity; brave and therefore we can be free from fear; and faithful and therefore be *free from meaninglessness in life.* As Krishnamurthy puts it, "the consummation of spirituality is to gradually move towards that perception which sees al beings in the Self and the Self in all beings and consequently hates none".[38] and, I am convinced, that is the type of *seasoned spirituality* is what our modern youth needs today.

---

36 V. Krishnamurthy, pp. 187 – 195.

37 The 25-volume cross-cultural series on World Spirituality where each volume concentrates on a particular faith is worth-mentioning - J. R. Hinnells (ed.), *A New Handbook of Living Religions* (Oxford: Blackwell, 1997; London: Penguin Books, 1998).

38 V. Krishnamurthy, p.198.

12

# Modern Science in India and the Emergence of a New Worldview

**Job Kozhamthadam SJ**

*Director, Indian Institute of Science and Religion, New Delhi*

**Abstract:** Serious study and reflection on the phenomenal developments in science and technology reveal that they have transformed not only the way we live – better home, health, means of travel and communication, etc. – but also in the way we think, act, shape our value system, frame our worldview, etc. This paper discusses these points in some detail, pointing out that the result has been a mixed bag of several well-effects and ill-effects. It suggests that the best strategy to deal with this situation is to focus on maximizing the well-effects and minimizing the ill-effects. It further points out that this noble task can best be achieved by blending harmoniously the latest findings of contemporary science the deepest insights of religions. The paper pays special attention to highlighting this important interplay in the context of the developments in India.

**Keywords:** Science-technology impact, worldview, science-religion interplay, science & technology in India

## Introduction

In the past science was very much looked upon as a provider of important but dispensable amenities and comforts of life. However, today it is being recognized that science has and does play a far deeper and wider role in our world and society, thanks mainly to recent developments in science and technology, particularly in the field of the biological sciences. It can be said that today modern science is in a position to have an important say in determining not only what we have and want to have, but also what we are and want to become. Not only is modern science an integral constituent of our culture, it also is slowly but surely reshaping our culture, paving the way for the emergence of new world order.

India has always been the home of an ancient and rich culture, noted for its wide variety and deep spirituality. Today modern science is daring to reshape India's deep-rooted values and time-tested customs.

This paper is a critical study of certain developments in modern science and technology which exert a profound influence on contemporary world culture in general and Indian culture in particular. After discussing briefly some of these important developments, I will point out that these changes have come to stay, and there seems to be no turning back. A new order is taking definite form in the world scenario, and a new culture is emerging in India, with all its 'well-effects' and ill-effects, offering serious and almost unavoidable challenges. It is for us to transform these challenges into genuine opportunities in order to usher in a more prosperous and nobler world. I will further argue that creative and constructive interaction between modern science and spirituality can be of considerable help in this laudable venture by maximizing the 'well-effects' and minimizing the ill-effects. Furthermore, India is in a privileged position to contribute substantially towards this dialogue since here both science and spirituality have always been taken very seriously.

## 1. Some Recent Developments in Science and Their Implications

A number of developments initiated or catalyzed by developments in science have played a pivotal role in bringing about the new world order. I discuss below some of the more important ones.

### a. Shift from the Age of Discovery to the Age of Mastery

Thinkers are pointing out that today science is moving from an age of discovery of nature to an age of mastery over nature. In the past scientists were pleased and felt fulfilled when they succeeded in revealing the secret laws of nature. Johannes Kepler, Isaac Newton, Albert Einstein, etc., were acclaimed as outstanding scientists because of their discovery of important laws of nature. Today scientists seem to be far more ambitious: Not only do they want to make new discoveries, they also want to have mastery over the operations of nature, but they also want to have a hand in determining the destiny of nature. A good illustration for this new focus is the Genetic Revolution and Neurological Revolution that is being unfolded before us, conspicuously from the second half of the 20$^{th}$ century onwards. Certainly, this revolution involves the discovery of new laws. However, today we see that these laws are being skillfully transformed into tools of mastery to reshape the nature and destiny of humans and the world around.

## b. Paradigm Shift in the Role of Science

Closely linked to the shift of focus is the transformation taking place in the role of science and the impact science has on society. As mentioned already, in the past the role of science was confined very much to providing certain amenities and comforts in life. Computers, TV sets, mobile telephones, etc., were some of the outstanding gifts of modern science to humanity. These contributions certainly helped to enhance the quality of life, at least for those who could afford them. But they remained optional: one could remain neutral towards them without being affected in any significant way. They touched humans from the outside; they concerned the world around humans. But today science is in a position to go deeper, to human persons themselves. For instance, the main actors of the Genetic Revolution – genetic engineering, the Human Genome Project (HGP), cloning, nanotechnology, etc. - touch human persons themselves in a significant way. We may say that so far science dealt with the conditions of life, but today, thanks to developments like the Genetic and Neurological Revolutions, science is in a position to deal with life itself. So far, science focused on what humans have and want to have, but in Genetic and Neurological Revolutions it focuses on what humans are and can be.

## c. The Narrowing of the Geographical Boundaries and the Formation of the Global Village

The term 'global village' is closely associated with Marshall McLuhan, who popularized it way back in the 1960s in his well-known books like *The Gutenberg Galaxy: The Making of Typographic Man* in 1962 and *Understanding Media* in 1964. Although in the past it was used as a metaphor to describe the amazing speed with which the electronic and internet media could interlink the different parts of the world, today it is becoming more and more literally true. Our globe has become a village in a true sense – whatever happens in any part of the world, however remote and inaccessible, is almost instantly made accessible to anyone, anywhere. This revolution cannot be passed over as a mere advance in the ease and efficiency of communication, it has very serious implications and far-reaching consequences – social, cultural, political, economic, religious, etc.

## d. Tension between Global and Local Interests: Emergence of Regional Nationalism and Power-Centres

The present world scenario is full of inconsistencies and contradictions, apparent as well as real, giving rise to tensions and uncertainties. One such instance is the tension between global and local interests. Never in the history of our globe has there been so much progress made in the process of globalization and widening of interests as well as concerns. At the same time one sees local groups with their own specific agenda clamouring for world attention and support. The aborigines ( *adivasis*, first settlers), the dalits and other disadvantaged groups in various parts of the world are raising their voices for sympathetic and decisive hearing. There is no doubt that the process of globalization has come to stay; there is no turning back. The challenge facing our world today is to discern and identify appropriate ways of responding to these local needs without jeopardizing the process of globalization.

### e. Greater Realization of the Need and Relevance of Collaboration and Teamwork

One area in which the positive impact of the globalizing tendency is noticeably seen is the growing awareness regarding the need and relevance of collaboration and teamwork. It is becoming more and more evident that great advances are brought about not so much by isolated efforts of individuals, however gifted, as by collaborative efforts of talented, committed and open-minded persons. The old paradigm of *"genius in isolation"* for serious, creative achievements is giving way to that of *"experts in collaboration."* Newton in the 17th century and Einstein in the 20th did outstanding, creative work almost as isolated individuals. But today the Human Genome Project, the Space Programme of NASA, God Particle discovery, Gravitational Wave discovery, etc., owe their success to the well-planned and meticulously executed collaborative efforts of experts from different fields.

### f. Greater Awareness and Recognition of the Power and Limitation of Science

Another apparent contradiction we find in our world of science today is the growing awareness of both the power and the limitation of science. Never before in the history of humankind have we witnessed the amazing power and capability of modern science. At the same time, never before have scholars exposed the inherent limitedness and inescapable weakness of modern science. Science, indeed, is the creation of humans and seems to share in the limitedness of humans. Gone are the days of scientism when many a megalomaniac scientist assumed that science was the panacea for all problems and the scientific approach the sure path to all success. Today, thanks to several groundbreaking developments in science itself and in the philosophy of science, it is becoming more and more accepted that, although science is mighty and potent, it is not omnipotent. Scientific findings and predictions are reliable, but can claim no inerrancy; Science has given us *the best knowledge,* but not *perfect knowledge.*

I refer to this turnaround as the "humbling experience" of science, wherein science has come to a genuine and realistic self-understanding, recognizing its real power and capabilities, acknowledging its clear limitations and shortcomings. This is a very healthy development that opens the door for greater enrichment. In particular, this opens the door for constructive and creative dialogue between science and other areas like religion.

### g. Shift from the Mechanical Philosophy of Nature with Its Mechanistic World to a Non-mechanistic, Complex World

One of the points emphasized by contemporary philosophy of science is that science is not just a collection of laws, theories and methodological rules, but brings with it a worldview that plays a crucial role in our understanding of the world and in the shaping of our value system. Classical science or Newtonian science was most successful from the 17th to the end of the 19th centuries and brought along with it a worldview known as the Mechanical Philosophy of Nature (MPN), according to which the universe was a gigantic machine following the rules and principles of mechanics with assured certainty and guaranteed predictability. Practically all the prominent scientists during this period subscribed to this view, to some degree or other, hoping that science would give us sure and absolute knowledge. However, later developments in science, particularly the advent of Relativity and the Quantum Theory, have exposed the poverty of MPN, revealing the complex, indefinite nature of the universe. The mechanistic view of the universe is not fully given up since even today it persists in many areas of science, particularly in the medical sciences. But the awareness is growing that pure mechanical principles alone cannot capture the complexity and diversity of our universe.

### h. Shift from a Deterministic, Static, Sure and Certain Universe to an Indeterminate, Dynamic, Uncertain and Unpredictable World

The mechanistic world was characterized by determinism according to which everything acted in accordance with strict laws of nature. It was also a static world prohibiting any radical change of the system itself, although within the system changes could take place. Furthermore, it claimed to yield sure and certain knowledge about the universe, including human actions. But more recent developments in science like quantum mechanics showed that ours was an indeterminate world; evolution showed that ours was an ever-evolving dynamic world; the Uncertainty Principle of Werner Heisenberg showed that ours was an uncertain and hence unpredictable world. These changes, far from being confined to the academic circles, were recognized as having far-reaching consequences in other important areas as well.

### i. Shift from Humans as Creatures to Humans as Co-creators: Human Dignity Enhanced

One of the positive results of these developments in science was the enhancement of human dignity. This was particularly true of the developments in the biological ad neurological sciences, like cloning, the Human Genome Project, genetic engineering, Artificial Intelligence, robotics, etc., which offered unprecedented powers to scientists to reshape and even alter the nature and function of living beings. In the past humans were mere creatures living helplessly subject to the creator. With these advances, humans have been elevated to the level of co-creators and collaborators empowered to chart the future course of creation.

### j. Reaffirmation of the Unity of the Universe

Another far-reaching consequence of the developments in science, particularly since the dawn of the $20^{th}$ century, is the reaffirmation of the unity of nature. In the first half of the twentieth century the different discoveries in particle physics revealed the unity in diversity of the non-living world, since, according to them, the whole material world is made up of the same fundamental particles like protons, neutrons, electrons, etc. In more recent times, the genome project and related developments show this unity in diversity of the living world. Just as atoms of different material elements are made up of the same fundamental particles, the DNA of different beings is made up of the same kind of nucleotides – A(Adenine), G(Guanine), C(Cytocine), and T(Thymine). Even in the sequencing one can see a remarkable similarity. The genomes of different organisms like yeast, nematode worm, fruit fly, mouse, etc., show remarkable similarity with the human genome. According to some estimates, humans share 99% of DNA with chimps. With cow the DNA shared is 90%, with mouse 75%, with yeast about 30%, with *E. coli* 15%, etc.[1] The human race has crossed the 7.5 billion mark in 2017. Despite such large numbers spread over many continents, cultures, and races, humans show a remarkable deeper unity in their biology. It is found that any two individuals differ on the average only in one nucleotide per one thousand.

## 2. Interconnectedness of the Universe – The Butterfly Effect

Many religious traditions, particularly the eastern ones, have always upheld the interconnectedness of the myriad of beings in the universe.[2] Today this is

1 For details see Michio Kaku, *Visions* (Oxford: Oxford University Press, 1998), pp. 152-153. Please note that the percentages given are only approximate, since different researchers give slightly different figures.

2 About eighty years later, as early as 1963, Edward N. Lorenz, using Poincaré's mathematics, described a simple mathematical model of a weather system that was made up of three

being confirmed by developments in contemporary science. Quantum theory, particularly as developed in the Copenhagen tradition, strongly endorses this view. The theory of quantum entanglement focuses precisely on this point. The "butterfly effect" in chaos theory, according to which, "a butterfly flapping its wings in Hong Kong can affect the course of a tornado in Texas" also carries the same message. The genomic data presented above show how deep the genetic connection is, not only between the different living beings but even more among the billions of human beings. In a real sense, we are brothers and sisters, having a real common origin and a common destiny.

This interconnectedness is not confined only to the quantum world or the genomic world. Today we find echoes of it in the world of our everyday experience too. The action of a single person, however insignificant, has the potential to affect the rest of the world. Think of what the action of Bin Laden, Abu Baker al-Baghdadi, etc., who were almost unknown and unheard of persons till recently, have done to the world. Today it is becoming clear that no person, whatever be his/her status and background, can be taken for granted.

## The Return of the Mystery Dimension of the Universe

It was hoped, mostly by the opponents of religion and God, that with the emergence and growth of science, all mysteries would be demystified, thereby banishing religion and God to the limbo of the superfluous and the superstitious. But this has not happened; on the contrary the mystery dimension has only reasserted itself, taking up more sophisticated forms. The human genome, recent findings about the human brain, etc., reveal the mastery and mystery of creation. They all bear testimony to the creator's mastery over creation. At the same time their complexity and intricacy has become a baffling mystery to us humans. The sheer number involved is staggering. The latest estimate show that in an average human body there are 37.2 trillion cells. In the nucleus of each cell there is DNA, which contains about 3.1 billion base units or nucleotides, each one of which has over 50 atoms. Now one can figure out how many atoms there are in each cell, how many in the whole human body! And all these trillions and trillions of atoms are arranged in the most orderly manner to make complex life possible. This is for just one human being, and

linked nonlinear differential equations that showed rates of change in temperature and wind speed. Some surprising results showed complex behaviour from supposedly simple equations; also, the behaviour of the system of equations was sensitively dependent on the initial conditions of the mathematical model. He spelled out the implications of his discovery, implying that if there were any errors in observing the initial state of the system (which is inevitable in any real system), prediction as to a future state of the system was impossible. Lorenz labelled these systems that exhibited sensitive dependence on initial conditions as having the "butterfly effect":This unique name came from the proposition that a butterfly flapping its wings in Hong Kong can affect the course of a tornado in Texas. This has become the emblem of chaos theory, following James Gleik.

there are over 7.5 billion of them walking around on the planet. These facts exposed by contemporary science simply astound us. The only answer Francis Collins, the director of HGP (Human Genome Project), could give to this, was "a sense of awe." His sincere and hard-headed science transformed Collins from an atheist in his younger days into a practising Christian today. Speaking of his most important work on HGP, he comments: "I experience a sense of awe at the realization that humanity now knows something only God knew before. It is a deeply moving sensation that helps me appreciate the spiritual side of life."[3] Collins is not the only scientist to have this kind of experience. The well-known British astronomer late Allan Sandage too had a very similar experience through his work in contemporary astronomy. Speaking of his turnaround from "almost a practising atheist as a boy" to a believer at 50, he says: "It was my science that drove me to the conclusion that the world is much more complicated than can be explained by science. It is only through the supernatural that I can understand the mystery of existence."[4] One can give many other similar cases. Decades ago, both Albert Einstein and Werner Heisenberg had voiced similar sentiments.

## 3. Scientific Developments and the Indian Scenario

India is a country that has always accorded great importance to science and technology, and hence these revolutionary developments cannot but have a serious impact on the situation in India. I discuss below briefly some aspects of it.

### a. Some Positive Aspects

#### i. Shift from a Backward, Primitive, Un-technical, Underdeveloped Country to a Technologically Advanced, Vibrant Nation

In the past, particularly during the colonial, and initial parts of the postcolonial times, the stereotype perception of India was that of a third-world, third-rate country, teeming with poverty, hunger, illiteracy and superstition – all leading to an underdeveloped nation of no serious significance. But today this questionable perception has taken a total turnaround. According to reliable reports, today:

- India has the second-largest pool of scientists and engineers in the world.
- India is among the top 10 most industrialized nations.
- India is ranked the sixth country in the world in terms of satellite launches.

---

3 John Cornwell, "Scientists Playing God," in *The Tablet*, 8 July, 2000, p. 920.

4 Sharon Begley, "Science Finds God," *Newsweek*, July 20, 1998, p. 47.

- India is the only country, other than US and Japan, to have built a supercomputer indigenously.
- India is ranked 2nd in the software industry.
- Four out of 10 Silicon Valley startups are run by Indians.
- Mangalyaan and Chandrayaan projects of ISRO (Indian Space Research Organization) have placed India among the top echelons of space science and exploration.
- There are almost 4 Million Indians in America. Their involvement in the field of science and technology in the US is impressive. For instance, according to some past records, 38% of doctors in America are Indians; 12% of scientists in America are Indians; 36% of NASA employees are Indians; 34% of Microsoft employees are Indians; 28% of IBM employees are Indians; 17% of INTEL employees are Indians; 13% of XEROX employees are Indians.

According to experts, "India finally has started acting as the technology superpower in the 'new world' where countries become superpower by virtue of technical strength and capability and not colonial wealth!" Albert Einstein has the following to say about India: "We owe a lot to the Indians, who taught us how to count, without which no worthwhile scientific discovery could have been made."[5]

## ii. Shift from a Poverty-Stricken, Impoverished Colony to a Potential Economic Giant

For centuries India was looked upon as a poverty-stricken, impoverished state, colonized by foreign masters. But today this situation has changed significantly.

- According to the latest data India is the world's 5th largest economy by nominal GDP and the 3rd largest by purchasing power parity (PPP).
- India has become an attractive centre for investors. As Bertie Ahern, former prime Minister of Ireland, says, "India's unprecedented economic growth over the past decade makes it an attractive prospect for companies seeking new markets for their products and services...."

5 https://www.goodreads.com/quotes/1128408-we-owe-a-lot-to-the-indians-who-taught-us, acceessed on 4 November 2019.

### iii. Shift from a Land of Diseases, Epidemics, Malnutrition and Other Health Hazards to an Attractive Centre of Medical Tourism

In the past India was often depicted as a land of high health hazards, abounding in diseases and epidemics. Foreigners, particularly from the developed, affluent nations, hesitated to come to India. But today the scenario has changed dramatically. India has become an attractive spot for medical tourism – India is placed 5th highest in the world and 2nd highest in Asia in the field of medical tourism. Of course, India has always been noted for Ayurvedic medicines, massage treatments, yogic meditation techniques and other ancient medical traditions. However, today she is at the forefront of modern medicine as well, attracting huge numbers to her state-of-the-art medical facilities in various parts of the nation. The records in these world-class medical institutions are impressive.

### iv. Increasing Food Production and Move towards Self-sufficiency

With regard to the production of food also India has made great strides. The statistics in this regard speak for themselves. For instance, the total area under the high-yielding-varieties programme was a negligible 19,000 km$^2$ in the financial year 1960. However, since then the growth has been spectacular, increasing to nearly 1,54,000 km$^2$ by the financial year 1970, 4,31,000 km$^2$ by the financial year 1980, and 6,39,000 km$^2$ by 1990.

## b. Some Negative Aspects

### i. Shift from Self-reliance to Techno-Reliance

Indian culture and tradition were noted for its simplicity, practicality, closeness to nature, and self-sufficiency. Mahatma Gandhi crystallized these effective, time-tested traits in his concepts of *swadeshi* and *swaraj* in which the aspect of self-sufficiency and self-reliance are fundamental. In his own words, "My idea of village *swaraj* is that it is a complete republic, independent of its neighbours for its own vital wants, and yet interdependent for many others in which dependence is a necessity."[6] This would mean that the epicentre of Indian culture and tradition are the villages. In Gandhi's vision "The true India is to be found not in its few cities, but in its seven hundred thousand villages. If the villages perish, India will perish too."[7] Furthermore, this would mean

6 M.K. Gandhi, "My Idea of Village, Swaraj," in *Harijan*, 26-7-1942, https://www.mkgandhi.org/panchayat_raj/village_swaraj.htm, accessed on 4 November 2019.

7 Satish Kumar, "Gandhi's Swedeshi – The Economics of Permanence," https://www.google.com/search?sxsrf=ACYBGNQClPll3J7Yl_UIHdBxf1HK6cam_g:1572886200694&q=Mahatma+Gandhi:+%22The+true+India+is+to+be+found+not+, accessed on 4 November 2019.

that we focus on production by the masses rather than mass-production. In Gandhi's view, mass production is only concerned with the product, whereas production by the masses is concerned with the product, the producers, and the process.

In contemporary India, thanks to the explosive growth of science and technology, this tradition is fading away, and a culture of techno-reliance is fast spreading. People become so dependent on machines that they cannot manage if the machine-system breaks down, as evidenced almost daily when we are afflicted with electricity power cuts. This change has serious consequences. The simplicity of life is lost; the use of the hands becomes rarer and rarer; unwanted and unnecessary dependence sets in. Speaking on this scenario Gandhi wrote: "It's a tragedy of the first magnitude that millions of people have ceased to use their hands as hands. Nature has bestowed upon us this great gift which is our hands. If the craze for machinery methods continues, it is highly likely that a time will come when we shall be so incapacitated and weak that we shall begin to curse ourselves for having forgotten the use of the living machines given to us by God."[8] Accompanying this disregard for nature and what is natural is the mechanical mentality which looks upon fellow-humans as machines, and which wants to analyse their life and behaviour mechanistically.

## ii. Economic and Cultural Exploitation

Another negative aspect of technological development is that it can quickly become an effective tool of exploitation in the hands of profit-hungry multinationals and technocrats. In fact, it has already become in many cases. This has come about because any technology, particularly the frontline ones, requires highly expensive infrastructure, which only very few can afford. Again, the nations and companies which are already ahead and well-established have a decisive advantage. Also, today technology and regulations are such that those ahead can claim a monopoly, and prevent others from coming up. For instance, today the genetic technology can produce terminator seeds that do not allow new seeds to be produced from them, forcing the farmers to purchase fresh seeds each time they want to cultivate. Since only the original company with a monopoly and copyright can produce and sell these seeds, the farmers are forced to buy the seeds from the parent company, often at an unjustly high price.

A number of instances of this kind of economic colonisation and exploitation have been reported and documented. It has been said that these companies with very good capital base, particularly in India because of the attractive Rupee foreign exchange rate, first buy up all possible local

8 Mahatma Gandhi, "Mahatma Gandhi Quotes, https://www.azquotes.com/quote/877358, accessed on 4 November 2019.

competition by offering a highly attractive and even disproportionate price. For instance, it was reported some years ago that in Brazil the Monsanto Company - a US multinational agro-product company, headquartered in St. Louis, Missouri - spent more than $1 billion to buy out 60% of all the seed companies in just two years. In India, it bought major holdings in the largest seed company. Once this is done, these multinational companies introduce their own product along with their production technology and monopolize the field. It may be noted that the seeds produced by these genetically engineered products either do not germinate or need for germination certain specific chemicals developed by these companies. This means that once farmers begin to use this product, they are permanently dependent on the companies, leaving these multinational giants full freedom to wantonly squeeze out money from the local people.

There is not only economic exploitation but also cultural exploitation, often introduced in a subtle, innocuous manner, as part of entertainment, advertisements, etc. Cultures and cultural values have specific contexts, and once detached from these contexts and introduced into another culture, they can become not only unhelpful, but even harmful. This is already happening in India today. For instance, family values are taking a strong beating in many parts of India, particularly in the urban areas. It has been pointed out that one of the sources of this tragedy is the invasion of the entertainment media from certain countries where family values have lost their centrality.

### iii. Tension between Material Prosperity and Spiritual Poverty

Progress in science and technology is often accompanied by material prosperity, particularly in the technologically advanced countries and groups. More food, better education, improved health, more leisure, longer lifespan, etc., are the usual indicators of this prosperity. However, it has been found that this material prosperity is not accompanied by any spiritual, or inner growth. In fact, in some cases, one can see a concurrent decline in the world of the spiritual. Commenting on this asymmetry in the growth of the material and spiritual worlds, Louis de Broglie lamented: "Our enlarged body clamours for an addition to the spirit."[9] "Now, in this extremely enlarged body, the spirit remains what it was, too small now to fill it, too feeble to direct it," he continued, "Let us add that this increased body awaits a supplement of the soul and that the mechanism demands a mysticism."[10] In his view, "Humanity groans half-crushed under the weight of the advances that it has made. It does

---

9 Ken Wilber, ed., *Quantum Questions,* 1984, p.121.

10 *Ibid.*, p.122.

not know sufficiently that its future depends on itself. It is for it, above all, to make up its mind if it wishes to continue to live...."[11]

This imbalance between material affluence and spiritual hunger cannot be brushed aside as something insignificant or irrelevant. This is a serious matter demanding our careful attention, since this mismatch exhibits itself in many ways like decline in the law and order situation, increase in the cases of depression and suicide, etc. Our contemporary society in many parts of the world, including India, is afflicted by this unhealthy situation.

### iv. Widening of the Gulf between the Haves and the Have-Nots

Another unhealthy outcome of the explosive growth in science and technology is the widening gulf between the rich and the poor. The economic growth, in many ways, has been a one-sided one, giving rise to a deformed monster rather than a well-balanced organism. The rich seem to be getting richer and richer, while the poor becoming poorer and poorer. Nowhere is this anomaly more conspicuous than in India which still has the world's largest number of poor people in a single country. Of its more than 1.3 billion inhabitants, an estimated 22% live below the poverty line, 75 per cent of them in the rural areas. The level of illiteracy is alarmingly high, particularly among women. More than 40 per cent of India's population is illiterate, with women, tribals and scheduled castes particularly affected. With regard to infant mortality also, the statistics are equally dismal. India is ranked 53 in the world with 55 deaths for 1000 births, and 78.6 deaths for 100-births in the case of children under 5.

### v. Rise in Environmental Degradation and Pollution level

Another unfortunate victim of all these developments triggered by an unprecedented advance in science and technology is mother-nature, particularly the environment. Much has been written on this problem under the heads of deforestation, acid rain, green house effect, ozone depletion, etc. Pollution in all its virulent forms – air pollution, water pollution and land pollution, has been inflicting serious health problems on India. A number of Indian cities have been listed among the most polluted ones. For instance, some reports in November 2019 say that Delhi is the most polluted city in the world. Many steps have been taken by governmental and non-governmental agencies, but much more needs to be done.

## 4. Some Serious Consequences of these Developments

### a. The Cultural Confusion

There is no doubt that the astounding developments in science and technology have played a significant role in bringing about the changes and shifts, with

11 Idem.

their accompanying blessings and curses, as discussed above. No doubt several other factors also have their share of responsibility. But since the capability of science with striking immediate results is far greater than that of many other influencing agents, the major responsibility rests with it. Moreover, since science's forward march is an ongoing one with ever-increasing pace, one can expect more surprises on the way.

Perhaps one of the immediate consequences is the cultural confusion these developments are giving rise to, presenting formidable challenges to various sections of our society. It is clear that many of the items in this package are good, and are to be encouraged. For instance, many aspects of globalisation with its broadening of vision and opening up of new vistas are beneficial. But the challenge is how to safeguard many legitimate local needs and concerns in this process of globalisation so that the individuality and uniqueness of local cultures is not sacrificed. So often we are saddened by the spectre of many abandoning their Indian cultural values in a mad chase after certain western fads.

The challenge is not something that will go away with time. In fact, it will only become stronger and more formidable since there is no turning back of this process. Nor is the traditionalists' solution of "retreat to the good-old-days" a healthy response to this challenge. Ours is an evolving world; evolution is not only a law of life, it is also a law of the universe. As Teilhard de Chardin and other thinkers have passionately and persuasively argued, no power on earth can stop this process of ongoing evolution. This world of ours will have to learn to deal with this situation constructively and creatively. Therein lies the path to future success.

## b. How to Meet this Challenge?

At the very outset, we need to admit that this challenge is only natural and to be expected since culture by nature is a dynamic, growing/evolving phenomenon. As the "Theme Overview" of this seminar puts it, culture can be looked upon as "the sum total of all the devices and methods that a society has at its disposal to control, direct, and modify the material conditions of its existence." In the case of such a complex, dynamic phenomenon, changes and challenges are to be welcomed as part of the growth process. History tells us that Indian culture is one of the most ancient and experienced ones, having had to face the onrush and impact of many outside alien influences, even destructive ones. India has faced them successfully and creatively in the past. No culture or outside influence that has come into close contact with India has remained unaffected by some aspects of her unique traits. The well-known British writer Mark Twain has remarked: "India is the cradle of the human race, the birthplace of human speech, the mother of history, the grandmother of legend and the great grand mother of tradition."

The present challenge seems to be rather formidable, having many apparently conflicting strands, defying any easy integration. We are called upon to do due justice to the different strands without undermining the essential elements of our own culture. Among other things:

- This would mean the challenging task of keeping our technological edge that is essential for growth, without sacrificing the human face.
- It would mean keeping the path of material prosperity open without marginalizing those below the poverty level.
- It would mean developing frontline medical treatment, without ignoring the basic medical facilities for the ordinary people.
- It would mean that India's economic plans should focus *not only on profit-making, but also profit-sharing*, particularly with the less-privileged ones.
- It would mean that science and technology be put primarily at the service of meeting the basic needs of humans, rather than making lucrative cosmetic items for the rich and famous.
- It would mean using the almost inexhaustible nuclear power for useful, peaceful programmes, rather than for the production of more and more sophisticated weapons of mass destruction.
- *It would mean transforming the national and multinational corporations from profit-hungry organizations to service-sensitive ones.*
- *In fine, a cultural, value-based restructuring is required in the light of these developments, giving rise to a new culture, a new world order, a new India.*

## 5. Science-Spirituality Dialogue and the New World Order

In this final section, I wish to point out that a creative and constructive interaction of science and spirituality is necessary for this cultural restructuring. This collaboration is only natural since science is today an integral part of any culture, particularly our Indian culture, and spirituality has always been a central part of it, although it is expressed in different ways.

This all-important process of value-based cultural restructuring is a long and complex process requiring judicious and skillful intermingling of many elements. This certainly involves adapting and integrating the emerging new trends into the cultural setting of India. Not all new trends can be assimilated wholesale; nor should all the traditional values be thrown overboard. Identification of the new items to be admitted and of old ones to be abandoned will have to be done with the utmost care and sensitivity.

### a. Certain Traditional Values to Be Reemphasized

This process also involves the reemphasizing of many of our traditional, time-tested values and principles. For instance, India was noted for her positive appreciation of other cultural values. History tells us that we accepted other cultures with a welcoming attitude. This spirit has to be preserved and further developed. Again, India was noted for her spirit of tolerance. In fact, many serious scholars have shown that Hinduism is the most tolerant among the major religions of the world. In the process of cultural restructuring this spirit will be of immense assistance. The spirit of *nishkamakarma*, selfless service, was another value very much emphasized by our Indian religious traditions. In today's profit-hungry, success-oriented world, driven by cutthroat competition and rivalry, this principle should play a central role. The spirit of the *mahatma*, large soul, is another treasured value in our rich tradition. This spirit too needs to be reemphasized. I leave the experts to extend this list further.

### b. New Values to Be Developed

This process involves also developing new values in the light of the developments around – a task demanding well-informed, discerning, creative, innovative, and daring persons. Here also a constructive interplay between scientific and spiritual values can be of immense help. To suggest a few possibilities, along with the scientific values of efficiency and expediency, concern and care for others are to be cultivated. Again, along with the scientific values of exactness and certainty, room will have to be provided for a certain imperfection and uncertainty. Furthermore, along with the scientific values of predictability and self-reliance, provision will have to be made for a certain unpredictability and reliance on other sources, particularly on divine providence.

## Conclusion

The challenge is clear, but the line of response awaits further clarity. But one thing is non-controversial: neither science alone, wherever its success may take us, is competent to meet this challenge, nor is spirituality left alone, whatever be its resources, competent to deal adequately with this situation. On the other hand, together they can meet the challenge more effectively, creatively and constructively. A serious, well-planned, and skill-fully executed dialogue between modern science and spirituality should be one of the principal players in the creation of new world order for the betterment of humans and the cosmos.

13

# Approaching Evil in Our Highly Complex World, Inspired by Cyril Desbruslais SJ

**Kuruvilla Pandikattu SJ**

*Dean of Philosophy, Jnana-Deepa Vidyapeeth, Pune 411014*

**Abstract**: Two prominent thinkers Desbruslais has been exploring in understanding the mystery of evil is Augustine and Irenaeus. The former represents the static view of the universe, while the latter a dynamic view. Irenaeus's understanding of sin and evil in a dynamic world makes better sense today, as pointed out by John Hick. At the same time, we need to admit that today, based on our scientific discoveries, we have moved further from the dynamic world. We are in a highly complex world where determined) chaos (so, not utter chaos) rules. Based on the assumptions of this complex world, the author attempts to outline a theodicy.

**Keywords**: Theodicy, Augustine, Irenaeus, John Hick, Sin, Evil, Chaos theory, Fuzzy logic.

All of us experience evil and ask the question, Why? We feel immense pain and try to make sense of it? We experience betrayal and try to cope up with it. Cyril Desbruslais has shown us the way to move from a static world to a dynamic world to make better sense of evil. By following his methodology, in this article, we need to move toward a new dimension on 'evil' in the complex world that we live in. In this article we accept that dependent on our contemporary scientific findings, our world, (remembering the evil present in it), can be better comprehended as a complex one, rather than to a dynamic one.

## 1. Evil: The "Question of Questions"

The agonising question as to how a world of so much suffering and pain could be reconciled with a God of love and power is one of such magnitude that many thinkers (particularly those of a mystical bent) suggest that perhaps the best response we can come up with – and one most worthy of a person of religious faith – would be a humble, trustful silence. On the other hand, a hasty retreat behind a bulwark of "mystery" and "blind faith" only puts many of our contemporaries off. We can hardly blame those who scoff at such a response as being a convenient form of escape to cover up our ignorance, our unfeelingness and our laziness. Finally, it would be a safe bet to argue that this matter is the greatest stumbling block to faith and that every day more numbers are added to the list of lapsed believers and drop-outs from the ranks of those whose naive religious formation has not been able to help them integrate a painful human experience of suffering and death into a personal conviction concerning a God who cares.[1]

### a. The Christian Difficulty

Any religious faith that implies belief in not just any kind of deity or vague force but a conviction that God is, at one and the same time, all-good and all-powerful is faced with a real challenge here. And since Christianity implies such an avowed creed, Christians have to come to terms with it in a particular way, sooner or later. Of course, belief in such a divinity is not the monopoly of Christianity alone. A similar conviction pre-dates our era and the sages of pre-Christian times had sought to wrestle with the matter long before we did. In fact, it is the philosopher Lactantius (260-340 AD) who has preserved for us the version of the objection as formulated by his master almost 600 years earlier:[2]

> God either wishes to take away evils, and is unable, or He is able and is unwilling; or He is neither willing nor able, or He is both willing and able. If He is willing and is unable, He is feeble, which is not in accordance with the character of God; if He is able and unwilling, He is envious, which is equally at variance with God; if He is neither willing nor able, He is both envious and feeble, and therefore not God; if He is both willing and able, which alone is suitable to God, from what source then are evils? Or why does He not remove them?

Faced with this dilemma, not a few of our contemporaries have suggested a belief in a kind of limited, non-almighty divinity, "far more human and closer

1 For this section I am indebted to Cyril Desbruslais Cyril Desbruslais, *Philosophy of God for Today,* New Delhi: Christian World Imprints, 2019, 95-112. It may be noted that he has elaborately dealt with this problem (or better, mystery) of evil in his writings.

2 Quoted by John Hick, *Evil and the God of Love*, Glasgow, Collins, 1978, 5.

to us", who, like any loving and caring person on earth, would yearns to put an end to all suffering and pain, but is quite unable to do so. Metaphysics aside, such a modification of our conception of the deity would involve such a radical, essential and total reworking of the Christian and biblical vision of God as to call into doubt the entire creed!

Desbruslais notes that the controversy has, indeed, spawned a specialised new word to refer to the quest, *theodicy*. It comes from two Greek terms, *theos*, which means 'God' (nothing new for us, there) and *dike*, which means 'justice'. In other words, *theodicy* would be fabricated in parallel with jurisprudence and the law courts, where a defence lawyer would try to "justify" (prove 'just' or 'innocent') someone who had been accused of some crime or the other. In effect, the philosopher would be trying to acquit God of the charge of 'colossal mismanagement of the cosmos'! This whole approach assuredly smacks of the arrogant and the presumptuous (not to say the blasphemous and the impious), inasmuch we seem to abrogate the right and power to stand in judgment of God and defend him against charges of negligence, perceived as per our human and limited capacities – a "justifying of God's ways to man" of the worst order.

However much we can sympathise which such reactions – and we cannot deny that, as John Hick recalls, "[such a] solution to the problem of evil must be worse than the problem itself" inasmuch as it claims access to God's secrets and hidden purposes and plans – we can't simply brush aside the whole project. Theodicy might be aimed not so much as "justifying" (in the legal sense) God's ways to man but *understanding* them. And if there can be proud and irreligious theodicies, there can also be approaches that are humble and sensitive to the mystery we are trying to apprehend (not comprehend)! This is all the more imperative when a major portion of the effort consists in trying to clear up and correct mistaken and misleading ideas about God and his action in the world.[3]

## b. Grappling with Difficulties and Dealing with Omnipotence

However, there still remain some radical questions. For instance, why is there within us a tendency to evil at all? Why couldn't God create us, like himself, as beings who only seek and do what is good? And if we want to say that sin and crime stem not from God but from the abuse of our freedom, why did God make us free at all, knowing that we could abuse this freedom? And what about other evils that have nothing at all to do with human wilfullness – natural calamities like earthquakes and cyclones, diseases and accidents due to natural frailty? After all, couldn't God have given us a world in which there were no viruses and tidal waves? Finally, why did he make us embodied at all? For,

3 Cyril Desbruslais, *The Philosophy of Liberation: Revisiting Genuine Religious Experiences with Special Reference to Christianity*, New Delhi: Christian World Imprints, 2016, 73-74.

had we no bodies and were pure created spirits "like angels" we should not be prone to pain, disease and death? We have to grapple, as best as we can, with these upsetting questions.

There is no question of denying God's almightiness. But, all too often, people think that it means "God can do anything at all!" They would imagine that God can make square circles or men that cannot die! But, as we have been reminded, time and again, this is not at all the case.

The fact that God cannot sin and we can don't make us, as it might seem at first sight, "freer than God", inasmuch as we can do something that he can never bring himself to do. The ability to sin is not an expression of freedom: it is the result of a lack of freedom. Freedom, that is to say, it is a means to an end: liberation because we are not fully liberated. It is possible for us to choose something which brings us fulfilment in only one isolated area of our many-faceted existence, but that harms our total personal growth (in other words, makes us less liberated).

We will have to show that God cannot, in effect, make finite persons who are not embodied, who are not placed in an evolutionary (non-finished product world) and so on, any more than he cannot sin or make square triangles. If God could have acted otherwise and yet did not, then one might raise doubts about his goodness or omnipotence. But such was not the case, as Desbruslais indicates.

## c. Approaching the Mystery of Evil

Many thinkers prefer to speak of the problem of evil, rather than call it as a mystery. This is because they are averse to the "easy-answer" approach that I alluded to above, whereby the whole gamut of agonised and agonising questions are covered up by a convenient cloak of pseudo-religiosity: "It's all a mystery. Ours not to question why, ours but to believe and die!"

However, Cyril Desbruslais still persists in referring to this issue as a mystery as the philosopher Gabriel Marcel ascribes to it. "I hereby seek to remind ourselves that evil is not 'a disorder which I view from outside,' but as a baffling reality that has its roots in me. Evil, then, is not just something that lies outside of me – the wicked world with all its unjust structures, false values, crimes and natural calamities. There lurks within me a selfish craving that battles against my better self: the call of evil outside of me finds a responsive chord within me." Here he recalls the insightful words of St Paul, the truth of which we all find verified in our own experience: "I cannot understand my own behaviour. I fail to carry out the things I want to do, and I find myself doing the very things I hate... In fact, this seems to be the rule, that every single time I want to do something good it is something evil that comes to hand" (Rom 7:14ff). It is a sobering and often-forgotten truth that when we wrestle with the horrendous fact of wickedness, we are struggling with a powerful aspect of ourselves. Indeed, serious plumbing into the depths of wickedness within ourselves will more likely throw a lot of light on its nature and origin than a detached survey of it, hypocritically, "from outside" as if it had no roots within us!

The way one approaches an issue cannot but have an impact on the kind of response one works out to it. The man who views something as a stumbling block will react to it in a totally different way from the one who sees it as a stepping stone! One may view a river as plainly and simply a bit of a nuisance, as something to be crossed, somehow or the other so as to get on with one's proper goal and purpose. Or one can dive in, enjoy the river and relish a swim!

So, it is with the mystery of evil. Of course, he is not at all suggesting that we try and view cancer, murder, war and train accidents as "nice things" (some theodicies try to do that – "nothing is evil in itself, but thinking makes it so!") Try telling that to someone wasting away from cancer or to a Dalit whose wife has been raped, stripped and paraded naked in the market place. And does anyone really believe that the only difference between Mother Teresa and Hitler is the perspective from which we view them? What I am saying is that the evil of cancer will be looked at differently by someone who sees it as a punishment for one's sins, or the sins of his parents or those committed in one's previous life and by someone who views it as not having been directly willed by God at all!

"The destiny of the human community has become all of a piece, where once the various groups... had a kind of private history of their own. Thus, the human race has passed from a rather static concept of reality to a more dynamic, evolutionary one." (*GS* – Vatican II, "The Church in the Modern World", No. 5) Evil viewed against a static understanding of reality will be understood – and responded to – in quite a different way from evil understood against a dynamic vision of reality. And this brings us up square with John Hick's observations on evil approached from the Augustinian (static) and more traditional angle and evil viewed from the Irenaean (dynamic) and less commonly known (yet real nevertheless) perspective.[4]

## 2. Phenomenology of Suffering

### a. Ills Unlimited

At first sight, it would appear that the world around us affords us naught but a sorry spectacle of things gone awry. And which one of us has not, at some time or the other, felt stirred (and perhaps still is stirred) to get up and do something about the mess the world is in. Like Hamlet of old, Desbruslais recognises that "something's rotten in the state of Denmark", or India or wherever. But soon our youthful ardour and before the immensity of the evil and injustice, we are

4 John Hick, *Evil and the God of Love*, 11 ff.

trying to take on. Once again, Cyril says that with Hamlet, we tend to cry out, in effect:

The time is out of joint. O, cursed spite,
That ever I was born to set it right!

And most of us, sooner or later, give up, in disgust, any attempt to venture into the lists against the powers of darkness and wickedness. "It's just a phase we all have to go through," we tell ourselves. And the majority of us resign ourselves sadly (and cynically) to the status quo. "Nothing can be done about it," we say as if to excuse out option out.

## b. Two Sources of Evil

As for "the mess the world is in", well that clearly seems to stem from two clearly defined and well separated immediate issues. There are things like the ill-treatment of Dalits in India or internecine tribal battles in South Africa, the invasion of Kuwait and the consequent Gulf War and such like. These are obviously the result of deliberate human choice. Human beings have – for whatever justifiable or non-justifiable reasons – wilfully decided to make these things come to pass. But there is a whole series of unpleasant things that no human being wished for nor caused: the earthquake that ravaged Uttar Kashi, the deformed little baby that is born to horror-struck parents, the sickness that carries off a youngster in the bloom of his or youth. Nobody wanted these things to happen, much less brought them into being!

There is a third class of painful events that are due to human causality, but not deliberately. This is the whole area of human error or accident. Due to a pilot's carelessness, a plane crashes and he and all the passengers are killed. A cricket player hits the ball and it zooms to the boundary... where it strikes someone on the temple and he dies. An enquiry might or might not exonerate the pilot from "culpable error" in the first place or not: it is certain that he didn't consciously and deliberately intend, will and carry out with grim efficiency the killing of himself and all his passengers. In other words, though this calamity was due to man's instrumentality (our "first source", above), it cannot be put down to a mere "abuse of human freedom", but rather to the unfortunate consequences of human frailty.

## c. "Nature, Red in Tooth and Claw"

However, a close look around us will make it strikingly evident that – whatever be Gandhiji's impressions on the matter – the world is hardly founded on non-violent principles. As Tennyson put it in *In Memoriam* (lvi), "Nature (is) red in tooth and claw". If one accepts Evolution (and there are more reasons in favour of accepting it than rejecting it), then we have to admit that "survival of the fittest" and "might is right" have been the bloody and brutal laws that governed its progress. One could, of course, point out that it was not sheer physical force and strength that decided things for, on that account, man would never have been able to prevail. If a timely and "providential" (?) fall of a flock of convenient meteors did wipe out the lumbering dinosaurs, still puny man had to contend with woolly mammoths, mastodons and sabre-toothed tigers – all more than a match for his pigmy capabilities: man survived because his emergent intellect made him overall superior to these powerful beasts, which he killed and devoured before they could render him like service!

Still, in the sea, the big fish swallow up the smaller fish and, on the land, the bigger animals prey upon the smaller ones, not to mention the fact that, at every turn and twist, we massacre millions of microbes. By virtue of a grim kind of poetic justice, a tiny germ or virus can snuff out the life of an organism vastly greater than itself. Then there is the colossal phenomenon of prodigious waste that governs the working of the laws of nature. Of the billions of sperms and ova that come into being, only a minuscule percentage go on to constitute an embryo. The rest are discarded and forgotten. Indeed, lower animals spawn their offspring in prolific abundance because only a tiny proportion has any hope of survival. There seems to be a curious logic (to say the least) in the fact that a huge animal like an elephant is satisfied with leaves and insensate life whereas the much smaller cat has to terrorise, hurt and kill a mouse to its appetite. Details such as these warn us against coming up with a naive, simplistic and glib justification of God's/Nature's ways!

## 3. Hermeneutics: A Dynamic Approach

### a. Augustine and Irenaeus and Their Differences

Desbruslais is indeed indebted to John Hick for drawing our attention to the fact that, historically, there have been two rival approaches to theodicy in the Christian tradition. The roots of one, the more commonly known and generally followed, the one that has received more conscious thematic elaboration, were laid by St Augustine of Hippo (354-430). It is to the lesser-known but earlier St Irenaeus of Lyons (140 202) that we owe the other. It was neither critically elaborated nor extensively passed on but it is significant to know that from almost within the first century of the Christian era, an alternative reading of the Genesis story was current – one whose implications would yield a far more dynamic and evolutionary vision of the human person and his destiny, one far more in keeping with contemporary patterns of thought! If the former view was more originally characteristic of (and prevalent in) Roman Christianity, the latter was, in more sense than one, the product of the Greek point of view. In the end, the Roman viewpoint won hands down and the Irenaean-Greek insight, though picked up a bit by St Clement of Alexandria (150-214), never really got the chance to develop into the full-fledged theory of a school. Nevertheless, from time to time, various Christian thinkers seized upon inspirations coming from their wrestling with Scriptures in the light of experience (and vice versa), came up with ideas and approaches that just as easily could have been direct elaborations of Irenaeus' pristine discovery.

Perhaps we should let John Hick's own words summarise this key contrast. After all, it is he who first shared this provocative insight with all of us!

> Instead of the (Augustinian) doctrine that man was created finitely perfect and then incomprehensibly destroyed his own perfection and plunged into sin and misery, Irenaeus suggests that man was created as an imperfect, immature creature who was to undergo moral development and growth and finally be brought to the perfection intended for him by his maker. Instead of the fall of Adam being presented, as in the Augustinian tradition, as an utterly malignant and catastrophic event, completely disrupting God's plan, Irenaeus pictures it as something that occurred in the childhood of the race, an understandable lapse due to weakness and immaturity rather than an adult crime full of malice and pregnant with perpetual guilt. And instead of the Augustinian view of life's trials as a divine punishment for Adam's sin, Irenaeus sees our world of mingled good and evil as a divinely appointed environment for man's development towards the perfection that represents the fulfilment of God's purpose for him.[5]

### b. Implications

The key issue here is not whether Augustine and Irenaeus took the Adamic myth for a true story and believed that Adam and Eve were historical personages (probably both of these seminal thinkers did). It is their implicit philosophy of man and his environment that interests us and that is relevant for its far-reaching implications.

In Augustine's vision, Adam and Eve were created as perfect as finite beings could be. They could not have been absolutely perfect, for that would require them to have been uncreated and infinite (and that would be obviously out of the question). But he saw them as endowed with "preternatural gifts", such as immortality and the fullness of all knowledge and wisdom. As a result of the "Fall" – whereby they failed "the test" God had given them – they lost ("fell from") the high estate which God had granted them, far above their natural deserts or exigencies. Their nature became corrupt and various evil tendencies and other pathways to sin opened up in them. Catholics and Reformers might differ here and there as to precisely the degree of corruption that had entered man and how much of his freewill still remained, but all seemed to agree that "concupiscence" (understood as the inner prompting to evil consequent upon his "sin") had begun to vitiate all man's efforts.

5 Hick, 220-221

Furthermore, not only had man's very nature become "wounded" by this action, his whole life, as punishment, was to be lived out in a vale of tears and no longer in the pleasant Garden of Eden which would have been God's original intention, had Adam and Eve been a bit more co-operative. More than that, because of Adam's "sin", all his descendants were to be barred from Paradise and locked out in this wicked world of pain and woe: this is the famous Augustinian doctrine of "original sin" which would become a dogma of the Church.

It should be noted that there is nothing in the *Genesis* story to necessitate belief in anything like the above-mentioned gifts being lavished on our "first parents" and consequently being wounded/corrupted after Adam and Eve sinned. If this is so, can we genuinely speak of a "Fall" (since there was no previous elevated "state" to fall from)? And let us not forget that the phrase "original sin" is found nowhere in the Old or New Testament and nothing in either (not even in St Paul's letters) would oblige us to hold that the affliction common to all of us was founded upon a common fault. It simply records the gradual universalisation of sin, as mankind freely and progressively turned his back upon God's call and values. We prefer to speak of "cosmic" or "universal" sin and the *development of the dogma* of original sin teaches us to dissociate it from the notion that our present condition is in any way a punishment for the revolt of an alleged person – someone other than ourselves – committed in the mists of pre-history! The Adamic myth, in other words, aims at throwing light upon the *nature* of sin and its immediate consequences (alienation from one's fellow humans and from nature): it is *not* interested in telling us about *origins* (that is, how sin began – apart from the fact that it was basically man's creation, not God's).[6]

## c. Two Understandings of Evil

The traditional Augustinian understanding of evil, which Aquinas also follows, sees evil as *privatio boni*, a privation of good. In other words, metaphysically speaking, evil is not a positive entity but, as Aquinas would put it, "a relative non-being". That implies, notes Desbruslais, evil, as such, does not exist. It is not so much as a being as an absence of a *due* perfection in some positive reality. Blindness is an evil in man, inasmuch as man is meant to see – the ability to see is a "due perfection" in the human person. But the "blindness" or inability to see a chair or a stone is not evil: it is not a *lack* in these things for neither of them is supposed to see! In other words, the more common scholastic theodicy would totally reject what Leibnitz called "metaphysical evil", that is, the mere fact of imperfection in itself, whether it referred to quality due

6 More can be found in look it all up in his anti-Gnostic polemic, *Against Heresies*. There is an excellent translation in Vol. I of *The Faith of The Early Fathers*. See St. Irenaeus, *Against Heresies,* tran. W. Jurgens, Bangalore, Theological Publications, 1984, pp. 84 – 102.

or undue. For instance, in Leibnitz's book, the finiteness of a creature is a metaphysical evil – quite irrespective of the fact that infinity is not a "due perfection" of creatures and cannot be! Just for the record, Leibniz "explains" metaphysical evil by pointing out that imperfect or limited existence is better than no existence at all. Still, it is not very meaningful to call something an "evil" when it doesn't indicate something that is missing and should have been there in the first place!

Following upon the above more traditional understanding, evil is subdivided into two main types: physical and moral. Physical evil would be the absence of some due tangible quality in some material being. Thus, the inability of an injured crow to fly or deafness in a human person would be examples of physical evils. Moral evil would be the absence of a due orientation in a free personal act. Moral evil is an another word for sin. A culpable lie is a moral evil inasmuch as it is an act of speech which lacks in its due orientation: the natural purpose (orientation) of speech is to reveal or share information/knowledge, but in a lie, speech is used to conceal – which is to go against its very *physis*, or nature.

In the Irenaean approach, however, evil would be understood as a kind of unavoidable possibility in the context of immature man's necessary environment for the process of person-making. In other words, Adam and Eve's sin would be seen not so much as an inveterately wicked and malicious act of adults who could – and should – have known and acted better, but the clumsy fault of immature, childish folk, stumbling towards adolescence: something that would elicit pity rather than wrath. Sin is seen as evil but recognised as a practically inevitable option open to humans in their finiteness at the start of the evolutionary process. Physical evils (pain, suffering, illness and death) are seen not as divine punishments unleashed upon hapless humans but as the necessary attendant circumstances for that evolving world which alone would enable us to attain growth and gradual maturity. Human "error" is the natural consequence of our inherent frailty as finite and embodied. All these have not "entered the world" as a result of our having sinned (in and through our ancestors) in an "original state of grace", where we were endowed with "preternatural gifts" in a paradisical somewhere which could not hurt us in any way!

So far Desbruslais has contributed to the phenomenon of evil from a dynamic perspective bringing in Irenaeus and John Hick. Even though the attempt is heroic, we cannot still fully make sense of evil. Even if we can better "understand" or interpret evil, we have not been able to "change" or improve it significantly. In the next section, we see how modern perspectives of the world can help us further.

## 4. From Complex Perspective

We know that sometimes evil is caused unwittingly by good people with good intentions. At other times evil bad may also cause good results. So there is no necessary connection that good causes always produce good results or the other way around. The real world around us too complex and difficult to comprehend. So we try to understand this world using two mathematical theories: fuzzy logic and chaos theory.

### a. Fuzzy Logic

It is a form of many-valued logic in which the truth values of variables may be any real number between 0 and 1 both inclusive. ... The term fuzzy logic was introduced in 1965 by Lotfi Zadeh, a mathematician and computer scientist from the University of California. In mathematics, fuzzy sets (aka uncertain sets) are somewhat like sets whose elements have degrees of membership. .Unlike the binary notions, fuzzy set theory permits the gradual assessment of the membership of elements in a set; this is described with the aid of a membership function valued in the real unit interval [0, 1].[7]

A fuzzy control system is a control system based on fuzzy logic—a mathematical system that analyzes analog input values in terms of logical variables that take on continuous values between 0 and 1, in contrast to classical or digital logic, which operates on discrete values of either 1 or 0 (true or false, respectively.

Fuzzy logic is extensively used in modern control systems such as expert systems. Fuzzy Logic is used with Neural Networks as it mimics how a person would make decisions, only much faster. It is done by Aggregation of data and changing into more meaningful data by forming partial truths as Fuzzy sets.

Fuzzy logic is an approach to computing based on "degrees of truth" rather than the usual "true or false" (1 or 0) Boolean logic on which the modern computer is based. It is employed to handle the concept of partial truth, where the truth value may range between completely true and completely false.[8]

### b. Chaos Theory

Like fuzzy logic, the theory of chaos is an interdisciplinary theory stating that, within the apparent randomness of chaotic complex systems, there are underlying patterns, constant feedback loops, repetition, self-similarity, fractals, and self-organization.

---

7 This is similar to the doctrines of anekāntavāda and syādavāda are often criticised to denying any certainty, or accepting incoherent contradictory doctrines.

8 For more details Pichalakkattu, Binoy. *Bridging Mathematics, Philosophy, and Theology: Fuzzy Logical Thinking for Science-Religion Dialogue*. New Delhi: Christian World Imprints, 2017.

This mathematical theory looks at certain systems that are very sensitive. A very small change may make the system behave completely differently. ... Some systems (like weather) might appear random at first look, but chaos theory says that these kinds of systems or patterns may not be. Propounded by the French mathematician Henri Poincare, this theory assumes that seemingly simple events could produce complex and confounding behaviours. It is a theory that was seen to have great potential for discovery among many fields.

Complexity theory focuses on complex systems involving numerous interacting parts, which often give rise to unexpected order. ... Collectively known as dynamical systems theory or nonlinear dynamics, neither chaos nor complexity theory is a theory in the ordinary sense of the word.[9]

## c. Our Highly Complex World

We are not competent to propose a better theodicy (understanding and elimination of evil) in our highly complex and sophisticated world. Still, some outlines may be proper. Drawing from the chaos theory, we have factals, which measures the "roughness of a surface." In the real world, there are no straight lines, no spheres and no smooth surfaces. The idealised smooth surface is present only in the mind of the observer. The actual world is a world of roughness and curvature, of different degrees, with an underlying homogeneity.

Similar to this analogy of smooth and rough surfaces, we can really hold that in the highly complex real-world the binary between light and darkness, love and hatred and goodness and evil does not exist.

At the same time, we need to admit that evil exists. It's real. But its relationship to goodness is much more complex. In the movement from evil (0) to good (1), we are confronted with the analogue (opposed to digital or binary) chaotic possibility of apparent randomness. Within the apparent randomness of chaotic complex systems, there are underlying patterns, constant feedback loops, repetition, self-similarity, fractals, and self-organization.

Can the degrees of reality, feedback loops, repetition, self-similarity, fractals, and self-organization help us to understand evil better and transform it? Can we affirm the unconditional love of God even when we acknowledge that evil exists, but is not absolute? Can we still make sense of the birth of a handicapped child and the death of a preborn? Are we better placed to understand evil in a complex world, rather than in a static or dynamic world? We need to dwell with these questions so that the answers may transform us making us better and more loving. Maybe the mystery of love can transform sinners to saints, evil to goodness, in ways we do not at the moment fully understand.

---

9 The classical book on chaos theory for non-specialists is Gleick, James. *Chaos: Making a New Science*. London: The Folio Society, 2015.

## Conclusion

We should acknowledge that when Desbruslais has moved from Augustine's static world to Irenaeus' dynamic world, he provides us with a better appraisal of the mystery of evil. Similarly, in the ever complex and evolving world, we need to formulate different theories to explain to ourselves the presence of evil in our hearts, in our communities and in the world. We need to recognise this evil in the presence of an ever-loving God, who is unconditionally on our side. Some hints we may draw from the highly complex world we are living in this world.

- The reality is rough and tough. Still, we can experience smoothness to various degrees. Similarly, life is hard and cruel. Still, we can experience the presence of love from our neighbours and its fullness from God.
- There is both love and hatred in our hearts. Just like there is darkness and light in our material world. We need to move through hatred to love, through the darkness to light. Only God can do, with the cooperation of human beings. We do not fully understand the evil among us. But we can hope to understand it by bringing in the ever-loving God.
- We can believe that we are collectively moving towards unconditional, absolute love (goodness through the complex and crooked world! The suffering and even death of that innocent child can only make sense if there is a loving God who will deal with the injustice in His own way.
- We need to go beyond the binary reward/punishment approach of human living and bring in elements of compassion and mercy into our discourse on human activities. Mercy can help us better understand the evil, since "All will be well and all will be well and every kind of thing shall be well" (Julian of Norwich) in spite of the felt experience of evil.[10] Such an optimism can come only after having experienced terrible tragedies and God's loving involvement in our world.

10 Mirabai Starr, "All Will Be Well: The Radical Optimism of Julian of Norwich," HuffPost, Jan 23, 2014. https://www.huffpost.com/entry/julian-of-norwich_b_4115736. She writes further: Sin, says Julian, turns out to be "no thing." Though controversial, she is quite clear: "Nowhere in all that was revealed to me did I see a trace of sin," she writes. "And so I stopped looking for it and moved on, placing myself in God's hand, allowing him to show me what he wanted me to see." In Julian's exceedingly practical view, "sin has no substance, not a particle of being, and can only be detected by the pain it causes." When we make mistakes and create suffering, we humble ourselves and God loves us all the more. For those of us non-Christian and post-modern types, try substituting the word *sin* for shame, or blame, or even karma. In other words, we screw up, but that only opens the tender heart of the cosmos where we can find refuge and come back into wholeness.

- We can hope that evil is somehow transformed into goodness and leads to its fullness. Just as Jesus transformed death to the fullness of life (through resurrection). After affirming the incredible and unexpected cruelty and evil, we can truly be open to the God of Surprises.[11] Joyfully and lovingly, in spite of the tragic situation around us.

We can finally pray with the Psalmist (Ps 13):

> O LORD, how long will you forget me? Forever?
> How long will you look the other way?
>
> How long must I struggle with anguish in my soul,
> with sorrow in my heart every day?
> How long will my enemy have the upper hand?
>
> Turn and answer me, O LORD my God!
> Restore the sparkle to my eyes, or I will die.
>
> Don't let my enemies gloat, saying, "We have defeated him!"
> Don't let them rejoice at my downfall.
>
> But I trust in your unfailing love.
> I will rejoice because you have rescued me.
>
> I will sing to the LORD
> because he is good to me.

---

11 Hughes, Gerard. *God of Surprises*. Luton: Andrews UK Ltd, 2010. The surprise, unexpected and complex dimension is easily perceived in the Holy Spirit.

14

# Hunger and Violence: A Contemporary Exploration of Social Responsibility to '*Live Life Being More Human...*'

**Joji Valli**
*Researcher and Publisher, Pune*

**Abstract:** Hunger and Violence are the two sides of the same coin throughout the history of human existence. As a progressive thinker and liberation philosopher Dr. Cyril Desbruslais throughout his career, vehemently voices the concern regarding social injustice and discrimination. He argues, "Violence is not the solution to violence, hunger to be alleviated, injustice to be addressed, violence to be overcome, wars to be stopped..." He believes that empowering the youth is the solution to develop a deep social sense and relationship, a sense of social responsibility and concern for the poor, the deprived and all victims of injustice, in our country and all over the world. "Give people context for relationships. Don't try to dominate any relation. Be open to differences and celebrate differences." Relationship and responsibility are hallmarks of human existence because life is a gift and a one time opportunity.

**Keywords:** Relationship, Responsibility, Social responsibility, Corporate Social Responsibility, Purpose of life, Hunger, Fully human-Fully alive

## Introduction

Around the globe, we wake up to the headlines and images of devastating violence. But beneath the headlines, there is another great challenge that is often the root cause of violence or its unintended consequences: increasing rate of hunger and an alarming lack of food. Often, hunger and violence go hand in hand. And as a consequence, millions of innocent people in poor countries suffer the burden. It is an alarming situation and a challenge permeated into humanity. Cyril Desbruslais who is a radical thinker and a champion of human liberation would say, "life is for being more human than for having more – having more things, having more money, having more power etc…"[1] Having implies the attitude of possessiveness and possession of materiality and not the attitude of sharing and caring. So he is of the opinion that we should develop or cultivate a 'be-attitude'[2] to share and care for the poor and marginalized sections of the society "to become more fully human and more fully alive,"[3] because life in any form is precious and invaluable. Life is something extraordinary.[4] The significance of life is *living*. Let it be human beings, animals, plants or any other species in the universe — life is nothing less than *living*. Many people live their lives without ever reflecting on life itself or its meaning for them. Their lives may be full of activities. They may marry, have children, run a business, or become professionals or artists, without ever obtaining any degree of understanding as to why they do these things. Their lives have no overall purpose to give meaning to separate events, and they may have no clear idea of their own nature or identity, of who they really are. So, Cyril wanted to help the youngsters to develop a deep social sense, a sense of social responsibility and concern for the poor, the deprived and all victims of injustice, in our country and all over the world – and do something about it. In his words, "For I am convinced that good philosophizing – like good prayer – always overflows into action."[5]

Human existence tops all other species with peculiar nature of reasoning. But if plants are the organisms that feed and grow, and animals are the organisms that feel and sense, what functions has man in these scheme of things? Aristotle's answer was that reason alone distinguishes human beings, and the good for man must in some way involve our reasoning faculty.[6] Descartes says, "Humans are the rational beings ('thing that thinks')."[7] Hence, he notes that human being's purpose in living must be connected with the

1 Cyril Desbruslais, *Postmodernity,* (JDV Philosophy Series, Pune, 1997).

2 Cyril Desbruslais, "The Indian Scene," *Vidyajyoti Journal of Theological Reflections* 65, no. 11 (2001), p. 796.

3 Cyril Desbruslais, *The Philosophy of the Human Person,* (JDV Philosophy series, Pune, 1997).

4 J. Krishnamurti, *What are You Doing with Your Life: Teen Books on Living*, (Krishnamurti Foundation of America, California, 2001), p. 60

5 Cyril Desbruslais, *Violence and Revolution,* (JDV Philosophy series, Pune, 1997).

6 Burton Frederick Porter, *The Good Life: Alternatives in Ethics*, (Rowman & Littlefield, Maryland, 2001), p. 137

7 *Ibid.*

proper use of this central and primary ability to become fully human and fully alive.

The meaning of life as a human being is deeply entrenched in the philosophical and religious conceptions of existence, social ties, consciousness, and happiness etc… The value of the question pertaining to the purpose of life as a human being may coincide with the achievement of ultimate reality, or a feeling of oneness, or even a feeling of sacredness.[8] Christianity postulates the purpose of human life as to love God and thereby attain heaven. Similarly, Hinduism postulates the purpose of human life as realizing the fundamental truth about oneself— "*Tat Tvam Asi.*" All religions and philosophers propagate spiritual or metaphysical ends to spell out the purpose of human life. But, for an existentialist point of view is to look where people find meaning in life because one's life arises only after one comes into existence (*existence precedes essence*).[9] To a pragmatist, the meaning of life is discoverable only via experience. "I suppose it's to help all people become more fully human, more fully alive. That would also imply recognizing that beauty is unity in diversity. Unity without diversity is uniformity, and that's boring; diversity without beauty is jarring and garish, and that's ugly,"[10] says Cyril Desbruslais. So, in order to unravel the human purpose of life, let us delve deeper into two specific concepts, 'relationship' and 'social responsibility'.

## 1. Life as Both a Question and Answer

Life is a question; life is an answer. The question is hidden in the answer and vice-versa. Life is the answer to life. Life is what happens between conception and death. A journey that starts in the womb and ends at the tomb – in the meantime whatever happens is nothing but, what we call as life.[11] From the time of the ancient Greeks, scholars have debated the proper moment at which human life comes into existence.[12] Many argue that human life begins at conception, which occurs when a human egg becomes fertilized with human sperm and becomes a zygote. Though, we all know it black and white, the question of 'what is life' bothers us every moment. So let us see what experts have to say about it.

Life is not a thing or a fluid any more than heat is. What we observe are some unusual sets of objects separated from the rest of the world by certain

8 *Ibid.*

9 Famous Existential dictum of Jean-Paul Sartre's lecture in 1946 on *Existentialism Is a Humanism.*

10 Cyril Desbruslais, *Violence and Revolution,* (JDV Philosophy Series, Pune, 1997).

11 Joji Valli, *The Canvas of Life*, (CreatiVentures, Pune, 2011), p. 39.

12 William A. Wallace, "*St. Thomas on the Beginning and Ending of Human Life*", in John P. Lizza (ed.), *Defining the Beginning and End of Life*, (The Johns Hopkins University Press, Baltimore, 2009), p. 470.

peculiar properties such as growth, reproduction, and special ways of handling energy. These objects we elect to call 'living things.' — Robert Morison[13]

What is life? It is surely one of the oldest questions. Richard Dawkins would describe life as genes. "They are inside you and me, they created us, body and soul; and their survival is the final reason for our existence."[14] Some other biologists would describe it as diffusion of atoms. The history of philosophical approaches about the concept of life, confirms this conception that rational man, who is constantly confronted with life, cannot distance himself from life. It is always life that happens to him, with him, through him.[15] The experience of life, therefore, is neither pure recognition of self nor merely reaction to outside stimuli. Reality can be understood only in living, not in escape. When you seek the purpose of life, you are really escaping and not understanding what life is.[16] Philosophers like Husserl, Wittgenstein and Habermas prefer to use the terms 'living world' and 'living experience' rather than life.[17] So I try to define life as an experience of living — living in the world; living with the world; living through the world. Life is a process, and the process is living. It is common to all organic beings. So life is *LIVING*.

## 2 Life is *LIVING*

All organic beings have a peculiar nature of coming into existence — living the life. We are born, mature, age, and die — life implies everyday actions, everyday thoughts, everyday feelings along with the struggles, the pains, the anxieties, the deceptions, the worries, the routine of the office, of business, of bureaucracy, and so on. So life goes for me, you, and just about everyone, allowing sort of small individual and cultural variations that affect the form but not the fact of routine. These activities constitute everyday life. Everyday life is, what life mostly is. Keeping it going, however, involves constant struggle. The struggle for existence or *living life* is inevitably common to all organic beings.[18] J. Krishnamurthy notes that no one has escape from this struggle instead understanding it.

> To understand the full significance of living, we must understand the daily tortures of our complex life; we cannot escape from them. The society

13 Quoted in Lynn Margulis, Dorion Sagan, *What is Life?,* (California University of California Press, 2000), p. 1.

14 Richard Dawkins, *The Selfish Gene*, p. 51.

15 Lynn Margulis, Dorion Sagan, *What is Life?*, (University of California Press, California, 2000), p. 26

16 J. Krishnamurti, *What are You Doing with Your Life: Teen Books on Living*, (Krishnamurti Foundation of America, California, 2001), p. 63.

17 Lynn Margulis, Dorion Sagan, *What is Life?*, p. 26.

18 Charles Darwin, *The Origin of Species*, (Forgotten Books, USA, 1965), p. 414.

> in which we live has to be understood by each one of us — not by some philosopher, not by some teach, not by a guru — our way of living has to be transformed, completely changed. I think that is the most important thing we have to do, and nothing else.[19]

Though each being lives its life, everything in the universe is interconnected. The entirety of organic and inorganic existence is interconnected that nothing escapes anything. The process of living entails cooperation between the living and non-living.

> Cooperation is the basis of life and of evolution — this already becomes clear on the lives of the simplest microbes. The American scientist James Shapiro found during his investigations that even bacteria form organized associations, go hunting for prey in teams, and are more similar to cells of an organism, than to autonomous loners. He came to the conclusion that most — if not practically all — bacteria live their lives in community.[20]

There is cooperation within and among the species. The vicious cycle of life is nothing but living in cooperation with everything around. It is said that ants have a 'social stomach,' because all the members of the colony of ants share their nourishment and feed each other if necessary.[21]

One species become food for the other. Organic beings, indeed, contain within themselves a special principle of dissolution.[22] In the process of living life with its struggles and complexities, all species irrespectively cooperate and undergo this evolutionary process — being the feed for each other. This grand fact of grouping of all organic beings under what is called the Natural System, is utterly inexplicable in the theory of creation.[23]

Perhaps, we humans who claim to be the top of all species with rationality are even subject to this evolutionary phenomenon. Though human beings claim to be the superior species in the organic plethora, we have no escape from admitting ourselves to the natural process and the law of nature. Thus, having a close glimpse at human being would positively help us to understand and to approximate the purpose of life as human being.

### 3. Life is LIVING a Relationship

Man cannot live alone. He must satisfy certain natural basic needs in order to survive. He has to enter into relationships with his fellowmen for living a life.

---

19 J. Krishnamurti, *What are You Doing with Your Life: Teen Books on Living*, p. 62.

20 Hans-Peter Dürr, Fritz Albert Popp, Wolfram Schommers (Eds.), *What Is Life?: Scientific Approaches and Philosophical Positions*, (World Scientific, Singapore, 2002), p. 17.

21 *Ibid.*, p. 16.

22 Martyn Paine, *Medical and physiological commentaries, Volume 3.*, (Collins, Keese, New York, 1844), p. 30.

23 Charles Darwin, *The Origin of Species*, p. 416.

No man can break the shackles of mutual dependence. This begins perhaps between the embryo and the mother; it continues till the last breath. The need of the embryo may be more physical than mental, but the mother's need is the other way round. "Society friendship and love/divinely bestow'd upon man," sang William Cowper, portraying the pangs of solitude of Alexander Selkirk who had been marooned on an uninhabited island for years. The words of the great philosopher Aristotle would substantiate how important relationship is:

> Man is by nature a social animal; an individual who is unsocial naturally and not accidentally is either beneath our notice or more than human. Society is something that precedes the individual. Anyone who either cannot lead the common life or is so self-sufficient as not to need to, and therefore does not partake of society, is either a beast or a god.[24]

Thus, man is by nature a social animal. He is born in society lives in society and dies in society. Society is indispensable for man. Man cannot live as man, without society. Isolation from society is regarded as a punishment. Ignoring the existence or alienating a person in the society is considered to be the cruelest punishment. Similarly, when I think from the perspective of Social Responsibility or Corporate Social Responsibility (henceforth abbreviated as SR/CSR),[25] it is clear that when people are ignored of the living conditions, they are being punished. Because their every life is simply ignored by the alienating conditions of their existence; this is because there are people to cooperate and collaborate in the everyday living. Solitary life is unbearable for him. Social life is necessary for man. The instinct for some form of social life is innate in human being where relationships play an indispensable role. Life is a relationship within and between organisms. The reality of relationship happens in living.

> Reality can be understood only in living, not in escape. When you seek purpose of life, you are really escaping and not understanding what life is. Life is relationship, life is action in relationship; when I do not understand relationship, or when relationship is confused, then I seek a fuller meaning.[26]

---

24 Aristotle, *Politics.*

25 Corporate Social Responsibility (CSR) is a type of international private business self-regulation that aims to contribute to societal goals of a philanthropic, activist, or charitable nature or by engage in or support volunteering or ethically-oriented practices. In this article CSR equates with Social Responsibility SR because Cyril Desbruslais philosophy of life is empowering individuals to develop a deep social sense and concern for the poor and marginalized.

26 J. Krishnamurti, *What are You Doing with Your Life: Teen Books on Living*, (Krishnamurti Foundation of America, California, 2001), p. 63-64.

Action is the crux of living a relationship. According to Cyril Desbruslais, "Sharing supposes a relationship of equals; it never makes others dependent."[27] Everything happens in life, when we are able to take that extra step in life. When we bottle ourselves within us or in an island, the possibility of relationship, to a certain extent is shut. That does not eliminate us from relating to the environment and other beings around. Life is relationship with things, people, and ideas; if we do not attend to these relationships rightly, and fully, conflicts arise from the impact of the challenge. [28]

Martin Buber speaks about the Other in his famous '*I-Thou*' relationship. For Buber, to be is to be in relation, in dialogue. "In the beginning," Buber writes, "is the relation."[29] This beginning is also a saying. To be human being, for Buber is to hold oneself in an attitude of relation by saying a 'basic word.' There are, Buber insists, two basic words, *I-Thou* and *I-It*.[30] One cannot utter the word I without relating to the world outside the self. These two basic words mark two ways of being in relation to the world. *I-It* relations are characterized by experiencing and using objects. These are one-way relationships. The *I* of *I-It* relation, understands and experiences the world as one composed of objects locatable in space and time. This way of relation to the world makes no distinction between people and things.

I-Thou relationships, on the other hand, are two-way relationships based in dialogue, one being encounters another with mutual awareness. Mutual awareness about the needs of the other and empathy towards the other is the pre-requisite for SR/CSR. The relations between the individual/corporate and the society are also coming in the purview of I-Thou relationships. Thus, such I-Thou awareness not only at the individual level but also at the corporate level I-Thou relationships are characterized by what Buber calls *presentness*. For Buber, the present is not "the abstract point between past and future," but "like the eternal now of the mystic, it is the present of intensity and wholeness" and "exists only insofar as meeting and relation exist."[31] I-Thou relationships live in what Buber calls "the between," the relational space created by the encounter.[32] Even in the corporate framework, I-Thou relationships live in the 'the between' and that relation can be very well fostered through CSR. The nature of the I-Thou relationship is best depicted in Buber's own poetic language:

27 Cyril Desbruslais, *Violence and Revolution,* (JDV Philosophy series, Pune, 1997).

28 *Ibid.* p. 194.

29 Martin Buber, *I and Thou*, (Scribner, New York, 1958), p. 18.

30 *Ibid.*, p. 20.

31 *Ibid.* p. 58.

32 Martin Buber, Ronald Gregor Smith, *Between man and man*. (New York: Routledge; 2002) p. 241.

> If *I* face a human being as my *Thou*, and say the primary word I-Thou to him, he is not a thing among things and does not consist of things. Thus human being is not He or She, bounded from every other He or She, a specific point in space and time within the net of the world: nor is he a nature able to be experienced and described, a loose bundle of named qualities. But with no neighbor, and whole in himself, he is Thou and fills the heavens. This does not mean that nothing exists except himself. But all else lives in his light.[33]

The experience of I-Thou is so powerful that it is not sustainable. In Buber's words, "It is not possible to live in the bare present. Life would be quite consumed if precautions were not taken to subdue the present speedily and thoroughly."[34] Therefore every *I-Thou* relationship must become an I-It relationship. In other words, once one experiences the *Thou* as a person with qualities that can be appreciated separately, the evanescent I-Thou relationship disappears. Once an *It* has been a *Thou*, however, it always has the potential to become a Thou again. Thus, when there has once been an I-Thou relationship with another, the ongoing relationship is characterized by a continuous alternation between *I-Thou* and *I-It*.[35]

For Buber, overemphasis our ability to use and experience comes at the expense of our power to enter into relation.[36] It is I-Thou relationship which gives meaning to our lives and make us fully human.[37] Thus, *I-Thou* and *I-It* relationships give meaning to SR/CSR and make it a fully human enterprise. Martin Buber's concepts of *I-Thou* and *I-It* provide a useful theoretical framework and a conceptual model of life as a living relationship in the larger context of purpose of life as a human being where SR/CSR plays a vital role for the progress of the society.

For Levinas, the Other is always 'higher' than me. I must serve the Other because the Other needs me. Thus, I have the responsibility to relate and serve as an ongoing connection between the human beings and the world. However, J. Krishnamurthi would encourage us to take a deep dip in the ocean of relationship than running away from it. He asserts:

> We never admit to ourselves that this life is all we know and that it should therefore be understood fully and completely. We prefer to run away from ourselves and that is why we seek the purpose of life away from relationship. If we begin to understand action, which is our relationship with people, with property, with beliefs and ideas, then we will find that

33 Martin Buber, *I and Thou*,. p. 8.

34 *Ibid*. p. 34.

35 *Ibid*. p. 17.

36 *Ibid*. p. 39.

37 *Ibid*. p. 34.

> relationship itself brings its own reward. You do not have to seek. It is like seeking love. Can you find love by seeking it? Love cannot be cultivated. You will find love only in relationship, not outside relationship, and it is because we have no love that we want a purpose of life.[38]

Of all the people you will know in a life time, you are the only one you will never lose. This relationship with the 'me' inside, is crucial; the better we know ourselves, the better we know others, since our perception of our own self provides us with our primary means of understanding all other humans.

C.H. Cooley's famous 'looking-glass-self' gives more clarity into the awareness of self and others. Cooley (1902), in his work *Human Nature and the Social Order*, his "looking-glass self" involved three steps: the imagination of our appearance to the other person; the imagination of his judgment of that appearance, and some sort of self-feeling, such as pride or mortification.[39] According to him, "society and individual denote not separable phenomena but different aspects of the same thing, for a separate individual is an abstraction unknown to experience, and so likewise is society when regarded as something apart from individuals."[40]

Cooley's theories were manifested in response to a threefold necessity that had developed within the realm of society. The first of which was the necessity to create an understanding of societal phenomena that highlighted the subjective mental processes of individuals yet realized that these subjective processes were effects and causes of society's processes. The second necessity examined the development of a social dynamic conception that portrayed states of chaos as natural occurrences which could provide opportunities for 'adaptive innovation.' Finally, a need to manifest publics that were capable of exerting some form of 'informed moral control' over current problems and future directions. Thus, for him there is no separate existence for individuals and society or apart from the close-nit relationship with the other. It is very evident from his own words, "just as there is no society or group that is not a collective view of persons, so there is no individual who may not be regarded as a particular view of social groups."[41] He has no separate existence. A person is bound into the whole of which he is a member, and to consider him apart from it is quite as artificial as to consider society apart from individuals.[42] The

38 J. Krishnamurti, *What are You Doing with Your Life: Teen Books on Living*, (Krishnamurti Foundation of America, California, 2001), p. 64.

39 Charles Horton Cooley, *Human Nature and the Social Order*, (Charles Scribner's Sons, New York, 1902), p. 152.

40 Charles Horton Cooley, *On Self and Social Organization*, (University of Chicago Press, Chicago, 1998), p. 132.

41 *Ibid.*, p. 133.

42 *Ibid.*

Looking-glass self is created through the imagination of how one's self might be understood by another individual. Thus, Cooley felt that each individual has to decide the boundaries for our concern for the society. In his word, "we find on the frontier: for plain dealing, love of character and force, kindness, hope, hospitality and courage."[43] So the relationship with the Other or the society is an inseparable conjunct in the life of an individual as well as in the SR/CSR framework of the 21st century.

Similarly, when we have no relationship with the self, with the Other and the world, life become purposeless. The essence of existence as a human being itself not accomplished and life becomes aimless. Hence, we are confronted with the question of 'why does it happen to human beings'? Understanding ourselves probably aids self-acceptance, self-control, and good relationships. But self-understanding comes only from interacting with others; we know ourselves in comparison to others. So, the two — self-awareness and insight into relationships — develop together. Indeed, we have a relationship with ourselves as well as with others. This paradigm calls for responsibility towards oneself, Other and the environment. According to Hans Joans, Our fundamental responsibility is towards that which allowed us to come into being, nature herself, but this responsibility is exercised first of all in our relationships to other human beings.[44] It is said that ants have a 'social stomach,'[45] because all the members of the colony of ants share their nourishment and feed each other if necessary. If human beings forget the element of relationship and their responsibility towards the other, I am sure there are enough reminders in the nature itself.

Life is living together – Living with each other, for each other, and from each other. Because, life is based on life, life lives on life – and above all by one living thing feeding on another living thing.[46] We cannot live as an island and end our life. Instead, living together in cooperation which requires responsibility and empathy.

> A man can live his whole life without struggle or battle or war — but not a minute without cooperation. Without the coordinated cooperation of its cells his body would be a single cancerous tumor. Without the symbiosis with the bacteria of his intestinal flora he would die of starvation.[47]

---

43 Charles Horton Cooley, *Social Organization: A Study of the Larger Mind*, (Transaction Publishers, New Jersey, 1983), p. 355.

44 Hans Jonas, Lawrence Vogel, *Mortality and Morality: A Search for the Good After Auschwitz,* (Northwestern University Press, Illinois, 1996), p. 15.

45 Hans-Peter Dürr, Fritz Albert Popp, Wolfram Schommers, *What Is Life?: Scientific Approaches and Philosophical Positions*, (World Scientific, Singapore, 2002), p. 16.

46 *Ibid.*,18.

47 *Ibid.*,18.

Indeed, these words are the upheaval of responsibility to the Self, Other and Nature.

## 4. Human Being: A Responsible Being

Kant, in his 'moral imperative' assigns being 'responsible' and 'being rational' as qualities of a human being.[48] To live implies, encountering the other and being part of the society. Thus, responsibility is woven into our created-ness and it precedes our subjectivity.[49] Responsibility for the self; responsibility for the Other; responsibility for the environment; responsibility for the society or let us say, in simple words, as social responsibility.

Responsibility can be defined as the desire of the person to respond to the other. It is the ability to respond to self, others, and environment. To be responsible is to be answerable. Now the question is, 'answerable to whom'? Answerable to myself. My ability to be answerable to myself before I answer anyone else in the world.[50] I would even go to the extreme and say that the foundation of SR/CSR is responsibility to the self that I am answerable to myself. Corporate who are not answerable to themselves do not care about the welfare of the society. They are neither answerable to themselves or to the society because they live in the utopian world of cut-throat business and accumulating profits. Nevertheless, it is clear that responsibility lies in the agent who stays with his action, who accepts the consequences in the form of reactions and looks forward in a present deed to the continued interaction.[51]

Responsibility for the other comes from encounter with the other and similarly for the self too. Not rules, regulations or order that directs me to respond to the need of the other, it is the face of the other that demands a response.[52] The face of the other, that element of the other that is the ground of interpersonal contact, indicates an immediacy with the other person that Levinas calls 'proximity'.[53] Proximity is felt as immediate contact. Levinas writes:

> ... the proximity of the Other is not simply close to me in space, or close like a parent, but he approaches me essentially insofar as I feel myself—insofar as I am—responsible for him. It is a structure that in nowise

48 Robert B. Louden, *Kant's Human Being: Essays on His Theory of Human Nature*, (Oxford University Press, Oxford, 2011), p. xxvi.

49 Thorukattil, *Becoming Human*, p. 66.

50 Joji Valli, *Melody of the Heart*, (CreatiVentures, Pune, 2010), p. 146.

51 Helmut Richard Niebuhr, The Responsible Self, (John Knox Press, Westminster, 1999), p. 64.

52 Michael L. Morgan, *Discovering Levinas (Cambridge University Press, Cambridge, 2007)*, p. 85

53 See Andrew Tallon, "Intentionality, Intersubjectivity, and the Between: Buber and Levinas on Affectivity and the Dialogical Principle," Thought 53 (1978): 304.

> resembles the intentional relation which in knowledge attaches us to the object—to no matter what object, be it a human object. Proximity does not revert to this intentionality; in particular it does not revert to the fact that the other is known to me.[54]

Responsibility is an inherent attitude in every human being. When I see the face of the other, I am moved to action as I have the feeling of being answerable to myself. The other's vulnerability originates from our relationship — relationship with self, other and environment. The relationship with other gives me the freedom to make a choice of responsibility.[55] The proximity of the other demands a response. Thus, Levinas claims that proximity is responsibility, or the ability to respond.[56] Though, I agree with Levinas, I would go a step further and say, proximity to myself, makes me more responsible. The more I am related to myself, the more I am connected to myself; my ability to respond, expands to the other. Gabriel Marcel argues that the 'to whom' of responsibility is both to oneself and everyone else.[57]

Responsibility should not be understood in an exclusive manner as if one were responsible only for the other who stands before me but also to every other. Thus, all others come under my responsibility who are near or far away. In other words, universal responsibility calls me away from myself unto the ends of the earth.[58] The challenge of the SR/CSR is the same. It reminds us to be responsible to the self, other and nature. In other words, it initiates us to an ongoing process of self to the universal responsibility.

Responsibility is inherent in every encounter that we have with the other. It is not reciprocal in nature. In view of SR/CSR there is no reciprocal approach as the individuals and corporations undertake the responsibility for maintaining the well-being of the society. They are responsible for others not because of any statutory polices of social structure. It is because their encounter with the 'face' that demands them to be responsible.[59] Thus, taking responsibility for the self and others, makes one a human. In the words of Levinas, the very identity of human starts from responsibility.[60] Hence, for him what makes life

54 Emmanuel Levinas, *Ethics and Infinity: Conversations with Phillipe Nemo,* translated by Richard Cohen (Duquesne University Press, Pittsburgh, 1985), p. 97.

55 Ibid. p. 95.

56 Emmanuel Levinas, *Otherwise than Being or Beyond Essence*, translated by Alphonso Lingis (Martinus Nijhoff Publishers, Boston, 1981), p. 139.

57 Gabriel Marcel, *Homo Viator: Introduction to a Metaphysic of Hope*, trans. E. Craufurd (Harper Torchbooks, New Yourk 1962), p. 21.

58 Rogger Burggraeve, ed. "No One Can Save Oneself without Others," in *The Awakening to the Other: A Provocative Dialogue with Emmanuel Levinas* (Leuven: Peeters, 2008), p. 20.

59 Emmanuel Levinas, *Otherwise than Being or Beyond Essence*, translated by Alphonso Lingis (Kluwer Academic Publisher, Netharlands, 1991), p. 114.

60 Levinas, *Ethics and Infinity*, p. 95.

is nothing but responsibility. Corporate Social Responsibility is the extension of one's life to the society and for the society.

### a. Nature of Responsibility

People want to know who is responsible for certain actions and who is accountable for the consequences of those actions. In other words, to be responsible means to be answerable and to be accountable for ones' actions. Business historian Vincent E. Barry has defined the term responsibility, when used in business affairs, as referring to "a sphere of duty or obligation assigned to a person by the nature of that person's position, function, or work."[61] Responsibility could thus be viewed as a bundle of obligations associated with a job or function. But Levinas argues that man is vested with responsibility even when he does not want to be. It is not man's choice to be responsible; he belongs to responsibility. It is an obligation of the person to respond to the need of the other. It is a responsibility to do something for the other.[62] Human beings' inherent desire to do something for the other or the society is the philosophical foundation on which the concept of SR/CSR has been rooted. So the responsibility to do something for the other is more important than to know him. Responsibility begins as absolute heteronomy. Thus, I am made responsible, I get in touch with other, and a reciprocal relation is established which becomes my responsibility. Be it individual or corporate, the aspect of responsibility does not change as it is inherent in the human nature.

> When I respond to natural events I do so as a social being; on the other hand, when I respond to my companions I do so as one who is in response-relations to nature. I do not exist as responsive self in two separate spheres or in two distinct encounters — with the Thou on the one, with the It on the other; with society on the one hand, with nature on the other. I engage rather in a continuous dialogue in which there are at least these three partners — the self, the social companion, and natural events.[63]

Thus, it is natural phenomenon that the self before nature remains a social self, responding to other selves in all responses to nature.[64]

### b. Responsibility for the Other — Sprouting of SR/CSR from the Heart

Responsibility is innate to human being. Responsibility for the other begins as an absolute heteronomy. Here the 'I' cannot be the yardstick of all things,

61 Vincent E. Barry, *Moral Issues in Business* (Wadsworth, Belmont, CA, 1979), p. 27.

62 Arokiam Stalin Dhanaraj, Levinas on the Vulnerability of Face." *Journal of Philosophy and Education*, Vol. 16/1 (2001): p. 68

63 Helmut Richard Niebuhr, *The Responsible Self*, p. 80.

64 *Ibid.*, p. 81.

but 'I' is there as a responsible person. Responsibility is not initiative of 'I'; rather, it conditions the structure of the subject itself. Responsibility conditions the structure of my being. The face inspires the 'I' to responsibility. 'I' comes in touch with the other and the other becomes the center of my spirituality. So I realize my responsibility through the other.[65] Hence, it is not the legal responsibility, rather the responsibility by and for the other should be understood in a wider perspective, especially when many corporations are working in transnational or multi-national scenarios. Thus, I, as a human being cannot eliminate anyone from my responsibility because the responsibility should not be limited to nation, culture, religion etc… The whole humanity is in need of my service. Universal responsibility calls me away from my selfishness and leads me to the freedom of worldwide responsibility.[66] Nothing evades my responsibility because as Indian philosophy very well put it, *aham brahmashmi* — I am Brahman. When this seed of responsibility sprouts in my heart, I become responsible to everything around entrusting me with universal responsibility for the well-being and welfare of the society or world. It also asserts the view of *tattvamasi* (That you are!) from the deep rootedness of perceiving everything around as the 'That,' in terms of a deeply rooted spiritual invitation to partake in the universal responsibility that we are endowed with as human beings and spiritual being in the phenomenon called *living*.

## 5. Responsibility becomes Accountability to Self

Responsibility becomes the expression of the self. "My responsibility is untransferable, no one can replace me."[67] This is the accountability I have towards myself. It cannot be transferred to anyone else. I am answerable to none but myself. I express myself before the other in terms of responsibility for which I am accountable to myself. Responsibility for the other is rooted in our subjective constitution.[68] This accountability is what Gita talks about as *nishkama karma*; Bible speaks about "love your neighbor as yourself;" Tilak speaks about *lokasangraha*; Buddha talks about *damma*.

> Accountability applies only to individuals, and is both a personal promise and obligation, to yourself and to others, to deliver specific, defined results. Being accountable within an organization means you agree to be operationally defined as the sole agent for an outcome, regardless of the

65 Arokiam Stalin Dhanaraj, Levinas on the Vulnerability of Face." *Journal of Philosophy and Education*, p. 71.

66 Burggraeve, *The Awakening to the Other*, p. 20.

67 Levinas, *Ethics and Infinity,* p. 100.

68 Roger Burggraeve, Proximity with the Other (Bangalore, Dharmaram Publications, 2009), p. 11

often-inadequate level of authority or control that you have been formally assigned by the organization.[69]

Corporations and individuals must transcend beyond the 'I' concept by understanding it dynamically as the responsibility. This 'responsibility to others' and the 'holding others responsible' is grounded on a radical and universal 'self-responsibility.' On the ground of self-responsibility, a communicative ethics flourishes. It absorbs every form of being responsible to others and for others.[70] This understanding will make us realize that there is a purpose for our life here on earth. It is not just living but that very understanding will make us to live that purpose responsibly. Thus, SR/CSR becomes the responsibility of every human being because I am accountable to myself and it is my responsibility to be responsible for the other. So development of the society becomes my priority irrespective of whether I am individual or corporate. When each human being takes responsibility for the self and for the other, earth becomes the happiest place to live. Thereby, each of us fulfills the very purpose of life as living in this paradise called earth. "*Lokaa samasta subkhino bhavantu*," let the entire world be happy.[71]

## Conclusion

The purpose of human life is nothing but *living*. It is not simply living but *living responsibly* as each of us is responsible for the self, other and nature. The responsibility inherent in me, calls for a personal accountability to myself. Thus responsible living becomes the nature of human life. It opens up a new paradigm for altruism where one helps another person for no reward, which Indian sages in their great wisdom called as *nishkamakarma*. This calls for the dawn of a new era which already Karl Marx had foreseen. Living a life as per the law of nature, reminds us to be responsible to Self and to the Other. SR/ CSR is an invitation to encounter the face of the other in responsibility for both as individuals and corporate. Thus, maintaining the equilibrium of nature, abiding the laws of nature as unwritten laws that help to sustain progress and well-being of all. In the words of Cyril Desbruslais, it is the "*be-attitude* to become more fully human and more fully alive."

69 Bruce Klatt and Shaun Murphy, Accountability. Getting a Grip on Results, Retrived on 25-07-2012 http://www.refresher.com/!accountabilitykb.html.

70 Bernhard Walden Fels, "Response and Responsibility in Levinas," *Rutledge Encyclopedia,* Vol.8, p. 39.

71 Quoted in R. S. Nathan, *Hinduism That Is Sanatana Dharma,* p. 23

# 15

# Physically Challenged: Coping with Life Effectively

**VM Jose SJ**
*Moral and Pastoral Theolgoy, Jnana-Deepa Vidyapeeth, Pune*

**Abstract:** The Preamble to the Convention on the Rights of Persons with Disabilities states that "Disability results from the interaction between persons with impairments and attitudinal and environmental barriers that hinder their full and effective participation in society on an equal basis with others." Again it emphasizes that "Persons with disabilities include those who have long term physical, mental, intellectual or sensory impairments which in interaction with various barriers may hinder their full and effective participation in society on an equal basis with others. Disability should be considered as an important issue by the Government so that this essential public health problem can be tackled in the community. The services should cover all types of disabled who need rehabilitation services and it should be part of mainstream development in the community. One of the biggest challenges is providing rehabilitation services to the unreached persons with disabilities living in rural areas and small towns. Efforts have to remain focussed on the prevention of disability and rehabilitation in our country; and, particularly in lower income countries, disabled people have to rely largely on informal systems for support. Disability should not be an obstacle to success.

**Keywords**: Sudha Chandran, Impairments, Rehabilitation, Malnutrition, Nuclear disasters, Psychological trauma, Bibliotherapy

*"The only thing worse than being blind is having sight but no vision."*
*–Helen Keller*

Miss Sudha Chandran was born in Kannur, Kerala to a Tamil family. She began learning classical dance at the age of 3 and by the time she was 15 she had already performed several major events. Then suddenly life took a different turn. She narrates, "I was travelling from Trichy by bus, when we met with a major accident that left me with a fracture and some cuts – I was probably the least injured there. However, because of the heavy influx of patients, I was attended to by a couple of interns who forgot to attend to the cut on my right ankle and went ahead to wrap it up. This resulted in my foot getting gangrene and because of the fear of it spreading throughout my body, my parents had to take the difficult decision of amputating my right foot. I was shattered because it was only then that I realized just how passionate I felt about dancing. I began to learn how to walk again and it took me 4 months to even walk straight. Once I got the Jaipur leg, it took me three years of physiotherapy to recover and feel normal again. I remember people would come home and say things like, 'it's so sad your dreams can't come true' or 'we wish you could dance' when I decided to re-learn what I had known my entire life – to dance."[1]

After a slow and painful process she learnt that her life was being fulfilled. She realized that she was ready for the performance. Her first performance after her accident was a grant success and the show was completely sold out. She danced with ease and received a standing ovation. It was after that show, that she received so much respect from the media, got an offer to act in a film based on her life, *Mayuri,* and received all of the opportunities that she has today. She understood that what her grandmother said was true: God was with her. Though she didn't see it then, he was with her all along and that's the irony of life that an accident so fatal, can still be a blessing in disguise.[2]

---

1 Sudha Chandran's story about her accident will leave you inspired, http://blogs.timesofindia.indiatimes.com/everything-social/sudha-chandrans-story-about-her-accident-will-leave-you-inspired/ accessed on 26.03.2016.

Cyril Desbruslai: My acquaintance with Cyril goes back to 1984, when I was doing my philosophy in JDV and residing at DNC. I had the opportunity to be in the same community for two years. We related closely to each other, as he was friendly with students and youth. His involvement in the social ministry regularly was something that inspired most of us. Moreover, he motivated the youth to be committed to the poor and marginalized of society. Every year he used to conduct a good theme based play and raise fund for a social cause. I feel very sad to know that he had a stroke and then he could not become as energetic as he used to be earlier. May God bless him to regain his full energy and health.

2 *Ibid.*

## 1. What is Disability or Physical Challenge?

As defined by the World Health Organization Disability "is an umbrella term, covering impairments, activity limitations, and participation restrictions. Impairment is a problem in body function or structure; an activity limitation is a difficulty encountered by an individual in executing a task or action; while a participation restriction is a problem experienced by an individual in involvement in life situations. Thus disability is a complex phenomenon, reflecting an interaction between features of a person's body and features of the society in which he or she lives."[3]

The Convention on the Rights of Persons with Disabilities (2006), the first legally binding disability specific human rights convention, adopted by the United Nations gives two descriptions of disability. The Preamble to the Convention states that "Disability results from the interaction between persons with impairments and attitudinal and environmental barriers that hinder their full and effective participation in society on an equal basis with others." Again it emphasizes that "Persons with disabilities include those who have long term physical, mental, intellectual or sensory impairments which in interaction with various barriers may hinder their full and effective participation in society on an equal basis with others." Both the expressions reflect a shift from a medical model to social model of disability.[4]

## 2. Disability: Census

The WHO estimated that more than six hundred million people across the globe live with disabilities of various types due to chronic diseases, injuries, violence, infectious diseases, malnutrition, and other causes related to poverty. People with disabilities are subject to multiple deprivations with limited access to basic services, including education, employment, rehabilitation facilities etc. Widespread social stigma plays a major role in hindering their normal social and economic life. To work towards an inclusive, barrier free society through raising awareness and policy actions, there is a need to have comprehensive reliable statistics on people with disability and their socio-economic conditions. According to CRIN (Child Rights International Network) over 150 million children worldwide have a disability. 50% of these children with a hearing impairment and 60% of those with an intellectual impairment are sexually abused. There are many medical professionals who kill children with disabilities and justify them as mercy killings. 90% of the children with disabilities will not even survive beyond the age of twenty. Children with disabilities face discrimination not only in services but also in the justice

---

3 Disability in India – A Statistical Profile, available from http://mospi.nic.in/Mospi_New/upload/disablity_india_statistical_profile_17mar11.htm, accessed on 08.05.2016.

4 *Ibid.*

system as they are often not considered credible witnesses.[5] This is the general scenario we find in the world today.

## 3. Disability in India

While estimates vary, at the turn of the new millennium about 21 million people in India were found to have disability as per the official statistics. These included persons with visual, hearing, speech and mental disabilities, who constituted about 2 percent of the population. However, some sources claim that the magnitude in actuality is more with at least 5 per cent of population suffering from one disability or other and the official statistics accounting for only the most severe ones. By and large, people with disability are further disabled through unequal treatment and denial of basic rights by the broader society. The voiceless disabled people are inseparable part of India's growing population of marginal, weaker and vulnerable sections of society. The roles and responsibilities of the Government of India are clearly identified in laws but there is a need to study the gap between the law and the practice.[6]

Children with disabilities in India mainly come under the purview of the Ministry of Social Justice and Empowerment. Some of the issues are dealt with by the health ministry. As no single ministry has been assigned the protection of these children there are varying data about occurrence of disability amongst children. In India 1.67% of the 0 – 19 age group of the population has a disability. 35.29% of all people living with disabilities are children. Other estimates say that India has 12 million children living with disabilities. Only 1% of children with disabilities have access to school and one third of these disabilities are preventable. Under-nutrition is a severe problem with children who suffer from cerebral palsy. In India 80% of children with disabilities will not survive past age forty. What we do not realize is that many of these disabilities in children are preventable if the mothers are looked after well before giving birth and after giving birth.

## 4. Causes of Disability in India

Some of the main causes of disability in children are: there are some women who have been disabled since birth. Some women become disabled suddenly, because of various reasons, including giving birth. In fact some babies form differently inside the womb and this can lead to disability both in the mother and the child. What is to be understood is that many disabilities in babies are caused by harmful conditions of the mothers' situations. If these women are given enough nutritious food and can get good health care, particularly during

---

5 Disability, available from http://crinarchive.org/themes/ViewTheme.asp?id=5, accessed on 03.04.2016.

6 Disability in India – A Statistical Profile.

the time of childbirth, then many disabilities may be prevented. One major factor we cannot forget is that disabled people have convincingly argued that disability is itself a social, not a natural category.[7]

## a. Poverty and Malnutrition

In the Third-World countries poverty is one of the biggest causes of disability. Poor people are exposed to very vulnerable situations and they are forced to live and work in unsafe environments with poor sanitation and crowded living conditions. Moreover they have little access to education, clean water, or enough good food. Such difficult situations can lead to diseases such as tuberculosis and polio that can cause severe disabilities and such diseases are transmitted from one person to another easily. Many babies in India die in their infancy or may be born with disabilities because of poverty. The reason for such deaths or disability may be because the mother did not get enough food to eat when she was pregnant. It is also possible she did not get enough food to eat when she was a girl. This grim reality of India is known all over the world; often girl children are less cared for in their childhood. As a result, she remains weak all her life and can later cause difficulty during childbirth, especially if she does not receive good health care. If a baby does not get enough good food to eat, there are possibilities that she or he may become blind or have trouble learning or understanding.[8]

## b. War and Nuclear Problems

In many parts of the world there are wars, conflicts and rivalry which cause disabilities like deafness, blindness and losing their limbs, as well as death. Many of these victims are women and children. No doubt in saying that their mental health is also badly affected by the violence. War also destroys homes, schools, health centres, and means of livelihood and the tragic effect of this is increased disability, poverty, and disease. Nuclear disasters (radiation) have also resulted in many forms of disability. Though many precautions are taken dangers are very serious. Such incidents cause widespread destruction and death from exposure to radiation. The people who survived nuclear tragedies and bombing attacks have suffered mainly from cancers, either tumours in various parts of the body, especially in the thyroid gland or leukaemia (cancer of the blood), all of which bring early death. Wherever the nuclear incidents

---

7 Eva Kitty, Disability, Equality Dignity and Care, in *Concilium*, (London: SCM Press, 2003), 2, 105.

8 Cf. Nilika Mehrotra, Disability, Gender & State Policy: Exploring Margins, (Jaipur: Rawat Publications, 2013), 187-90.

happened, there has also been an increase in the number of children born with learning difficulties, such as Down syndrome.[9]

### c. Poor Health Care and Illness

Many disabilities can be prevented if good health care is provided. Difficult labour and birth can cause a baby to be born with a disability such as cerebral palsy. When there are no trained people to take care of pregnant women there can be risks of such disabilities. Some medicines and drugs taken during pregnancy can cause disability in the baby. Some other difficulties in the villages are, vaccines are not available, or people who are poor or live far from cities cannot afford them, or there is not enough medicine for everyone. For example if a woman gets German measles (rubella) during the first 3 months of pregnancy, it is possible that her child may be born deaf. Sometimes even medicines and injections cause diseases instead of healing. It is known all over the world that here is a worldwide epidemic of unnecessary injections and each year these unnecessary injections sicken, kill, or disable millions of persons, especially children. Unclean needles or syringes also can cause infection and can pass the germs that cause serious diseases such as HIV/AIDS or hepatitis. Unclean injections are also a common cause of infection that can lead to paralysis or spinal cord injury or death.[10]

### d. Other Causes of Disability

There are many other reasons for disabilities, especially mental disabilities. In India, there are many children who are trafficked, abused and sexually exploited and they are at risk for psychological effects as well as physical retardation. Other forms of violence against children can also lead to disabilities, such as corporal punishment in schools, children living on the streets, and purposefully created disabilities for begging. Almost all these children come from poor families.

Disability in India is not properly dealt with as a serious issue of a rights perspective. Teachers are not trained and schools do not have the infrastructure to deal with children with disabilities. There are not enough well equipped hospitals to take care of such cases. There is not enough data on the number of children living with disabilities to allow the government to provide the necessary services. Naturally it becomes a problem to deal with disability.

## 5. Some Authors on Disability

In India a lot of literature has pointed to the importance of the concept of karma in attitudes to disability, with disability perceived either as punishment for

9 Causes of disability, available from http://en.hesperian.org/hhg/A_Health_Handbook_for_Women_with_Disabilities:Causes_of_disability, accessed on 25.05.2016.

10 Cf. Nilika Mehrotra, Disability, Gender & State Policy: Exploring Margins.

misdeeds in the past lives or the wrongdoings of their parents. Many authors have related this to divine justice. In our day to day life people with disabilities are perceived as somehow inauspicious. This has led to considerable social marginalization of people with disabilities in India. Literature plays a powerful role in society purporting truths and values, reflective of the time in which it was created. Literature is particularly important and influential as a cultural force because of its commonplace presentation. Lacking the sensationalism of other media formats this type of text provides more fully developed and readily accepted versions of reality. It is known that fiction plays an important place in the communication of values and ideas and in the sharing of common culture and unspoken tradition. Some authors say that stories, lore, myths, legends, jokes, and proverbs act as cultural authorities passing on moral lessons, values, and understanding of right and wrong, and good and bad in a less filtered manner than provided by other historical mediums. With this ability to influence, literature becomes a powerful force.

Literary study of disabilities has relevance in our society as it can help physically or mentally impaired people to come into the mainstream society and at least partially establish their equality and enhance their self-esteem. It is worth pursuing for further research to have a better understanding of the lives of people with disability and generating not sympathy but empathy for the people with disability.

## a. Anita Desai (born 1937)

One of the famous Indian novelists, Anita Desai, addresses female psychological trauma at the sites of colonial and postcolonial clashes. Her preoccupation is with the modern Indian woman's psyche, and the isolation of the physically ill and the psychiatrically othered. It is depicted in some of her novels such as, *Voices in the City* (1965), *Clear Light of Day* (1980) and *Fire on the Mountain* (1977). There are endless conflations of psychiatric disabilities as symbolic of national fissures, cultural crises, states of corruption, internal strife, and ethnic violence. The social framing and ideological work of disabled characters in *Clear Light of Day* and inclusion of a disability perspective in post-colonial and feminist critiques can enrich our understanding of the dialectic between colonizers and colonized and refigure our consideration of hybridity.[11]

In her novel *Clear Light of Day*, Anita Desai portrays Indian women as marginalized characters facing challenges and burdens imposed by a patriarchal society. They resemble colonial subjects whose lives are fractured. Among the female characters Bim, Tara, their mother and Aunt Mira are subordinated by a male-dominant culture which underestimates female subjectivity. It is

11 Glimpses of Disability in the Literature and Cultures of East Asia, South Asia, the Middle East & Africa, available from, http://www.independentliving.org/docs7/miles200807.html#south_asia, accessed on 23.05.2016.

important to note how these women manage their precarious situation and stand up to a society controlled by men. They really have to struggle in different ways to assert their existence. As these women are unable to improve their circumstances, their attempts to be active members in society force them to hybridize their identity. Accordingly, they employ the oppressors' language and culture in order merely to cope with and to adjust themselves for survival.

### b. Rohinton Mistry (born 1952)

In his award-winning novel, *Family Matters* (2002), Nariman Vakreel, an aging professor living in Bombay, becomes the object of both pity and derision by his family when he becomes bedridden following a fall. His recovery time was significantly prolonged because of Parkinson's and osteoporosis. Thus Nariman becomes a source of contention to his children who argue intensely over who should assume care giving responsibilities. It is interesting to note that he sympathizes with their reluctance to take care of him and asks 'can caring and concern be made compulsory?' At the same time, when Nariman temporarily moves in with his daughter and her family, he contributes to the well-being of his grandchildren by providing them with love and support when their parents quarrel, teaching them about their Parsi heritage, and encouraging family harmony in general. Mistry aptly puts the frustration of such people: Like trapped animals struggling to break free. What a curse was damned Parkinson's disease, as cruel as torture.[12]

### c. Chellappa & Pitchamurthi

Chelleppa's *The Lame Child* and Pitchamurthi's *The Blind Girl* are rather typical of the disabled short story genre. Chellappa illustrates the desperate efforts of lame six-year-old Gnanam to discover some way to be included in the neighbourhood children's hide-and-seek games, against their fear of his 'ugly' and 'dangerous' feet. One girl briefly risks some involvement. Others follow, with continuing doubts. Gnanam rejoices to find a 'stationary' role that he can play, and which the others are happy for him to take; but disaster soon follows. Pitchamurthi has a more subtle, negotiatory play between a house owner, a tenant, and a disabled child. The house owner wishes to relieve himself of the care of the twelve-year-old orphan blind girl (whom he had inadvertently acquired through the death of a former tenant), by sending her to an orphanage; or if that failed, to a Christian missionary, though the latter idea was unpalatable. The tenant is trying to give notice of quitting his room. Neither listens to what the other is saying. The blind girl approaches unnoticed, and apologises for being a nuisance and burden. Two men connected with the orphanage turn up, and written notes are exchanged, signed and witnessed, for

---

12 *Ibid.*

handover of the girl. She hears her fate being sealed, learns that her two skirts and one torn blouse have been packed, and that she must leave immediately with a stranger from North India. Does he speak Tamil? At last, she bends to pick up her little bundle, and two tears are seen hitting the floor. A moment of illumination. The men unexpectedly discover that they have hearts.[13]

## 6. Remedies: Bibliotherapy for Disabilities

If teachers are to effectively use children's literature on disabilities to teach empathy, acceptance, and understanding of diversity, then it stands to reason that there should be instructional activities that are part of their professional teacher preparation program that provide insights into the effectiveness of the literature and the use of bibliotherapy (an expressive therapy that involves the reading of specific texts with the purpose of healing. It uses an individual's relationship to the content of books and poetry and other written words as therapy[14]) in their classrooms. One such activity is a review of children's and young adult literature that addresses issues associated with disabilities. Teacher candidates in this course are at the beginning of their professional programme and as such may have had limited experiences with disabilities. They have to gradually learn the art of dealing with the situation properly.

We need to consider some of the following criteria when reviewing books on disability: Promotes empathy not pity; Depicts acceptance not ridicule; Emphasizes success rather than, or in addition, to failure; Promotes positive images of persons with disabilities or illness; Assists children in gaining accurate understanding of the disability or illness; Demonstrates respect for persons with disabilities or illness, Promotes attitude of "one of us" not "one of them"; Uses language which stresses person first, disability second philosophy; Describes the disability or person with disabilities or illness as realistic (i.e., not subhuman or superhuman.); Illustrates characters in a realistic manner.[15]

## 7. Constitutional Rights of the Disabled

When we deal with the topic of disability, we should be also aware of the constitutional provisions that are available in a country. The Preamble of the Charter of the United Nations affirms the dignity and worth of every human being and gives primary importance to the promotion of social justice. Persons with disabilities are, de-facto, entitled to all the fundamental rights upheld by the Charter. Article 25 of the Universal Declaration states that each person

13 Bisgaard, Daniel J., Social Conscience in Sanskrit Literature, available from, http://ijellh.com/representation-disabilities-indian-english-fiction-viewpoint/, accessed on 09.05.2016.

14 Bibliotherapy, available from https://en.wikipedia.org/wiki/Bibliotherapy, accessed on 10.05.2016.

15 Joan K. Blaska, Ph.D., Children's Literature That Includes Characters With Disabilities or Illnesses, in *Disability Studies Quarterly,* (Winter 2004), Volume 24, No. 1.

has, the right to security in the event of unemployment, sickness, disability, widowhood, old age or other lack of livelihood in the circumstances beyond his control. The United Nations declared, 1981 the International Year of Disabled Persons, and adopted the World Programme of Action concerning Disabled Persons (1982). The UN also declared the decade (1983-1992) as a decade of Disabled Persons. Since then, the attention towards the disabled people and the need to promote their welfare came into the forefront. The Asia Pacific Region was the first to follow up with a regional Decade of Disabled Persons in 1993 since approximately 400 million of the world's 600 million disabled people live in the region.[16]

The Right to Education Act (amendment ) Bill passed in the Rajya Sabha to widen the beneficiary net for children with disabilities is a retrogressive step since it defeats the very purpose of the Act, which is to promote social inclusion in elementary schools. The amendment is in contradiction of the United Nations Convention on the Rights of Persons with Disabilities and the recent Supreme Court judgment (April 2012) on RTE, since it seems to suggest that home-based education may be the best option for children with 'severe disability.'[17]

The very notion of what constitutes 'severe disability' is a contested term and the assumption that 'certain children' may be best educated at home rather than schools, defeats the very premise of inclusive education that espouses the belief that every child, including those with differing abilities have an entitlement to study with their peers and not be excluded from mainstream education. Even if we were to presume that certain parents 'choose' home-based education for say their child who has severe medical complications with impairment, how would the state governments find the human resources to make home-based education a reality? Currently, there are 415 institutions, which are recognised by Rehabilitation Council of India (RCI) to run rehabilitation councils, and the total number of registered rehabilitation professionals in the country are approximately 35,000, with special educators included in this figure.[18]

## 8. Challenges and Opportunities

The major challenge includes understanding the concept of disability and acceptance of CBR (Community Based Rehabilitation) as a valid intervention. Hospital-based rehabilitation services will lead to mystification of knowledge with social isolation and low efficiency of services which will benefit fewer disabled. Prioritization of resources like finance, human power, and materials

16 Cf. Nilika Mehrotra, Disability, Gender & State Policy: Exploring Margins.

17 Renu Singh, Rights of children with disabilities, in *The Times of India, 30.04:2012.*

18 *Ibid.*

will be another important issue to be considered. Poor planning and management of CBR with lack of inter-sectoral coordination lead to poor functioning of the services to disabled. Non-availability of evidence-based facts, lack of co-ordination between the Government and NGOs, the absence of a coherent community level strategy, limited competence and capacity of decentralizing services, limited models of good practices are the other lacunas in the system. Disability should be considered as an important issue by the Government so that this important public health problem can be tackled in the community. The services should cover all types of disabled who need rehabilitation services and it should be part of mainstream development in the community.[19]

A multi-sectoral approach including social integration interventions, health, education, and vocational programmes are important issues related to rehabilitation services. Primary health care system must play a major role both as a provider and supporter, and should engage with initiatives such as early identification of impairments and providing basic interventions, referrals to specialized services such as physical, occupational, and speech therapies, prosthetics and orthotics, and corrective surgeries. The educational sector should be more inclusive by adopting newer techniques with respect to content of the curriculum, methods of teaching and ensuring that classrooms, facilities, and educational materials more accessible. Children with multiple or severe disabilities who might require extensive additional support may access education through the use of innovative methods best suited to their context. Collaboration with the employment and labour sectors is essential to ensure that both youth and adults with disabilities have access to training and work opportunities at the community level. Productive and decent work in a conducive environment is essential for the social and economic integration of individual persons with disability (PWDs).[20]

Monitoring and Evaluation in the service delivery should be strengthened with information dissemination related to impact on disabled, community mobilization, an opportunity for education, an opportunity for work, transfer skills to the community level, program activities, and involvement of disabled people. Research with respect to services, fund allocation, cost-effectiveness, human power, training, and technical aid of disabled people should be strengthened. One of the biggest challenges is providing rehabilitation services to the unreached persons with disabilities living in rural areas and small towns.

**Happy in Life**: There are examples of several disabled people who have succeeded in life because they have tried to learn as much as possible about their disability. While obsessing over negative medical information is

19 Cf. Dr. P. Prayer Elmo Raj, Disability, Theology and Mission, in *CSI Life*, Vol XIII/Issue 8, Augsut 2015, 10-12.

20 Cf. Nilika Mehrotra, Disability, Gender & State Policy: Exploring Margins.

counterproductive, it is important to understand what they are facing. There is no use comparing oneself to others (or to the past self). They do not discourage themselves by comparing where they are today to where they were pre-disability. The healthy way to judge the progress is by comparing where they are today to where they were yesterday. Stress is hard on the body and can make many symptoms worse, so it is important to find ways to manage the stress, such as practicing relaxation techniques, carving out a healthy work-life balance, and learning healthier coping strategies. By the personal effort, organization of self and exercise these people have succeeded in coping with their disability courageously. They are polite and stay calm particularly with strangers. They do not complain if others do not notice them and show much concern for them. They have managed to establish wider and stronger social network and friends. Many of these people have realized that they could be happy even in a "broken body". Though some of them could not walk, hear or see as others do, they could find their life happy and meaningful for them. The real life stories of many people who lived before them inspire them because they have set good and motivating examples for others. It does not mean that they have not mourned the losses, but they have moved on in life bravely. They focussed on what you could do and what they could hope to do in the future. This attitude of looking hopefully to the future is a motivating factor. There is no use dwelling on what they can no longer do.

## Conclusion

Efforts have to remain focussed on prevention of disability and rehabilitation in our country; and, particularly in lower income countries, disabled people have to rely largely on informal systems for support. The detrimental effects of broadly applied institutionalization policies are recognized, and there is an emphasis on integrating the disabled into existing programs, appropriate technology, self-reliant schemes, and participatory approaches, including community based rehabilitation (CBR). Increased public effort is needed, particularly in strengthening prevention measures, i.e., promoting maternal and child health care, and primary health care, including immunization programs, but also in making information on prevention, treatment, and rehabilitation more widely available.[21]

"Disability need not be an obstacle to success," Stephen Hawking wrote in the first ever world disability report back in 2011. As one of the most influential scientists of modern times, the wheelchair-bound physicist is certainly proof of that. Mexico's most famous artist was born with *spina bifida*, a condition that can cause defects in the spinal cord. At six, she contracted polio, which left one leg much thinner than the other. In spite of these challenges, she was

21 Cf. Eva Kitty, Disability, Equality Dignity and Care, 105-115.

an active child, but at 18, a bus accident left her with serious injuries. It was while recovering from the accident that Frida discovered her love of painting. She would go on to be one of the most famous Surrealists in the world. All that has to be done is, being out there to strive to succeed in order to live life the way you want to and never let anyone tell you that you cannot do something because of your disability.

So Helen Keller is right in saying: "Science may have found a cure for most evils; but it has found no remedy for the apathy of human beings!"

# 16

# Lord Ayyappa and the Feared Feminine: A Socio-Psychoanalytical Explication of the Sabarimala Temple Controversy

**Sacaria Joseph**
*St. Xavier's College, Kolkata*

**Anuradha Mazumder**
*Prafulla Chandra College, Kolkata*

**Abstract:** This article attempts to explicate one of the most scintillating religious controversies in contemporary India – the Sabarimala Temple controversy in 'God's own country,' Kerala, the south-western coastal state of India, from a socio-psychoanalytical perspective. The issue grabbed national as well as international attention as the contentious question of the entry of women of menstruating age into the Sabarimala temple, a supposedly religious issue, not only became a legal, political, gender and justice issue, but also an agenda for campaign in the parliamentary election of 2019 in India.

The article stitches together the various legends surrounding Ayyappa, the Hindu deity enshrined at the temple; elucidates the narratives regarding his 'naishtika brahmacharya' (eternal celibacy), the controversial religious as well as traditional foundation for prohibiting women of menstruating age from entering the temple; examines the narrative of the supposed sacrilege caused by the entry of these women into the temple from a socio-psychoanalytical perspective in terms of the deep-seated male fear of the feminine and 'womb envy' prevailing in our patriarchal society.

The article expounds why and how the 'fear of the feminine' and 'womb envy' lead society to interpret the fecund feminine as polluting, desecrating, annihilating and emasculating the masculine. In its concluding arguments it explains how the adverse patriarchal narrative on the feminine internalised both by the male and female members of society snowballs into a polygonal controversy and, unfortunately, becomes a powerful tool in the hands of people keen on dividing a religiously sensitive nation along the lines of religion and gender for their own vested interests.

**Keywords:** Ayyappa, Sabarimala, Menstruation, 'Naishtika brahmacharya,' Fear of the feminine, 'Womb envy,' Gender politics.

## Introduction: The Sabarimala Temple Controversy

It is rather difficult to ascertain exactly when the prohibition of the entry of the women of menstruating age (aged between ten and fifty) came into effect at the Sabarimala temple in 'God's own country,' Kerala, the south-western coastal state of India. Even though those who support the prohibition argue that it has existed since time immemorial, the actual practice of restricting the entry of women into the temple had been rather lenient till 1991, and except on the festival days of 'Mandalam,' 'Maharavilakku' and 'Vishu,' women of all ages were permitted to enter the temple. Therefore, customarily, on the days of monthly pooja (worship), women of all age groups visited the temple, especially to participate in the first rice-feeding ceremony of their children. The receipts that used to be issued to women by the Travancore Devaswom Board that manages the temple against the payment of fees for conducting the ceremony are proof of that practice. (S. Mahendran v/s Secretary, Travancore Devaswom Board, Thiruvananthapuram)

The scenario changed with the filing of a Public Interest Litigation in the Kerala High Court in 1990 by the then twenty-year old S. Mahendran, seeking a ban on women of menstruating age entering the temple. Mahendran was inspired to file the litigation after he saw in a local newspaper the photograph of the first rice-feeding ceremony of the grand-daughter of S. Chandrika, a former Devaswom Board commissioner, being conducted at the Sabarimala temple in the presence of the girl's mother. Based on rule 3(b) of the '*Kerala Places of Public Worship (Authorization of Entry) Rules, 1965,*' the court upheld the prohibition. The rule states that "Women at such time during which they are not by custom and usage allowed to enter a place of public worship" will be barred from entering the holy shrine of Ayyappa (Indian Young Lawyers' Association & Ors. vs The State of Kerala & Ors.). While upholding the prohibition, the court stated the following:

(1) The restriction imposed on women aged above 10 and below 50 from trekking the holy hills of Sabarimala and offering

worship at Sabarimala Shrine is in accordance with the usage prevalent from time immemorial.

(2) Such restriction imposed by the Devaswom Board is not violative of Articles 15, 25 and 26 of the Constitution of India.

(3) Such restriction is also not violative of the provisions of Hindu Place of Public Worship (Authorisation of Entry) Act, 1965 since there is no restriction between one section and another section or between one class and another class among the Hindus in the matter of entry to a temple whereas the prohibition is only in respect of women of a particular age group and not women as a class.(S. Mahendran v/s Secretary, Travancore Devaswom Board, Thiruvananthapuram).

The court maintained that if a custom does not permit women to enter certain religious places, such a custom shall be upheld. In its verdict, the Court quoted the testimony of Puthumana Narayanan Namboodiri (the 'Thantri', 'the head priest' of the temple recognised by the Travancore Devaswom Board) who argued, "Since the deity is in the form of a Naisthik Brahmachari, it is therefore believed that young women should not offer worship in the temple so that even the slightest deviation from celibacy and austerity observed by the deity is not caused by the presence of such women" (S. Mahendran v/s Secretary, Travancore Devaswom Board, Thiruvananthapuram). The court verdict resulted in the complete prohibition of women of menstruating age entering the temple. The court directed the Travancore Devaswom Board to implement the verdict.

Fifteen years after this verdict, in 2006, the 'India Young Lawyers Association' filed a Public Interest Litigation in the Supreme Court of India, challenging the 1991 High Court verdict that favoured the prohibition. It argued that Rule 3(b) of the *Kerala Hindu Places of Public Worship (Authorization of Entry) Rules, 1965* violated the right to religious freedom, equality and non-discrimination enshrined in Articles 14, 15 and 25 of the Constitution of India. The petition argued that Rule 3(b) not only violated the Fundamental Rights of citizens, but also went against the *Kerala Hindu Places of Public Worship (Authorisation of Entry) Act, 1965* itself. The further filing of affidavits and counter-affidavits by the successive governments in Kerala, some favouring and some challenging the prohibition, becomes an interesting case study of India's long and dubious tradition of politicising religious issues.

The United Democratic Front (UDF) government filed an affidavit in the Supreme Court of India in the same year, upholding the prohibition of the women of menstruating age entering the temple, quoting the testimony of the 'Thantri' recorded in the 1991 verdict of the Kerala High Court. It further stated that matters of religion such as this is not the prerogative of the court and the government was duty-bound to protect the rights of the devotees to practice their religion and faith. In 2007, when the Left Democratic Front (LDF) government came into power in the state, it filed a counter affidavit in the Supreme Court, stating its stance in favour of allowing all women to enter the temple. In 2016, when the UDF government was re-elected, it withdrew the LDF government's affidavit, stating that "the restriction on women between the age of 10 and 50 has been prevailing in Sabarimala from time immemorial. This is in keeping with the unique 'pratishtasangalp' or idol concept of the temple" (Das and Paul). In its latest judgement on 28 September 2018, however, the Supreme Court of India maintained that women of all ages must be permitted entry into the temple. The judgement stated that the Rule 3(b) of the *Kerala Hindu Places of Public Worship (Authorization of Entry) Rules, 1965* that authorised the prohibition violated the rights of women to practise their faith. (It is, however, significant to note that the only dissenting voice in the five-judge Constitution Bench that gave the judgement was the sole woman judge on the bench, Justice Indu Malhotra). The latest Supreme Court judgement created much debate and a certain degree of social unrest in the country. As one takes a closer look at the passionate argument in support of the continuance of the restriction on the entry of women into the temple, one realises that there is much more to the issue than meets the eye. This apparently religious and spiritual issue seems to have a complex social and psychological underpinning that becomes clearer as one meanders through the hazy legend of Ayyappa, his 'naishtikabrahmacharya,' and the fear and envy of the feminine internalised and manifested by his exclusively male devotees.

## 1. The Ayyappa Legend and its Counter-Narrative

No classical Hindu scripture talks of the Hindu deity, Ayyappa, enshrined at the temple at Sabarimala surrounded by eighteen hills of the Western Ghats falling in Pattanamthitta district of Kerala. The legend of Ayyappa, as we have it now, has evolved over the centuries out of many unrecorded beliefs, traditions, stories and legends centred on the deity. One such legend regarding the birth of Ayyappa relates that when Vishnu took the form of the beautiful enchantress Mohini in order to vanquish the demon, Bhasmasura, Shiva became irresistibly enamoured of her, and out of their union was born Ayyappa from Vishnu's thigh (O'Flaherty, 228). Since "he was not of womb born, Ayyappa is free from the mundane cycle of reincarnation and has magical powers to solve problems beyond human control" (Bardon, 122). Hence, he is one of the most popular deities in South India, especially in Kerala. The legend has it that soon after his birth, Ayyappa's divine parents tied a 'mani' (a bell) around his 'kandam' (neck); hence, he is called Manikandan (the bell-throated). Ashamed of the event of their same-sex union, both Shiva and Vishu discarded the baby on the bank of the river Pampa. The baby was discovered by the twelfth century king

Rajashekhara of the Pandya Dynasty (who ruled the kingdom of Panthalam situated once in the present-day Patthanamthitta district in Kerala) and was adopted as his son. Therefore, Ayyappa grew up as the prince of Panthalam.

As he came of age, Ayyappa left his home and reached Sabarimala, where he achieved his divine form of 'Dharma Sastha' (meaning, 'teacher and enforcer of righteousness'). In fact, Ayyappa is believed to be the human incarnation of the deity, Dharma Sastha (often referred to simply as 'Sastha'), one among the eight Sasthas. 'Sastha' is a generic term for 'teacher' and several deities in the southern part of India are associated with Sastha. Since Dharma Sastha is often referred to as Sastha, the mention of Sastha as Hariharaputra in *Brahmanda Purana* holds that he is the son of Vishnu (Hari) and Shiva (Hara). Hence, Ayyappa and Dharma Sastha could be understood as one and the same. Originating from two Tamil words, 'ayya' (revered) and 'Appa' (father), the word 'Ayyappa,' meaning, 'revered father,' is often regarded as an honorific term referring to Dharma Sastha, who is also believed to be "Buddha professing his doctrine" (Sadasivan, 122). That explains why the Sabarimala temple dedicated to Ayyappa had been known as 'Sree Dharma Sastha Temple.'

Parashurama, the sixth avatar of Vishnu and the supposed legendary creator of the state of Kerala, is believed to have founded five temples dedicated to Dharma Shasta in different parts of the state, namely, at Kulathupuzha and Aryankavu in Kollam District, and at Achankoil, Kanthamala and Sabarimala in Pathanamthita District. Owing to the supposed union of Ayyappa with Dharma Shasta, all these five temples honour Ayyappa in different stages of his life. At Kulathupuzha, Ayyappa is honoured as a child, 'Manikantan;' at Aryankavu as a young man seated on an elephant with his lover Prabha; at Achankoil as a family man with his two wives, Poorna and Pushkala; at Kanthamala (where there is only an imaginary and not a real temple) as a yogi; and at Sabarimala as a 'naishtika brahmachari' (eternal celibate).

Legend has it that when Ayyappa was twelve years old, his foster father, King Rajashekhara, wanted to coronate him, instead of the King's biological son, as heir to his throne. At the advice of her evil counsellor, the furious queen feigned an illness, which, according to the councillor, could only be cured if the queen drank leopard's milk brought by Ayyappa from the tigers in the forest. The queen's wicked design in collusion with her counsellor sent Ayyappa on his fatal mission to the jungle in search of leopards. However, as Ayyappa entered the forest, "at Shiva's command, the gods became leopards, and Indra himself a tiger. And Ayyappa rode back to Panthalam on the tiger's back and announced to Rajashekhara that the leopards carried all the milk needed for the queen's cure" (Adluri and Bagchee, 485). Recognising the divine nature of his son, the king is believed to have built a shrine at Sabarimalain in honour of him. The present-day Sabarimala temple, in all probability, was thus built sometime in the twelfth century.

However, there is a counter-narrative to the legend. The members of the Dravidian Mala Araya tribe, who once lived on the eighteen hills surrounding the Sabarimala temple until they were forcefully evicted from there in the early nineteenth century by the Pandalam royal family (to which Ayyappa is believed to have belonged), claim that Ayyappa is not of divine origin. They maintain, instead, that he was the son of Kandan and Karuthamma, a couple belonging to the Mala Araya tribe. He was born in a cave at Ponnambalamedu near the present Sabarimala temple site after his childless parents undertook a forty-one-day fast at the suggestion of a priest. As the son of Kandan, he was called Manikandan. Ayyappa was born at a time when the people of the area were constantly attacked by the Cholas. Ayyappa who is believed to have had his training in martial arts, is said to have united the tribe and fought against the Cholas (Abraham and Bhat).

The two Malayalam words, '*mala*' (hill) and '*arayan*' (king) from which the name, 'Mala Araya' derived, are suggestive of the social status of the tribe in the eighteen hills surrounding Sabarimala. This tribal community of over thirty-thousand members, and spread over the districts of Idukki, Kottayam and Pathanamthitta in Kerala, claims that until they were evicted by the Pandalam royal family from the hills they originally inhabited, they managed the Sabarimala temple along with other temples in the hills and performed the religious rituals. After their eviction, the royal family brought their Brahmin priests belonging to the ThazhamonMadom family to manage the temple and the rituals. With the arrival of the Brahmin priests, the temple went through a process of Brahminisation. One among the many instances of Brahminisation process was the change in the libation ritual. When the Mala Araya tribe managed the temple, they performed the libation of honey on the idol of the deity. However, when the Brahmin priests began to manage the temple, they changed it into a libation of ghee.

Ever since the appointment of a member of the Thazhamon Madom family as the head priest (Tantric) of the temple in 1904, the post of the head priest of the temple has always remained with the family. However, the erstwhile royal family continues to hold the right over the performance of the rituals in the temple. Since 1950 the temple has been managed by the Travancore Devaswom Board. The tribal community that was eventually silenced and eclipsed, built Ayyappa temples wherever they went, and they continue to worship the deity following their Dravidian rites and rituals. The 'Aikya Mala Araya Maha Sabha', the organisation for the welfare of the tribe, insists that the Sabarimala temple should be given back to the tribe which, it claims, was the original manager of the temple. Along with the Sabarimala temple, it asks for three other neighbouring temples, namely Ponnambalamedu, Karimala, and the Nilakkal Mahadeva temples (Abraham and Bhat).

## 2. Ayyappa and His 'Naishtika Brahmacharya'

'Brahmacharya' is the first among the four 'ashramas' (stages) in the life of an ancient Hindu male belonging to any of the twice-born caste groups. 'Brahmacharya' is the student stage. The other three are 'grihastha' (the house holder stage), 'vanaprastha' (the hermit stage) and 'sannyasa' (the wandering ascetic stage). Rather than being a prevailing practice, these four stages are seen as the ideals of life by which one is expected to live.

In Sanskrit, '*Brahma*' refers to the Ultimate Reality or the Ultimate Truth; and 'charya' means 'proceeding,' 'seeking after,' 'going after, 'questing after' and so on. Therefore, 'brahmacharya' means seeking or questing after the Brahman, the Supreme Being. "Brahmacharya properly and fully understood means search after Brahma ... Therefore Brahmacharya signifies control of all the senses at all times and at all places in thought, word and deed" (Gandhi, 53). As the first of the four 'ashramas' in the life of ancient twice-born Hindu males, 'brahmacharya' was a stage of learning, characterised by the search for knowledge and 'Truth,' for about the first twenty-five years of their lives, during which they took refuge in the Brahman without getting distracted by the stimulations of the senses, without succumbing to the cravings of the body and without being caught up in the cares and snares of the material world. During this time, they went to live with their gurus, who taught them the Vedas and imparted all other practical knowledge necessary for their future life. They lived a disciplined and austere life at this stage.

After the 'brahmacharya' stage, one would ordinarily leave his guru, get married and begin one's 'grihastha' stage. However, one may also voluntarily choose to remain a 'brahmachari' for life. Such a person is referred to as a 'naisthika brahmachari' (perpetual student) as opposed to 'upakurvana brahmachari' (preparatory brahmachari) who practices 'brahmacharya' only until he completes his studies. 'Naisthika brahmcharya' qualifies one for 'sanyasa.'

Legend has it that a beautiful woman, an avatar of the goddesses Saraswati, Laxmi and Parvathi combined, had been under a curse to live the life of a buffalo-headed demon, Mahishi, until the curse could be reversed by the vanquishing of the demon. After Ayyappa accomplished this mission of vanquishing the demon in a battle, she emerged out of the body of the demon requesting him to marry her. Ayyappa could not grant her request, on account of the vow of 'naishtika brahmacharya' he had taken. A 'naishtika brahmachari' is expected to live an austere life "'destroying' (finishing) the body and subduing the senses; i.e., taking special care to conquer his senses, that Brahmachari attains the 'region of Brahma' or immortality and is never again born here" (Vidyarnava, 88). Therefore, Ayyappa's 'naishtika brahmacharya' demands that he does not come in contact, not even in visual contact, with women of menstruating age. However, he promised his newfound lover that he would marry her the day his male devotees stop coming to visit him at Sabarimala, the shrine his father had made for him to ensure 'dharmashasan' (righteous rule) in the world. As his eternal lover, the woman is believed to be still waiting for Ayyappa to marry her in a neighbouring temple that king Rajashekhara made for her. She is now worshipped as Malikapurathamma (mother goddess at the tower) at a shrine close to the Sabarimala temple. In order to mark their visit to Ayyappa at Sabarimala, the devotees customarily stick arrows on a peepal tree. At the end of the season of pilgrimage, the statue of Malikapurathamma is taken to the tree in a procession, in order to make her see for herself the evidence of the coming of the devotees to Sabarimala. "Thus, the devotees actively participate in keeping the god free from marriage. Their presence is crucial to enable him to remain unmarried" (Vanita, 97).

It is believed that Ayyappa does not receive women of menstruating age in his temple on account of his 'naishtika brahmacharya,' and also as a mark of respect for Malikapurathamma, his eternal lover. As a mark of devotion to the deity, "Ayyappa's celibacy is imitated by his devotees who take a forty-one-day vow to refrain from sex and other indulgences such as animal food while preparing for and undergoing the pilgrimage. During this period, they live a simple life, sleeping on the floor and trying to be courteous and helpful to everyone" (Vanita, 96).

## 3. Fear and Envy of the Feminine

Deliberating on his theory of sexuality in children, Sigmund Freud hypothesises how male children come to terms with the fact of the absence of penis in their female counterparts. According to him, in the early stages of their life, children of both sexes think that all human beings have penis. By means of their reasoning, eventually, the male children come to associate the absence of penis in their female counterparts with castration — an association that gives rise to their fear of, and aversion to, the feminine:

> little girls too had a penis, but it was cut off and in its place was left a wound. This theoretical advance already makes use of personal experiences of a distressing kind: the boy in the meantime has heard the threat that the organ which is so dear to him will be taken away from him if he shows his interest in it too plainly. Under the influence of this threat of castration he now sees the notion he has gained of the female genitals in a new light; henceforth he will tremble for his masculinity, but at the same time he will despise the unhappy creatures on whom the cruel punishment has, as he supposes, already fallen (Freud, 88-89).

To show 'interest' in the penis plainly and openly is to indulge in the forbidden activity, namely, masturbation, which little boys assume, would result in the punishment of their penis being cut off, leading to their emasculation. Herein lies the assumption that the females have their penis cut off owing to the explicit expression of and indulgence in their sexuality. The collective unconscious of traditional patriarchal society that expects men to be the initiators and performers of the sexual games and women to be the passive participants, cannot but associate the absence of penis in women as punishment for their attempt to reverse the 'assigned' gender roles. The absence of penis in women and the sight of their menstrual blood can reinforce the fear of the possible castration on account of the association of the bleeding vagina with the scary image of the archetypal "vagina as devouring mouth, or vagina dentate, the jaws of the giant cannibalistic mother, a menstruating woman with the penis bitten off, a bleeding trophy" (Brown, 63). This deep-seated fear finds its manifestations in most cultures in varying forms.

> The myth about woman as castrator clearly points to male fears and phantasies about the female genitals as a trap, a black hole which threatens to swallow them up and cut them into pieces. The *vagina dentata* is the mouth of hell — a terrifying symbol of woman as the 'devil's gateway'... The *vagina dentata* also points to the duplicitous nature of woman, who promises paradise in order to ensnare her victims. The notion of the devouring female genitals continues to exist in the modern world; it is apparent in popular derogatory terms for women such as 'man-eater' and 'castrating bitch'" (Creed, 106).

Perhaps it is this fear of the feminine that makes menstruation a taboo and menstrual blood a pollutant in different cultures and societies. Unfortunately, such beliefs are often sanctioned and reinforced by legends and religions. For instance, the *Bhagavata Purana* (one of the sacred literary works of Hinduism) talks of how Indra, the king of the gods, was once angered when he realised that Visvarupa, the Brahmin guru of the gods and goddesses, was secretly helping the demigods against his wish and interest, and became afraid of being defeated by the demigods. In a fit of rage, he killed Visvarupa even though he was aware that 'brahmahatya' (killing a Brahmin) would have serious consequences for him. After the murder, Indra distributed one-third of these consequences to land (which made land to be lacerated by means of digging), one-third to trees (which made trees undergo pruning) and one-third to women (which made them menstruate). The colour of the menstrual blood is the colour of the blood of the Brahmin Indra killed (Smith 218-19). Therefore, "one should not converse with [a woman] with stained garments, nor should one sit with her or eat her food when she has emitted the colour of *brahmahatya*" (Keith, 188).

As per the *The Law of Manu* (the most authoritative text on ancient Hindu laws), a menstruating woman is impure, and she can overcome her impurity only “by bathing after the bleeding has stopped” (Doniger and Smith, 112). Since she is a pollutant, a man who even touches her becomes impure and he “becomes pure by bathing” (85). She is stripped of her human dignity when Manu says, “Neither a ‘Fierce’ Untouchable, nor a pig, a cock, a dog, a menstruating woman, or an impotent man should be watching the priests dine” (86) and even if a man is “out of his mind (with desire) he should not have sex with a woman who is menstruating; he should not even lie down in the same bed with her;” worse still, he “should not carry on a conversation” with her (95) and not eat the food “touched” by her (103).

That explains why a purification ritual was performed at Sabarimala temple after two women of menstruating age entered the temple on 2 January 2019, subsequent to the verdict of the Supreme Court of India permitting women of all ages to enter the temple. Owing to the supposed inherent ‘impurity’ of women, their presence is believed to have defiled the deity and the temple. The restriction on women’s entry into the temple, based on menstruation as the yardstick of impurity, is a form of untouchability which holds that certain classes of individuals are impure, and hence, pollutants. Since this restriction is discriminatory in nature, it is a violation of the Fundamental Rights guaranteed under Article 25 of the Constitution of India.

Being born of the feminine, the supposedly ‘polluting agent,’ is to be born ‘polluted,’ at least partially. Ayyappa’s pedigree, thus, bypasses the issue of impurity by identifying his parents as two male gods, Vishnu (Hari) and Shiva (Hara), which earns him the name, Hariharaputra (son of Vishnu and Siva). Born of two male parents, Ayyappa is free of the supposedly ‘polluting feminine,’ and hence, free of pollution itself from birth. He would remain free of pollution by embracing ‘naishtika brahmacharya’ that prohibits any form of contact with the feminine. Almost all his devotees are males who are free of the ‘polluting feminine’ during their forty-one-day preparation for their visit to the temple. The female devotees, if any, will also be people who are free of the polluting menstrual blood. As per the traditional belief, Ayyappa does not approve of the presence of the women of menstruating age (i.e. women who have the potential to be sexually active, and hence, are a prospective danger to his status as a celibate) in his temple, lest it should adversely endanger his status as a ‘naishtika brahmachari.’

Ayyappa’s disapproval of the presence of the women of menstruating age is symbolic of patriarchal society’s fear of the supposedly ‘alluring,’ ‘tempting’ and ‘destructive’ feminine. As this fear of society is projected on to Ayyappa, he becomes the alienated male self of the society that fears the feminine. This fear seems to have been internalised by both the male and female members of society equally. The prohibition also underscores the assumption that women are incapable of practicing celibacy. The words of the ‘Tantric’ that were quoted by the Kerala High Court while delivering its verdict on the question of women's entry into temple — a stereotypical male chauvinistic discriminatory narrative internalised — prove how women are looked upon as objects of temptation and agents of sexual provocation by both the celibate deity and his male devotees. This prohibition of women in the temple is a form of their annihilation. Ayyappa is the annihilator of the feared mythical feminine — the buffalo-headed female demon, Mahishi. Being the cousin of Mahishasura, she had usurped the throne of Indra, and threatened to avenge the death of Mahishasura. Mahishi's annihilation was of supreme cosmic importance, but she could be annihilated only by an offspring of Vishnu and Shiva (Khan, 80). This made Ayyappa, born of two male parents and endowed with the powers of both, the rightful vanquisher of the buffalo-demon. Interestingly, none of these myths provides a credible answer to the question why the deity, who had voluntarily embraced lifelong celibacy, should feel threatened by the mere presence of women of menstruating age. Is not the human effort to protect and ensure Ayyappa's celibacy the greatest irony on the deity's vow of eternal 'brahmacharya?' The entire Sabarimala controversy, thus, may be read as one that stems from the collective, deep-rooted, fear of the feminine internalised by society over centuries.

The fear of the feminine had prevailed in the West as well, cutting across the waves of Enlightenment feminism and re-surfacing prominently at the turn of the nineteenth century that witnessed the emergence of the independent 'New Woman' in the West. The 'New Woman' was "clearly a product of industrial culture insomuch as its economic and educational effects created opportunities for women outside the domestic sphere and the outworn marriage plot of middle-class respectability" (Childers, 94). She would assert her independence in every way and refuse to be satisfied with her confinement to the private space of the home. She would refuse to be subjugated by man intellectually, socially, economically or sexually. The apprehensive Victorian patriarchy responded by labelling her "as a highly sexual creature," who with her "permissiveness" could undermine their long-cherished "social stability by breaking down the vital bonds of state and culture" (Rogers, xii). Mid-Victorian England witnessed the clash of contradictory discourses on women; while the dominant discourse eulogized woman as the epitome of virtue, the Victorians feared the fallen woman who subverted the concept of ideal womanhood. The fear of the feminine, however, has continued unabated till date, not just in Europe but in all corners of the world, cutting across spatiotemporal boundaries; myths, legends and folklores in different cultures and corners of the world thus abound in the figure of the 'femme fatale.' From Succubus, Circe and Helen of Troy to Jezebel, Delilah and Salome, to their Indian counterparts like Mohini and the Visha Kanyas, there are numerous examples.

The fear of the feminine could also be understood from another psychological perspective, through the intriguing concept of 'womb envy', a term developed by the neo-Freudian psychologist, Karen Horney. 'Womb envy' refers to the male envy of pregnancy, nursing and motherhood, i.e. of women's primary role in creating and sustaining life. In a forthright rejection of such concepts as 'penis envy' and other manifestations of male bias in psychoanalytical theory, Horney argued:

> [T]he essence of sexual life lies in its biological creative powers; a greater role in sexual life belongs to the female because she is the one who is able to bear and nurse children. This superiority is recognized by the male and is the source of intense envy. Womb envy, rather than being openly acknowledged by most males, has often taken subtle and indirect forms, such as the rituals of taboo, isolation and cleansing that have frequently been associated with menstruation and childbirth, the need to disparage women, accuse them of witchcraft, belittle their achievements, and deny them equal rights (Engler, 128).

On account of their sense of inferiority, Horney argues, men have the psychological need and compulsion to establish their superiority over women in other fields. Hence, according to Horney, "the impressive achievements of men in work or other creative fields may be seen as compensations for their inability to bear children" (Engler, 128). Therefore, it is understandable why the patriarchal voices arguing in favour of the ban on the entry of menstruating women in the Sabarimala temple hold that apart from the fact of women's menstrual blood polluting the temple, the deity and the devotees, women are also not capable of observing the forty-one-day penance expected of an Ayyappa devotee before he or she undertakes the pilgrimage. The physiological nature of women, they argue, renders them incapable of doing so. Besides, they say, women are physically not strong enough to undertake the arduous trek through the mountainous terrains to the temple — arguments that hold no water. Such arguments seem to arise, from what Brian Luke would call, the need for a "realm of pure male activity that men can compare favourably to women's essential reproductive work" (Luke, 113). Luke argues that the reason why sacrifice, which is considered to be important for the wellbeing of a society, is almost always performed by men is because it is seen as a compensation for their 'womb envy' (113).

In the predominantly masculine world of Sabarimala, every pilgrim of this primarily male fraternity seeks not only the blessing of the hyper-masculine deity, Ayyappa, but also a mode of spiritual identification with him. He prays for the wellbeing of his spouse, children, family and relatives; he prays for his domestic concerns that indirectly affirm his role as father, husband and brother – his gendered identity, his superiority and his control. With his prayer on his lips to his deity, with whom he already feels a spiritual communion, he is thus "dissolved within and connected to a sea of men who, by their sheer numbers, seem to suggest the entirety of male" (Osella, 747). The narrative in support of the restriction on the entry of women in the temple seems to gain its impetus as much from the unarticulated male fear and envy of the feminine as from the male desire for the affirmation of his male identity and control over the feared feminine.

## Conclusion

One of the ways in which patriarchal society has traditionally attempted to alleviate its deep-seated fear of the feminine is by taking control of the feminine. Restricting the entry of women into a place of worship – an important public space in any society since time immemorial – is certainly a way of taking control of the feminine and of gendering space. However, the Sabarimala temple is as much the hot seat of gender politics as it is the hot seat of identity politics, as borne out by the different attempts to change the name of the temple by people or groups with vested interests. Since one's name is an inextricable part of one's identity, changing one's name is tantamount to changing one's identity. By the same logic, changing the name of a temple may be read as an attempt to alter the identity of the deity enshrined in the temple. It is interesting to note that in the recent past, the name of the temple at Sabarimala was changed twice, in an attempt to bolster the argument either favouring or banning women's entry into the temple premises: first in 2016, when the name was changed from 'Sri Dharma Sastha Temple' to 'Sabrimala Sree Ayyappa Swamy Temple;' and once again in 2018, when it was rechristened back to 'Sri Dharma Sastha Temple.' The politics of the name change can be grasped only against the backdrop of the myth surrounding the identities of the gods, Dharma Sastha and Ayyappa.

As per traditional belief, though Dharma Sastha is a 'brahmachari' he is not regarded as a 'naishtika brahmachari' like Ayyappa, because, in his previous incarnation, he is believed to have had two wives – Pushkala and Poorna. Hence, Dharma Sastha could neither be averse to the presence of women, nor opposed to the entry of women of all ages into the temple. The case is, however, different for Ayyappa, the eternal celibate and the supposed human incarnation of Dharma Sastha, who is believed to have merged with Dharma Sastha after the completion of his earthly mission. Therefore, it is not surprising that as the UDF government in Kerala declared its stance favouring the ban in 2016, the Travancore Devaswom Board renamed the temple as 'Sabarimala Sree Ayyappa Swamy Temple,' precluding women's entry in the temple altogether.

The decision to change the name of the temple from 'Sree Dharma Sastha Temple' to 'Sabarimala Sree Ayyappa Swami Temple' was clearly a move to influence the Supreme Court of India in giving a verdict banning women of menstruating age from entering the temple. The rechristening the temple in

2018 with its original name was definitely in view of establishing a counter narrative. In any case, the September 2018 verdict of the Supreme Court of India, unequivocally ending the ban on women of menstruating age entering the temple, has emerged as the latest gendered religious controversy in India. Emboldened by the ruling of the highest court and escorted by police, two women – Kanaka Durga (39) and Bindu Ammini (40) – made history early this year by becoming the first women to enter the Sabarimala temple ever since the emergence of the controversy related to the entry of women in the temple. A massive protest erupted following their entry into the shrine; Hindu outfits in the state called a dawn-to-dusk hartal, and protesters burned the effigy of the Chief Minister, Pinarayi Vijayan, for allowing the women to defy the ancient custom. This controversy, understandably and unfortunately, will go on for some time to come and will be used as a political weapon by people who keep looking for opportunities to gain political mileage by dividing the religiously sensitive nation along the lines of gender and religion.

## References


Abraham, Korah and Prajwal Bhat. Sabarimala. Wednesday November 2018. 15 March 2019. <https://www.thenewsminute.com/article/sabarimala-belonged-us-kerala-s-mala-araya-tribe-challenge-thantri-family-91167>.

Adluri, Viswa and Joydeep Bagchee, *When the Goddes was a Woman: Mahābhārata Ethnographies - Essays* by Alf Hiltebeitel. Vol. 2. Boston: Brill, 2011.

Bardon, Edward J. *The Knowledge Drive: Confronting Mythological Beliefs*. Indianapolis: Dog Ear Publishing, 2008.

Brown, Norman O. *Love's Body*. Berkeley: University of California Press, 1990.

Childers, Joseph W. "Industrial Culture and Victorian Novel." *The Cambridge Companion to the Victorian Novel.* Ed. Deidre David. Cambridge: Cambridge University Press, 1991. 77-96.

Creed, Barbara. *The Monstrous-Feminine: Film, Feminism, Psychoanalysis*. London & New York: Routledge, 2015.

Das, Usha Rani and Lilly Paul. *Outlook*. 28 September 2018. 14 February 2019. <https://www.outlookindia.com/newsscroll/obama-warns-against-racial-nationalistic-politics/1392899?scroll>.

Doniger, Wendy and Brian K. Smith. *The Laws of Manu.* New York: Penguin, 1991.

Engler, Barbara. *Personality Theories.* Boston & New York: Hougton Mifflin Harcourt Publishing Company, 2009.

Freud, Sigmund. "Beyond the Plea sure Principle: Leonardo da Vinci and a Memory of His Childhood." *Philosophers on Art: from Kant to the Postmodernists.* Ed. Christopher Kul-Want. New York: Columbia University Press, 2010. 74-95.

Gandhi, M. K. *Self Restraint V. Self Indulgence*. Ahmedabad: Navajivan Publishing House, 1928.

Indian Young Lawyers' Association & Ors. vs The State of Kerala & Ors. No. Writ Petition (Civil) 373 of 2006. Supreme Court of India. 2006.

Keith, Arthur Berriedale. *The Veda of the Black Yajus School, Entitled Taittirīya Sanhita.* Cambridge: Harvard University Press, 1914.

Kerala Places of Public Worship (Authorization of Entry) Rules, 1965. No. 373 OF 2006. Kerala High Court. 28 September 2018. English.

Khan, Dominique-Sila. "Lines in Water: Religious Boundaries in South Asia." *Vawar Swami: A Hindu-Muslim Saint of Kerala.* Ed. Eliza Kent and Tazim R Kassam. New York: Syracuse University Press, 2013. 78-100.

Luke, Brian. *Brutal: Manhood and the Exploitation of Animals.* Urbana and Chicago: University of Illinois Press, 2007.

O'Flaherty, Wendy Doniger. *Siva: The Erotic Ascetic.* Oxford: Oxford University Press, 1981.

Osella, Filippo Osella and Caroline. "'Ayyappan Saranam:' Masculinity and the Sabarimala Pilgrimage in Kerala." *The Journal of the Royal Anthropological Institute* Vol. 9.No. 4 (2003): 729-754.

Rogers, David. "Introduction." Stoker, Bram. Dracula. Hertfordshire: Wordsworth, 1993. V-XIX.

S. Mahendran v/s Secretary, Travancore Devaswom Board, Thiruvananthapuram. No. O.P. No. 9015 of 1990. Kerala High Court. 5 April 1991. English.

S. Mahendran v/s Secretary, Travancore Devaswom Board, Thiruvananthapuram. No. O.P. No. 9015 of 1990. Kerala High Court. April 1991.

Sadasivan, S. N. *A Social History of India.* New Delhi: APH Publishing, 2000.

Smith, Frederick M. *The Self Possessed: Deity and Spirit Possession in South Asian Literature and Civilization.* New York: Columbia University Press, 2006.

Vanita, Ruth. "Ayyappa and Vavar: Celibate Friends." *Same-Sex Love in India: Readings from Literature and History.* Ed. Ruth Vanita and Saleem Kidwai. New York: Palgrave, 2001. 94-99.

Vidyarnava, Rai Bahadur Srisa Chandra, trans. *Yajnavalkya Smriti.* Allahabad: Sudhindra Nath Vasu, 1918.

17

# Refugees and Religion: Exploring their Multi-faceted Relationship in Our World Today

**James Ponniah**
*University of Madras*

**Abstract:** Our present decade in 21st century is marked by sharp increase in the number of displaced people. i.e., 70 million according to United Nation's report. From its previous peak in 1992 at 3.7 per 1,000 of the population, the number of the displaced had more than doubled to 9.3.in in 2018. It is an alarming trend. At this juncture, the most pressing question to ask is: how does the rest of humanity respond to this new category of people called 'stateless people' who have been pushed to this miserable status involuntarily and unwillingly? What role does religion play to address their plight? Is religion's engagement confined to humanitarian assistance? Do religions place the refugees merely at the receiving end? Or do they facilitate their agency to reconstruct their lives and to aspire for a hopeful future? These are questions raised and answered in this essay.

**Keywords**: Refugees, Religion, Identity Construction, Agency, Liberation

We live in a paradoxical world today. On the one hand, we proudly call our contemporary world a global village, a place in which humans enjoy the freedom of mobility and interaction across national borders. On the other hand, certain movements of people across borders has become a matter of great concern for the nation states as the quantum of people who are displaced due to conflict, war, persecution and human rights violation has significantly increased in recent times as per UNHCR's statistics. It clearly indicates more and more humans are pushed to the state of insecurity, vulnerability and homelessness in our contemporary era. It is against this background that this essay seeks to understand the complex phenomenon of refugees in our world today and explores its relationship with religion from different perspectives.

## 1. Complex Phenomenon of Refugees Today

A 'refugee,' according to 1951 UN Convention, is a "person who has a well-founded fear of persecution because of his or her nationality, race or ethnic origin, political opinion, religion or social group; is outside the country of his or her nationality and owing to such fear is unable or unwilling to seek the protection of the authorities of his or her own country." (Mckay 2009: 12). This definition, in spite of its merits to recognize the vast number of people displaced due to various reasons, is still inadequate to capture the complex reality of refugee situation in our world today. UNHCR in recent years has shifted to the usage of the term 'persons of concern' to include various categories of people such as Asylum-seekers, Internally displaced persons (IDPs), Returned refugees, Returned IDPs and Stateless persons. Asylum-seekers are individuals who have sought international protection and whose claims for refugee status have not yet been determined, irrespective of when they may have been lodged. Internally displaced persons (IDPs) are people or groups of individuals who have been forced to leave their homes or places of habitual residence, in particular as a result of, or in order to avoid the effects of armed conflict, situations of generalized violence, violations of human rights, or natural or man-made disasters, and who have not crossed an international border. Returned refugees are former refugees who have returned to their country of origin spontaneously or in an organized fashion but are yet to be fully integrated. Such return would normally only take place in conditions of safety and dignity. Returned IDPs refer to those IDPs who were beneficiaries of UNHCR's protection and assistance activities and who returned to their areas of origin or habitual residence. Stateless persons are defined under international law as persons who are not considered as nationals by any State under the operation of its law. In other words, they do not possess the nationality of any State. According to 2018 statistics, the people of concern at the global level are estimated to be 74.79 million out of 7.5 billion people in the globe.

## 2. Refugees as Interrogators of the Nation State

Refugees and asylum seekers are unfortunately perceived as desireless and unfit everywhere. While their own home country treats them as unwanted because of their ethnic, linguistic or religious background, not all host countries welcome them with open arms. More often than not, there are groups, peoples and political parties in the host country who regard them not only as culturally unfit but also as burden and drain on the state purse. But when we ask why there are being treated as unwanted and unfit, we may get new perspectives to the issue. In the first place, it indicates that a nation which renders its own citizens as refugees and stateless has become a land of discrimination, injustice and partisanship that perceives certain people with certain background as disruptions to the public order and social harmony or dangerous to national security as we see in the case of Rohingya Muslims in Burma or the Bengali Muslims in Assam. Such treatments not only reveal the new developments in the home country such as religious nationalism, ethnic conflicts or civil unrest but also expose the real or hypercritical stance of the national government that side with the religious, ethnic or linguist majority and overlook, if not permit, the persecution and violence on the minority population.

Secondly, refugees' relationship with the potential refugee receiving nations which either reject or tolerate the refugees from other nations is also symptomatic of the inhuman and self-centered world we live in. The fact that people with certain background are not welcome to a country while others are is clearly indicative of discriminatory refugee policies of the host country. For instance, Muslim refugees from other south Asian countries are not welcome to India while the Hindu refugees are received and looked after gladly by the Indian state. While some of the western countries follow rigorous refugee policies that generally look at refugees with suspicion, others tend to single out Muslim refugees as trouble makers and potential terrorists. The sad story of Rohingyas, the Bangladeshi Muslim minority, declared illegal migrants in Myanmar and not accepted by any of the neighboring nations including Bangladesh and India is the recent case in point. Refugees have become a problematic category of people to the nation states not because the nation states lack resources to accommodate them but primarily because the nation states have their own ideological, ethnic, racial and religious preferences that prevent them to treat the refugees humanly and justly. When the refugees cross borders and go to the neighbor states in search of safety and security, they—like other critics of nation state—express their distrust in the very existence of nations that divided people by the stroke of a pen on the maps by creating nations but at the expense of cultural ties, ethnic unity and religious solidarity of the people living in a geographical location. They call into question the very existence of nation states which in the name of national unity not only divide humanity but also pursue the interests of a few and wages war of different forms to advance their agenda. In doing so, the refugees join voices with Tagore, Tolstoy and other humanists who interrogated the concept of nation state in the aftermath of World wars I and II and campaigned against its vested interests so that humanity can be saved.

## 3. Refugees and Religion: Exploring their Multiple Relationship

When we think of religion's relationship with refugees, what immediately comes to our mind are religious organizations such as the Anglican Communion, Caritas International, Church World Service, HIAS (Hebrew Immigrant Aid Society), International Catholic Migration Commission, Islamic Relief Worldwide, Jesuit Refugee Service, Lutheran World Federation, Rabbis for Human Rights – Israel, the World Council of Churches, and World Vision International which have done commendable work among the refugees, asylum seekers and the displaced including climate refugees. When the refugees and displaced people are forced to move to unknown places, who come to their immediate help are the church networks, monastery-run organisations or mosques that provide not only food and shelter but also offer resettlement help and legal advice. No doubt they also help them to overcome trauma, facilitate worship practices, take care of their spiritual needs and enable their integration into host nations. In this regard, Alexander Horstmann and Jin-Heon Jung observe, "Humanitarian aid provided by missionary networks or professional relief organizations has become increasingly important. Under hostile circumstances that make it impossible to return home, stateless migrants and refugees often depend on religious congregations and missionary networks, with their ability to reach areas and fulfill needs unreached and unmet by other humanitarian organizations, to prepare and develop the routes and imaginaries that they travel." (2015: 1) Various popular and scholarly literatures are being written and published to highlight the significant humanitarian works done by religion-based institutions across the world.

In these traditional modes of humanitarian works, human agency lies with the religious groups who take various sincere efforts to make the refugees feel welcome, safe and secure. In such contexts, religious organizations become care-givers and refugees care-receivers. In other words, religious groups function as agents of humanitarian works while the refugees become recipients and beneficiaries. We can also look at religion's role in the lives of the refuges beyond this equation. New roles of religion will emerge when we look at the other sets of data that call for and provide new perspectives to understand the relationship between religion and refugees. In the new set of data discussed below refugees are viewed not as mere recipients and beneficiaries but as agents and religious actors who with the help of religions aspire to make a new life for themselves. In this regard, authors like Lubkemann (2002) discuss the central role religion plays in the home-and-place-making of vulnerable refugees who have fled humanitarian crises and natural disasters. Besides, Alexander Horstmann and Jin-Heon Jung (2015), Thomas Tweed (2006) hold that religion is capable of offering a "sanctuary and space of relief for vulnerable people, to be a 'compass' and 'itinerary'"(Horstmann and Jin-Heon Jung 2015: 1) and can function as a lens to understand "the kinetics of homemaking in often hostile environments."(ibid.) As mentioned earlier, when refugees are forced to go to a new place, more often than not, it is religion which provides them not only community centres but also community help to establish new homes in alien environments. "Religion can thus be a lens through which to view the hopes and aspirations that make reorganized lives more comfortable and bearable." (ibid.) Religion as an "itinerary" refers to its ability to facilitate involuntary mobility. "It assists in crossing boundaries and is part of a process of self-settling, self-organization, and reconstruction, of self-transformation and reidentification. It is a tool with which displaced people rebuild a sense of homeland, belonging, and engagement with other religious spaces and movements in diaspora." (ibid.: 1-2). It is with the help of religion that the refugees assume ownership over their lives, rebuild their future and "sacralize spaces while placing themselves in and outside of the international regime of refugee protection." (ibid.: 2) While providing locus for allocating resources for social support, religious networks make all the difference for physical survival in some contexts and just for spiritual benefits in other contexts. In this regard Horstmann (2014) also discusses how religion can become an integral part of refugees' public space making.

Religion also plays a significant role in the construction of refugee's identity. Various studies undertaken by scholars in different sites of refugee life-world have offered interesting insights into how this process of construction pans out. They demonstrate "the interplay between religion and the identity constitution of refugee migrants in the processes and practices of searching for and making a home in the context of displacement." (ibid.: 15)

For instance, Janet Hoskins (2015), making a study on Vietnamese refugees, draws our attention to the new avatars of two Vietnamese indigenous religions, namely, the modernist Caodaism and Dao Mau (the Mother Goddess tradition) among the Vietnamese refugees in California. While the latter offered a performative ritual religion "based on an imperial pantheon of warriors, ladies of the court, and impish baby princes familiar to the ancestor worship,"(21) its ritual repertoire became a way of "returning" to an ancestral homeland. Displaced from their homeland, the refugees felt a stronger need to evoke these spirits specifically to get the guidance of their ancestors in a new world thereby they stayed connected to their far away land. Caodaism originally emerged in the 1920s during the French colonial period as a response to the great dislocations and upheavals experienced by the of the colonial period. "Caodaism emerged in response to the "loss of country" during the colonial period. The earliest spirit medium séances asked for divine guidance to deal with the loss of sovereignty to the French."(32) During the French rule, while the catholic missionaries had considerable success in northern Vietnam in the sixteenth and seventeenth centuries, they were not received well into the southern Vietnamese colony of Cochinchina. Instead of converting to

Christianity, the educated elite in and around the city of Saigon forged a new modernist syncretic religion built on Sino-Vietnamese secret societies (the "Minh") and claimed sanction from the Jade Emperor himself. Their goal was "to erect an alternative apparatus of power (a "Vietnamese Vatican") that would have to be respected by the secular colonial regime."(ibid.) Caodaist believers drew upon essential elements from Buddhism, Taoism, and Confucianism and incorporated Jesus Christ and biblical narratives into their new framework to innovate a new syncretic religious phenomenon. In this new anti-colonial religion, "Christ himself was, paradoxically, less important in this scheme than a number of Christian ideas about history and popular emancipation—the notion of the Vietnamese as God's chosen people, the idea of a prophet who would fight for the independence of his people against an empire based in Rome, and the erection of an intricate administrative hierarchy blending Confucian titles with Catholic ones (a Pope, female and male cardinals, bishops, and so on)." (ibid.)

After the fall of Saigon in 1975, many Caodaists fled to different parts of the world including USA. Since the 1990s, a new generation of Vietnamese refugees in the US sought to establish Caodaists as a transnational community of faith and have linked Caodaists in the United States to their coreligionists in other countries and in Vietnam especially after the Socialist Republic of Vietnam has officially recognized the religion. In the last three decades, Caodaists have done well economically, erected new temples, formed new communities in different parts of USA. They became "simultaneously active in proselytizing vigorously by means of media technology and multilingual materials in envisioning a glorious future of Vietnam." (ibid. 15) In the backdrop of such developments, Caodaists began to interpret the fall of Saigon in 1975 and their subsequent eviction as part of God's plan to spread and to globalise their religion. They stopped seeing their fleeing from Vientnam in 1970's as a trauma but rather as "God's way of forming new missionaries in countries like the United States, Australia, Canada, and France. They came to see that it was their role to help create a global religion of unity, not merely a religion in exile that would serve the Vietnamese community." (ibid 35)

Other studies on refugees elsewhere point to the emergence of new possession cults and practices in the context of displacement and refuge. As Jalison Hoskins (2015) observes, "spirit possession is a survival strategy developed by religions that suffer displacement, since it allows the deities of the land and of origins to move into the bodies of their disciples." (24) In fact, in the absence of native and indigenous lands, "the body of the possessed person becomes a new sacred space, the "seat" on which the spirits come to sit, and the platform through which they can come to teach."(ibid.) Spirit possession cults are quite prevalent among the refugees and the displaced as evidenced in the works of Brown (2001) Matory (2005) on African slaves who formed Vodou, Candomblé, and Santeria cults, Stoller (1992, 1995) on urban migrants or climate refugees in Africa among whom developed the West African Hauka cult, Boddy (1988, 1994) on Sudanese *zar* and Morris (2000) on the northern Thai villagers among whom emerged Chiang Mai. In her work, Hjorleifur Jonsson (2015) has demonstrated how Iu Mien refugees who fled to the United States, Thailand, and France after Second Indochina War in Laos (1962–1975) have changed the methods of engaging with the world of spirits. It is noted that "as a response to the crisis and suffering, they went beyond the realm of ancestor spirits, and came to practice syncretic forms of religion, including, for instance, worshipping soldier spirits, wearing Buddhist amulets, translating the Bible, and further establishing international and interreligious networks" (Horstmann and Jin-Heon Jung 2015:18). This example illustrates how exposures to new contexts and new predicaments can make the refugees adopt new religious beliefs and practices that can transcend their traditional religio-cultural customs. In doing so, they can broaden their horizons and widen their frameworks and worldviews. This study also highlights the capacity of religion, in the context of refugee life-world, to engage across social, spiritual, political, and linguistic differences.

Leonardo Schiocchet (2015) in his work on Palestinian refugee camps differs from most of the works on refugees that consider them as mere recipients of host country's patronage. His work like that of Alexander Horstmann demonstrates that the refugees are not just passive objects of tutelage but function as important agents of the imagined community. The social belonging processes of Palestinian refugees is as much defined by ascription to an imagined ("transnational") Palestinian nation as they are by the local urban symbolic space surrounding them. For outsiders the refugee camps may seem as a marginal space of exception especially from the lenses of the urban landscape. But for the refugees it is the very core of an imagined community. The agency of the refugees is also evident from the fact that different camps in the same host country can vary in their organizational structure and symbolic configuration, and relate differently to their surroundings. Thus, refugee camps, even in the same host country, can be thus *more* "open" or "closed" depending on the way refugee camp dwellers interact with and relate to the surrounding populations, religious leaders, the host state, humanitarian relief agents, local grassroots movements, and other local and international social actors. The work also investigates how Palestinian refugees make use of the religious concept of *al-ṣumud* (steadfastness). This notion which had once acquired secular connotation to guide their time management has become more Islamized today and has helped them to construct what he calls as "hyper-expression of identity". This Islamised notion results in ritualization of mundane activities in the Palestinian refugee camps and facilitates the production of Palestine nationalism.

Religion also provides both means and a goal for refugees to move forward resolutely with self-respect in spite of having to face crisis situations. Elizabeth McAlister's work (2015) for instance describes how a network of conservative evangelical Christian refugees dealt with the natural disaster of Haiti earthquake and the subsequent humanitarian relief that came their way rather negatively. No doubt they adopted a conservative outlook of punitive theodicy to understand the natural disaster of earthquake as God's punishment. But they took a radical stand when they rejected American aid when possible, and interpreted the aid they did accept as having been sent by God. "Their strict moral order allowed the congregation to formulate an uncompromising critique of the Haitian government, the UN peacekeeping mission, and foreign humanitarian relief. They developed a stance of Christian self-sufficiency, anti-foreign aid, and anti-dependency." (ibid. 183) This stance made the community to tap from within both the material and spiritual resources required to overcome their immediate needs, to rebuild themselves internally and to reconstruct their lost lives materially. Commenting on this surprise move, Elizabeth McAlister observes "Their critique of foreign aid and dependency mirrored the critique of humanitarian aid launched by both Haitian intellectuals and Haitian and American anthropologists; however, the church members expressed it in a Christian moral register. Theirs is a local, evangelical, grassroots iteration of a similar critique that anthropologists have made of humanitarian aid and NGO involvement in the country, from a very different ideological site." (Ibid.).

As Peter Schalk (2007) notes in this study of Sri Lankan Tamil refugees in Europe, the involuntary refugee situation of the Sri Lankan Tamils can transform certain highly localized form of conservative vernacular Hinduism, such as Tamil Saivism of Jaffna, into a religious project of emancipation or liberation. In exile, Tamil Saivism, like any other refugee religion, not only provides psychological and emotional sustenance to the Tamil speaking refugees but also "allows them a connection with their culture and traditions and the ability to resist assimilation and create a separate ethnic identity while giving them the strength to deal with the loss of their rightful place in their own country." (1) In other words, Sri Lankan Tamils are able to uphold this identity only by their deliberate choice to maintain this temple as Tamil Temple disallowing the use of Sanskrit or Hindi in those temples and by refusing to accept other South Asian Hindus into temple membership and administration. This move actually meant that the economic onus of making and maintaining the Siva temples is totally on the Tamil-speaking Sri Lankans as it would also make them inelibgle to access the local state grant to the places of worship as the state officially recognizes and supports only those Hindu temples that are meant for all the

Hindus, not a section of them. For almost all Tamils in exile who aspire for the birth of an independent Tamil state called Eelam, Tamil Saivism "is an expression of these hopes, symbolised, above all, by two gods, Vinayakar and Murukan, sons of Civaṉ (*sic*), who act as liberating deputies."(1) Peter Schalk describes how these two gods came to be accepted as liberator deities in the refugee religion of Sri Lankan Tamil Saivism. In Tamil Saivism, Murukan is regarded as a true war god who solves problems by overcoming the enemies. With his powerful symbol *Vel* (lance) which he holds in his hand, Murukan appears as a hope for a future victory in the present conflict. His power of victory is celebrated by his devotees when they praise him through the lance by shouting "lance, lance, beautiful lance – sharpened lance, lance of valour, and lance of victory!" Tamils believe Vinayakar to be a remover of obstacles especially for the household. Hence, unlike his brother, his duty seems to be civilian. He is regarded either as a bachelor or as platonically married to two wives who both represent spiritual qualities. He is a preferred God for women as he is a symbol not only for warm relation of devotion, affection, and well-wishing but also for imagining and reproducing prosperous household. Some of these household women foster a second generation of refugee Tamils, some of them already born in exile and they have observed closely the consequences of war including the killings of their husbands, sons, daughters, and relatives. Hence they promote the worship of Vinayakar, the Remover who stands as "as representation and preserver of an idealised pacifist pre-or post-war culture. Murukaṉ is the victor over the enemy who is a threat to tradition. The Remover is the preserver of the same tradition. Both are regarded as needed in the exile situation." (Ibid. 107)

## Conclusion

To sum up, this essay has explored the relationship between religion and refugees beyond the traditional scope of humanitarian aid provided by the religious organisations which generally place them at the receiving end. Departing from this dated perspective, this essay has put together data from recent research works to argue a case for refugees' exercise of agency across the global to rebuild a new life for themselves. Their endeavours everywhere seem to revolve around identity construct through religious means and idioms. It involves production of new sites of religious strategies that include not only the creation of new centres of worship, pilgrimage destinations, meditation centres, and places of spiritual healing but also the generation of innovative ideas, practices and actions. They also instrumentalize religion for political project to aspire for a homeland which "is not only a physical place but also a concept and a desire – a place to return to through the imagination through a kind of simultaneous doubling of psychic space – the possibility of living here in body and elsewhere in mind and imagination, or doing a ritual in order to collapse together these doubled spaces, and bring the distant homeland back into the body located" (Hoskins 2015:3) in exile.

## References

Boddy, Janice. 1988. "Spirits and Selves in Northern Sudan: The Cultural Therapeutics of Possession and Trance." *American Ethnologist*, 15 (1): 4–27.

Boddy, Janice. 1994. "Spirit Possession Revisited: Beyond Instrumentality." *Annual Reviews in Anthropology*, 21: 407–434.

Brown, Karen McCarthy. 2001. *Mama Lola: A Vodou Priestess in Brooklyn*. 2nd ed. Berkeley: University of California Press.

Horstmann, Alexander and Jin-Heon Jung 2015. "Introduction: Refugees and Religion" in *Building Noah's Ark for Migrants, Refugees, and Religious Communities*, eds. Alexander Horstmann and Jin-Heon Jung, 1-22. New York: Palgrave Macmillan.

Horstmann, Alexander. 2014. "Stretching the Border. Confinement,Mobility and the Refugee Public among Karen Refugees in Thailand and Burma." *Journal of Borderlands Studies*, 29 (1): 47–61.

Hoskins, Janet 2015. "What Is a Refugee Religion? Exile, Exodus, and Emigration in the Vietnamese Diaspora" in *Building Noah's Ark for Migrants, Refugees, and Religious Communities*, eds. Alexander Horstmann and Jin-Heon Jung, 23-44. New York: Palgrave Macmillan.

*Jonsson, Hjorleifur 2015.* "Conversion and Community among Iu Mien Refugee Immigrants in the United States" in *Building Noah's Ark for Migrants, Refugees, and Religious Communities*, eds. Alexander Horstmann and Jin-Heon Jung, 235-256. New York: Palgrave Macmillan.

Lubkemann, Stephen 2002. "Where to be an Ancestor? Reconstituting Socio-Spiritual Worlds among Displaced Mozambicans." *Journal of Refugee Studies*, 15 (2): 189–212.

Matory, J. Lorand. 2005. *Black Atlantic Religion*. Durham, NC: Duke University Press.

*McAlister, Elizabeth 2015.* "Humanitarian Ad-Hocracy, Transnational New Apostolic Missions, and Evangelical Anti-dependency in a Haitian Refugee Camp" in *Building Noah's Ark for Migrants, Refugees, and Religious Communities*, eds. Alexander Horstmann and Jin-Heon Jung, 181-208. New York: Palgrave Macmillan.

Mckay, Sonia 2009. "The Commonalities of Experience: Refugees and Recent Migrants" in *Refugees, Recent migrants and employment: Challenging Barriers and Exploring Pathways,* ed. Sonia Mckay, 11-22. New York: Routledge.

Morris, Rosalind. 2000. *In the Place of Origins: Modernity and Its Mediums in Northern Thailand*. Durham, NC: Duke University Press.

*Schalk, Peter 2007.* "Caivam – A Religion Among Tamil Speaking Refugees From Sri Lanka," *Refugee Survey Quarterly*, Vol. 26, Issue 2, 91-108. DOI:10.1093/rsq/hdi0230.

*Schiocchet, Leonardo 2015.* "Palestinian Steadfastness as a Mission" in *Building Noah's Ark for Migrants, Refugees, and Religious Communities*, eds. Alexander Horstmann and Jin-Heon Jung, 209-34. New York: Palgrave Macmillan.

Stoller, Paul. 1992. *The Cinematic Griot: The Ethnography of Jean Rouch*. Chicago, IL: University of Chicago Press.

Stoller, Paul. 1995. *Embodying Colonial Memories: Spirit Possession, Power and the Hauka in West Africa*. New York: Routledge.

Tweed, Thomas A. 2006. *Crossing and Dwelling: A Theory of Religion*. Cambridge and London: Harvard University Press.

# PART THREE

# OPEN TO DIFFERENCE AND DISSENT

# 18

# Religious Pluralism, Dissent, and Empowering Peace: A Subaltern View

**Gnana Patrick**

*Department of Christian Studies, University of Madras*

**Abstract:** In this article the author argues that religious pluralism cannot be grasped deeply in a-historical manner; it needs, on the other hand, a context-specific exploration in order to make meaningful statements upon it. It has to be anchored context-sensitively on social reality as it obtains in different instances of situatedness, the *sitz-im-leben* of life. Accordingly, this reflection would like to pursue a socio-religious approach, anchoring on a subaltern location.

This agonistic experience of religious pluralism takes place in a dialectics of dissent and ascent. It is a dissent to the dominating other, and an ascent to the dominated self; it is an acute moment of experiencing distinction and identity, in an on-going process of negotiation with the other. This negotiation takes place within a deeper experience of the divine dialectics of transcendence and immanence, a spiritual experience which transcends the historical experience of domination, even while affirming and assuring a new emancipatory identity to the dominated.

**Keywords:** Religious pluralism, Dissent, Religious diversity, *Sitz-im-leben*, Empowering peace.

## Introduction

Discourse on religious pluralism is being pursued from different angles today.[1] A theological angle looks into the theological value of plurality of religions and their mutual relationship; a philosophical perspective explores the way religious pluralism deals with such ultimate questions as ontology of religious pluralism, one and many, universality and particularity, and the like. These perspectives tend to treat religious pluralism in a-temporal and non-spatial manner. In this paper, I would like to present an argument that religious pluralism cannot be grasped deeply in a-historical manner; it needs, on the other hand, a context-specific exploration in order to make meaningful statements upon it. It has to be anchored context-sensitively on social reality as it obtains in different instances of situatedness, the *sitz-im-leben* of life. Accordingly, this reflection would like to pursue a socio-religious approach, anchoring on a subaltern location.

## 1. Locating the Context

The contemporary western Euro-American world speaks of religious pluralism, by and large, in a post-Enlightenment context. Among others, there are two core sets of changes which have characterised the context there: One, the dismaying or dissipation of the modernist framework, and the other, the experience of globalisation, which has brought forth, a 'reverse colonisation', or a new experience of communities, especially of religio-cultural communities. The former, against the development of certain saturation in secular modernist discourse, has tended to steer its orientation away from objectivist positivist thinking which, with its instrumental rationality, as the critical theorists would have it, strived to bring diversity under its ambit of universality, and projected the universal citizen as its sublime practitioner. The other, quite consequentially, mediated an experience of the presence of the other, especially the erstwhile third world other(s) along with their religio-cultural identities. These two currents of changes seem to serve as the typical Euro-American context from which the discourse on religious pluralism emerges. As a consequence, the discourse is informed by a new sensitivity to community, characteristically

1 Whenever I remember Dr. Cyril Desbrulais, a wind of youthfulness passes by my mind; he came across to me as a person for the young generation. The plays he staged, the roles he acted out, the way he went about, and the brilliant classes he took – all have an air of youthfulness. There was also an aspect of critical dissent in his youthfulness. Once when he had dressed up for an inaugural mass, he had tucked portions of an oversize alb around the cincture like a lump, and joined the procession. I noticed it and smiled, and he said in a quiet voice, "that's my way of showing the dissent." Not only in an instance like this, but in the very way he lived out his priestly calling there was an air of dissent, a very substantive and meaningful one at that. My present essay, therefore, is dedicated to that fine aspect of the person of Dr. Cyril Desbrulais.

different from the previous *Gemeinschaft* type. It is a new sensitivity in that the community is not looked as a pre-given overarching paradigm of life for an individual, but, as a necessary constitutive process in the construction of selfhood and identity of individuals; It is a sensitivity which, within the broad political framework, treats the cultural rights of individuals. In this sensitivity, the religious identity becomes one of the salient forms of the cultural community or the predominant cultural right of the individual, serving as the 'sources of the self' as Charles Taylor would have it.[2] Religious pluralism in this context is therefore a post / advanced modernist or post-secularist discourse.

The context is characteristically different in most of the countries of the Southern and Eastern continents. Indian context has its unique characteristics, and its discourse of religious pluralism today needs to be situated within its experience of a 'fractured modernity', which is a skewed modernity, producing post-secularist / post-modernist discourses among a certain section, leaving a vast majority of the population still under the grip of feudal forces. The fractured modernity impacted differentially upon different social worlds, causing the emergence of a mixture of the traditional *Gameinschaft* and the modern *Geselleschaft* types of societies. Differentiality goes with systemic ambivalence and complexity, which are perhaps the characteristic features of the discourse on religious pluralism in India today.

One way out of this systemic ambivalence is locating the discourse within a particular social world and exploring it from that location. This short reflection, accordingly, endeavours to locate it within the subaltern world and argues that religious dissent is integral to a substantive religious pluralism in the Indian context. By 'religious dissent' I mean a religious experience, which articulates an alternative or a counter to an existing religious tradition that has obtained hegemonic proportions. The alternative or counter religious tradition is characterised by a deep sense of egalitarianism, anti-hierarchy, participation, interrogation and contestation of the dominant tenets and practices that legitimise a hegemonic tradition.

## 2. Religious Dissent

When a specific form of religiosity, epitomised in the consecration of *Ezhava Shiva*, was manifest in Sri Narayana Guru movement (of Travancore), a mystic in South Travancore, known as Vaikuntacami, was mediating a religiosity which centred around a contextual interpretation of Dharma, the paradigmatic religious ideal in India. He said: "...uplift of the lowly is dharma". He said this against a background wherein Travancore, called by some historians as the land of Charity, had attempted to live up to the *varnashrama dharma* ideal, and,

2 Cf. Charles Taylor, *Sources of the Self: The Making of the Modern Identity*, Cambridge, Mass: Harvard University Press, 1989.

accordingly, considered serving the Brahmin as its *dharmic* virtue. The life and activities of Vaikuntasamy became the hub of a process of reinterpretation of the classical dharma. The hermeneutical endeavour was impregnated with the social experience of the subaltern people, who lived a broken life, characterised by several inhuman forms of oppression. Rituals, symbols, and oral teachings emerged out of this hermeneutical task, which mediated a new religiosity for the subaltern people. Phenomenologically, it was a religious dissent whose site of origin was simultaneously the mystical experience of Vaikuntasamy as well as the experience of social subordination of the subaltern people. Both personal as well as collective experiences converged into the manifestation of this alternative religious tradition in the South Travancore context of the nineteenth century.

There is immense literature produced or being produced on similar religious traditions which emerged in many parts of the Indian subcontinent during the eighteenth-nineteenth and early twentieth centuries. It was an era of religious transformations, enkindled by a process of innovation as well as reinterpretation of some of the dominant religious ideals of the time. There was a churning of the ocean, so to say. One of the key contributors to this churning was the phenomenon of western modernity as introduced, in its ideological dimension, by western antiquarians, ethnographers, educators, Christian missionaries, and several other agents. The churning went with the emergence of waves of religiosity or religious experience which found differential manifestations among the different socio-cultural groups. That which I speak here as 'religious dissent' was a particular form of religiosity which was found in this churning; It was a religious experience that exhibited such dynamic features as critical consciousness, spirit of interrogation and reinterpretation, and the will to forge alternative identity for the religious actors. Dissent here is not a negative energy, but, a positive potentiality for emancipation. As Peniel Jesudason Rufus Rajkumar would have it, it is a "resilient vitality which threatens hegemony by maintaining a persistent presence in the very forms of life which hegemony seeks to thwart."[3] Sree Narayana Guru movement, Ayya Vazhi, Vallalar movement, Varkari movement, Devi movement, and Chamar movement are only few examples of the hundred and odd such religious phenomena. Many more of similar religious phenomena are being unearthed today. Works carried out by pioneers like MSA Rao, Stephen Fuchs, the Subaltern Studies Project, Kenneth Jones, Gail Omvelt, G. Aloysius, Lawrence Babb, David Hardiman, and several other scholars point to the presence of such phenomena.

3 Peniel Jesudason Rufus Rajkumar, "The Diversity and Dialectics of Dalit Dissent and Implications for a Dalit Theology of Liberation", in Sathianathan Clarke et al., *Dalit Theology in the Twenty-first Century: Discordant Voices, Discerning Pathways,* New Delhi: OUP, p. 55.

Not that these movements of religious dissent arose only during the modern era; we already see features of them in the forerunners like Buddhism, Jainism, Ajivakam, bhakti traditions and so on. However, those of the modern era helped extend the experience of an integration of religiosity and critical consciousness among wider sections of people. These newer traditions, according to several studies, are the very manner in which the subaltern people integrated modernity in their lives and sought to fashion a new emancipatory identity for them. By constructing a mythography with a respectable past, a dynamic present and a bright future wherein full freedom would reign, these religious traditions served to construct a transformative self for their followers.

## 3. Dynamic Religious Diversity

This experience of the religious dissent arose from within the experience of the dynamic religious diversity this subcontinent experienced for a very long time in history. Folkloristics, in the recent decades, has captured and continues to capture it descriptively and analytically. The innumerable variety of folk deities, male and female, which form the object of worship; the fascinating diversity of ritual practices and beliefs; the rich region-specific oral traditions which are performed in the ritual ambience – all these are only the traces of the deep-seated richness of the religious experience of the people living especially at the margins of the society. These folk traditions are said to function in diverse manners – as collectivising strategies, as community catharsis, as sites of communication of sacra, as liminal spaces generating creative freedom and equality, as rituals of resistance, as weapons of the weak, as sites of popular religiosity, as identity markers, and so on. Their innumerable forms and functions are only indicators of the richness of religiosity, and its context-specific diversity.

This diversity is dynamic in that it is not just a notional diversity, but one characterised by social, economic, and cultural experiences of different communities. And, in sharing these attributes, it also becomes a negotiating diversity, which keeps negotiating differences, contesting dominances, interrogating hegemonies, and so on. All these features of the dynamic diversity bring forth innumerable cults, beliefs, ritual practices, performances and so on. As Romila Thapar opines, "[T]he religious reality in the past for the majority of Indians had been the recognition of a multiplicity of religions ... rooted in local cults, beliefs and rituals and identified less by religion and more by *jati* or by *zat*... They maintained a distance from the *brahmanas* and the *ulema* for they were essentially unconcerned with norms of the *sastras* or with *fatwas*, governed as they were by their own customary observances..."[4]

4 Romila Thapar, "Secularism and History", in Romila Thapar, *Cultural Pasts – Essays in Early Indian History*. OUP, 2004, p. 1021.; T.N. Madan would clearly point out that,

Unfortunately, the history of this dynamic diversity is not recorded, and they do not find a place in the public discussion of the Indian religious landscape.

The dynamic religious diversity is enriched by its embodied religious experience, which combined the bodily presence with transcendence in many unique ways. These religious traditions took less to the rejection of this-worldly duties, much less to a soul-body dualism which characterised the western process of degrading the body as the terrain of the materialist domain. Body as a site of life was less antagonised against the site of a soul. Body was perhaps not treated as polluting as against a pure soul. However, it must be noted here that the bodies of the lower castes were treated as polluting. It was therefore in the recognition of a social hierarchy that the body came to be treated as polluting and impure, but not so much against a pure soul/spirit.

It is also the case that religious diversity and dissent, as they became representations of acute disputations on social hierarchy, were sought to be neutralised either through open conflicts or by subtle religio-cultural mechanics. Open conflicts between religious sects were engendered by the developing strain in relationships between social groups. The other method is more subtle. It is one of co-option by the dominant tradition into its symbolic world of the different or differentiating traditions. It means that the usual cliché that Indian religions are tolerant towards the other cannot be taken in a face value.

## 4. The Changing Context Today

One today speaks of religious revival taking place all over the globe. One of the chief experiences of this revival is presencing of religion in the public sphere, associating it with identity discourse. This revival could be explained from several angles. However, the revival in the Indian context cannot straightaway be explained as, for example, Gianni Vattimo would do in a western context as the 'return of the repressed'. It needs more context specific explanations. Certainly there is a revival of religion in the Indian public sphere. But, it is not something that comes after a process of secularisation. It occurs against the globalising context, wherein facilities for public representation and communication are more to count. This revival is not as natural as it is presented to be. A strenuous effort is being made to give an orientation to this revival, and effort is being made by the steadily growing middle class of India. The growing middle class is in need of an identity, which can be presented as specifically their own in contrast to other religious traditions that they experience in the global arena. The middle class therefore vigorously promotes *a* religion for India, in a homogenous form. This urge of the middle class ventures to do away with all dissent and diversities present in the grassroots of Indian religio-

"Hinduism is a federation of faiths with a horizontal as well as vertical distribution rather than a single homogenous religion." (Religions of India, 42)

cultural terrain. It projects, as explained by Romila Thapar, a syndicated Hinduism, along the lines of the semitic religions which are more organised. This dynamics of syndicating takes place against the growing interest of the middle classes for identity, which are linked with their opportunities in the global scenario. As Thapar suggests, "[T]here is inevitably a search for new identities and in the Indian situation of recent times, encouragement has been given to religious identities, on the basis of a particular interpretation of what is regarded as the Indian tradition and Indian history."[5] It is this interest which provides the specific tone and pitch to the demands raised by the forces of cultural nationalism.

The cultural nationalist forces (read Hindutva forces) have a project that intends to include all religio-cultural differences within their fold. The trajectory of this inclusive project begins from the time when India began to experience the fractured modernity. A section of the Indian population, spearheaded by the 'modern makers' of India, began, with the help of the resources generated by the colonial and Christian missionary scholarship, to construct a cultural nationalism based on the sanskritic religious traditions. This inchoate nationalism, later on, within the impulse of electoral politics, began to organise itself as politico-cultural movement and political parties. This stream today presents itself with a strong inclusive paradigm of religious pluralism. It forcefully imposes the idea that different religions are to be allowed their spaces only within a core cultural nationalistic vision. This inclusive paradigm goes against the very grain of religious pluralism and it strives to stifle the space for religious dissent.

This inclusivist project of Hindutva forces has also a hidden script. The middle class interest of the Hindutva works also to hide those factors which are uncomfortable for recognition. It is nothing but the actual socio-economic reality of India. That the level of poverty, as per the Tendulkar committee, has increased to 41% against the UN multi-dimensional poverty index, that the Muslims cut a very appalling figure in terms of economic and educational development as per the Sachar committee report, that civil liberties of the Dalits are continued to be denied in the public sphere, etc are uncomfortable facts which the upstart middle class of India does not want to recognise. The projected cultural nationalism does much to help them in hiding this dismal face of India in their global playing field. Thapar points it out clearly, as "[T]he intensification of Hindutva has acted, as intended by its followers, to divert attention from the fact that almost half the population of India is at or below the poverty line and is denied even the most basic rights and amenities."[6] The

5 Romila Thapar, "Secularism and History", p. 1023.

6 Romila Thapar, *Historical Interpretations and the Secularising of Indian Society*. Bangalore: Visthar, 1999, p. 27

hidden script is not merely to hide the uncomfortable facts from the public gaze, but in a very typical Indian fashion, it is also a vigorous attempt at maintaining the hegemony of the sanskritic tradition over the multiple religious traditions, and contributing to the maintenance of the social hierarchy associated with it.

One finds a convergence between the market-led cultural homogenisation and the cultural nationalism which seeks to steamroll myriad forms of culture into one cultural framework. The logic of the market is to make every culture and even religion to play to the tune of the profit-making market, and try to marginalise and destroy that culture which does not become market-friendly. Similar is the dynamics with which the forces of cultural nationalism are functioning in our country today. 'Do not tolerate radical differences, much less radical dissents in culture and religion' is the mantra being chanted both by market and cultural nationalist forces. What does it mean to speak of religious pluralism in this context? Religious pluralism, which contributes to empowering peace, would preserve a radical religious dissent, which would stand apart prophetically, without falling victim to the forces of the market as well as the hegemonic cultural nationalist forces.

## 5. Concluding Thoughts: Avenues for Empowering Peace

Religious dissent and diversity are, phenomenologically speaking, unique forms of religious experiences which contribute to maintain a healthy pluralism and peace. They are manifest in contexts which are characterised by creative agency of the subaltern people in a dialectical relationship to their experience of social subordination and hegemony. They emerge at the meeting point of an agonising emptiness and a creative will to respond to this experience of emptiness; it is an agonistic moment wherein an acute sense of emptiness, socially imposed, is responded with a creative urge for self-construction and selfhood. This agonistically creative moment articulates itself symbolically in the form of religious traditions. This symbolic articulation is simultaneously the way in which subaltern people experience transcendence and hope in their lives.

This agonistic experience takes place in a dialectics of dissent and ascent. It is a dissent to the dominating other, and an ascent to the dominated self; it is an acute moment of experiencing distinction and identity, in an on-going process of negotiation with the other. This negotiation takes place within a deeper experience of the divine dialectics of transcendence and immanence, a spiritual experience which transcends the historical experience of domination, even while affirming and assuring a new emancipatory identity to the dominated. When this experience gets articulated symbolically, it presents itself as a healthy alternative, which transforms agonistically the antagonism generated in the social suffering of the subaltern people into an empowering alternative. Herein religion occurs in its positive potentialities, as creative and emancipatory experiences of life. It is the occurrence of such moments of religious experience that has intimated and continues to mediate an experience of substantive and empowering peace in the society.

It implies that we create space for dissent in our society. This task of 'creating space' is not a passive toleration of the other, but an active and agonistic negotiation with the other which opens a rupture for the religious dissent to burst forth. Such moments inform the life and traditions of subaltern people and they ensure substantive peace in our society.

## Bibliography


Ahmad, Aijaz. 2005. "The Making of India" *Social Scientist*, vol. 33, nos. 11-12, Nov-Dec.

Das, Veena et al. 1999. *Tradition, Pluralism and identity*. SAGE.

Eck, Diana L. 1999. "The Imagined Landscape: Patterns in the Construction of Hindu Sacred Geography." in Das, Veena et al. 1999. *Tradition, Pluralism and identity*. SAGE, pp. 23-46.

Gottschalk, Peter. 2001. *Beyond Hindu and Muslim – Multiple Identity in Narratives from Village India*. OUP.

Mauffe, Chantel. 2007. "Religion, Liberal Democracy and Citizenship." Vries, Hent de and Lawrence E. Sullivan (eds). 2007. *Political Theologies – Public Religions in a Post-secular World*. New Delhi: Social Science Press and Orient Longman.

Menon, Dilip. 2004. *Blindness of Insight – Why Communalism in India is about Caste?*. Navayana.

Rajkumar, Peniel Jesudason Rufus. 2010. "The Diversity and Dialectics of Dalit Dissent and Implications for a Dalit Theology of Liberation." in Sathianathan Clarke et al. *Dalit Theology in the Twenty-first Century – Discordant Voices, Discerning Pathways,* OUP, pp. 55-77.

Thapar, Romila. 2007. "Is Secularism Alien to Indian Civilization?" in Srinivasan, T.N. (ed). 2007. *The Future of Secularism*. OUP.

_______ 2004. "Secularism and History", in Romila Thapar, *Cultural Pasts – Essays in Early Indian History*. OUP.

_______ 1999. *Historical Interpretations and the Secularising of Indian Society*. Bangalore: Visthar.

19

# Epistemic Injustice and Indian Social System: A Strategic Epistemic Harm Done to the 'Other'

**M.X. Gnanadhas Joseph Raj**
*Research Scholar, University of Innsbruck, Austria*

**Abstract:** This article identifies and analyses the varieties of epistemic injustice, which are prevalent all over the world especially in the arena of gender and race. This article deals not on distributive injustice of any epistemic good, rather it deals with injustice, which is, as Miranda Fricker identifies, "distinctively epistemic in kind". The social system in India allows now for all the categories of people to attend school, college, or universities. Therefore, the distribution of epistemic goods, like information and education, is very well carried out. Does it, however, really allow certain categories of people to acquire or to provide knowledge or to be intelligible? Epistemic injustice is done to them, as Fricker characterizes it as "a wrong done to someone specifically in their capacity as a knower", because of the prejudicial stereotypes created by people of the first three ritual classes. This article is an attempt to identify and to analyze the epistemic injustice, which is prevalent in the Indian social system so that we can find some solutions for the same without damaging the dignity of the speaker and the knower in any given context.

**Keywords:** Epistemic Injustice, Testimonial Injustice, Hermeneutical Injustice, Identity-prejudicial Credibility Deficit, Hermeneutical Marginalization, Epistemic Isolation.

## Introduction

Humans, as social and interacting beings, engage in epistemic practices of giving information to others and of interpreting their own experience. These epistemic practices are integral to our rationality, identity, agency and dignity. It is evident that, when injustice is done to our epistemic practices, then it may be a source of deep harm (Kidd 2017). The epistemic injustice damages the epistemic life of a person or a group. Where there is oppression, there is resistance to oppression. In the same way, where there is epistemic injustice, there is resistance to epistemic injustice. Analyzing and identifying epistemic injustice done to a person or a group are also forms of resistance to epistemic injustice (Pohlhaus 2017). Many social and virtue epistemologists identified the varieties of epistemic injustice.

India is a subcontinent, having 29 states and 7 union territories including two islands. It celebrates "unity in diversity". Elements of social diversity can include ethnicity, lifestyle, religion, language, tastes, and preferences. It means understanding that each individual is unique, and recognizing our individual differences. Unfortunately, the country also carries a frightening burden for many centuries, which is called *Varnashramadharma* (Duty of the Class) of *Manu Sashthra* (Law of Manu is the most important of *Smritis* or *Dharmasastras*). This *Varna System* was later turned into the social caste system (Ellwood 2007:200-201). It hinders particular classes of people to come up in their lives, especially in their epistemic life. Consequently, it curtails their freedom to acquire or to provide knowledge, because of the prejudicial stereotypes created by people of the first three ritual classes.

In this article, I will discuss elaborately the two kinds of epistemic injustices identified by Miranda Fricker and by some other philosophers such as David Coady, Gaile Pohlhaus Jr., Rabecca Mason, and Alvin Goldman. I will also analyze and identify kinds of epistemic injustice, which are prevalent in India, through the manifestation of some cases in the Indian social system. I will propose a scope of further study on the varieties of epistemic injustice in Indian Context.

## 1. Epistemic Injustice

Miranda Fricker introduced the notion of 'Epistemic Injustice' in her book Epistemic Injustice*: Power & the Ethics of Knowing* (2007). She generally characterizes epistemic injustice as "a wrong done to someone specifically in their capacity as a knower" (Fricker 2007:1). She makes it clear that the epistemic injustice is not "distributive unfairness in the distribution of epistemic goods such as information or education". Instead, it is "distinctively epistemic in kind". She attempts to find the distinctive forms of personal wrong that are both epistemological and forms of injustice. David Coady clearly differentiates the concept of epistemic good of Alvin Goldman from that of Fricker, when he explains it through a critique of Golman's veritistic social epistemology. For Goldman, a single intrinsic epistemic good is "knowledge". Goldman's concern is that knowledge should be distributed justly, if not, then it incurs epistemic injustice (Here knowledge is to be understood as true belief, which requires no further conditions even justification. Coady 2010:102).

Fricker distinguishes two main kinds of epistemic injustice, namely testimonial injustice and hermeneutical injustice. The root cause of both is prejudice. The former is caused by prejudice in the economy of credibility. The latter is caused by structural prejudice in the economy of collective hermeneutical resources. When harm is done to the testimonial and hermeneutical capacities, it is clear that an injustice is caused. The forms of injustice which are intrinsically epistemic, she claims, can only be understood by studying their manifestations in cases that involve epistemic phenomena or knowledge.

## 2. Testimonial Injustice

Testimony is one of the sources of acquiring knowledge. Testimonial injustice need not strictly be in respect of testimonial speech acts, but rather "any speech act whose acceptance depends on its receiving sufficient credibility" (Fricker 2007:60). The Testimony, here Fricker means is "our everyday phenomenology of informal testimonial exchanges, which presents learning something by being told as distinctly *un*-laborious and spontaneous" (Fricker 2007:63). The epistemology of knowledge and belief based on testimony "help to reveal one of the ways in which the human mind is constitutively a social phenomenon, one of the ways in which being the kind of minded being that we are involved participating in interpersonal and social relationships" (McMyler 2011:3). Testimonial injustice is mainly caused by *Identity-Power prejudice* which is related to social identity group (Fricker 2007:27).

## 3. Identity Power

Identity power is one of the kinds of social power in the social world. Power operates actively or passively. Power, as a capacity, exists even if it is not exercised. Power is exercised by social agents on other social agents. A social agent may be a person or a group or an institution. There are agential operations of social power. For example, traffic police have power over a driver who exceeds the speed limit while driving. There are operations of power that are purely structural. For example, there is voting power. It can be exercised by a citizen or not. Any operation of power is dependent upon the context of a functioning social world. For example, student-professor co-ordination is maintained in the context of a university. A professor can exercise her power in grading her students. This co-ordination constitutes the requisite social alignment. Then, social alignment constitutes partly the power relation. Therefore, social power for Fricker is "a practically socially situated capacity to control others' action, where this capacity may be exercised (actively or passively) by particular social agents, or alternatively, it may operate purely structurally" (Fricker 2007:13). According to Fricker, social power in itself is neutral. If we consider social power as 'controlling' then the questions arise who or what is controlling whom, and why?

Social power may require, in some cases, not only practical social co-ordination but also imaginative social co-ordination. An operation of power depends upon shared imaginative conceptions of social identity. Whenever there is an operation of social identity, identity power is at work. Gender is one arena of identity power. Fricker takes gender identity power as an example to explain the notion of identity power, since it is prevalent all over the world. As the social power, so identity power is also exercised actively or passively. When a man is silencing a woman by drawing from the collective conception of femininity as insufficiently rational because it is excessively intuitive, then it is active. When a woman is silenced by a man by the mere fact that she is a woman, then it is passive.

Caste is another arena of identity power. For example, a report was submitted with ample pieces of evidence on 5th May, 2007 by the Prof Thorat committee regarding caste discrimination. This committee was instituted by the Government of India itself. The report brings to light the facts of discrimination against a particular group of people who are not allowed to acquire or to provide knowledge. It explains the nature and horrors of discrimination suffered at every level not only by the students but also by a handful of members of faculties. Still it attracts no attention either on the facts provided or on the recommendations given by the committee. In 2016, on the eve of Independence Day, Pranab Mukherjee, then the President of India, had called the violence against "weaker sections" that militate against the national ethos as "aberrations". He said that an attack on Dalits should be dealt with "firmly". Recently, Mukherjee said in a video conference, "Every time an individual, a child or a woman is brutalized, the soul of India is wounded" and "Violence not only perpetuates physical harm but mental, intellectual and socio-economic destruction as well" (Indian Express, Oct. 23, 2019).

Whether an operation of identity power is active or passive, it depends very directly on imaginative social co-ordination. Identity power typically operates in conjunction with other forms of social power. It often takes a purely structural form. Here the concern is, how the identity power is involved in the sort of discursive exchange in which knowledge can be imparted from speaker to knower (testimonial exchange). Depending on the use of social stereotypes, the knower's assessment of the speaker's credibility changes negatively or positively.

## 4. Identity-Prejudicial Credibility Deficit

According to Fricker, testimonial injustice "occurs when prejudice on the part of the knower leads to the speaker receiving less or more credibility than he or she deserves" (Fricker 2007:154). The prejudice results in the speaker receiving more credibility than one otherwise would have is called *a credibility excess*. When it results in one's receiving less credibility than one otherwise would have is called *credibility deficit* (Fricker 2007:17). In other words, the testimonial injustice is the injustice of receiving a degree of credibility that has been reduced or puffed up by some kind of prejudice. This kind of epistemic injustice consists in an unjust deficit or excess of credibility (Fricker 2017:268). Both equally endanger the function of the knower in testimonial practice. Normally we think that the credibility excess is advantageous, and the credibility deficit is disadvantageous. But it does not seem so in all the cases. For example, it creates unwanted ethical burden when a medical doctor receives credibility excess from a patient. In this case, credibility excess is disadvantageous.

Fricker focuses mainly on the prejudice caused by a credibility deficit. For, though receiving unduly high credibility may cause injustice, it is not the injustice of 'epistemic in kind' but distributive injustice. Credibility is not considered here as a good to be distributed properly. On the contrary, one may fail to capture the distinctive respect in which the speaker is wronged. The idea is to explore testimonial injustice as distinctively epistemic injustice. It means that testimonial injustice is a kind of injustice, in which someone is "wronged specifically in her capacity as a knower" (Fricker 2007:20). This ethical poison leads someone to the ethical poison of testimonial injustice. In the long run, this ethical poison creates prejudice. Then, prejudice causes credibility deficit in some social agents. Fricker picks up some examples of prejudice from history, namely "women are irrational, blacks are intellectually inferior to whites, the working classes are the moral inferiors of the upper classes, Jews are wily," and so on (Fricker 2007:23).

Apart from the above-mentioned prejudices, we have some prejudices particular to India. Sudras, Dalits, and tribal are not meant to give or to acquire knowledge. They are only meant for physical labour to serve the upper classes. They can acquire sufficient working knowledge through the instructions of their fathers. By their very birth, they are not allowed to do any other studies or acquire knowledge. They should not opt to become a priest, or an IAS officer, or politician or a scientist, and so on (as a cow is for milking and a horse for riding). Animals have an instinct to do their respective work. But why should a carpenter's son be a carpenter, a canal worker's son a canal worker and so on? This question remains unanswered.

The testimonial injustice is caused sometimes incidentally or systematically. It is incidental, when, for example, a panel of scientists, having a dogmatic prejudice on a scientific method, rejects the project of a candidate. It is systematic in the cases of gender and of racial prejudices. For example, if a female politician's policy proposal receives a low level of credibility from the electorate owing to gender prejudice, then she has been subjected to a testimonial injustice (Fricker 2017: 268). The knower suffers here because of the prejudice related to social identity. Fricker calls this prejudice as *identity prejudice*. This identity prejudice can be negative or positive. But, Fricker takes up the negative identity prejudice. Therefore, the central case of testimonial injustice is *identity-prejudicial credibility deficit,* since "(T)he speaker sustains such a testimonial injustice if and only if she receives credibility deficit owing to identity prejudice in the knower" (Fricker 2007:28).

## 5. Prejudice and Prejudicial Stereotypes

Fricker emphasizes that prejudice must be taken broadly to include situations in order to understand the kinds of epistemic injustice properly. Fricker claims that prejudices and stereotypes are neutral, partly because they can be benign and sometimes advantageous, and partly because they serve an essential pragmatic cognitive and social role. She also clarifies that a prejudicial stereotype may not cause any injustice in some cases. She calls these types as *innocent error* and *honest mistake*.

*Innocent Error*: The knower may have some negative preconceived opinions of a speaker. She is also aware of some other prejudicial stereotypes about the same speaker. However, she has an open mind to hear the speaker's testimony. After listening to the speaker's testimony, she realizes that the negative opinions and the prejudicial stereotypes that she had earlier on the speaker are false. Here the knower does not fail as a knower. The prejudice does not affect the judgment of the knower on the credibility of the speaker (Fricker 2007:21). For example, a medical doctor is invited to present a paper in a seminar on ethics. A participant has a prejudicial stereotype that all medical doctors have no knowledge of ethics. As a consequence, she wonders why a medical doctor is invited or on what she is going to speak. However, she hears the testimony of the speaker. The medical doctor clarifies some ethical concepts professionally, since she has studied medical ethics. After the testimony of the medical doctor, the knower changes her prejudicial stereotype about medical doctors. Here, testimonial injustice is not done. The knower does not fail as a knower; on the contrary, she acquires knowledge.

*Honest Mistake*: A knower has identity-prejudicial credibility deficit towards a speaker. But the testimony of the speaker is not interrupted by the knower's prejudice. On the contrary, the incapability (shyness, language, fear, anxiety, and complex) of the speaker impedes her from testifying what she knows. In this case, the knower is not culpable (Fricker 2007:33). Thus, it is an honest mistake. For example, in a classroom context, a student is always keeping quiet because of her shyness. A teacher has a prejudice that a student comes from a particular place or belongs to a particular group, is not rational but intuitive. Here, the *identity-prejudicial credibility deficit* of the teacher does not hinder the student to testify the knowledge that she has. However, the shyness of the student impedes her from testifying the knowledge that she has. Though there is a prejudice on the part of the teacher, she is not culpable, since she does not harm the student's testimony.

Therefore, Fricker explains that prejudices "are judgments, which may have a positive or a negative valence, and which display some (typically, epistemically culpable) resistance to counter-evidence owing to some affective investment on the part of the subject" (Fricker 2007:35).

So, we can summarize as follows: In cases of Testimonial Injustice a knower K fails to acquire knowledge or the belief that $p$ because K does not trust the speaker S and gives less credibility to S because of prejudicial stereotypes.

The most obvious case of this would be when the prejudice in question leads a knower to disbelieve what she is told, even though a speaker deserves to be believed. The concern about testimonial injustice arises when a person or a group is subjected to a *negative identity-prejudicial stereotype*. It involves a disparaging association between a social group and one or more attributes. It is also closely connected to an ethically objectionable investment such as disdain for the relevant social group. It has the character of generalizing the attribute to the entire group or a person. Fricker finds three categories of *generalization*, namely universal, very dilute form and something in between (Fricker 2007:31). There is a vast difference among "*all* blacks are liars", "*many* blacks are liars", and "*most* blacks are liars" (Fricker 2007:25). The first type of generalization distorts credibility judgment of a knower completely. In a court, imagine, a jury thinks that all blacks are liars in racial stereotypes of the day. As a result of her negative identity prejudice, she pays no attention to the speaker's testimony. When it comes to the verdict, she goes along with the automatic distrust delivered by the prejudices. On the contrary, there is at least a remote possibility to hear a speaker's testimony in the second and third types of generalization.

Therefore, a negative identity-prejudicial stereotype is: "a widely held disparaging association between a social group and one or more attributes, where this association embodies a generalization that displays some (typically, epistemically culpable) resistance to counter-evidence owing to an ethically bad affective investment" (Fricker 2007:35). Such is the sort of prejudice that is at work in systematic testimonial injustice.

## 6. The Epistemic Harm

There is of course a purely epistemic harm done "when prejudicial stereotypes distort credibility judgments: knowledge that would be passed on to a knower is not received" (Fricker 2007:43). Basically, prejudice causes direct and indirect obstacles to truth. It is direct when a prejudice causes a knower 'to miss out on a particular truth'. It is indirect when a prejudice creates 'blockages in the circulation of critical ideas'. Sometimes a prejudice can prevent speakers from successfully putting knowledge into a public domain. In all cases testimonial injustice is incurred.

The harm that concerns us here is not the epistemic harm incurred by the error or to the epistemic system. It is neither any implied damage done to the foundations of the polity and its institutions. Rather, the immediate wrong that the knower does to the speaker who is on the receiving end of a testimonial injustice.

Fricker deals with two aspects of harm, namely primary and secondary. The former is intrinsic and the latter is extrinsic in its nature. It is intrinsic because, basically the subject is wronged in her or his capacity as knower, wronged in a capacity essential to human value by insulting, undermining or preventing to provide one's capacity as giver of knowledge which makes a deep wound in the speaker. The latter aspect is further divided into two broad categories namely *practical* and *epistemic*. An example for practical is that a person losing a promotion or an award because of the identity prejudicial credibility deficit in context of a job in an industry or in a factory or in a university. Another example for an epistemic harm is that a person loses hope and confidence in the epistemic life. These primary and secondary harms can cause "we now have a portrait of an injustice that shows it to be capable of running both deep and wide in a person's psychology and practical life" (Fricker 2007:58). Here the testimonial injustice is not only persistent but also systematic. It presents a face of oppression.

## 7. Hermeneutical Injustice

In every society, there exist collective social understandings. The powerful have an unfair advantage in structuring collective social understandings. If anyone has money power or muscle power or mind power, then she or he may have the tendency to influence the process by which social meanings are generated. As we have mentioned earlier the hermeneutical injustice is caused by structural prejudice in the economy of collective hermeneutical resources. This structural prejudice blocks a socially powerless agent from being intelligible. A powerless agent could not be understood by others when that agent interprets her or his own social experiences. Since the social power has skewed shared hermeneutical resources towards the powerful agents they tend to have appropriate understandings of their social experiences. On the contrary, the powerless agent has ill-fitting meanings to draw on in the effort to render them intelligible. We have already discussed the formation of social identity. The identity power controls who can or cannot participate in the pooling of social knowledge. Identity power is any operation of power that depends on shared imaginative conceptions of social identity. Those conceptions are alive in the collective social imagination that govern, for instance, "what it is or means to be a woman or a man, or what it is or means to be gay or straight, young or old, and so on" (Fricker 2007:14). There are attempts made to resist against hermeneutical injustice, especially in gender and racial context. Turning back the pages of history, we can say that women were collectively able to overcome extant routine social interpretive habits to some extent. For example, a woman after giving birth to a child understands female depression after maternity through participating in a group discussion. We can sense two grounds, which cause a woman not to protest against gender identity prejudice. One is a general lack of frankness about the harassment and another is a structural inequality of power. In some of the cases related to sexual harassment, some women decided that they also have to speak-out in order to break the silence about this (Fricker 2007:150). A question is unanswered here. Why is the epistemic wrong suffered only by her and not also by the harasser? Fricker argues "for the lack of proper understanding of women's experience of sexual harassment was a collective disadvantage more or less shared by all" (Fricker 2007:151). Here, harasser and harassee are cognitively handicapped alike by the hermeneutical lacuna. In order to find out the relevant hermeneutical lacuna we need to focus on the background social conditions. There we can find the collective social meanings. For example, the position of women is one of the unequal hermeneutical participations.

It is very hard to detect unequal hermeneutical participation, since the existing meaning veils the real meaning of hermeneutical resources. When there is unequal hermeneutical participation with respect to some significant areas of social experience, members of the disadvantaged group are hermeneutically marginalized. Hermeneutical marginalization is always a form of powerlessness, whether structural or one-off (incidental but not systematic). There is also another possibility that a person might be marginalized in one area and have fuller participation in another area. For example, a person can be intelligible at her working place and not in her neighborhood or in her family. The complexity of social identity also matters a lot in this connection. Hermeneutical marginalization need not be the result of identity power or plain material power, but it often will be. This kind of hermeneutical marginalization renders the collective hermeneutical resource structurally prejudiced. A hermeneutically powerful group may interpret the social experience of the powerless agent negatively and create biases. These biases make the collective hermeneutical resources as discriminatory. Consequently it affects the social identity of the powerless. This leads to identity prejudice. Fricker calls it structural identity prejudice. Thus, hermeneutical injustice is "the injustice of having some significant area of one's social experience obscured from collective understanding owing to a structural identity prejudice in the collective hermeneutical resource" (Fricker 2007:155). Fricker argues that when an individual's ability to render her experiences communicatively intelligible can be constrained, then "the subject suffers from one or another sort of prejudice against them *qua* social type" (Fricker 2007:155).

Imagine, for example, the distinctive social experience of a physically challenged person is understood by her or him, by her or his family and friends, and also by some other social groups to which she or he belongs. However, she or he may not be intelligible to members of other groups, such as her or his employer or her or his neighbor. "Such a person is frustrated in her or his attempts to render her or his experiences intelligible to those significant others. When this happens, her or his communicative frustration exemplifies hermeneutical injustice" (Fricker 2017: 268).

Another way in which hermeneutical injustice can arise, is through what Ian James Kidd calls *epistemic isolation*: situations where a person or group lacks the knowledge of, or means of access to, particular information (Kidd 2017:183-184). For example, when sudden the electricity is cut in a particular area so that no one can come to know about any mass protest against the injustice done against farmers, millworkers, etc.; or blocking websites or outlawing certain literature; or especially attempting to change the word 'secularism' in the preamble of the constitution of India; or directing the entire media to telecast the live showing of some events while simultaneously doing some injustice.

Gaile Pohlhaus Jr. highlights through the lens of the racial contract the degree to which the knowers are intersubjectively constituted. He argues that the feminist philosophers identify how social contract theories eclipse the degree to which nurturing relations are necessary. The feminist philosophers also identify the struggles of those who raise up the knowers (oppressed) and teach them how to know, that they are oppressed, through which knowers become real knowers. Through this lens, epistemic injustice falls into two broad categories: First, exclusions that keep epistemic agents isolated from one another without warrant and, second, fractures in epistemic trust (Pohlhaus 2017:18-19). For example, many Christian missionaries were attacked and were killed because they disclosed the knowledge about the rights and the privileges of the oppressed. Where there are serious and systematic breakdowns in trust, epistemic injustice still prevails. In the case of Christian missionaries, the trust of the oppressed towards missionaries is broken by generating a false message about conversion. In some cases, not only mistrust is created but also self-trust is distorted (epistemic harm as mentioned by Fricker).

## Conclusion

It may be noted that the varieties of epistemic injustice can be further identified in educational system, health care, castism, media, journalism, multicultural situation, multi-linguistic situation, multi-religious context, (post)colonial literature, etc.

Each of the above mentioned and yet to be identified examples of epistemic injustice leads us to different ways of categorizing and understanding varieties of epistemic injustice. It is very evident that when we pay attention to the different aspects of epistemic life we can bring varieties of epistemic injustice into the light. We also should keep in mind that in the process of identifying and analyzing the epistemic injustice, whether it is in the form of epistemic violence or epistemic oppression, we should not fuel the issues and thereby aggravate more problems for the oppressed. Kristie Dotson warns that "when addressing and identifying forms of epistemic oppression one needs to endeavor not to perpetuate epistemic oppression" (Dotson 2012: 24). We will provide a proper analysis of epistemic injustice without claiming the superiority over the finding of one's own list of epistemic injustice and without devaluing or skipping the history of resistance to the epistemic oppressions. It will help us to delve deeply into the matter and to find solutions for the same without damaging the dignity of the speaker and the knower in any given context.

## Bibliography

Coady, David. 'Two Concepts of Epistemic Injustice', *Episteme*, 7 (2010): 101-113.

Dotson, K. "A Cautionary Tale: On Limiting Epistemic Oppression," *Frontiers: A Journal of Women Studies*, 33(1) (2012): 24–47.

Ellwood, Robert S., and Gregory D. Alles, (2007) "Hinduism" in *The Encyclopedia of World Religions* (Revised Edition), DWJ Books LLC: New York, 199-203.

Fricker, Miranda (2007). *Epistemic injustice: power and the ethics of knowing*. Oxford. Oxford University Press.

Fricker, Miranda and Katharine Jenkins (2017) "Epistemic Injustice, Ignorance, and Trans Experiences" in Ann Garry, Serene J. Khader, and Alison Stone eds., *The Routledge Companion to Feminist Philosophy* (NY: Routledge) 268-278.

Fricker, Miranda. 'Replies to Alcoff, Goldberg, and Hookway', *Episteme* 7 (2010): 164–178, especially pp.174f.

Hookway, Christopher. 'Some varieties of epistemic injustice', *Episteme* 7 (2010): 151–163.

Kidd, Ian James & Havi Carel, "Epistemic Injustice and Illness", *Journal of Applied Philosophy.* 34 /2 (2017): 172-190.

Mason, Rebecca 'Two Kinds of Unknowing', *Hypatia* , 26/ 2, (2011): 294-307.

McMyler, Benjamin (2011). *Testimony, Trust, and Authority*. New York, Oxford University Press.

Pohlhaus Jr., Gaile (2017), "Varieties of Epistemic Injustice", in Kidd, Ian James, José Medina, and Gaile Pohlhaus Jr. (eds.), *The Routledge Handbook of Epistemic Injustice*. NewYork: Routledge, 13-26.

*Prof Thorat Committee Report on Caste Discrimination in AIIMS,* New Delhi (2007).

20

# "Temple and Image are a Scandal:" Stories as Condition for Meaningful Lives

**Paul Thelakat**

*Chief Editor, Light of Truth, Ernakulam*

**Abstract:** We may distinguish between two different modes of representation: verbal and non-verbal languages. Among the non-verbal are those languages without words: songs, tears, and laughter. What is revealed on the borderline between the non-verbal and the verbal, where the word is devoid of semantic content and becomes pure sound? These languages begin where words leave of and their purpose is not to close but to open. They are the rising up of the void. Therefore, at times they overflow and sweep us of in the irresistible multitude of their waves; therefore, at times they cost a man his wits, or even his life. Only pre-languages can bear witness to this void, a dangerous realm that reverberates with horror and death. At the same time, however, "every creation of the spirit which lacks an echo of one of these three languages is not really alive"[3]. There are important authors and mystical thinkers who demonstrate various ways of transforming theological tropes and transcendental concepts into the aesthetic realm—poetic and musical. In "absolute music", a symphony, for example, gives listeners emotional insight into and access to divine spheres by letting them experience what cannot be described. Being linked to the "absolute", music, art, literature and rituals become part essential part of religion. Music has been given shape to the divine Name.

Religious language in turn is a form of poetic discourse. In it the human imagination is at work, creating new forms of response to God's actions upon us. The truth claims of religious texts are more like those of the poet than of the historian or the scientist. Jesus is the Parable of God. Heavenly is imprisoned in the earthly, the opposition of heaven and world is reconciled in the incarnation. Can an adequate realization of the spiritual in the sensuous be achieved without tension? Life gives language to the Holy but tongue can only stammer. In Ephesus of St. Paul's time, "temple and image are a scandal."

**Keywords:** Scandal, Image, Religious language, Poetic discourse, Modes of representation, Name of God, Aesthetics, Living through stories

## 1. The Violence of Idol-Breaking

"Now when the Lord spoke to Moses in Egypt, he said to him, "I am the Lord. Tell Pharaoh king of Egypt everything I tell you." But Moses said to the Lord, "Since I speak with faltering lips, why would Pharaoh listen to me?" His tongue is not flexible. Thought is easy; speech laborious. Then the Lord said to Moses, "See, I have made you like God to Pharaoh, and your brother Aaron will be your prophet. You are to say everything I command you, and your brother Aaron is to tell Pharaoh to let the Israelites go out of his country" (Exodus 6:28-&: 3). Aaron will be enlightened; he shall be your mouth! From him will your own voice then issue, as from you come my voice! But when the people saw that Moses was so long in coming down from the mountain, they gathered around Aaron and said, "Come, make us gods who will go before us. As for this fellow Moses who brought us up out of Egypt, we don't know what has happened to him." Aaron answered them, "Take off the gold earrings that your wives, your sons and your daughters are wearing, and bring them to me." So all the people took off their earrings and brought them to Aaron. He took what they handed him and made it into an idol cast in the shape of a calf, fashioning it with a tool. Then they said, "These are your gods, Israel, who brought you up out of Egypt" (Exodus 32: 1-3).

"Moses turned and went down the mountain with the two tablets of the covenant law in his hands. They were inscribed on both sides, front and back. The tablets were the work of God; the writing was the writing of God, engraved on the tablets"(Ex.32:15-16).The ecstatic dance and singing around the golden calf infuriates Moses, he ground it to powder, scattered it on the water and made the Israelites drink it. He ordered the Levites to kill and in one day about three thousand of the people died.

Arnold Schoenberg (1874–1951), an Austrian Jewish composer, converted to Protestantism, before returning to Judaism in the 1930s composed his Opera *Moses und Aron.* He wrote the Confession of the Jew: "It is our thinking of the one, eternal, God who is invisible, who forbids imitation, who forbids to make a picture and all these things, which you perhaps have realized when you read my *Moses und Aron* ...The miracle is, to me, that all these people who might have forgotten, for years, that they are Jews, suddenly facing death, remember who they are"[1]

Aaron asks Moses in Schoenberg's opera, "Can you Worship what you dare not even conceive?" Moses retorts "Dare not? Not conceived because unseen, can never be measured, everlasting, eternal, because ever present, and almighty. The one God is almighty." The distinction between the concrete image (Aaron) and the abstract idea (Moses) is conveyed through the use of different musical styles. Moses' words serve as the motto of the whole opera: "Only one, infinite, thou omnipresent one, unperceived and inconceivable God."[2] God is characterized as the one and only, which emphasizes the revolutionary aspect of monotheism relative to the polytheistic religions. Other characteristics are the infinity of God, his omnipresence and finally the inability to conceive and perceive him.

We may distinguish between two different modes of representation: verbal and non-verbal languages. Among the non-verbal are those languages without words: songs, tears, and laughter. What is revealed on the borderline between the non-verbal and the verbal, where the word is devoid of semantic content and becomes pure sound? These languages begin where words leave of and their purpose is not to close but to open. They are the rising up of the void. Therefore, at times they overflow and sweep us of in the irresistible multitude of their waves; therefore, at times they cost a man his wits, or even his life. Only pre-languages can bear witness to this void, a dangerous realm that reverberates with horror and death. At the same time, however, "every creation of the spirit which lacks an echo of one of these three languages is not really alive"[3]. There are important authors and mystical thinkers who demonstrate various ways of transforming theological tropes and transcendental concepts into the aesthetic realm—poetic and musical. In "absolute music", a symphony, for example, gives listeners emotional insight into and access to divine spheres by letting them experience what cannot be described. Being linked to the "absolute", music, art, literature and rituals become part essential part of religion. Music has been given shape to the divine Name.

Here, there lies the danger of music, as conveyed, for instance, through the singing of the mythological sirens. An act of violence to which the listener must surrender, for the soul is incapable of resisting its sensual temptations, music also embodies a powerful threat: elevation and surrender become two sides of the same coin. This danger is inherent in all forms of art and expression. The formless truth of Moses can become violence of dictatorship. The expressions of Aaron can degenerate to paganism of idolatry and irresponsible ecstasy.

## 2. He Shall be Your Mouth

Where Moses accuses Aaron of enslaving the people with images while it is Aaron who is standing, before them and before us. To take the prohibition of graven images to its extreme—at least in the way Moses does—is to become one of the world's great taskmasters. So Aaron asks Moses, "What are the tablets in your hands but idols?" In that bitter anger he threw the tablets, breaking them to pieces at the foot of the mountain. Later Moses was commanded to cut two stone tablets like the first ones in which God "wrote the words that were on the first tablets" (Ex.34:1-2). This indicates not a radical questioning that, in the case of Moses and Aron, can be seen to break into the claims of the Absolute's unrepresentability.

We are now in a position to say why Aaron builds the idol. His message explains why he becomes master of ceremonies at the orgy, fanning its flames until Moses can witness it to break the idols. And the message is not merely that we cannot do without images, a fact that Aaron takes for granted and on which he builds. Moses sees himself as liberating the people from lies, as he has liberated them from Egypt; Aaron, in the calf, points to the perils of liberation, to the fact—to continue the lesson—-that the desire to rid ourselves of idols is equivalent in experience to the ultimate idolatry. Aaron suggests it, but Moses does not hear. In breaking the tablets, he has come as close as possible to the "nothing" that is the modern ambition to create, a nothing that is nevertheless not nothing, since it is a representation of nothing, but he is not comfortable in this position; he rushes too fast to deconstruct; he cannot live with the fact that "the image is constantly reborn"; he will thus destroy and destroy again.

Religion can never break its link with art, literature and music. These are venues of man's value creation. The language any religion employs is poetic. The poetic experience, the musical experience, and indeed the experience of the work of art embodies strife and calls attention. This poetic, musical, artistic experience is thus a transformation not of the world, but man, and thus of the world. "In music sounds resound; in poems vocables, material of the said, no longer yield before what they evoke, but sing with their evocative powers and their diverse ways to evoke, their etymologies."[4] "Music, feelings of happiness, mythology, faces worn by time, certain twilights and certain places, want to tell us something, or they told us something that we should not have missed, or they are about to tell us something; this imminence of a revelation that is not produced is, perhaps, 'the aesthetic event'."[5] To undergo this experience is to re-attune to the origin of being, and this transformation is a musical one. As man comes to embody the song whose instrumental properties withdraw during use like the hammer, poetry becomes the 'pointer' toward a musicality which is in constant withdrawal. The poetic (musical) experience with language reveals a nexus in which sound, organization and signification meet in the place of man. As man is both the common origin and the point of convergence for these ontic manifestations, the experience of this point intrinsically implicates a systemic abstraction which in turn 'calls' the implementation of a technique into play. "The function of art is expression"[6]. Art, however, expresses itself in different ways, speaks in different languages, and employs different modes of expression. "An artist—even a painter, even a musician—tells. He writes of the ineffable." [7]

## 3. Original Sin of Art

Adorno describes beauty as the "original sin"[8] of art; it is that which makes art a "permanent protest against morality." [9]. By opposing beauty to the living and to morality, and by characterizing it as a source of violence and of guilt, Adorno closely approximates Levinas's indictment of beauty in "Reality and its Shadow." Levinas, by comparison, treats the beautiful work as "essentially disengaged" [10] and "a dimension of evasion."[11] According to Levinas's view, fundamentally opposes engagement and the demands of responsible action; when experiencing art, one feels "as though everything really can end in songs."[12]

"The artist has given the statue a lifeless life, a derisory life which is not master of itself, a caricature of life."[13] The artwork imprisons its characters, locks them in, thereby substituting an immobile plasticity for a living history. During Hitler's regime, Adorno reminds us, the beautiful was exploited in the service of the most barbaric ends. "The more torture went on in the basement," Adorno writes, "the more insistently they made sure that the roof rested on columns."[14] Despite employing very different terms, Levinas recognizes a similar problem with aesthetic enjoyment and binds pleasure in beauty to a feeling of guilt and shame: "There are times when one can be ashamed of it, as of feasting during a plague."[15] "If in modern artworks cruelty raises its head undisguised, it confirms the truth that in the face of the overwhelming force of reality art can no longer rely on its a priori ability to transform the dreadful into form. Cruelty is an element of art's critical reflection on itself; art despairs over the claim to power that it fulfils in being reconciled."[16] Adorno explains: "His poetry is permeated by the shame of art in the face of suffering that escapes both experience and sublimation. Poems want to speak of the most extreme horror through silence. Their truth content itself becomes negative. They imitate a language beneath the helpless language of human beings, indeed beneath all organic language: It is that of the dead speaking of stones and stars."[17]

Aaron's final answer in Opera is as follows: "Image of your idea / they are one, as all is that emerges from it . . . / Yet the knowing ones surely will I ever again discover it" words at ease with a multitude of images, a variety of representations. "It is just as much a property of language to sound and ring and vibrate, to hover and to tremble, as it is for the spoken words of language to carry a meaning. But our experience of this property is still exceedingly clumsy, because the metaphysical-technological explanation gets everywhere in the way, and keeps us from considering the matter properly."[18] Any person, whether musician, philosopher, or both, who embarks upon the formidable task of writing about music will encounter the inherent impossibility of writing about it and encountering it at the same time. We are always just before it, or just after it. We chase its traces and spectres. Perhaps the problem confounds itself in the case of generative music. We seek here to textually explore an experience, and furthermore wish to transcend the subjective nature of this from within. We thus arrive in a space which is perhaps best describable through analogy.

## 4. Aesthetics Inseparable from Ethics

Art is substituting the object with its image, not its concept. Art kills reality producing its images. Image in itself is not art, but art utilises the image. Conceptless, substanceless relation is pure sensation, and thus the whole world can be perceived aesthetically. To Levinas, an image is not transparent like symbols and signs are, but it is connected to its object in resemblance. Intention does not reach an object within a picture. Yet image is not an independent entity, as reality is the cause of the image. "A being is that which is, that which reveals itself in its truth, and, at the same time, it resembles itself, is its own image."[19] As this cause, reality includes its own shadow, its image. "To say that an image is an idol is to affirm that every image is in the last analysis plastic, and that every artwork is in the end a statue—a stoppage of time, or rather its delay behind itself…the artwork does not succeed, is bad, when it does not have that aspiration for life which moved Pygmalion. But it is only an aspiration…a caricature of life."[20]

Art is not representation but materialisation. Art immerses us in an idolatry of pleasure. The idea of idolatry is returned into below. A critic is useful for breaking the public's passivity in receiving the art, as the critic does not contemplate in silence. The critic integrates the artwork and the artist to the real world and calls out the artist's irresponsibility. Art is not completely useless nor unethical as it may act as a useful tool for philosophy and thought. Levinas uses his religiously imbued language to describe what art is not: it is not part of creation, nor is it revelation. God can be represented in language, because unlike art, language can render absence, - - it does not allow any blurring of the representation and the thing represented, the signifier and the signified; while one cannot take words for things, one can be deceived into confusing pictures of things with the things themselves."[21] "One might think that art is limited to rendering what is finite and present. Aniconic art seeks to render the infinite and to put presence in question."[22]

Instead of sacred, there is holiness. Things and spaces, the holy Land, may be holy but people are holier.[23] Derrida describes a conversation he had with Levinas, and how Levinas told him, "You know, one often speaks of ethics to describe what I do, but what really interests me in the end is not ethics, not ethics alone, but the holy, the holiness of the holy."[24] Ethics is a religious experience. To turn this logic backwards, religious experience is ethics. Levinas himself tells an example of this "I am reminded of a visit I once made, as part of a religious ceremony, to the church of Saint Augustine in Paris. It was at the beginning of the war, and my ears were still burning from the 'new morality' phraseology that for six years had been circulating in the press and in books. There, in a little corner of the church, I found myself placed beside a picture representing Hannah bringing Samuel to the Temple. I can still recall the feeling of momentarily returning to something human, to the very possibility of speaking and being heard, which seized me at that moment"[25]. Bible cannot be read literally as science text. The scriptures play their part in the "naming of God" reframed as "the logic of equivalence" and the "logic of abundance". They act as mutual correctives, although Ricoeur does not offer an equivalent to *phronesis* (ethical sense) in the economy of the gift. According to Levinas, aesthetics is inseparable from ethics, which requires us to enhance the tools of artistic judgment within the ethical discussion. In one of the few articles which he dedicated to the subject of art, Levinas expresses the concern that art leaves man alone with himself. "There is something wicked and egoist and cowardly in artistic enjoyment"[26]. He writes, leaving us to contend with the question of whether artistic creation is indeed an egoistic action. Is the act of artistic creation a re-entry into "the cave"?

## 5. Bible Prohibits the Bible

Prohibition of graven images should be taken further than it was originally intended, meaning that it should be turned on the Bible itself. We are surely aware that this is a parasitical position, not only because the critique of the Bible relies on the existence of the Bible, but because, the prohibition is already taken this far in the biblical text. The Bible shows us the prohibition of the Bible. The sacred fragment given to us can be grasped as long as, at the same time as we resist the enthusiasm that would marry us to the image, we also resist the countervailing enthusiasm that would have us smash the image the moment it arises. "Language which has become Holy Scriptures, and which maintains its prophetic essence—probably language par excellence—the Word of God that is already audible or still muffled in the heart of every act of speech, is not solely a matter of the engagement of speaking beings in the fabric of the world and History, where they are concerned with themselves—that is to say, with their perseverance in being."[27] Biblical text demonstrate how the various modes of discourse disclose "styles" of faith. "The 'confession of faith' that is expressed in the biblical documents is inseparable from the forms of discourse, by which I mean the narrative structure."[28]

These various forms include prophecy, parable, or hymns, and each constitutes a "style" of confession of faith that creates a "polyphonic language." Sometimes God appears "as the hero of the saving act, sometimes as wrathful and compassionate, sometimes as the one to whom one can speak in a relation of I-Thou type, or sometimes as the one whom I meet only in a cosmic order that ignores me."[29] Because these forms for discourse do not establish a unified style of faith, one's "theological significations" will be "correlatives of forms of disclosure."[30] Religious discourse adopts the same creative dimensions active in poetic texts. The text solicits the readers, allowing a possible world to manifest and challenge him or her to project their own possibilities within this world.[31].

Jesus Christ himself, exegesis and exegete of Scripture, is manifested as logos in opening the understanding of the Scriptures. But secondly, and already within the New Testament, a correspondence is effected between "the interpretation of the Book and the interpretation of life." Levinas concludes: "It is one thing to answer a question, in the sense of solving a problem that is posed; it is quite another to respond to a call…"[32.] So we begin to stutter, to murmur, or to mumble; then the entire language reaches the limit that sketches the outside and confronts silence. "The artist refuses to be only an artist," Levinas asserts, "…because he needs to interpret his myths himself."[33]

## 6. Lifting the Veil: Epiphany

The Temple of Isis expressed a sublime thought: "I am all that is and that was and that shall be, no mortal has lifted my veil". Is revelation of art higher than all wisdom and philosophy? How to gaze "the starry heaven above and moral law within" of Kant and attain the epiphany? "What we call sublime in nature outside us… becomes interesting," writes Kant, "only because we present it as a might of the mind to rise above certain obstacles of sensibility by means of moral principles."[34] For Kant, sublime experiences make "intuitable for us the superiority of the rational vocation of our cognitive powers over the greatest power of sensibility."[35] By directing the subject toward those aspects of humanity that go beyond the level of the merely sensible, in other words, toward the dictates of practical reason, Kant describes the experience of the sublime as raising the "soul's fortitude,"[36] and keeping "the humanity in our person from being degraded."[37]

Marion uses the metaphor 'screen' to convey the sense of what he thinks is the mediating nature and the conditionality of the Heideggerian Being. The only way to escape idolatry altogether, Marion proposes, is to break the 'screen', to think God without any condition, not even the condition of Being. The task is twofold, corresponding to the double meaning of Being, that is, Being understood in the tradition of metaphysics, and Being in the Heideggerian non-metaphysical sense. The first step of the task is to free God from metaphysical Being, which is precisely the theological significance he finds in Heidegger's criticism of onto-theology. Beyond the idolatry proper to metaphysics, another idolatry, the second idolatry, proper to the thought of Being as such. By idolatry Marion means any regionalization of the divine. The solution to this second idolatry, therefore, is to dissolve or break the 'screen', to abandon the anteriority of Being, to de-centre Being, or as Marion puts it, 'to think God without any condition, not even that of Being' and 'to think God without pretending to inscribe or describe him as a being.'[38.] Obviously 'screen' is used by Marion as a condition in its negative sense. It makes God visible to human eyes, but at the same time closes our access to His invisibility and reduces His infinity.

*Book of Questions* by Edmond Jabes states: 'All faces are His; this is why He has no face'?" Richard Kearney said in an interview "This is one of the dangers of monotheism, and arguably, principally of Christian and Islamic monotheism, both of which appeal to one special face, Jesus and Mohommad. It is particularly an issue for Christianity. Yahweh has no face, but all faces are Yahweh's face." "Now as I understand it, this refusal by Jesus as *prosopon*, to be reduced to a singular face/person, is the refusal of possession. It is the refusal to be made into an idol or property of any particular church. This refusal by Jesus proclaims that, as much as we may try, we cannot latch on to him as the unique *Noli me tangere*. He must go, so that the spirit may come. Now what is the spirit? Well the spirit for me is other faces." "Then the face of Jesus becomes—potentially at least—every face. That is very different from saying there is only one Jesus."[39]

"The first I see of the other is his face, not as one among other visible aspects of him, but that which I see first. It's to his face that my plight is addressed, his face that holds my attentive gaze. The face is visible. But the face has a peculiar status in the visible: it is at the same time expressive. It does not remain trapped in a plastic form. It overflows its expressions. It is irreducible to a grasp, a predatory perception."[40]

"For the presence before a face, my orientation toward the Other, can lose the avidity proper to the gaze only by turning into generosity, incapable of approaching the other with empty hands". "The face of the Other at each moment destroys and overflows the plastic image it leaves me, the existing to my own measure and to the measure of its ideatum the adequate idea ... To approach the Other in conversation is to welcome his expression, in which at each instance he overflows the idea a thought would carry away from it. It is therefore to receive from the Other beyond the capacity of the I, which means exactly: to have the idea of infinity. But this also means: to be taught. The relation with the Other, or Conversation, is a non-allergic relation, an ethical relation; but inasmuch as it is welcomed this conversation is a teaching [*enseignement*]. Teaching is not reducibile to maieutics; it comes from the exterior and brings me more than I contain. In its non-violent transitivity the very epiphany of the face is produced."[41] I can never fully grasp the Other's own unique relationship with language. It involves 'no more than the most elementary of gestures: "from self to Other"; not a mode of thinking or observation, no inner intention but responsibility –a going toward, a being for the Other, responding to his or her turning, his or her face –giving.'[42]

## 7. We Live in Stories, Rituals and Metaphors

The storyteller 'tells stories of the gods, but his yarn is spun from the ungodly, human heart'.[43] Every story is also an idol we have to retell and deconstruct. Unnarrated life is not worth living. A society is inspired by narrative imagination rather than doctrinal sermons or abstract treatises. We live in stories, in metaphors and idols. By imitating 'the exemplary acts of mythic deities and heroes', writes Mircea Eliade, 'man detaches himself from profane time and magically re-enters the Great Time, the Sacred Time.'[45] We belong to history before telling stories or writing histories. The historicity proper to story-telling and history-writing is encompassed within the reality of history. 'For whomever [the story] becomes the truth it does so ... by hammering out a shape of life patterned after its own shape ... the shape of the story being mirrored in the shape of our life is the condition of its being meaningful for us.'[46]

Liturgical acts are showings of faith and hope and love. Silence of love is transformed into a new showing, a showing that involves words. Action and multivalent words mutually shape and correct each other, dancing in constant tension so that neither becomes stagnant or faded in the Christian imagination. Faith, hope, and love cannot be said; they are not subject to proof or scientific investigation. They are altogether different from anything that could be subject to empirical inquiry. Language and the acts into which language is woven form the language game, which is dynamic; it changes and acquires variations as often as people grow and progress through the ages. For the Christian theologian it may serve as a reminder of the *via negativa*, that in everything we affirm about God (and ourselves in relation to God), we also deny. Ricoeur understands these stories as a species of religious language. Religious language in turn is a form of poetic discourse. In it the human imagination is at work, creating new forms of response to God's actions upon us. On Ricoeur's view, the truth claims of religious texts are more like those of the poet than of the historian or the scientist. Jesus is the Parable of God. Heavenly is imprisoned in the earthly, the opposition of heaven and world is reconciled in the incarnation. Can an adequate realization of the spiritual in the sensuous be achieved without tension? Life gives language to the Holy but tongue can only stammer. Hölderlin writes in a later version of the elegy "*Brot und Wein*": "But in Ephesus temple and image are a scandal."[47]

## End Notes

1. Arnold Schoenberg, *Self-Portrait: A Collection of Articles, Program Notes and Letters by the Composer about his Own Works*, edited by Nuria Schoenberg Nono. Pacific Palisades: BelmontMusic Publishers, 1988, p.105.
2. A. Schoenberg, *Moses und Aron. Opera*, edited by Christian Martin Schmidt. London: Ernst Eulenburg Ltd, 1984, p.8.
3. Haim Nahman Bialik, *Revealment and Concealment in Language. In Revealment and Concealment in Language*, translated by Jacob Sloan. Jerusalem: Ibis Editions, 2000, p. 26.
4. E. Levinas, *Otherwise than being,* trans. A. Lingis, Pittsburgh: Duquesne University Press, 2011, p.40.
5. Jorge Luis Borges, *Labyrinths: Selected Stories and Other Writings,* Donald A. Yates and James E. Irby (eds.),New York: New Directions, 1962, p. 168.
6. E. Levinas, *Reality and its shadow*, In S. Hand (Ed.), 1989, *The Levinas Reader*, Oxford: Basil Blackwell, 1989, p.130.
7. *Ibid.*, p. 130.
8. Adorno, *Aesthetic Theory*, eds. Gretel Adorno and Rolf Tiedemann, Minneapolis: University of Minnesota Press, 1997, p.65, 405.
9. *Ibid.* p. 260.
10. Levinas, "Reality and its Shadow," p. 12.
11. *Ibid.*
12. *Ibid.*
13. Levinas, "Reality and its Shadow," p. 9. I.
14. Adorno, *Aesthetic Theory*, p. 64.
15. Levinas, "Reality and its Shadow," p.12.
16. Adorno, *Aesthetic Theory*, pp. 65. 277.
17. Adorno, *Aesthetic Theory*, p. 405.
18. Martin Heidegger, *On the Way To Language*, Peter D. Hertz (trans.), San Francisco: Harper and Row, 1982, p .98.
19. Levinas, The Levinas Reader, p.135.
20. *Ibid.,* p. 138
21. Anthony Julius, *Idolizing pictures: idolatry, iconoclasm and Jewish* art, London: Thames & Hudson, 2001, pp.35-36.
22. *Ibid.*, pp. 41-42.
23. Levinas, *The Levinas Reader*, p297.
24. Jacques Derrida, Jacques. *Adieu: To Emmanuel Levinas*. Trans. Pascale-Anne Brault and Michael Naas. Stanford: Stanford University Press, 1999. p.4.
25. E. Levinas, *Difficult Freedom: Essays on Judaism*, Baltimore: The Johns Hopkins University Press,1997, p.12.
26. Levinas, *The Levinas Reader*, p. 142),
27. E. Levinas, *Beyond the verse: Talmudic readings and lectures*, trans. G. D. Mole, Bloomington, IN: Indiana University Press, 1994, p.xii

28. P. Ricoeur, "Philosophy and Religious Language," *Figuring the Sacred: Religion, Narrative, and Imagination*, ed., Mark I. Wallace, Minneapolis: Augsberg Fortress, 1995), p. 39.
29. *Ibid.*
30. *Ibid.*
31. Paul Ricoeur, "Naming God," *Figuring the Sacred*, ed., Mark I. Wallace, (Minneapolis: Augsberg Fortress, 1995), 221. Reprinted with permission from Union Theological Seminary Quarterly Review 34 (1979) pp. 215-27.
32. P. Ricoeur, *Oneself as Another* ,transl. Kathleen Blamey, Chicago, London, The University of Chicago Press, 1992, pp. 24-25.
33. Oneself as Another, pp. 24-25
34. I. Kant, Immanuel, *Critique of the Power of Judgment*. New York: Cambridge University Press, 2000, p.271.
35. *Ibid.*, p. 257.
36. *Ibid.*, p. 261.
37. *Ibid.*, p. 262.
38. Jean-Luc Marion, God Without Being, translated by Thomas Carlson (Chicago and London: The University of Chicago Press, 1991, p. 72
39. An Interview with Richard Kearney "Facing God" Liam Kavanagh, *Journal of Philosophy and Scripture* Vol. 1 Issue 2, page 17 Volume 1, Issue 2 | Spring 2004.
40. A. Gerin, Report made in application of article 145 of the ruling in the name of the mission of information on the practice of the wearing of the full-face veil in the national territory]. Paris: Assemblée Nationale. Retrieved from http://www.assemblee-nationale.fr/13/rap info/i2262.asp#P4357_1361685Kenaan, H. (2013). 2010, p. 117.
41. E. Levinas, *Totality and infinity: An essay on exteriority*, transl. A. Lingis, Pittsburgh, PA:Duquesne University Press, 1969, pp.50-51.
42. *Ibid.*, p. 136.
43. Arundhati Roy, *The God of Small Things*, London, Flamingo, 1997, pp. 229–30.
44. H. Frei, *The identity of Jesus Christ: The hermeneutical bases of dogmatic theology*, Philadelphia: Fortress, 1975, pp. 156,170-171.
45. Mircea Eliade, Myths, Dreams, and Mysteries, New York: Harper & Row Publishers, 1967, p.23.
46. P. Ricoeur , *Time and Narrative*, vol. 1, transl. K. McLaughlin & D. Pellauer, University of Chicago Press,. Chicago, IL.1983, p.10.
47. Jochen Schmidt, *Hölderlins geschichtsphilosophische Hymnen:* 'Friedensfeier'— 'Der'Einzige'— 'Patmos', Darmstadt: Wissenschaftliche "Buchgesellschaft, 1990, p. 135. See Acts 19:26,27.

# 21

# Specters of Hinduism: A Postmodern Appraisal of Contemporary Hindutva

**Victor Ferrao**
*Dean of Studies, Rachol Seminary, Goa*

**Abstract**: Drawing inspiration from Derrida's specters of Marx the author tries to understand the Specters of Hindutva. This work may uncloak the innocent child-like fancies of its adherents, as well as open the hauntologies of those who fear it the most. These fantasies and hauntologies afflict both the sheep and the wolves in our society. It may open to us the wretchedness of the real condition of our society. Somehow everyone vampirizes each other while an elite takes hold of the resources of our country. In many ways Hindutva is a political economy and is a form of capitalism in capital letters. Its capitalist's foundations remain ghostly and have to be expelled to fully emancipate India. The spectral reality of Hindutva has to be unmasked for the love of India and its people. Hindutva is a hiding place of virulent political economy but doubles up as the opium of the masses. Under its reign its shadowy political economy is growing by leaps and bound making the people of India poorer by the day.

With Hindutva, cannibalising Hinduism has opened an empty place and closed it at the same time. There is no room for Hinduism in Hindutva. Hindutva has occupied its space. Therefore, it is our task to continue the work of mourning. The dead live in its other and beyond, concludes the author.

**Keywords**: Hinduism, Hindutva, Spectrality, Hauntology, Paradox of fidelity, Mourning Hinduism

Are we mourning the imminent death of Hinduism[1] and its space being usurped by Hindutva[2]? Has the afterlife of Hinduism already arrived? Derrida opens the issue of mourning in his book specters of Marx around Hamlet and the ghost of Hamlets father and provides the occasion to imagine what would be the ghost of Marx would be like. Following the lead of Derrida, we ask similar question. In the wake of Hindutva what would be the ghost of Hinduism look like? Does Hindutva echo Hamlet's cry: 'the time is out of joint.'[3] We not just mourning the loss of Hinduism but also it place being taken over by Hindutva. Hindutva is a ideology that has invaded a vibrant religion. But Hinduism and Hindutva have become ghostly to the extent we take one for the other. Somehow Hinduism has dissolved into Hindutva. Marx wanted to do away with every shade of ideology. He may have lost as Marxism itself may have become an ideology. Communist in today's societies cannot do without ideology. Derrida seems to bring this home when he makes a distinction between the tradition of Marxism and the spirit of Marxism.[4] While choosing Marx's dislike for ideology and marking some distance with Marxism, if this is possible here I attempt to draw an inspiration from Derrida's specters of Marx[5] to understand the Specters of Hindutva. This work may uncloak the innocent child-like fancies of its adherents, as well as open the hauntologies[6] of those who fear it the most. These fantasies and hauntologies afflict both the sheep and the wolves in our society. It may open to us the wretchedness of the real condition of our society. Somehow everyone vampirizes each other while an elite takes hold of the resources of our country. In many ways Hindutva is a political economy and is a form of capitalism in capital letters. Its capitalist's foundations remain ghostly and have to be expelled to fully emancipate India. The spectral reality of Hindutva has to be unmasked for the love of India and its people. Hindutva is a hiding place of virulent political economy but doubles up as the opium of the masses. Under its reign its shadowy political economy is growing by leaps and bound making the people of India poorer by the day.

---

1 To get an insight into how Hindutva is afflicting and assimilating Hinduism, see Shashi Tharoor, *Why I am a Hindu* (New Delhi: Aleph Book Comapany, 2018).

2 For a detail understanding of Hindutva, see Joytirmaya Sharma, *Hindutva*: *Exploring the Idea of Hinduism* (London: HarperCollins, 2015).

3 Jacques Derrida, *Specters of Marx*: *The State of Debt, the Work of Morning and The New International*, trans. Peggy Kamuf (London: Rutledge 1994), 1.

4 Michael Sprinker, *Ghostly Demarcations*: *a Symposium Jacques Derrida's Specters of Marx* (London: verso 2008), 2.

5 Jacques Derrida, *Specters of Marx.*

6 Hauntology is a term coined by Derrida to articulate a tensive relation with time and carry eschatological and teleological relation with space. See Jacques Derrida, *Specters of Marxs*: *The State of Debt, the Work of Morning and The New International*, 10.

## 1. Understanding Spectrality of Hindutva

Spectrality has become a common experience. It has become everyday experience of the masses. The world is on a fast lane on the wings of mobile, flexible, computerised and immaterial. The labour has become spectral.[7] Spectrality has become a common experience as clear as a sun. We seem to being having nothing but the Lila and Maya of 'the dancing Shiva'. Spectrality is something like a real illusion that is surrounding us. There is nothing outside this real illusion. We are all immersed into it like fish in the ocean. It transforms our place as well as time. Our world is fully meshed into it. Hindutva binds us to this world of spectrality in a powerful way. It has become our illusive Indra's net.[8] The hegemonic order of Hindutva has transformed our experience.

## 2. Hindutva and Space

Hindutva belongs to the space in the past and space in the future. It remains always displaced in the present. It makes us feel unlocate-able and root-less in the present and we have to belong to the present by belonging to the golden place of the past and by longing for the future making of the ancient glorious place. But this future glorious place has no place for the minorities, the tribals and the dalits. Thus, the space in which we live has become ghostly. It really does not exist unless it links itself to the past and longs for its future fuller coming. India has become spectral. We seem to be living in a 'no man's land' of the past and the coming future. We cannot inherit the land that we live as it is. We cannot pass it to our future generations as it is. It has to be transformed by the sacred glories of the ancient past. All this has put our mother land India into the spectral world. There is no ontology for India for now. It has become a haunted place. It is afflicted by a hauntology.[9] It has to devolve into its ancient past. That is the road ahead. Somehow a descent into the old has become our ascent into the future. The hermeneutic of the past colours our present and envisions our future. We have become spectral beings lost in an Alice's world of spectrality. We are provisionally in a place for now, we are all longing for the future to become our present. We Indians are living as an Eschaton. But it alludes us and leads as to the Armageddon hopping for its fuller coming. The land in the present can be stained with innocent blood. The stains do not stick to it as its future is coming on the drops of the blood of the innocent.

---

7 Antonio Negri, "The Specter's Smile' in Michael Sprinker," *Ghostly Demarcations*, 8-9.

8 It is a metaphor used to denote Buddhists concepts like sunyata, dependent origination. See https://en.wikipedia.org/wiki/Indra%27s_net accessed on 28/08/2019.

9 Hauntology is opposite of logocentrism. Logocentrism is present-centrism. Hauntology is about absent-centrism. It is about absence and the manner in which it afflicts us. See Tom Lewis, "The Politics of 'hauntology' in Derrida's Specters of Marxs' in Michael Sprinker, *Ghostly Demarcations*, 141.

## 3. Hindutva and Time

Hindutva has a seismic relation with time. Being a promissory note, it is always dislocated with time. It remains unstable and oriented to a promised future. This means it does not have its feet on the ground in the present. But its dis-locatedness is hidden by the aura of the promised future. We all experience a disjointed time. Without such a dis-adjusted time, no change is possible. Hindutva successfully conveys us that time is out of joint. This is where deconstruction of Derrida is 'in joint' or profoundly relevant. Deconstruction has the power to hook it to the hermeneutics of the present and future. India may not need a regressive pause that offers us an anxious present and ancient future. We need emancipation from hauntology of Hindutva. It's psychic as well as temporal relation to time is enslaving. The end of time or the end of history has already arrived for us . We belong to the future. The future has merged with our now. We are experiencing a spectral time. There is a kind of emptying out of meaning of time. There is only a singular past and a singular future destiny. Our future is an appointment with the past. The present has no meaning. It is empty and has to be filled with the golden past and the coming future. All ontology has died. What is left is only a hauntology.[10] We are haunted by the past as well as by the coming future. Hindutva has closed our experience of time. It is an impoverishment. Open experience of time is our deepest longing. This longing is also killed by Hindutva for now.

## 4. Hindutva and the Sources of Self

Hindutva forces us to embrace the specters of the past. We cannot belong to the present without linking the past as the source of our self. Hindutva makes us hospitable to past while it remains hostile to the present. It makes us open to the heroes and spirits of the past and commit us to incarnate them into the present and the coming future. The self is not stable unless it roots into past to belong to the coming future. Self without belonging to its glorious past is fragile and anxious. Even by drawing upon the ancient sources of self, it does not get out of anxiety. It enters a new commitment to reach its fuller manifestation in the coming future. Hence, the self lives angst. Hence, present becomes performative[11] of the past, a desire to draw upon the source of self from the past and inaugurate the future of the past in the coming future. As displaced in this manner, the self becomes extremely political. The self thinks

10 Derrida Asserts the need to replace ontology with its near homonym, hauntology. It represents instability of the real as well as the fear and panic provoked by an a recognition of a flawed nature of the state of affairs. See Tom Lewis, "The Politics of 'hauntology' in Derrida's Specters of Marx' in Michael Sprinker, *Ghostly Demarcations*, 140.

11 Judith Butler has expanded the concept of performative first developed in philosophy of language by J. L. Austin to gender and identity. See https://faculty.georgetown.edu/irvinem/theory/Salih-Butler-Performativity-Chapter_3.pdf accessed on 28th/08/2019.

that it is born to but right that time that is out of joint. This means politics becomes the medium of making of one's self. In many ways the self does not belong to the discourse of being of beings or ontology. It is always in the making. But this making is closed upon itself. It is not an open self making. It is unfolding into a past and is never at home in the present. It belongs to a new discourse of being that Derrida calls hauntology.[12] It lives always into a perfomative mode, the mode of becoming a Hindutvavadin. It is a jubilatory, maniac and triumphant self seeks its plenitude in the realisation of Hindutva in the form of Hindu Rashtra.

## 5. Understanding Hauntolgy of Hindutva

Hindutva promises a promised land that is at once close to it as well as disassociated with it. It is haunted in its very being. It has become a messianic hauntology/ eschatology and as such it exists as being out of joint and becomes an imperative to bring it up to date. It converts the promise of the Promised Land into a land of promises. The land that we call India has promises to keep. It is haunted by these promises to bring about the coming future. The Coming of this promised future is almost like the coming of God into the world. It is tomorrow, point where history will come to an end and we will live happy ever after. This means our hauntology is also our ecstasy.

## 6. Ghostly Logic and Hindutva

Hindutva follows the logic of the ghost. It is a ghostly logic because it exceeds the binary or dialectical thought. Dialectical thinking is platonic in character. It marks the difference and opposes effectivity or actuality (present, empirical, living or not) and ideality (regulating or absolute non-presence).[13] The present of being a Hindu is opposed with an ideality of being a sanskari Hindu. Thus, logic of Hindutva disqualifies every Hindu and renders them not Hindu enough until they become a sanskari Hindu. This logic does not leave other Indians too. Every Indians are opposed with the ideality of brahminical Hinduism and have to live on the rope that is tied between being what they actually are and what they ought to be, an Indian Hindu. This logic de-historicizes every Indian. No Indian is Indian enough in their actual present. They have to change in order to belong to India. We have truly stepped into a new India that is often announced by the PM Modi . It is as if we have reached the end of History in India. We cannot be Indians in other ways. The future is closed to a singularity. We are already heading towards a Hindu singularity. This is why we may say that every Indian is haunted today. He/she has to change to belong to a new

12 Jacques Derrida, *Specters of Marxs: The State of Debt, the Work of Morning and The New International*, 63.

13 Jacques Derrida, *Specters of Marxs: The State of Debt, the Work of Morning and The New International*, 78.

India. We seem to have fully surrendered our thinking to what Derrida calls ghostly logic. It is this logic that keeps us all out of joint. This is why most Indians seem to imagine only a closed future that is going to converge on a Hindu singularity. In some way this logic summons Indians into being and has become their hauntology. As long as we Indians will never match the idealism of Hindutva, It will always be a hauntology. The future will never occur. We will forever be longing and blindly waiting for its coming. This is the danger of the logic of teleological singularities. It just tends to a point and closes all other possible futures.

## 7. Hindutva and Recognition

Hindutva is a drive and a struggle for recognition.[14] It seeks recognition from everyone. It begins with a self recognition of a flawed and incomplete nature of being an Indian. The plural India and ways of being Indians have to die. They cannot be recognized as genuinely Indian. They are only fake and counterfeit. Once pushed into the dungeons of impurity, these other Indians can then be killed or done away with. Thus, to recognize oneself as a sanskari Hindutva, often a good Hindu is led to kill an innocent Muslim. The persistent need of recognition awakened by Hindutva is a hauntology. It is blood thirsty and may not rest till it smells blood. This is why its other also haunts it. It is haunted by what it excludes, combats and represses. It is in this context that we can read the desire of Hindutva. It seems to be a megalothymia or maniacal excessive need for recognition. It is fulfilled in the very act of heralding as well as being in a self-performative mode. It is a sense of inheritance that keeps the fire in its belly. This inheritance is never given. It has a force of an imperative. It is in its self-performative mode that the self becomes an heir of the promises of Hindutva. It is this task that the self recognizes itself and is recognized by others as having a filial relation to Hindutva. The legacy of Hindutva is inherited in the performative mode. It always remains in a mode of being in an unfinished business.

## 8. Hindutva a Messianic Eschatology

There is a theological dimension of Hindutva. The utopian aspect of Hindutva translates into messianism. It is laden with an arche-teleology. It belongs to the 'already and not yet' zone. It does this through an undetectable time movement from one locus and temporality to another temporality that is deemed as perfect and endowed with plenitude. This movement puts our experience of the lived present into an imbalance and nurtures angst. The temporalities evoked by it remain in the past, past perfect and the future anterior time mode. They

14 Recognition has moral foundations. See https://cristianorodriguesdotcom.files.wordpre accessed on 29/08/2019.

remain in a tensive relation of co-presence. In a way, hauntology fragments the totalizing elements of ontology and theology. It creates a hope, an expectation of the return of the sacred presences like the glorious past of Hindutva as well as cherished absences, like the absence of the demonised minorities. It entangles the present experience of time and fuses it with a mingled anticipation of a glorious future. It has a retroactive sense of the victory of the eschaton.[15] The spectral future lingers in the present and energizes it to move towards its fuller flowering. In some way the absent future draws the present to move to the actualization of it. It is a kind of metaphysics of absence. The absent presence that haunts us is cast in the mode of messianism of Hindutva. This means the Hindutva future returns to haunt the present and produce us as subjects. The eschatological future that gravitates our subjectivation has performative-mystical moorings. In psychoanalytic terms, it presents the present as castrated and wounded and leads us to think that it can only be healed to the perfomative enactment of a Hindutva self.

## 9. Mourning the Fate of Hinduism

Since the publication of 'mourning and melancholia' of Sigmund Freud,[16] there has been a lot academic attention to mourning. It has gone through different re-definitions. In the contest of this study, we continue with Derrida's re-definition of the ethical configuration of the work of mourning. Like Derrida,[17] Judith Butler[18] has elaborated the ethical task of mourning and melancholia. I see mourning as booth an ethical and a political critique. Hindutva is fast assimilating/ cannibalising Hinduism. Hinduism has entered the spectral zone of being in-between. It does not seem to have it's own being. It lives into Hindutva. The being of Hinduism is dead. It is dislocated into Hindutva. It is living a borrowed life. Hence, our ethical task becomes urgent. The ethical task of mourning the death of Hinduism is a way of making space for its return.

## 10. Posthumous Infidelity

If we do not take up the task of mourning we will fail Hinduism forever. We shall commit what might be called posthumous infidelity. Hinduism is fast dying into Hindutva. Maybe it is already dead and we do not know about it. We

15 We can trace similar parallel in Derrida with regarding to the death of Marxism. See Aijaz Amhad, "reconciling Derrida: Specters of Marx and the Deconstructive Politics" in Michael Sprinker, *Ghostly Demarcations*, 92 95.

16 Sigmund Freud, *on History of Psycho-Analytic Movement: Papers on Metaspsychology and Other Works*, Trans., James Strachey (London: The Hogath Press) 243-258.

17 See Derrida, *The work of Mourning*, trans., Pascal Anne-Brault and Michael Naas (Chicago: Chicago University Press, 2001).

18 https://journals.sagepub.com/doi/abs/10.1177/0090591712444841?journalCode=ptxa accessed on 29/08/2019.

have come to reckon with its fate. We have to take stock, recount and account for our silence or active role in the fading away of Hinduism into Hindutva. Therefore, we cannot risk being impolitical. We have to take up the humble but noble task of mourning of the death of Hinduism.[19] We have to participate in the codes and rites of mourning. Our silence, our abdication or refusal to mourn the death that is occurring right in front of our eyes is unforgivable. This mourning is always with responsibility to the other. It is not narcissistic or ego-logical. It is what we have to first come to reckon within the task of mourning. This will allow the dead to speak in us. Hinduism can no longer speak through Hindutva. It is only in us that it can speak. This mourning is letting it speak again. This letting it trace it's voice in us is a way of preparing the space for its return. Mourning thus takes us on the road of mimetism without becoming the other. To let Hinduism speak through us, we have to somehow be like it. It is in this way of mourning that lets the dead become alive in us and between us, we can let Hinduism resists its assimilation into Hindutva. We have the task of keeping Hinduism alive in us and beyond us without becoming posthumously unfaithful to it. Hinduism is in us and in you. Let us all strive to let it live.

## 11. Facing the Unbearable Paradox of Fidelity

Hinduism no longer lives in itself. Hindutva has replaced it. It is now living in it's other. It is living in the minoritized, the demonised other of Hindutva. This is an unbearable paradox of fidelity. What faces us as a source of our responsibility cannot be fully interiorized. Hinduism is living outside itself in its other. We cannot fully become Hindu. But its other is not a Hindu. This is cost of mourning its death. It is in its other and beyond it too. It is not same as its other. It is characterized by infinite alterity. Death has entrusted it to us but it has also marked a distance between us. We cannot see Hinduism dying. But not mourning its dying is not a choice. It is an ethical imperative. To a Hindu of today there is no difference between Hindutva and Hinduism. He/she does not know that Hinduism is dead. To him/her the rise of Hindutva is the rise of Hinduism. He/she cannot see how Hinduism is dying in him or her. This is why our ethical responsibility to undertake the task of mourning and embrace the unbearable paradox of fidelity is urgent and inevitable. It is a moral imperative to allow Hinduism to talk in and through its minor other. It is a challenge to die to self so that Hinduism can rise in its other. This is the call to live the excess of fidelity. It is an invitation to take our inter-being seriously. The dead is always within us and outside us. Dead is inter-living. Hinduism that is dying in Hindutva can rise in the condition of inter-living.

---

19 We imitate Derrida's Mourning of his friends as well as mourning of the demise of Marxism. See Derrida, *The work of Mourning.* Sean Gaston, *The Impossible Mourning of Jacques Derrida* (New York: Continuum, 2006).

## 12. Fidelity to the Other and the Self

We die in the death of the beloved. The other teaches us ethics, responsibility and assists us to develop our own relationship to our death. We can only experience death through the death of the other. Dying Hinduism in Hindutva has many lessons to all minorities in our country. With death of the other, something unique and singular in the world dies. This something unique and singular is irreplaceable. It is in the death of the other we learn to survive. This is why the death of the other is not just a eu-thanatology. It not about learning to die well but it is also about learning to survive and live. This is why in the death of the Hinduism, not only does the other learn to die honourably, but also it teaches us how to survive and live. This is why the work of mourning Hinduism is also a service to oneself. Hence, in this task of mourning, we become faithful to the other as well as oneself. In a way the work of mourning leads us to face the coming future. In many ways those that we mourn for shape us. Maybe this is why Derrida emphatically said, 'I mourn therefore, I am'. [20] We have to mourn the death of Hinduism ethically. We cannot cannibalize it. We have to make room for it beyond ourselves. If we also cannibalize Hinduism there is nothing to choose between us and Hindutva. Hindutva is cannibalizing Hinduism. We cannot eat or incorporate the other. Ethical mourning is a challenge of fidelity to the other and the self.

## Conclusion

With Hindutva, cannibalising Hinduism has opened an empty place and closed it at the same time. There is no room for Hinduism in Hindutva. Hindutva has occupied its space. Therefore, it is our task to continue the work of mourning. The dead live in its other and beyond. This is why Hinduism exists in its others and beyond. It is an ethical task to let it come alive once again. Hence, we have an imperative to save Hinduism from the jaws of Hindutva.

---

20 Derrida J (1995) *Istrice 2: Ick bünn all hier*, trans. Peggy Kamuf, In Weber E (ed) *Points... Interviews, 1974-1994*, (Stanford, CA: Stanford University Press), 321.

# 22

# Satire and Blake: Image, Symbol and Anti-Text

**Suchetana Banerjee, Gayatri Mendanha & Ananya Dutta**
*Symbiosis School for Liberal Arts, Symbiosis International (Deemed University), Pune*

**Abstract:** We live in troubled times, in a country that is evolving into a beast we may no longer be able to recognise. If we are to build a 'Jerusalem' in our county's 'green and pleasant land', we need a visionary prophet to find our way out of chaos to enlightenment in unification with the creator. This paper is an exploration of William Blake's symbolic use of language, the images and symbols used in his poetry, to seek answers to questions of ultimate concern. In particular, it examines the use of satire in the *Songs of Experience* to probe Blake's deliberate subversion of text in lyrical poetry.

**Keywords:** Symbolism, Satire, Poetic Imagination, Traditional Images, Blake as visionary

Martin Heidegger's study of Holderlin's, lyric poetry is to be taken as a metaphor for language's birth, he claims: "Poetry is the naming of the gods. But poetic language can only receive its naming power if the gods bring us to language."[1] Lyric poetry then is both the producer and the produce of the gods. This paper will discuss how the poetry of William Blake (1757 1827) makes and breaks the notion of God, religion, church, and state in a language

1 Heidegger, Martin (1988). "Hölderlin and the Essence of Poetry." *In Existence and Being*. Kampmann.

that according to Heidegger shapes the essence of human beings. Through an analysis of poems from Blake's *Songs of Experience*, this essay will expand on the use of symbols and images through the form of satire in Blake's poetry. Satire is a literary device which criticises and ridicules established power structures and its vices. The doctrine of contraries and of complementarity is Blake's proclamation of the gospel. The string of irony, unrelenting satire and bitterness that mark the *Song of Innocence* and *Song of Experience* align Blake to the tradition in which authors like Erasmus, Fielding, Rabelais and Swift belongs. So powerful is Blake's handling of the weapons of criticism, as Northrop Frye points out "One may wonder... Blake's sense of the grotesque, of broad caricature and ribald parody, was really a minor quality, and good only for an occasional *tour de force*. One may wonder whether satire was not his real medium."[2] Blake's affinity with this tradition is very deep. His use of the metaphor of innocence and experience, though not rare among Romantic poets, is most complex and bold. This metaphor has the relevance to Blake not merely as a literary device but through philosophical naturalism of Locke and the belief that mind is a passive receiver, Hume's denial of the positive existence and his rejection of traditional doctrines and that a relationship exists between the individual mind and its perceptual universe had resulted in a great epistemological shift.[3] Blake, like Wordsworth and Coleridge was influenced by the prophets and the mystical of the *Old Testament*, which asserted the primacy of imagination. Blake believed in mind's power to alter a world of its perception, to affect its own perceptual destruction by recognising its active role. Hence, the extensive use of innocence and experience in Romantic literature. The triumph of Blake's satiric art lies in the fact that he achieves a mixture of intellectual satire and prophecy, and thus, as Harold Bloom points, fuses the classical with the Biblical tradition.[4]

## 1. Blake's Use of Symbols and Metaphors

Blake manipulates traditional images and in the process recasts established images into symbols expressive of his own philosophy. As a result, his work often becomes a kind of critically evaluative anti text which ironically or satirically comments on and subverts past symbolic associations. This process breaks horizons of expectation of the readers as their expectations from the poet is subverted and responses manipulated by his rebellious use of traditions.

2 Northrop Frye, *Fearful Symmetry: A Study of William Blake* (Princeton; Princeton University Press, 1974), p.193.

3 William Crisman, "'Song' and the Bind of Self-Conscious Lyricism in Blake," *ELH*, Vol. 61, No. 3 (Autumn, 1994), pp. 619-633. The Johns Hopkins University Press, stable URL: https://www.jstor.org/stable/2873337.

4 David Erdman and Harold Bloom, ed., *Introduction, Poetry and Prose of William Blake* (New York: Doubleday Anchor, 1965).

Blake uses traditional motifs as thematic gestures but alters or combines them with others so as to surprise the reader into a profound awareness of his own, often subversive in meaning. This blend of satire and symbol, of traditionalism and revolt, is the unrecognised axis on which much of Blake's work moves.

Blake's poems especially are based neither on dramatic action nor lyric effusion, his paintings neither on literal illustration nor private fantasy, but on the unexpected, deliberate juxtaposition and modification of traditional images. Both in his designs and texts, Blake manages to unite diverse, even clashing symbolic elements and to arrange them into coherent, richly suggestive wholes greater than the sum of their disparate parts. Their success of communication depends, in part, on the reader/viewer's ability to recognize the traditional images Blake uses as well as his manipulation of their original values. In the fullest sense, then, Blake's work is "re-visionary", expressing his own startling vision but doing so primarily through the audacious transformation of pre-existing icons taken from widely (and wildly) divergent sources. Blake gives us clusters of symbolic imagery that we must, in a sense, choreograph for ourselves if the seemingly unstructured mass of Blake's bizarre imagery is to take firmer shape as an intricate yet coherent pattern of symbolic relationships.

According to Abrams: "Some symbols are 'conventional' or 'public'; thus 'the Cross', 'the Red, White, and Blue', 'the Good Shepherd' are terms that signify symbolic objects of which the further significance is fixed and traditional in a particular culture. Poets, like all of us, use such conventional symbols; many poets; however, also use 'private' or 'personal symbols', which they develop themselves .... Some poets, however, often use symbols whose significance they mainly generate for themselves, and these set the reader a more difficult problem in interpretation."[5]

William Blake employed a central group of related symbols to form a dominant symbolic pattern – the child, the father, and Christ, representing the states of innocence, experience, and a higher innocence. These major symbols provide the context for all the minor, contributory symbols in the *Songs*. Blake often used symbols to express increasingly subtle and complex intellectual distinctions. However, as his system developed, he found it necessary to emphasize the symbolism with an elaborate mythology, which does not easily explain itself. The problem for readers of Blake's poetry is to maintain a balance between what he is trying to say and what the words commonly convey. The symbolism of the *Songs of Innocence* and the *Songs of Experience* is successful, because Blake is able to maintain this balance.

5 Meyer Howard Abrams, Jack Stillinger, *The Correspondent Breeze: Essays on English Romanticism, Introduction*, Replica Books, 1999. p. 23.

Despite simple rhyming patterns and the images of children, animals and flowers, the *Songs* are argumentative or satirical, and reflect Blake's deeply held political beliefs and spiritual experiences. Blake's vision embraces radical themes like poverty, child labour and abuse, the repressive nature of state and church, as well as right of children to be treated as individuals with their own desires. Many of the poems in *Songs of Experience* respond to counterparts in *Songs of Innocence*. Appearing in *Songs of Experience*, 'The Tyger' is understood as the companion piece of 'The Lamb' in *Songs of Innocence*; both poems ask the same question: where do we come from? In 'The Lamb', an answer is given: God made us – an affirmation of faith. 'The Tyger' only implies the answer by posing the rhetorical question:

'Did he who made the lamb make thee?'[6]

Indeed, one of the most noticeable features of 'The Tyger' is that it takes the form of a series of questions, none of which are answered, but it circles around the reader in just the same way as a tiger stalks its prey. 'The Lamb' posits the process of creation as natural and harmonious, 'The Tyger' stands for something much more ferocious, wild (that which is not natural) and mysterious; the tiger comes from 'the forests of the night' and its eyes burn in 'distant deeps and skies'. Its creation is an act of audacity. The poem has references to different narratives associated with rebellion: to Satan's revolt in *Paradise Lost* ('the stars threw down their spears'), to Prometheus, a favourite of the Romantics ('What the hand dare seize the fire?'), and, perhaps to Icarus ('On what wings dare he aspire?' – though this line might also suggest Milton's Satan). These images and associations have led some critics to read 'The Tyger' as a metaphor for revolution.

Another aspect of Blake's metaphor is, unlike the lamb, who is 'made' by God, the tiger owes its life to a combination of human labour and industrial process. 'And what shoulder and what art, could twist the sinews of thy heart' focuses on human effort, the next stanza conceives of the tiger's creation in terms of industry, using a series of metonyms for the blacksmith's forge: 'hammer', 'chain', 'furnace', 'anvil'. While, like all the Romantics, Blake was repelled by the Industrial Revolution and its objectification of human beings, this stanza has undeniable energy and a fascination with what industry can produce: "What dread grasp, Dare its deadly terrors clasp?" It is interesting to note that both the worker and the tiger are represented by a strange combination of body parts ('shoulder', 'heart', 'sinews', 'hand', 'feet', 'brain').

Characters inhabiting the *Songs of Experience* cling to the earth in attitudes of sorrow as in a 'Poison Tree' lying flat on the ground. In *Songs of Experience* we are frequently involved in monologue or soliloquy: dynamic

6 William Blake, "Tyger" *Songs of Innocence and Experience* (London: Chatto and Windus, 1938): 33.

communication is replaced by thought out statement. In 'Infant Sorrow' we hear the cerebral click of cogs as the child's brain forms its decisions: "I thought best, to sulk upon my mother's breast."[7] The child decides to "sulk" upon the breast of the mother, almost in a manner that allows the child to enjoy what little comfort it has left. It is the counter poem of 'Infant Joy'. The poem suggests that childbirth is not always joyful and happy but can bring sorrow and pain. The response of the child itself may be different from that of the child in 'Infant Joy' when the infant is being brought helpless and naked to the "dangerous world", it expresses a wilful consciousness in the intentionality of 'sulk' and 'leapt' and the knowingness of its allusiveness both Biblical and classical.

## 2. Towards the End of the Golden String

Blake as spiritual, imaginative and artistic visionary sees so naturally a better world and his fight is towards creating that city of God, that 'Jerusalem' on earth. As a social radical he sees the everyday filth of baser materiality which births an imperfect world of cruelty and injustice. In response, he interweaves the social and the spiritual in a tapestry of art and literature that points to freedom. Blake wanted his message to be known. It was almost a duty and a calling to break the "mind-forg'd manacles" and change society through his poetry.[8] His mystical experiences and divine visions are not treasures that he hoards for himself in contemplative solitude, but experiences that he wants to share, for he wants us all to *see*. Thus, In *Jerusalem* Blake reaches out to the reader, inviting them to step into this world.

I give you the end of a golden string;
Only wind it into a ball,
It will lead you in at Heaven's gate,
Built in Jerusalem's wall.

In according agency to the reader, the text and its symbolic meanings are co-created by poet and reader as they journey towards the 'end of a golden string'. In making this journey with Blake, in engaging spiritually and intellectually with the text, the reader will make discoveries that are both the poet's and their own.

In Blake's recognition of the sacred in all, he declared that everything that lives is Holy. According to him, there is no other God, other than the one within us and honouring the God within the other is an act of worship. Thus, "Blake's metaphysics may best be described as a kind of pantheistic

7 William Blake, "Infant Sorrow" *Songs of Innocence and Experience* (London: Chatto and Windus, 1938): 52.

8 William Blake, "London" *Songs of Innocence and Experience* (London: Chatto and Windus, 1938): 55.

idealism".[9] The Creator is in the created, the created exists in the Creator, and thus there is no distinction between the Creator and the Created. Hence, for Blake everyone equally has divine potential and the ability to reflect the divine image, as do all religions that spring from the same source.

While Blake celebrated divinity in all, he harshly attacked the oppressive teachings that were being imposed by false preachers on lamb-like congregations. This corruption is expressed in 'The Human Abstract' where the virtues of delight and the "unifying forces of Mercy, Pity, Peace and Love have become tools of repression – wielded by hypocritical priests and moralists".[10] For Blake the union of the soul with God was of ultimate concern and anything that came in the way of that, leading us away from freedom and imposing earthly bondage was to be fought against. "Blake believed that the only kind of revolution which could succeed was the revolution within the mind."[11] This battle was not of bloodshed and war, but a much more challenging destruction of 'mind forger manacles'. Thus, in the preamble to *The Four Zoas*, he states from the Ephesians, "For we wrestle not against flesh and blood, but against principalities, against powers, against the rulers of the darkness of this world, against spiritual wickedness in high places"

Although, Blake rebelled against the theology of his time, he saw himself as a true Christian, creating his own faith-system. Thus, unlike many radicals of his time, he was not anti-Christian. However, he guarded his personal freedom and through his creative imagination forged a path of his own, through the application of his own mind to his own principles. He stated that "No bird soars too high, if he soars with his own wings"[12]. Thus, he approached received wisdom with a questioning attitude and could not subscribe to systems laid down by others. In his characteristic voice, he stated, "I must Create a System or be enslav'd by another Man's". He encouraged the exercise of the "Divine Arts of the Imagination" so that the people could become "priests, monarchs, and artists in their own homes", rather than submitting to the false image of a God that expected oppressive religious morality. Thus, while he was drawn to religion, he made it bend to his own abstract spirituality, intellectually challenging established beliefs and standard interpretations of scripture, he boldly stated:

---

9 Peter Marshall, "William Blake Revolutionary Romantic" in *Revolutionary Romanticism,* ed Max Blechman (San Francisco: City Light Books, 1999): 42.

10 Timothy Vines, "An Analysis of William Blake's Songs of Innocence and of Experience as a Response to the Collapse of Values" *Cross Sections* I (2005): 118.

11 V. de S. Pinto, "William Blake: The Visionary Man" *Journal of the Royal Society of Arts* 106, No. 5018 (Royal Society for the Encouragement of Arts, Manufactures and Commerce, January, 1958): 88.

12 Peter Marshall, "William Blake Revolutionary Romantic" in *Revolutionary Romanticism,* ed. Max Blechman (San Francisco: City Light Books, 1999): 40.

Both read the Bible day & night
But thou readst black where I read white

Blake's experience of the world, through a visionary gleam, was unique and we can only attempt to understand it. He could see the illusory nature of the material, apparently solid universe through symbolic visions, accessing the purer forms of the eternal world. These distinct visions allowed him to hermeneutically engage in meaning-making, as he sought answers to questions of ultimate concern. They guided his spirit and being out of chaos and complexity to a greater universal spiritual and social destiny. Thus, they were not an escape from reality, but a deeper engagement with it. In offering the world deep original insights into the 'life of things', he is a visionary prophet and as visionary, set apart and marked out for genius, moving beyond the ordinary to greatness. Thus, as depicted in the 'Auguries of Innocence', he was he able:

To see a World in a Grain of Sand
And a Heaven in a Wild Flower,
Hold Infinity in the palm of your hand,
And Eternity in an hour

## 3. A Critique of Abstract Reason

Blake's attack on abstract false reason and its power to govern and destroy all it holds is represented in his mythology, by the tyrant Urizen. "Urizen falls into this world of his own making and attempts to organize it with laws generated in his own psyche".[13] It is this rationality that powers industrialization and colonialism, and constructs an oppressive morality that separates the human being from God. In holding onto the fixed principles, and rejecting imagination and innocence, the 'free thinkers' of his day had allowed themselves to be bounded in slavery. He displayed confident self-assertion and clarity of thought in expressing his own philosophy in direct opposition to the dominant worldview of the time. "Blake rejected the rationalism of Newton, the empiricism of Bacon, and the sensationalism of Locke which presented the external world as matter in motion governed by universal laws" and as a philosophical idealist he believed "that the world is not made of matter but of organized spirit".[14] Thus, Blake "not only questions many fundamental assumptions in moral and political philosophy but threatens the materialist and rationalist premises of Western civilization itself."[15] It is important to

13 Robert N. Essick, "William Blake, Thomas Paine, and Biblical Revolution" *Studies in Romanticism* 30, No. 2 (Boston University, 1991): 200.

14 Peter Marshall, "William Blake Revolutionary Romantic" in *Revolutionary Romanticism,* ed Max Blechman (San Francisco: City Light Books, 1999): 43.

15 *Ibid.*, 41-42.

note however, that Blake was not denouncing reason and the intellect as whole, he specifically challenged the exalting of abstract reason which, in its divorce from the imagination, infects the modern world with its mechanical, reductionist worldview.

## 4. Imagination's Way

"The God in whose name Blake prophesies is Imagination, and it is this God who inspires artists: Jesus and his Apostles and Disciples were all artists."[16] Blake's spiritual and artistic journey are intertwined and it is in fulfilling himself as artist that he reveals himself as Christian. It is through this faculty of the creative imagination, which itself was divine grace, that he pierces the veil to see beyond the surface to what exists eternally and immutably. As poetic genius this faculty is highly developed and it was his imagination that offered him profound insights. "Blake saw his visions in a visionary or pictorial way which was the way of the ancient Hebrew prophets, Isaiah, Ezekiel and the author of the Book of Job".[17] Thus, in the *The Marriage of Heaven and Hell*, Blake imaginatively reconstructs himself as prophet, propounding his own revolutionary beliefs. Blake wages his battle through his imagination, which is a superior to reason and it is through art and poetry, aimed at the reader that the battle is to be won in the reader's head, as he believed that all human beings possessed the ability to see creatively and imaginatively. All Blake wanted us to do was cleanse "the doors of perception" and "everything would appear to man as it is: infinite".

## 5. Power and Priesthood

Blake bore witness to the abject misery of the working classes, especially impoverished children who worked as bonded labourers. In this state of despair, one is cut off from the divine goodness and fullness of a life in God. He confronted the shocking indifference of their exploiters and began to question the myth of a glorious England. Blake painted a bleak picture of 'London' where everywhere he observed, "Marks of weakness, marks of woe".

"Blake believed that the political is the personal, and called for individual rebellion in everyday life even while working for a total transformation of society."[18] However, he lived in times when radicals were hunted down and sentenced. His poetry and imagination was viewed as potentially dangerous,

16 Paul Grimley Kuntz, "William Blake and the Ten Commandments" *Soundings: An Interdisciplinary Journal* 83, No. 2 (Penn State University Press, 2000): 436.

17 V. de S. Pinto, "William Blake: The Visionary Man" *Journal of the Royal Society of Arts* 106, No. 5018 (Royal Society for the Encouragement of Arts, Manufactures and Commerce, January, 1958): 80.

18 Peter Marshall, "William Blake Revolutionary Romantic" in *Revolutionary Romanticism,* ed Max Blechman (San Francisco: City Light Books, 1999): 62.

it was a time, he wrote, when "The Beast [of the State] & the Whore [of the Church] rule without control."[19] However, Blake re-worked language and symbol to continue to create subversive art and poetry. Language is a living, breathing thing, its meanings can change; symbols can be fashioned to hold prophetic messages and calls to freedom. Thus, in the garb of mythology, he attacked and painted visions of a future society, free of the rigid shackles of old. Thus, "his approach is the vigorous action of the iconoclast smashing the idols."[20]

The "priest and king," whose praises are routinely sung in Sunday Church, are central to Blake's criticism of the existing social order, not just in 'The Chimney Sweeper' where the phrase appears, but in several of the poems in *Songs of Experience.* If his criticism of the State is crystalized in the figure of the king, the priest is the embodiment of the evils of the Church. Blake reserves his sharpest words for the ministers of the Church; their appearance, motives and actions all closely scrutinised by his pen. The "black gowns" they are robed in no longer representing their vows of austerity, but something much more sinister.

Significantly, there are no priest figures in the *Songs of Innocence*. The closest we come to an encounter with the men involved in the affairs of the Church is in 'Holy Thursday' where we meet "the aged men wise guardians of the poor," who are unable to soar to the same spiritual heights that the orphans are able to reach.[21] The reference to the "beneficent patrons of charity schools" who rejoice in the spectacle of parading these children through the streets of the city also deploys irony, but it is in the *Songs of Experience* that the attack becomes explicit and relentless.[22]

The satirical tone of the poems in *Songs of Experience* is also evident in Blake's treatment of the priest figures, with irony frequently deployed in these descriptions. Often, the contradiction between appearance and actuality is explored via the juxtaposition of the text and the accompanying visuals. Thus, in 'The Garden of Love' we see a beatific image of a priest in grey kneeling before a grave while the text describes the priests "walking their rounds" as if they were prison guards "binding with briars my joys and desires."[23] This

19 *Ibid*, 57.

20 Paul Grimley Kuntz, "William Blake and the Ten Commandments" *Soundings: An Interdisciplinary Journal* 83, No. 2 (Penn State University Press, 2000): 432-433

21 William Blake, "Holy Thursday" *Songs of Innocence and Experience* (London: Chatto and Windus, 1938): 18.

22 Robert F. Gleckner, "Irony in Blake's "Holy Thursday"" *Modern Language Notes* 71, No. 6 (The Johns Hopkins University Press, 1956): 414.

23 William Blake, "The Garden of Love" *Songs of Innocence and Experience* (London: Chatto and Windus, 1938): 50.

contrast between the serenity of the image and the severity of the imagery of the poem creates different layers within the same text.

Perhaps the most strident attack on the clergy appears in 'The Little Boy Lost' where we bear witness to a scene of extreme cruelty. When a child poses a rational challenge to "our most holy mystery," instead of addressing the boy's query, the priest responds through gratuitous violence and public humiliation.[24] This is the fate of the child at the hands of the priests:

They stripped him to his little shirt,
And bound him in an iron chain,
And burned him in a holy place
Where many had been burned before[25]

While there is certainly hyperbole involved in the extreme torture meted out to the child, but two key points emerge. Firstly, the priests have veered so far off the course of love and kindness at the heart of the Christian gospel that they wouldn't think twice before crushing innocence with brutality. Secondly, this is not an anomaly – the "holy" spot where the immolation occurs is one "Where many had been burned before."[26] This is not the suppression of an individual challenge to the Church's doctrine, but a part of a cycle of violence that the priests partake in emphasized by the confusion of his parents in that final rhetorical question, "Are such thing done on Albion's shore?"[27]

We find a third kind of priest figure in 'The Little Vagabond,' where Blake's speaker reimagines the Church as an Alehouse and tries to prophesize what the substitution would achieve. Blake's rejection of puritanical remonstrations against the consumption of alcohol presents us the vision of a parson who "might preach, and drink, and sing" in this new vision of Church-as-Alehouse.[28] In this imaginary Church, we are shown the first happy priests. Thus, the alteration would not only achieve a happier congregation than the one that currently attends service in a Church that is physically and emotionally cold, but also effect a transformation of the clergy from the "poor parsons with wind like a blown bladder swell" to merrier ones that drink and sing.[29] The visual gag of the present clergy as windbags also sets up a contrast with the alternative situation, where the drunk priests may now truly "preach."

24 William Blake, "A Little Boy Lost" *Songs of Innocence and Experience* (London: Chatto and Windus, 1938): 51.

25 *Ibid.*

26 *Ibid.*

27 *Ibid.*

28 William Blake, "The Little Vagabond" *Songs of Innocence and Experience* (London: Chatto and Windus, 1938): 40.

29 *Ibid.*

Is Blake again resorting to irony when he says that a drunk parson may preach better than the present lot of priests? Or does Blake really believe that a Church with fewer "“Thou shalt not,” writ over the door" would allow its priests and parishes achieve higher levels of spirituality?[30] The *Songs* don't have easy answers to the questions they raise. The figures of the priests, whether real or imagined, are themselves symbolic codes that we can use to investigate the meanings that the poetry has to offer.

Jesus, as liberator and revolutionary, represents freedom from oppressive religious morality as is evident to Blake in Jesus' statement about the Fourth Commandment: The Sabbath was made for man, not man for the Sabbath. Jesus preached the doctrine of love not rules, which for Blake was the essence of Christianity. Thus, "The tablets of the law themselves, placed by the Established Church of England above the altar, are, Blake protests, a golden calf – as are the institutions of state and church, particularly when combined, and as are all in authority."[31]

## Conclusion

We live in troubled time, in a country that is evolving into a beast we may no longer be able to recognise. If we are to build a 'Jerusalem' in our county's 'green and pleasant land', we need a visionary prophet to find our way out of chaos to enlightenment in unification with the creator. We go to Blake because he was able to never let go of the golden thread. Rooted in the experience of the divine he made sense of a complex world, offering songs of love and rebellion, as a way to freedom. Through his songs he raises questions, taking on the form of the Tyger, however he allows the reader to struggle for understanding and does not offer answers on a golden platter. The world is not always bright and beautiful, and as we feel the world shift under our feet, abstract reason cannot provide lasting meanings.

What is remarkable about Blake, is inspite of having to witness deep seated misery, injustice and hypocrisy, he did not despair and instead, "offered an alternative system of values and believed that it was possible to create a new society which would be both free and fulfilling."[32] The Bard, as spiritual essence, guides individuals towards paradise, calling to fallen man to walk again in Eden, in union with God.[33]While he depicts the "dark satanic

30 William Blake, "The Garden of Love" *Songs of Innocence and Experience* (London: Chatto and Windus, 1938): 50.

31 Paul Grimley Kuntz, "William Blake and the Ten Commandments" *Soundings: An Interdisciplinary Journal* 83, No. 2 (Penn State University Press, 2000): 433.

32 Peter Marshall, "William Blake Revolutionary Romantic" in *Revolutionary Romanticism,* ed Max Blechman (San Francisco: City Light Books, 1999): 54.

33 Timothy Vines, "An Analysis of William Blake's Songs of Innocence and of Experience as a Response to the Collapse of Values" *Cross Sections* I (2005): 117.

mills" in 'London', he also offers us visions of Jerusalem and while he terrifies us with the despotic Urizen, he offers us Albion who dances naked, free of oppression. These spiritual and social Jerusalems have to be built both within every human being and without in all lands, in an attitude of respect for individuality and diversity, in universal brotherhood.

23

# *The Satanic Verses:* Ruminations on Freedom of Speech and Expression

**Sacaria Joseph SJ**
*St. Xavier's College, Kolkata*

**Abstract:** Even three decades after the publication of Salman Rushdie's satiric novel, *The Satanic Verses*, the controversies regarding the novel has not come to an end. While many praise novel for its literary merits, the Muslim community across the world regards it as offensive, blasphemous and as an anti-Islamic propaganda. They see the novel as a direct attack on and a conspiracy against Islam by the use of distortion and scorn, which have the effect of alienating Muslims from their faith.

This article analyses Rushdie's satire on the sacred in Islam, namely, the controversial 'satanic verses' that permitted intercessory prayers to three Meccan deities, the Muhammad event, the concept of divine revelation and the birth of Islam. Rushdie's narrative progresses by re-telling and re-imaging matters of history and faith by fantasising and fabulating them. The result is that Rushdie's novel becomes a catalogue of multiple layers of conflict; it sets the long-cherished Islamic beliefs against the imaginative and satiric re-interpretation of those beliefs.

Rushdie's handling of the sacrosanct issues of the Islamic faith does not seem to resonate with the spirit of the 'freedom of speech and expression.' In the process, Rushdie overstretches the limits of the freedom of expression. Rushdie's satire in *The Satanic Verses* on what is sacrosanct in Islam does not seem to contribute to any form of constructive or reformative thinking in society; it has only resulted in division and disturbance. Therefore, the article argues that it not only goes against the intent and spirit of satiric literature, but also tends to become spiteful in nature.

**Keywords:** Freedom of speech, Fatwa, Monotheism, Polytheism, Revelation, Sacrosanct in religion, Re-imaging, Satire.

## Introduction

Deliberating on the concept of the 'freedom of speech and expression,' article 19 of the 'Universal Declaration of Human Rights' states that "everyone has the right to freedom of opinion and expression; this right includes freedom to hold opinions without interference and to seek, receive and impart information and ideas through any media and regardless of frontiers" (Morsink, 333). However, one must remember that one's freedom is never absolute; it is to be exercised with utmost respect to other people's right to the same. 'Freedom of opinion and expression' does not embrace the freedom to offend anyone in any way based on religion, faith, gender, race, social class, appearance, nationality, sexual orientation and so on. With the publication of Salman Rushdie's, novel, *The Satanic Verses* on 26 September 1988 by Viking/Penguin, the issue of the 'freedom of speech and expression' was discussed and debated by the intelligentsia across the world, perhaps as never before. Today, even after three decades, opinions on this novel continues to remain divided. Those who endorse the novel argue that it's narrative is well within the bounds of the author's right to 'freedom of speech and expression.' Those who condemn the novel, on the other hand, argue that it's narrative has overstepped the boundaries of 'freedom of speech and expression' and deliberately offended the religious sentiments of the Muslim community owing to its sacrilegious satirical treatment of the Quran, Prophet Muhammad and Islam.

Satire may be defined as "a literary manner which blends a critical attitude with humour and wit for the purpose of improving human institutions. True satirists are conscious of the frailty of institutions of human devising and attempt through laughter not so much to tear them down as to inspire a remodelling" (Holman, 398). It aims at exposing society's follies and vices in all their manifestations wittily and humorously so as to bring about a much-needed reform in society. For instance, by means of his characteristic Juvenalian satire in his literary works, Jonathan Swift in the early eighteenth century aimed at exposing the follies and vices of humankind in general and thereby curing them of the same, and in doing so, reforming and renewing society. Reforming or renewing society being a supposedly no easy task, Alexander Pope, a contemporary of Swift, through his literary works, tried to deter society from being tainted by follies and vices. Satiric writers make use of literary devices such as parody, caricature, wit, humour, irony, sarcasm, derision, burlesque, exaggeration, juxtaposition, comparison, analogy, and double entendre in order to ensure that satire achieves its noble end. With its overarching vision and responsibility of reforming society and reaffirming its long cherished values, satire essentially is therapeutic, reformist and progressive in its approach. It is never otherwise. Therefore, one needs to examine whether or not Rushdie's satire in *The Satanic Verses* is in consonance with the honourable aim of the satiric genre. This article will analyze the credibility of the satiric intent of the novel with respect to the author's right to 'freedom of speech and expression.'

## 1. Fatwa and *The Satanic Verses*

Regardless of how many people may have read *The Satanic Verses* (which, in fact, is not only difficult to procure, but also difficult to read), many have praised it for its literary merit. However, the larger sections of the Muslim community across the world have condemned it for its satiric narrative which they argue is offensive to their religious sensibility. Those who condemn the book, regard it as a blasphemous anti-Islamic propaganda. Since there is nothing more sacred for a Muslim than the Quran, Prophet Muhammad and Islam, the scathing satire on all the three in the novel offended as well as enraged the Muslim community in general.

The reaction of the Muslim community against *The Satanic Verses*, culminated in a fatwa (religious edict) calling for the assassination of its author as well as his publishers on charges of blasphemy. It was issued on 14 February 1989 by Ayatolla Ruhollah Khomeini, the then Supreme Leader of Iran, who unfortunately had not read the novel himself. This extreme reaction, as many argue, was certainly neither in conformity with the spirit of Islam, nor in agreement with the universal human rights to freedom of speech and expression. Therefore, the fatwa was condemned by people from across the world, some of whom were Muslims themselves. It was rather shocking that Khomeini invested himself with authority to condemn a citizen of a foreign country to death without trial.

This fatwa backed by the Iranian Government would be lifted officially only ten years later in 1998 by the then President of Iran, Mohammad Khatami. However, since a 'fatwa' is a religious decision made by a 'mufti,' an Islamic scholar authorized to interpret and promulgate Islamic law, no secular authority can actually lift or nullify it. Therefore, even today, Rushdie continues to be under the sway of the fatwa which today is backed by several Islamic organizations in different parts of the world.

## 2. The Provocative Narrative of *The Satanic Verses*

Rushdie's controversial novel, *The Satanic Verses*, is named after the apocryphal verses that came to be called 'satanic verses,' which purportedly permitted intercessory prayers to three Meccan deities – al-Lat, al-Uzza and Manat. The author makes his satiric intent obvious in the title of the novel itself. The verses in question were supposedly prompted by Satan to Prophet Muhammad, which the Prophet uttered as the 'word of God,' but later retracted. One finds references to the contentious event of the 'satanic verses' in the Quran, Hadith and in the writings of the early Muslim scholars and biographers of Muhammad, such as, Ibn Jarir al-Tabari, Al-Wakidi, Ibn Sa'ad and Ibn Ishaq. Many among the Muslim community, however, regard this apocryphal story not only as being at variance with Quran, but also disrespectful to the testimony of the Quran. Different verses from the Quran support the theory that this discomforting episode related to the contentious 'satanic verses' in the Quran was a malicious fabrication. For instance, verses 41:42 that says, "No falsehood can approach it / From before or behind it / It is sent down / By One Full of Wisdom / Worthy of all praise." The Muslim community often quotes this verse in defense of the impeccability of the Quran. Yusuf Ali's footnote to this verse notes that it means that "God's truth is fully guarded on all sides. No one can get the better of it by attacking it from before or behind it, openly or secretly, or in any way whatever" (The Holy Quran, 1299).

Islamic tradition and faith hold that the Quran, the eternal 'word of God,' existed in heaven, and the Archangel Gabriel revealed it to Prophet Muhammad over a period of twenty-three years. Under the direction of Muhammad, his scribe wrote these revelations down, and thereby, eventually gave it a physical existence in the form of a book for the sake of the believers. Quranic verses like, "We have, without doubt / Sent down the Message / And We will assuredly Guard it (from corruption)" (15:9) are seen as upholding the authenticity and sanctity of the revealed book.

People of the pre-Islamic polytheistic Arab world worshipped Hubul also referred to as Allah (the god). Hubal who was believed to be a moon-god was also considered to be the creator god and the leader of the three-hundred and sixty other gods worshipped by various tribes in Arabia. The meaning of the original Arabic word, 'al-ilah,' being 'the god,' from which came the term Allah, possibly, the term Allah might have been used as a title rather than as the name of a god. Hence, Hubul being the specific name of a god, he being referred to as Allah (the god) is understandable. Hubul (Allah) was worshipped as the lord of the Arabian city of Mecca (the birthplace of Muhammad) and Kaaba (House of God). The three Arabian deities, al-Lat and al-Uzzan (named after Allah) and Manat were regarded as his daughters. Each of them had a separate shrine near Mecca and its adjoining places. "Hubul (Allah) along with 360 others were being worshipped before and during the days of Muhammad. It looks like Muhammad declared Allah (using the title) to be the only God to be worshipped from then on. With Muhammed using the title Allah, the true name Hubul would be lost" (Jackson, 17).

Those who defend the legitimacy of the 'satanic verses' episode argue that owing to a misguided revelation, or, expediency if one might say so,

Muhammad seems to have uttered (as part of the revealed message) that the three Arabian deities — al-Lat, al-Uzza and Manat — are the exalted cranes (intermediaries) whose intercession can be sought. However, by means of another revelation, Allah is believed to have informed him that these verses that accept polytheism should be retracted. In an interview on 27 January 1989, Rushdie said that in the case of Muhammad, there seems to have been "a brief flirtation with a possible compromise – about monotheism – which was very rapidly rejected" (Appignanesi & Maitland, 22). One among the different dream sequences though which the narrative of the novel unfolds is the sequence containing the inventive re-telling and re-imaging of the story of Muhammad, the birth of Islam and Muhammad's alleged short-term flirtation with polytheism. This re-telling and re-imaging through dream sequences becomes for Rushdie a powerful means to launch his satire. Creative re-telling, re-imaging and re-valuing of past narratives are not new; Rushdie has many illustrious predecessors in this field such as James Joyce, Gabriel Garcia Marquez, Thomas Pynchon Gunter Grass and so on.

Whenever an issue is linked to history as well as faith, it becomes highly complex and extremely sensitive. Secular, free and imaginative interpretations of such an issue invariably lends itself to controversies. For Muslims, Muhammad is the mediator of God's revelation — the uncreated word of God, the Quran; the voice that speaks in the Koran is the voice of God; and "The prophet's own speech and action are the agents of revelation and thus charged with divine power and sanctity" (Thomsom, 117). However, with his creative imagination, Rushdie burlesqued the story of Prophet Muhammad, the episode of the divine revelation, the birth of Islam and many other fundamental issues of the Islamic faith, as a believer would argue, with scathing scepticism and disdain. On his handling of the contentious aspect of the Muhammad event in the novel, Rushdie says:

> The one thing you learn as a historian is just how fragmented and ambitious and peculiar the historical record is. So, I thought, well, let's not try and pretend to be writing a history, let's take the themes I'm interested in and fantasise and fabulate them and all that, so that we don't have to get into the issue: did this really happen like this or did it not (Appignanesi & Maitland, 22).

Though it is difficult to arrive at the truth regarding the controversial verses in the Quran, one may look at the issue from historical and sociological perspectives. While Muhammad advocated strict monotheism, worship of Allah, the Quraysh tribe to which Muhammad actually belonged continued to worship al-Lat, al-Uzza, Manat and many other deities compliant with their tradition. Muhammad's stringent monotheism came in conflict with the prevailing polytheism of his tribe. This conflict alienated Muhammad from his tribe. He realized that by compromising his absolute monotheism in favour of the local deities he could not only end the rift between the Quraysh tribe and himself, but also bring in many more from the tribe to the new faith. Muhammad's supposed utterance of the command to worship the pagan deities (though not mentioned in the Quran) may have been a compromise formula that he worked out at a moment of weakness, or, in other words, at a moment of the supposed 'demonic temptation.' From an Islamic religious point of view, it may be seen as Satan's alleged promptings to insert into the divine revelation the command to seek the intercession of the three pagan deities and thereby lead the faithful astray. In *Sacred Places of Goddess,* Karen Tate notes how "Jibril, or Gabriel, the angel of revelation, informed Muhammad that Satan had used Muhammad's desire for reconciliation with the pagan leaders to insert into the revelation of God the verses about the interceding cranes, otherwise called the 'satanic verses' (Tate, 167).

Rushdie was fascinated by the paradoxes inherent in the revealed word of God. "At the very beginning of Islam," says Rushdie in an interview, "you find a conflict between the sacred text and the profane text, between revealed literature and imagined literature. For a writer, that conflict is fascinating and interesting to explore. So that's what I am doing, exploring" (Appignanesi & Maitland, 23). Rushdie's novel is a catalogue of multiple layers of conflict; and it sets some of the long-cherished Islamic beliefs against his imaginative and satiric re-interpretation of those beliefs.

Though polytheism is strictly prohibited in the Abrahamic religions – Judaism, Islam and Christianity – Islam underwent a conflict between monotheism and polytheism in its infancy after which monotheism prevailed. "In the Muslim view … the most heinous sin against God that a human can commit is that of *shirk*, 'associating' some other thing or being with the Almighty and Omnipotent himself. Thus, idolatry, or any kind of polytheism is abhorred …" (Neusner, Chilton, & Graham, 248). As mentioned earlier, even though the questionable utterance of Muhammad regarding the three goddesses seems to have originally been accepted as divine revelation, following a supposed instruction from God, it is argued that Muhammad soon retracted this command. Accordingly, the revelation in Surah 53:19-20 reads, "Have ye seen / Lat, and Uzza / And another / The third (goddess), Manat?" instead of the supposedly original verses known today as the satanic verses that say, "These are the exalted cranes (intermediaries) whose intercession is to be hoped for" (Tate, 167). Verses 22:52-53 in Quran refer to the satanic verse episode:

> Never did We send /An apostle or a Prophet / Before thee, but, when he / Framed a desire, Satan / Threw some (vanity) / Into his desire: but God / Will cancel anything (vain) / That satan throws in / And God will confirm / (And establish) His signs / For God is full of knowledge / And Wisdom.

> That He may make / The suggestions thrown in / By Satan, but a trial / For those in whose hearts / I a disease and who are / Hardened of heart: verily / The wrong-doers are in a schism / Far (from the Truth) (The Holy Quran, 22:52-53).

Though Quran and Islam do not approve of the worship of any deity other than Allah, in Rushdie's novel, when Grandee Abu Simbel, the leader of Jahilia (Mecca), realizes that the monotheism proposed by Mahound (Muhammad) would be the future religion, he cajoles Mahound to accept with the permission of Allah the worship of "three of the three hundred and sixty idols" that "are worthy of worship" in the city (Rushdie, 105). The Arabic word, 'Jahilia,' meaning 'ignorance' connotes to the Islamic notion of the 'Age of Ignorance' prevailing in Arabia before the birth of Islam. Since Jahilia, in the novel, stands for the holy city of Mecca, Grandee Abu Simbel's suggestion gains a symbolic significance in the narrative. Through the mediation of the controversial Gibreel (when Gibreel Farishta, a Bollywood actor and a character in the novel sleeps, he dreams that he is Archangel Gabriel and utters divine revelations to Mahound), it is revealed to Mahound that the deities – Lat, Uzza, and Manat – are "the exalted birds, and their intercession is desired indeed" (Rushdie, 114). If one of the fundamental prohibitions of Islam is the worship of idols and deities, in the novel, ironically enough, Allah seems to approve of this worship. For the Muslim community, this supposed divine approval is an insult against Allah and his Prophet. "The wronging of God or his Prophet must be far more serious than any offence Rushdie might have committed against ordinary mortals" (Fletcher, 322).

The novel tells us that with the adoption of the pagan goddesses into Islamic faith, the number of the followers of Islam began to increase; Abu Simbel himself and his wife, Hind, embraced Islamic faith. However, as Mahound realizes that Abu Simbel may abandon Islam, he declares, after consulting the Archangel, that the first revelation regarding the pagan deities was the work of the Devil. He says, "'It was the Devil ... 'The last time, it was Shaitan'" (Rushdie, 123). The omniscient narrator comments saying, "This is what he has *heard* in his *listening*, that he has been tricked, that the Devil came to him in the guise of the archangel, so that the verse he memorized, the ones he recited in the poetry tent, were not real thing but its diabolic opposite, not godly, but satanic" (Rushdie, 123). In place of the 'demonic revelation,' Mahound comes up with verses that ask, "Shall He have daughters and you sons? ... That would be a fine division! These are but names you have dreamed of, you and your fathers. Allah vests no authority in them" (Rushdie, 124). In the process, Rushdie seems to reduce the issue of divine revelation to Muhammad's opportunistic pragmatism for gaining religious, social and political mileage — an idea a believing Muslim would find hard to accept. Describing the novel as an attempt to address the migrant experience in Britain, M. D. Fletcher argues, "Rushdie's interests centrally include explorations of how migration heightens one's awareness that perceptions of reality are relative and fragile, and of the nature of religious faith and revelation, not to mention the political manipulation of religion" (1).

With much sarcasm, Rushdie makes the divine revelation wear the garb of opportunism yet again as Mahound and his followers reach Yathrib after having fled from Jahilia on account of the persecution of Muslims there. Salman, the scribe to whom the Prophet dictates the revealed verses, says, as Mahound finds Muslim women being influenced by the progressive women of Yathrib, "bang, out comes the rule book, the angel starts pouring out rules about what women must do, he starts forcing them back into the docile attitude the Prophet prefers…" (Rushdie, 367). Thus, the Archangel seems to be revealing what the Prophet wants him to reveal and what would cater to his patriarchal mindset and society. Therefore, Salman calls Quran, "those revelations of convenience" (Rushdie, 365).

When Gibreel wryly says (about the conflicting revelations regarding the worship of the three local deities), "*it was me both times, baba, me, me first and second also me*. From my mouth, both the statement and the repudiation, verses and converses, universes and reverses, the whole thing, and we all know how my mouth got worked," (Rushdie, 123) Rushdie makes the Quran appear as the most absurd religious book one can think of. Furthermore, Rushdie not only puts into the mouth of the Archangel the vulgar language of the streets, but also depicts the Archangel like a fraud. Satire such as this, irrespective of the intention of the writer, strikes hard at the foundations of the long cherished Islamic faith.

In the background of the controversy of the 'satanic verses,' the name of the novel, *The Satanic Verses,* suggests that Prophet Muhammad was unable to distinguish the angel from the devil, the divine revelation from the demonic interpolation, and that the Quran as the revelation of God is questionable. By turning the name, Muhammad, into a "Devil's synonym: Mahound," which is a "demon tag," and calling him "the medieval baby-frightener" (Rushdie, 93), Rushdie establishes Muhammad's demonic association, and thereby underscores the theme of the satanic verses. Muslims regard the wives of the Prophet as mothers of the entire Muslim community. By giving the prostitutes in a brothel called 'the Curtain,' the names of the wives of the Prophet, Rushdie depicts the Prophet as a cuckold and Muslims as the illegitimate children of their fallen mothers. To add insult to injury, the term, 'the Curtain' itself is a reference to the 'hejab' or veil worn by Muslim women.

The process of revelation itself is thoroughly lampooned. On the one hand, the revelation seems to emerge from the tormenting and recurring day slumber of Gibreel Farista, the Bollywood actor who in his dreams metamorphoses himself into the Archangel Gibreel (Gabriel). This is no respectful depiction of the Archangel of God. What is ironical and even farcical is that "Gibreel feels paralyzed by the presence of the great Prophet and thinks, "I can't make a sound I'd seem such a goddamn fool" (Rushdie, 111). On the other hand, this hallucinatory dream is dreamt together with Mahound as they lie together in a homosexual embrace, a sort of "wrestling match" between Mahound and the Archangel Gibreel (Rushdie, 123). It is difficult to ascertain who among them is the actual dreamer. In fact, neither of them knows who the dreamer is and who the dreamed. This infamous process of revelation is depicted mixing the third and the first person narrative in a stream-of-consciousness style in order to fuse the boundaries between the dreamer and the dreamed.

> But when he has rested he enters a different sort of sleep, a sort of not-sleep, the condition that he calls his *listening*, and he feels a dragging pain in the gut, like something trying to be born, and now Gibreel, who has been hovering-above-looking-down, feels a confusion, *who am I*, in these moments it begins to seem that the archangel is actually *inside the Prophet*, I am the dragging in the gut, I am the angel being extruded from the sleeper's navel, I emerge, Gibreel Farista, while my other self, Mahound, lies *listening*, entranced, I am bound to him, navel to navel, by the shining cord of light, not possible to say which of us is dreaming the other. We flow in both directions along the umbilical cord (Rushdie, 110).

What is revealed appears to be the promptings of Mahound's own mind. Mahound tells Salman, "Often when Gibreel comes, it's as if he knows what's in my heart. It feels to me, most times, as if he comes from within my heart: from within my deepest places, from my soul." The exceedingly caricatured Archangel of God is afraid of Mahound the businessman, who comes to receive the revelation. "Gibreel's fear, the fear of the self his dream creates, makes him struggle against Mahound's arrival, to try to put it off … and the archangel hold his breath" (Rushdie, 109). The angel's thoughts at this moment are rather discourteous. *"Mahound comes to me for revelation,"* says Gibreel, *"asking me to choose between monotheist and henotheist alternatives, and I'm just some idiot actor having a bhaenchud nightmare, what the fuck do I know, yaar, what to tell you, help. Help"* (Rushdie, 109). Rushdie depicts the Archangel of God as an ineffectual charlatan with a vulgar tongue. The archangel's use of demeaning language in order to parody the fundamentals of Islamic faith is an enormous embarrassment for the Muslim community. As Richard Webster argues, "It is such extreme language, which is potentially the most violent and the most insulting registers available to Western writers, which, in the pages of *The Satanic Verses*, is brought into conjunction with some of the most sacred traditions of Islam" (93).

Rushdie makes fun of the concept of divine revelation in the Quran further by making Salman surreptitiously tamper with what the Prophet dictates to him, and by depicting the Prophet as absolutely incapable of identifying the deliberate falsification of the original. Salman says:

> Little things at first. If Mahound recited a verse in which God was described as *all-hearing, all-knowing,* I would write, *all knowing, all wise.* Here's the point: Mahound did not notice the alterations. So there I was, actually writing the Book, or re-writing, anyway, polluting the word of God with my own profane language. But, good heavens, if my poor words could not be distinguished from the revelation by God's own Messenger, then what did that mean? What did that say about the quality of the divine poetry? … So the next time I change a bigger thing. He said *Christian,* I wrote down *Jew.* He'd notice that, surely; how could he not? But when I read him the chapter he nodded and thanked me politely … So I went on with my devilment, changing verses …. (Rushdie, 367-68).

He further reports that the longer he worked as the scribe for Mahound the worse it got. It would take the Prophet some time before he discovers that Salman has been setting his own "words against the Words of God" (Rushdie, 374). Such delay in discovering the malicious interpolation questions the credibility of the Prophet to engage in the most holy enterprise – giving a written form to the revealed word of God. The Quran being an infallible book for the Muslims, lampooning the Quran, the angel who mediated the revelation, the prophet who uttered the revelation and the very process of revelation itself, Rushdie derides the foundation of Islamic faith. The question is whether the right to freedom of speech and expression gives the author liberty to distort and ridicule the religious faith and practices that a community considers as sacrosanct.

While the author may argue in favour of creative freedom, it is important for him to know how far is too far. Rushdie's satire on the laws laid down in the Quran as guidelines for the faithful is certainly impudent. The omniscient narrator of the novel says, in Yathrib as the faithful lived by lawlessness, "Mahound – or should one say the Archangel Gibreel? – should one say Al-Lah? – became obsessed by law" (Rushdie, 363). This statement suggests that the laws laid down in the Quran might as well be the laws of the Prophet himself or of the Bollywood actor-turned-Archangel Gibreel rather than the laws of Allah. Furthermore, these laws are the result of an obsession with law itself rather than a heavenly intent. With total disrespect to these laws, Salman says with disdainful humour that out of this obsession came, "rules about every damn thing" (Rushdie, 363). As Gibreel specifies rules for every aspect of human life, Salman wonders what "manner of God this was that sounded so much like a businessman" (Rushdie, 364). He loses his faith as he realizes that before becoming a religious leader and a prophet, Mahound had been a successful businessman, and therefore, "organization and rules came naturally" to him and he would obviously employ a "businesslike archangel, who handed down the management decisions of this highly corporate, if non-corporeal, God" (Rushdie, 364).

## Conclusion

Ali Khamenei who succeeded Ayatollah Ruhollah Khomeini as as Supreme Leader of Iran in 1988 asked Rushdie to apologize and disown the novel as a mark of regret, and in doing so, seek forgiveness for his offence against Islam from the enraged Muslims across the world. However, the fatwa would remain effective even if he apologized and disowned the novel. At this juncture, Rushdie issued the following carefully worded response.

> As author of *The Satanic Verses I* recognize that Muslims in many parts of the world are genuinely distressed by the publication of my novel. I profoundly regret the distress that publication has occasioned to sincere followers of Islam. Living as we do in a world of many faiths this experience has served to remind us that we must all be conscious of the sensibilities of others (MacDonogh, 132).

Rushdie's response while appeasing some, enraged some others further, for some interpreted the response as only a tactic of adding insult to the already injured Islamic sensibility. Even before the publication of the novel, Rushdie was aware that the novel would meet with extreme reactions from the Muslim community. "I expected," he said, "that the mullahs wouldn't like it. But I didn't write it for the Mullahs … obviously I have a view of the world which is not theirs. I insist on my right to express it as I think fit" (Appignanesi & Maitland, 21). Rushdie's re-telling and re-imaging of the sacrosanct issues of Islamic faith, however ingenious it might be, does not resonate with the spirit of the 'freedom of speech and expression.'

Article 295 A of Indian Penal Code states that whoever deliberately and maliciously tries to outrage or insult the religion, religious feelings or religious beliefs of any class of citizens of India, by words either spoken or written or otherwise shall be punished with imprisonment, or with fine or with both. When India banned the novel in defense of the religious sentiments of its Muslims, Rushdie wrote to Rajiv Gandhi, the then Prime Minister of India, "that the book isn't actually about Islam, but about migration, metamorphosis, divided selves, love, death, London and Bombay" (Fischer & Abedi, 388). The Muslim community was not satisfied with this explanation.

Rushdie was incensed by the fact that "Almost all the people who are being so insulted and provoked and disgusted have not really read the book" (Appignanesi & Maitland, 32). Reacting to Rushdie and foreshadowing the sentiments of the Indian Muslim community, Syed Shahabuddin, a member of the Indian parliament in the Government headed by Gandhi, who initiated the ban on the novel in India said:

> Yes, Mr. Rushdie, we are a religious people …. Call us primitive, call us fundamentalists, call us superstitious barbarians, call us what you like, but your book may serve to define, what has gone wrong with the western civilization — it has lost all sense of distinction between the sacred and the profane …. Yes, I have not read it, nor do I intend to. I do not have to wade through a filthy drain to know what filth is" (Fischer & Abedi, 388-89).

One should certainly not get carried away by the emotional outbursts like that of Shahabuddin against the novel. Instead, one should come up with an informed and mature stand on the matter, which unfortunately seldom happens when a complex literary work such as *The Satanic Verses* from a writer as famous as Rushdie is wrapped in a controversy based on its religious content. The Muslim community across the world continues to regard *The Satanic Verses* as a direct attack on and a conspiracy against Islam by the use of "distortion and scorn, which have the effect of alienating Muslims from their faith" (Pipes, 127). Attempt to discredit Islam and to tamper with its doctrines, they argue, had been made before, "but the Rushdie book exceeded all others in its audacity and in its scope" (Pipes, 127). I think, there is certainly some truth in the observation of the Muslim community regardless of the fact that few among them may have read the novel. Rushdie's satire in *The Satanic Verses* on what is sacrosanct in Islam does not seem to contribute to any form of constructive or reformative thinking in society. At least, even three decades after its publication it has not done so. Instead, it has only resulted in division and disturbance in society. Therefore, I think it goes against the intent and spirit of the satiric genre. This is where Rushdie's novel seems to overstep the boundaries of the author's right to 'freedom of speech and expression.'

## References

Ali, A. Yusuf, trans. *The Holy Quran*. Leicester: Islamic Foundation, 1975.

Appignanesi, Lisa and Sara Maitland, *The Rushdie File*. New York: Syracuse University, 1990.

Fischer, Michael M. J. and Mehdi Abedi. *Debating Muslims: Cultural Dialogues in Postmodernity and Tradition*. Madison : University of Wisconsin Press , 1990.

Fletcher, M. D. "Introduction: The Politics of Salman Rushdie's Fiction." Fletcher, M. D. *Reading Rushdie: Perspectives on the Fiction of Salman Rushdie*. Ed. M. D. Fletcher. Amsterdam: Rodopi, 1994. 1-22.

Holman, C. Hugh. *A handbook to literature:Based on the original edition by William Flint Thrall and Addison Hibbard*. Indianapolis: Bobbs-Merrill Education Pub, 1980.

Jackson, Montell. *Islam Revealed: The Hidden truth*. Maitland: Xulon Press, 2003.

MacDonogh, Steve, ed. *The Rushdie Letters: Freedom to Speak, Freedom to Write*. Lincoln: University of Nebraska Press, 1993.

Morsink, Johannes. *The Universal Declaration of Human Rights: Origins, Drafting, and Intent.* Philadelphia: University of Pennsylvania Press, 1999.

Neusner, Jacob, Bruce Chilton and William Graham. *Three Faiths, One God: The Formative Faith and Practice of Judaism.* Boston: Brill Academic, 2002.

Pipes, Daniel. *The Rushdie Affair: The Novel, the Ayattolla, and the West.* 2nd . New Brunswick: Transaction, 2003.

Rushdie, Salman. *The Satanic Verses.* London: Viking, 1988.

Tate, Karen. *Sacred Places of Goddess: 108 Destinations.* San Francisco: Consortium of Collective Consciousness, 2006.

Thomsom, William. "Muhammad: His Life and Person". *The Muslim World.* xxxiv (1994): 96-137.

Webster, Richard. *A Brief History of Blasphemy: Liberalism, Censorship and 'The Satanic Verses'.* Southwold: The Orwell Press, 1990.

# 24

# Ambiguity in Sartre's Notion of "Bad Faith"

**Keith D'Souza SJ**
*Rector, St. Xavier's College, Mumbai*

**Abstract:** In his magnum opus *Being and Nothingness*, Jean-Paul Sartre provides us with a detailed phenomenological analysis of the tenuous features of the human existential situation, and the vexatious contours of human relationships. One of his claims is that a vast majority of human attitudes and relationships are founded on what he called "bad faith." Sartre provides several examples of "bad faith," in order to substantiate his claim that this disposition is widely prevalent in society. However, there is a methodological as well as programmatic problem with this claim. Sartre is not methodologically clear and consistent in his demonstration of "bad faith," as there are several ambiguities and inconsistencies in his presentation and argumentation. More fundamentally, it seems that while *Being and Nothingness* is an attempt to highlight the features of false consciousness which governs human attitudes and relations, in his subsequent works Sartre himself alludes to more authentic modes of human relations as well as fulfilling modes of "being-with-others"—modes which transcend the somewhat narrow and pessimistic presentation of "bad faith" as constitutive of the human predicament in *Being and Nothingness*.

**Keywords:** Bad faith, Inauthenticity, Authenticity, Good faith, Sincerity, Lying, Anguish.

The phenomenon of inauthentic modes of functioning in human society is indeed a common experience of human reality. Of the many themes that Sartre addresses, perhaps the one on bad faith—related to inauthenticity—is the one for which he is popularly most famous.[1] Besides, his concern with bad faith fits in with his obsession to philosophically preserve the radical nature of human freedom. For Sartre, bad faith is "bad" because it only serves to minimize our very "nature" as freedom itself.

Yet, as we shall see, while Sartre's concern to uphold freedom and protest against any tendency to escape from our existential situation is noble, the ontological and epistemological presuppositions with which he operates leave much to be desired. He wants to militate against the phenomenon of bad faith, but his ontology will not allow him to do so consistently and unambiguously. At every consideration of the different forms of bad faith which Sartre portrays for us we meet with serious problems as to the very possibility of its occurrence. Finally, the very explanation for the possibility of bad faith in the first place limps badly for want of adequate ontological presuppositions.

The scope of this paper is to systematically present the phenomenon of bad faith in the writings of the early Sartre—more specifically, in *Being and Nothingness*[2]—and to point out areas of ambiguity and inconsistency with regard to the presentation of this phenomenon by Sartre. My basic thesis is that the explanation of the phenomenon of bad faith in terms of Sartre's phenomenology and ontology as presented in this *magnum opus* of his leaves much to be desired in terms of clarity and consistency and is thus an inadequate treatment of the issue.[3]

I shall begin by presenting the most significant descriptions of bad faith in *Being and Nothingness* (and the description of the possibility of bad faith in the first place), and then go on to indicate problems of ambiguity or inconsistency with regard to each of these descriptions. I shall conclude with a brief section indicating significant shifts which Sartre undertook in his later philosophical journey, thereby calling for a personal revision of his understanding of bad faith.

---

1 David Detmer, in *Sartre Explained: From Bad Faith to Authenticity* (Chicago: Open Court, 2008), p.88, states that "Sartre suggests that bad faith is very pervasive indeed, and many readers take his overall message to be that it is virtually inevitable and inescapable."

2 Jean-Paul Sartre, *Being and Nothingness*, trans. Hazel Barnes (New York: Philosophical Library, 1956).

3 Ronald Santoni, in *Bad Faith, Good Faith, and Authenticity in Sartre's Early Philosophy* (Philadelphia: Temple University Press, 1995), xviii, points out that, "although Sartre's notion of bad faith has engaged the interest of academics and laypersons alike—and has even become a kind of watchword for many seeking to understand Existentialist thought—it has hardly been free of conceptual confusion, controversy, and lack of detailed understanding."

## 1. The Notion of "Bad Faith" in *Being and Nothingness*

Towards the end of the first paragraph in the section on bad faith, Sartre asserts that "there is one determined attitude which is essential to human reality and which is such that consciousness instead of directing its negation outward turns it toward itself. This attitude, it seems to me, is *bad faith (mauvaise foi)*."[4]

This notion of bad faith being "essential to human reality" and at the same time being something of a private nature in its construction is introduced even before the section on bad faith *per se*, in the section on "The Origin of Negation," where Sartre explains that the "nature" of a human being is existential anguish, and that bad faith results from a desire to escape the unique constitution of human "nature" as a being-for-itself. Let us begin, then, with Sartre's preliminary notion of bad faith before going on to describe the other instances of bad faith in the section on bad faith *per se*.

### a. Bad Faith as an Escape from Existential Anguish

Chapter One of Part One of *Being and Nothingness* is concerned with the demonstration that "nothingness lies coiled in the heart of being—like a worm."[5] This recognition leads to a state of existential anguish, because we are faced with the fact that in reality we have no identity.[6] The obvious thing is to flee such a situation and to attempt to fill this existential void that consciousness generates with some identity or the other. On the other hand, Sartre seems to deny the very possibility of an escape from existential anguish. He asserts that "we cannot overcome anguish, for we *are* anguish," and "anguish, properly speaking, can be neither hidden nor avoided."[7] Thus,

> If I am my anguish in order to flee it, that presupposes that I can decenter myself in relation to what I am, that I can be anguish in the form of "not-being it," that I can dispose of a nihilating power at the heart of anguish itself. This nihilating power nihilates anguish in so far as I flee it and nihilates itself in so far as I am anguish in order to flee it. This attitude is what we call *bad faith*. There is then no question of expelling anguish from consciousness nor of constituting it in an unconscious psychic phenomenon; very simply I can make myself guilty of bad faith while apprehending the anguish which I am, and this bad faith, intended to fill up the nothingness which I *am* in my relation to myself, precisely implies the nothingness which it suppresses.[8]

---

4 Sartre, *Being and Nothingness*, 48.

5 *Ibid.*, 21.

6 Or, in other words, the nature of consciousness "simultaneously is to be what it is not, and not to be what it is" (Ibid., 70).

7 *Ibid.*, 43.

8 *Ibid.*, 44.

Bad faith in this case, then, consists in a futile and unsuccessful attempt to flee our existential situation. From the quotation above and in these two pages immediately preceding the Chapter on "Bad Faith" *per se*, Sartre seems to question whether the outcome of bad faith is at all possible. He promises to address this issue, though (on the conditions for bad faith to take place successfully), in the next Chapter, a promise that he will not entirely and satisfactorily fulfill, as we shall see.

### b. Bad Faith as "Lying to Oneself"

In the phenomenon of lying, one person is aware of the truth but wishes to conceal it from the other, and tries to do so in words and deeds: "The liar intends to deceive and he does not seek to hide this intention from himself nor to disguise the translucency of consciousness."[9] Bad faith, on the contrary, involves a lie to oneself: "what changes everything is the fact that in bad faith it is from myself that I am hiding the truth. Thus, the duality of the deceiver and the deceived does not exist here. Bad faith on the contrary implies in essence the unity of a *single* consciousness."[10]

Sartre's famous example of the woman who goes out on a date with a man with dubious intentions seems to fit into this characterization of bad faith. But in this example, it is the *woman* who possesses dubious intentions, for Sartre, and is thus in bad faith: "She knows also that it will be necessary sooner or later for her to make a decision. But she does not want to realize the urgency."[11] Sartre concludes his analysis of the woman's behavior by saying that what unifies the different acts that go to make up the bad faith of the woman "is a certain art of forming contradictory concepts which unite in themselves both an idea and the negation of that idea."[12] He goes on to explain this by adding that in bad faith it is either transcendence or facticity that is affirmed of the individual consciousness, but never a "valid coordination" of the two: "Bad faith seeks to affirm their identity while preserving their differences. It must affirm facticity as *being* transcendence and transcendence as *being* facticity, in such a way that at the instant when a person apprehends the one, he can find himself abruptly faced with the other."[13]

Sartre admits that this appears to be an impossibility: the act of lying to oneself is not possible given the nature of consciousness as translucent.

---

9 *Ibid.*, 48.

10 *Ibid.*, 49.

11 *Ibid.*, 55. On the other hand, a few lines later Sartre mentions that "she does not quite know what she wants," implying a state of ambiguity rather than pure translucency of consciousness.

12 *Ibid.*, 56.

13 *Ibid.*

"We must agree in fact that if I deliberately and cynically attempt to lie to myself, I fail completely in this undertaking; the lie falls back and collapses beneath my look."[14] Sartre promises to address the issue of the conditions for the possibility of lying to oneself later, and in fact does raise the issue again in the last section of this Chapter, but in a manner of argumentation that still leaves the question very unsettled, as we shall see.

### c. Sincerity as an Example of Bad Faith

The word 'sincerity' usually has a positive connotation, but Sartre gives it a negative one, because in trying to "be" someone (or in trying to "be sincere"), I deny the very nature of consciousness as a unity both of facticity and transcendence. I turn facticity into a transcendent quality, and vice-versa. In the case of sincerity, I treat a factual quality (a courageous act) as if it is a transcendent one ("I am courageous"). The goal of sincerity is that "a man be *for himself* only what he *is*. But is this not precisely the definition of the in-itself—or if you prefer—the principle of identity?"[15] Sincerity, in fine, then, results in the attempt to diminish our status as a being-for-itself.

This is brought out in Sartre's illustration of the waiter in the café,[16] one of his more popular examples. In this caricature, Sartre points out that there is both, social pressure to assume a given role, as well as individual initiative in assuming the role. Both of these influences arise on account of the desire to "be someone."

On the other hand (somewhat confusing the issue even further) Sartre asks, "What then is sincerity except precisely a phenomenon of bad faith? Have we not shown indeed that in bad faith human reality is constituted as a being which is what it is not and which is not what it is?"[17] Sartre goes on to give yet another example of the homosexual who refuses to be identified as one (true to his transcendental status), yet should not, but does, refuse to accept that he engaged in homosexual activity in the past (and thus is a homosexual, from the point of view of his factual status).

But, just like an escape from anguish is a futile one, so is an attempt to be sincere or to try to be a being-in-itself, because I am *conscious* of this intention as not being a properly human one. "Thus in order for bad faith to be possible, sincerity itself must be in bad faith."[18] Not only is the act of being sincere a case of bad faith, but even *trying* to be sincere is in bad faith (if at all it is possible). One wonders, however, how Sartre would have reacted if the waiter

14 *Ibid.*

15 *Ibid.*, 58.

16 Cf. *Ibid.*, 59, for the detailed caricature of the waiter.

17 *Ibid.*, 63.

18 *Ibid.*, 67.

in the café insisted that he mainly discuss philosophy with Sartre instead of serving him coffee.

## d. Good Faith as an Example of Bad Faith

Sartre tries to draw a distinction between good and bad faith, but as the explanation progresses, it becomes apparent that good faith is merely a form of bad faith, as he has described bad faith earlier. Good faith is understood to be the disposition to operate from bad faith while assuming that it is good to do so (while bad faith stops short of making such an assumption), i.e., good faith is persuaded by evidence pertaining to some issue (that, for example, Pierre likes me), while bad faith is not persuaded by such evidence (or any evidence, for that matter). Good faith is willing to commit itself to some belief, while bad faith refuses to do so and so suspends belief.

Like sincerity, then, good faith, while it seems to be an antithesis of bad faith (in our ordinary understanding of these terms), is really not so, according to Sartre: "The ideal of good faith (to believe what one believes) is, like that of sincerity (to be what one is), an ideal of being-in-itself."[19] This is because "good faith seeks to flee the inner disintegration of my being in the direction of the in-itself which it should be and is not."[20] But here too, Sartre questions the possibility of good faith:

> The nature of consciousness is such that in it the mediate and the immediate are one and the same being. To believe is to know that one believes, and to know that one believes is no longer to believe. Thus, to believe is not to believe any longer because that is only to believe–this in the unity of one and the same non-thetic consciousness . . . Thus belief is a being which questions its own being, which can realize itself only in its destruction, which can manifest itself to itself only by denying itself . . . To believe is not-to-believe.[21]

The possibility of good faith, like any other form of bad faith, is intertwined within the discussion of the possibility of bad faith in general. In what follows, Sartre will try to demonstrate (finally, but alas, not definitively) that bad faith is indeed possible.

## e. The Possibility of the Enterprise of Bad Faith

As we have seen thus far, Sartre only presents us with different attempts at bad faith, and different illustrations to clarify these attempts. At every point, though, he has questioned whether the different forms of bad faith are at all possible *in principle*, given his ontological presuppositions about human consciousness.

19 *Ibid.*, 69.

20 *Ibid.*, 70.

21 *Ibid.*, 69.

While a primary condition for the possibility of bad faith is the suspension in belief in the unique nature of human consciousness as being a complex of facticity and transcendence, a more necessary condition for its possibility is that one is able to successfully *lie* to oneself (about the nature of one's facticity and transcendence), given the *translucency* of consciousness. We need to keep in mind that Sartre refuses to accept any appeal to the subconscious in order to explain bad faith (i.e., that it is due to subconscious forces that we suppress one aspect of our consciousness—either the factual or the transcendent). He finally addresses this issue in the last section in the Chapter on bad faith, along with his description of good faith. He asserts here that the only way that bad faith is possible (and explainable) is to consider it as an instance of "faith" or "belief":

> The true problem of bad faith stems evidently from the fact that bad faith is *faith*. It can not be either a cynical lie or certainty—if certainty is the intuitive possession of the object. But if we take belief as meaning the adherence of being to its object when the object is not given or is given indistinctly, then bad faith is belief; and the essential problem of bad faith is a problem of belief.[22]

We have seen already how he distinguishes good and bad faith. His explanation for the very possibility of bad faith rests on this distinction. In bad faith, one does not commit oneself to believing persuasive evidence (as in good faith), but one is confronted with, and so *believes in the presence of non-persuasive evidence* (i.e., evidence that is "not given or is given indistinctly"):

> Bad faith apprehends evidence but it is resigned in advance to not being fulfilled by this evidence, to not being persuaded and transformed into good faith . . . Thus bad faith in its primitive project and in its coming into the world decides on the exact nature of its requirements. It stands forth in the firm resolution *not to demand too much*, to count itself satisfied when it is barely persuaded, to force itself in decisions to adhere to uncertain truths . . . Let us understand clearly that there is no question of a reflective, voluntary decision, but of a spontaneous determination of our being. One *puts oneself* in bad faith as one goes to sleep and one is in bad faith as one dreams. Once this mode of being has been realized, it is as difficult to get out of it as to wake oneself up.[23]

With this strange statement about the nature of bad faith, Sartre seems to have considerably qualified his understanding of bad faith as taking place within the normal circumstances of the translucency of consciousness. Furthermore, bad faith turns out to be a strange form of belief, because instead

22 *Ibid.*, 67.

23 *Ibid.*, 68.

of committing itself to the *evidence* presented to consciousness, "it has become content with itself as belief."[24]

## 2. Problems Connected with Each of These Descriptions of "Bad Faith"

While Sartre's intentions are noble, in that he wishes to provide a phenomenological analysis of the prevalence of bad faith in normal human relations, his methodological and ontological presuppositions or commitments do not allow him to easily demonstrate the validity of the nature of bad faith itself. We will examine each of the types of bad faith presented above, in order to highlight a few ambiguities and even inconsistencies in Sartre's argumentation while presenting these cases.

### a. Bad Faith as an Escape from Existential Anguish

As the main feature of bad faith here is to suppress the transcendent nature of one's consciousness and to try to reduce oneself to an in-itself, this description of bad faith is very similar to the one of "sincerity." Hence the arguments versus Sartre's presentation of existential anguish as a form of bad faith will be found among those pertaining to the notion of sincerity.

### b. Bad Faith as "Lying to Oneself"

One of the most problematic issues within the bad faith problem is the one about the nebulous nature of lying to oneself given the fact that Sartre subscribes to the full translucency of consciousness, as well as his reluctance to have recourse to subconscious drives as being responsible for our bad faith decisions and actions. For Sartre, the mixed motives that we have when we operate from bad faith seem to be crystal clear, because of the "psychic unity" that goes to make up the consciousness of the for-itself.

Thus, asserts Santoni, "in the strict sense of successfully and completely hiding a truth from oneself, within the unity of a single consciousness, "lying to oneself" is not possible for Sartre."[25] However, Santoni believes that in the last section on the possibility of bad faith, Sartre makes room for a *modified* version of "lying to oneself," hinged on Sartre's statement that "it is precisely

24 Allen Wood, "Self-Deception and Bad Faith," in *Perspectives on Self-Deception*, ed. Brian P. McLaughlin and Amelie Oksenberg Rorty (Berkeley: University of California Press, 1988), 221. This author gives a very lucid description of the contents of the last section of the Chapter on bad faith, far clearer than the dense and convoluted one that Sartre himself provides. The explanation by Santoni too, in *Bad Faith, Good Faith, and Authenticity in Sartre's Early Philosophy*, 37-46, is very readable.

25 Santoni, 42. I will examine the possibility of the operation of bad faith in more detail a little later.

as the acceptance of not believing what it believes that it is bad faith."[26] This acceptance allows one to "not believe while "believing" and presumably believe while "not believing"."[27]

The problem, however, is that lying to oneself may now only be understood in a *weak* sense,[28] rather than the strong one that Sartre would have us commit ourselves to, if he could.

> As such, it seems to be a lie of "half-persuasion," which Sartre earlier characterizes as a common, degenerate form of the lie and rejects as an instance of bad faith.[29] Either there is an inconsistency here, or Sartre, without having specifically expressed it, has altered his approach to "half-persuasion" while developing his account of bad faith.[30]

Secondly, this involves cynicism on the part of the person who is lying, because there is a "*deliberate* intention to accept as persuasive what is not fully persuasive, and to "believe" (according to criteria that one "knows" are inadequate for *full* persuasion) what one consciously does not fully believe."[31] However, on a number of occasions (as Santoni indicates) Sartre expressly rules out cynicism as part of bad faith.[32]

Sartre himself realized that the definition of bad faith as "lying to oneself" cannot be entirely acceptable. He promises to explain, though, how it may be possible, but doesn't live up to his promise to the extent that he himself would have desired. He is faced with two alternatives: either to retain his notion of the translucency of consciousness, in which case "lying to oneself" is only possible in a weak sense, and thereby the person living in bad faith may be considerably less responsible than may appear at first, or on the other hand to accept that consciousness may not be entirely translucent, and that there may be either inattention on the conscious level or non-conscious forces at play. He is unwilling to accept the second alternative because of his ontology. Thus, he seems more willing to present us with an unclear picture of bad faith rather than abandon his ontological presuppositions.

---

26 Sartre, *Being and Nothingness*, 70.

27 Santoni, 43.

28 Santoni thus concludes his Chapter on "Bad Faith and "Lying to Oneself"" by asserting that "it is a far cry from the view of bad faith (suggested in the early part of Sartre's analysis) that requires a *successful* concealment of truth from consciousness in the full translucency of consciousness" (p. 46).

29 Sartre, *Being and Nothingness*, 48.

30 *Ibid.*, 45.

31 Santoni, 45.

32 Sartre, *Being and Nothingness*, 67, 70. Santoni, however, devotes an entire Chapter of his book (Ch. 3) to demonstrate that Sartre has to commit himself to defining bad faith in terms of cynicism.

## c. Sincerity as an Example of Bad Faith

In his analysis of sincerity as a feature of bad faith, Santoni contends that Sartre indulges in a bit of equivocation in his description, and this equivocation leads to the false association of sincerity with bad faith: "he seems to be juxtaposing an ordinary-language formulation of sincerity with his own idiosyncratic philosophical view of human reality as consciousness."[33] In other words, Sartre takes the ordinary language understanding of sincerity as "being true to oneself," and applies it to a specific manner of the functioning of *consciousness* according to Sartrean ontology. When Sartre asks, "how can he *be* what he is when he exists as consciousness of being?,"[34] he asks an illegitimate question, because he is confusing the normal understanding of being with his own understanding of consciousness as not being able to be described only in terms of being (as it has to be described in terms of non-being as well).

Furthermore, Sartre seems to indulge in more equivocation when he identifies consciousness and bad faith when he says, "Have we not shown indeed that in bad faith human reality is constituted as a being which is what it is not and which is not what it is?"[35] But, asserts Santoni, "if to be sincere is, as Sartre says, *to be what one is*, it obviously does *not* have the structure of *being what it is not and not being what it is*."[36] Sartre, then, cannot have it both ways: either he defines bad faith in two ways (and indulges in equivocation), or he defines it in one way, but it doesn't then apply to sincerity.

The difficulties with the example of the waiter as manifesting bad faith in trying to be sincere are obvious. For Sartre is not just trying to say that the waiter who *acts* excessively waiter-like is thus sincere and in bad faith. He seems to be making a far stronger claim[37] and asserting that *any* waiter (or any person who takes his or her job seriously), by acting out their social roles well enough, live in bad faith. Sartre's ready label of "bad faith" over any social

---

33 Santoni, 10. See 10-16 for his critique of Sartre's identification of sincerity as an instance of bad faith, from where I have culled out these objections to Sartre's argumentation.

34 Sartre, *Being and Nothingness*, 58-59.

35 *Ibid.*, 63.

36 Santoni, 14-15.

37 That he seems to be making a stronger claim is borne out by the fact that the example of the waiter is presented within the context of the nature of identity-descriptions. Keep in mind that Sartre *accepts* that the waiter is not *only* a waiter: "the waiter in the café can not be immediately a café waiter in the sense that this inkwell *is* an inkwell" (ibid., 59). Joseph Catalano, on the other hand, in "Successfully Lying to Oneself: A Sartrean Perspective," *Philosophy and Phenomenological Research* Vol. L, No. 4 (1990): 673-93, tries to redeem Sartre by asserting that "*our* waiter has chosen his job precisely in order to avoid the responsibility of questioning his role in society" (p. 692). The problem is: if Sartre is indeed making such a tame observation, then his allegations about the bad faith status of "sincerity" should also be similarly tame–but they are not.

role-playing thus seeks to call into question any and every human occupation taken seriously and responsibly.

D. Z. Phillips complains that in the waiter example, "Sartre speaks in terms of ceremony and dance, but does not take them seriously enough. The words and gestures of the waiter must be taken in the context of that ceremony and dance."[38] Phillips is arguing against what he feels to be Sartre's "general contention that there is nothing in the waiter's profession which has any dignity and which could provide any satisfaction worthy of a human being."[39]

This notion of sincerity as being an example of bad faith, then, as we have seen, is not without ambiguity and grounds for critique, in terms of both illustration as well as explication.

### d. Good Faith as an Example of Bad Faith

The basic equivocation Sartre indulges in here is that he begins his analysis of the possibility of bad faith by clearly *distinguishing* between good and bad faith, and ends his analysis by reducing good faith to a form of sincerity, and as sincerity is a form of bad faith, good faith too may be said to be a form of bad faith.

Santoni, though, gives us a redeemed understanding of good faith that need not fall under the category of bad faith. Good faith, by committing itself to believing in something is better off than "bad" faith which refuses to do so, and thereby doesn't deserve the name of "faith." Furthermore, good faith "*assumes responsibility* for the authorship of its beliefs and actions . . . While the attitude of bad faith is to flee its freedom and its anguish, the attitude of good faith is to face its freedom of consciousness; that is, the autonomy and responsibility to which consciousness is condemned."[40]

From this we can see that Sartre cannot have it both ways: either he accepts that good faith is different from bad faith (and hence cannot be qualified as a form of bad faith), or that good faith is the same as bad faith (but then how may one distinguish the two, as Sartre would wish us to do, in order to explain the very possibility of the phenomenon of bad faith?). Sartre, of course, argues that the *ideal* of good faith (to commit oneself entirely to a belief) is to be in bad faith, but this is not satisfactory, as then we will not be able to distinguish between good and bad faith, and hence not be able to explain how bad faith is possible in the first place.

---

38 D. Z. Phillips, "Bad Faith and Sartre's Waiter," *Philosophy* 56 (1981): 28.

39 Ibid., 29. Phillips, on the other hand, considers a number of the things a waiter would find worthwhile in his or her profession (p. 29).

40 Santoni, 80-81. This criticism of Sartre's notion of good faith as bad faith I owe to Santoni.

Good faith does not metamorphose into an in-itself state precisely because *epistemologically* it remains "faith" and not certainty, claims Santoni. Furthermore, on the *ontological* level,

good faith is precisely the human being's (freedom's) project of accepting its abandonment to freedom and the anxiety of its ontological distance . . . it is the basic attitude of accepting ourselves—without regret, remorse, despair, or excuse—as anguished "freedom" and of taking responsibility for our choices, projects, attitudes. Good faith, as an ontological attitude, is, we might say, the "*acceptance*" *of our abandonment to both freedom and responsibility.*[41]

Hence the notion that Sartre presents of good faith as yet another mode of bad faith is not without its problems. Let us go on to examine whether at the very least Sartre's description of the very possibility of bad faith meets some degree of clarity and consistency.

## e. The Possibility of the Enterprise of Bad Faith

We have observed that all Sartre's notions of a translucency of consciousness have almost disappeared by the end of his description of bad faith. After building up "the conditions which render bad faith conceivable, the structures of being which permit us to form concepts of bad faith,"[42] he is now not able to provide us with the possibility for this conceptual schema to take off the ground in the first place (i.e., given his ontological presuppositions).

According to Allen Wood, "in bad faith, I disbelieve what I believe to the extent that I recognize my belief as an imperfect attempt to produce an integral response to the world. But bad faith is not a case in which I disbelieve what I believe in the stronger sense of *knowing* that what I believe is false while nevertheless believing it."[43] Hence Sartre, to be consistent with his description of bad faith as a form of faith, should have said that there are *degrees* of consciousness of bad faith, or *degrees of believing or non-believing non-persuasive evidence.* Wood goes on to add that,

the devices available to Sartrian bad faith seem, on the whole, to be restricted to what Harry Stack Sullivan calls "selective inattention." In bad faith, I maintain my belief by consciously attending to those aspects of the world that my belief integrates, and directing my attention away from those aspects that clash with my belief . . . Some sort of "divided

41 Ibid., 86-87, original italics. Santoni is aware that this definition of good faith may seem to come close to the description of "authenticity" found in Sartre's later work titled, *Notebooks for an Ethics*, trans. David Pellaeur (Chicago: University of Chicago Press, 1992). Santoni distinguishes between sincerity, good faith and authenticity in the later Chapters of his book.

42 *Ibid.*, 67.

43 Wood, "Self-Deception and Bad Faith," 222.

> mind" explanation, most likely involving unconscious knowledge and unconscious choices, seems required to account for this conduct.[44]

Even if we do not need to have recourse to the unconscious[45] to explain the phenomenon of bad faith, there is no doubt that the process of "selective inattention" is operative in the person operating with bad faith: he or she pays greater attention to some beliefs while neglecting others. Of course, Sartre could still argue that at one point in time the person makes a conscious choice in deciding to which beliefs he or she should pay greater attention.[46] But this is a considerably muted allegation of bad faith, and does considerably damage to Sartre's notion of consciousness being entirely translucent.

Kathleen Wider, in her short but thorough-going analysis of Sartre's presentation of the different modes of self-consciousness, raises a much more fundamental objection with respect to Sartre's epistemological presuppositions connected with bad faith.[47] She points out that in connection with the nature of belief in the last section on bad faith, "Sartre argues that once I know I believe, I see my belief as purely subjective, and so my belief is undermined; it is no longer directed outward toward its object."[48] But Sartre accepts that, according to his own ontology, "non-thetic consciousness is not to *know*."[49] Yet, Wider adds, "he dismisses this inconsistency on his part by simply repeating his claim that pre-reflective consciousness, in its translucency, is at the origin of all knowledge."[50] In other words, Sartre admits that knowledge of the belief of bad faith destroys the specific belief in question as a *belief* (it loses its status as

---

44 *Ibid.*

45 Wood himself goes on to illustrate a case of a person engaging in an act of bad faith on the conscious level. However, there is certainly no translucency of consciousness demonstrated on the part of the person in the illustration. See Wood, "Self-Deception and Bad Faith," 223-25.

46 In the words of Santoni, 40, "The faith of the coquette, for instance, in "deciding" in advance not to be fully convinced in order to convince itself (*sic*) that she is not what she is (a flirt) is in *bad* faith from the start." The moot question, however, is: can she be said to be in bad *faith all through* (given that consciousness is continuously translucent)?

47 Kathleen Wider, "The Failure of Self-Consciousness in Sartre's *Being and Nothingness*," *Dialogue: Canadian Philosophical Review* 32 (1993): 737-56. In fact, she tries to (successfully, in my opinion) point out a number of ambiguities and inconsistencies in Sartre's presentation of self-consciousness. She concludes by saying, "If my criticisms of Sartre's account of self consciousness are correct . . . the ontology developed in *Being and Nothingness* has been seriously undermined" (p. 753).

48 *Ibid.*, 750.

49 Sartre, *Being and Nothingness*, 69.

50 Wider, 750.

belief),[51] yet he sees no harm in going on all the same to uphold the function of this known belief as providing for the possibility of bad faith.[52]

## 3. Beyond the "Bad Faith" of *Being and Nothingness*

We have examined both Sartre's presentation of the phenomenon of bad faith, as well as problems connected with this presentation. The general picture which emerges is that while Sartre is keen to demonstrate the constant temptation towards the many modes of bad faith and thereby the minimizing of our basic ontological status as free beings, his ontological and epistemological presuppositions themselves seem to restrict his ability to demonstrate the possibility of these modes of bad faith adequately. At best he presents us with an inadequate and ambiguous presentation of bad faith. At worst, this presentation is inconsistent or internally incoherent. In either case his presentation on bad faith seems to require either serious revision of his ontological and epistemological presuppositions, or a much more coherent (and by implication a far less incriminatory) approach towards the explication of the possibility and the operative preponderance of bad faith as part of our human experience.

At various points in *Being and Nothingness*, Sartre seems to define the nature of human consciousness itself as being plagued with bad faith. We have to keep in mind, however, that almost the entire work of *Being and Nothingness* is directed towards the explication of what constitutes *false consciousness.*[53] Sartre himself mentions the distinct possibility of authenticity or the "self-recovery of being,"[54] as well as almost contemporaneously wrote material that would later appear in *Notebooks for an Ethics*. This material seems to allow more easily for an authentic mode of human functioning, a far cry from the bad-faith-ridden-consciousness description of human reality with which *Being and Nothingness* is replete.

The binary or dualistic ontological understanding of nature in *Being and Nothingness* seems to constitute an ontological bias or assumption rather than a phenomenological description. In reality, consciousness is not as translucent and controllable as Sartre would like us to believe. There are a good number of psychological, sociological and cultural forces at play which condition

51 Sartre, *Being and Nothingness*, 69: "To believe is to know that one believes, and to know that one believes is no longer to believe."

52 Or, in the words of Santoni, 38: "the initial enterprise of bad faith is to be seen as a decision made in bad faith about the nature of bad faith."

53 See Thomas Anderson, *Sartre's Two Ethics: From Authenticity to Integral Humanity* (Chicago: Open Court Publishing Company, 1993), Ch. 3, Section 1, which is titled, "The Ontological Structure of Human Relations: Alienation, Degradation, Conflict."

54 In *Being and Nothingness*, 70, n. 9, Sartre refers to, "a self-recovery of being . . . [which] we shall call authenticity, the description of which has no place here." In reference to this, Anderson comments that "Apparently a treatment of authenticity belongs in ethics, not in a work of ontology" (p. 16).

consciousness, even though they may not determine action in a certain direction. Sartre does not make philosophical space for sub-conscious theory in his works, but in his later writings, already in the early 1960s, especially in *The Critique of Dialectical Reason,*[55] he is sympathetic to the Marxist emphasis on the fulfillment of transcendental human needs, in the context of the many socio-economic restrictions to human freedom. Sartre delineates the many common human needs which bind us into a common humanity– this is still not an essential description of what it means to be human, nor an ideological justification for praxis, but rather a phenomenological realization that human beings share a particular set of material, intellectual, social and communicative needs. At this stage, Sartre is also more appreciative of the need for inter-subjective and group efforts to bring about social change, in order that these fundamental human needs are met.

Thomas Anderson designates the focus of the early Sartre as *authenticity*, while that of the later Sartre as *integral humanity*. It is a pity that Sartre did not work out his understanding of bad faith with regard to his later understanding of what it means to be authentically human. It would seem that bad faith for the later Sartre would entail a conscious forgetting of our social responsibilities stemming from this new sense of social concern and human solidarity.

According to Anderson, Sartre had arrived at a *third* phase in his ethical theory, in which he allowed for substantive or *ontological* claims with regard to a primary '*we*' consciousness as the foundation for human striving.[56] In this third and controversial phase – controversial because De Beauvoir did not seem to accept that these were indeed Sartre's developed views – Sartre seemed to have clearly moved beyond his earlier repulsion in terms of formulating substantive claims. Based on this primordial 'we' consciousness, bad faith would seem to now constitute a refusal to recognize our fundamental connectedness and continue to live as if we are separate monads, each seeking to create his or her own set of values, apart from a consensual dialogue based upon this ontological commonality. While one can trace a thin line of continuity between the concerns of the early Sartre and this last Sartre in terms of retaining the nature of human *freedom*, this revised understanding is indeed a far cry from that presented in *Being and Nothingness*, at least in terms of how the problem of bad faith is depicted. However, it is an approach with which we can more easily identify, as well as an approach which we badly need in our contemporary world of individual and social fragmentation.

---

55 Jean-Paul Sartre, *Critique of Dialectical Reason: Theory of Practical Ensembles*, Vol. 1, new ed., trans. Alan Sheridan Smith (London: Verso, 2004) and *Critique of Dialectical Reason: The Intelligibility of History,* Vol 2 (unfinished), trans. Quintin Hoare (London: Verso, 1991).

56 See the Appendix of Anderson, *Sartre's Two Ethics*, titled, "Sketches of the Third Ethics," 169-172.

PART FOUR

# TOWARDS FULLER LIVING

# 25

# Teleology and Meaning of Life: Re-visioning Pragmatic Insights of William James

**Libin Joseph CST**
*Pontificia Università della Santa Croce, Rome*

**Abstract:** Prospection is a key concept in Positive Psychology which captured attention and appreciation over the last few years. Martin Seligman and companions, who analyze how the thought about the future guides human action and enables human flourishing, acknowledge William James as their inspiration. James integrated his view of teleology in his psychology, philosophy and religious thought. His teleological perspective was an immediate response to the Darwinian revolution which questioned the purposiveness of the organism. James interpreted Darwinism in favour of teleology accommodating the role of an Intelligent Designer and upholding an internal purposive nature of the organism. His future-oriented teleology highlights the possibility of creating a new future with human initiatives. He highlighted the higher value of ethical, aesthetic and religious motives criticizing Herbert Spencer's narrow teleology which considered survival as the supreme purpose of human existence. His teleological perspective is a guiding map for a meaningful life. For James, 'the meaning of life' consists in responding optimistically and creatively to the struggles of life with purposes. The believe in a supernatural order gives a better guarantee to foster this optimism.

**Keywords**: Teleology, Prospection, Meaning, Darwinism, Intelligent Design, Future, Survival, Supernatural

## Introduction

Martin Seligman, the founder of Positive Psychology, and his companions undertake scientific study of human flourishing and the positive aspects of the human experience that make human life successful and meaningful. In the last couple of years, the focus of their research is on prospection.[1] Martin Seligman, Peter Railton, Roy Baumeister and Chandra Sripada, the authors of *Homo Prospectus*, see prospection as "a label for mental process of projecting and evaluating future possibilities and then using these projections for the guidance of thought and action."[2] Their account is called 'teleological' as it is an "explanation by selection in light of values and goals."[3] Their theory of prospection draw cues from William James. *Homo Prospectus* begins by quoting James: "My thinking is first, and last, and always for my doing."[4] Baumeister qualifies prospection as 'pragmatic prospection' indicating its affinity with James' pragmatic approach.[5] However, beyond this acknowledgements, they have not gone to the roots of James' teleological perspectives. This article, divided into three parts, attempts to explore James' proposal of teleology and meaning of life. The first part overviews teleology in philosophy leading to James' significant contribution. The foundation and proposal of his teleology is analyzed in the second part. In the final section, his insights for a meaningful life is illustrated.

## 1. Teleological Perspectives in Philosophy

The term 'teleology' traces its origin from the Greek *telos* meaning end, goal or result and *logos* meaning logic or reason.[6] Hence, etymologically teleology means "the science of ends."[7] In a wider sense it is defined as an "explanation

---

1 See, Martin E. P. Seligman, et al., *Homo Prospectus* (Oxford; New York: Oxford University Press, 2016), 3.

2 Seligman, et al., *Homo Prospectus*, 6. The proponents adopt the term 'prospection' from Daniel D. Gilbert, Timothy D. Wilson, Randy L. Buckner and Daniel C. Carroll who define it as "the mental simulation of future possibilities." See Martin E. P. Seligman, et al., "Navigating into the Future or Driven by the Past," *Perspectives on Psychological Science* 8, no. 2 (2013):120.

3 Seligman, "Navigating into the Future," 120.

4 William James, *The Principles of Psychology,* II (New York: Henry Holt and Co., 1890), 333. It is cited in Seligman et al., *Homo Prospectus*, 3.

5 See, Roy F. Baumeister, Kathleen D. Vohs, and Gabriele Oettingen, "Pragmatic Prospection: How and Why People Think About the Future," *Review of General Psychology* 20, no. 1 (2016): 4.

6 "Teleology" *Online Etymology Dictionary*, https://www.etymonline.com/word/teleology (accessed on November 15, 2019).

7 Felix Adler, "The Problem of Teleology," *International Journal of Ethics* 14, no. 3 (April 1904): 265.

by reference to some purpose, end, goal or function."[8] Purpose, end and goal are often interchangeably used but function stands out separately in the literature on teleology.

The functional teleology involves "achievement of a goal without effort or intention, as a natural outgrowth of the thing's nature or of the arrangements of its parts."[9] A river flowing to the sea and a leaf turning towards sunshine are examples of it. In this sense, everything in the nature has a function, goal or end which is naturally oriented without any reference to human intention, consciousness or choice. The purposeful teleology implies "achievement of goal with persistence and sensitivity to surrounding conditions"[10] and it involves "consciousness with its power to anticipate, motivate and select."[11] It is related to human intention, consciousness and choice.

The idea of teleology was traditionally emerged, in opposition to materialism, as an explanation for the existence of complex designs. Materialists, sometimes called naturalists, saw all natural phenomena as "the product of the causal interactions of matter."[12] They saw all complex items and material arrangements as the product of non-purposive natural forces, matter and cause, instead of any purposive agent. They explained even human intentions, goals and consciousness materially, without any reference to goal-directed processes. Teleologists, in opposition to the materialists, explained the existence of complex machines in terms of goal-directed arrangements.[13]

Traditionally there had been roughly two alternative views of teleology: Platonic teleology (external teleology) and Aristotelian teleology (internal teleology).[14] The Platonists held that the materialist explanation for the simple motion satisfactorily explained astronomical patterns but it was insufficient to explain beauty, orderliness and good arrangement of the cosmos.[15] They

---

8 "Teleology," *Encyclopaedia Britannica*, https://www.britannica.com/topic/teleology. (accessed November 2, 2019).

9 See, Paul Croce, "A Future-Oriented Teleology: Evolutionary Biology, Jamesian Philosophical Psychology, and Sufficient Design," http://www.metanexus.net/future-oriented-teleology-evolutionary-biology-jamesian-philosophical-psychology-and/. (accessed November 15, 2019).

10 Croce, "A Future-Oriented Teleology," cit.

11 Croce, "A Future-Oriented Teleology," cit.

12 André Ariew, "Teleology," in *The Cambridge Companion to the Philosophy of Biology*, ed. David L. Hull and Michael Ruse (Cambridge: Cambridge University Press, 2007), 161.

13 See, Ariew, "Teleology," 161.

14 See, James G. Lennox, "Teleology," in *Keywords in Evolutionary Biology*, ed. Evelyn Fox Keller and Elisabeth Lloyd (Cambridge, MA: Harvard University Press, 1992), 324-333; Richard England, "Natural Selection, Teleology, and the Logos: From Darwin to the Oxford Neo-Darwinists, 1859-1909," *Osiris* 16 (2001): 275.

15 See, Ariew, "Teleology," 161.

supposed that an agent outside the nature arranged material within nature for its own purposes.[16] The Aristotelians explained the biological arrangements and functions without reference to the intentions of an external agent. It upheld "an inherent purposive or goal-directed force that resides in the material properties of living entities."[17] For Aristotle the activity originates from the capacity of a living being rather than any ingested material or external element. The active principle and "orderer" is always internal to the living being.[18]

Charles Darwin's *On the Origin of Species* (1859) challenged many traditional ideas in biology and philosophy including the teleological perspectives. A debatable question was whether Darwinism promoted a teleology. The answer was not so easily found because Darwin himself did not directly speak about teleology. In fact, it was not his area of investigation.[19] However, he envisioned a new worldview of the origin and growth of organism giving impetus to explain teleology in a new framework. Thus, the interpretations of his theories brought the question of teleology to the forefront.

Scientific naturalists challenged religious claims to "ultimate worldly purpose" and proposed that creatures evolve "without purpose" responding to naturalistic forces.[20] Many religious, cultural and philosophical traditions tried to find purposeful action in original creation and in on-going natural functions. They regarded natural selection's inattention to these as a sign of "the poverty of Darwin's theory."[21] Some religious people appreciated Darwinism for its scientific merits. They claimed that Darwinism left "religion's affairs of the spirit" untouched and they interpreted its endorsements of natural selection as "God's means of creating and sustaining the natural world."[22] William James

---

16 See, Philip Sloan, "The Question of Natural Purpose," in *Evolution and Creation,* ed. Ernan McMullin (Notre Dame, Ind.: University of Notre Dame Press, 1985), 125; England, "Natural Selection, Teleology, and the Logos," 275-276.

17 Ariew, "Teleology," 161-162. See also, J. D. Logan, "The Aristotelian Teleology," *The Philosophical Review* 6, no. 4 (July 1897): 394.

18 See, Aristotle, *De anima* 1.1 404a1-b18, as given in Juan Andrés Mercado, "Origin of the Metaphysics of the Living," *Acta Philosophica* 1, no. 22 (2013), 52. See also, Ariew, "Teleology," 161-162.

19 See, James G. Lennox, "Darwin was a Teleologist," *Biology and Philosophy* 8 (1993): 418.

20 See, Croce, "A Future-Oriented Teleology," cit.

21 Croce, "A Future-Oriented Teleology," cit. See also, Seymour Garte, "Teleology and the Origin of Evolution," *Perspectives on Science and Christian Faith* 69, no. 1 (March 2017): 42; Alister McGrath, "The Ideological Uses of Evolutionary Biology in Recent Atheist Apologetics," in *Biology and Ideology from Descartes to Dawkins*, ed. Denis R. Alexander and Ronald L. Numbers (Chicago, IL: University of Chicago Press, 2010), 339; Daniel C. Dennett, *Intuition Pumps and Other Tools for Thinking* (New York: W. W. Norton, 2013).

22 Croce, "A Future-Oriented Teleology," cit.

developed his teleological perspective in response to some of these debates on Darwinism.[23]

## 2. William James' Teleological Perspective

### a. Darwinian Basis of James' Future-Oriented Teleology

William James was born and brought up in an orthodox religious culture, holding a belief in a purposeful life derived from God. His interests in teleology evidently began at the time of his higher education especially during the Thayer Expedition[24] with Lois Agassiz. Agassiz was an anti-Darwinian who upheld teleology as a comfortable feature of his idealistic science. In fact, James spent more time with the scientists who accepted Darwin and tried to clarify many doubts about the teleological dimensions of nature. He was reflecting on the philosophical and religious implications of Darwinism in the discussion of the Metaphysical Club.[25] Through these activities, he tried to discover "evolution" as "an essential teleological conception."[26]

James found a couple of challenges in Darwinism and in the new worldview it projected. The confidence and claims of scientific naturalists to exhibit the authority of science as the only positive knowledge and their prospect of 'a purposeless world' disturbed him. He could not digest the adherents of traditional religion and idealism who perceived Darwinism as neglecting spiritual and idealistic aspects of human nature.[27] Science presented a confident picture of the world that could be explained through its natural systems with methods improving steadily. Therefore, the notion of "an intelligent Planner of the material Universe" struck him as "a tissue of absurdities." [28] They made him restless with their certainty bordering on faith in their approach to science.

---

23 Paul Croce identifies three principle sources of inspiration for James in proposing his view on teleology: (1) his observation of the progressive path of science; (2) his work in psychology where he tried to understand the reflective and planning consciousness of the mind; and (3) Darwinism where he encountered others with contrasting views.

24 Thayer Expedition was a natural history expedition of a group of scientists from the Museum of Comparative Zoology at Harvard University led by Louis Agassiz embarked for Brazil in April 1865. The purpose of the expedition was to study the fauna and flora of that country.

25 The Metaphysical Club was a group of a dozen Harvard-educated men who met for informal philosophical discussions during the early 1870s in Cambridge, Massachusetts.

26 See, Croce, "A Future-Oriented Teleology," cit.

27 See, Croce, "A Future-Oriented Teleology," cit. See also, Paul Jerome Croce, *Science and Religion in the Era of William James*, vols. 1 2 (Chapel Hill: University of North Carolina Press, 1995).

28 See, William James, "Review of Huxley," in *The Works of William James: Essays, Comments, and Reviews,* ed., Frederick H. Burkhardt, Fredson Bowers and Ignas K. Skrupskelis (Cambridge, MA: Harvard University Press, 1987), 205.

He could notice the role of an adaptive teleology within the theory of natural selection in spite of its associations with naturalism.[29] Instead of resigning to a life without purpose, he upheld a teleology emerging from "continuing thought in a certain direction."[30]

The future-orientation, with all its contingencies, places the outlook of Darwin and James in contrast with the anti-Darwinians of natural theology and intelligent design, and with the advocates of scientific naturalists such as Spencer and his intellectual descendants.[31] The natural theologians and scientific naturalists focus on the past with a concern for 'origins' even though there are sharp differences in their positions. The former group explains the origin of the designs in nature resulted either as from "a creator God" or "an initial anthropic imprint on the world." The latter group considers identity as shaped by origin and claims that the attention to the evolutionary beginnings of things can lead to reduction of new experiences in terms of the past and the familiar. It is an undoubtable fact that the origin has a large influence. However, they cannot explain the whole, particularly "at the moment of choice when the future is about to be created."[32]

In *The Principles,* while discussing the purposive actions in physical world and intelligent beings, James mentions the debated question about the 'final purpose' of the universe and Intelligent Designer. He states that the question, "Is the Kosmos [Cosmos] an expression of intelligence rational in its inward nature, or a brute external fact pure and simple?" is "the deepest of all philosophical problems."[33] He responds further:

> If we find ourselves, in contemplating it, unable to banish the impression that it is a realm of final purposes, that it exists for the sake of something, we place intelligence at the heart of it and have a religion. If, on the contrary, in surveying its irremediable flux, we can think of the present only as so much mere mechanical sprouting from the past, occurring with no reference to the future, we are atheists and materialists.[34]

This response does not explicitly reveal his choice among these two alternative positions. However, his later philosophy and a holistic outlook of his entire philosophy give more clarity about his view on intelligent design and purpose of the universe.

29 See, Croce, "A Future-Oriented Teleology," cit.

30 William James to Charles Eliot Norton, November 14, 1864 and December 9, 1864, in *Correspondence of William James*, eds. Skrupskelis and Elizabeth Berkeley (Charlottesville: University Press of Virginia, 1995): 93-94.

31 See, Croce, "A Future-Oriented Teleology," cit.

32 Croce, "A Future-Oriented Teleology," cit.

33 James, *The Principles of Psychology*, II, 8.

34 James, *The Principles of Psychology*, II, 8.

In *Pragmatism*, James explains the possibility of accommodating intelligent design in the Darwinian framework with an analogy of making shoes. Shoes are designed to fit with one's feet. They are made by the machines. However, these machines are designed by intelligent beings to fit the shoes with the feet.[35] Hence, he states, "Without nature's stupendous laws and counterforces, man's creation and perfection, we might suppose, would be too insipid achievements for God to have designed them."[36] He views Intelligent Designer in a wider perspective: "The designer is no longer the old manlike deity. His designs have grown so vast as to be incomprehensible to us humans. The what of them so overwhelms us that to establish the mere that of a designer for them becomes of very little consequence in comparison."[37]

The future-oriented teleology of James stands between "lack of purpose" of nihilists and the "fixed purpose" of the idealists.[38] Michael Polanyi, admiring this position, states that while most modern thinkers committed themselves to the polarities of blind mechanical necessity and total freedom, James remained in a smaller group of thinkers who offered "the first-rate teleological alternatives." For him, James upholds a "looser view of teleology" accepting the operation of the intelligible directional tendencies in the world without restricting them as the only determining factor.[39] The future-oriented teleology that James articulates in his psychology, philosophy and religious thought enables one to appreciate the religious impulses and to commit oneself to professional scientific practices.[40]

## b. James' Critique of Spencer's Narrow Teleology

James developed his philosophy critiquing Herbert Spencer. The central feature of Spencer's philosophy that James criticized was Spencer's teleological position which he formulated by wrongly interpreting Darwin. Spencer was the chief proponent of an evolutionary naturalism who associated the theory of natural selection to a materialistic philosophy with the assumption that the laws of evolution implied a deterministic and predictable set of behaviours for all creatures of the natural system. James found defects in Spencer which he did not find in Darwin due to Spencer's tendency to build a bold "materialistic

---

35 See, William James, *Pragmatism: A New Name for Some Old Ways of Thinking: Popular Lectures on Philosophy* (New York: Longmans, Green and Co., 1919), 57.

36 James, *Pragmatism,* 57.

37 James, *Pragmatism,* 57-58. The italics in the citation is from the original source. Such italicized citations in this work signify James' own emphasis.

38 See, Croce, "A Future-Oriented Teleology," cit.

39 Michael Polanyi and Harry Prosch, *Meaning* (Chicago: University of Chicago Press, 1975), 162-163.

40 See, Croce, "A Future-Oriented Teleology," cit.

monistic" philosophy based on a selective reading of evolution.[41] Spencer claimed that his definition of mental correspondence was purely scientific but James detected it also as "frankly teleological."[42]

In one of his earliest essays, "Remarks on Spencer's Definition of Mind as Correspondence," James critically analyzes Spencer's philosophy. In Spencer's *Principles of Psychology*, the answers to the questions, "How does the mind evolve?" and "What is the relationship between consciousness and environment?" are found in a central evolutionary principle. Spencer defines mental life as *"adjustment of inner to outer relations,"* which comprehends also "the entire process of mental evolution."[43] It implies many things such as the physical could explain the mental; the mind was a product of its physical surroundings; and the mind was essentially passive, receiving the impress of environmental influences.[44] When the mind accurately cognizes the way things exist in the world outside and adopts to such environmental demands, one moves towards mental perfection.[45]

Spencer takes the example of a polyp[46] to prove his theory of correspondence. He claims that polyp tries to adjust itself to the environment for its self-preservation and survival. James disagrees, first of all, with Spencer's belief that a more primitive form of life will yield greater insight in the working of human consciousness. He disproves Spencer, secondly, by arguing that even the polyp defies Spencer's correspondence principle. He comments, "He [Polyp] is as innocent of scientific as of moral and aesthetic enthusiasm; he is the most narrowly teleological of organisms; reacting, so far as he reacts at all, only for self-preservation."[47] He claims further that when the polyp moves around, avoids obstacle and tries to survive, it is due to an implicit teleology of the need to stay alive. Hence, "mere correspondence with

41 See, William James, "Notes on First Principles" and "Spencer's Law of Intelligence," *William James Papers*, given in Croce, "A Future-Oriented Teleology," cit.

42 William James, "Remarks on Spencer's Definition of Mind as Correspondence," *The Journal of Speculative Philosophy* 12, no. 1 (January 1878): 5.

43 James, "Remarks on Spencer's Definition of Mind as Correspondence," 2. This idea is restated in the later writings of James. See, William James, "What the Will Effects." In *The Works of William James: Essays in Psychology*, vol. 13, eds. Frederick H. Burkhardt, Fredson Bowers and Ignas K. Skrupskelis (Cambridge, MA: Harvard University Press, 1983), 217. The original publication of the article is: William James, "What the Will Effects," *Scribner's Magazine* 3 (February 1888): 240-250; See also, James, *The Principles of Psychology,* I, 6.

44 See, Croce, "A Future-Oriented Teleology," cit.

45 See, James, "Remarks on Spencer's Definition of Mind as Correspondence," 1-2.

46 Polyp or coral polyp is a tiny, soft-bodied organism related to sea anemones and jellyfish.

47 James, "Remarks on Spencer's Definition of Mind as Correspondence," 4.

the outer world" does not say anything about the way in which creatures even primitive as the polyp conduct their lives.[48]

James criticizes the position of Spencer concerning 'interest.' Spencer regards the creature as "absolutely passive clay." Experience rains down upon this clay and it becomes impressed most deeply where the drop falls thickest. The final shape of the mind is moulded in this way.[49] In the concluding chapter of *The Principles,* he states: "Mr. Spencer's opinion that our consciousness of classificatory, logical, and mathematical relations between ideas is due to the frequency with which the corresponding 'outer relations' have impressed our minds, is unintelligible."[50] In the observation of Ralph Barton Perry, the main object of James is "man the organism, saving himself and asserting his interests within the natural environment."[51] He considers human interests as the irreducible "teleological factor," which has to be centre and point of reference in any account of mind. Spencer's idea of mind as correspondence of *"adjustment of inner to outer relations"* fails to realize such correspondence as "relative to the organism's interests."[52]

James notes that Spencer's evolutionary formula which covers the "entire process of mental evolution," leaves out aesthetic impulses, religious emotions and personal affections.[53] He clarifies that "the ascertainment of outward fact constitutes only one species of mental activity."[54] Hence, Spencer's framework is extremely reductionistic. Regarding human consciousness, James argues that there is a plurality of purposes in human beings and "survival is only one out of many interests."[55] He pointedly states, "If ministry to survival be the sole criterion of mental excellence, then luxury and amusement, Shakespeare,

---

48 See, James, "Remarks on Spencer's Definition of Mind as Correspondence," 6.

49 See, William James, "Brute and Human Intellect," in *The Works of William James: Essays in Psychology*, vol. 13, eds. Frederick H. Burkhardt, Fredson Bowers and Ignas K. Skrupskelis (Cambridge, MA: Harvard University Press, 1983), 19. The original publication of the article is: William James, "Brute and Human Intellect," *Journal of Speculative Philosophy* 12 (July 1878): 236-276. See also, James, *The Principles of Psychology,* I, 403.

50 James, *The Principles of Psychology,* II, 676.

51 Ralph Barton Perry, *Present Philosophical Tendencies: A Critical Survey of Naturalism, Idealism, Pragmatism and Realism together with a Synopsis of the Philosophy of William James* (New York: Longmans, Green and Co., 1925), 350.

52 Perry, *Present Philosophical Tendencies,* 350.

53 See, James, "Remarks on Spencer's Definition of Mind as Correspondence," 2.

54 James, "Remarks on Spencer's Definition of Mind as Correspondence," 2.

55 See, James, "Remarks on Spencer's Definition of Mind as Correspondence," 7. Survival is a key idea in Spencer's Philosophy. It was Spencer who coined the expression "survival of the fittest." See, David Weinstein, "Herbert Spencer." *The Stanford Encyclopaedia of Philosophy.* https://plato.stanford.edu/archives/sum2018/entries/spencer (accessed October 16, 2019).

Beethoven, Plato, and Marcus Aurelius, stellar spectroscopy, diatom markings, and nebular hypotheses are by-products on too wasteful a scale."[56]

James did not call Spencer's view of consciousness as completely wrong but he charged it as being limited, one choice among many.[57] James indicates that there are other ends higher than survival and worldly success: "Vainly, too, would you talk to a Christian, or even to any believer in the simple creed that the deepest meaning of the world is moral. For they hold that mere conformity with the outward – worldly success and survival – is not the absolute and exclusive end."[58] He affirms further that "Spencer merely takes side with the τέλος [*telos*] he happens to prefer, whether it be that of physical well-being or that of cognitive registration. He represents a particular teleology."[59] For Spencer 'origin' was destiny but for James 'origin' was simple, elementary and it was simply just origin. Origin could suggest direction but he did not agree that "the embryologic line of appeal can alone teach us the genuine essences of things."[60]

## 3. Prospect for a Meaningful Life

### a. Struggle and Meaning of Life

William James' insights on the meaning of life is seen in most of his writings, precisely in some of his essays like "Is Life Worth Living?" and "The Sentiment of Rationality." William Hurrell Mallock had published a book *Is Life Worth Living?* fifteen years before James published his essay in 1895 with the same title. Even though the question was the same, the answer was different for both. Mullock answered that "it depends on the *liver*"[61] but James answered that life can be *made* worth living by imparting to it the quality of bold and strenuous

---

56 James, "Remarks on Spencer's Definition of Mind as Correspondence," 10.

57 See, Croce, "A Future-Oriented Teleology," cit.

58 James, "Remarks on Spencer's Definition of Mind as Correspondence," 12. James explans similar idea in the essay "Are We Automata?" See, William James, "Are We Automata?" in *The Works of William James: Essays in Psychology*, vol. 13, eds. Frederick H. Burkhardt, Fredson Bowers and Ignas K. Skrupskelis (Cambridge, MA: Harvard University Press, 1983), 57. The original publication of the essay is: William James, "Are We Automata?" *Mind* 4 (January 1879): 1-22.

59 James, "Remarks on Spencer's Definition of Mind as Correspondence," 13.

60 James, "Remarks on Spencer's Definition of Mind as Correspondence," 4.

61 William James, *The Will to Believe and Other Essays in Popular Philosophy* (London; Bombay; Calcutta: Longmans, Green and Co., 1909), 32. "Is Life Worth Living?" was an Address to the Harvard Young Men's Christian Association. It was published in *International Journal of Ethics,* October 1895. It has become integral part of *The Will to Believe.* See also, William Hurrell Mallock, *Is Life Worth Living* (London: Chatto and Windus, 1879).

action.[62] For the former, one's perception and attitude to life determines the meaning of one's life but for the latter, one's creative response determines it.

James articulates that struggles and sufferings of human life can give meaning to life. He argues, "It is, indeed, a remarkable fact that sufferings and hardships do not, as a rule, abate the love of life; they seem, on the contrary, usually to give it a keener zest. The sovereign source of melancholy is repletion. Need and struggle are what excite and inspire us; our hour of triumph is what brings the void."[63] He illustrates it further through two contrasting examples. The pessimistic words in the Bible come from the days of Solomon's glory rather than from the captivity of the Jews. In contrast, Germany produced the most optimistic and idealistic literature at the time when it was trampled under Bonaparte's troopers.[64]

In *The Principles* James evaluates how far pleasure and pain are motivating factors in human life. He includes pleasure and pain, both felt and anticipated, as important motives of human action, but not the exclusive ones.[65] He clarifies that the thought of a pleasure need not be always pleasurable and the thought of a pain painful. He recalls the words of Dante and Homer to illustrate it. Dante says, "*nessun maggior dolore*" meaning "not that the thought of pain be a pain."[66] Similarly Homer says, "griefs are often afterwards an entertainment."[67] However, present pleasures are "tremendous reinforcers" and present pains are "tremendous inhibitors" of whatever action leads to them. Hence, the thoughts of pleasure and pain take rank amongst the thoughts which have most impulsive and inhibitive power.[68]

In the essay "The Sentiment of Rationality" James notes that an optimistic human response to the hard realities of life can transform the reality for a better state and make one's life more meaningful. When one looks at the world and

---

62 See, James, *The Will to Believe, 32.* See also, Ralph Barton Perry, *The Thought and Character of William James: Briefer Version* (New York: George Braziller Publisher, 1954), 225.

63 James, *The Will to Believe, 47.*

64 James, *The Will to Believe, 47.*

65 See, James, *The Principles of Psychology,* II, 555. See also, Gerald E. Myers, *William James: His Life and Thought* (New Haven and London: Yale University Press, 1986), 213-214.

66 Cited in James, *The Principles of Psychology*, II, 549-550. No reference is given. It is taken from Dante's *The Divine Comedy* written between 1308 and 1320. In Italian, *"Nessun maggior dolore che ricordarsi del tempo felice nella miseria..."* is popularly translated as "No greater pain than to remember happy time in misery…." Dante, *Divine Comedy* – Hell – Song 5, nos. 121 123.

67 Cited in James, *The Principles of Psychology*, II, 549-550. No reference is given. It is taken from Homer's *The Odyssey* written between 800 and 700 BC in Greek language. A translation from Greek to English is: "Even his griefs are a joy long after to one that remembers all that he wrought and endured."

68 See, James, *The Principles of Psychology*, II, 550.

sees full of misery, old age, wickedness, pain and unsafe future in it, one may make a pessimistic conclusion, cultivate disgust and dread, cease striving, and end one's life. If one adds the subjective complement x to the mass M of mundane phenomena, it makes of the whole an "utterly black picture" without being illumined by any gleam of good. M + x expresses a state of things totally bad.[69] The result can be changed entirely by reversing the human reaction x with the same evil facts M. Instead of giving way to the evil, if someone confronts it bravely, finds a sterner and more wonderful joy than any passive pleasure, the bad character of the M will be diluted by the good character of the x.[70]

In the same essay James quotes the words of James Hinton to illustrate the significance of struggles in making life meaningful: "Little inconvenience, exertions, pains, – these are the only things in which we rightly feel our life at all. If these be not there, existence becomes worthless, or worse; success in putting them all away is fatal. So, it is men engage in athletic sports, spend their holidays in climbing up mountains, find nothing so enjoyable as that which taxes their endurance and their energy."[71] He concludes with the following words: "We have not got our proper life. So you perceive pain is no more necessarily an evil, but an essential element of the highest good."[72] It is, in fact, not an invitation to passively accept one's pains and struggles of life or to perceive some good in them but to transform oneself and the world through one's active response to them.

### b. Will to Believe and Meaning of Life

The emphasis on human action in transforming the world has the risk of limiting one's life to the material world and to some kind of activism. Limiting the scope of life to them is dangerous. James optimistically hopes for a supernatural order which exists beyond the visible world. The order of nature which constitutes the experience of this world is only one portion of the total universe. There is an unseen world beyond this visible world. Even though humans do not know anything concretely about it, the significance of the present mundane life consists in relation to the invisible world.[73] He shows further how one's belief in the supernatural order helps one to find meaning in life. He articulates, "I wish to make you feel [....] that we have a right to believe the physical order to be only a partial order; that we have a right to

69 See, James, *The Will to Believe, 101.*

70 See, James, *The Will to Believe, 101.*

71 James Hinton, *Life of James Hinton*, 172, as cited in *James, The Will to Believe, 101-102.*

72 Hinton, *Life of James Hinton*, 173, as cited in James, *The Will to Believe, 102.*

73 See, James, *The Will to Believe, 51.*

supplement it by an unseen spiritual order which we assume on trust, if only thereby life may seem to us better worth living again."[74]

For James, the essential function that human lives in this world have to perform 'maybe' to believe in the supernatural world. The 'maybe' is critically seen by the positivists. They argue that 'maybes' have nothing to do with a scientific life. James refutes this claim and argues that the scientific life has much to do with it. The vital productive and originating functions of human beings have to deal with 'maybes.'[75] He points out, "Not a victory is gained, not a deed of faithfulness or courage is done, except upon a maybe; not a service, not a sally of generosity, not a scientific exploration or experiment or textbook, that may not be a mistake. It is only by risking our persons from one hour to another that we live at all. And often enough our faith beforehand in an uncertified result is the only thing that makes the result come true."[76] His assumption is that one's faith in an invisible order inspires one's efforts. His advice at the end is motivating: "Be not afraid of life. Believe that life is worth living, and your belief will help create the fact."[77]

## Conclusion

William James' teleological perspective contains dynamics to make one's life meaningful. In nutshell, life has higher goals than mere survival; life has meaning when it has a purpose; struggles with goals constitute the meaning of life; and a belief in a supernatural order gives assurance of a meaningful life. This essay is only a miniature form of his philosophical vision on teleology and meaning of life based on a selective reading of some important works. More explanations and applications are scattered in his works such as *The Principles of Psychology, Pragmatism, The Will to Believe, A Pluralistic Universe and Some Problems of Philosophy.* The function of consciousness, volition, habits, instincts and emotions, and the dynamic aspects of novelty, creativity, optimism and hope are some specific areas where his teleological vision is manifested. They give a 'guiding map' for a meaningful life. The attempts of Seligman and companions to promote prospective thinking enables human beings to look at the future with possibilities and to act concretely at the face of the obstacles of life. Analyzing the creative applications of prospection in the light of James' teleology will establish a solid foundation for prospection. Simultaneously, having an impetus to revise James's teleological vision will re-discover the unforgotten value of his thought. This mutual exchange of ideas will enrich human beings to find the meaning of life in a new and profound way.

---

74 James, *The Will to Believe, 52.*

75 See, James, *The Will to Believe, 59.*

76 James, *The Will to Believe, 59.*

77 James, *The Will to Believe, 62.*

## Bibliography

Adler, Felix. "The Problem of Teleology." *International Journal of Ethics* 14, no. 3 (April 1904): 265-280.

Ariew, André. "Teleology." In *The Cambridge Companion to the Philosophy of Biology*, edited by David L. Hull and Michael Ruse, 160-181. Cambridge: Cambridge University Press, 2007.

Baumeister, Roy F., Kathleen D. Vohs, and Gabriele Oettingen. "Pragmatic Prospection: How and Why People Think About the Future." *Review of General Psychology,* 20, no. 1 (2016): 3–16.

Croce, Paul Jerome. *Science and Religion in the Era of William James*, vols. 1-2. Chapel Hill: University of North Carolina Press, 1995.

Croce, Paul. "A Future-Oriented Teleology: Evolutionary Biology, Jamesian Philosophical Psychology, and Sufficient Design." http://www.metanexus.net/future-oriented-teleology-evolutionary-biology-jamesian-philosophical-psychology-and/. (accessed November 15, 2019).

Dennett, Daniel C. *Intuition Pumps and Other Tools for Thinking.* New York: W. W. Norton, 2013.

England, Richard. "Natural Selection, Teleology, and the Logos: From Darwin to the Oxford Neo-Darwinists, 1859-1909." *Osiris* 16 (2001): 270-287.

Garte, Seymour. "Teleology and the Origin of Evolution." *Perspectives on Science and Christian Faith* 69, no. 1 (March 2017): 42-50.

Jacobs, Jonathan. "Teleological Form and Explanation." In *Current Issues in Teleology,* edited by Nicholas Rescher, 49-55. Langam, New York and London: University Press of America, 1986.

James, William. "Are We Automata?" In *The Works of William James: Essays in Psychology*, vol. 13, edited by Frederick H. Burkhardt, Fredson Bowers and Ignas K. Skrupskelis, 38-61. Cambridge, MA: Harvard University Press, 1983.

_________. "Brute and Human Intellect." In *The Works of William James: Essays in Psychology*, vol. 13, edited by Frederick H. Burkhardt, Fredson Bowers and Ignas K. Skrupskelis, 1-37. Cambridge, MA: Harvard University Press, 1983.

_________. "Remarks on Spencer's Definition of Mind as Correspondence." *The Journal of Speculative Philosophy* 12, no. 1 (January 1878): 1-18.

_________. "Review of Huxley." In *The Works of William James: Essays, Comments, and Reviews,* edited by Frederick H. Burkhardt, Fredson Bowers and Ignas K. Skrupskelis. Cambridge, MA: Harvard University Press, 1987.

_________. "What the Will Effects." In *The Works of William James: Essays in Psychology*, vol. 13, edited by Frederick H. Burkhardt, Fredson Bowers and Ignas K. Skrupskelis, 216-234. Cambridge, MA: Harvard University Press, 1983.

_________. *Pragmatism: A New Name for Some Old Ways of Thinking: Popular Lectures on Philosophy.* New York: Longmans, Green and Co., 1919.

_________. *The Principles of Psychology,* vols. 1-2. New York: Henry Holt and Co., 1890.

_________. *The Will to Believe and Other Essays in Popular Philosophy.* London; Bombay; Calcutta: Longmans, Green and Co., 1909.

James, William to Charles Eliot Norton, November 14, 1864 and December 9, 1864. In *Correspondence of William James*, edited by Ignas Skrupskelis and Elizabeth Berkeley, 93-94. Charlottesville: University Press of Virginia, 1995.

Lempert, Michael P. "Pragmatic Constructivism: Revisiting William James's Critique of Herbert Spencer." *Paideusis* 11, no. 1 (Fall 1997): 33-50.

Lennox, James G. "Darwin was a Teleologist." *Biology and Philosophy* 8 (1993): 409-421.

_________. "Teleology." In *Keywords in Evolutionary Biology,* edited by Evelyn Fox Keller and Elisabeth Lloyd, 324-333. Cambridge, MA: Harvard University Press, 1992.

Lenoir, Timothy. *The Strategy of Life: Teleology and Mechanics in the Ninetieth-Century German Biology.* Chicago: University of Chicago Press, 1982.

Logan, J. D. "The Aristotelian Teleology." *The Philosophical Review* 6, no. 4 (July 1897): 386-400.

Mallock, William Hurrell. *Is Life Worth Living.* London: Chatto and Windus, 1879.

McGrath, Alister. "The Ideological Uses of Evolutionary Biology in Recent Atheist Apologetics." In *Biology and Ideology from Descartes to Dawkins*, edited by Denis R. Alexander and Ronald L. Numbers, 329-351. Chicago, IL: University of Chicago Press, 2010.

Mercado, Juan Andrés. "Origin of the Metaphysics of the Living." *Acta Philosophica* 1, no. 22 (2013): 35-56

Myers, Gerald E. *William James: His Life and Thought.* New Haven and London: Yale University Press, 1986.

Perry, Ralph Barton. *Present Philosophical Tendencies: A Critical Survey of Naturalism, Idealism, Pragmatism and Realism together with a Synopsis of the Philosophy of William James.* New York: Longmans, Green and Co., 1925.

Polanyi, Michael, and Harry Prosch. *Meaning*. Chicago: University of Chicago Press, 1975.

Ruse, Michael. “Teleology and the Biological Sciences.” In *Current Issues in Teleology,* edited by Nicholas Rescher, 56-64. Langam, New York and London: University Press of America, 1986.

Seligman, Martin E. P., Peter Railton, Roy F. Baumeister, and Chandra Sripada. *Homo Prospectus*. New York: Oxford University Press, 2016.

_________. “Navigating into the Future or Driven by the Past.” *Perspectives on Psychological Science* 8, no. 2 (2013): 119-141

Sloan, Philip. “The Question of Natural Purpose.” In *Evolution and Creation,* edited by Ernan McMullin, 121-150. Notre Dame, Ind.: University of Notre Dame Press, 1985.

Weinstein, David. “Herbert Spencer.” *The Stanford Encyclopedia of Philosophy*. https://plato.stanford.edu/archives/sum2018/entries/spencer/>. (accessed October 16, 2019).

Woodfield, Andrew. *Teleology.* Cambridge: Cambridge University Press, 1976.

“Teleology.” *Encyclopaedia Britannica*. https://www.britannica.com/topic/teleology (accessed November 2, 2019).

“Teleology.” *Online Etymology Dictionary*. https://www.etymonline.com/word/teleology (accessed November 15, 2019).

26

# Life is Not a Problem to be Solved but a Mystery to be Lived

**M.D. Joseph**
*Research Scholar, Jnana-Deepa Vidyapeeth, Pune*

**Abstract**: Existentialism is not a system of philosophy rather it is way of philosophizing. There is no common pattern of thinking in this style of philosophizing. Though Søren Kierkegaard is called the father of existentialism, this style of philosophizing came to the fore during and after the World War I & II, when the human life was on the verge of extinction. At the same time what makes these thinkers similar in view is that they all begin their works centered on human life and its existential situation. Thus, Existentialism came a reaction to logical positivism with its emphasis on sensory empiricism, objectivity, and science with emphasis on individualism, subjectivity, introspection, and feeling. It is a philosophy of the situation-the actuality of existing and not the concept of existing In reaction to idealism it is an objection to be liberal doctrines of optimism and progress that man is not an object to be understood, or a problem to be solved and grasped but a subject and a mystery to be lived as brought out by Gabriel Marcel in his writings. With their outcry of subjectivism, existentialism is a champion of the concrete against the abstract, of life as opposed to logic, of the non-intellectual and irrational in contrast to intellectualism, and of freedom as against mechanism and determinism. It has much in common with romanticism, pragmatism, personalism, Bergsonism, voluntaristic and vitalistic philosophies in general. This article brings to light that life is not a problem to be solved but a mystery to be lived, a thought central to the writings of the French writer Gabriel Marcel.

**Keywords:** Søren Kierkegaard, Gabriel Marcel, existentialism, humans, God, world, problem, and mystery

## Introduction

As Rev Dr Cyril Desbruslais SJ, writes, "when we take a brief glance at contemporary Western philosophy, we are filled with new interest and it seems to confirm our all too human penchant for constructing neat "national stereotypes" and over-simplified generalizations. Thus, German philosophers turn out to be "characteristically," abstract and obscure as they elaborate vast system of thought which, in 'an all-too-orderly fashion, assign a neat place to everything according to a pre-planned scenario, Idealism, culminating in Hegel, appears to be precisely that kind of thing.[1] He says that as for the French, most obligingly, they offer us Existentialism, a philosophy which, in "typical Gallican" spirit, wears its heart on its sleeve and writes melodramatically about anguish and anxiety in a hyperemotional vein that would make us "traditionally inexpressive Orientals" blush.[2] For him Sartre is a good example of this and it is a pity that Kierkegaard is Danish; his outpourings would fit in well with the type of stuff we'd expect a Frenchman to produce. The British, with their usual English phlegm, guard a stiff upper-lip and raise their eyebrows at the sentimentalism of "those wretched frog-eaters" and serve us up the philosophy which cause us no surprise at all; cold, detached analysis of "words, words, words."[3] While linguistic philosophy is "so thoroughly English, y'know" and the average professor of philosophy in Indian Universities of today will hasten to sit at the feet of Wisdom and Ryle (we are still culturally colonialised by the British).[4] Prof. Desbruslais asks: "and the Americans?" The reply is simple: "What else can we demand from them but pragmatism-that rough and ready way of reviewing things which is so stamped with the "American way of life' and actually pontificates in philosophical terminology what the Great American Dream has always proclaimed: the important thing is to succeed? The true is what works. After all, isn't that 'in a nutshell' what William James was trying to say?"[5]

Pro. Desbruslais reminds us that we should be more than cautious about all kinds of stereotypes, nutshell-summaries and hasty generalizations and at

1 Cyril Desbruslais, SJ, *Contemporary Western Philosophy* (Pune: Jnana-Deepa Vidyapeeth, 2000), 1.

2 *Ibid.*

3 *Ibid.*

4 *Ibid.*

5 *Ibid.*

best these are but exaggerations. At the same time let us not forget that, if they are authentic exaggerations, as they can only be so by underscoring a solid vein of truth.[6] According to him it is not too startling to note that philosophers, like everyone else, are as much makers of their age as they are shaped by their cultures. He points out that nowadays, when we are more than aware of the conscious and unconscious undercurrents of the will to power that infiltrate all manner of national and international structures.[7] Keeping in mind of this nature of the background of all philosophies, systems and patterns of thought that this article titled, "Life is not a problem to be solved but a mystery to be lived," is being brought out. This, I believe that it is a common experience of every one of us that life is often a problem to be solved rather than a mystery to be lived and contemplated. But as humans whatever be the problems one has to face in life, one comes to realization at one time or other that life is not merely a problem to be solved but a mystery to be lived, which makes us to live our life as authentic and responsible human persons. Such approach to life will help us to see the preciousness our life as humans in this world.

## 1. Basics of Existentialism

Thus, at the opposite pole of logical positivism, with its emphasis on sensory empiricism, objectivity, and science, Existentialism has been a reaction in favour of individualism, subjectivity, introspection, and feeling.[8] It is a philosophy not of things, but of the situation, the actuality of existing and not the concept of existing.[9] Against the philosophy of idealism it is an objection to be liberal doctrines of optimism and progress that man is not an object to be understood, or a problem to be solved and grasped but a subject and a mystery to be lived. With their outcry of subjectivism, existentialism as a champion of the concrete against the abstract, of life as opposed to logic, of the non-intellectual and irrational in contrast to intellectualism, and of freedom as against mechanism and determinism. Existentialism has much in common with romanticism, pragmatism, personalism, Bergsonism, and voluntaristic and vitalistic philosophies generally.[10]

Though existentialism is not a system of thought, but a way of philosophizing, has its historical roots deep in the culture, with an ancient heritage, the outlines of which have become plain especially since the work of its chief technical philosophers such as Martin Heidegger, Socrates, the

---

6 *Ibid.*

7 *Ibid.*

8 B.A.G. Fuller (ed), *A History of Philosophy*, (Calcutta: Oxford & IBH Publishing Co, 1955), 603.

9 *Ibid.*

10 *Ibid.*

psalmists, Paul, Augustine, and Pascal who contributed to its foundations.[11] But it came to its modern technical form, grounded in the psychology and theology of Søren Kierkegaard, the philosophy of Nietzsche, and the method and ontology of the phenomenologist Husserl.[12]

It should be noted that there is no single existentialist position in their philosophizing but they all begin their philosophizing with man (humans) from their act of existing. Thus, the philosophy varies with its proponents, some of whom insists that they are not existentialists at all.[13] But there is a common stream of doctrine that identifies them, nevertheless, and indicates quite clearly their relation to the classical philosophic tradition with their major and differentiating thesis that "existence is prior to essence," while in the established tradition, "essence is prior to existence."[14] By this the existentialist means that human nature is determined by the course of life rather than life by human nature.[15]

In political philosophy, in the present, epoch, the submerging of the individual takes other forms than that of absolute idealism, in the powerful tendency towards political and social totalitarianism with its reduction of personal responsibility, and its evaluation of personal value in terms of service to the collectivity.[16] Existentialism, in some of its forms, can be considered, in part that is to say, as a reaffirmation of the free individual in the face of this powerful tendency.[17] Frederick Copleston points out that one of the reason why Marxists have represented the existentialism of M. Sartre as being the philosophy of the dying bourgeoisie, the last convulsive effort of an outmoded individualism.[18] He says that again, existentialism, by insisting on the individual, on the free subject, is also a protest against the general tendency in our civilization to resolve the individual into his (her) social function or functions, such as taxpayer, voter, civil servant, engineer, trade unionist, etc.[19] According to Copleston this theme has been developed by Gabriel Marcel in particular, who believes that the tendency towards the functionalization of man (humans) involves degradation of the human person.[20] As he writes that in general, therefore, we can say that existentialism represents the

11 *Ibid.*

12 *Ibid.*

13 *Ibid.*

14 *Ibid.*

15 *Ibid.*

16 Frederick Copleston, *Contemporary Philosophy* (London: Search Press Ltd., 1972.), 138.

17 *Ibid.*

18 *Ibid.*, 138-139.

19 *Ibid*, 139.

20 *Ibid.*

reassertion of the free man (humans) against the collectivity or any tendency to depersonalization, and in this respect it is akin to personalism and has some affinities with pragmatism.[21]

Existentialism is more than a protest of the free individual against totalitarianism and impersonal functionalization. For as in certain forms it seems to be being presented, tacitly at least, as a way of salvation, which is partly true of Marcel's philosophy; for as a convinced Catholic, he believes that man's salvation is achieved by other means than by man's unaided effort and choice.[22] For example, it seems to be verified not only in the case of Jaspers' philosophy but also in those of Sartre and Camus.[23] As Copleston writes that it may, indeed, appear to constitute a gross paradox if one speaks of a way of salvation in connection with an atheistic philosophy such as that of Sartre.[24]

In the ancient world history we find people looking to philosophy for a way of life, for reasoned guidance in conduct and belief, which was not provided by the official cult. It does not mean great numbers of people turned to philosophy for moral guidance and for religious belief.[25] According to Copleston serious philosophy is scarcely a popular pastime; and the number of people who pay much attention to philosophers is at any time comparatively restricted.[26] He points out that even in the earlier phases of Greek thought we find the tendency to look to philosophy for a way of life: we have only to think of the Pythagorean "society." In the Hellenistic and Roman periods we find the tendency taking definite forms as in Stoicism and Neo-platonism.[27] Copleston points out that the former offered a moral doctrine which was supported by rational argument: the latter offered, besides ethical teaching, a deeply religious view of the world and of human life, a view which was capable of attracting those who had no real belief in the ancient anthropomorphic mythologies and who at the same time looked, in the uncertainty and bewilderment of 'human existence,' for some message of personal salvation which was at once intellectually respectable and satisfying to the religious impulse.[28] In many a time, the individual (human), thrown back on himself (herself) in the great cosmopolitan society of the Empire and only too consciousof the forces threatening his personal security, could find in Stoicism the ideal of the self-

21 *Ibid.*

22 *Ibid.*

23 *Ibid.*

24 *Ibid.*

25 *Ibid.*

26 *Ibid.*

27 *Ibid.*

28 *Ibid.*

sufficient virtuous man or in Neo-platonism a religious doctrine of liberation and salvation.[29]

While in the mediaeval world the situation was very different. For them the way of salvation was provided by the Christian religion and, whether they practiced it or not, men accepted the Christian code as the norm of moral action. In the mediaeval world, philosophy, therefore, tended to be a purely academic pursuit, a matter for university professors and their students.[30] It was the view of the general circumstances, that mediaeval man should not have expected from philosophy, as distinct from Christian theology and Christian moral and ascetic teaching, what Marcus Aurelius, for example, had looked for in Stoicism.[31]

Coming to modern Europe not however, mediaeval Europe, here, belief, in the Christian religion has waned, and this has been followed as Nietzsche saw that it would, by doubt concerning the absolute character and universal applicability of Christian values and of the Christian moral teaching.[32] Copleston says that at the same time it is now realized more clearly than it was in the last century that we cannot expect science to provide us with a normative morality or with religious belief.[33] He points out that it is no matter for surprise that some at least should look to philosophy to provide them with what, in their opinion, neither Christianity nor science can give them.[34] In such human situation where one finds himself (herself), Copleston says that whether we think that existentialism meets the need or not, it seems to him that it is one of the forms of philosophy which attempts to do so.[35] Thus existentialism lays special emphasis on the free individual that is why existentialism finds its relevance even today.

Existentialism in its theistic form has been an important factor in the neo-orthodox awakening that has marked theology since the first war with its emphasis on the negative qualities of man, on human estrangement and the tragedy of human existence, have supported the resurgence of the dogma of original sin and the entire structure of eschatological theology.[36] While secular, or what is often called atheistic, Existentialism has popularized especially since the second war by numerous in fiction, drama, and poetry,

29 *Ibid.*, 139-140.

30 *Ibid.*, 140.

31 *Ibid.*

32 *Ibid.*

33 *Ibid.*

34 *Ibid.*

35 *Ibid.*

36 B.A.G. Fuller (ed), *A History of Philosophy*, 603-604.

particularly by its French partisans under the leadership of Jean Paul Sartre.[37] Existentialism in its recent technical formulations is largely a German product, its foremost representatives being the Protestant theologian Paul Tillich and the philosophers Karl Jaspers and Martin Heidegger.[38] In the post-war scene, to some extent the rise of Existentialism must be attributed to the destruction and human desolation attending the two world wars and the anxieties that stem from the continuing unrest in both world and domestic affairs and as such it is a product of large-scale social failure.[39] It is also an expression of the psychological and moral tensions that hold the individual in their grip in any age and in any society, for as humans we are the same irrespective of place and time.[40]

## a. Gabriel Marcel

Gabriel Marcel, (in full Gabriel-Honoré Marcel, born December 7, 1889, Paris, France—died October 8, 1973, Paris), is a French philosopher, dramatist, and critic who was associated with the phenomenological and existentialist movements in 20th-century European philosophy and whose work and style are often characterized as theistic or Christian existentialism (a term Marcel disliked, preferring the more neutral description "neo-Socratic" because it captures the dialogical, probing, and sometimes inchoate nature of his reflections).[41] He is considered as the advocate of Christian existentialism in France, who was also a personal thinker like Kierkegaard, whose thought springs from personal experience. Marcel was opposed to abstract system building and absolute capacity of reason to resolve human difficulties.[42]

According to him evils, hatred and mass hysteria of modern times are the result of unwarranted abstraction. He says that the need of day is to react with our whole strength against that dissociation of life from spirit which a bloodless rationalism has brought about, which reflects his 'obstinate and untiring battle against abstraction.[43] According to Marcel such abstraction not only leads the philosopher away from the truths of one's own experience but also leads to fanaticism and violence.[44] Marcel sees the limitation of excessive claims of thinkers who place everything in the wheel of reason. For him reason

---

37 *Ibid.*, 604.

38 *Ibid.*

39 *Ibid.*

40 *Ibid.*

41 Brendan Sweetman, "Gabriel Marcel," https://www.britanica.com/biography/Gabriel-Honore-Marcel (accessed September 10, 2019).

42 M.N. Sinha, *A Primer of Existentialism,* (Delhi: Capital Publishing House, 1982), 18.

43 *Ibid.*

44 *Ibid.*

is always inadequate in explaining existing individual.[45] He says that it causes evils in society and obstructs natural flow of life and, as such brings man into the chain of determinisms.[46]

Thus, at times, it catches hold of the individual person and fastens him (her) so tightly that he (she) feels immense pressure in participation.[47] It is for this that Marcel emphasizes the recovery of personal value not through reason but through art, contemplation and friendly association.[48] Thus, this personal value culminates in the existential unity of every creature and in the love of Being.[49]

## Being

Marcel's spirit of his thought, as revealed in his concern with exploring the realm of "Being," is more "metaphysical," than the spirit of Sartre's thought, which is turned dramatically towards action.[50] At the same time as Copleston points out that we can hardly read Marcel's writings without realizing his concern with exhibiting that it means to be a human person in the fullest sense of the term and with bearing witness to what he regards as the truth with a view to enabling others to appropriate it freely, not only by intellectual recognition, but also on the plane of being.[51]

## The Existent

Marcel analyses the existent reality. The existent reality for him cannot be known rather can be encountered through communion. Thus he is against the dichotomies of thought and being, subject and object, self and God, the individual and the society, set forth by different thinkers in the history of thought.[52] According to him these dichotomies are epistemological rather than ontological and, as such, they are contingent. For him, even knowledge is contingent and being so, it fails to explain the existent reality.[53] He says that it does not account for participation in being. Thus, his statement, knowledge is contingent on a participation in being for which no epistemology can account because it continually presupposes it, bears testimony to this fact.[54]

---

45 *Ibid.*

46 *Ibid.*

47 *Ibid.*

48 *Ibid.*

49 *Ibid.*, 18-19.

50 Frederick Copleston, *Contemporary Philosophy*, 136.

51 *Ibid.*, 136-137.

52 M.N. Sinha, *A Primer of Existentialism*, 20.

53 *Ibid.*

54 *Ibid.*

Thus, Prof. Desbruslais points out that Gabriel Marcel was an existentialist before the term became fashionable. According to him Marcel was the first to use the word to describe his own approach to philosophy-though he rejected it afterwards because of Sartre's appropriation of the label into his atheistic system.[55] He says that Marcel was also a phenomenologist before phenomenology became a central concern for European philosophy.[56] Prof. Desbruslais points out that finally, he was a religious thinker at a time when religious was not a respectable thing in philosophy.[57] For him, no wonder Seymour Cain called him "a herald of our times."[58] Marcel lived in a time when the world was shaken by the two great earthquakes viz., World War I & II. So his life was one of sufferings, pain, hunger and thirst, alienation, anxiety, despair and death. Thus his world was a world of problems. From the midst of such a situation he develops his philosophy of life that 'life is not a problem to be solved but a mystery to be lived.'

## Being in a Situation

It is the experience of any of us as humans in the world that we are always in a situation or in a predicament, which could be called as in an existential situation. Thus, Prof. Desbruslais writes that Marcel's is indeed, a very "concrete approach," to man (humans).[59] He says that rather than approach him abstracting man's ego from out of its context and then grappling with the pseudo-problem of how to bring the context back again-via the "problem of the bridge" bogey or attempts to "prove" the reality of the world-he takes a realistic, down-to-earth approach which takes men (women), as he (she) is, a being in situating.[60] This also means to what am I? Or what does it mean to be a person? This situation also implies the world, the spactio-temporal reality that surrounds me (us). Thus it is not the self-enclosed ego but myself (ourselves) in the world, present in a situation, participating in Being and open to Being.[61] Prof. Desbruslais says that according to Marcel this insertion into the cosmos is through my body. He points out that through my body I am "incarnating into the world and my relation to my body is, thus, mysterious. Thus neither statement does justice to the facts – neither have "I had a body," nor I am a body".[62]

---

55 Cyril Desbruslais, SJ, *Contemporary Western Philosophy*, 102.

56 *Ibid.*

57 *Ibid.*

58 *Ibid.*

59 *Ibid.*, 103.

60 *Ibid.*

61 *Ibid.*, 101.

62 *Ibid.*

According to Marcel it is a unique type of relationship; it can be properly compared or likened to none other.[63] Thus Marcel avoids the fatal dichotomy of "me and the body," trying to put the proverbial Humpty Dumpty together again after having separated what was inextricably joined together.[64] For him the postulate that the primary philosophical-and psychological concept is not the isolated "I" but the "I-in-situation" which, in the context of persons, broadens into an "I-in-communion" is certainly a healthy corrective to the usual individualistic thrust of many an existentialistically inclined author.[65] Being human always implies that we are always in a situation. This is also what we mean when we say, 'life is not a problem to be solved but a mystery to be lived,' particularly when we are faced with life's problems and anxieties.

### b. Problem and Mystery

Prof. Desbruslais points out that this well-known distinction of Marcel is the key to his whole philosophical development.[66] He says that in his own words, metaphysics is essentially a 'reflection bearing on a mystery[67] for Marcel to speak of ontology as a problem is an abuse of language, which, in the last analysis invalidates the whole process of philosophizing.[68] Thus by making the distinction between 'problem' and 'mystery,' he intends to explain the true position of existential philosophy which does not explain the concepts rather unfolds the mystery and reveals deeper implications of our existence.[69] This is one of the distinctive mark of Marcel when we say, 'life is not a problem to be solved but a mystery to be lived.'

### Problem

For Marcel, a problem relates to things that can be resolved by intellect objectively and does not involve the being of the questioner.[70] For example, in a problem, the involved object is an epistemological subject who can be replaced by a machine as a computer solving the problem of calculation.[71] But as humans we are, most of us today are faced with daily problems of life such as basic necessities of life like shelter, food and clothing. Even in these utter human necessities of life one does not get lost in the stark realities of life such as these problems of life. But in the midst of all these, there is always a

---

63 *Ibid.*

64 *Ibid.*

65 *Ibid.*

66 Cyril Desbruslais, SJ, *Contemporary Western Philosophy*, 100.

67 *Ibid.*

68 *Ibid.*

69 M.N. *A Primer of Existentialism*, 20.

70 *Ibid.*

71 *Ibid.*

ray of hope which makes us go on with our life joyfully and with hope and love which raises us from problem to life as a mystery. This could be what in Marcel's philosophy when he says that life is not a problem to be solved but a mystery to be lived.

## Mystery

Aristotle says; "one fine day, the mind comes up against not this or that aspect of being but being itself-being as being."[72] For Marcel in mystery, the being of the questioner, the human person, is involved. Therefore, is a problem which encroaches upon its own data, which invades them, as it were.[73] And finally, it transcends itself as a simple problem. For Marcel ontological reality is a mystery and not a problem as it cannot be solved like problem by intellect but can be revealed directly through participation or encounter.[74] Thus the work of philosophy, according to him, relates, to the realm of revelation of mystery underlying human existence and not the mere explanation of the concepts related to it.[75] This is the outstanding contribution of Marcel to the thought of philosophizing in the history of philosophy. For him, the existential philosophy does not or should not undertake the explanation of concepts or resolution of problems related to these concepts but attempts or should attempt to unfold the mystery of human existence and reveals the deeper implications underlying it.[76] This is what we mean when we take Marcel's pattern of thought that life is not a problem to be solved but a mystery to be lived.

## Conclusion

Marcel is noted for describing man's (humans') place in the world in terms of such fundamental human experiences such as relationships, love, fidelity, hope, and faith.[77] He is a survivor of the two great earthquakes – World War I and II that shook the whole world. Among his contributions to the history of thought is his description of human life with regards to problem and mystery which can be summarized in these words that life is not a problem to be solved but a mystery to be lived. His whole philosophy can be said to be centered on this theme. His brand of existentialism was said to be largely unknown in the English-speaking world, where it was mistakenly associated with that of Jean-Paul Sartre. Marcel's view of the human condition was that "beings"

72 Cyril Desbruslais, SJ, *Contemporary Western Philosophy*, 100.

73 M.N. Sinha, *A Primer of Existentialism*, 20.

74 *Ibid.*

75 *Ibid.*

76 *Ibid.*

77 "Gabriel Marcel," https://www.encyclopedia.com/people/philosophy-and-religion-philosophy-biographies/gabriel-marcel (accessed September 10, 2019).

are beset by tension, contradiction and ambiguity.[78] He was also interested in life's religious dimension and was considered the first French existentialist philosopher.[79] At times it may seem that Marcel offers an anthropocentric philosophy with regards to human life where metaphysics seems to be absent or alien.[80] To this Copleston himself says that Marcel's thought centres round the human person; round the person as related to other persons and to God, it is true, but still round the human person[81], which Marcel calls 'intersubjectivity.' It is from this background that Marcel develops his theme that life is not a problem to be solved but a mystery to be lived, where oneself, others, God and the world are intimately related.

## Bibliography

Copleston, Frederick. *Contemporary Philo*sophy, London: Search Press Ltd, 1972.

Desbruslais, Cyril SJ.*The Philosophy of Human Person: An Introduction to Philosophical Anthropology,* Pune: Jnana-Deepa Vidyapeeth, 1997.

_______. *The Philosophy of Be-ing: Introduction to Metaphysics for Today*, Pune: Jnana-Deepa Vidyapeeth, 1997.

Fuller, B.A.G.*A History of Philosophy,* Calcutta: Oxford & IBH Publishing Co., 1955.

Gaur Prakash Ved, *Indian Thought and Existentialism with Special Reference to the Concept of Being in Gabriel Marcel and the Upaniṣads,* Delhi: Eastern Book Linkers, 1985.

Joseph, M.D. *Thrown into the World: An Existential Approach to Life.* Guwahati (India): EBH, 2016.

Pandikattu, Kuruvilla SJ, (ed). *Metaphysics: Philosophy of Be-ing for Today*, Pune: Jnana-Deepa Vidyapeeth & New Delhi: Christian World Imprints, 2019.

_______. (ed) *Postmodernity: An Indian Christian Philosophical Appraisal,* Pune: Jnana-Deepa Vidyapeeth & New Delhi: Christian World Imprints, 2019.

Sinha, M.N. *A Primer of Existentialism*. Delhi: Capital Publishing House, 1982.

---

78 *Ibid.*

79 *Ibid.*

80 Frederick Copleston, *Contemporary Philosophy*, 133.

81 *Ibid.*

## Unpublished Material

Cyril Desbruslais, SJ.*Contemporary Western Philosophy*, (Pune: Jnana-Deepa Vidyapeeth, 2000).

## Electronic documents from Internet/World Wide Web site

Sweetman, Brendan. "Gabriel Marcel," https://www.britannica.com/biography/Gabriel-Honore-Marcel, (accessed September 10, 2019).

"Gabriel Marcel," https://www.giffordlectures.org/lecturers/gabriel-marcel, (September 10, 2019).

"Gabriel Marcel,"https://www.encyclopedia.com/people/philosophy-and-religion/philosophy-biographies/gabriel-marcel, (accessed, 10, 2019).

"Gabriel Marcel," March, 2016, https://plato.stanford.edu/entries/marcel/, (September 10, 2019).

"Gabriel Marcel: Ethics within Existentialism," https://link.springer.com/chapter/10.1007/978-94-015-9924-5_14, (accessed September 10, 2019).

Hernandez Graper, Jill. "Gabriel Marcel," https://www.iep.utm.edu/marcel/, (accessed September 10, 2019).

27

# Right Rites and Rite Rights
# Some Critical Reflections on Community Worship

**Subhash Anand**
*Professor (Emeritus), Dept of Indian Studies, JDV, Pune*

**Abstract:** Being embodied, humans need sensible signs to communicate. Certain inner experiences cannot be described but only evoked symbols and symbolic actions. Though out symbols are shaped by your environment, our environment is not static, nor given once for all. Hence, we need other symbols even though what we wish to communicate—the symbolized—is the same. The rites and rituals that constitute our cult are narrative actions using symbols.

While we need symbols, they need not always be adequate to communicate the symbolized. Human rights and greater than rites and rituals. Hence nobody can be obliged to follow some particular rites and rituals. These are legitimate if they promote values and deepen our commitment to human wellbeing. Abiding and discerning commitment can only be nurtured by contemplation. Hence rites and rituals have a right to continue only if the foster contemplation.

**Keywords:** commitment, community, contemplation, cult, environment, existence, history, rite, ritual, symbol, symbolized, time.

As embodied beings, humans communicate through signs and symbols they can perceive with their senses. A rite or ritual is a chain of signs and symbols that has acquired some legitimacy and continuity within a community. Rites and rituals are an essential part of organized religions: they constitute its cultic life. They are especially important when the community gathers for worship.

People know what is going to take place and so they can participate with ease. They are familiar with their rites and understand them—at least that is what most cultic leaders claim. Rites and rituals emerge from within the religious experience of the community and so function as a bond not only with the members today, but also relate them to their past, and give them a sense of responsibility for the future.

I am not sure whether the historical Jesus ever spoke affirmatively about rites and rituals. The parable of the Good Samaritan (Lk 10.30-37), which portrays a Samaritan fulfilling the Law, and the priest and Levite ignoring it, is "something of an anticlerical joke."[1] Jesus' attitude to the Temple and its cult "helps to explain why the priestly class and the lay aristocracy in Jerusalem... was most prominent in bringing Jesus before Pilate. The mortal struggle between Jesus and his opponents has elements not only of Galilean versus Judean...but also of the laity versus the priests."[2] Yet the tragic paradox is that no Christian Church is as cultic as the Roman Church. Hence, the persistence of rites and rituals needs to be understood; only then any remedial action is possible.

## 1. Being in History

Depth psychology has helped us arrive at a better understanding of religion. Religious beliefs and practices are intimately connected to our fears and anxieties related to our most fundamental concern: survival, especially those that go back to our individual and collective childhood. If necessity is the mother of invention, then our struggle for survival is the source of great inspiration; pushing us towards newer and newer inventions. Cult too is rooted in our survival project.

Our ancestors moved from place to place in search of food. Whenever we leave behind a familiar terrain and move into a new place, we experience some unease, if not real fear. Then life was very fragile: wild animals, hostile weather, marauding aliens, etc. Sickness, natural calamities and other tragedies were taken to be signs of divine wrath. This explains the origin of rituals.

> The primitive seeks by his rituals to save himself from starvation, from death by storm, from disease, from wild animals, and from enemies and to sufficiency of food and shelter, to freedom from danger and disease, and to human fertility. Implicit in this context, and in the realm of mental and emotional malaise, is salvation from mysterious and even malign powers and forces of evil. The achievement of salvation in all these areas is striven

1 John P. MEIER, "Jesus", in Raymond E BROWN, Joseph A. FITZMYER & Roland E. MURPHY (eds.), *The New Jerome Biblical Commentary*, Bangalore: Theological Publications in India, 2005, pp. 1316-1328, p. 1319a.

2 *Idem*. History continues to provide evidence of the proximity of the clergy to its lay aristocracy.

> for by all possible physical means with the superadded power of ritual, charm and magic.[3]

All cultic forms are human creations, an expression of their survival instinct. This also explains why some cultic actions that were once very popular gradually disappear.

## a. Being in Body

Once at a railway station I saw many children begging. Suddenly I noticed a *chapati* flying out from the window of my coach. Many kids ran for it. There was one girl among them a little older than the others. Let us call her Preeti. She outran them all, picked up the chapatti, sat down, and smiled at the other kids. It was not an arrogant smile; it was a compassionate smile, an inviting smile. The smaller kids understood her. They all came and sat near her in a circle. What followed left me speechless. Preeti then made small pieces of that one chapatti and shared it with her friends. She was aware that like her all her companions were hungry. That chappati was just not enough. But love made up for it. She was still a small child, but truly a great person. I wish I too had been blessed by her bounty. Nourishment takes care of our physical survival. When we share food, we help others to live. We are concerned for them. Sharing of food becomes a communication of love and concern. This is one reason why when we celebrate the different moments of life of somebody we love, we eat together in love and communion. This is one reason why the family meal is so important.

Slowly the sharing of food becomes a symbolic gesture: an enacted narration. The primary function of food recedes into the background and its evocative function takes over. For instance, the birthday 'baby' (BB) cuts a birthday cake. Then a senior person places a piece of that cake in the mouth of the BB. On behalf of all present, the senior person assures the BB of the love and care of all present; it is an assurance for the years to come. The symbolic function of food can also remind us of the past. At one birthday party, the ten-year-old BB had tears in her eyes. She was reminded of her mother, whom she lost soon after her last birthday.

Sometimes a meal brings the past and the future together in the present. Two thousand years ago, a teacher gathered his disciples for a farewell meal. He wanted it to be a parting message as well. He took bread, broke it into pieces and gave it to them, saying: "Take and eat, this is my body broken for you." Similarly, he took a cup, filled with wine, and gave it to them, saying: "This is my blood poured out for you." Looking back, Jesus gathered his life:

---

3 Winston L. KING, "Religion", in Mircea ELIADE (ed.-in-chief), *The Encyclopedia of Religion*, 16 vols, New York: Simon & Schuster Macmillan, 1993, vol. 12, pp. 282a-293a, here pp. 287b-288a.

his person (body), his life (blood) was totally for others. He also looks towards the future; he hopes his disciples too will be like him: willing to lay down their life for others.

I am inclined to believe that most of our rites and rituals are related to our struggle for survival not only as embodied beings, but also as beings who are aware of being embodied. Love is the greatest survival force. It is easy to break bread and share wine; it is crucifying to love. Slowly the powerful symbolic gesture loses it evocative function, its prophetical challenge. It becomes a lifeless ritual; people continue performing it without feeling it. It ceases to be lifegiving; it degenerates and becomes a source of income. This, perhaps, is the greatest tragedy of all organized religions. They promote superstitions: rites and rituals that have no meaning. They cease to communicate to and challenge the people involved in them.

### b. Being in Space

To be in body is to be in space. Our space is not the same everywhere. Our food habits are shaped by our geography. In Kerala, tapioca may be the food most easily available for the common people. For people in north India, it will be bread made out of wheat or some other cereal. When Keralites travel north in search of jobs, they soon get acclimatized to the food available there. The question is not what they eat, but whether what they eat is adequately nourishing. Wherever we go, we will always need food, but what we eat will be determined by our geography. We humans have been blessed with a special gift: we can adjust to different food patterns. For this reason, we can survive in any part of the world.

Our symbols too are related to our environment. They will have an evocative function for us if they have been part of our survival struggle, of our life milieu. A ritual exclusively using grape wine will be totally strange to people who have never seen grapes. They may enjoy the wine, but it will not speak to them. Meaningful rites and rituals emerge from life-experience. Life-experience helps us to interpret symbols. But our environment is not given once for all. We move beyond geographical and cultural boundaries.

### c. Being in Time

Humanity travels through history. As an infant, I was nourished by my mother's milk. Then, she began to feed me, placing the food in my mouth. Things are significantly different now. I would not mind her placing food in my mouth were I to be sick, or on some special occasion as an expression of her maternal love. I would be uncomfortable were she to insist on doing it every time I sat down for a meal. I would even resent her treating me like a child. No doubt, I am her child, but I am no longer a child. I have travelled in time. Our primal ancestors ate not only raw fruits and vegetables, but also uncooked meat and fish. The food they relished may not appeal to us. Today we have a highly pluralistic and sophisticated cuisine. Given the sedentary life-style of many today, people might suffer from indigestion were they to eat raw meat and fish in memory of their ancestors. It is good to remember our ancestors, but we need to be realistic.

Our symbolic consciousness is to a great extent shaped by our history. At a particular time in history, the ritual of circumcision was viewed within a religious frame. Today, some may find it meaningful only as a medical procedure. In the past, animal sacrifice was an essential component of a community's cult. Today, many would find it crude and cruel. Here again, we need to distinguish between what we wish to communicate and how we communicate. The former may always be legitimate, but the latter may need constant revision. Even though the symbols that constitute our cultic activity may belong to the childhood experience of humanity and thus be fairly universal, the narrative accompanying those actions may have to be repeatedly contextualized.

Rituals that may make sense in our childhood may give adults the impression that the priestly class wishes that they continue to be children. That definitely makes life more comfortable for them. History necessarily implies change; but it does not guarantee that the change is always for the better. Jesus broke bread to share it with the poor; he and his disciples served at table; the first disciples felt an intense call to be broken for others. Now that bread is transubstantiated and carried in vessels made out of precious metals. The disciples who claim the honour for this think they are sharing in God's omnipotence; they imagine themselves to be little gods—the source of clericalism.[4] The bread is placed in a very costly box; people sit comfortably in front of it lost in adoration! A horrible caricature of what Jesus did, and a pastoral disaster. The doctrine of transubstantiation

> *led to the further sacerdotalization of priesthood.* According to the long-standing consensus, the priest was ordained for the *corpus Christi*, or "body of Christ" (Paul's term for the church)...Once the *corpus Christi* for which the priest was ordained was understood to be Eucharist, *his transition from the minister of the gospel to the cultic servant of the altar was complete.*[5]

Without ongoing discernment, the cult of a community deteriorates; it is seen more and more as magic. It does not call for competence and credibility. What Gandhi wrote in 1937 is still applicable today: "At the present moment

---

4 See Aloysius PIERIS, S.J., "Two Root Causes of Clericalism: A Theological Fallacy and a Formational Deficiency", *JIVAN*, April 2019, pp. 18-19.

5 John Jay HUGHES, "Christian Priesthood", in ELIADE, *The Encyclopedia of Religion*, vol. 11, pp. 536a-539b, here p. 538; emphasis added.

the most deplorable thing is that the temple priests are, as a rule, ignorant men often devoid of character."[6] My perception is that the situation today is still worse.

Gradually other items are added to the original symbolic action and it becomes very elaborate. This tends to distract people from the original symbol and its meaning. Before and during the ritual, people are taken up by the secondaries. Certain additions may be the need of the time. If so, with the change of time if the need ceases, then those additions should be dropped. For instance, in the past when we did not have electricity, we needed oil lamps or wax candles so that we could read the ritual text correctly.[7] Today we have electricity, but the candles continue to burn without any need, but only adding to our atmospheric pollution. To add to the waste of resources, we have many more electric lamps than we actually need. Thus, without ongoing discernment, our cult becomes more and more consumer. In some communities, there is a ritual for almost every occasion. I have a hunch that organized religion was the earliest form of consumer industry. It created jobs for many, jobs that were not really needed.[8] Today organized religion, with its multifarious rituals, has been successfully co-opted by the consumer market; it has become an ancillary industry of the corporate world.

## d. Being in Communion

Being embodied necessarily links us to other humans. We come from them. We can only survive with them. One function of cult is to sacramentalize the communion that is expected to unite the believers. The cultic assembly is the incarnation of the scattered community, particularly in a pluralistic society, wherein we can become anonymous individuals.[9] The more the assembly actively participates in the cult, the deeper is their experience of being a community, the greater is their sense of being in communion that leads to love, care and concern.

In its earliest stages, no religion is organized. The ritual is very simple. There are no rules and rubrics; no special vessels and vestments; no special place of worship. The head of the family or the senior most member present,

---

6 *Collected Works of Mahatma Gandhi*, 98 vols., New Delhi, Publications Division Government of India, 1999, gandhiashramsevagram.org/gandhi-literature/collected-works-of-mahatma-gandhi-volume-1-to-98.php; accessed on 31-01-2019, vol. 71, p. 299.

7 Before Vatican II, when during Mass, a bishop had to read a text, an assistant would hold a candle close to him, even if the place was adequately lit up. Possibly the bishops then had poor sight and not enough insight.

8 In the Old Testament, the tribe of Levi was given no land for cultivation. The Levites were to be provided from the revenue of the temple. They had to create a narrative to make sure that the other tribes brought many offerings.

9 This is one explanation, why in the Third World, cultic functions continue to attract crowds.

and on some special occasions, the leader of the tribe or the village, officiates at the cult. This was true also of the first Christians.[10] Slowly the ritual gets more and more complex. Some people are given special initiation so that they can serve as priests. Gradually the priestly class succeeds in monopolizing the cult. They generate a theological discourse to justify and perpetuate the hierarchical order: the cult and the priesthood are divine institutions. This did not create any particular problem in the past because, as a rule, the society too was governed by a single person. Also, the vast majority of the believers were not much educated. Postmodern ideas and democratic ideals are bound to affect our religious thinking. The mushrooming of 'charismatic' groups is one reaction to the dominance and legalism of the clergy.

Slowly the cult tends to be become one more source of power. prestige and property. This is bound to generate some problems. The temple of God becomes a den of thieves (Mk 11.17). Many want a share in the booty. Factions emerge, mobilized by ambitious leaders. As a result, the police have to intervene to maintain the law and order situation.[11] Within the Roman Church in India, official spokespersons play down the source of conflict between the

---

10 It is time that Christians, particularly the Roman Church, take very seriously the findings of modern New Testament studies.

The older blueprint supposition, by which Jesus had the church clearly in mind and had already planned its structure, sacraments, etc., has little or no textual support; for the very few passages to which appeal may be made (e.g., Mt 16.18: "You are Peter, and on this rock…", Lk 22.19: "Do this in commemoration of me") have no parallel in the other Gospels and probably represent postresurrectional understandings specifying Jesus' intentions. In what are commonly accepted as historical memories from Jesus' ministry, he is singularly silent on foundational or structural issues. This is understandable, if we see Jesus interested not in founding a separate religion but in renewing Israel, which already had worship, priests, sacrifices—Jesus did not need to plan such structures (Raymond E. BROWN, Carolyn OSIEK & Pheme PERKINS, "Early Church", in Raymond E BROWN, Joseph A. FITZMYER & Roland E. MURPHY (eds.), *The New Jerome Biblical Commentary*, Bangalore: Theological Publications in India, 2005, pp. 1338-1353, here p. 1339b-1340a. The scholars mentioned here are all Catholics. The book has a *Nihil obstat* and an *Imprimatur*.).

In other words, the Roman claim that Jesus founded a church which has the charism to define dogmas and the canon of the Bible, the seven sacraments, the ministerial priesthood and the three-tiered hierarchy, is a human construction very much constricted by a hidden agenda. The contemporary New Testament findings give us abundant postmodern options. Our cult can be renewed in ways unthought of before. We will be more open to God who works in ways beyond our expectations. These conclusions will mean a radical rethinking of being Church. This will mean that many will lose their power, prestige and property. *But only truth can save us.*

11 This is happening in Udaipur and some other towns, where there are two Bohra groups (See Ashgar Ali ENGINEER, "History of Reform Movement in Udaipur". http://www.dawoodi-bohras.com/about_us/jamaats/udaipur/udaipur_history_1/; accessed on 01-11-2019). This is also seen in Kerala, where two Orthodox groups are claiming ownership

Orientals and the Latins: the need to maintain the apostolic origin of those churches. This explanation sounds good, but it fails to convince many. The conflict and tension are primarily the fallout of a struggle for power. Cult has become a source of division.

## 2. Being Beyond History

All embodied living creatures in some way or the other journey through time and space. Their journey is guided by their nature or instinct. We humans too have our instincts; but we are also gifted with freedom. This difference explains why existentialist philosophers reserve 'existence' only for humans. The other creatures are totally defined by their nature; they journey within the boundaries determined by their instincts. Humans, on the other hand, can 'stand out' (ex-ist), go beyond and at times even against their nature and instincts. As for other creatures, "their nature or essence is already given to them. The human being exists actively, by standing out or emerging through the decisions and acts that make this individual the unique person that he or she is."[12] If cult is to be legitimate, then we need to ask ourselves again and again: "Is it helping us to be free in a responsible manner, or are we enslaved by it?" If the answer is in the affirmative, then those rites and rituals have a right to be; they fulfil their function.

### a. Symbol and Symbolized

If cult is a symbolic narrative, then it is crucial that we differentiate between what we wish to narrate and how we do it. The mystery symbolized should remain the *norma normans* and the symbol *norma normata*. The symbol will function affectively if it effectively conveys the mystery symbolized. The failure to follow this rule can lead to major religious conflicts. The "Azyme Controversy that finally divided Eastern and Western Christianity in 1054,"[13] was whether we should use leavened or unleavened bread when we commemorate the Last Supper. Whether Jesus himself used leavened or unleavened bread is peripheral to the discussion. If Jesus wanted to portray his life as broken for others, inviting us to be like him, it would matter little whether the bread he used was leavened or not.

As Christians move away from the Middle East, they face a new set of problems. Today they find themselves in many lands where wheat and grape are not known, or at least not part of the common food. We constantly need to

---

of the same properties (https://indianexpress.com/article/india/kerala/kerala-malankara-syrian-church-ownership-piravom-tense-6027576/; accessed on 01-11-2019.

12 John MACQUARRIE, "Existentialism", in ELIADE, *The Encyclopedia of Religion*, vol. 5, pp. 222a-225a, here p. 223a.

13 James E. LATHAM, "Leaven", in ELIADE, *The Encyclopedia of Religion*, vol. 8, pp. 490b-491a, here p. 490b.

discover new symbols. If we continue to use food items that are not really part of our normal meal then we will continue to use imported symbols. We are forgetting that the more natural a symbol the more evocative it is. A symbolic meal with imported items is very artificial and leads to ineffective or even distorted communication. Then it is more of "an ideology: a suspect sign,"[14] the relict of a colonial past. The Lord's Supper is a narrative of sharing life, life nourished by food. That food could be wheat bread and grape wine; it could equally be rice and curds. What is primary is not what the historical Jesus did, but what he intended by what he did. The intention norms the expression.

## b. Rite and Right

Some organized religions engage in proselytization, trying to attract members of other communities to their own. In the history of India, many Hindus were converted to Islam and Christianity. When this shift takes place, the most visible difference is that the new members accept the beliefs (creed), rules (code) and rituals (cult) of their new religion. But in most cases the real difference is cultic: a new set of rites and rituals.[15] In the recent years, some militant Hindus have engaged in reconverting the converts, bringing them to their original community, to their parental home (*ghar waapsi*).[16] Naturally, this reconversion move agitated the minority communities. They accused the militant Hindus of using unethical means to wean people away from their present community. They contended that persons have their freedom to choose. This ought to be respected by others. We cannot use intimidation or monetary allurement to win over former converts. The individual is not bound to belong to his ritual community all his life. The original ritual community cannot claim a right over him.

If we concede that the freedom of the individual is greater than the rights of rites, then, ritual communities cannot oblige individuals to return to their original rites. Yet we must humbly admit that even within the Roman Church we have a *ghar waapsi* movement. During the last fifty years some Syro-Malabar dioceses have been erected outside Kerala. Syro-Malabar Christians (SMC) living outside Kerala were then pressurized to stop attending services at Latin churches and go to the Syro-Malabar parish for their needs. "Although,

14 Edward SCHILLEBEECKX, *The Church with a Human Face: A New and Expanded Theology of Ministry* (London, SCM Press, 1985), p. 223.

15 Recently an African theologian said that in Africa they are producing many baptized persons, but very few Christians. I am afraid the situation in India, particularly in the North, is very much the same. We have Catholic lay people, priests and bishops, men and women religious, but not enough Christians (see https://international.la-croix.com/news/africa-is-producing-baptized-people-not-christians/9200; accessed on 31-10-2019).

16 See Subhash ANAND, "The Pastoral Challenge of 'Ghar Waapsi'", *Third Millennium*, 18/1 (January - March, 2015), pp. 47-72.

these families trace their roots to SMC ancestors in Kerala, several of them have settled in Delhi [and in other major cities of India] for decades and are more familiar with the Latin rites. Most of the children have lost touch with Malayalam and, unlike the Latin rite, which conducts services in several languages, SMC services are only in Malayalam."[17] Most of them are fairly well-to-do and their children are studying in English medium schools. Many of them cannot read the Malayalam script. They are not too keen to attend services at Syro-Malabar churches. Yet they were emotionally pressurized to return to their roots. If they do not then the implication would be that they are not "proud of their tradition and culture."[18] I myself have heard people sharing their anxieties arising from this kind of unchristian tactics.

The Sabbath was one of the most important religious institutions of the Jews. The writer of *Jubilees*, a Jewish text from the second century B.C., says that on the Sabbath a person should not even light a fire. Anybody violating the holy day ought to be put to death.[19] Yet, Jesus is reported to have said: "The sabbath was made for man, not man for the sabbath; so the Son of man is lord even of the sabbath" (Mk 2:27-28). Only God is absolute; only God can made non-negotiable demands on us. All our rites and rituals, and therefore all our ritual churches, are human constructions. They are in the service of individuals. They do not have rights over individuals, unless individuals freely accept them. If need be, rites must die so that human rights may thrive.

Unlike other living organisms that migrate to survive, humans journey not just to survive, but to find deeper meaning in their life. If our most evocative symbols are related to our environment, then the more our rites incorporate native symbols, the more they become evocative. The evocative function of rites and rituals are foundational to their legitimacy. God understands all our signs and symbols. We do not need to stick on to some signs and symbols to worship him. To do so, would be to reduce God to a tribal totem. To hold on to some imported symbols would mean that to be Christian we need to abandon

---

17 http://www.thehindu.com/todays-paper/tp-national/tp-newdelhi/syromalabar-catholics-oppose-transfer-to-new-eparchy/article6293586.ece (accessed on 31-01-2015). This report also states:

> An official survey among Delhi's Catholics in 2002 recorded that only 12 per cent of SMC Catholics wanted a separate diocese and 75 per cent of them wanted freedom of choice in choosing the rite of worship. The dissenters, who have also invested in the Latin rite archdiocese by virtue of their contributions in building the community, banded together to form the "Syro-Malabar Faithful of Delhi Archdiocese" —to oppose their transfer.

18 http://www.ucanindia.in/news/no-compulsion-on-rites:-faridabad-archbishop/26695/daily (accessed on 31-01-2015).

19 Gerhard F. HASEL, "Sabbath", in David Noel FREEDMAN (ed. in chief), *The Anchor Bible Dictionary*, 6 vols., New York (NY): Doubleday, 1992, vol. 5, pp. 849a-856b, here p. 854a.

our ecological and cultural roots. When this happens in relation to the central ritual of a community, it results in a profound alienation, even though the members of that community may not be aware of it. Their lack of awareness of that alienation only indicates the depth of their alienation.

## c. Cult and Commitment

Traditional religions may be characterized by three Cs: creed, code and cult. The creed finds its symbolic expression in the cult. The cult, in turn, is supposed to generate a certain ethical frame of mind. Gradually, as the clergy succeeds in monopolizing the cult, they make it their livelihood. They project it as the primary expression of religion. This makes religion very easy for all, but a challenge to none. Speaking of the Christians whom he knows closely, José Antonio Pagola says:

> Many of them, good women and men, live on the 'epidermis of faith', nourished by a conventional Christianity. They find religious security in the beliefs and practices that are within their reach…I know how tempting it is to live correctly within the Church, without worrying about the one thing Jesus sought: the kingdom of God and its justice.[20]

When cult becomes dominant, then people go by infantile beliefs, often bordering on the superstitious; they are satisfied with the minimum of religious praxis that is demanded by law, but not promoted by love.

As cult becomes powerful it leads to blind faith, which in turn becomes a useful tool in the hands of an exploitative clergy. Hence in the history of every religion which has given great importance to rites and rituals, there have been moments of revolt and rejection. We find this among the prophets of the Old Testament. They pass a very severe judgement on religion dominated by cult but devoid of ethics. Through Amos, God tells his people:

> I hate, I despise your feasts and I take no delight in your solemn assemblies. Even though you offer me your burnt offerings and cereal offerings [offertory processions], I will not accept them, and the peace offerings of your fatted beasts I will not look upon. Take away from me the noise of your songs, to the melody of your harps I will not listen. But let justice roll down like waters, and righteousness like an ever-flowing stream (5.21-24).

We hear a similar verdict from Isaiah:

> What to me is the multitude of your sacrifices? says the Lord; I have had enough of burnt offerings of rams and the fat of well-fed beasts; I do not delight in the blood of bulls, or of lambs, or of goats…Bring no more

20 José Antonio PAGOLA, *Jesus: An Historical Approximation*, tr. Margaret Wilde, Bangalore: Theological Publications in India (TPI), 2013, p. 27.

> vain offerings; incense is an abomination to me. New moon and Sabbath and the calling of convocations—I cannot endure iniquity and solemn assembly. Your new moons and your appointed feasts my soul hates; they have become a burden to me; I am weary of bearing them (1.11-14).

The Israelites had forgotten the most important aspect of the Covenant: God had compassion on them in their suffering. This should make them compassionate towards their weaker and poorer sisters and brothers (1.15-17).

This kind of prophetical rejection is found in the history of Hinduism too. Already in the Upaniṣads, we find a shift, "a focus not so much on the details of the ritual as on its internalization and universalization…[ritual action] can no longer be regarded as a positive means to the constitution of a permanent self. Rather, it is ultimately negative."[21] Rituals lead to rebirth. Basava (12th century), a reformer from Karnataka, was very critical of priests, temples and the cult dependent on popular icons.[22] He directed his followers not to visit temples, but to carry on their person the *iṣṭaliṅga* (a small pebble in the shape of the *liṅga*), and to make it the focus of their prayer and worship.[23]

The situation in the Church today does not seem to be much different. Not only our numerous rituals, but also our Sunday sermons are more soft pastoral options than real challenges to our people. Pope Francis says:

> It needs to be said that in preaching the Gospel a fitting sense of proportion has to be maintained. This would be seen in the frequency with which certain themes are brought up and in the emphasis given to them in preaching. For example, if in the course of the liturgical year a parish priest speaks about temperance ten times but only mentions charity or justice two or three times, an imbalance results, and precisely those virtues which ought to be most present in preaching and catechesis are overlooked (*Evangelii Gaudium*, 38).

How true, our people rarely hear a good homily on justice. This may partly be because we need greater justice in the Church of God! A cult that does not promote human values and deepen the humanity of those who officiate and participate in it, is a very convenient escape. It can only dehumanize its followers, while they continue to think that they are very religious. This sort of religion can only alienate the educated and committed people. This is actually happening today.

---

21 Alf HILTEBEITEL, "Hinduism", in ELIADE, vol. 6, pp. 336a-360a, here p. 341a.

22 BASAVA, *Vacanas of Basavanna*, ed. H. DEVEERAPPA, tr. L. M. A. MENEZES & S. M. ANGADI, Srigere: Annana Balaga, 1967, pp. 26-37.

23 As the temple and its icon have become so much a characteristic of Hinduism, the question has been raised whether the Liṅgāyata tradition is part of Hinduism. M. R. SAKHARE, *History and Philosophy of Liṅgayat Religion*, Dharwar: Karnatak University, rep. 1978, pp. 425-39.

## d. Commitment and Contemplation

If cult is to nurture commitment, it has to bring about an inner conversion. Slowly, rituals become routine actions: they do not touch us. The poet-saint Kabir Das (15th century) is said to have composed the following verse:

| | |
|---|---|
| *mālā pherat jug gayā,* | Ages have gone by my chanting the beads; |
| *gayā na man ka pher.* | the crookedness of my heart has not gone away. |
| *karkā mankā chāḍī kar,* | Stop chanting the beads with your hands; |
| *mankā mankā pher.* | chant the beads of your heart. |

To experience conversion, to forget our ego and turn towards others is far from easy. We need interior prayer. Kabir is only echoing the advice Kṛṣṇa gave to Arjuna:

> viṣayā vinivartante nirāhārasya dehinaḥ,
> *rasavarjam raso 'pyasya param dṛṣṭvā nivartate.*
> A person who is fasting stands at a distance from food,
> the desire for food, however, persists in him.
> This desire too will abandon him,
> only after he has a vision of the Supreme.[24]

Only contemplative prayer—not cult—can free us from the hankering after things of this world, so that our hearts have some more space for others. There is, however, a deeper need for contemplation. Without contemplation, our cult is bound to be consumeristic.

Humans need symbols because, unlike other living creatures, they have a depth dimension that cannot be adequately described. We use symbols to evoke in others the experience we have. Hence if religions use symbolic actions and narratives in their cult, then these actions and narratives are legitimate if they help the devotees to discover and slowly actualize the real purpose of religion. "The essence of religion is the relation of man beyond himself to the unknown reality that faith calls God. It is man's capacity to go beyond all tangible, measurable reality and to enter into the primordial relation… This relationship itself, I would say is, properly speaking, the content of religion."[25] Religion is the depth dimension of human existence.

God does not need our religion with its worship. It is we who need it. It should be an inspiration for pilgrims who are journeying beyond themselves. The symbols it uses are meant to be points of departure. Our pilgrimage unto transcendence demands that every point of arrival be a point of departure,

24 *Bhagavad-gītā*, 2.59.

25 Joseph RATZINGER, *Salt of the Earth: The Church at the End of the Millennium* (an interview with Peter Seeward), San Francisco: Ignatius, 2007, p. 22.

because God is beyond all our created images, signs and symbols. This is why we are forbidden to make lifeless statues of him (Lev 19.4). Only humans, who choose to be alive as human and humane, can in some way be unto his image and likeness. Only the struggle to see God can bring us life. *Gloria enim Dei vivens homo, vita autem hominis visio Dei.*"[26] Humans who try live a deeply humane life are the real glory of God, the only worship fitting God. Humans can discover that depth within them by becoming aware of the depth enwombing them. Without contemplation humans can live only superficially. Hence all cultic rites and rituals have a right to be only if they eventually take us beyond cult; only if they promote contemplation.

26 https://en.wikiquote.org/wiki/Irenaeus; accessed on 04-10-2019.

28

# Wherein Lies Human Dignity? Inadequacies of Rational Capacities and Requirements of Bodily Criteria in Sciences and Humanities

**J. Charles Davis**
*Humboldt Research Fellow, Albert-Ludwigs University of Freiburg, Germany*

**Abstract**: Human dignity is inseparable from the human condition. It is the most fundamental principle to weigh human acts and protect human lives. It is neither earned through qualifications and positions nor can it be stripped off or lost. Dignity is the equal value of every human being without grades irrespective of age, gender, culture and health condition. Dignity does not lie in the realization of rational capacities but belongs to the whole person of body-soul integrity. That is why, when any aspect of human being is humiliated and misused, his or her dignity is said to be violated. Spiritual, physical, psychological, socio-political and economic needs are rights for a dignified life.

***Keywords***: Human Dignity, Rationality, Freedom, Morality, Human Body, Basic Needs, Bioethics,

## I. Dignity is Inseparable from Human Condition

Dignity, the intrinsic value of humans, is inseparable from the human condition. Human dignity (*Menschenwürde*) is the norm ultimatum to respect and protect human life and to assess human acts. What do we understand by norm? A norm has the ability to state whether an act is right or wrong, and if an act is wrong, it entails a duty not do it; and if it is right, it entails a duty to do it. Honnefelder[1] makes a distinction between normativeness and descriptiveness: (i) constitutional status is biological, ontological or descriptive and reveals something innate and (ii) positional status is normative, attributive or conventional and is an external recognition of something what is intrinsic. Value judgements may thus consist of (a) the recognition of an intrinsic good and/or (b) the attribution of the extrinsic good. The extrinsic good can be added to something by the society, whereas the intrinsic good exists in the very nature of the thing whether we recognise it or not; or whether we are able to empirically know it or not. Something that is intrinsic to humans can be not only descriptively but also normatively expressed.

A descriptive statement designates a human being as someone belonging to the species of *homo sapiens.* The statement "All human beings are members of the species *homo sapiens*" is a descriptive expression. When we speak of human beings in our daily interactions, we use the term "human being" not only descriptively but also normatively recognizing him/her with dignity. Normative statements consist of expressions that would explicate its inner nature. In a sense, the inner nature is something that is already there and based on which we make a value judgment to be a norm. It is simply a recognition of a value that a being intrinsically has by its very nature. Let us look at this statement: "The human being is of absolute value." Such expressions are *indexical*, that means, they constitute in the basic character of a natural species a status which exists even prior to human recognition. Such constitution is not a language convention, but an expression of reality and of natural laws specified by it.[2] When we speak of humans in normative terms, we think of them with certain inherent value. Such assertions consist in the very nature of humans. Cicero spoke of such an intrinsic dignity of human nature [*in natura excellentia et dignitas]*.[3] It is the intelligence or excellence that keeps them above animality of other creatures signifying a specific moral status or value or dignity of humans. Among all animals, only humans have intelligence intrinsically. It is neither attributed nor granted to them by a third party. More normative statements can be drawn from this intrinsic value. That which is normative is binding and common to all. Thus, we can argue plausibly,

1 See Ludger Honnefelder, "Die Frage nach dem moralischen Status des menschlichen Embryos," in: Otfried Höffe et al (eds.), *Gentechnik und Menschenwürde: An den Grenzen von Ethik und Recht* (Köln: 2002) 79-110. This article is dedicated to our dignified teacher, colleague and philosopher Prof. Dr. Cyril Desbruslais SJ who is an epitome of service to the youth as a symbol of honour on his 80th birthday.

2 see Ludger Honnefelder, "Die Frage nach der Einheit des Menschen: Bioethik und Hylemorphismus," in: Konrad Hilpert und Dietmar Mieth (eds.), *Kriterien biomedizinischer Ethik,* 50-65 (Freiburg: 2006) 60-61.

3 Cicero, *De Officiis,* Walter Miller (ed.), Liber primus Nr. 106: "And if we will only bear in mind the superiority and dignity of our nature, ...".

P1 : A human being has a moral status and demands protection against any harm. (normative)

P2 : A human life starts at conception and ends at death. (biological and descriptive)

P3 : A human life from conception to death is that of a human being. (descriptive and normative)

P4 : A human being has a full moral status from conception to death. (normative)

P5 : All humans have full moral status from conception to death. (normative)

C : All humans from conception to death demand protection against any harm. (normative)

While empirical science of developmental biology informs us the starting and ending point of human life, normative science (ethics) requires the biological information to be authentic and to apply norms to the whole human species. The normative content of human dignity depends on essential features that demand moral claims. Whether only humans or non-human animals, too, have dignity relies on those features partially or fully present in them. Making a sharp distinction between humans and non-human animals, Kant says, "Morality, and humanity, insofar as it is capable of morality, is that which alone has dignity."[4] According to him, it is the capacity that counts and not its actual functioning. Among living beings, humans are the only beings who have the ability for morality on account of rational capacity. Friedo Ricken says that the ability for morality lies in the invisible noumenal order and the visible phenomenal proof is the belongingness to the biological species homo sapiens.[5] Ricken explains:

That the ability for morality is an idea does not mean that it is not real feature; it belongs to the noumenal order, which is real, even if it is beyond the empirical knowledge. However, we need a practical idea, one criterion (and as such it can be only an empirical sign), by which we can recognize which creature belongs not only to the phenomenal, but also to the noumenal order, i.e. to which creature the ability for morality is due. The only criterion, which is at our disposal, is the belongingness of an individual to the biological

4 Immanuel Kant, *Groundwork of the Metaphysics of Morals,* trans. & ed.: Mary Gregor (Cambridge: Cambridge University Press, 2011) 42. GMS IV: 435.

5 See Friedo Ricken, "Mensch und Person," in: Konrad Hilpert and Dietmar Mieth (eds.) *Kriterien biomedizinischer Ethik* (Freiburg: 2006) 66-86, 72-73 and "Homo Noumenon und Homo Phenomenon: Ableitung, Begründung und Anwendbarkeit der Formel von der Menschheit als Zweck an sich selbst," in: Otfried Höffe (ed.), *Grundlegung zur Metaphysik der Sitten. Ein kooperativer Kommentar* (Frankfurt a. M.: 1989) 234-252.

species Homo sapiens. It is the "humanity" as a biological species, which is capable of morality, and therefore has dignity.[6]

The capacity for morality can be conceived as an "idea," but "idea" does not mean that it is not real. This idea is the expression of the noumenal self of every human being. So, the only empirical criterion that every human is a bearer of morality is his/her belongingness to the biological species *Homo sapiens*. For Ricken as well as Kant that a human (person) comes into existence from the moment of conception.[7] Thus, this capacity for morality, therefore dignity, exists in humans from the moment of conception.[8] It was meaningless for Kant to ask when or at what stage of the biological development a human turns or begins to be a being of moral capacity, since a person comes into existence from the moment of conception.[9] On the Right of Domestic Society under the title II "Parental Right" §28 Kant says:

> For the offspring is a *person*, and it is impossible to form a concept of the production of a being endowed with freedom through a physical operation. So from a *practical point of view* it is a quite correct and even necessary idea to regard the *act of procreation as one by which we have brought a person into the world* without his consent and on our own initiative, for which deed the parents incur an obligation to make the child content with his condition so far as they can. They cannot destroy their child as if he were something they had *made* (since a being endowed with freedom cannot be a product of this kind) or as if he were their property, nor can they even just abandon him to chance, since they have brought not merely a worldly being but a citizen of the world into a condition which cannot now be indifferent to them even just according to concepts of right.[10]

It is beyond doubt that Kant applied the criterion of belongingness to the biological species *Homo sapiens* as bearers of an absolute moral worth from conception to explain the parental obligations towards the legal rights of children. This same criterion can become the decisive measuring scale to assess decisions on bioethical issues, for example, to guarantee dignity to embryos, foetuses and infants. It is the capacity for morality that authenticates a moral value and it is not a speciesist statement as if mere belongingness to the species *Homo sapiens* makes its members valuable or worthy of protection.

---

6 Ricken, "Mensch und Person," 72-73. GMS IV: 435.

7 Immanuel Kant, *The Metaphysics of Morals,* trans. & ed.: Mary Gregor (Cambridge: Cambridge University Press, 2011) 64, 330.

8 Ricken, "Mensch und Person," 73. Kant, MS VI: 280f.

9 Ricken, "Ist die Person oder der Mensch Zweck an sich selbst?" in: Mechthild Dreyer und Kurt Fleischhauer (eds.), *Natur und Person im ethischen Disput*, 147-168 (Freiburg: 1998) 154. GMS VI: 435.

10 Kant, *The Metaphysics of Morals*, (trans. & ed.: Gregor), 64. MS VI: 280f. Italics mine. Ricken, "Mensch und Person," 73.

Honnefelder says that a value judgement is simultaneously attached with the descriptive characterization of the human as a member of a species whose nature has the property of reason:[11] Honnefelder explains:

We call human a living creature, to which the *life* is the manner, in which it exists, of reason-talented. To be a reason-talented creature is the manner in which man exists, so we say then, if the human is it [reason-talented creature] no more, that he no longer exists. This does not mean in any case that [hu] man exists only, insofar as he currently operates his reason. Power of reason alone is used as a species-specific property that is characteristic of these types of organisms.[12]

Humans, by virtue of being members of the species *Homo sapiens*, are end in themselves because of their *specific* capacity for rationality, and thus for autonomy and morality. This rational faculty of humanity resides in the noumenal self (as *Anlage*) and expresses its existence and capacities through the phenomenal (empirical) self and commands "dignity" to its whole self. In this sense, "every human is a person on account of his nature,"[13] and is a bearer of an absolute moral worth from the moment of conception.[14] In other words, "every creature, that has the nature of humans, is also a person."[15] Thus, the concepts of 'human' and 'person' have the same extensional meaning.[16] The concept of person has been mistakenly used to exalt the property of reason, as if humans do not yet possess reason until they become persons, or humans who do not exercise reason are not persons. This has led to unclarity and confusion in bioethical discussions.[17] Thus, Ricken comes to a simple conclusion:

---

11 Honnefelder, "Die Frage nach der Einheit des Menschen: Bioethik und Hylemorphismus," 63.

12 Honnefelder, "Die Frage nach der Einheit des Menschen: Bioethik und Hylemorphismus," 62. "*vivere viventibus est esse, intelligere intelligentibus est esse* [...]." (Aristoteles, *De anima* II 4, 415b 13).

13 Ricken, "Ist die Person oder der Mensch Zweck an sich selbst?" 152.

14 Kant, *The Metaphysics of Morals*, (trans. & ed.: Gregor), 64, MS VI: 280f.

15 Ricken, "Ist die Person oder der Mensch Zweck an sich selbst?" 152-53.

16 See Ricken, "Homo noumenon und homo phenomenon," 234-252.

17 Eberhard Schockenhoff, "Pro Speziesargument: Zum moralischen und ontologischen Status des Embryos," in: Damschen and Schönecker (eds.), *Der moralische Status von Embryonen: Pro und Contra Spezies-, Kontinuums-, Identitäts-, und Potentialitätsargument,* 11-33 (Berlin/New York: Walter de Gruyter, 2003) 31: "Die in der philosophischen Tradition angelegte Verdoppelung der Begriffe 'Mensch' und 'Person' erzeugt, in der gegenwärtigen Ethikdebatte oftmals unnötige Konfusionen." See also Tom L. Beauchamp, "The Failure of Theories of Personhood," *Kennedy Institute of Ethics Journal* 9 (1999): 309-24; Jane English, "Abortion and the Concept of a Person," *Canadian Journal of Philosophy* 5 (1975): 233-43; Similarly, M. Warnock says, "I believe that we would do better to remove the concept of ´person´ altogether from the debate. It is both confusing and redundant." See

The danger of the term 'person' lies therein that it does not refer to the natural species in contrast to the 'human' as such. Is, therefore, the human or the person an end in himself? If we understand the term 'human' contrary to all naturalistic tendencies in the fullest sense, which it has in the great tradition of the West, then the answer can only be: the human being.[18]

Mere affiliation of an individual to the species *Homo sapiens* necessitates and suffices for recognition of inviolable dignity which demands unrestricted protection-worthiness. Whether a human individual is healthy or a comatose patient or a dementia patient or in an embryonic stage or an infant or an adult or a dying person, each one of them is human, a complete human organism, an individual belonging to the human species of rational nature with intrinsic powers of autonomy and is thus an end in himself or herself. A human as a possessor or as a potential (*active potency* for flourishing)[19] possessor of a rational nature is sufficient to command due respect and demand dignity and protection. Medical biologist Fritz Baumgartner rightly says, "it is not potential to become a person that entitles a human embryo to legal and moral status. It is part of the fabric of natural and biological law that the human embryo's actuality of being human entitles him or her to legal and moral status."[20] In this sense, if we can do away with the term person, we will still be able to do bioethics and all sciences of humanities. The concept of person (personhood) is a surplus term. All humans are persons. No human can be said to be a non-person.[21] Distinctions made between humans and persons by René

---

M. Warnock, "In vitro fertilization: the ethical issues (II)," *The Philosophical Quarterly* 33 (1983): 238- 249, 241.

18 Ricken, "Ist die Person oder der Mensch Zweck an sich selbst?" 168.

19 See Robert E. Joyce, "Personhood and the Conception Event," *New Scholasticism* 52 (1978) 97-109. Robert Joyce states: "To be a human organism is to be a whole living member of the species *Homo sapiens,* with a human present and a human future evident in the intrinsic potential for the manifestation of the species typical form," … "No living being becomes anything other than what it already essentially is." Quoted in William Hurlbut, "Stem Cells, Embryos and Ethics: Is There a Way Forward?" in: Lars Østnor, ed. *Stem Cells, Human Embryos and Ethics: Interdisciplinary Perspectives* (Oslo: Springer, 2008) 71-87, 78. Hurlbut adds that "the act of fertilization is a leap from zero to everything" and "as a living being, an organism is an integrated, self-developing and self-maintaining unity under the governance of an immanent plan."

20 Fritz Baumgartner, "Human embryos: potential persons?" *Science* 296 (2002): 1967-8.

21 During my lectures, classes, seminars and conferences on bioethics, I raise the following question invariably: "If we are not persons from the beginning, do we turn to become persons from the assumed status of being mere humans?" Nobody has responded satisfactorily but with many arbitrary answers, such as, after brain growth, at or after birth. Actually, there is only one non-arbitrary answer that all humans are persons from the moment of conception, during every developmental phase and even after losing activities of rational faculties. This fact is a matter of biological, logical and philosophical enquiry to substantiate the essential

Descartes (1596-1650 CE), John Locke (1632-1704 CE), Tristram Engelhardt (1941-2018 CE), Michael Tooley (b.1941 CE), John Harris (b.1945 CE), Peter Singer (b.1946), Jeff McMahan (b.1954 CE) and Ralf Stoecker (b.1956 CE) on account of rational capacities are arbitrary and discriminatory.[22] According to them, humans are essentially thinking things and those humans who lack self-consciousness, self-awareness, self-reflection and activities of rational faculties are not yet or no longer persons and hence do not deserve the same value of dignity due to persons. Actually, all rational capacities such as autonomy and morality are due to all humans from conception to death, not only when humans are mistakenly thought to become persons. Humans grow always as humans and never unto humans or persons. Some may find it difficult to call an embryo or the fertilized egg a person, but it is merely a cultural problem.[23]

---

nature of humans. All that meets the eye empirically need not be true and may require reflection.

22 Davis, *The Ethics of Human Embryonic Stem Cell Research,* 48-68, 73-80, 81-84. See "Ego sum res cogitans, id est dubitans, affirmans, negans, pauca intelligens, multa ignorans, volens, nolens, imaginans etiam & sentiens," in: *Meditationes De Prima Philosophia,* Meditation III. According to Descartes, "a person is a thinking thing." His understanding of human is purely dualistic and the real person is only the thinking mind. He does not value the bodily existence; John Locke, *Essay Concerning Human Understanding: with Thoughts on the Conduct of the Understanding,* Book II, Chap. 27 on: "Of Identity and Diversity," (Edinburgh: Mundell & Son, Royal Bank Close, 1801), 54, 62, 156-57; Michael Tooley, *Abortion and Infanticide*, (Oxford: Clarendon Press, 1983),167; Peter Singer, *Practical Ethics,* Second ed. (New York: Cambridge University Press, 1993), 87-90; Tristram Engelhardt, "Some Persons are Humans, some Humans are Persons, and the World is What we Persons Make it," *Philosophical Medical Ethics* (Boston: Reidel, 1977) 183-194; J. McMahan, "Cloning, Killing, and Identity," *Journal of Medical Ethics* 25 (1999) 83; John Harris, *The Value of Life: An Introduction to Medical Ethics* (London: 1985) 57f; John Harris, "The Concept of the Person and the Value of Life," *Kennedy Institute of Ethics Journal* 9 (1999) 293 – 308; Ralf Stoecker, "Contra Identitätsargument: Mein Embryo und Ich," in: Damschen and Schönecker (eds.), *Der moralische Status von Embryonen*, 129-144; Derek Parfit, *Reasons and Persons,* (Oxford/New York: 1984); Beauchamp, "The Failure of Theories of Personhood," 309-24; Jane English, "Abortion and the Concept of a Person," 233-243.

23 Some may argue that people do not mourn the death of an embryo as they do when a child or an adult dies. The quality or quantity of mourning is a cultural factor. It is not to be ignored either that every mother mourns at heart when a preborn embryo is naturally lost or artificially aborted. Mourning of death of any human/person can vary according to various cultures. Such arguments have serious problems in using human emotions as criteria for moral decisions, as Hume has pointed out: Cited in Lars Østnor (ed.), *Stem Cells, Human Embryos and Ethics: Interdisciplinary Perspectives*, Ch. 10, pp. 137-147 (Norway: Springer, 2008), 139: "The strength of our feelings is no reliable measure of the ethical rightness or wrongness of an act." Using feelings as a measure in ethical rightness or wrongness is a fallacy and blinds the deliberations in making moral judgements. Emotions can vary from person to person and increase when tragedies meet people personally. Unlike a philosopher, a physician would have a stronger feeling towards the embryo when

In Hinduism and Indian culture, a human being is called *atman* (human or person) at all stages. No one finds it difficult to call an embryo an *atman*. In Tamil language and culture, a human being is called *manithan* at all stages of development and there is no term corresponding to person.

If there exists a developmental stage when we turn to be persons and again non-persons in a coma, then questions arise: Are we at times persons and at times non-persons? How could we ever become persons if we were not persons from the beginning? How could non-persons ever turn to be persons? How could ever persons turn to be non-persons? Is it not an internal contradiction that today we say to our existence as an adult "we" on the one hand and therefore (must and should) maintain continuity from our embryonic existence to our dying stage; on the other hand, we deny humanity, personhood and dignity to our embryonic existence or to the dying patients or people in coma stage?[24] Robert Joyce states: "To be a human organism is to be a whole living member of the species *Homo sapiens,* with a human present and a human future evident in the intrinsic potential for the manifestation of the species-typical form,"[25] and "no living being becomes anything other than what it already essentially is."[26] Any right, protection and dignity that are due to grown-up humans must, therefore, apply to embryos, fetuses and dying, suffering and coma patients too, as they/we belong to the same species. Lack of biological knowledge and of embryological development of human body has caused a lot of the harm to humans themselves.[27] Noble laureate geneticist Jerome Lejeune says that biological characteristics are necessary and sufficient for the membership in the human species:

> Each of us has a unique beginning, the moment of conception… As soon as the 23 chromosomes carried by the sperm encounter the 23 chromosomes carried by the ovum, the whole information necessary and sufficient to spell out all the characteristics of the new [human] being is gathered… a new human being is defined which has never occurred before and will never occur again… [it] is not just simply a non-descript cell, or a ′population′ or loose ′collection′ of cells, but a very specialized individual.[28]

---

he examines its development in the womb with the emergence of eyes, fingers, etc. His feelings are not the same as that of a philosopher or politician who has not seen it with his own eyes.

24 Günter Rager, *Die Person: Wege zu ihrem Verständnis, Studien zur theologischen Ethik* 115 (Fribourg i. Ue: Academic Press Fribourg/Freiburg i. Br.: Verlag Herder, 2006) 192.

25 Cited in Hurlbut, "Stem Cells, Embryos and Ethics: Is There a Way Forward?" 78. See Joyce, "Personhood and the conception event," 97-109.

26 Hurlbut, "Stem Cells, Embryos and Ethics: Is There a Way Forward?" 78.

27 The joining of gametes (sperm and egg) brings into existence an entire living organism.

28 Jerome Lejeune gave his testimony in *Davis* vs *Davis*, Circuit Court for Blount County, State of Tennessee at Maryville, Tennessee, 1989. Reprinted in: Martin Palmer (ed.), *A*

Beauchamp and Childress concluded that "to be a living member of the species *Homo sapiens* is a necessary and sufficient condition of moral respect."[29] The concise statement of two members of the President's Council of Bioethics makes the point clear very evidently:

> Fertilization produces a new and complete, though immature, human organism. ... A human embryo is a whole living member of the species Homo sapiens in the earliest stage... Human embryos possess the epigenetic primordial for self-directed growth into adulthood... We were then, as we are now distinct and complete.... To deny that the embryonic human being deserves full respect, one must suppose that not every whole living human being is deserving of full respect... As humans, they are members of a natural kind – the human species.... Since *human beings are intrinsically valuable and deserving of full moral respect in virtue of what they are*, it follows that they are intrinsically valuable from the point at which they come into being.[30]

The intrinsic human dignity is due to humans not from the mere fact of belonging to a particular species either,[31] but from the rational capacity of the species for morality whose author he himself is.[32] It is the capacity for morality that makes the moral status of humanity normative. Highlighting the distinctive moral capacity of humans, Wolfgang Wieland says:

Human dignity cannot be based on empirically leviable facts, neither on the interests for life of the human, nor on the ability for sensitivity and

---

*Symphony of the preborn child: Part Two* (Hagerstown, MD: NAACP, 1989), 9-10. Similarly, Baumgartner says, "I am not a philosopher or theologian but a student of medicine and surgery. I can speak to you with authority that from a pure, unadulterated biological and embryological standpoint, *there is no greater pivotal moment in our growth and development than when 23 chromosomes from our father join with 23 chromosomes of our mother to form a unique, new biologic entity who heretofore simply had not existed.*" Fritz Baumgartner, "Life Begins at the Beginning," *Pro-Life America* (April 12, 2005).

29 Tom L. Beauchamp and James F. Childress, *Principles of Biomedical Ethics,* Sixth Edition (New York: Oxford University Press, 2009) 67.

30 Robert P. George and Alfonso Gomez Lobo, "The Moral Status of the Human Embryo," *Perspectives in Biology and Medicine* 48 (2005) 201-05.

31 Kant avoided the naturalistic fallacy in his argument, as Ricken explains, "'Der Mensch ist Person' ist ein Werturteil. Er wird durch den Hinweis auf die Natur des Menschen begründet, ohne dass diese Begründung ein naturalistischer Fehlschluss ist, weil die Natur des Menschen nicht bestimmt werden kann, ohne die unbedingte Norm zu nennen, unter welcher er steht. Er ist Person 'als Subjekt einer moralisch-praktischen Vernunft'[a] als ein Wesen 'unter moralischen Gesetzen'[b] oder als ein Wesen, das de Sittlichkeit fähig ist."[c] Frido Ricken, "'Mensch' und 'Person'", 70. [a)] MS VI: 434; [b)] Kant, *Kritik der Urteilskraft,* Akad. Ausg. Vol. V (Berlin: 1968), 448; [c)] GMS IV: 435.

32 Wolfgang Wieland, "Pro-Potentialitätsargument: Moralfähigkeit als Grundlage von Würde und Lebensschutz," in: Damschen and Schönecker, *Der moralische Status von Embryonen*, 162.

experience, neither on his reason or his intelligence or his ability to develop desires, not even on his self-consciousness, but ultimately only on the fact that he is a creature that is not wrapped up in its naturally given physical, psychological and mental faculty, but stands out above all through his moral capacity.[33]

Not to rely merely on rational capacities in order to give greater protection to vulnerable humans, the new Bioethics in Europe introduced dignity, integrity and vulnerability, in addition to the four bioethical principles of Beauchamp and Childress, namely, autonomy, beneficence, non-maleficence and justice,[34] to be guiding (protective) values (alongside autonomy).[35] The exalted freedom or autonomy is not given up but takes a back seat in the new bioethics. The idea behind this is that no vulnerable individual is to be sacrificed for the greater good of medical progress, even if one is not able to give an informed consent or has not yet developed the rational faculties, which are equal and same at all phases intrinsically. Ultimately, it is the belongingness to the species with a normative claim that gives the basis for dignity of/for all humans, which according to Otfried Höffe, is the highest moral and legal principle that gives humans an absolute value against other highlighted natures of rationality and freedom.[36] The recognition of rights of equality and freedom is bound by no other characteristic than that of being human, in which *all* human beings agree beyond social, political or cultural differences.[37] The very basis of humanity does not allow anyone to claim privileges over each other. Human dignity is directly attached to humanity itself.[38]

---

33 Wieland, "Pro-Potentialitätsargument," 161.

34 Beauchamp and Childress, Principles of Biomedical Ethics, 2009.

35 Beyleveld and Brownsword, *Human Dignity in Bioethics and Biolaw,* 41-42. Beyleveld and Brownsword consider that "modern bioethics has its origin in the Nuremberger Code of 1947 and gathers pace with the Declaration of Helsinki in 1964. Central to these developments is the idea that human beings should not be subjected to scientific and medical research without their free and informed consent. To the extent that human dignity has a role to play in such thinking, it is as the foundation for human rights, specifically the right of human beings to decide whether or not they will subject themselves to medical trials or treatments" (29). See also Henk ten Have, "Respect for Human Vulnerability: The Emergence of a New Principle of Bioethics," *Bioethics Inquiry,* 12 (2015) 395-408.

36 Höffe, "Prinzip Menschenwürde," 49.

37 Schockenhoff, *Ethik des Lebens*, 227: "Die Anerkennung der Gleichheits- und Freiheitsrechte is an kein anderes Merkmal als das des Menschseins gebunden, in dem alle Menschen vor jeder sozialen, politischen oder kulturellen Differenzierung übereinstimmen."

38 Schockenhoff, *Ethik des Lebens*, 227: "Die Achtung vor der Würde *jedes* Menschen ist deshalb unabhängig davon gefordert, ob die einzelnen gesellschaftlichen Gruppen in der philosophischen Begründung des Personseins oder gar in der Anerkennung seines theologischen Hintergrundes übereinstimmen oder nicht. Sie gilt einfach deshalb, weil

Certainly, the moral content of any concept must lie within itself and should not be loaded on to it from outside. If dignity is intrinsic, its moral content to be a norm must also be intrinsic. The agreement on its ability to be a normative principle must be realistic and should not be a mere attribution, though recognition of any value requires a human attribution. If a principle is able to state that a certain act is right or wrong, it automatically becomes a norm. In addition to intuition, the principle of dignity is able to state that certain acts, such as rape or unjust imprisonment, are wrong. Human dignity is a moral term because it is able to state that a certain act is right or wrong. The term "stone" and its shape or weight, on the contrary, does not say anything about morality. The stone has a material value and is available for any instrumental use. On the contrary, humans as ends-in-themselves (*Selbstzwecklichkeit*), have an intrinsic moral value that commands respect and mutual recognition, and, therefore, everyone exists for his or her own sake and can never be used as a mere means even for any noble use, such as the health of the future generations. The Kantian formula of *Selbstzwecklichkeit* has been effective to enact laws that would negatively prohibit instrumental uses of humans but has not given us a catalogue of positive claims,[39] though it can be positively used as a right to respect and protect humans.[40]

## 2. Inadequacies of Rational Capacities and Requirements of Bodily Criteria

Rational-moral capacities help us substantiate the uniqueness of humans and their worth of human dignity, but they are inadequate. Human dignity cannot be accorded completely to these capacities alone,[41] as Kass says, "Not all of dignity consists in reason or freedom."[42] A rational-moral dignity is unique but not sufficient. If we squarely focus only on reason, then bodily-physical, spiritual-psychological and socio-political aspects of human life get ignored. It would be as if the deprivation of basic human needs such as a minimum

wir auf der Basis unseres Menschseins keine Vorrechte voreinander in Anspruch nehmen dürfen."

39 See Schockenhoff, *Ethik des Lebens*, 239, from W. Wolbert, *Der Mensch als Mittel zum Zweck,* 115-117.

40 Schockenhoff, *Ethik des Lebens*, 239: "Als *negatives* Bewertungskriterium, das uns die schrankenlose Instrumentalisierung menschlichen Lebens untersagt, gibt uns die Berufung auf die Menschenwürde noch keine erschöpfende *positive* Zielvorgabe an die Hand, an der abzulesen wäre, in welche Richtung wir die künftige biomedizinische Forschung lenken sollen."

41 Nussbaum, for example, in "Human Dignity and Political Entitlements," (363), says that "There is dignity not only in rationality but in human need itself and in the varied forms of striving that emerge from human need."

42 Kass, "Defending Human Dignity," 313.

subsistence would not affect the deeply spiritual and metaphysical dignity of humans. Therefore, there is a greater need to pay attention to the bodily needs for the wholistic understanding of humans. We must therefore take the basic needs of humans into ethical consideration in addition to the rational capacities, for humans are embodied beings and not mere rational spirits. This makes us revert back to the so-called age-old problem of "body-soul" dichotomy. Dignity of humans should not be centered only on the "soul" aspects ignoring the "body" aspects, for it is only in and through the "body" that the "soul" can exist and act. The human needs an existence of bodiliness in physicality and temporality in the first place to talk at all about mental properties and metaphysical qualities that the individual possesses. It would not be possible for us to talk about rationality and morality, unless we existed in some stature (Gestalt). Thus, Schockenhoff says:

As corporeality and temporality are necessary conditions of subjectivity and capacity of moral acts of the human, the respect for personal dignity should be not only brought to the complete expression of self-consciousness, rationality, and actual self-disposition, but it must also include the entire time continuum and the space of corporal expression, which bears and allows the spiritual self-expression of the person.[43]

We can only regard another human, if we are able to recognize him in a concrete Gestalt (e.g. human body).[44] The importance of human life and human body (Leib) with its "Leiblichkeit" (bodiliness) and "Zeitlichkeit" (temporality) needs therefore an emphasis as a *prima facie* criterion, for it is in and through the body that a human is able to express or perform an act which is *art specific.* Such an act specifies the art of the human species and signifies the nature of the act, namely, (ir)rational, (im)moral, etc. As Schockenhoff points out:

The body is the concrete medium of expression, in which the human person presents himself necessarily in all his records, including the self-performance of the spirit. The human-being must therefore also be considered

43 Eberhard Schockenhoff, "Pro Speziesargument: Zum moralischen und ontologischen Status des Embryos," in: Damschen and Schönecker (eds.), *Der moralische Status von Embryonen,* 11-33, 31: "Da Leiblichkeit und Zeitlichkeit zu den notwendigen Bedingungen der Subjekthaftigkeit und moralischen Handlungsfähigkeit des Menschen gehören, darf der Respekt seiner Personswürde nicht erst der vollen Ausprägung von Selbstbewußtsein, Rationalität und aktueller Selbstverfügung entgegengebracht werden; er muss vielmehr auch das gesamte zeitliche Kontinuum und das leibliche Ausdrucksfeld umfassen, das die geistigen Selbstvollzüge der Person trägt und ermöglicht."

44 Schockenhoff, "Pro Speziesargument," 31: "Wir achten einen anderen Menschen nur dann, wenn wir ihn in der konkreten Gestalt anerkennen, in der er uns begegnet, sei dies als gesunder Mensch auf der Höhe seiner persönlichen Attraktivität und beruflichen Leistungsfähigkeit, sei es als kranker, behinderter, sterbender oder noch ungeborener Mensch in der äußersten Verletzlichkeit seines leiblichen Daseins."

under the aspect of his capacity for moral acts as corporal-spiritual unity, because he can express himself in his ability for moral self-determination only *in* and *through* his body. The accusation of speciesism thus fails to capture the meaning, which carries our belonging to the human nature for our concrete personhood.[45]

We must admit that the person needs his body to carry out his acts. It is in and through the body that a human individual is able to exercise his capacities. The human is a unity of body-soul. The soul is inseparable from the body and carries out his rational and moral actions as a body-soul entity. Therefore, this "*leib-seelische Einheit*" [body-soul unity] is human, whether born or unborn, whether the "*Leib*" has some defect or the "*Seele*". Therefore, the virtue of belonging to the human species makes every human individual an owner of all capacities of "*leib-seelische Einheit*," and the dignity of humans must also consist in the unity of the spiritual and corporeal existence.[46] The body-soul integrity exists from conception, when all the biological and spiritual properties for a human life begin to inhere fully in the new organism. It is only a matter of gradual development of the given properties. The Aristotelian-Aquinas's theory of delayed ensoulment is not tenable anymore. The theory of brain development is also not valid anymore. Identity and integrity of body and soul are all the time present continuously in every human being. All that one requires is to extend human dignity retrospectively and prospectively to the vulnerable stages of beginning and end of an individual human life, namely, conception and death respectively.[47] Human body [*Leib*] is a prerequisite for a human life. The foundation of a human life on earth is the human body, which functions as a concrete whole uniting the spiritual, physical, psychological, socio-political and economic aspects of human life. Social, economic, cultural and political rights are demands for a dignified life. However, the concept of human dignity

---

45 Schockenhoff, "Pro Speziesargument," 30-31: "Der Leib ist [...] das konkrete Ausdrucksmedium, in dem sich die menschliche Person in allen ihren Akten, also auch im Selbstvollzug des Geistes, notwendig darstellt. Der Mensch muss daher auch unter dem Aspekt seiner moralischen Handlungsfähigkeit als leib-seelische Einheit betrachtet werden, weil er sich in seinem Vermögen zur moralischen Selbstbestimmung gar nicht anders als *in* seinem Leib und *durch* seinen Leib gegeben ist. Der Speziesismus-Vorwurf verkennt daher die Bedeutung, die unsere Zugehörigkeit zur menschlichen Natur für unser konkretes Personsein besitzt."

46 Davis, The Ethics of Human Embryonic Stem Cell Research, 92-95.

47 Adolf Laufs says that dignity exists in the body-soul unity, see "Die Künstliche Befruchtung beim Menschen: Zulässigkeit und zivilrechtliche Folgen," in. V. Braun, D. Mieth and K. Steigleder (eds.), *Ethische und rechtliche Fragen der Gentechnologie und der Reproduktionsmedizin,* Gentechnologie, Chancen und Risiken 13 (München: 1987) 188: "Die Würde des Menschen besteht in der Einheit seines geistigen und leiblichen Seins, die ihn zu seinem geschichtlichen Dasein befähigt." Quoted in Schockenhoff, *Ethik des Lebens*, 244.

cannot quantify the fundamental rights universally, but practical reason (*geschichtlich-gesellschaftliche Vernunft*) can help in defining and sharing them equally under the principle justice within a particular society. However, participation in these rights hangs in the air, unless the right to life and bodily integrity are upheld. Since the human life per se is the fundamental good of all rights and freedoms, the right to life is strictly owed to every individual, particularly, to the unprotected, the dependent and the weak persons, who cannot depend against the violation of their fundamental rights.[48] Martha Nussbaum deserves appreciation for her emphasis on physical existence and basic needs or capabilities or opportunities, which must be available as a hallmark of minimum social justice, to live, function and celebrate life in concrete forms. Nussbaum considers ten "capabilities" to be threshold conditions necessary for a life worthy of human dignity.[49] In critique of the

48 Seee Schockenhoff, Die Ethik des Lebens, 242.

49 Martha Nussbaum, *Frontiers of Justice: Disability, Nationality, Species Membership* (Cambridge, Mass.: Harvard University Press, 2006). In her article on "Human Dignity and Political Entitlements," 351-380, 377-378: in the Appendix: The Central Human Capabilities, she mentions: *1. life, 2. bodily health, 3.bodily integrity, 4. senses-imagination-thought, 5. emotions, 6. practical reason, 7. affiliation*, social interaction and provisions of self-respect and non-discrimination on the basis of race, sex, sexual orientation, ethnicity, caste, religion, and national origin, *8. other species:* concern for and in relation to animals, plants and the world of nature, *9. recreation* and *10. control over one's environment*: socio-political participation and mutual recognition. Nussbaum repeatedly says that it is not the actual striving or functioning rather than the basic capabilities which are conditions which need opportunities for development and expression. They are flexible and pluralistic and respectful of human dignity. Yet the political goal is single and demanding to shape capabilities into entitlements for equal treatment of humans, at the same time, the state and the political goal is to impose any single metaphysical morality upon them. The state cannot punish people if they are not actualizing their entitlements because of their free choice. This is where Nussbaum differs from Aristotle that unlike his comprehensive doctrine of human flourishing toward a political doctrine, Nussbaum says the political goal is to ensure opportunities for capabilities leaving lots of space for different individuals, cultures and religions toward self-actualization in a way they want. This, according to her, will respect pluralism and thus she believes her capability approach is appropriate to the basis for political principles in a pluralistic democratic society. For a fuller discussion of the Aristotelian and Marxian themes in her writings, she suggests, "Nature, Function, and Capability: Aristotle on Political Distribution," in: *Oxford Studies in Ancient Philosophy*, Supplementary Volume (1988): 145-184, reprinted in: George E: McCarthy (ed.), *Marx and Aristotle* (Lanham, Maryland: Rowman and Littlefield, 1992) 175-212; "Aristotle on Human Nature and the Foundations of Ethics," in: James E. J. Altham and Ross Harrison (eds.), *World, Mind, and Ethics: Essays on the Philosophy of Bernhard Williams* (Cambridge: Cambridge University Press, 1995) 86-131; "Aristotelian Social Democracy," in: R. Bruce Douglass, Gerald R. Mara and Henry S. Richardson (eds.), *Liberalism and the Good* (New York and London: Routledge, 1990) 203-252, reprinted in: Aristide Tessitore (ed.), *Aristotle and Modern Politics* (Notre Dame, Indiana: University of Notre Dame Press, 2002) 47-104.

Stoic account of the intrinsic dignity that is due to every human being without any distinction of male or female, slave or free, king or peasant on account of the rational-moral capacity irrespective of their moral attainments, Nussbaum points out the neglect of external goods such as money, honour and status, and of basic goods such as food, health and education.[50] There are lacunae in the otherwise beautiful concept of the Stoic form of dignity that ensures equality. There might be indifferences to slavery, rape, poverty and all sorts of misfortune, since they cannot remove or damage the dignity. Nussbaum wants the world to get rid of a docile sort of false spirituality, pleads for a practical, political attitude towards "human capacities [that] require support from the world (love, care, education, nutrition) if they are to develop internally, and yet other forms of support from the world if the person is to have opportunities to exercise them (a suitable material and political environment)."[51] She says that "we need a picture of human dignity that makes room for different levels of capability and functioning and that also makes room for unfolding and development."[52] Nussbaum explains her position:

> The basic idea in my own version of this tradition is that *human beings have a worth that is indeed inalienable, because of their capacities for various forms of activity and striving*. These capacities are, however, dependent on the world for their full development and for their conversion into actual functioning. I use the term *basic capabilities* for the untrained capacities, the term *internal capabilities* for the trained capacities, and the term *combined capacities* for the combination of trained capacities with suitable circumstances for their exercise.[53]

However, Nussbaum seems to depend on the precious gift of individual conscience in realizing these capabilities. She cites Roger Williams (1603-

---

50 Nussbaum, "Human Dignity and Political Entitlements," 354: "Stoics not only split humans off from other animals more sharply, ... but also denied without argument that there is any dignity or end-like worth inherent in those human capacities in which animals also partake, such as sentience, everyday (non-moral) practical reasoning, emotion, and the capacity for love and care."

51 Nussbaum, "Human Dignity and Political Entitlements," 357.

52 Nussbaum, "Human Dignity and Political Entitlements," 357.

53 Nussbaum, "Human Dignity and Political Entitlements," 357: "Thus, someone might have fully developed internal capabilities without having the associated combined capabilities, if, for example, she is an educated person capable of free speech and association but is living in a repressive regime that denies those freedoms." Nussbaum agrees that "capacities have to be evaluated. Not all capacities that inhere in nature are the source of moral/political claims," and suggests that we must develop only those capacities that are "necessary for living a life that is worthy of the dignity that human beings possess."

1683 CE) in her defense of liberty of conscience,[54] which according to him, is each person's capacity to search for meaning in life and a precious jewel kind of worth which is inalienable and grounds political claims. Roger Williams had given two imageries of "unjust imprisonment" (denied free activity) and "soul rape" (denied free speech, subjected to forced conversion, etc.) to prove his point that they are wrong not because they would sully the worth of the concerned individual but because they violate the bodily, mental and emotional life depriving him/her of the opportunity to exercise good capacities. Nussbaum takes these images to show why the denial of religious liberty is wrong and connects to her neo-Aristotelian claim for all major human capacities such as sentience, imagination, emotions, reason and choice, which possesses dignity. Lacking in respect for these capacities/capabilities goes against the dignity of the possessor. Nussbaum attempts to clarify her position against Stoics and makes it clear that it is the duty of the political liberalism to ensure that opportunities turn capabilities into flourishing:

So the Stoics are wrong if they think that respect requires only a reverential attitude. It requires more: it requires creating the conditions in which capacities can develop and unfold themselves. Respect for human dignity is not just a lip service, it means creating conditions favorable for development and choice. … Whose task is it to create the conditions? [I]t is the task of the "basic structure" of society to put in place the necessary conditions for a minimally decent human life, a life at least minimally worthy of human dignity, expressive of at least minimal respect. [G]overnment (meaning the basic structure of society) should support the central human capabilities. [55]

Nussbaum's political theory seems to anchor on conscience, and the State has the duty only to create opportunities for living, dynamic, striving beings (human and non-human animals as well) for decent life. However, she restricts the State to make any consistent rules that would permit or restrict acts of citizens. She says that people have the freedom to choose what they want. The State must be open to the conscience of the people and celebrate differences in respect for pluralism. Thus, the single political goal of the State should focus on ensuring capabilities rather than actual functioning, leaving spaces for consciences of citizens to determine whether or not they wish to avail themselves of opportunities for functioning that politics give them. She gives a series of examples: (i) a member of the Old Order Amish will not vote or participate in politics, but s/he can accept the right to vote as a fundamental entitlement of all citizens, (ii) an atheist would object to any required religious functioning, but s/he can happily accept religious liberty as a central political

54 Nussbaum, "Human Dignity and Political Entitlements," 359. Roger Williams, *The Blouday Tenet of Persecution for the Cause of Conscience* (London: 1644).

55 Nussbaum, "Human Dignity and Political Entitlements," 359-360.

good.[56] While objecting the Aristotelian or any metaphysical sort of political arrangement on a single comprehensive (ethical or religious) doctrine of the flourishing life, Nussbaum draws ideas from Aristotle for basic capabilities and from Kant for rational capacities.[57] She justifies her non-metaphysical position with respect for pluralism:

> But in modern pluralistic democracies, it is appropriate to base political principles on any particular comprehensive doctrine not shared by reasonable citizens, because that would itself be a failure of respect and a type of soul rape. If all consciences require space to search for meaning in their own way, then a state that builds its principle on a single religious (or secular, e.g. Kant's) fails to accord conscience the right sort of space. Or rather, worse, it accords to some, [i.e.] those who accept the preferred creed, and not to others.
>
> I think we ought to seek political principles that have a moral content but that avoid contentious metaphysical notions (for example, the notion of the soul) that would make them incompatible with some of the many reasonable comprehensive doctrines that citizens hold.
>
> To make a dignity-based approach appropriate to the basis for political principles in a pluralistic democratic society, then, we must first work to develop it in a non-metaphysical way, articulating the relevant idea of dignity in a way that shows the ethical core of that idea but that does not insist on linking it to involved metaphysical or psychological doctrines concerning which the major religions and secular conceptions differ.[58]

What is missing in Nussbaum's position is the intrinsic worth of humans prior to human capabilities, flourishing or perishing, prior to the society and the State, prior to those who socially or religiously formed their own conscience. Is there no dignity in humans apart from capabilities? Nussbaum fights for dignity of capabilities, such as, conscience, sentience, practical reason, choice, emotions, senses, body, health and life, but she fails to give dignity to the possessor *per se* of these capabilities. Her own critique against Stoic dignity is applicable to herself, too. Ensuring capabilities can authenticate the intrinsic dignity of humans. Why should the State ensure capabilities in the first place?

---

56 Nussbaum, "Human Dignity and Political Entitlements," 360-361.

57 The framers of the UN's Universal Declaration of Human Rights had a profound agreement on an intuitive (metaphysical) idea that the human being is an end and not merely as means for a practical political unity. Jacques Maritain's defence of the shared intuitive idea of humans as ends (which Kant substantiated on capacity for autonomous action) and John Rawl's "overlapping consensus" are in my opinion metaphysical notions. See Jacques Maritain, *Man and the State* (Washington, D.C.: Catholic University of America Press, 1951), John Rawls, *Political Liberalism* (New York: Columbia University Press, 1996), Nussbaum, "Human Dignity and Political Entitlements," 360-361.

58 Nussbaum, "Human Dignity and Political Entitlements," 360, 361.

Is it merely to establish a social order or political peace with a minimum social justice? Or is there more to it, namely, in the nature of humans? Justice itself needs justification.[59] What is the purpose of the very humanity? In the attempt to appreciate and uphold democracy and pluralism in respect of human capabilities and political entitlements, Nussbaum wants the State to permit its citizens to decide for themselves in the (formed, relative, right or wrong) conscience pro or contra abortion, suicide, euthanasia, embryonic stem cell research, etc.[60] Nussbaum's idea of political entitlement is commendable for the emphasis on human needs and entitlements but not without drawbacks in the ethical and spiritual arena. She does not address the question: what is the purpose of humanity? Democracy and pluralism do not mean only celebration of differences. They do not demean the underlying unity either. Is there nothing intrinsic in and common among humans? Can we ever speak of one single humanity without metaphysics? Can a bridge stand without foundations or a common thread holding it? Democracy and pluralism must respect the fundamental right to life. That is why, especially in areas of bioethics, while dealing with the issues of right to life, such as, abortion, euthanasia, killing, etc., it is tellingly clear that humanity and its value of dignity are universal-able and at least minimally common. Is it enough to talk about individual humans and leave out humanity as a species? Politics, too, stand on a metaphysical premise of duties to protect humanity and other species.

There is certainly a revival of Aristotle in Nussbaum with a modified view of the pluralistic attitude towards claiming fundamental political entitlements coupled with the economic materialism of Karl Marx. For Nussbaum, any being that has the capacity for activity and striving would have some sort of dignity. But any being that has the capacity for activity but has no striving is without worth and is not entitled to rights. Thus, she puts the life of an anencephalic child or a person in a persistent vegetative state at risk of abandoning, because there is "no striving" at all.[61] Although Nussbaum wants "an account of the basis of human dignity that is respectful of the many different varieties of humanity and that doesn't rank and order human beings," and insists that "the political entitlements of all citizens are equal and the same," and includes children and adults with severe physical and mental disabilities to be sharers of human dignity and approves of guardians and legal guardianship for them,[62] she has unfortunately excluded the non-

59 Rawls says that "each person possesses an inviolability founded on justice that even the welfare of society as a whole cannot override." Rawls, *Theory of Justice* (Oxford: Oxford University Press, 1973), 3. I think it is other way round that justice is founded on inviolability [of human dignity and human life].

60 Nussbaum, "Human Dignity and Political Entitlements," 367-377.

61 Nussbaum, "Human Dignity and Political Entitlements," 363.

62 Nussbaum, "Human Dignity and Political Entitlements," 363, 364.

striving humans. Are they "rocks"? Acknowledging the uniqueness of human life, reason, language and imagination, Nussbaum holds that humans under a species norm have a unique and equal dignity different from the dignity of an animal.[63] She writes, "Animals other than human beings possess dignity for the very same reason that human beings possess dignity: they are complex living sentient beings endowed with *capacities for activity and striving.* It seems to me morally unacceptable to harp on the importance of human dignity while denying this dignity to other animals."[64] Nussbaum deserve appreciation for combining rational or striving (alive) capacities and bodily needs in moral claim for dignity of any species with life. However, Nussbaum put the onus on "*striving*," which has unfortunately become the biggest drawback of her theory. In fact, she rightly gave moral weight and political entitlements to the "undeveloped basic capabilities" (which included all human beings without any discrimination) initially, but she changed her position and reformulated "developed" major capabilities. She says that "we do have political obligations to human beings and not to rocks," and immediately thereafter mentions that "we would not accord equal human dignity to a person in persistent vegetative state, or to an anencephalic child, since it would appear that there is no striving here, no reaching out for functioning."[65] She is wrong here. We would not discard a human being in whatever stage or state s/he is, as we would throw a damaged computer. The human being is a living being even without striving. Non-striving humans do not turn to be a piece of lifeless flesh. Humans, at all stages and in different states, even in a coma, are humans and have dignity. Is there fairness in her theory of political justice that people must be able to

63 Nussbaum says that "to protect the capabilities of animals, ... we will surely have to stop the factory farming industry and lots of other cruel abuses of animals. We have to stop hunting and fishing for sport, the desecration of the habitat of animals "in the wild," and lots of other practices in which our world currently engages. ..., while ending the unnecessarily cruel treatment of animals in research." Nussbaum, "Human Dignity and Political Entitlements," 366-367.

64 Nussbaum mentions a couple of difficulties: "I argue that one can reasonably be agnostic about the painless killing of some animals for food, after a decent life, on the grounds that most animals don't have the type of interests that are frustrated by death, an argument proposed by both Bentham and Peter Singer, though still controversial," and "we could rescue ourselves from inconsistency if we were to return to the Stoic account, arguing that dignity resides in rationality. I have argued, however, that such an account is unacceptable even if we focus only on the human community. If we do accept the Aristotelian account I recommend, it seems very difficult to draw a sharp line between our species and other species, and much more ethically responsible to reflect long and hard about the reasons we have to change our behaviour to other species." Nussbaum, "Human Dignity and Political Entitlements," 366-367.

65 Nussbaum, "Human Dignity and Political Entitlements," 363.

exercise their basic capabilities, and thus political entitlements on their own?[66] What happens, when a coma patient returns to normal life? We need scientific integrity and respect with a sense of awe for miraculous happenings even in science. There is another drawback in Nussbaum`s theory: while heavily relying on two major basic capabilities of *practical reason* and *free choice*[67] that help human individuals realize their own capabilities and to have concern for other species, Nussbaum gives freedom to individuals to live a life of their own choice. This is nothing more than equating dignity with autonomy. Nussbaum thus makes a series of arbitrary conclusions to justify prostitution, abortion, suicide, euthanasia, embryonic stem cell research, cloning, enhancements, etc.[68] While including most of the human physical, spiritual, social and political aspects of human life to assess a dignified life of flourishing, Nussbaum seems to have lost herself in a new form of reductionism or Aristotelian materialism[69] without reflecting on the very purpose of the human species and on the intrinsic human dignity prior to capabilities.

Capabilities are actually indicators of dignity and not the source of dignity. Respect for dignity means respect for capabilities, and it demands opportunities for capabilities. However, similar to Kass, I would say, "Not all of dignity consists in capabilities alone either." Respect for dignity means respect for the vulnerable and palliative care for terminally-ill patients. In fact, we are not respecting the capabilities *per se* but human beings with capabilities. Respect for dignity actually means respect for the being with dignity. We do not actually (though we do) adore the abstract concept of dignity but the human being inherent with dignity. In the Kantian term, humanity is synonymous with dignity, which is an inseparable value. In his sense, respecting dignity means respecting humanity. While championing against ethical universalism in favour of multiculturalism to be flexible and

---

66 In her single conception of political justice, she includes people with disabilities that may be helped to the point at which they are able to exercise these entitlements on their own. But what happens, if a mentally disabled person is not at all able to exercise them?

67 Practical reason and choice are extremely important capabilities that have an architectonic function, pervading an organizing all of the others. Without opportunity to exercise practical reason and choice in the use of adequate nutrition, one has not been shown respect for dignity. Nussbaum states categorically that it is the *opportunity*, not its actual exercise. See Nussbaum, "Human Dignity and Political Entitlements," 368.

68 See Nussbaum, "Human Dignity and Political Entitlements," 362-377.

69 L. S. Carrier, "Aristotelian Materialism," *Philosophia* 34 (2006) 253-266, 266: "Martha Nussbaum [is] mistaken in saying that Aristotle was not a materialist, but a functionalist. His functionalism should instead be given a materialistic interpretation, since he holds that only the appropriate sort of matter can realize the human psyche. Aristotle's functionalism is therefore best viewed as a "causal functionalism," in which functional descriptions enable us to find the right sort of material embodiment." We do not enter into discussion on Aristotle in this matter.

pluralistic, respectful of human diversity,[70] Nussbaum denied the intrinsic dignity to the non-striving (for example, brain dead) humans. A member of the President's Council of Bioethics and a Professor of Political Science at Loyola University of Maryland, Diana Schaub rightly says, "The repellent results of a focus on developed quality-of-life capabilities without an acknowledgement of either the equality of human rights or the unique dignity of the human being are on display in Martha Nussbaum's essay."[71] I believe that Nussbaum could still include those non-striving or ever non-strivable humans, since her theory actually speaks of capabilities and opportunities, and not of actual functioning, as she supports the rights and guardianships of children and adults with severe physical and mental disabilities. Her theory requires consistency.

Many worldviews attempt to include spiritual-material wellbeing and socio-political entitlements for a life worthy of dignity. Expectations of a dignified life summarize a maximum definition (*Maximaldefinition, Geltungsbereich*) expanding its horizons but what belongs to the essence of humanity (*Genese, Gattungszugehörigkeit, Erkenntisprinzip*) without any cultural ascription is the minimum concept (*Minimalbegriff, Kerngehalt*) of human dignity that means an inviolable worth beyond economic value and social use.[72] The maximum definition refers to moral demands of basic needs and social justifications for a dignified life, while the minimum definition refers to the natural dignity, which is universal and normative. The former requires consensus, whereas the latter is independent of cultural ethos and religious precepts for a fulfillment of human existence. Thus, the binding content of human dignity can only be in its minimum definition (i.e. the inviolable worth of humanity) to be enforced democratically and protected legally by the constitutional states.[73] Many expectations and meanings in

---

70 Martha C. Nussbaum, *Cultivating Humanity: A Classical Defense of Reform in Liberal Education* (Cambridge, MA: Cambridge University Press, 1997).

71 Diana Schaub, "Commentary on Nussbaum, Shell, and Kass," in: *Human Dignity and Bioethics. Essays Commissioned by the President's Council on Bioethics* (Washington, D.C.: 2008) 381-386.

72 See Schockenhoff, *Ethik des Lebens*, 237, 233: "Die eigentliche epistemologische Aufgabe, eine rationale Rekonstruktion des Wissens, kann … nur durch eine *interne* Darlegung des Rechtfertigungszusammenhangs geleistet werden, die von seinen *externen* (historischen, soziologischen, psychologischen, etc.) Entstehungsbedingungen absehen muss." See Hans Reichenbach, *Experience and Prediction: An Analysis of the Foundations and the Structure of Knowledge* (Chicago: University of Chicago Press, 1938).

73 See Schockenhoff, *Ethik des Lebens*, 237: "Der harte Kern der Menschenwürde-Vorstellung zielt auf nichts anderes, als was den Menschen zum Menschen macht: seine Fähigkeit zum freien Handeln und zur eigenverantwortlichen sittlichen Selbstbestimmung. Dieses letzte, unhintergehbare Residuum des Selbstseins begründet, warum der Mensch nicht nur ökonomischen Wert und gesellschaftlichen Nutzen, sondern auch eine Würde besitzt, die ihm als Zweck an sich selbst zukommt."

justification of a dignified life do not automatically mean a contradiction of a universal meaning of human dignity. There is always an underlying human dignity that is open to cultural and religious interpretations in application. The ability of varied uses of human dignity may be a blessing in pluricultural and multireligious societies without a compromise on the intrinsic value of humans. In fact, natural dignity means inherent human dignity. It subsists in the essence of humans. It belongs to the humans as humans. It does not have grades. It is the equal value of all human beings. This value qualifies humans inviolable and respects humans as subjects and never as objects or mere means, since they are end-in-themselves (*Selbstzwecklichkeit*) and possess the capacity of self-determination (*Selbstbestimmung*). Respect for human dignity means respect for autonomy, too. However, dignity does not consist in the individual realization of rational qualities alone but the very existence of humans irrespective of their physical, mental and moral conditions demand respect for humans. Autonomy has limits, when justice sets boundaries. Justice is the outer layer of inner equal dignity. Thus, natural human dignity is the foundational norm to address bioethical and socio-political problems, to value humans above science, society and state and to prohibit their instrumentalization even for a noble goal (*Verbot der Totalinstrumentalisierung*).

The understanding of human dignity is a mixed bag of biology, theology, anthropology, philosophy, ontology, existentialism, phenomenology, epistemology, hermeneutics, metaphysics, sociology, morality, ethics and law. Even psychology is not away from it, for humiliation affects the dignity of the individual. In brief, it deals with humans, and so we need an anthropology that respects body-soul elements. Finally, the question "why humans at all are there?" leads us to the very question of the creation and the purpose of humans. I tend to think intuitively that humanity as a whole or any individual human are not accidents. Thus, above all, the question of human dignity is a matter of creation theology and religions. This sublime thought needs attention in the dignity debate. Taking all elements of human life into consideration, Robert Spaemann thus says that there can be only one criterion of personality and dignity: the biological belongingness to the human generation.[74] Affiliation to the human species is a sufficient condition to qualify its members as humans or persons with dignity and claims for equal rights. This fundamental principle of ethics of human life is sufficient and abundantly rich to protect all the members of the human species standing out beyond and above any culture.[75] A strong

74 Quoted in Friedo Ricken, "Mensch und Person," 67. Robert Spaemann, *Personen: Versuche über den Unterschied zwischen etwas und jemand* (Stuttgart: 1996), 264.

75 Schockenhoff argues in: "Pro Speziesargument," 31: "Deshalb beruht auch *das Grundprinzip einer humanen Lebensethik*, nach dem wir dem menschlichen Leben von seinem Anfang bis zum Ende in jeder Form, in der es uns entgegentritt, die gleiche Achtung schulden, nicht auf einer partikularen religiösen Einstellung, sondern auf dem Respekt, den

species norm is an urgent need today more than ever 'in the face of the soul-flattening and dehumanizing dangers of a Brave New Word,' at a time when commodification of human bodily parts, commercialization of human bodies, enhancement of human life, manipulation of aging genes, designer babies are considered human goals. Thus, besides claiming political entitlements, the concept of human dignity is able to prevent humans not only from disfiguring the human image (from killing the creature made in God's image) but also from trying to "redesign humans after our own fantasies."[76]

---

wir in unserer demokratischen Rechtskultur der Freiheit und der Selbstbestimmung jedem einzelnen Menschen entgegenbringen."

76 See Kass, "Defending Human Dignity," 303, 304, 305. Kass says that "we cannot evaluate any proposed enhancements or alterations of our humanity unless we have some idea of human dignity, some notion of what is estimable and worthy and excellent about being human. In order to know whether change is progress rather than degradation, we need a standard of the *un*graded and the admirable. We need to understand the nature and worth of human flourishing in order to recognize both the true promise of self-improvement and the hazards of self-degradation.... We need, in short, wisdom about human dignity and what sustains and enhances it and what destroys it" (303-304). Friends of human dignity can easily have concern for the dignity of (mere) human aliveness as well as for the dignity of human flourishing. We can and should defend both the dignity of human *being* and the dignity of being *human* (306).

# 29

# Interfacing Discourse Ethics with Ethics of Liberation: A Creative Reading of Apel-Dussel Dialogue

**Prof Nishant A Irudayadason**
*Professor, Moral Philosophy, Jnana-Deepa Vidyapeeth, Pune*

**Abstract:** In this paper, we present the dialogue between discourse ethics and ethics of liberation. Although born in different contexts, both approaches to ethics work for a universal ethics preoccupied with global problems. This paper is an attempt to show how both models of ethics though conflictual are mutually enriching.

**Keywords:** communication, consensus, discourse, environment, ethics, exclusion, exteriority, foundation, intersubjective, liberation, universal

The dialogue between the discourse ethics of Karl-Otto Apel and the ethics of liberation of Enrique Dussel began in 1989 at the International Seminar organized by Raúl Fornet-Betancourt in Freiburg (Germany) entitled *Philosophie der Befreiung. Begründungen von Ethik in Deutschland und Lateinamerika heute* (Philosophy of Liberation: Foundations of Ethics in Germany and Latin America Today). The purpose of this seminar is to stimulate intercultural dialogue in philosophy as a "method" for overcoming dependence, asymmetry and colonial force in economics and politics. The thematic focus of this first International Seminar was the foundation of ethics and it was addressed from the perspective of Apel and Dussel, the former representing European moral philosophy and the latter Latin American ethics.

(Dussel 2013) These meetings gave Apel the opportunity to reflect explicitly on the problems of the Third World, as well as the challenge that the ethics of liberation represents for discourse ethics. Their philosophical dialogue was guided by the problems of global poverty and was aimed at the realization of justice in the international order. (Fornet-Betancourt 2002)

Karl-Otto Apel and Enrique Dussel led their philosophical reflections from their respective historical-political contexts. It is therefore important for us to know the different contexts in which the discourse ethics of Apel and the ethics of liberation of Dussel were born in order to better understand the differences between these two approaches. Despite different historical and political roots, these two philosophers have a clear vision for an authentic universalism that goes beyond methodological solipsism and totalitarian universalism. The world today is facing two major global problems: socio-economic problems and the environmental crisis. Philosophy must be able to respond to these global issues. To confront these two challenges, any attempt for universal ethics must be based on principles of responsibility and solidarity.

## 1. Two Different Contexts

Both the discourse ethics of Apel and the ethics of liberation of Dussel emerged in 1970s at a shared moment of political instability although it was due to different historical-political realities. Apel belonging to a generation that had experienced the catastrophe of National Socialism in Germany had an experience of the destruction of moral conscience. Dussel had a different historical experience, one of political dependency and economic underdevelopment.

Apel's experience in the German army led him to wonder how the Germans in the Third Reich were able to fulfil their obligations to their nation, despite the fact that they were serving an immoral regime, which has appalling consequences. He wanted to reconstruct moral conscience, in an effort to discover universally valid criteria though from a specific German point of view.

Having returned from the war with an immense thirst for knowledge, Apel began his studies in political history and philosophy. Though Apel's historical condition had some influence on the starting point of Apel's philosophy, his discourse ethics cannot in any way be reduced to it in a relativistic way. The central concern of Apel's philosophy was to move beyond Kant's transcendental philosophy to look for a rational foundation for an intersubjective validity of universal ethics, which seemed more urgent than before, in an era of scientific and technological progress.

Apel wanted to work out a universal paradigm for ethics moving beyond the conventional moral stages of development propounded by Köhlberg. His war experience along with his awareness of poverty and environmental crisis made him reflect on inescapable moral challenges posed by these realties. His need to find an ultimate philosophical foundation of universal moral principles was to ensure the survival of humanity.

However, Apel felt that a rational foundation for an intersubjective ethics has never been so difficult as it is today because reducing ethical conflicts seems impossible thanks to modern science that has claimed monopoly over rationality. (Apel 1996, 43) Thus, in in the age of science, to found a universally valid ethics on reason seems paradoxically both necessary and impossible: necessary because the co-existence of many different forms of life needs the norms of universal ethics capable of co-responsibility in solidarity; impossible because modern science monopolised the concept of a rational foundation, thus rendering all value-neutral theoretical elaborations as irrational ideologies. The greatest challenge for Apel was to find a *fundamentum inconcussum*, a firm foundation for a rational and objective ethics. He had to counter moral scepticism that holds the validity of normative statements as purely subjective.

Ethics of liberation emerged in the context of political dependency and economic underdevelopment in Lain America. It takes into account environmental problems and different types of exclusion from Eurocentric thinking of other peoples especially Latin Americans who are both victims and collaborators of colonial oppression. Dussel wanted to show how their political dependency has deceived them of economic development. The ontological experience of belonging to an exploited community by the capitalist world imposed a philosophical demand on Dussel to surpass this alienating ontology. (Dussel 2013, 238)

The discovery of Levinasian ethics offered new philosophical insights that were appropriated by ethics of liberation. Thus, the Levinasian philosophy of the Other enabled ethics of liberation to better understand the experience of exploited existence by realizing the fact of being massively dominated by colonial powers on which they depended for their economic development. Levinasian philosophy of the other and exteriority made it possible to think of a trans-ontological philosophy of liberation. Dussel understood exclusion and domination as a negation of the constitutive and historical exteriority of the Other.

Dussel made a radical critique of universalist pretensions of European reason and oppressive structures found in the rationality of communication. By his deliberate choice for the poor, liberation of the Third World countries became the central theme of his ethics. He considered cynicism as the principal obstacle to his ethics of liberation. Cynicism, according to him, is the affirmation of the power of a system as the foundation of reason, which controls strategic reason to mediate of its own realization towards absolute power. (Dussel 2013, 238) The first moment of cynical reason is the affirmation of universality without otherness; it is negation of the Other right from the beginning.

## 2. Two Approaches to Universal Ethics

According to Apel, we feel an urgent need to create a post-traditional universal morality. This urgency is due to the fact that today humanity is confronted with conflicts whose scope extend well beyond the borders of States. In this context, traditional morals preoccupied with guaranteeing the internal security of nations remain insufficient. Today, we need an ethics that can enable us to coexist and cooperate within and outside national borders, and to address ecological crisis. This is possible through a communicative organization of collective responsibility for the consequences of collective activities in science and technology. Unequal international relations and ecologically catastrophic consequences of contemporary industrial societies are two major concerns of a universal macroethics. (Apel 1996, 277-278)

This universal macroethics is not possible within the presuppositions of the Western system of complementarity which maintains dualism between value-neutral instrumental reason, specific to science and technology, and values-laden decision, specific to moral conscience. Therefore, the possibility of an ethical rationality or a rational foundation of intersubjective valid norms is a crucial question for a universal macroethics. If the objective interest of theoretical reason is truth and knowledge, the objective interest of practical reason is to elucidate subjective interests in the individuals of a community. Apel lays the need for this new foundation of ethics on a transformed transcendental philosophy, thus making a passage from a monological subject to a dialogical subject of a community of communication. This passage allows surpassing modern methodological solipsism.

Discourse ethics does not offer a concrete normative content, but gives formal conditions required for a norm to be able to legitimately oblige the members of a community of communication. The Düsseldorf philosopher asserts that only ethical rationality of consensual communication presupposes rules or norms which are common beyond the individual interests. (Apel 1996, 185) This rationality alone can constitute the basis of a universal ethics. In Apel's view, the opportunity to ground ethics is the result of becoming aware of the inevitability of a reasoned discourse as well as the normative and ethical conditions of possibility required by rational arguments.

The fundamental moral norm is a mutual recognition of all members of the community having the same rights and obligations to fulfil the demands of a reasoned discourse. Therefore, any attempt to exclude real or virtual interlocutors by limiting their argumentative capacity, ignoring their interests, or inviting them for a dialogue in a situation of inequality destroys the proper end of rational arguments. The community of communication is the key to universal ethics because it categorically demands the fulfilment of certain universal formal moral standards. Discourse ethics, therefore, consists of a formal procedure for ultimate foundation which, in turn, provides justification for concrete norms through consensual communication. (Apel 1996, 332)

Dussel does not deny Apel's position, but his perspective is different. According to him, the point of departure for a universal ethics cannot be found in the rational arguments of a community of communication since historically three-fourth of the world's population is excluded from participating in the discourse. If there is no symmetry and justice in the community of communication, it is impossible to arrive at the intersubjective validity of norms. Apel himself concedes that discourse ethics has limits in its because in the actual historically conditioned community of communication, we cannot start from the assumption that the conditions for the application of discourse ethics can naturally follow the insights of discourse ethics. (1996, 207) Dussel departs from this limit and places the ethical point of departure in the basic needs of the miserable majority. A philosophy that affirms the community of communication is not enough when many are excluded from the possibility of participating in the discourse. Dussel is aware of the importance and creativity of Apel's thought, but at the same time he considers it insufficient because, as a formal morality of intersubjective validity, it has failed to integrate the material moment of practical truth, which, in the eyes of the Argentine philosopher, is indispensable especially from the moment when the consequences of the system that inevitably produces victims become intolerable. As a result, Dussel's universalism gives importance to the revalorization and prioritization of the material aspect of ethics as different from the formal universalism of discourse ethics. But the universalism of Dussel is not only material but also formal because the poor are at the same time materially oppressed and formally excluded. So the universalism of Dussel, unlike that of Apel, includes a prior moment of content, which is expressed in the form of a universal ethical material principle.

After the eighth meeting at the Symposium held in Mexico City in 1997, Dussel presents in his essay titled "Principles, Mediations and the 'Good' as synthesis: From 'Discourse Ethics' to 'Ethics of Liberation'" (Dussel 1997, 55-66) the summary of the architectonics of ethics of liberation. (Dussel 2003) He states three universal principles that underlie the universalism of the ethics of liberation. First, the principle of discursive validity or principle of formal morality, which recuperates the discursive transformation of Kantianism: an action will be valid if it is decided thanks to the rational and symmetrical participation of all concerned in a community of communication. It is here that discourse ethics admits its limits because, empirically, there is no symmetry in the real community of communication. This leads Dussel to state the second principle, the universal material principle or practical truth, which will be anterior to the first. This principle is proposed against the formalisms but also against former versions of material ethics, which are not universal. If human life—which includes not only biological survival, but also cultural wholeness and integral dignity—is the mode-of-reality (*Realitätsmodus*) of the human person and the criterion of practical truth, the universal material ethical principle consists of the ethical obligation for production, reproduction and development of human life in a community. (Zúñiga 2020, 3) Dussel then introduces the third universal principle, namely the principle of feasibility which sets out the ethical obligation to perform an action that is possible from an empirical, technical, economic, political and historical point of view, within the framework of the two previous principles.

These three principles have critical counterparts defined from the negative effects of the system because, as soon as the effects of a system are considered unbearable, the project of the system becomes untenable and illegitimate for the victim who judges it as the cause of injustice he or she suffers. This is the moment of critical ethics and Dussel proposes the negative version of the three previous principles. While addressing the subject of life, who is denied life, the universal critical material principle presents it as a duty to criticize any institutional system that prevents life. To the subject of rationality, who cannot participate in the argumentation or discussion on the reproduction of his or life, the critical principle of validity or critical discursive principle affirms a symmetrical organization of the victims in a community of life and of communication, aiming at the projection of an alternative future. Finally, while addressing the subject of action, who has the obligation to change victimizing institutions, the critical principle of feasibility or liberation principle, upholds the duty of the critical community to effectively deconstruct the system so that the victims can live and can have equal right to participation in discussions leading to decisions.

What is essential for ethics of liberation is not primarily a community of communication, but the recognition of the excluded Other, the transcendental exteriority to the ontology of community. From this perspective, what is urgent is not so much the conditions of possibility of rational arguments to be able to participate in the public discourse as the transition from being excluded to becoming participants. This liberation process, according to Dussel is prior to Apel's community of communication.

The main obstacle to Dussel's authentic universalism is not methodological solipsism as in the case of Apel's universal ethics, but totalitarian universalism, because ethics of liberation is based on the suspicion that the community of communication can be a hegemonic society in reality and when it dominates cultures, nations, classes and genders it imposes its own particularity. (Dussel 1996, 39) In this context of material domination and formal exclusion from which most of humanity suffers, the starting point or the original source of any possible discourse has to be in the interpellation of the Other from exteriority to the community of communication. The Other becomes the a-priori condition for the possibility of any rational argument. This is because, before being affected by rational consensus, the Other is excluded from the discourse in which consensus are reached. Therefore, the transcendental absolute condition of possibility of any argument can only be in the recognition of the Other as a person, who through his interpellation demands the possibility of being part of the historically possible community of communication. The demand of the poor challenges the established consensus of the totalitarian universalism and calls for authentic universality.

## 3. Relation between the Two Approaches

Rather than focusing on the radical opposition between these two approaches to ethics, we would like to discover a possible relation between them, while recognizing the different emphasis each approach has made based on different historical contexts. Apel's architectonics is constituted of three principles: the first is the ideal conditions for formation of consensus through rational argument; the second is the duty of political leaders to preserve the real conditions of democracy; and the third is the modification of real circumstances to meet the ideal conditions. The last principle shows that Apel was aware of the impossibility of an immediate application of the first principle. Thus, Apel emphasizes that we must recognize our belonging to the community of communication, in which we find injustices as revealed by Dussel. The dialectical tension between the first and the last principle would contribute to a long-term transformation of relations aimed at alleviating the tension between the ideal of consensus and the political reality and to gradually get closer to the ideal conditions for the possibility of a consensual settlement of conflicts. (Apel 1996, 208)

In Apel's architectonics of three principles, we find a parallel to Dussel's ethics of liberation marked by three moments: (a) a formal moment of validity of norms though participation in discourse, (b) a material moment to ensure the political conditions for all, and c) a third moment, a long-term realization of human dignity and of community free from injustice and domination. This third principle is considered by both thinkers as a regulative idea of practical reason in the Kantian sense, that is, a normative principle having the force of obligation to the long term realization of ideal conditions. (Apel 1996, 208) A regulatory idea, unlike a utopia, expresses the idea that nothing at the moment of experience fully corresponds to the ideal. (Apel 1996, 237) The difference between the two thinkers appears in the order of these three moments. For Apel the formal moment is fundamental and must be applied in the material context later, but for Dussel, it is the contrary, namely the material moment must precede the formal moment.

For Dussel, ethics of liberation departs from the alleged inapplicability of the first and the fundamental principle of discourse ethics: the factual non-participation of nearly three-fourth of the world population is an undeniable exclusion of those in misery. In this reality of exclusion, responsibility for the Other obliges us to identify the causes of victimization in the system, which constitutes the true critical moment of ethics. (Dussel 2013, 343) Dussel makes it clear that he speaks of responsibility not in the Weberian sense, namely responsibility for the effects of our actions but in the Levinasian sense, that is to be responsible for the Other to liberate him or her from oppression. His understanding of responsibility, therefore, is both a critique and a call to eradicate the causes in the system that leads to misery, domination and exclusion suffered by the victims. It is also the practical condition of the possibility of any rational argument, which allows the Other to be part of a new community of communication paving way for an authentic universalism. Responsibility precedes any rational argument and in this sense anterior to Apel's understanding of responsibility for the consequences of consensual decisions made through rational argument in the community of communication.

Apel often speaks of the practical urgency for a universal macroethics in the face of environmental crisis caused by collective activities in the era of science and technology. Besides addressing the environmental problems, he also recognizes the need to work for justice on a global scale, through a process of progress towards social emancipation. The obligation of progress is at the same time an obligation to transform real relationships so that the fundamental norm of discourse ethics can be applied in the future.

Apel introduces a three-norm system in response to the main thesis of Hans Jonas, which states that in a crisis situation found in the industrialized societies of the 1980s, we must abandon all utopia of progress. What was needed in those industrial societies of 1980s, which began to face environmental crisis, was an "ethics of preservation and prevention, not of progress and perfection". (Jonas 1994, 139) Apel considers that in order to save human existence and dignity, it is not enough to have an ethics of preservation and, consequently not be contended with a simple a-posteriori responsibility for the consequences of collective activities. If we want "*humanly dignified social relationships come to be established throughout the world*", (Apel 233) it is also necessary to consider a regulative idea of technological and social progress "*in the real, human* community *of communication the ideal community of communication must always remain to be realized—progressively*". (Apel 236) Apel then introduces his third principle applicable to strategic plan which will contribute as much as possible to a long-term transformation of relations: a transformation aimed at alleviating the tension between the ideal norm of conflict resolution and the political reality and, thus, gradually getting closer to the ideal conditions for a consensual settlement of conflicts. (Apel 1996, 208) This third principle is therefore a principle of progress and social emancipation that acts as a regulative idea aiming at achieving social and political conditions for an ideal community and therefore for justice on a global scale. Apel thus escapes at the same time the possible Social-Darwinist solutions to the ecological crisis which affirm that, from a strictly biological point of view, the survival of humanity, in the face of overpopulation and scarcity of resources could well be ensured by starving population in the Third World countries. This type of response is incompatible with a universal ethics of Apel that tends to realize global justice.

Apel's mediation between ethical rationality and strategic rationality is the new element in discourse ethics, which distinguishes it from all traditional forms of "ethics of conviction". This mediation also constitutes a new idea for an ethics of co-responsibility. Thanks to this third principle, discourse ethics can be shown to be an ethics of collective responsibility of solidarity vis-à-vis the collective activities, making it different from Jonas' Responsibility Principle. Moreover, discourse ethics can be understood as an ethics not only of *a-posteriori* responsibility for the consequences of consensus, but also as an ethics of transcendental responsibility, that is co-responsibility as transcendental precondition for human community and reciprocal interaction. Therefore, for Apel, responsibility arising from the consequences of collective activities is guided by two criteria:

a) a *restrictive condition* for the preservation and guarantee of the survival of humanity, in the sense of Jonas,
b) the regulative idea of progress or "long-term, approximative realization of an ideal" (Apel 237)

The second criterion seems to resemble Dussel's understanding of responsibility which seeks to transform the real community of communication and build anew a future community of communication in which victims can participate and in which the fundamental norm of rational argument of discourse ethics can be applied so that the resolution of conflicts is done by the formation of a consensus between all the parties concerned. Consequently, it seems to us that both discourse ethics and ethics of liberation, despite their differences, support similar ideas, while accentuating different aspects depending on their fundamental concerns.

## Conclusion

Throughout various interventions that constitute the dialogue between Dussel's ethics of liberation and Apel's discourse ethics, both thinkers have attempted to place their ethics in relation to each other. According to Apel, the demands of ethics of liberation manifest a concrete case of part B of his discourse ethics, and according to Dussel, discourse ethics represents a moment of his ethics of liberation. In spite of their methodological differences arising from different starting points, we find their ethics mutually enriching though sometimes conflictual as recognized by both of them.

From the time of his first meeting with Apel in Freiburg on 25 November 1989, Dussel recognized the importance of Apel's approach to the discovery of the community of communication to overcome modern solipsism. Nevertheless, in Dussel's eyes, Apel's thought is insufficient in the context of domination and negation of the Other. He then proposes an extension of the definition of Apel's community of communication by explicitly including the exteriority of every person, the Other whom Dussel characterizes as not only different but also distinct. Dussel distinguishes "difference", defined from the perspective of identity, internal to the totality and "distinction" from the point of view of exteriority that represents the otherness of the Other. Ethics of liberation thus starts from the discursive proposition, while transforming it in order to be able to finally articulate the formal principle of Apel with the material principle. Consequently, the irruption of the Other who questions the totalitarian universalism of a real community of communication is a condition of the possibility of any new argumentation. In this sense, both interpellation and responsibility are anterior to argumentation. As a result, the fundamental principle of discourse ethics becomes a secondary moment in the architectonics of ethics of liberation.

On his part, Apel recognizes that ethics of liberation is a challenge to his discourse ethics, but only to the part B of his ethics, that is, the part of ethics dealing with those situations in which the conditions for the application of part A of discourse ethics are not yet realized in this world. As a result, exclusion is a specific issue in part B of his ethics and can be resolved within discourse ethics. Given the fact that we cannot apply the fundamental norm of part A of discourse, we must fulfil the complementary principle of part B of ethics. This is a regulative principle of responsibility that contributes to a long-term policy of changing the global situation in the world. Therefore, "while part A corresponds to the transcendental justification of the procedural principle of universalization, part B corresponds to the articulation of an ethics of responsibility". (Apel 1996, XIV) As a result, the interpellation of the Other excluded from the discourse does not challenge the pragmatic and transcendental approach of discourse ethics; it challenges only the articulation of an ethics of responsibility.

Nevertheless, the exclusion of which Dussel speaks is not only an exclusion from participation in the discourse but also an exclusion from life. Apel recognizes the importance of life as an ultimate reference, for example when he talks about overpopulation, hunger or ecological destruction as threats to human life. But, unlike the philosophy of liberation, he does not make this the starting point of his ethics. Although Apel recognizes that the interpellation of the excluded Other is a challenge to his discourse ethics, he considers that a foundation of ethics beginning from an encounter with the Other is not possible. Thus, in the sixth meeting held in Eichstätt in April 1995, Apel states that we cannot compare and confront bodily existence with transcendental discussion of philosophy; since, to express it emphatically, we can reflect on a valid or invalid discussion about human life and its conditions, but we cannot live on thought or discussion. This linguistic experience shows that what is unsurpassable in the transcendental sense cannot be life or bodily existence, even though it is the fundamental ontological or anthropological point of view.

Dussel holds that his ethics of liberation cannot be reduced to a specific case of part B of discourse ethics, namely the part concerning the application of fundamental norm. Thus, Dussel repeatedly asserts that the recognition is prior to the foundation of ethics in argumentation. Dussel also insists that for ethics of liberation, the starting point is the suffering corporeality of the excluded, namely the otherness of the Other. According to Dussel, it is not a question of the application of the fundamental norm, as is the case in discourse ethics. He reverses the order to conclude that in reality the material principle is prior to the former principle and it is the formal principle of the fundamental norm which has the function to apply the material principle.

By reading the successive interventions that constitute a dialogue between discourse ethics and ethics of liberation, we come to the conclusion that each of these two ethics represents a challenge for the other but they are mutually enriching. The conflicting positions are largely due to methodological differences. The dialogue between discourse ethics and ethics of liberation holds a particular interest because it represents an initiative in favour of a dialogue between the Occidental philosophy and the philosophy of the "peripheries".

## References

Apel (1996). *Selected Essays Volume Two: Ethics and the Theory of Rationality*, New Jersey: Humanities Press.

Dussel (1996). *The Underside of Modernity: Apel, Ricœur, Rorty, Taylor and Philosophy of Liberation*. New Jersey: Humanities Press.

Dussel (1997). "Principles, Mediations, and the 'Good' as Synthesis: From 'Discourse Ethics' to 'Ethics of Liberation'". *Philosophy Today* 41 (Supplement): 55-66

Dussel (2013). *Ethics of Liberation in the Age of Globalization*. Durham: Duke University Press.

Fornet-Betancourt (2002) *Interaction and Asymmetry between Cultures in the Content of Globalization*. IKO.

Zúñiga (2020). "Ethics of Liberation and Discourse Ethics: On Grounding the Material Principle of Life". In Mendieta and Allen (eds.). *Decolonizing Ethics: Enrique Dussel's Ethics of Liberation*. Penn State: Penn State UP (Critical Theory Series).

30

# Role of Humans in Universe: Ecological Understanding of A.R. Peacocke

**Isaac Parackal OIC**
*Systematic Philosophy, JDV, Pune*

**Abstract**: New discoveries have enriched the scientific understanding of the universe and corrected the age-old misconceptions about it. This article is an elaboration of A.R Peacocke's vision of the human being in the light of evolution and his/her relation with the world. The humans have in this universe a significant role to perform. In this understanding, God, humans and the world are interconnected and interrelated. The role of a human person as priest, prophet, symbiont and co-creator is very well established and God works through humans to sustain and preserve the world. Human work becomes the genuine Opus Dei for the betterment of the whole universe.

**Keywords**: Person, Unfulfilled Paradox, Priest of creation, Steward, Symbiont, Prophet, Co-Creator, Opus Dei, Liturgy-Offering of the World

## Introduction

Our age has witnessed marvellous discoveries in the field of science and technology. The tremendous success in the field of science has given a new face to humanity and profoundly transformed human life. Today we know more about the origin not only of our human race but also of the universe. New discoveries have enhanced the scientific understanding of the universe and corrected the age-old misconceptions about it. We shall see in detail A.R Peacocke's notion of the human being in the light of evolution and his/her relation with the world. Humans have in this universe a great role to perform. His relationship with the world is not a kind of 'domination' but as of priest who has the sacred duty to offer the world back to God. In this context, human work is conceived as collaboration in the creative act of God. Human work as *Opus Dei* should contribute to the betterment of the cosmos. The human person as co-creator protects nature and implement the plan of God in this universe which is the sacrament of God, a concept so dear to Dr Cyril Desbruslais.

## 1. Human Beings in the Light of Evolution

Scientific endeavour unveils the fact that human being is the product of evolution and s/he is a part of the material structure of the world. Though human being is a part of the material structure s/he is only partially describable in terms of atoms and molecules. Peacocke points out the indescribability concerning human brings:

> The level of organisation of matter which we call a man is thus as much as and as little describable in terms of physics and chemistry of his constituent atoms and molecules as any other organism. Moreover, in a man new properties and activities of matter emerge which cannot be subsumed or described in terms of languages and concepts used for the forms which preceded him."[1]

According to Peacocke the mental activities are "activities which emerge distinctively and characteristically in matter organized at the level we call man."[2] This points to the fact that humans are distinct and unique in the evolutionary chain of his/her emergence. Peacocke observes that these physical and mental activities are of the same entity which he prefers to call 'person'.[3]

### a. Human Being as Person

Peacocke thinks that 'person' is the appropriate name for Man. He observes:

> This way of describing man does justice to human's evolutionary origins out of the matter of the world, on which he is still dependent for life; and on the truly emergent mental activities which characterize man specifically. Man has been said to be a psychosomatic unity: perhaps one would rather say he is one person possessing both physical and mental attributes, each explicated by appropriate sets of predicates.[4]

1 A.R. Peacocke, *Science and the Christian Experiment*, (London: Oxford University Press 1971), 141.

2 *Ibid.,* 142.

3 *Ibid.*, 142.

4 *Ibid.,* 142.

For him, there is a close relationship between human mental activities and physical organization. We see 'diversity-in-unity' in human being concerning the mental and physical activities which are interrelated and interconnected. "Man remains a diversity-in-unity and neither the diversity nor the unity can be properly denied as being characteristic of man, who standing at the summit of the evolutionary process, himself reflects on the ladder by which he has climbed out of insentient matter."[5]

Compared to animals, humans have something more that requires autonomous concepts for its description and elaboration. In human beings a number of cognitive functions are integrated into a system of higher order.[6] According to Peacocke our capacity for self awareness is the root of our personhood. He states: "Human beings furthermore have a capacity for self-awareness–we use the word 'I' of ourselves in semantically peculiar ways – which is the root both of our capacity for inter-subjective communication and the integrating activity which gives each of us our sense of personhood, of being particular person."[7] We need appropriate concepts and language to describe the interrelatedness of mental and physical activities of Man as person.[8]

## b. Human Being as Unfulfilled Paradox

According to Peacocke, like any other terrestrial mammalian vertebrate Man needs food, rest, shelter, sex etc.[9] However, even when the basic needs are satisfied and met, many a time humans are not content. "He (human being) has a restlessness which stems from his failure to satisfy other needs, which he seems not to share with other animals."[10] Human awareness of these failures and shortcomings make him/her tragic and desperate. Peacocke points out that this is actually the paradox of being human:

> We have the paradox of man as the summit of the cosmic development so far, for his mental activities transcend all, yet at the same time he is tragically aware of his personal and social shortcomings and subject to the tension between the awareness of the finitude of his individual life and infinity of his longings. He is aware of both of that from which he has

5 *Ibid.,* 144.

6 Human beings exceed all other living organisms in the complexity of their intelligent apprehension, storage and processing of information from their environment; cf. A.R. Peacocke, "The Kindling of the Divine Flame", *Teilhard Review*, 25(1990), 9.

7 A.R. Peacocke, "The Kindling of the Divine Flame", *Teilhard Review*, 25(1990), 9.

8 Cf. A.R. Peacocke, "The Nature and Purpose of Man in Science and Christian Theology" *Zygon,* 8 (1973), 378.

9 Cf. A.R. Peacocke, *Creation and the World of Science* (Oxford: Clarendon Press, 1979), 179.

10 *Ibid.,* 179.

> evolved and of his tendency always fall short of the full realization of his own individual and corporative potentialities. Thus the incompleteness of the actualisation of the potentialities inherent in the stuff of the universe is, in man, a result of his own decisions, or lack of them, and is quite different from the situation of unrealized potentiality in the molecular or cell which is eventually expressed in, *inter alia,* living organisms.[11]

This dichotomy in human experience and the resulting tension and the sense of incompleteness is specific to human being.[12] This situation always creates a confusion and perplexity in human life and makes it confounded and flummoxed. Peacocke presents this difficulty very nicely:

> Man's dilemma is real, for how is he to know, which way to go, to which challenge he should respond, what is his real potentialities might be? What does it involve to be a human being, to be fully human person? What should constitute personalness in its richest manifestation? What should human beings strive to become?...The evolutionary sequence clearly shows that the answers to these questions are vital for man and his future but, at the same time, provides nothing from within the process itself which will tell us what human beings *ought to become*, how they should achieve their ends in a way which recognizes their personalness, that psychosomatic unity which differentiates them from the rest of the cosmos.[13]

Humans are tragically aware of their failure to become what they might be and what they ought to be. "Man has always been aware of the potentialities for achievement and fulfilment of his individual life and only too well aware of his inability to attain to his highest aspirations. This is a common place of all tragic literature and also the underlying theme of comedy."[14] There is always a misfit between human being and his/her environment. Peacocke observes that human being alone in the biological world, it seems, individually commits suicide; Humans alone in their prehistory give evidence by their burial rituals of the sense of another dimension to existence; they alone go through their lives with a sense of incompleteness evidenced by contemporary quests for self-realization and personal growth. Human beings seek to come to terms with death, pain, and suffering, and we need to realize our own potentialities and learn how to find our way through. The natural environment cannot satisfy such aspirations, nor can the natural sciences describe, accurately discern, or

---

11 A.R. Peacocke, *God and the New Biology*, (Gloucester: Peter Smith, 1994), 92; also cf. A.R. Peacocke, "The Nature and Purpose of Man in Science and Christian Theology", 380.

12 A.R. Peacocke, *Science and the Christian Experiment*, 144.

13 A.R. Peacocke, *God and the New Biology*, 92.

14 A.R. Peacocke, *Creation and the World of Science*, 183.

satisfy them.[15] This shows a kind of 'dis-ease' which calls for explanation and even cure.[16]

Human, for Peacocke, is conscious to both of that from which s/he has evolved and of his/her leaning always to fall short of the fulfilment of his/her own individual and corporate potentialities. "Thus," he writes, "the non realization of the potentialities inherent in the universe has, in man, become the responsibility of that creature himself."[17] This points to the fact that humans are free to respond to the challenges presented to them.[18]

## c. Human Being is Free

Human person for Peacocke, is a free being who is capable of accepting or refusing the challenges in the realization of his/her potentialities. He can consciously say a 'no' to the 'call' to 'become'. "The evolution of man now depends on his freely willed conscious response to the challenge of what he might become."[19] Peacocke observes that s/he is the first organism to be conscious of the possibilities and potentialities which are open to him/her and is aware of his freedom to choose by changing him/herself and the environment.[20] In human person, the evolutionary process has given rise to a creature conscious of his/her origin and capable of seeing where s/he might go and capable of accepting or refusing the challenge. Human person is challenged by an immense variety of calls–but s/he is tragically aware of the possibility of his/her not responding to his/her vocation and fulfilling the potentialities.[21]

## 2. Humans' Role in Creation

The human person has a privileged role in creation as s/he is the only creature in the world capable of relating with the Creator. The traditional term 'dominion' means exploitation. It does not adequately convey the 'caring' component inherent in the Biblical understanding.[22] Since God is immanently

15 A.R. Peacocke, "Biology and A Theology of Evolution", *Zygon*, 34 (1999), 702; cf. A.R. Peacocke, *Creation and the World of Science*, 180ff.

16 A.R. Peacocke, "Biology and A Theology of Evolution", 703.

17 A.R. Peacocke, "The Nature and Purpose of Man in Science and Christian Theology", 380.

18 *Ibid.*, 381.

19 *Ibid.*, 380.

20 *Ibid.*, 380.

21 Before human freedom even God is helpless because God cannot contradict his love by restraining it. God respects the freedom of man because there is no love without respect. Vladimir Lossky, an Eastern thinker writes that love of God for man is so great that it cannot constrain, for there is no love without respect. cf. Vladimir Lossky, *Orthodox Theology: An Introduction*, tran. Ian and Ihita Kaesarcodi- Watson, Crestwood, St. Vladimir seminary Press, 1978, 73.

22 A.R. Peacocke, *God and the New Biology*, 103.

present in the world, the world is to be seen as the manifestation of God's action. "God is everywhere and at all times in the processes and events of the natural world which are to be seen as the vehicle and instrument of God's action and as capable of expressing his intentions and purposes –as our bodies are agents of ourselves."[23] Then, human attitude towards nature should show respect.[24] Humans' role in nature should not be a 'dominion' but a 'caring' which promotes the betterment of the created world. He is not dominator but priest, trustee or vicegerent of creation.[25]

## a. The Human Being as Priest of Creation

According to Peacocke human role in creation can be seen as that of priest of creation. He observes that the complex of proper responses of human person to nature suggests that his/her role may be perceived as that of priest of creation, as a result of whose activity, the sacrament of creation is reverenced and dignified.[26] Since s/he alone is conscious of God, him/herself and nature, "can mediate between insentient nature and God – for a priest is characterised by activity directed towards God on behalf of others."[27] Humans alone, for Peacoke, can reflect on the purposes of God and they alone can fulfil those purposes cooperating with God. "Man alone can contemplate and offer the action of the created world to God. But a priest is also active towards others on God's behalf and in this sense too, man is the priest of creation."[28] S/he alone, having reflected and contemplated on God's intentions and plans, can be active in and with the created world consciously seeking to enhance and fulfil God's purposes. S/he is to live with reverence for all creation and giving equal value to all.

Peacocke suggests that human person should have the respect for the nature in the same way s/he has respect for his/her own body or those of other persons. We do not consider the body of the other as mere aggregates of flesh, but as a person. He explains:

> This immediately suggests that man should respond to nature with respect of the same kind as a man accords to his own body and those of other people –as agents of those other 'selves'- a respect which does not treat them simply as mere aggregates of flesh, hair, bone protein, haemoglobin, etc. For a human person respects the body of another person as being the

23 A.R. Peacocke, *Creation and the World of Science*, 295.

24 A.R. Peacocke, *God and the New Biology*, 104.

25 All these are the terms used by Peacocke to show human role in creation. Cf. A.R. Peacocke, *God and the New Biology*, 103.

26 A.R. Peacocke, *God and the New Biology*, 104.

27 *Ibid.,* 104.

28 *Ibid.,* 104.

> expression of that other 'self'–the body is seen as the mode and arena of the agency of that other self.[29]

So likewise, Peacocke suggests further:

> In the case of the natural world, if it is God who is the agent who is expressed therein, man's attitude to nature should show a respect which is transmuted into reverence at the presence of God in and through the whole of created order, which thereby has, as it were, a derived sacredness or holiness as the vehicle and instrument of God's own creative action.[30]

In other words, human person has the sacred duty to revere the nature as s/he does to other persons. According to him, to be a priest means to be a mediator. So a priest has the sacred duty to gather together the offering of creation and present it to God. In this sense, the human person is an intermediary between God and Man. He is cooperating with God in the creative activity and fulfils God's purposes within it.[31]

## b. The Human Being as Steward and Manager of Creation

According to Peacocke, in the myth of Genesis human person is presented as having 'dominion' over creation. Though the terms like vicegerent, steward, trustee or manager could be appropriate, these terms "introduce a nuance of 'domination' into the Biblical concept of 'dominion' and, in modern English, do not adequately convey the 'caring' component inherent in the Biblical understanding."[32] The term 'dominion' has got a kingly reference. However, caring and preserving are part of kingly qualities. A king is supposed to look after his Kingdom and the subjects. He is not expected to exploit his people for his own purposes. Human person would fail in his royal office of dominion over the earth, were he to exploit the earth's resources to the detriment of the land, plant life, animals, rivers and seas etc. What is decisive is the responsibility of humans for the conservation of what has been entrusted to them. They can show this responsibility by exercising their royal office of mediator of prosperity and well-being, like the kings of the ancient world.[33]

Explaining the Genesis myth Peacocke points out the secondary meaning of the term 'dominion':

> Although 'dominion' has the kingly reference, it is a caring 'dominion' exercised under the authority of the Creator, and so it is a more accurate reflection of the meaning of the Genesis myth to say that it describes

29 A.R. Peacocke, *Creation and the World of Science*, 295.

30 A.R. Peacocke, *Creation and the World of Science*, 295.

31 *Ibid.*, 296.

32 *Ibid.*,103.

33 C. Westermann, *Creation* (London: SPCK 1974), 61.

man as vicegerent, or steward, or manager, or trustee (as of property, or a charity) as well as exercising the leadership of king of creation. He is, in the myth, called to tend the earth and its creatures in responsibility to its Creator. He is accountable. He is responsible.[34]

In this sense, the creation is entrusted to the proper care and concern of humans and they are answerable and accountable to God for the faithful preservation and maintenance of it.

### c. The Human Being as Symbiont with Reverence for Creation

The world, for Peacocke manifests God's continuing presence and so it commands admiration and awe. "God is present 'in, with, under' (a set of prepositions usually used with a sacramental reference) all the world processes which, as an aspect of God's being and action, therefore command respect and reverence and have value."[35] Emphasizing the interdependent, symbiotic character of life Peacocke suggests that our attitude to nature should not be manipulative. Peacocke proposes a partnership between human person and the world and he says that "man as *symbiont* does not injure his partners in living."[36]

Peacocke affirms that humans have the sacred duty to conserve and protect nature which is unique and irreplaceable.[37] The Earth is a precious home for all of us and it deserves our love. It is our duty to preserve it from degradation and destruction "just as trustees of an art gallery preserve the works of human creative art for future generations -who may, indeed appreciate and understand their significance better than any those responsible for the preserving at any given time."[38] Since God created nature for its own sake not just for humans' exploitative purposes it is the duty of human person as trustee to care for what is of value to God.[39]

### d. The Human Being as Interpreter, Prophet, and Lover of Creation

For Peacocke, God as creator "is expressing his intentions and purposes, is unveiling his meaning, in the various and distinctive levels of the created natural world and in its processes, which thereby have the meaning with which he endows them."[40] In this way God is recognized as self communicating agent actively unveiling his meanings to human being who is capable of seeing and

34 A.R. Peacocke, *Creation and the World of Science*, 283.

35 *Ibid.,* 298.

36 *Ibid.,* 299.

37 *Ibid..,* 303.

38 A.R. Peacocke, *Creation and the World of Science*, p. 303.

39 *Ibid.,* 303.

40 *Ibid.,* 300-301.

hearing it. The natural world is seen as the symbol of God's meaning and it is conceived as the means whereby God's intentions and purposes are made known. In other words, the world is seen as a sacrament.[41]

This concept of sacrament, according to Peacocke "serves to emphasize another aspect of Man's functions, namely, Man as *interpreter* of creation's meaning, value, beauty and destiny."[42] Peacocke views human person as an evolutionary product who can read and articulate the divine meaning. He clarifies:

> Man alone in the natural world reads, articulates, and communicates to others the meanings he reads. If those meanings are correctly and surely discerned, the we may say that in man God has created through evolution a creature who is able to be aware of his (God's) purposes and to discern them and articulate them consciously. In man creation becomes conscious of itself as created and the emergence of man's consciousness and intelligence, whereby he is capable of reading God's meaning, must be seen as an intention of God's work.[43]

In other words, God meant the creation to be able eventually to respond to the meaning of his Self that he had communicated through his creation.

As interpreter of God's meaning in creation Peacocke attributes to humans the prophetic function which is a complementary aspect of the priestly role. A prophet is one who reads the sign of the present times and interprets it for the future. "So man is," writes Peacocke, "the interpreter of God, and as such, he acts *prophet*, a role which historically has always complemented the priestly in man's corporate relation to God."[44] Human person as prophet reads the signs of the nature and interprets them for the betterment of the world. Further Man is depicted as the lover of nature when Peacock brings the idea of "I-thou" relationship between human person and nature. Nature is conceived as the 'beloved' of human person and so she must be treated with love and affection in the same way a lover treats his or her partner.[45]

## e. The Human Being as Co-Creator and Co-Explorer with God

In the scene of creation Man stands with his creative energies within himself and in relation to nature through his newly acquired technologies. Here, Man according to Peacocke is faced with a choice: "does he join in with the creative work of God harmoniously integrating his own material creations (which

41 *Ibid.,* 301.

42 *Ibid.,* 301.

43 A.R. Peacocke, *Creation and the World of Science*, 301.

44 *Ibid.,* 301.

45 *Ibid.,* 300.

are never *ex nihilo*) into what God is already doing? Or does he introduce a discordant note, an entanglement and confusion within the dance?"[46]

To these questions human person responds by cooperating with God in the continued creative processes. In this sense, s/he is acting as a creative participant in creation "as it were the leader of the orchestra of creation in the performance which is God's continuing composition."[47] Moreover, human person is offering him/herself with dedication in the creative process. In short, s/he has the opportunity of consciously becoming *co-creator* and *co-worker* with God in his work on Earth.[48]

According to Peacocke if one recognizes that God is always active 'making things new', then one's response to created nature should be flexible and open-minded. One should then expect change and adjust him/herself to modifications in the world's ecosystems as he observes sensitively the changing processes.[49] Peacocke suggests:

> Man thus could become that part of God's creation consciously and intelligently cooperating in the ongoing processes of creative change, taking due account both of man's and of nature's proper needs, with duly assigned priorities for each. And, in a small way, is it not precisely this that every good gardener and farmer concerned to maintain the fertility of his land has always practised?"[50]

Peacocke views technology positively and he understands it as the progeny of science.[51] Technology, for Peacocke, helps humans fulfil their personal and social development in cooperation with God. "Man would then", writes Peacocke, "through his science and technology, be exploring with God the creative possibilities within the universe God has brought into being. This is to see man as *co-explorer* with God."[52] This cooperation of human person in the creative processes is not a passive involvement but an intelligent and active participation. In order to do this one has to discern God's meaning.[53]

## 3. Human Work as Genuine *Opus Dei* (Work of God)

From the idea of Peacocke that human person is the co- worker of God, follows the notion of work as the genuine *opus Dei*. Human person being the co-creator derives his/her creativity from God to build his reign of love. Peacocke argues:

---

46 *Ibid.,* 304-305.

47 A.R. Peacocke, *Creation and the World of Science*, 305.

48 *Ibid.,* 305.

49 *Ibid.,* 305.

50 A.R. Peacocke, *God and the New Biology*, 106.

51 A.R. Peacocke, *Creation and the World of Science*, 306.

52 *Ibid.,* 306.

53 A.R. Peacocke, *Creation and the World of Science*, 306.

"Man has derived creativity from God and all genuine activities of man which attain excellence, and are in accord with God's intentions to build his reign of love (his kingdom), may be regarded as man exerting his role as *co-creator* with God."[54] Peacocke views this as the 'building up of Jerusalem'.[55] Here, he proposes a Christian humanism, "in which all human excellence is seen as man making his distinctive human contribution as *co-creator* to that ceaseless activity of creation which is God's action in and for the world."[56]

Here, the work of human person for the betterment and progress of the society and the environment is seen as the work of God himself (*Opus Dei*). The human civilization and technology are also seen positively. Basing himself on the Christian doctrine of humans in Genesis Peacocke observes:

> Such an apprehension of life of man engraced by God now allows us to make a more positive assessment of human civilisation, in general, and technology in particular. For it is not without significance that the Biblical account of man begins in a garden in the book of Genesis, but is consummated in the new Jerusalem-a city, symbol of culture. For one who believes in, is committed to God as Creator can affirm that it must have been God's intention that human society must have attained its present economic and technological complexity since he created man, through evolution, with just those abilities which made such complexities inevitable and he, at least must have known that it would be so. Such a believer could thus see his work in a technological society as genuine *opus Dei* of its own; in building up human society one is joining in that creative activity of God which brought man and society into existence– and this could give human work a new significance and counteract the pointlessness and vacuousness which so many feel about it."[57]

In this perspective every work in the human society can be seen as God's work for the development and progress of the human society and of the whole creation. Even an unimportant job in the society has got a great significance and it serves for the upliftment and better shaping of the human society. Peacocke argues that one, "taking seriously the scientific perspective, can see his work not as being a kind of sacrificial offering for God, but actually as a genuine *opus Dei* of its own; for in building up human society one is joining in the creative activity of God who made it all possible."[58] Peacocke continues: "Even the humblest job in the complex society created by scientific technology in satisfaction of real and legitimate needs would take on a new point, if seen as

54 A.R. Peacocke, *God and the New Biology*, 106-107.

55 *Ibid.,* 107.

56 *Ibid.,* 107.

57 A.R. Peacocke, *God and the New Biology*, 107.

58 A.R. Peacocke, *Science and the Christian Experiment*, 194.

part of that creative process which brought man and society into existence."[59] In other words, even the smallest job in the society is the work of God by and through the hands of human person and it serves to the ongoing creation of God for the building up of the kingdom of God based on love.

## 4. Human Work as Liturgy: Offering the World Back to God

Peacocke envisages human work as liturgy which connects all beings in nature. According to Peacocke, human life and nature are interrelated:

> The energy source for all living organisms, including man, is the sun whose energy is absorbed through green plants, on which animals depend ultimately for food and which themselves depend on the activities of bacteria decomposing dead organisms and making nitrogen available. So all life is interdependent–indeed many creatures can only live in concert with, and often literally on, particular other organisms (symbiosis).[60]

So all things in the world are interdependent and humans cannot think of acting independently without taking into consideration the rest of the world. All animals and plants live in complex systems consisting of many cross flows and exchanges of energy and matter in a variety of chemical forms of such baffling complexity that only the advent of computers and the development of systems theory have given any hope of analysing them.[61] "Modern man is misguided if he thinks he can live and operate independly off the rest of the living world."[62] The whole human life is in one way or the other is related to nature. Although human person is capable of living in many habitats, s/he is still just as dependent on plants and bacteria, and on other animals, as was primitive Man.[63]

All these show the inseparable relationship between humans and nature. In this context, Peacocke states that the primary duty of a human person is to work for the betterment of nature, and the future of the whole world is in the hands of human beings. But unfortunately, humans are not aware of this fact as they destroy and exploit the environment for their own selfish motives. Peacocke says:

> Ever since man has emerged as *homo sapiens* he has been having a distinctive impact on natural ecosystems, from the time he first employed fire-drive methods to hunt game, thereby destroying forest and expanding grazing land –to the development of agriculture, which liberated at least some of the human population from food gathering to make things, build

59 *Ibid.,*194.

60 A.R. Peacocke, *Creation and the World of Science*, 258.

61 *Ibid.,* 258.

62 *Ibid.,* 258.

63 *Ibid.,* 258.

> cities, and to create the arts of civilization –to the destruction of forests of Lebanon and North Africa and the enclosure of common land in eighteenth-century –England –right up to the present century.[64]

Analysing these aspects of human exploitation, Peacocke shows that the Earth is getting weaker and crippled because of the manipulating attitude of humans.[65] He observes that "almost everything man does to natural ecosystems for his own benefit is of such a kind and has such global effects that he is forced into becoming the manager of the Earth."[66]

In this context, Peacocke puts forward the idea of human work that is for the consecration of the whole world and offering the world back to God.[67] Here, the world is seen as not only a gift from God but also a task to be fulfilled by Man. Being a priest of creation it is human's primary duty to do service of God - to offer the world back to God. In this sense, whatever s/he does for the betterment of the world is a sacred service or liturgy, and thereby, s/he becomes celebrant of nature.[68] This model of human work, according to Peacocke, is "able to provide motivation for people to act for the future good of humanity and the whole ecosystem."[69] All these ideas point to the fact that a human person can only worship God (genuine liturgy)[70] in and through his/her work in the world by cooperating with the creative activity of God.[71]

## Conclusion

In this article, we have analysed Peacocke's understanding of the human person and the world in the light of the new scientific discoveries and evolutionary theories. In this understanding, God, humans and the world are interconnected and interrelated. The role of a human person as priest, prophet, *symbiont* and co-creator is very well established and God works through humans to sustain and preserve the world. So, human actions become genuine *Opus Dei* when it is done with devotion and dedication. In this way, the humblest job in the society becomes a liturgy-an offering of the world back to God in thanksgiving. The world is the altar in which humans are to offer the sacrifice of thanksgiving to the creator by integrating their own scientific discoveries and inventions with the divine creative work for the betterment of the whole cosmos and humankind.

64 *Ibid.*, 261.

65 *Ibid.*, 263.

66 *Ibid.*, 263.

67 *Ibid.*, 274.

68 *Ibid.*, 297.

69 *Ibid.*, 274.

70 *Ibid.*, 318.

71 *Ibid.*, 316.

## Bibliography

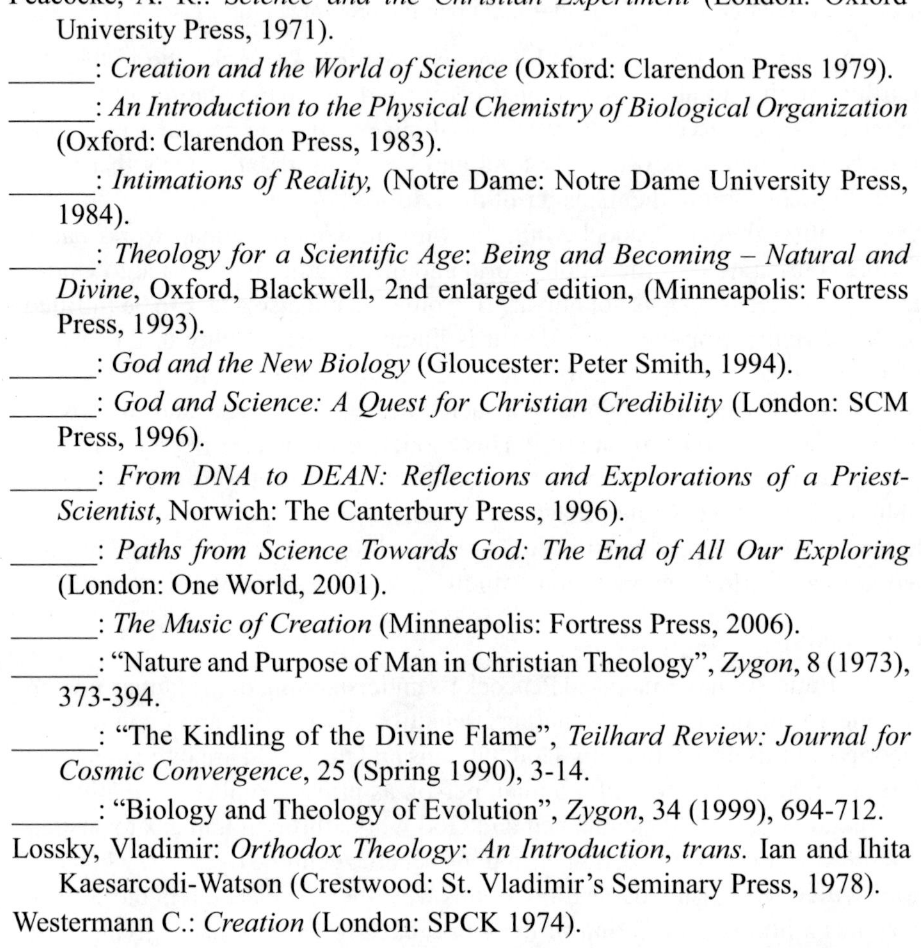

Peacocke, A. R.: *Science and the Christian Experiment* (London: Oxford University Press, 1971).

______: *Creation and the World of Science* (Oxford: Clarendon Press 1979).

______: *An Introduction to the Physical Chemistry of Biological Organization* (Oxford: Clarendon Press, 1983).

______: *Intimations of Reality,* (Notre Dame: Notre Dame University Press, 1984).

______: *Theology for a Scientific Age*: *Being and Becoming – Natural and Divine*, Oxford, Blackwell, 2nd enlarged edition, (Minneapolis: Fortress Press, 1993).

______: *God and the New Biology* (Gloucester: Peter Smith, 1994).

______: *God and Science: A Quest for Christian Credibility* (London: SCM Press, 1996).

______: *From DNA to DEAN: Reflections and Explorations of a Priest-Scientist*, Norwich: The Canterbury Press, 1996).

______: *Paths from Science Towards God: The End of All Our Exploring* (London: One World, 2001).

______: *The Music of Creation* (Minneapolis: Fortress Press, 2006).

______: "Nature and Purpose of Man in Christian Theology", *Zygon*, 8 (1973), 373-394.

______: "The Kindling of the Divine Flame", *Teilhard Review: Journal for Cosmic Convergence*, 25 (Spring 1990), 3-14.

______: "Biology and Theology of Evolution", *Zygon*, 34 (1999), 694-712.

Lossky, Vladimir: *Orthodox Theology*: *An Introduction*, *trans.* Ian and Ihita Kaesarcodi-Watson (Crestwood: St. Vladimir's Seminary Press, 1978).

Westermann C.: *Creation* (London: SPCK 1974).

31

# Social Progress Index: Human Well-Being Quantified

**Ginish Cheruparambil**

*Asst. Prof. of Economics, Christ University, Lavasa*

**Abstract**: Human wellbeing a highly debated topic from many disciplines have been tried to quantify by the usage of Social Progress Index, which has taken into account fifty-four indicators. This can be considered as the best possible way of quantifying it from quite many angle. This analysis has compared often known indicator with the SPI. Currently many have come up with the view that GDP has to retire. This can be seen as a probe into the same category. The outcome seems to be quite disgusting from an economic perspective.

**Keywords**: SIP, GDP, HDI, Rank Correlation Coefficient, Progress Indicator

The reason why Richard Ainley Easterlin, as an economist at the University of Southern California, is worried with happiness is that he unambiguously identifies it with welfare. He accepts the English economist Arthur Cecil Pigou's dissimilarity between social (or total) welfare and economic welfare. In Easterlin's view: "Happiness corresponds to the broader of the two concepts, that of social welfare, or welfare at large". Unfortunately, he does not propose a more accurate definition of happiness.[1] To examine whether higher income is linked with greater happiness, Easterlin performs three diverse comparisons.

1 In 2001, Easterlin writes: "Throughout this article, I use the terms happiness, subjective well-being, satisfaction, utility, well-being, and welfare interchangeably" (Easterlin 2001), p. 465.

Third, he compares the happiness of Americans at unlike points in time. This to the point arrangement of Easterlin's article illustrates that he adopted the innermost assumptions underlying psychological measures of well-being. First, the technique he uses to determine welfare presupposes that wellbeing is a matter of a psychological state, in this case happiness.

In the above, I have traced the chronological roots of subjective course of well-being. There is no doubt that subjective method of well-being appeared in functional branches of psychology and other fields. Even though the questions given to subjects in the early studies consistently referred to happiness – of individuals or of marriages – the conclusions were often framed in terms of contentment as well as happiness. Over time, psychologists in full swing started asking questions about satisfaction together with questions of happiness, and they realized that answers to questions of satisfaction were not as highly correlated with answer to questions about happiness as they would have thought. Some ask about happiness, others about satisfaction. At the same time, the correlation between answers to questions about happiness and satisfaction suggests to the researchers that for many purposes, a measure of either one can serve as a measure of both. Anyway, this passage certainly gives the impression that psychologists and economists working on subjective well-being simply assume that people are reliable judges of their happiness.

The concept of well-being, as it is used here, needs to be sharply distinguished from the concept of financial well-being, or economic welfare, in the sense of access to economic resources.[2] For the purposes of understanding, I divide accounts of well-being into three main classes: mental state accounts, preference-satisfaction accounts, and objective list accounts. Welfare, rather, is like physical fitness. Although Keller does not offer a complete account of welfare, he does put forward that one aspect of welfare is the accomplishment of goals. Second, Keller maintains, goals be different from simple preferences or desires.

In this section we take into account the three different indicators and the relationship between these are checked over here. Once these relations are established it can help us to know the real facts about freedom and capability establishment in an economy. When we speak of an economy it takes into account a concept of nation. Gross Domestic Product, Social Progress Index and Opportunity are the three indicators taken into account in the analysis.

## 1. GDP or HDI as Progress Indicator

The two measures of GDP and HDI has remained as the majority commonly used standards by which experts assessed whether a country is making

---

2 Amartya Sen, *Commodities and Capabilities (*New Delhi: Oxford University Press, 1987), p.16.

improvement better than in the past. Sometimes GDP has also been regarded as a representative indicator for by and large development and progress in all-purpose. However, with the succeeding insight that GDP does not put across information on social inclusion, environmental sustainability or social progress in its intend and function, the need to harmonize and substitute GDP with some enhanced development indicators has been progressively more recognized. The indispensable concern that emerged from this discernment raises the question whether the GDP measure evaluates progress precisely, while progress could take account of not only the material progress but the standard of life aided by health care, education and basic amenities of life. In fact, the development of Human Development Index (HDI) in 1990 is recognition to the information that per capita income levels are not satisfactory to denote overall development. According to Anand and Sen[3], income or wealth do put up with importance but cannot constitute a direct measure of the overall well-being and therefore the HDI is constituted approximately a broader concept of development by combining health, education and per capita income into a composite index. On the other hand, it is also argued that at the same time as composite indices broaden the dimensions of development they also compromise on the fact that all the components in a composite index are not evaluated at market prices.[4] In fact, it has in recent times been claimed that GDP bears a noteworthy advantage over other indicators of development in the sense that it only uses information that are generated by the market processes.[5]

One may for that reason be apprehensive about deliberating the appropriateness of using the GDP measure as an alternate indicator for wellbeing and in general development as opposed to the HDI. It may be mentioned that several studies have earlier indicated high correlation between economic indicator of per capita GDP and other aggregate social indicators of development, thereby suggesting that GDP can be used as a proxy measure of development. It may be well-known that the values of development index like the HDI have been shown to show evidence of positive and statistically significant correlation with the GDP or GNP per capita. Some researchers have consequently recommended that since the HDI is so intimately correlated with GDP or GNP per capita, it is a redundant index. The argument that is forwarded is that since additional dimensional indicators like health and education outcomes often advance with income, then the HDI measure would

3 S. Anand, and Amartya Sen, "The Income Component of the Human Development Index", *Journal of Human Development* (2004)

4 G. E. M. Santos, "Composite Indices of Development", in Bruce Currie-Alder, Ravi Kanbur and D.M Malone (eds) *International Development: Ideas, Experience and Prospects* (New York:Oxford University Press, 2014), p.11

5 J. Weimann, A. Knabe and R. Schob, *Measuring Happiness: The Economics of Well-Being*, (Cambridge:MIT Press, 2015), p.103.

consistently be closely connected with the per capita GDP and therefore no additional information can be gained from the HDI index.

It may likewise be noted that the features of higher economic growth have often been found to be associated with performance in cumulative or dimensional human development indicators like health and education attainments. According to Sen[6], economic development holds a innermost orientation for the human capability expansion, since improvements in per capita income provides superior opportunities for people to benefit from long, healthy and creative lives. On the converse, the responsibility of human and social capital accumulation has critically been acknowledged in accounting for differences in growth rates across countries. Investments in health and education have been emphasized in the development literature for its positive contributions. A series of papers by Boozer, Ranis, Ranis and Stewart, Ranis, Stewart and Samman explored the two-way relationships between economic growth and human development, and argued that human development is not only an end product of the development procedure but also a means to generate future economic growth. It is argued that strong economic growth advances human development through the increased domestic consumption expenditure as well as public expenditures, which unswervingly benefit the poor. Thus, while economic growth increases a country's tax base, it becomes possible for the government to spend more on the key public services of health, education and other items that contribute to their capabilities and raise the standard of living. The employment opportunities created by robust growth levels can also create incentives for families to expend in education and health. On the other hand, the impacts from human development to economic growth works as people turn out to be healthier, better nourished and educated and to contribute more to economic growth.

Although, per capita GDP growth can continue as an important mechanism for achieving a higher standard of life, the impact of economic growth on human development level significantly depends on aspects, such as the allocation of income. Thus, the same level of GDP can be found to distribute very different development performances depending on the allocation of income across income classes. In fact, a key message enclosed in various Human Development Reports remains that economic growth alone does not automatically translate into human development progress. For instance, the 1996 edition of the Human Development Report identified five ways in which economic growth can be problematic, viz.,

i. Jobless growth, where economic growth does not expand employment opportunities.
ii. Ruthless growth, where growth benefits only the rich.

6 Amartya Sen, *Development as Freedom* (New Delhi: Oxford University Press, 2000), p.28.

iii. Voiceless growth, where economic growth is not accompanied by democracy or empowerment.
iv. Rootless growth, which causes minority cultures to be swamped by the dominant culture.
v. Futureless growth where resources for future growth are exploited (UNDP 1996)[7].

The elevated economic growth rates may not convert into development unless appropriate distributional policies and well-designed delivery instruments are accompanied to translate the benefits of growth into the lives of the under-privileged.

## 2. HDI to SPI

Most wellbeing indices, such as the Human Development Index, the Better Life Index, and Bhutan's Gross National Happiness measure integrate GDP or other economic measures directly. Most of these either comprise only a modest portion of social progress, such as the environment or basic needs, conflate social measures with economic ones, or make use of more subjective contribution measures rather than outcomes. The Social Progress Index is the primary holistic measure consisting of only observable outcomes that focuses exclusively on social and environmental performance. These are commendable efforts to measure wellbeing that have laid important groundwork in the field. However, because they conflate economic and social factors, they cannot explain or discharge the relationship between economic development and social progress. The Social Progress Index measures social progress unswervingly, independently of economic development, in a way that is both holistic and rigorous. The Social Progress Index can be used to measure a country's performance on social and environmental factors relative to its economic peers in a more meaningful and rigorous way than when economic performance is incorporated as a component. The Social Progress Index is the first holistic measure consisting of only observable outcomes that focuses exclusively on social and environmental performance.

## 3. SIP as a Progress Indicator

Economists created the Social Progress Index to enlarge how country achievement is measured, beyond economic indicators like GDP per capita. Social progress is about gathering everyone's basic needs for food, clean water, shelter, and security. It is about living healthy, long lives, and protecting the environment. It is about education, freedom, and opportunity. Social progress has become a more and more serious agenda for leaders in

7 United Nations Development Programme, *Human Development Report* (New York: Oxford University Press, 1996).

government, business, and civil society. Citizens' demands for enhanced lives are obvious in uprisings such as the Arab Spring and the emergence of new political movements in even the most prosperous countries, such as the United States and France. Since the financial crisis of 2008, citizens are increasingly expecting business to play its role in delivering improvements in the lives of customers and employees, and protecting the environment for us all. This is the social progress imperative. Advancing social progress requires a new model of development, because economic development alone has been found wanting.

Economic growth has had an astonishing impact on our world. Not only has global Gross Domestic Product (GDP) per capita more than doubled since 1970 but, according to World Bank estimates, the percentage of the world's population now living in extreme poverty has fallen from nearly 40% to less than 10%. However, the gains from this growth have been uneven. Most of the worlds extremely poor now live in countries considered middle income. Progress on social issues does not automatically accompany economic development. Rising income usually brings major improvements in access to clean water, sanitation, literacy, and basic education. But on average, personal security is no better in middle income countries than low-income ones, and is often worse. "Too many people – regardless of income – live without full rights and experience discrimination or even violence based on gender, religion, ethnicity, Traditional measures of national income, such as GDP per capita, fail to capture the overall progress of societies. This limitation has been well documented in reports such as *Mismeasuring Our Lives*, but solutions have been slow to emerge. The question of when and how economic development advances social progress (and when it does not) has become central due to concerns about inequality and environmental limits to growth, but the answers have been absent."[8] The Social Progress Index is the first wide-ranging framework for measuring social progress independently of GDP, and gives us the ability to understand the relationship between economic and social progress. Our vision is a world in which social progress sits together with GDP as a core standard for national performance. The Social Progress Index provides a methodical, empirical foundation for this yardstick and a guide for comprehensive growth strategies.

## 4. Analytical Examination

This section explores whether the SIP and Opportunity ranks countries differently from the way the popular economic indicator of per capita GDP ranks them. To deal with this issue we draw together a 100 country data set at

8 Michael E. Porter , and Scott Stern, *Social Progress Index 2017* (Washington DC: www.socialprogressimperative.org., 2018), p. 8.

two dissimilar points of time, i.e., 2014 and 2017. The gap between per capita Gross Domestic Product, Social Progress Index and Opportunity is examined for the full sample of 100 countries, as well as for diverse income groups of countries. Our analyses make use of the SIP and Opportunity scores and per capita GDP (current values in USD) data consistently for the full sample 100 countries as well as three sub-samples of high, middle and low-income groups of countries for the duration of two points of time. We have used the World Banks' per capita income categorization in each definite year to group economies according to the high, middle and low income countries. The information of the income categorization and the number of countries falling in each group throughout specific years are provided in Table 1.[9]

**Table 1: Classification of Countries in Income Groups, 2014 and 2017.**

| Years | Income Range for Country Classification (2014 and 2017) | | | |
|---|---|---|---|---|
| | **High Income Countries** | **Middle Income Countries** | **Low Income Countries** | **Total Countries** |
| 2014 | 12806.56 USD and above (32 Countries) | 12593.7 -1052.13 USD (52 Countries) | 1031.11 USD and below (16 Countries) | 100 Countries |
| 2017 | 13429.41 USD and above ( 32 Countries) | 11856.8 - 1139.57 USD (50 countries) | 998.201 USD and below (18 Countries) | 100 Countries |

*Source*: World Bank (various years).

9 Considering the aspect of data availability on a comparable basis, we could find uniform data for 100 countries, which are Afghanistan, Albania, Algeria, Argentina, Armenia, Australia, Austria, Bangladesh, Belgium, Benin, Bolivia, Botswana, Brazil, Bulgaria, Cambodia, Cameroon, Canada, Central African Republic, Chile, China, Colombia, Congo, Costa Rica, Côte d'Ivoire, Croatia, Cuba, Cyprus, Czech Republic, D.R. of the Congo, Denmark, Dominican Republic, Ecuador, Egypt, El Salvador, Estonia, Fiji, Finland, France, Gambia, Germany, Ghana, Greece, Guatemala, Guyana, Honduras, Hungary, Iceland, India, Indonesia, Iran (Islamic Republic of), Iraq, Ireland, Israel, Italy, Jamaica, Japan, Jordan, Kazakhstan, Kenya, Kuwait, Kyrgyzstan, Lao People's DR, Latvia, Lesotho, Malawi, Malaysia, Mali, Malta, Mauritania, Mauritius, Mexico, Mongolia, Morocco, Mozambique, Myanmar, Namibia, Nepal, Netherlands, New Zealand, Nicaragua, Niger, Norway, Pakistan, Panama, Paraguay, Peru, Philippines, Poland, Portugal, Romania, Russian Federation, Rwanda, Saudi Arabia, Senegal, Serbia, Sierra Leone, Singapore, Slovakia, Slovenia, South Africa, Spain, Sri Lanka, Swaziland, Sweden, Switzerland, Tajikistan, Thailand, Togo, Tonga, Trinidad and Tobago, Tunisia, Turkey, Tanzania, Uganda, Ukraine, United Arab Emirates, United Kingdom, United States, Uruguay, Venezuela, Yemen, Zambia and Zimbabwe.

**Figure 1: SPI versus GDP Per Capita Rank in High Income Countries, 2014**

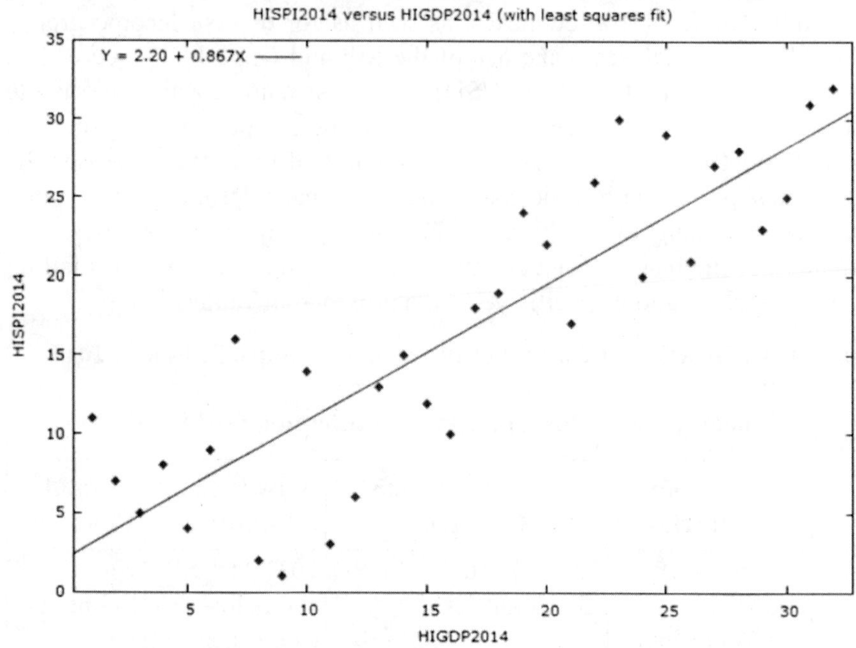


**Figure 2: SPI versus GDP per Capita Rank in Low Income Countries, 2017**

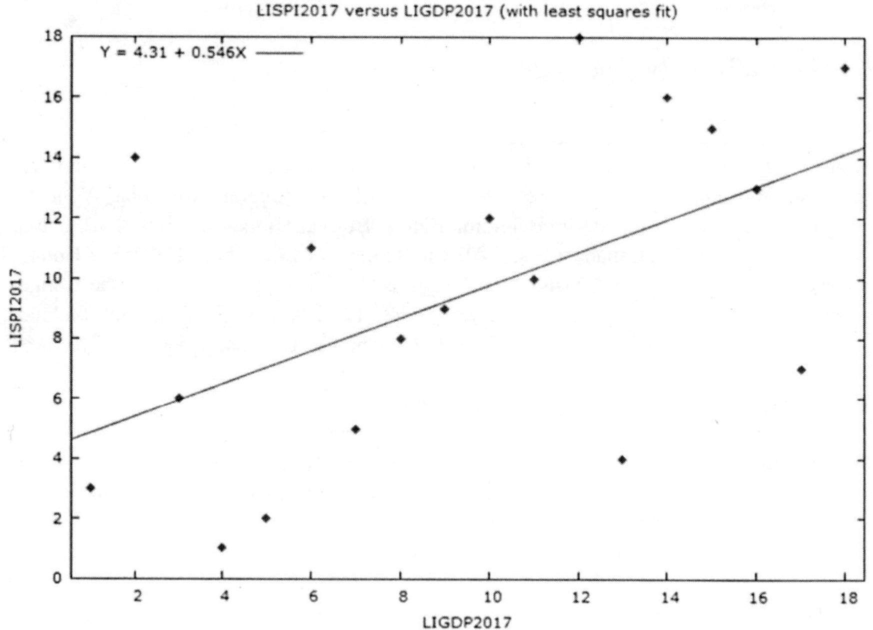

**Figure 3: Opportunity versus GDP per Capita Rank in Low Income Countries, 2017**

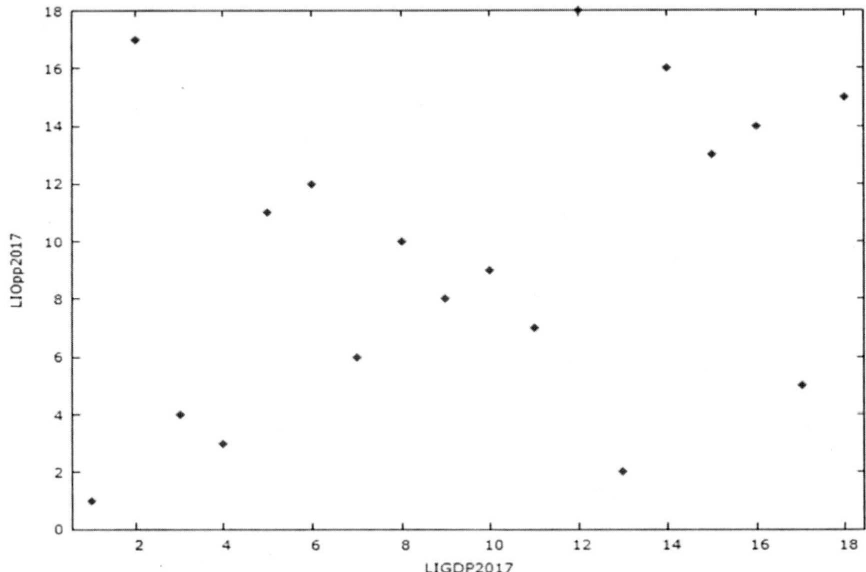


The statistics on per capita GDP, SPI and Opportunity level for the section of 100 countries have been defined and sourced as follows. The per capita gross domestic product in current U.S. dollars is defined as country's gross value added by all occupant producers in the economy plus any product taxes and minus any subsidies not incorporated in the value of the products divided by the midyear population. This information has been derived from the World Bank and Social progress Index Annual reports of two years. The SPI and Opportunity scores for countries are derived from Social Progress Index Report.

The assessment of the differentiation in the rankings between SPI, Opportunity and per capita GDP is first attempted by a contrast of scatter plots for like chalk and cheese income group of countries during two specific points of time. Consequently, we compute the Spearman's rank correlation coefficients between the SPI, Opportunity values and current per capita GDP level for the full sample 100 countries as well as the sub-samples of high, middle- and low-income countries.

## 5. Scatter Plots and Regressions

The assessment of the rank differences between SPI scores, Opportunity scores and per capita GDP (current levels in USD) is performed by plotting the GDP per capita ranks in the horizontal axis and other ranks in the vertical axis from our cross-sectional country data. The analysis is performed for different income group of countries and time after time during two points of time, viz., 2014 and 2017, so as to establish whether the experimental association is undergoing any change over time. The first four figures (Figures 1 to 3) demonstrates how closely the SPI, Opportunity and per capita incomes were connected during the year 2014 in high- and middle-income countries, while the same for all income groups of countries are depicted in Figure 7 & 8. We observe a high positive correlation between the per capita SPI, Opportunity and GDP rankings for all the 100 countries, so that the fitted regression line also yielded a positive sloped line. The same line of analysis but disaggregated over different income groups, however, disclose that positive correlation is the highest in the case of High income countries (Figure 1 to 2), which is followed by the middle income countries (Figure 3) and no relation for the low income group of countries. Thus, the fitted regression lines are upward sloping for high- and middle-income countries in the year 2014. No relation established between the low-income countries in the year 2014.

Similarly, the relationships during the year 2017 are graphically represented through a scatter-plot of the two series for three specific income groups and all countries in Figures 8 to 16. While the fitted regression lines are still upward sloping, the degrees of correlation vary substantially among different income groups in the sample. The positive relationship remains more pronounced in the high-income group of countries. Although the observed correlation remained the lowest for the low-income group, it registered higher degrees of correlation than the correlation in 2014. We can study the link between the rankings of SPI, Opportunity and per capita real GDP during the 2017. The regression lines are positively sloped for all the income groups, but the positive relationship remains more evident in high income countries. One can notice that the positive association between the rankings of SPI, Opportunity and per capita GDP remains the highest for the high- and middle-income group of countries in comparison to the association in other income group during all the two time periods. Overall these results seem to indicate that although the SPI and Opportunity ranking of countries is not very different from the ranking of per capita GDP in the full sample of all countries except from low income countries, there remain substantial differences in the results for sub-samples of countries containing different income groups. The opportunity which is taken in this case gives a clear picture about the fact of Amartya Sen's concept of freedom of choice, which seems to be influenced by many other factors than income alone.

## 6. Rank Correlation Tests

The rank correlation coefficient measures the degree of similarity between the two rankings, and can be meaningfully used to assess the significance of the relation between SPI, Opportunity and GDP per capita. The rank correlation coefficients are calculated using the full sample comprising 100 country observations, together with sub-samples that comprise countries classified by their income groups according to the World Bank classification as low, middle- and high-income countries. The total sample of 100 countries has been reorganized for three income groups depending on the range of incomes in each year group. The results on the rank correlation coefficients are reported in Table 2 & 3 for the full sample of 100 countries as well as for the subsample of different income group of countries. One can observe positive and high rank order correlation (in the range 0f 0.94 to 0.95) between the SPI and per capita GDP, Opportunity and per capita GDP (0.88 to 0.89) for the full sample in each specific year. All these coefficients are statistically at significant level. We also observe positive rank-order correlation coefficients for the sub-samples consisting of high, middle- and low-income countries in all the years, but the degrees of rank correlation remained different across various income groups of countries. For instance, the rank correlation coefficients between SPI and per capita GDP recorded values of (0.86, 0.76, 0.17 and 0.94) for high, middle, low- and all-income groups of countries in the year 2014. The degrees of rank correlation increased in successive years and reached to (0.85, 0.77, 0.54 and 0.94) in the year 2017 for high, middle, low- and all-income groups of countries. When we take the case of the rank correlation coefficients between Opportunity and per capita GDP recorded values of (0.80, 0.67, 0.07 and 0.88) for high, middle, low- and all-income groups of countries in the year 2014. The degrees of rank correlation increased in successive years and reached to (0.79, 0.58, 0.33 and 0.89) in the year 2017 for high, middle, low- and all-income groups of countries.

**Table 2: Spearman's Rank Correlation Coefficient between SPI and GDP per Capita (Sample: 2014 and 2017).**

| Rank Correlation Coefficient | Income Group of Countries | | | |
|---|---|---|---|---|
| Years | High Income Countries | Middle Income Countries | Low Income Countries | All Countries |
| 2014 | 0.867 (32 Countries) | 0.765 (52 Countries) | 0.176 (16 Countries) | 0.941 (100 Countries) |
| 2017 | 0.857 (32 Countries) | 0.779 (50 Countries) | 0.546 (18 Countries) | 0.949 (100 Countries) |

**Table 3: Spearman's Rank Correlation Coefficient between Opportunity and GDP per Capita (Sample: 2014 and 2017).**

| Rank Correlation Coefficient | Income Group of Countries | | | |
|---|---|---|---|---|
| Years | High Income Countries | Middle Income Countries | Low Income Countries | All Countries |
| 2014 | 0.803 (32 Countries) | 0.675 (52 Countries) | 0.074 (16 Countries) | 0.881 (100 Countries) |
| 2017 | 0.794 (32 Countries) | 0.588 (50 Countries) | 0.335 (18 Countries) | 0.892 (100 Countries) |

It may be noted that the correlation coefficients between ranks of SIP and per capita GDP remained comparatively high for high income countries all along, even though a reasonable re-grouping of countries occurred among income groups over the years. Ehen we compare the correlation we understand that though there is a slight change happened in 2017 low income group but it can be considered as a rather good move between SIP and GDP Per Capita (0.17 to 0.54). a substantial growth is brought about in this aspect. But when we consider Opportunity and GDP Per Capita there no substantial growth present over there. There is no positive correlation between then in low income group. As we have observed the value (0.074 to 0.33) this is not considered as a substantial positive growth. So we can conclude by saying that both in the case of SPI and Opportunity in relation with GDP Per Capita the low income countries are never in tune with the GDP. There should be another means to measure the development. This actually contradicts the study done on GDP Per Capita and HDI.

## Conclusion

Human life without a purpose to live is meaningless. The ultimate purpose and meaning in life are viewed by different people in different ways. The analytics shows a very different aspect of the freedom and capability approach. It explains that the practical approach of these philosophical aspects. Also, at the same time the speciality of variations which takes place with the countries in terms of relation with GDP, SIP and Opportunity. These relationships undergo various changes as the countries change from high income to middle income and low-income groups. These changes revel a greater truth about the hidden factors in the whole economy or nation taken together.

PART FIVE

---

# CONCLUDING ARTICLES

32

# The Minor Stage: Brecht and Liberation as Means of Decolonization in the Plays of Cyril Desbruslais SJ

**Rajan J. Barrett**
*Department of English, Maharaja Sayajirao University of Baroda Vadodara – 390 002*

**Abstract:** This paper tries to trace the development of Cyril Desbruslais S.J. as a playwright who has a predilection for Brecht, probably because of his roots in Kolkata. It also looks at what I term as 'Minority Theatre' because it works for a minority community and put up by a select group of young people who engage with the notions of being from complex perspectives. The insights of the plays spring from an engagement with notions of Liberation Theology, Existential Philosophy, events that shake the World inside and outside the Church. Thus, decolonization is a major process towards freedom and away from oppression both of Church and State. In technique, form, and theme, a postmarxist, postfeminist, postcolonialist and a posthumanist reading of the plays is attempted.

**Keywords:** Liberation, Postmarxist, Postfeminist, Postcolonialist, Posthumanist, Brecht, Culture-studies.

This paper examines the plays of Cyril Desbruslais SJ [1] and consider how the plays function[2] as an expression of minority[3] communities and their stance

---

1 Harry Kreisler in his interview with Sashi Tharoor Feb 8,1999 titled "Shashi Tharoor Interview: Conversations with History, Institute of International Studies, UC Berkeley" records Tharoor's statement about his background and Cyril Desbruslais figures in it as a Jesuit of the Calcutta Provence teaching at St. Xavier's School. I include the excerpt here:

**Kerisler:** Who were your influential teachers?

**Tharoor:** There were a number of them. I should have mentioned that the schools I went to had an interesting thing in common: they were all Jesuit schools. The Jesuits have developed an interesting vocation for educating the privileged of the Third World. I don't mean that in a disparaging way. I just mean that because they have these excellent schools in the English language in countries like India, they tend to attract members of the Indian urban educated professional classes and their children. And while there were in fact some relatively less well-off children, we didn't actually have a great cross-section of Indian society. What we had was the urban elite. But having said that, the schools were very good, all of them.

The school in Calcutta, St. Xavier's, was unquestionably in my day the best school in the city, particularly in terms of its intellectual rigor. I and a couple of my friends in school came out with the highest possible grades in the school system in the state largely because of the quality of the teaching. I don't want to rattle off names that will mean nothing to those not in India. A number of the priests at these schools are very well trained themselves. I remember a young Jesuit Father, Cyril Desbruslais, who actually took us through an epistemological argument for the existence of God, which certainly impressed my fourteen-year-old imagination no end because I was just beginning to flirt with the idea of atheism. When you discover rationality, your religion doesn't seem so impressive anymore, and when you discover the limitations of rationality it all comes back, but in between I had this very rational, structured philosophical argument from a Jesuit priest. And that was very striking. The values the Jesuits imparted were vital, too: I especially admired Father Remedios, an excellent teacher who visited prisoners in his spare time. http://globetrotter.berkeley.edu/people/Tharoor/tharoor-con1.html (Downloaded on 27/09/2013)

2 Cyril Desbruslais SJ originates from Kolkata. He is an Indian by nationality. He had his primary education in Asansol, West Bengal. Is currently Prof. Emeritus at Jana Deepa Vidyapeeth, Ramwadi, Pune. He is an alumnus from the Department of English, University of Pune, while having degrees from France and other parts of India, besides JDV and De Nobili College, Pune.

3 I.P. Massey "Nation is a socio-psychological concept-based common ethnic and cultural affinities and shared perceptions of these affinities coupled with political consciousness. Minority groups or collectivities are people who have not achieved such national consciousness but are nevertheless united through race, religion, language, or culture of which their members are conscious and which forms the basis of a common identity and distinguishes them from others on that basis. Such collectives or groups are generally called minorities when they are less numerous than the other groups or when they occupy a subordinate, economic, political or special position in the state, or both. Therefore, it is possible to speak of numeral or sociological minorities. There are numerous criteria used in defining and classifying minorities. However the distinguishing factor is the relationship to the majority or the dominant ethnic group." *Minority Rights Discourse in India* (Shimla, IIAS) 2002, 15.

towards decolonization. The issue being that for the Indian Roman Catholic there are complex layers of colonization though the one by the state (British /Portuguese/ Dutch/ French) seems apparent, there is also a question of the denomination: Syrian-Christian, the Latin-Christian, etc. and questions of caste, race and language associated with being Roman Catholic in India.[4]

## 1. Locating Cyril Desbruslais SJ's Plays

None of these plays have been published, though Cyril Desbruslais SJ has been writing plays from 1966 and putting them up in various parts of India. While the messages of the plays begin from the motivation of liberation theology[5] they also address the question of being Christian and Roman Catholic in India (a multi-religious country).

Desbruslais' plays seem to address the question of colonialism not only from philosophical, sociological and cultural positions but the question of religion and the interface between theology and politics. They take on the question of 'Being Christian' and 'Indian' together. In the process of his growth as a playwright Desbruslais as a Professor of Philosophy[6] has kept being an organicist and considers liberation philosophy[7] reaching out not only to the

4 I.P. Massey in *Minority Rights Discourse in India* says: "Minorities may come into existence either as a result of conquest and subjugation or breakup of a multinational empire or process of amalgamation or integration of ethnic groups or immigration or political, social and economic inequalities or combination of these various factors. In India minority environment is a combination of these various factors. Minority groups are not eternal they are dynamic social units that may emerge, metamorphose and dissolve over a period of time according to changing historical circumstance. " (Shimla, IIAS) 2002, 16.

5 Roman Catholic movement that originated in the late 20th century in Latin America and seeks to express religious faith by helping the poor and working for political and social change. It began in 1968, when bishops attending the Latin American Bishops' Conference in Medellín, Colom., affirmed the rights of the poor and asserted that industrialized nations were enriching themselves at the expense of the Third World. The movement's central text, *A Theology of Liberation* (1971), was written by the Peruvian priest Gustavo Gutiérrez (b. 1928). Liberation theologians have sometimes been criticized as purveyors of MARXISM, and the Vatican has sought to curb their influence by appointing more conservative prelates. http://www.merriam-webster.com/dictionary/liberation%20theology (Downloaded on 27/09/2013)

6 Cyril Desbruslais S.J. is currently Professor Emeritus at Jnana-Deep Vidyapeeth(JDV) and De Nobili College, Pune. He formerly held the posts of Professor and Dean. He was born in 1940.

7 "One of the best known and most interesting contributions of modern Latin American intellectual life is liberation philosophy. The philosophical movement originated in Argentina, although many of its practitioners reside in other Latin American countries. Philosophy of liberation should not be confused with liberation theology. Philosophy of liberation attempts to explain philosophically the theoretical underpinnings of social and political phenomena, such as dependency, and reinforces theology of liberation. These movements are responses to significant events in twentieth-century Latin America such

Catholic community but to everyone at large and hence in his later works considers this as an important message as opposed to the narrow confines of liberation theology from which he begins.[8] It might be important to consider Lancy Lobo SJ's position on liberation theology to get a clearer picture of where another Jesuit stands on this matter:

---

as the Cuban Revolution (1959), the Argentine 'Dirty war' (1976–1983) and repressive regimes which began in Guatemala in 1954, Brazil in 1964 and Chile in 1973. Other political topics for these writers included populism, Marxism and Peronism. Philosophy of liberation differs from theology of liberation, Latin Americanist philosophy and Marxist philosophy especially in terms of its more limited accessibility. Philosophers of liberation employ a complex and specialized vocabulary which requires initiation on the part of readers. In addition, philosophy of liberation is not a unified movement: it is more appropriate to speak of philosophies of liberation. Such fragmentation in this field can be partly explained by the political orientations of thinkers whose views range from the extreme left to the extreme right. Their philosophical influences vary widely and include Francophone, German and other Latin American thinkers.

Philosophical activity in Latin America is characterized by a tremendous diversity of focus and methodologies. Latin Americans are keenly aware of philosophical developments in the rest of the world and thus entertain a variety of philosophical stances: progressive and conservative, pragmatist and idealist, materialist and spiritualist. Numerous philosophical interests and projects exist in Latin America because of a diversified and active philosophical profession, an interested public, some government support, a cultural awareness of other continents among the educated and noneducated alike and a widespread faith in education as a key to development." OLIVER, AMY A. (1998). Latin America, philosophy in. In E. Craig (Ed.), *Routledge Encyclopedia of Philosophy*. London: Routledge. Retrieved September 27, 2013, from http://www.rep.routledge.com/article/ZA009

"Philosophy of liberation tries to formulate a metaphysics (2.4.9.2)—not an ontology(2.4.9.1) —demanded by revolutionary praxis (3.1.7-8) and technologic-design poiesis (4.3) against the background of peripheral social formations. To do this it is necessary to deprive Being of its alleged eternal and divine foundations; to negate fetishist religion in order to expose ontology as the ideology of ideologies; to unmask functionalisms—whether structuralist, logico-scientific, or mathematical (claiming that reason cannot criticize the whole dialectically, they affirm it the more they analytically criticize or operationalize its parts); and to delineate the sense of liberation praxis. Post-Hegelian critics of the European left have explained it to some extent. Only the praxis of oppressed peoples of the periphery, of the woman violated by masculine ideology, of the subjugated child, can fully reveal it to us (5.9) ." Enriqe Dussel *Philosophy of Liberation* tr. from the Spanish by Aquilina Martinez and Christine Morkovsky (New York: Obis Books) 1985. 15.

8 The message of Cyril Desbruslais S.J. "Give yourself generously to the service of the people. Inspire others also to take care of, and reach out to, the "little ones". Make good use of the energy and resilience of your youth in the service of the people. Never write anyone off as a "gone case", or irredeemable. Learn languages and how to make better use of the media. Sts Ignatius and Francis Xavier would have, if these precious blessings had available to them in their ministry." Posted by De Nobili College at 10:12 on 3rd July 2012 downloaded from http://dnctimes.blogspot.in/2012/07/jubilarian-cyril-desbruslais-sj-speaks.html (Downloaded on 27/09/2013)

"... Intellectual inputs in terms of social analysis, and greater exposure of the religious personnel to the economic problems of the lower strata, have indirectly furthered the cause of inculturation in India.

However, the contribution of the liberation theology thrust to inculturation is limited. By excessively leaning towards the classical Marxian orientation, liberation theology cannot appreciate the width and depth of the inculturation debate. Culture itself is taken in a narrow sense. By focusing merely on poverty, exploitation, oppression and de-humanisation, a lot of other elements of the total culture of a group are overlooked. This is understandable: the main concern of liberation theology is not inculturation but liberation. But we must record that its contribution even to inculturation consists in turning the attention of the church to the lower strata, composed of Christians and non-Christians. Moreover, of late an evolution in the thinking of liberation theologians has taken place. They have found their exclusive focus on the economic concerns of the lower strata wanting. They have seriously begun taking cognizance of the religious dimension. For instance, the efforts in the Basic Christian Communities to incorporate day-to-day life experiences in their liturgy and worship, in the local idiom, has been a welcome change." 'Towards an Inculturation in the Non-Sanskritic Tradition' *Vidyajyoti,* XLIX (January 1985) 22-23.

## 2. Brecht's and Desbruslais' Theatre

Though Desbruslais is known for his use of the Brechtian '*Verfremdungseffekt*'[9] which brings in the political dimension of space into the plays, his plays also derive from the Ibsenite 'Theatre of Ideas'. Cyril Desbruslais SJ being a

9 "**alienation effect,** also called **a-effect or distancing effect**, German **Verfremdungseffekt or V-effekt**, idea central to the dramatic theory of the German dramatist-director Bertolt Brecht. It involves the use of techniques designed to distance the audience from emotional involvement in the play through jolting reminders of the artificiality of the theatrical performance.

Examples of such techniques include explanatory captions or illustrations projected on a screen; actors stepping out of character to lecture, summarize, or sing songs; and stage designs that do not represent any locality but that, by exposing the lights and ropes, keep the spectators aware of being in a theatre. The audience's degree of identification with characters and events is presumably thus controlled, and it can more clearly perceive the "real" world reflected in the drama.

Brecht conceived the alienation effect not only as a specific aesthetic program but also as a political mission of the theatre. Inspired by the philosophies of G.W.F. Hegel and Karl Marx and by Viktor Shklovsky's theory of *ostranenie* ("making it strange," or defamiliarization), Brecht regarded his method as a way of helping spectators understand the complex nexuses of historical development and societal relationships. By creating stage effects that were strange or unusual, Brecht intended to assign the audience an active role in the production by forcing them to ask questions about the artificial environment and how each individual element related to real-life events. In doing so, it was hoped that viewers would distance

professor of Philosophy, ideas are what he works with. However, his message is not of the hunky-dory kind. As the Brechtian Theatre expects the audience to do their homework, and also does not offer comfort at the end, but a problem to go home with. Thus the plays are meant to disturb, search and rethink one's own stand to society. Sometimes, the plays seem to be a culmination of group work derived from searching for notions of being. Desbruslais has run his Group the SSU (Searching and Serving in Unity) mainly single handedly.[10] As far as theatre productions go with amateur actors, there has been consistent production, growth and change; hence the productions require to be considered more seriously. Besides all this, there has to be a documentation of a minority theatre speaking to a minority community with messages that are not always comfortable.

---

themselves emotionally from problems that demanded intellectual solutions." http://www.britannica.com/EBchecked/topic/15423/alienation-effect (Downloaded 27/09/2013)

10 Cyril Desbruslais says: "*A few words about the SSU, the Youth Group I formed in 1971*
I started this group in 1971, when I was beginning my Theology studies at DNC. I had faced a lot of problems and confusion in my own youth and I wanted to help other youngsters not to make the mistakes and blunders I did. I wanted to reach out especially to youngsters who normally don't feel drawn to join any youth groups, who seemed to be interested only in "freaking out" and drifting along. I also wanted to set up an inter-denominational youth group, one made up of young people of different religious and ethnic backgrounds – and I wanted us to celebrate our differences, not just sweep them under the carpet (through inter-faith celebrations of our major feasts, and the like). Finally I wanted to help youngsters to develop a deep social sense, a sense of responsibility and concern for the poor, the deprived and all victims of injustice in our country and all over the world – and do something about it. In the SSU we have Outreach programmes where we visit and/or help Institutions doing this (mainly NGOs), as well as put on plays with a social message, giving them the lion's share of the profits. Yes, the group is 40 years old this year and we're having a three day celebration of this in December, with past SSU members over the years (many of whom have their own teenage children following their footsteps in the SSU). We meet twice a week on Thursdays (a more serious activity) and Sunday (a fun and games session) after having animated the Sunday evening Mass at the Jesuit parish of St Xavier's in Pune, Camp. Then there are our regular Outreaches, the Annual one week leadership training Camp, at Kune, and the yearly fund-raiser dramatic venture by which we help some needy social work organization and give ample practical experience to our members." http://dnctimes.blogspot.in/2012/07/jubilarian-cyril-desbruslais-sj-speaks.html (Downloaded on 28/09/2013)

## 3. Minority Theatre in Operation

The plays of Cyril Desbruslais SJ should have been published a long time ago.[11] The play's are perhaps of greater interest for culture studies[12] as they concentrate on a minority community in a multi-religious country that has kept moving from colonialism to globalization, and has seen both local and national movements be they the rise of the Shiv Sena, Marxism, socialism, the emergency and the cultural emergency, etc. Most societies in a post-globalized world have little time for self-reflection and a self-critique in the process of getting and staying 'middle class'. The portion of the Catholic community, which inherits this tendency perhaps, suffers to some extent, from this insufficiency. Though there are sermons in the Church, and reflections

11 The author of this paper Dr. Rajan J. Barrett has a photo copy of the plays in typed/manuscript form and quotes from them wherever necessary hoping that one day they get published. The fact that they are not published calls for what is called 'theatre studies' as opposed to 'drama studies.'

12 While the term 'culture studies' may be used broadly, to refer to all aspects of the study of culture, and as such may be taken to encompass the diverse ways in which culture is understood and analysed, for example, in sociology, history, ethnography and literary criticism, and even sociobiology, it may also more precisely, be taken to refer to a distinctive field of academic enquiry. IN this second use, its historical roots can be traced back to the work of Raymond Williams and Richard Hoggart in the late 1950's and early 1960's, and thus to the formation of the Birmingham Centre for Contemporary Cultural Studies in 1964, originally under the directorship of Hoggart and then of Stuart Hall. From the body of work there emerged a multi-disciplinary approach to culture, drawing not merely on the orthodox approaches derived from the social sciences, but also on more radical approaches suggested by, for example, feminism, Marxism, and semiotics. This miscellany of approaches facilitated the asking of new questions, and thus to a reconceptualisation of exactly what was entailed by the term 'culture'. In particular, cultural studies can be seen to have set itself against the preconceptions about culture found in the traditional critical disciplines, such as literary criticism, aesthetics and musicology. While such traditional disciplines predominantly treated cultural products as objects or texts that could be legitimately or even exhaustively, studied in isolation from the social and historical context of their production and consumption, the exponents of cultural studies sought to situate cultural products explicitly in relation to other social practices, and particularly in relation to political structures and social hierarchies such as race class and gender. An implication of this approach was that the cultural products to be studied could not merely be those selected and celebrated by an intellectual and artistic elite but would rather be the material and symbolic products encountered in all strata and sections of society.

Cultural studies can therefore be seen to be situated between an approach to culture that is explicitly opposed to the celebration of high or elite culture, as represented for example, in the canonical texts studied in English Literature, or the subject-matter of traditional musicology, and an approach that is more positively derived from the social sciences, and particularly from cultural anthropology and the sociology of culture. [AE]" *Key Concepts in Cultural Theory* eds. Andrew Edgar and Peter Sedgwick (London: Routledge) 1999, 100-101.

on the Christian way of life, they have most often the markers of self-preservation, tradition, and conservativism. A critique, which challenges the basic assumptions of a society, can make a community grow culturally and socially by virtue of reflection. Cyril Desbruslais SJ as a priest however, is one of the persons among the Catholic community who has taken the trouble to reflect on the development of the community with an understanding and vision that springs from scholarship, reflection and involvement, besides being majorly anti-establishmental in orientation his reflection is shared with a theatre audience.[13] It might seem that there is a limitation with this kind of theatre in as much as it is 'for' and 'by' a local Pune based community, and the idealism of the plays of Desbruslais do not reach out to the larger masses of Christians. However, the fact that his productions have been consistent for the last forty years with youth who are a part of his group the SSU (Searching and Serving in Unity), and its performances twice a year, cannot be brushed aside.[14] What Judith Butler says regarding minority practices (though in the context of gender) might still be important here: 'This doesn't mean that all minority practices are to be condoned or celebrated, but it does mean that we ought to be able to think them before we come to any kinds of conclusions about them.'[15]

I think it might be important to be conscious that at first this is minor theatre because it springs from a minority community. Secondly, the plays are in English, which is a language that is not really a major language in India, there are of course occasional Hinglish words used for topical allusions. Thirdly, the plays establish that though there are Roman Catholics in India their unique position in a multi-religious world, with a plurality of languages and culture have to be considered. This accounts for the unique political stance to the Vatican, the World and the Country. Fourthly, the plays have a message which spring form a distinct movement in the Catholic Church, which is associated with the well known Second Vatican Council (Called Vatican II) and the subsequent movement of liberation theology.

---

13 There are of course priest and scholars who study the Catholic Community from various angles. One such person is Lancy Lobo SJ whose scholarly output of sociological studies cannot be denied. However, Cyril Desbruslais SJ's Theatre reaches out to those who are not used to such scholarly reflection. The monastery one might say is brought to the market place.

14 There are elements of the shared theatre here, especially when the production is out of reflection on discussions and engagements of the group. Though the plays are said to be written by Desbruslais and performed under his direction the plays also are an output of his reflection and engagement with young people.

15 *Gender Trouble: Feminism and the Subversion of Identity* (New York: Roultedge) 1999, viii.

## 4. The Post-Vatican II Engagement

That this is minority theatre of a sort that is rare and hardly gets much publicity outside the city of Pune[16] because the plays were meant initially for a Catholic community, grew in their ecumenism and then are distinctively for a larger interreligious audience, shows the organic development of both Desbruslais and the plays. The theological background, which is not available to most lay persons, is something that the plays make available, in an oblique manner. This is a point to take note of as the Church until Vatican II[17] had services in Latin with a hermeneutics to make religion accessible. This might ring a bell with our own brahminical culture (Sanskritic practices) minus the hermeneutics. However in spite of Vatican II with its opening up of the Church to non-

16 There have been productions in Mumbai and Hyderabad as there were collaborations with youth groups in both these cities.

17 "When Pope John XXIII was elected at the age of 76 in the fall of 1958, he was expected to be an interim or transitional pope. In other words, people expected him to maintain the status quo and to conduct business as usual.

What a surprise it was, then, when only three months later John XXIII met privately with a group of cardinals and announced his intent to convene an ecumenical council, meaning a legislative gathering that was worldwide in scope. His announcement was met with stunned silence from the cardinals.

Calling for an ecumenical council was a major undertaking, and a possible indication that sweeping changes for the Church were on the horizon. Many of the cardinals at that time thought of the Catholic Church as a flawless institution and resisted the idea that anything inside the Church was in need of change. Pope John XXIII explained, however, that his intent was not to change any of the doctrines of the Church, but rather to modify the way they were presented—to better equip Catholics to live and worship in a rapidly changing world.

In the past, popes had convened ecumenical councils only to refute errors or condemn heresies. For example, the Council of Trent (1545-1563) was convened in response to the Protestant Reformation, and the First Vatican Council (1869-1870), which defined papal infallibility, was convened to counteract the principles of the Enlightenment and the French Revolution of 1789.

But John XXIII's purpose in calling the world's bishops together this time was different. To illustrate his intention to one particular cardinal, he walked over to the nearest window, thrust it open wide and said that the Church needs to let in some fresh air."

He would later expand on this idea, saying, "We are not to be museum keepers, but to cultivate a flourishing garden of life." In other words, John XXIII intended not to change major doctrines and teachings, but to update the way they were presented, thus honoring the Church as a dynamic, living, breathing entity.

He had previously spoken about this approach as looking at "the signs of the times" in order to meet today's needs. He often used the Italian word *aggiornamento*, which means "a bringing up to date." The image of the open window and the term *aggiornamento* have served as Vatican II's signature symbols ever since." From 'Vatican II for Gen-Xers' By Renée LaReau http://www.americancatholic.org/Messenger/Nov2005/Feature2.asp (Downloaded 28/09/2013)

clerical participation, there is little by way of theological and philosophical understandings of religion among the laity of the Church. One does not negate the outreach and spread of the movement by the laity, but as far as scholarship and research, which lead to self-reflection and direction are concerned, a lot of the laity are still like the proverbial sheep who are dependent upon 'the good shepherd' also called 'the pastor'. The pastoral notion is more in tune with a romantic world, which seems at odds with the modern world.[18] Thus there has to be some way by which the advances between the theoretical understandings of the scriptures and the world have to be made available to the laity. If that does not take place, which is sadly the case, the question of self-reflection and a dynamic identity cannot take place.

## 5. Locating the Laity and the Clergy

The fact that a community is dynamic and interacts with the world at large is something that perhaps seems forgotten by the clerics. Thus the plays are important in as much as they offer at least a vent for such ponderings and questionings by the laity. The laity's views and opinions too have to be considered and perhaps very little of this takes place in molding the clergy to such a democratic understanding, which leads to a rift that has its own brahminical divide owing to the brahminical culture of Indian Christianity.[19] Desbruslais' plays seem to be addressing a number of these issues including the laity's take on the clergy, the church and the scriptures as they confront themselves. Lancy Lobo SJ deals with the complexity of the position of Indian

---

18 'The Pastoral' is a literary form which is associated with the shepherds and the sheep and said to have originated with Theocritus in 3BCE. 'Pastor' is the Latin for shepherd. Virgil too in his *Eclogues* works with the pastoral. The English poets including Shakespeare, Shelley, Wordsworth etc. are taken up with the notion of the pastoral and it can be seen either wholly or in part in some of their poems. T. S. Eliot's *Wasteland* (1922) too is taken up by William Empson in *Some Versions of Pastoral* (1935) as a pastoral poem when the rest of the critics hail it as city poetry. Unfortunately the pastoral mode is ironically what seems to be the mode in which the Church operates which implies that modernism has not quite arrived though however, it uses it as a symbolic resource to romantically connect with the emotions of the congregation. It also perhaps works with biblical imagery which includes the piscolateral pastoral as the apostles have a large number of people of the fishing community.

19 Lancy Lobo S.J. uses the term 'sanskritic' which perhaps covers the politics of what Thornstein Veblin calls 'brahminical cultures' and also the practice by Brahmins of their religious practices when he says: " It now becomes obvious, perhaps, that the religious personnel exposed basically to the sanskritic tradition of Hinduism and great tradition of Christianity is ill-equipped for dealing effectively with the people of the non-sanskritic tradition, either in developmental or in evangelisational matters. But a recent call within the church has given a certain amount of re-orientation to the church personnel: back to the masses, back to the villages, back to the lower strata of society; back to the oppressed, exploited and de-humanized humanity!" *Vidyajyoti,* XLIX (January 1985) 22.

Christians and considers the elite, brahminical role of Christianity when he defines 'non-sanskritic inculturation' saying:

> "Exclusive concentration on the part of the church on its own great tradition and the Hindu sanskritic tradition, and the near total absence of scholarship on its own little tradition and the Hindu non-sanskritic tradition, has not helped to discover the common structural categories of each religion. External inculturation is perhaps easy, viz., life style, habits, dress and so on. But for any meaningful and depth level inculturation, one must uncover the common structural categories. An awareness of the complexity of the superimposition of one religious culture on another is greatly desirable. "Conversion" does involve the super imposition of the traditions of the new religion over the old one. The osmosis that has taken place as a consequence needs sociological analysis. The situation is complex as believers are often caught in a barrage of crossmessages. Culture as we said earlier, is a design for living and the convert is continually faced with designs and traditions that conflict. Rarely does a convert completely opt out of the old design and tradition to the new.[20]

Both Vatican II and liberation theology happen when Cyril Desbruslais SJ is still in religious formation in the nineteen sixties. These movements seem to have had a major impact on his plays. It might be important to consider the plays are possible because of the liberal spirit that Vatican II happened to bestow the Church with, which brought about a questioning of areas of religious life and humanity that were taken for granted by priests and laity alike. Liberation theology now exists as a movement that was potentially creative under the Papacy of Pope Paul VI, though the changes in the world after him namely the pro-Capitalism of Pope John Paul II, the collapse of the Berlin Wall and the Soviet Block along with the concomitant of globalization which neutralizes difference, worked to minimize its radicalism as a force of liberation.

## Locating Liberation

While Vatican II brought about tremendous changes in the Catholic Church throughout the world and also in India it had many detractors and an exodus of conservatives who find it more convenient to join other fundamentalist Christian groups, churches and movements. The rise in fundamentalism I attribute to the postmodern condition in the world where there is loss of identity on one hand and a leaning not to engage with complex questions because quick answers and surety is what everyone in an Americanized (read as postglobalized) world wants. These fundamentalist Christian groups of course rise not without the funding of capitalist agencies for which a right

20 *Vidyajyoti,* XLIX (January 1985) 23.

wing fundamentalist organization's help in the lack of questioning of agency and agents provide identitarian and emotional support.

However, to be in the Church that is conservative is tantamount to near medievalism. This would imply an exodus out of the Church for all those who have access to scientific rationality and the thinking deriving from the age of enlightenment. This is something that the Church suffered from before Vatican II and which is a problem for the French Jesuit and scientist, Pierre Teilhard de Chardin, the protagonist of Desbruslais' *The Pilgrim of the Future* (1973). This French Jesuit thinker, who dies in 1955, is constantly in trouble with the Church as his methods of thinking are well beyond his time and space and the medievalism of the Catholic Church. Modernity is something that the Church is not prepared for and the scruples, rituals, superstitions, traditions and customs of the Church help it become insular.[21] Teilhard de Chardin in his life, work and encounter with the world; questions and puts into perspective the notions of modernity, and posits a new way of thinking and being for the Church. The play shows how his very progressive ideas are the points which isolate him in more ways than one: his books are put on the index, he is stopped from teaching, and he is constantly in exile though a working scientist and thinker. The treatment given him stops short of the medieval world, where in the church plays a dark role, while the progressive elements of modern culture and civilization brew under the surface.

It might be important to note that the play *Pilgrim of the Future* is almost an Aristotelian play and would perhaps fit neatly into Freytag's pyramid with the complication, climax and denouement. However, Desbruslais' play seems to have something in common with Bertolt Brecht's *Galileo Galilee* (1943). The point of commonality being that one is made to think about the question of freedom for the scientist-priest and his research and ideas, which are interdisciplinary and hence whether it is more important to be in the Church or leave it in spite of the opposition and pressure. This becomes the pivotal point similar to Galileo's (in the play) as he recants before an inquisition court but does his scientific work, when he might have chosen to die and be a martyr for science. Teilhard de Chardin SJ does not have to recant but affirms that the Church and the Society of Jesus (the Jesuits) have been his support and his inspiration, which is the ending of the play. Teilhard de Chardin says:

21 In his feedback and discussion about this paper, V. Sebastian S.J. of Sneh Joyti, Sevasi, commented about modernity and the Church as a long discourse with its confrontations and contestations saying: "There is a very long history behind the confrontation between the Church and Modernity—and it crystallized in a crisis called the "Modernist Crisis" in the Roman Catholic Church in the opening decades of the 20th century. Alfred Loisy and Bernard Tyrrel. S.J. were excommunicated. New thinking was generally discouraged and suspected. Teilhard de Chardin SJ's censure needs to be located within this attitude of the Church."

> "Have I ever told you of the three women that have brought so much light and joy into my life? Marie, l'Église, la Compagnie: in French they are all feminine, Mary, the Church, the Society of Jesus!" (Act III Sc.iii.)

The Church has by the time of Teilhard de Chardin SJ learnt more sophisticated ways in which to contain, limit and nullify people. While Brecht's play uses his *Verfremdungseffekt*, which Desbruslais uses elaborately in other plays, Brecht's play also leaves the audience thinking and does not offer the catharsis that an Aristotelian play would afford. The *Pilgrim of the Future* does the same: Teilhard de Chardin is confronted by friends and foe about his freedom and with the opposition, restrictions and difficulties he stays within the Church and produces his work. This, one might attribute to his shrewdness as a Jesuit. Had he been less sophisticated, more emotional and less patient he might have opted out of the Church. However, his commitment to the Society of Jesus and his vows of poverty chastity and obedience; keep him questioning, suffering and accepting himself and the Church with a hope of transforming its understanding of itself and the world. The voice of Teilhard de Chardin SJ is heard in the prelude, before the beginning of the play before the curtain rises saying:

> "I am taking the vow of poverty; never before have I more clearly realized to what extent money can be a powerful means for the service and glory of God. I am making a vow of chastity; never before have I understood so well how a husband and wife complete each other in order to advance better towards God. I am taking the vow of obedience; never before have I been so overwhelmed by the depth of the freedom of the children of God… So far as my strength serves me, because I am a priest, I wish to be the first to seek, to be aware of what the world loves, and pursues and suffers; the first to seek, to sympathize, to grieve; the first to offer myself and sacrifice myself and to be more broadly human, more nobly of this world, than any of those who serve this world…"[22]

The message, however, for an Indian Catholic audience watching the play is that it brings in the question of other religions being respected in a democratic manner, as equally true in their seeking after the infinite, which is perhaps shocking and disturbing to orthodox believers. Mr. Ting's position in the play expounds the idea that conversion is a constant and that one is born in one religion and keeps changing one's religion as s/he grows and changes. One of the items in the list of beliefs one is converted to is agnosticism. This links up obliquely with the Aristotelian and the Church view of the perfectibility of nature. However, in practice conversion is something that does not go down well with most conservative people be they Christians in India; or

22 Prelude from *Pilgrim of the Future.*

conservatives of other religions who want to preserve the idea of their religion being right and unchanging. Ting thus stands as a person from another culture, which should be an inspiration for the ideal of liberation from a dogmatic understanding of an essential self, limited by being born into one faith, and living and dying in it. This conservativism, as we know in India, transforms itself into serious consequences, which lead to riots and violence that show disrespect for other people, because of their beliefs, when the Constitution of India guarantees freedom of religion. It is true however, that with people in groups, communities and cultures, change takes a long time, and sometimes painfully never happens.

## 6. Liberation and Its Responsibility

While the community may not be happy with Desbruslais' liberal and enlightened viewpoint, there is a didacticism which forces the audience to think against the grain. Teilhard de Chardin is accused of being a Marxist or at least thinking like one in the play. This too is an important dimension which all of Desbruslais' plays display: a left thinking radical philosophy, designed to make the audience a thinking audience, just as Brecht would want it to be. However, there seems to be the element of the Christian existentialist, Søren Kierkegaard, who expects Christians not to take their faith for granted but to be in 'fear and trembling' with regards to being a Christian, and one has to question oneself every moment of one's life whether one is a Christian or not if one wants to live authentically. Kierkegaard is not a Catholic, and yet becomes important for Christian existentialist thinking, especially as in the modern and postmodern world the world comes closer and closer; one has to define oneself, one's faith, one's value and one's community as one is confronted with advances in the world of science, technology and politics.

## 7. Liberation Theology

The other more important element that came in post Vatican II was Liberation Theology, which considered *the Bible* and the Christian message of Christ from a Marxist perspective, this approach simplistically meant: reading *the Bible* as a Marxist text. More complexly it would imply, radical action, which would often mean violence and death for the people who protested against regimes that were oppressive.[23] The period of liberation theology in the Church had

23 V. Sebastian S.J. commenting on this element of the paper says: "There are larger questions about social change here. What constitutes social change? What are the methods? There can be also non-violent social changes but it requires long period of time. Social changes are hugely complex precisely because it involves not only structural changes but also mind-sets. Both structures and mind-sets take enormous time to develop and to evolve. See, Hervé Ott, 'Principles of Non-Violent Action,' *Theology Digest*, Vol. 35, no. 3 (Fall 1988) pp. 213-217, here, pp. 214-15"

been perhaps the most creative phases in the history of the Church, because the priests and laity tried to understand themselves and their faith in a more complex and creative manner as they confronted their own political position and location in the world, along with their position as Christians. With the Papacy of John Paul II and Cardinal Joseph Ratzinger, who later became Pope Benedict XVI, the movement gets killed off and a pro-capitalist Church asserts itself. However, like the existentialist movement, the effects of Liberation Theology in Latin America and other third-world and developing nations, become an important way for understanding the Christian Community both politically and spiritually.

## 8. Modern Oppressive Systems and the Position of the Christians

The question of faith was never simple in the world, but now the challenge is far greater and more complex. This is because along with the Marxist is the coming in of the totalitarian and the capitalistic worlds. There are many who risk their lives and Desbruslais' plays *Esperanza*, and *A.T.*[24] are two important plays in which the bearing of liberation theology on the lives of Christian priests and people become important, *Against the Tide* confronts right wing totalitarianism namely Nazism. The thrust of liberation theology, which is seen in the message of these plays, is that a Christian cannot sit quiet and watch injustice done to the poor as the God of *the Old Testament* and *New Testament* is a God of the poor who is a God of the absolutes of Justice, Love and Peace. It might be important to note that the Jesuit General Pedro Arrupe SJ in 1968 formulates an initial understanding of what is a political and religious position called 'Option for the Poor.'[25]

*Against the Tide* is a play which is about an incident in 2003 in a village in Austria, which is to a large extent a memory play. Desbruslais himself witnesses the event in a village in Austria and mentions himself as the playwright from

---

24 The dates of these plays is difficult to find as they do not appear on the manuscript copy that the author of this paper has.

25 Desbruslais' reference to Fr. Pedro Arrupe S.J. is important, when he speaks of who inspired him the most: "***The Jesuit who inspired me most:*** That's easy. Apart from St Ignatius, Pedro Arrupe SJ. He helped the Society come alive for me. He taught me about the inseparable link between faith and justice. He was a true contemplative in action. I was able to meet this charismatic personality twice, when he visited DNC and one of my treasured possessions is a book with his signature in it. Just to re-read one of his writings (especially "On Our Way of Proceeding") fires me with enthusiasm and fervour all over again. I'm also deeply impressed by Adolfo Nicolas sj, whom I met before he became General, at the "Asian Identity Seminar" in Delhi and who reminds me in so many ways of Pedro. Nicolas has an infectious joy and sense of commitment. I could also mention Teilhard de Chardin SJ, who taught me about the holiness of matter and the divine milieu." http://dnctimes.blogspot.in/2012/07/jubilarian-cyril-desbruslais-sj-speaks.html (Downloaded 28/09/2013) DNC stands for De Nobili College, Pune.

Pune in the play. While this might be an element of *Verfremdungseffekt* which gives a moment of comic relief to the play, because of the auto-referential topical allusion, it also asserts the notion of testimony and lived experience. This play is also written with the values mentioned above in mind though it is set against the Nazi Reich. In fact is seems to echo the "Judgment on Two Standards" which is an important element in the *Spiritual Exercises of St. Ignatius* where Christ and his disciples are unarmed and calm while the Devil and his army are moving about with a lot of fanfare and might. Here in the play we have a parody of the 'Battle Hymn of the Republic' transformed for the Nazi's view of a thousand year Reich vs. the poor helpless villagers of Sankt Radegund who sing 'Peace is flowing like a river,' which is a hymn. Franz Jagerstatter is killed because he believes in standing up against the Nazi régime by refusing to fight in Hitler's imperialistic wars.

The play is a lesson for all Christians and people at large that one has to fight against totalitarian regimes, even if one is alone and has to pay for it with one's life. This is a value that seems to be disappearing with the onset of totalitarianism and in a capitalistic world in which one has to survive economically and become an economic fascist or totalitarian seeing that no other way but the capitalist is right.

Michael Foucault and Paulo Freire perhaps seem to be asking the same question about the position of the human subject and his/her subjectivity in a world that is becoming more and more conforming to one principle or way of thinking and being. Thus the play shows that if one has to live a Christian life of commitment and conviction one would have to face insults and abuses like Franzeska the wife of Franz and his children have to face because of his stand, even when there are people within the village and church who concede to the Nazis. Franz dies at the hands of the Nazis.

Just as Tielhard de Chardin SJ finds communion with the communists and others on his scientific journey, Franz finds communion with the communists, the Seventh Day Adventists and the Jehovah Witnesses who also resist the Nazi's with conviction leading to their death, when he is in prison. This brings in the idea of ecumenism, which is the attempt to get different Christian Churches together; in as far as the Christian faith is concerned. However, the commonality with the communist who resist Hitler becomes a position to engage with both for the liberation theologian and a believing Catholic; as a staid notion of *communitas* on one hand is what Christianity affirms, but the agnosticism of the communist is perhaps unacceptable. Here a communist and Catholic both resist a totalitarian and racist, positioning the meaning of what it means to be a Catholic as different from a communist and yet having a common enemy, the implications of which has to be worked out with care and complex critical thinking.

## 9. Confronting the Audience

The Play *A.T.* is about a Jesuit, Anchanical Thomas, who is killed in Bihar for fighting for the Adivasis against the powerful landsharks and landlords in 1997, he was a student of Jnana Deepa Vidyapeeth, Pune from 1971-73.[26] The notion that one cannot be a Christian and remain politically neutral but one has to be alive and awake and have a political stand which might imply dying for your faith unlike Galileo who recants when he sees the instruments of torture in Brecht's play discussed above. *Against the Tide* and *A. T* are closer to Ibsen's *Enemy of the People* (1882) except that both are people from real life and in the plays the protagonists pay with their lives for standing up for what they believe. Teilhard de Chardin SJ , *The Pilgrim of the Future*, too has to pay for his ideology with sanctions, exiles etc. like Dr. Stockman from *Enemy of the People.* All this points back to important statements made in real life and in the plays with the assassination of Archbishop Romero SJ of Latin America who is killed in 1980 for his position that is anti-establishment and pro-poor. There are nuns and priests and common people too who are killed in this exchange but die for their conviction something that is called martyrology that is inherited by the Christians from the Jews. Of course this becomes more complex in a world where in, one does not die for the faith alone, but for an interpretation of one's religion, based on a rather sophisticated set of propositions that lead to the reading of the tenets as laid down by *the Bible.* That this is relevant, when one stands up for ones political convictions, be it against the Nazis or the capitalist establishment in San Salvador, or the land mafia in Bihar is a bitter, difficult and challenging position that Desbruslais' plays place before the Christian community, which seems quite smug and complacent if not comfortably numb.

This Christian community, middle class probably, perhaps follows the principle of self interest in earning money, looking after the family, going to Church and enjoying life; when members of the same community in other parts of the world are taking on unjust regimes and people even if it means death.

26 On October 24 th 1997, Fr. Thomas then at the age of 46, went to visit these Dalits at the Sirka village. When he arrived, he found a group of policemen beating one of the villagers. These people where actually not the police, but insurgents dressed in police uniforms. Fr Thomas recognised that they were the same people who some years ago were trying to grab the land of the Dalits unjustly. Likewise, these land-grabbers too recognised Fr. Thomas. They immediately surrounded him and took him away at gunpoint; the villagers were helpless and powerless even though they tried to protect Fr Thomas. Three days later, Fr Thomas body was found floating in a nearby stream; clearly battered and decapitated. A visiting Jesuit from India who knew Fr. Thomas told me that, Fr. Thomas' body was covered with cigarette burns and disfigured by other marks of extreme torture; clearly inflicted before he was beheaded; it also took them several weeks to find the missing head of Fr. Thomas. (Downloaded on 29th September 2013 http://www.jesuit.org.sg/html/prayer/homilies/2010.yearc.23ordsun.php)

The interpretation of the Christian message in the modern idiom be it in Latin America, India or Austria is certainly more complex than the martyrology of the Jews and the Early Christians—it means reading and thinking critically which Franz Jaggerstatter, Teilhard de Chardin SJ , Anchanical Thomas and Romero have to do in a post-globalized world, where the power of the gun and the power of capital over rule any kind of human values and are therefore dehumanizing. The characters showing heroism of a kind that is supernatural, and seems to be of a kind of divinely inspired strength in the plays, do not advocate superstition or irrationality, but a question of political action. Resistance to the establishment, to totalitarianism, to injustice, to ill-treatment of the poor is the political message of Desbruslais' theatre.

## 10. For an Alternative World

A direct statement against the domination of the neo-colonial world is seen in the play *Excelsior* (2000) where there is the G8 summit and the role of the Indian delegates to it. The question of blind support of the exploitative nations and economic bullying of the stronger nations of the weaker nations is seen in tandem with a group of college students, their love life and family values no less affected by the conservative and establishmental values that the global world inflicts upon people as they stop thinking and reacting. The ironic reference of the world leaders to being 'one family' and at the same time exploiting the less powerful is seen in opposition to a fiancé who understands that an arranged marriage is a marriage that is loveless and the fiancée is amicably allowed to choose the one she loves instead of him. Thus the values that are in for questioning are machismo and the patriarchy.

The culture of the elite and powerful and the culture of the poor and marginalized are pitted against each other. This is a constant in Desbruslais' plays as the contrast between 'the haves' and 'the have-nots' asserting the notion that God is on the side of the 'have-nots' who are the politically powerless. However, there is an emphasis on being together in the struggle against the powerful in spite of the results pointing to death and defeat. This of course lifts the protagonists up to the level of the Greek classical heroes, which Hemingway in *Old Man and the Sea* (1952) articulates as 'A man can be destroyed but not defeated.' Teilhard, Franz, Romero, Anchanical Thomas and the Indian Delegates at the WTO are those who are destroyed but not defeated and that seems to be the reward, if one can call it so, that they achieve.

## 11. Considering Gender

One has to notice that there is an optimism of standing up for ones conviction and paying the price for it. Besides the human fear for one's life there is the question of the higher good, the greater good and the question of the principle, which one is willing to die for. While *Excelsior* is a play which is more a conscientizing play about the state of world affairs; it asks the Christians to think about their own position in such a world. It is again associated with the community and the resistance to power. However, it also goes against the grain of the Christians to find that the role of the Holy Spirit is played by a woman just as God in *Two by Two* (2011) is acted by a woman on stage. This is positing a resistance towards the typical patriarchal values of the Church and the world at large. Gender is a political category as has been asserted by Butler, Spivak and others. However, Desbruslais' treatment of the subject is sometimes iconoclastic but often he treats the subject gently as is seen in Teilhard who talks about three women in his life as quoted above. This moves Cyril Desbruslais' plays closer to liberation philosophy rather than liberation theology though the themes and force of liberation theology are markedly noticed in the plays.

While the political events of Desbruslais' plays are actual and have taken place in real life one finds that the political treatment given to them are more interesting. The politics of getting rid of Uriah in *No No Jeremiah! Or The Perils of Being a Prophet* (1982) is a stunt that one can see happening in India more and more and has been used politically everywhere when resistance of the people is difficult for the corrupt powers that be.[27] Desbruslais' *Eschaton* (1978) is a play based on the life of Christ and has a political reading to the life and death of Christ and the message of Christianity, which is not comfortable to the traditional priestly class the Pharisees. The death of Christ is thus a political murder of an innocent man who stands up against the hypocrisy and falsehood of a Pharisaical Jewish system. The play parodies the well known carol 'Silent Night'[28] and while the tune is the same the words show that the

---

27 One notices that Shakespeare writes plays both about his own country and about other countries often with a political message for the people and the rulers of the land. Thus Venice, Verona, Denmark are often plays which have a reference to England and the politics of England. Though Desbruslais is more outspoken and forthright there is often prudence which tempers his depiction of political reality.

28 "Christmas historian Bill Egan writes. Father Joseph Mohr wrote his six-stanza poem *Stille Nacht! Heilige Nacht!* in 1816 when he was assigned to a pilgrim church in Mariapfarr, Austria. Two years later, after a transfer to St. Nicholas Church in Oberndorf, Austria, the Catholic priest decided he wanted his poem set to music. On Dec. 24, 1818, he asked his friend Franz Gruber to create a melody and guitar accompaniment. The two men sang the carol at Christmas Mass in St. Nicholas Church with Fr. Mohr playing his guitar and the choir repeating the last two lines of each verse.

The man who translated *Stille Nacht* into *Silent Night* was John Freeman Young, While assigned to New York's Trinity Church, he translated European hymns into English as a hobby. Later in life he became the second Episcopal Bishop of Florida. Bishop Young is buried in Jacksonville, Florida, forgotten by the city he loved and ignored by the church he served, yet his words are sung by millions of people in English-speaking nations." http://www.bbc.co.uk/religion/religions/christianity/christmas/carols_1.shtml#section_2 (Downloaded 28/09/2013)

Christians are unconcerned about the poor and the oppressed. As one line goes: "Christians dine of their dainties and sweets while a poor babe dies in Pune's Streets. Christ the savior is born in a poor slum he is born."

Desbruslais' use of Brechtian *Verfremdungseffekt* during the crucifixion scene in *Eschaton*[29] incorporated the horrors that humans have done to other human beings in the name of Christ and otherwise by stage hands coming in placing placards with genocides and wars that have taken place in the name of Christ and otherwise, from after his death 2000 years ago till the present. Judas is looked at with sympathy as he makes a mistake thinking that he would push Christ into a miracle and when that does not work he shoots himself because he cannot forgive himself. There is a scene where Christ dances at the Wedding Feast of Cana, which is disturbing to a humdrum middle class audience for whom the deification of Christ is associated with purity and dancing with the common people would be not what Christ should be. That Christ dances with sinners and prostitutes is what the Pharisees in the play object to and so do the audience, silently at least. Thus Desbruslais attempts to demolish the brahminical and purist notions that people have about Christ and posits a Christ that is politically conscious, active and human.

## 12. Brechtian Effects

The Brechtian in a number of plays of Cyril Desbruslais is often not appreciated by audiences at large because perhaps it implies breaking down the illusion of theatre, besides the safety of the line demarcating the audience space and the stage space, or actor space, which itself becomes threatening. Desbruslais' plays bring in large crowds in crowd scenes, get the audience up on to the stage to break down the division between actor and audience space, often the actors sit in the audience and are often picked up by a stage manager, or narrator to dress up on stage and take up the roles that they are given. While this breaks down the illusion it also instills a deep theological message of being chosen for a role and responding with a vocation: a good example being *No No Jeremiah!*

Thus, the actor on the stage implies the actor in real life who is forced into roles that s/he is given and not always chosen but in struggling with the role and the commitments to it. The disinclination to take the role, as it does not keep to the personality fit, is often what is seen in the plays of Cyril Desbruslais SJ. However, the actor or person playing the role often 'finds himself' while he is grappling with the role and thus the role becomes meaningful. It is almost like the play *Fire and the Rain* (1995) of Girsh Karnad where in the mask becomes the face and one is forced to play it. While this emanates from the hackneyed Shakespearean lines: 'all the world's a stage' *As You Like It* Act II, Sc.vii. and

29 *Eschaton* is derived from the theological term 'eschatology' which is associated with the end of the world and the destiny of the human race. In Christian terms it is associated with the second coming of Christ, the Last Judgment etc.

'a poor player who struts and frets and hour upon the stage' *Macbeth* Act V, Sc.v., Desbruslais' players might accept the collapsing of the world and the stage but will not strut and fret upon the stage as the role is given to them to change the world and look at everything with hope no matter however dark, cruel and cynical the world may be. A political act cannot by its very nature be defeatist and dark, as Judith Butler draws attention to the proximity of theatre and politics saying "as if theatre and politics are always distinct".[30] One has to consider that there is a conscious and concerted effort at didacticism, which is not easy as the message and praxis is not easy and follows the conventional and establishmental path but stands *Against the Tide.*

The Brechtian might be useful for the epic dimensions of Desbruslais' plays like the crowd scenes, the loose plot structure, the use of a narrator or stage manager, the direct utterances about the opening and closing of the play, the tea breaks, the structure of the play and the setting which is constructed and demolished before the audience to break the illusion. But Desbruslais' plays also work at the level of demolishing the hunky dory nature of the Christian community, the illusion of being comfortable and the detached attitude of the Christian community. In essence this is what Brecht had aimed for in his notion of theatre: to have a platform that addresses people and make them go home with a problem that concerns them and society.

## 13. Praxis of Decolonization

We have briefly looked at the nature of the minority stage and it genesis with liberation theology, Vatican II and the techniques largely of Brecht, though expressionistic elements are also seen in Desbruslais' plays. However, one has to consider how Desbruslais' praxis is an attempt at decolonizing the stage. We might consider the efforts at Brechtian theatre an attempt to challenge a mindset brought up on plays of Shakespeare, which is the staple of most Christian Schools and institutions. The Church has a long tradition of morality and mystery plays, which we know of. There is a living tradition of Christian Drama in Kerala called *Margamkali*[31] which one would consider as pre colonial and some would even venture to say of organic growth from

30 *Gender Trouble: Feminism and the Subversion of Identity* (New York: Routledge) 1999, xx.

31 "In the year 345 A.D. a certain merchant Thomas Cana (Kana Thommen) migrated with 400 Syrian Christian families to Malabar and Cranganore. These are called Knanaya Syrian Christians. The worship pattern, art-forms, Church architecture etc. of the aforesaid groups of Christians were similar to those of the Hindu Brethren of that time. Their art-forms were least affected by the foreign influence and were very much Indian in Form and Spirit. Dance-forms such as Magamkali, Vattakali and Parisumuttukali practiced by these Christians survive to the present day. " *Christianity in Indian Dance Forms* by Francis Peter Barboza (Delhi: Sri Satguru Publications) 1990,3.

the subcontinent. Desbruslais' plays raise political issues that are concerned with a population of Christians: who are a product largely of the postcolonial establishment be it Portuguese, Dutch, French or British and sometimes even have identified with the colonizers in their attitudes and politics even though the colonizers are not around. Desbruslais' plays locate issues that are world issues and looks at the identity of the Christian community in a multi-religious India. That the Christians have a right to their own Indian Christian/ Catholic Church with a rich diverse culture and has to relate to it in various ways in the spirit of Justice, Love and Peace is a difficult synthesis to achieve. Besides, the plays strive for a political purpose of being considered as Indian, politically, and therefore asserting difference from the European, but at the same time integrating the values of the Roman Catholic Church. It is important to observe that while Cyril Desbruslais' plays work on the constructed identity of the Roman Catholic Indian, there are the developments both within India, which are political and those outside with demand a new and different identity of Christians in a decolonized/decolonizing land.

## Conclusion

In conclusion it would be appropriate to say that the plays of Cyril Desbruslais SJ are varied in theme and perhaps see lesser variation in technique. However, the political message of the plays is linked up to a kind of political commitment of Christianity and a reading of *the Bible* which calls for engagement, action, and taking a stand even if it means death. Desbruslais seems to be negotiating Christianity and decolonization (of the Latin American variety) together as he uses leftist readings of the world and the word often using the techniques of the Brechtian Theatre to stand against a world that is neocolonizing fast; post globalization. This of course is done for a minority community with purposes that are within the notions of 'community building' and 'service' that the Catholic Church prescribes. However, in the process, his plays confront and challenge the minority audience, who come to engage with them, and also the pro-capitalist, by default, understandings of what it is to be middle class and also Roman Catholic. Though there are non-sanskritic and non-elite who are members of the Roman Catholic Church, the urban Christian; caught in the post-globalized, pro-capitalist world is often made by the plays of Cyril Desbruslais SJ to reflect upon where s/he and the Church are heading. This reflection gives a direction of decolonizing those who are guided by larger forces of economics, culture, imperialism and more importantly for India sanskritic or brahminical tradition.

33

# Embodied, Enabled and Empowered: Struggles in Encountering Virtues and Values according to Cyril Desbruslais

**G. Lazar SVD**
*Director, Sanskruti, Hyderabad*

**Abstract:** By nature, human being has intrinsic goodness in herself. Throughout the history of humankind, one of the struggles of human being is to live a morally accepted life. In this world of rapid change and technocratic growth, the terms like virtue and value are not a matter of concern. This is a holistic attempt to affirm the basic philosophical certitude of human goodness and inner order achieved by authentic life. It is true that human being experiences struggle in doing so. In fact, human being is a being in and through struggle.

By unconditional and non-mutual relationship, human being can take her neighbour to excellence. Then, the hindrances to a life of excellence like those of the existential abnormality, animalism in human nature (*homo hominu lupus* of Thomas Hobbes) selfishness pre-established dualistic ideological tendencies and contradictory human consciousness will wither away.

**Keywords:** Human struggle, Virtues and Values, Erroneous Conscience, Responsible Choice, Moral Relativism, Natural Law

***Yada yada hi dharmasyaglanirbhavatibharata***
***Abhythanamadharmasyatadatmanamsrijamyaham***

***Paritranayasadhunangvinashay cha dushkritam***
***Dharmasangsthapanarthaysambhabamiyugeyuge***

Whenever there is decay of righteousness, O Bharata,
And there is exaltation of unrighteousness, then I Myself come forth.
For the protection of the good, for the destruction of evil-doers,
For the sake of firmly establishing righteousness, I am born from age to age.

"Whenever virtue subsides and wickedness prevails, I manifest Myself. To establish virtue, to destroy evil, to save the good I come from Yuga (age) to Yuga."
–Swami Vivekananda's translation

"You can tell the value of a man by the way he treats his wife, by the way he treats a subordinate, and by the way he treats someone who means nothing for him"
–Cyril Desbruslais[1]

## Introduction

Human being struggles to lead a virtuous life. By nature, human being has intrinsic goodness in himself/herself. Throughout the history of humankind, one of the struggles of human being is to live a morally accepted life. In this world of rapid change and technocratic growth, the terms like virtue and value are not a matter of concern. This is a holistic attempt to affirm the basic philosophical certitude of human goodness and inner order achieved by authentic life. It is true that human being experiences struggle in doing so. In fact, human being is a being in and through struggle.

This short essay is an attempt to reflect the intrinsic goodness of human being as visualised by Dr. Cyril Desbruslais S.J. as a philosopher and educationist who in many ways opened the floodgates of radical thinking in our postmodern world. In contrast to Christianity, Islam believes in human person as a total entity. According to him, human person is neither purely spiritual nor purely physical. His philosophy does not divide the person into body and soul. He would emphasise that we are spiritual-corporeal units, when one part of us hurts, all are hurt. In each case, metaphorically or literally, these images evoke sympathy and intend to modify our behaviour accordingly.

To start with, struggles in encountering values and virtues would take us back to the discussion of the basic human nature and its culture. There is a relentless war between human nature that is constant and human culture that is changing. In philosophy human nature is understood by its essence and existence. According to Phenomenological school of philosophy, human nature by essence is of consciousness, intentionality and meaning-giving system. Whereas Existential philosophers like Sartre, would insist on the existential nature of human being. The interplay between these human nature and culture confronts us with the problem of virtues and values today. One is inclined to ask how values and virtues can ever be anything but a set of moral

1 Collections from the class lectures, 1978, JDV, Pune.

beliefs and behaviour that relate to each other. Can we really even imagine a God that announces to its followers, "God exists" as part of its world-view but then recommends that they live as if there were no gods, or God, or makes no recommendation on a pattern of life? Can we really conceive of an ancient Chinese sage who might have said, "The Tao holds the secret of life" but then recommended that people live as if no such thing as the Tao existed?'

## 1. Historical Analysis of Human Conduct

Albert E. Avey, in his book *Hand Book in the History of Philosophy,*[2] brings out the deepest interests that underlie the actions of human beings. Human beings evolved, civilization flourished across the globe. Avey is certain that human beings have always thought of the final destiny of individual. The remains of the greatest civilizations like the Egyptian, the Mesopotamia, the Indus, the Mandarin and the Inca reveal this thought as prevalent. For the Egyptians, there is always a connection between the accepted conduct of human life and the final destiny of the individual. Thus, their theology was also concerned with final destiny along with appreciating the Divine Goodness. Every activity of life was expected to be a virtue-centred activity. The same was with the Hebrew ethical conduct. Ethics and moral life have meaning only in relation to the existence of the Divine Being.[3]

Parallel to these statements, the materialist schools sternly affirmed that ethical conduct does not lead to any metaphysics. There is no need for a divine order or metaphysical postulation to be moral. Life is to be lived here and now. Human being is just being out of material composition. Nevertheless, pursuing a good life is expected of every human being.

Thus, the historical analysis brings out a certain ideology that at every level of human progress, there was a desire to lead to a morally accepted life to reach the final destiny of human being. At the same time, human being is always choked by the overwhelming struggle to define what is virtue and value. A critical discussion on virtue and value enables the theme to evolve coherently. To explain what virtues and values without trying to grasp the system of meanings it conveys is not unlike trying to explain a computer without mentioning a programme, or a book without referring to words. It cannot be done.

## 2. A Philosophical Discussion on Virtues and Values

Values and virtues date back to antiquity. It means to say that understanding of virtues and values was that they were co-constitutive. It leads to moral excellence and takes away from depravity. Virtue is something that is excellent

2 Avey, Albert E. *Handbook of Philosophy*. New York: Barnes & Noble, 1970.

3 Avey, *Handbook of Philosophy*., 4.

at its task Many philosophers contributed critically for the development of virtue as a central part of the philosophy of morality. For **Socrates,** virtue is a matter of intellectual mastery. Socrates stated that man wishes to lead a virtuous life, but inscribed by struggle. Virtue, according to him, is the mastery of living a human life, but the degree of virtue changes. Therefore, virtue can be traditionally defined as the firm disposition of the soul. Socrates gave virtue an epistemological and anthropological stand, his dictum, "know thyself" as the perfect realization of virtue in life. For knowledge can be gained by human being only when human beings are conscious to sense and in mind.

Plato's virtue is highly personalised, attainable by the individual who controlled his/her passions and make constructive use of his/her ambition through the exercise of disciplined intelligence. In addition, Plato's virtue consists of the harmonious interaction of the virtues of self-control, courage and wisdom, which together constituted the civic virtue of justice. His virtue is confined to philosopher-king alone.

According to Aristotle, "Virtue is a certain kind of habit, a good habit". He made virtue and values a collective term when he said human being is social animal therefore virtue through good habits and actions builds a strong relationship between human being and the nature. In addition he enumerates the human struggle due to corruption, contrary habits, by negligence and laziness. He called them vices. Aristotle said it is possible to know the good and yet to choose contrary to it. Thus there arises the problem of the weakness of will. He gave virtue a metaphysical and ethical framework. The daily life and grounded imperfections stand at the root cause of struggle.

The nineteenth century has taken turn around in approaching moral philosophy and specially the concept of virtue. The existentialist philosophers name virtuous life as life of authenticity. The quest for authenticity becomes especially significant in extreme situations. Kierkegaard, Sartre, Nietzsche and Camus struggle for personal destiny. For them, a virtuous human being is one who writes his /her own story and navigates his/her life. They attempt to transcend this ethos and attain a personal and subjective pathos, which empowers their individuality as human beings. They embody the contradictions of trying to be outside society's accepted norms.

Thus the discussion on virtue started as an individual affair, at its first philosophical origin with Socrates ran down the centuries and accumulated greater importance. Now, virtue is a sign of co-existence and concerned-existence with the advent of existentialism. At last, the virtue ethicists interpret virtue as a collective and a societal issue leading to moral perfection. Moral perfection is the logical sequence of the acquisition of virtue. Virtue makes human action moral.

## 3. Struggle 1: Struggle with Erroneous Conscience

Struggle with the mistaken (erroneous) conscience is an anthropological struggle. It is a struggle that a human person experiences as a human being. Human person struggles with the erroneous conscience due to erroneous perception and uncertainly. An erroneous conscience is one, which is malformed due to various socio-psychological problems. When someone is acting consciously, it is intentional. So, the spontaneity and intentionality judge the actions when human being does something uneven. Unintentional and unconscious abstractions, deductions and generalizations contribute a lot in formatting an erroneous conscience and all other factors flow from these. Knowledge process is blind folded by unjust judgements over the experience and perception. In this way occurs the death of conscience, for one dictates one's own conscience falsely instead of being dictated by the conscience, which works under authentic human reason and will. There exists a tendency to picture reality as it is with perfect proportionality. Thus in doing so, human beings acquire knowledge of facts that one perceives probably but registered in mind erroneously.

Henry Bergson puts forth two distinctive forces that are at work in life. They are social pressure and personal aspiration. Social pressure includes rules, society, and security. Development and growth, freedom and power include the personal aspirations. The social pressures cause closed morality. The phenomenon of closed morality is natural to all. Human beings are struggling to break out of closed morality to open morality that is characterized by dynamism, progress and creativity. This struggle is an existential virtue and in this lies the path to moral perfection.

The consequences of an erroneous conscience are varied and they lead to fatal destructions, as the wrong data does in a computing machine. The malformation of conscience leads to weak and closed moral behaviour. Public piety and private pleasure as Pope Francis said. This limits human person to a set of rules to be followed making one's life an icon of orthodox conformity. It is reluctant to change, while being conservative and authoritative. (Bishops and parish priests and some theologians) When human being is confined only to a set of rules to epistemological struggle of freedom and choice. (abuse of fellow servants and religious sisters in parishes and institutions yet behave as pious servant of YHWH building the kingdom of God. A prominent theologian drank heavily to the point of death, yet the next day he continues his conservative teaching on the dogmas of the Church).

Talking about erroneous conscience about violence and religion today Cyril Desbruslais would contend that the connection between violence and poverty does really exist in our world and that the phenomenon of globalization increases its explosiveness. Further, he supposes there will be no controversy about the ethical assessment of this fact. However, it is not easy to come to a consensus about solutions to this scandalous situation in practice because effective solutions could require sacrifices from the members of affluent societies. Such renunciation will require strong external pressure on agents of powerful ethical convictions.

Cyril further states that millennial or fundamentalist extremism has raised in many nearly every cultural tradition where there are pronounced in equalities of wealth, power and status. The only way to create a safer world is to ensure that it is more just. He presumes that the state being impoverished supports the tendency to look for comfort within fundamentalist religious movements and therefore strengthens the inclination to violent behaviour.

## 4. Struggle 2: Blockade of Free and Responsible Choice: Epistemological Struggle

The struggle of free and responsible choice is an epistemological struggle. Epistemological struggle is the struggle that a human person experiences as a **rational being**. It is true that human beings acquire knowledge in varied forms like sense knowledge, inference, comparison, postulation, and so on. All these must help the human beings to arrive at right judgements of the reality. Where proper valid human judgement is lacking, there arises the epistemological struggle. Human beings face the epistemological struggle in the form of the blockade of free and responsible choice.

Human actions presuppose certain degree of freedom and responsibility. When human actions are not inscribed by freedom and responsibility, human beings experience an inner struggle. Blockade of free and responsible choice add fuel to the fire to human struggle.

## 5. Struggle 3: Subjective Moral Relativism: Struggle with Natural Law

Human being has the knowledge of the natural law by nature. Natural law is the dictate of right reason, which indicates the inclination of rational nature towards its end in the moral level. It is a law inherent in human nature. It guides human beings to moral good. This law is known through right reason. Moral law is expression of natural law, which is the expression of Eternal Law.

In the post-modern world of globalisation it is evident that different cultures of the world have various moral codes. All these moral codes are good in themselves. However, when compared with those that of other modes of morality, some moral codes may appear contradictory to human nature. This leads to subjective moral relativism. Then human beings judge falsely in their subjective moral relativism that whatever he/she does is morally accepted and valid.

It is true that there are divisions in values and it is fundamental. A wrong understanding of the word 'relativity' would lead one to degrading relativism. One of the concluding statements of a critique of Einstein's theory of relativity says that the theory of relativity does not hold good for the moral principles. Virtues and values may be acquired as per one's own religious requirements and beliefs, because a good and a choice that a human person desires is virtue. Here there is the problem of the subjective relativism and the question of subjective destiny. A member of ISIS (Islamic state of Iraq and Syria) might think that his destiny is by his choice to suffer. In his/her view, he/she is suffering, not that he/she is making others suffer. There comes the blockage of free and responsible choice, in which one's freedom is regulated by his/her religion and other external factors.

Another tension, the conflict between the ends and means is a consequence of moral relativism. Gandhi said the ends cannot justify the means. Even if the end is good, if the means are faulty and corrupt, and end cannot justify the means. It is wrong to use other people as means to end. Moral perfection is a human spiritual and psychological capacity. Human moral perfection, in its widest sense, is to mean an ideal that satisfies human beings' deepest needs or fulfils his/her being. All these grounded struggles tailor each other and flow into the problem of evil.

## 6. The Challenge: Based on Desbruslais' Philosophy of Human Person

### a. Desire to be the Transcendent

By the fact that human being is the conscious being in the world, he/she is concerned with life in the world. At the same time, there is a desire in human beings to transcend this empirical world. Human being expresses desire to transcend this empirical world is evident in the questions that he asks, and especially very tangibly evident in his ***metaphysical anxiety over death and destiny***. For this reason, Cyril would go along with Kant who calls human being a ***metaphysical animal.***

In many of his lectures Cyril would insist that human being is a composition of many layers in his essence. Some of the layers are rationality, spirituality, inter-subjectivity, morality, religiosity and so on. These layers are intrinsic to human being. Lack of any of these layers would make human beings deviant and abnormal. Only when all the necessary layers of human existence are present, human beings can be called human persons. Therefore, the layer of religiosity is important in entering into a trans-empirical world. To be a person of religiosity, it is not established that one needs to be part of an organised religion. The nature of religiosity in human being leads him/

her to the experience of the transcendent. Therefore, a deep longing for the transcendent paves the way for excellence.

### b. Thought-Word-Deed Oriented Existence

According to Cyril, knowledge had an eternal bearing on excellence, thus proposing knowledge as necessary for human existence. Excellence presupposes virtue and moral perfection, as virtue prerequisites knowledge and certainty in action. The ancients describe excellence as the skilful performance for anything. Ancients attributed excellence to virtuous actions.

Excellence is defined as the highest intellectual and moral functioning of a human being. For Greeks excellence was synonymous with virtue, meaning that the effective performance of a thing's proper functions with virtue. Excellence is the ideal towards which humans should strive in order to fulfil their unique capacities of moral deliberation and reasoned action.

Aristotle, almost rebuking his master, believed that excellence was achievable by anyone with sufficient experience and rational judgment. Genuine human excellence consists of being intelligent enough to judge correctly how to do the right thing at the right time in the right place in the right manner, and to do so consistently and deliberately. His excellence was basically a 'mean' - balance, a point of equilibrium between extremes - a mean, yet an extreme, between the vices. For Aristotle, like Plato, excellence is inextricably linked to enlightened citizenry, intending conscious political actions.

### c. Being Anonymous

Human excellence lies in being anonymous. Kant's *The Groundwork of the Metaphysics of Morals* has profound contribution to human excellence. While stressing the concept of duty, the book brings about the idea of anonymity. Kant's specialty of morality is that duty must be performed only for duty's sake. It is to go beyond the craving for the personal identity. Human beings are guided by the observance of the other human beings. It seems that if one dos not identify the actions of the other, there would be no more action or the exercise of the one's own duty. Moreover, life becomes devoid of action. When human duty is performed without any expectation, it becomes the supreme motto of human life. At this point Cyril would go a step ahead to ascertain that when human being tries to grow out of this crave for personal identity, human being is already in the realization of excellence.

## Conclusion: Being What a Person Actually Is

Finally, in the words of Cyril, 'a self-realization that persons complete one another culminates the process of excellence'. Being a person is the perfect way to excellence, yet an unending struggle that requires continuous personal effort. A human person by becoming a person, paves the way to excellence and happiness. It is an action-oriented endeavour. Thus what has been said earlier that is to shift from Egoism to Altruism becomes the need of the hour. It is neither neglecting the self nor exaggerating the other; neither renunciation nor pure selflessness; neither suffering nor over exuberance. Egoism is a deficient approach to life. On the other hand, altruism and concern for the welfare of others and nature often results in what is best for oneself and are important parts of the way.

Life is inter-woven with genuine and authentic relationships. The metaphysics of human relationship must help us reflect deeply into the reality of relations and relationships. A clear motto could be, "Be what you are, what a person is, and what a community is" The realization of this motto requires Carl Jung's concept of 'unmasking the self' and the existentialist's notion of 'authentic life'. By unconditional and non-mutual relationship, human being can take his/her neighbour to excellence. Then, the hindrances to a life of excellence like those of the existential abnormality, animalism in human nature (*homo hominu lupus* of Thomas Hobbes) selfishness pre-established dualistic ideological tendencies and contradictory human consciousness will wither away. Thus human vocation to life is the realization of a project inscribed in all human beings and which must be deciphered, loved and realized make it come true. This process has no end. When the hindrances sprout again, there is a need to go back, repair oneself and continue. The finality of human act has come true in experiencing life as it comes which is the expression of wonder.

## References


Adler, Mortimer (Ed), *Great Books of the Western World: Aquinas II,* Chicago, University of Chicago, 1990.

Avey, Albert E. *Hand Book in the History of Philosophy*. New York: Barnes and Noble Inc. 1954.

Beckwith, Francis J. *Do the Right Thing*. Massachusetts: Jones and Barnett Publishers, 1996.

Braunt, Richard (Ed). *A Cambridge Companion: Plato*. Cambridge: The University of Cambridge, 1992.

Teilhard de Chardin, Pierre. *The Phenomenon of Man*. New York: Harper and Row, 1959.

Chidamandjee, Sriravindra Brahmachari. *Buddhism and Ethics*. New Delhi; Asian Publishers, 2002.

Composta, Dario. *Moral Philosophy and Social Ethics*. Bangalore: Theological Publications, 1998.

Curd, Martin. *Philosophy of Science: Central Issues*. New York: W.W. Norton and Company, 1998.

Durant, Will. *The Story of Philosophy*. London: Pocket Books, 1961.

Golomb, Jacob, *In Search of Authenticity: From Kierkegaard to Camus:* London: Routledge Publishers, 1995.

Gratsch, Edwards, J. *Aquinas Summa*. Bangalore: Theological Publications, 1990.

Kant, Immanuel, *The Moral Law: The Groundwork of the Metaphysic of the Morals*, Translated by H.J. Paton, London: Routledge, 1991.

Kolnai, Aurel, *Ethics, Values and Reality:* London: University of London, 1997.

Mercier, Jean L. *Being Human.* Bangalore: Asian Trading Corporation, 1998.

Swinburne, Richard. *Is There a God?* Oxford: University of Oxford, 1995.

34

# A Philosopher with Angel's Wings: A Jesuit Vision of Art and Theatre (Inspired by Cyril Desbruslais)

**V. Y. Dasappan SJ**
*Principal, St. Xavier's College, Thumba, Thiruvananthapuram*

**Abstract**: Cyril Desbruslais is a mystery and an inspiration, a rare combination of a philosopher and theatre artist. Cyril's devotion and commitment to the training of the youth through theatre is in fine tune with the Jesuit tradition. The development of the Jesuit theatre - in the West as part of academic curriculum and in the East as part of the Jesuit Order's missionary task – is discussed. The Jesuit vision of art and theatre are discussed through the perspectives of Ignatius of Loyola and Pedro Arrupe. Art, including theatre, is not a priority, though it is considered useful to the extent it helps the Jesuit mission. Sadly but truly, the Jesuit artists and poets of the past were denied due recognition during their life time. The article concludes establishing that Cyril is a fine synthesis of the new and the old, the revolutionary and the traditional, the philosopher and the artistic-creative.

**Keywords**: Mystery, Freedom, Art, Jesuit theatre, Spiritual Exercises, Pedro Arrupe, Synthesis of tradition and modernity

On 8 December 2018, at the Press Club Hall, Thiruvananthapuram, Dr. Shashi Tharoor, after releasing my book on G. M. Hopkins, was addressing a large gathering of mostly teachers and other erudite personalities in his usual brilliant eloquent style. Almost half way through his speech, Tharoor began to speak of Hopkins' God and he quoted:

> Be adored among men,
> God, three-three numbered form;
> . . . . .
> Beyond saying sweet, past telling of tongue,
> Thou art lightning and love, I found it, a winter and warm;
> Father and fondler of heart thou has wrung" ("The Wreck of the Deutschland").

After reciting these lines, Tharoor quite spontaneously said,

> Oh. . . . . I cannot but recall with sweet memories how much I was influenced and inspired by the Jesuit Fathers in my school life. Among them, I always love to mention Dr. Cyril Desbruslais' name. I had a wonderful rapport with him. While studying at St. Xavier's School, when I was the editor of the school magazine, a precocious 14, I wrote an essay about why God doesn't exist, and of course the school magazine didn't publish it. But my essay was passed on to Fr. Cyril Desbruslais, who then proceeded to deliver a brilliant lecture detailing the epistemological justification for the existence of God, which subsequently put an end to my brief frustration with atheism.

## 1. Desbruslais: Mystery and Freedom

Cyril Desbruslais comes across to me as a mystery. In fact he taught me to look at everything and everyone as a mystery. 'Mystery' was a word he loved much and often used in the class. He was not an admirer of St. Augustine's theology or spirituality but he often quoted the Augustinean expression, '*Si comprehendis, non est* (*Deus*) - if you think you have understood (someone), it is not what he or she is'. More than three decades have passed since I studied under his guidance at Jnana-Deepa Vidyapeeth, Pune and lived with him under the same roof of De Nobili College, Pune. But having rubbed shoulders with him for years and having read almost all his works, apart from sitting in his class for two years, I am still left with the same wonder at the mystery that Cyril Desbruslais is!

Another favourate word for Cyril is 'freedom'. He has a philosophy of his own on freedom. He lives in total freedom and respects the freedom of others. He also manifests this freedom by weeping with those in agony and dancing and celebrating with those in joy. Once, during class, this left-handed Jesuit drew on the blackboard the picture of a kestrel with long wings spread. Then he recited the following lines from the Jesuit poet G. M. Hopkins' "The Windhover":

> ". . . striding high there,
> How he rung upon the rein of a wimpling wing
> In his ecstasy! . . . . "

Having recited the lines, he added: "We should be as free as this kestrel". Looking at Cyril's pointer finger which was on the right wing of the bird, I made a rather sarcastic comment, "this is a class on philosophy and as Keats said, "philosophy will clip an angel's wings". Immediately my teacher retorted, "Hell with philosophy! But look at the ecstatic flight of the falcon! ". . . As a skate's heel sweeps smooth on a bow-bend: the hurl and gliding / Rebuffed the big wind."

## 2. A Theatre Artist

Cyril, at the core, was an artist and a theatre man. In the class he was not merely teaching philosophy but was almost enacting it. Anyone interested in art, literature, theatre or music, who passed through the portals of Jnana-Deepa Vidyapeeth (JDV), Pune, cannot but have some encouraging experience from Cyril. The annual theatrical presentations, as part of the celebration of the feast of St. Ignatius of Loyola, almost always contained a play directed by him. Theatre is the vehicle through which he communicated his philosophy. In his artistic creation, Cyril throughout makes the fullest use of all his senses to bring home the subject dramatically with its joys or sorrows or terrors – to his imagination. The outcome of such a theatrical creation is his priestly prayer as a reflection of his meditations on the Holy Bible or the Ignatian Exercises or the socio-cultural issues of serious concerns in the world. I remember how I enjoyed acting as the tempter of Ignatius in the play "***Inigo***" directed by Cyril. The days we, the scholastics, spent rehearsing the play in the company of Cyril were certainly quite exciting and aesthetically rewarding. With a sense of humour, he corrects the body movement and action of each character. And the beauty of it is that he himself enjoys when, at times, the actor/ student makes fun of the director/ teacher The young boys and girls of Pune in SSU (Searching and Service in Unity) who got training in theatrical performance under Cyril and staged a play every year in the city have volumes to narrate of their similar or more profound experiences concerning their mentor. Cyril's devotion and commitment to the training of the minds of the youth through theatre is in fine tune with a long tradition of the Jesuit Order.

The need to be open to the good use of theatre for the sake of entertaining the students and their parents can be seen in the words of Ignatius himself as he dictated to Polanco, his secretary:

> In the schools, . . . to make things more interesting for the students, and to afford them and their parents pleasure at times during the year orations

should be delivered, and verses and dialogues recited, as is done in Rome. This will also add to the prestige of the school (Pachtler 472).

*Ratio Studiorum*, an educational directive for the Jesuits, endorses the view that art and literature, including drama and poetry, could be a powerful means to stir up pupil's interest in learning, development of talent and study of the humanities. The 1591 edition of *Ratio Studiorum* enjoins, "the public distribution of prizes is to be held annually and plays are not to be neglected, for poetry perishes when drama disappears. But the endless labour of training the actors, providing costumes and money, arranging the stage and other theatrical necessities, should not be imposed wholly on the professor of poetry since it is only right that others should help him" (Pachtler 27). *Ratio Studiorum* prescribed that the professors of humanities write and present a comedy each year at carnival time and that professors of rhetoric write and present tragedy at prize days at the term's end. Such was the importance the Jesuits gave to art, literature and theatre in their mission of education that Voltaire, their star pupil, who was to prove more an agony to his educators than ecstasy, declared that the best part of education he received from the Jesuits in Paris came from the theatrical performances.

## 3. The Jesuit Theatre

The Society of Jesus founded by St. Ignatius of Loyola has for its motto *Ad Majorem Dei Gloriam* (For the Greater Glory of God), and so in the mind of St. Ignatius anything that would contribute to the greater glory of God was taken as a means to attain the purpose of the Society. Among these means art, particularly theatre, was considered of no less important than the other means of promoting faith, education, culture, science, etc. As a result, Jesuits all over the world made their own unique contributions in the field of art, architecture, theatre, music, opera, and dance. Jesuits in the 16th, 17th, and 18th centuries were known as the educators of Europe. In order to train the youth in Christian faith and values, the Jesuits evolved theatre as an integral part of their educational programmes during this period. The Jesuit theatre was originally the stage where a variety of plays mainly in Latin were acted out by pupils of Jesuit colleges. In their widespread system of college and school theatres, some 350, that took by storm continental Europe for more than two centuries, the Jesuits conducted the first chain of theatres in history. This was the first educational theatre ever to aim consciously at reaching not only the student body but the entire population. Great artists were urged on in their works by Jesuitism. Many of the famous European poets, thinkers and dramatists were much influenced and inspired by the Jesuits. Being educated in their schools and colleges, distinguished men like Moliere, Corneille, Voltaire and Diderot in France and Lope de Vega, Tirsode Molino and Calderon in Spain received their first artistic stimulus in the Jesuit schools.

As the leader of a religious Order, Ignatius of Loyola was very flexible, especially in matters related to the mission of the Society. This flexibility is well reflected in the very Formula of the Institute which was approved by Pope Paul III on 27 September 1540:

> He (the Superior General of the Society) should be ever mindful of the kindness, meekness, and charity of Christ and of the pattern set by Peter and Paul, a norm which both he and the council should keep constantly in view. Particularly let them hold esteemed the instruction of children and the unlettered in the Christian doctrine of the Ten Commandments and other similar rudiments, whatever will seem suitable to them in accordance with the circumstances of persons, places, and times (De Aldama 1989: 11-12).

This evidently expresses the freedom a Jesuit has in fulfilling the mission entrusted to him according to circumstances of time, place and persons. The early Jesuit missionaries to India knew well this flexible attitude of the Society. As a result we see Francis Xavier, the man who knew best the mind of Ignatius and yet most loyal to his spiritual master, adapting himself to the special situation in Indian culture and boldly making significant changes in his approach to missionary works after his arrival in Goa in 1542. In his letters to the Jesuits in Rome, the Second Apostle to India takes great pride and enthusiasm in describing these cultural adaptations in his missionary works: "In Asia dancing and singing seemed indispensable for celebrations of any solemnity, as noted for Easter in Goa in 1563. In Cochin in 1569, boys dressed as angels danced and sang as participants in an Easter procession under Jesuit supervision" (O'Malley 2005: 7).

## 4. Openness to the Indian Heritage

The early Jesuit missionaries who came to India realized the rich culture and heritage of India and so they presented the Christian doctrine in the language and culture of this country. In India, particularly in the South Indian states of Kerala and Tamil Nadu, the Jesuits, as part of their propagation of faith, got involved in theatrical activities making use of the theatre and the art forms that were already existing in this country. While the Jesuit theatre in Europe evolved and developed as part of the academic curriculum, in India it was considered as an effective way of fulfilling the Jesuit Order's professed missionary task. Chummar Choondal, the eminent scholar and pioneer folklorist of Kerala says, "the western stream (of theatre) that came from the western Christendom paved the way for a new theatre development in India, mainly in the coastal lines. The missionaries from France, Spain, Italy and Germany brought the theatre to the Asian countries with their evangelization and religious propaganda programme" (Choondal 25). The Jesuits put Christian themes in the indigenous arts of the Indians which had folkloristic features. Biblical themes and incidents from the lives of the saints were given a 'local habitation,' and were presented in a form that was appealing to the people of the land. *Muuvarasu naatakam*, *Mar Allesu naatakam* and other religious dramas were popularized in places where the missionaries had concentrated their activities, such as Madurai, Tirunelveli, Palayamcottai, Salem, Coimbatore in Tamil Nadu.

The Portuguese Jesuit missionaries who arrived in Kerala found that *Kathakali*, a classical dance-drama rooted in Hindu mythology was very popular among the people. The Jesuit missionaries collaborated with Malayalam scholars and composed heroic poetry narrating the adventurous life of legendary Christian warriors. These long narrations in verse were a mixture of colloquial Tamil and Malayalam. Thus came into existence the Christian folk theatre called *Chavittu Nadakam* (stamping drama) which continues to be popular even today among the Latin rite Christians of Kerala. In Tamil Nadu this art form assumed a different style from that of Kerala and came to be called *Therukoothu*. The tradition of such kind of Christian plays goes back to several centuries and owes its existence to the efforts of the early Jesuit missionaries, that is to say sometime after the middle of the 16th century. In Goa the Jesuits set up a stage in front of the church, on which pupils performed plays based on the life and work of St. Francis Xavier. The strategic moves of the Jesuits in theatrical activities were enthusiastically welcomed by the people of India. Therefore the Jesuit missionaries reported: "Nothing has attracted the poetry-loving Indians more than our plays" (qtd. in Fulop-Miller 1930: 411).

## 5. Pedro Arrupe

Pedro Arrupe, the Superior General of the Society of Jesus from 1965 to 1983 was a modern Jesuit spokesman for Jesuit art, poetry and drama. Cyril was so great an admirer of Arrupe that he even wrote and directed a play on him in 1995. During one of our conversations, Cyril spoke about Arrupe as "one of my choicest and favourite gurus". Cyril considers it as one his greatest blessings to have met in person this most charismatic and inspiring Jesuit, after Ignatius of Loyola. Arrupe was one of the few who closely understood the mind and spirit of Ignatius. He elucidates the Principle and Foundation in the Spiritual Exercises, relates it to the Jesuit vision of art, including poetry and drama, and says that for Ignatius everything had 'a local habitation and a name'. The habitation was the Kingdom of Christ and the name was one before which everything bowed in heaven, on earth and under the earth. Arrupe is of the view that a Jesuit makes use of art to enrich humanity. One of the purposes of Jesuit art, according to him, is the formation of youth to a Christian life. Arrupe stresses here that the aim of the Society is not purely didactic or moralistic. It is also cultural. Dwelling further on the role of the

Jesuit artists, Arrupe says that they should have the higher aim of bringing art itself to Christ. He does not mean that the Jesuit themes have necessarily to be Christian. Whatever be the theme, Christ should be its inspiration and goal. In this connection, Arrupe quotes Hopkins' 'Pied Beauty' to show how from a bird, or a flower, or the marks on a fish in the river, the Jesuit poet Hopkins is able to lift our souls to God.

Cyril's plays, although primarily an individual's effort, are a great contribution in this great tradition of Jesuit theatre. He has written and directed more than two dozens of plays on themes as diverse as nuclear disarmament, globalisation, terrorism, capitalism and consumerism, religious commitment, etc. In almost all these plays what is remarkable is a fine fusion of his faith, his love for music and his philosophy of the beauty of an other-centred life. Cyril is a profound optimist and he communicates his optimism for a better and newer world through his characters. In his address to the Jesuit Institute of the Arts on June 16, 1972 at Mondragone Frascati, Italy, Arrupe, the 27th successor to Ignatius as Superior General, was honest, as true to his nature, when he said, "we have, I think, to face the fact that neither within the Society nor without, has the dedication of Jesuits to art, or even the association of Jesuits with art, been readily accepted" (Arrupe 1973: 83).

## 6. Jesuits and Art

In this context of the discussion on Jesuit contributions in many educational fields, one may be surprised to know that art and literature had not been a priority either for the Society of Jesus or the Catholic Church until Vatican Council II, 1962-65. As far as the Jesuit Order is concerned, art, including theatre, is not a priority, though such means are considered useful to the extent they help the Order's mission. The traditional attitude of Jesuits towards art was perhaps first framed by Jacobus Pontanus, a Bohemian Jesuit professor of humanities, in his treatise called *Institutiones poeticae*, according to which poetry is justified only in so far as it promotes virtue. His view is clearly opposed to the 'art for art's sake' school. Surprisingly the renowned Jesuit theologian of 20th century, Karl Rahner, in his essay "Priest and Poet" also speaks of art and poetry in a language not much different from that of Jacobus Pontanus. Rahner says, "if ever art is pursued exclusively for the sake of the aesthetic, it ceases to be art" (Rahner 1967: 316). In many ways today the Jesuit artists and writers are blessed. The most important of these blessings is the freedom the Jesuit Order bestows upon them since the Second Vatican Council. Cyril too, as a theatre artist, enjoyed this freedom to some extent. The greatness of this freedom a Jesuit artist or writer enjoys today can be well understood only if one knows also an important aspect of the same Jesuit Order's traditional attitude towards art or music.

Ignatius of Loyola and the other nine first original members of the Society of Jesus were all well educated in the University of Paris but no one among them showed any special interest in literature or any form of art. Having agreed upon among themselves to form a religious Order they decided to study theology and become priests in the Church. The syllabus of the priestly formation they underwent or the education they imparted to future Jesuits consisted chiefly of Aristotle's natural philosophy or science and the texts of Peter Lombard and other scholastic writers such as Aquinas. There was no scope for the study of art and literature. The major concern of the founding Fathers of the Jesuit Order was the missions, in the peculiar context of the Reformation movement in the Church they took upon themselves Counter-Reformation as their immediate and most important mission and so they rightly thought that the kind of education the Jesuits required most should be solely and entirely intellectual in nature and content. Although it might look funny today especially on account of the significant contribution the Jesuits have made in history in the field of art, architecture and music, the fact is that, in their obsession with a formation that would suit them most for the missions, they even considered a musical instrument, say for example an organ, and the singing of choir that existed in all the religious Orders of the time as a hindrance to engage themselves fully in their mission. O'Malley quoting the founding leaders of the Jesuit Order says,

> They should use neither organs nor singing in their masses and other religious ceremonies. Although these laudably enhance the divine worship of other clerics and religious and have been found to arouse and move souls by bringing them into harmony with the hymns and rites, we have experienced them to be a considerable hindrance to us because of the nature of our vocation (O'Malley 2005: 5).

These statements were later removed from the Constitutions of the Order, but the spirit of such a view continued to remain with the Jesuits of the time. People in general often have a suspicion of the Jesuits' sense of music, art and poetry. Juan Plazaola Artola, the Jesuit author of *The Sanctuary of Loyola*, remarks that Miguel de Unamuno, alluded to Felix Samaniego's well-known fable about the ant and the grasshopper, and affirmed that a singing grasshopper could never be comfortably harboured in that anthill of regular clergymen. Yet, only fifteen years before the Basque thinker expressed this view, the great Jesuit poet Gerard Manley Hopkins, whose works today have attracted a bibliography comparable to that of any other nineteenth-century British poet, died in Dublin (O'Malley 2005: xi).

Thus art, including poetry and theatre, was considered something a Jesuit could not afford to spend time on, so they had to be excluded from the life and ministry of the Jesuits. It is in this context that Hopkins says, "I cannot in conscience spend time on poetry", because he thought that the poetic art in him was in conflict with the Ignatian Principle and Foundation. Therefore he tells Bridges, "my works would interfere with my state and vocation" (Abbott 24).

Today the Jesuit Order is proud of the remarkable contributions some Jesuits have made in the past in art and literature. However, sadly but truly, they were not given the recognition and the appreciation they deserved during their life time. Hopkins' great poetry only came to be known to the public when his friend Robert Bridges, who did not share Hopkins' Catholic faith, published it in 1918, almost three decades after his death; similarly it was through a Carmelite priest, Paulinus of St. Bartholomew, O. C. D. that Arnos Padiri, the Malayalam poet and scholar came to be known in 1799, about 66 years after Padiri's demise. In the case of Constantius Beschi too, not a single poem, including the epic *Thembavani*, his greatest poetic work, was published until his death in 1747. The poetry of the English poet G. M. Hopkins as well as some other Jesuit poets including Constantius Beschi, Thomas Stephens and Arnos Padiri in Indian languages is recognized today as some of the best in world literature. However, the fact is that their poetry is the outcome of the efforts of individual Jesuits who struggled hard against all odds, as they had neither the support of the official Jesuit Order nor the support of the Jesuit communities in which they lived.

Although more than eight decades after Hopkins' death, Pedro Arrupe, the Superior General of the Jesuit Order, honestly confessed what sadly lacked with the Jesuit superiors concerning Hopkins as well as many a Jesuit with special talents: "In all honesty, let it be confessed that men with special talents are special cases. This is true of every human activity, but it is especially true of the arts. Even in the world this is recognized to be so. Artists are out of the common mould; they are a cause for concern, even apprehension, among those who have to deal with them - including, sometimes, their religious superiors" (Arrupe 1973: 84). Arrupe further says why Hopkins was frustrated in life: "an artist wants to be understood. When he is not, he is a prey to frustration. Both these hazards of an artist – the apprehension he elicits in others and the frustration others elicit in him – are illustrated in that famous *cri de coeur* (cry of the heart) of Father Gerard Manley Hopkins: "Brilliancy does not suit us" (Arrupe 1973: 84-85). In this honest confession lies the greatness and the spiritual depth of a religious superior like Pedro Arrupe. Rightly Cyril has adopted him as his favourite guru.

## Concluding Remarks

Cyril's daring conviction and its unswerving practice make him an energizing influence for generations after generations of his students. He is a fine synthesis of the new and the old, the revolutionary and the traditional, the religious and the artistic-creative. As was mentioned earlier, in a class on the philosophy of freedom, the evocative presentation of the powerful and graceful movements of the falcon in Hopkins' poem was possible for Cyril because he is an artist who is also at the same time a philosopher. Cyril is a gentle but firm person who opens his eyes wide to find the One ablaze in the many – a teacher who refuses to believe that 'philosophy will clip an angel's wings'.

## References

Abbott, Claude Colleer, ed. *The Letters of Gerard Manley Hopkins to Robert Bridges*. 1935; rpt. London: Oxford University Press, 1970.

Arrupe. Pedro. "Art and the Spirit of the Society of Jesus", *Studies in the Spirituality of Jesuits*. Vol. 5, No. 3, April 1973.

Choondal, Chummar. *The Christian Theatre in India*. Trichur: Kerala Folklore Academy, 1984.

Da Camara, Luis Goncalves. *Testament and Testimony: The Memoirs of Ignatius of Loyola*, trans. Parmananda R. Divarkar. Anand: Gujarat Sahitya Prakash, 1994.

Dasappan, V. Y. *Journey of a Poet: The Agony and the Ecstasy of G. M. Hopkins*. Kottayam: Expressions, DC Books, 2018.

De Aldama, Antonio M, ed. *The Constitutions of the Society of Jesus: The Formula of the Institute*, tr. Ignacio Echaniz. Anand: Gujarat Sahitya Prakash, 1989.

De Guibert, Joseph. *The Jesuits: Their Spiritual Doctrine and Practice, A Historical Study*. tr William J. Young. ed. George E. Ganss. 1964. St. Louis: The Institute of Jesuit Sources, 1972.

Fulop-Miller, Rene. *The Power and Secret of the Jesuits*. New York: Viking Press, 1930.

Gardner, W. H., and N. H. MacKenzie, eds. *The Poems of Gerard Manley Hopkins*. Fourth Edition. 1967; London: Oxford University Press, 1970.

Loyola, Ignatius. *The Spiritual Exercises*. tran, .George E. Ganss, S. J. Missouri: Institute of Jesuit Sources, 1992. rpt. Anand: Gujarat Sahitya Prakash, 1992.

O'Malley, John W, S. J. "Saint Ignatius and the Cultural Mission of the Society of Jesus",*The Jesuits and the Arts*. Philadelphia: Saint Joseph's University Press, 2005.

Pachtler, G. M.. *Ratio Studiorum et Institutiones Scholasticae Societatis Jesu per Germaniam Olim Vigentes*. 3 Vol. Berlin: A. Hofmann, 1887.

Rahner, Karl. "Priest and Poet", *Theological Investigation*, Vol. III. Baltimore: Helicon Press, 1967.

__________. "Poetry and the Christian". *Theological Investigations*, Vol. III. London:Darton, Longman & Todd Ltd, 1967a.

35

# Cyril Desbruslais, a 'Life-World' Explorer Par Excellence

**Babu Joseph Karakombil SVD**
*Director, Satprachar Press, Indore, M.P*

**Abstract**: The article explores the eventful life and noteworthy contribution of Dr Cyril Desbruslais in the field of philosophy and performing arts. The method he has adopted is phenomenological which attempts to describe his life journey as a philosopher guide to his thousands of students who passed through the portals of Jnana-Deepa Vidyapeeth, Pune and the numerous young men and women who have been closely associated with him in his social engagement through the stage shows.

His social engagement was with a purpose: it was designed to ignite the minds of young men and women to find adequate solutions to their personal problems as well as to reform society of its retrograde customs and practices. In this effort he was successful in coming up with novel ways of forging fellowship among people of diverse religious and cultural background. Consequently, he brought about a much needed new definition of human person beyond his religious and cultural affinities – something that would define the future of our country.

**Keywords**: Desbruslais, Existentialism, Merleau-Ponty, Husserl, Life-World

It is a matter of sheer joy for me to join the former students of Dr Cyril Desbruslais SJ in bringing out a Festschrift to relive the happy memories of a great teacher and philosopher who influenced scores of students in ways more than one. I for one would vouch for his intellectual acumen displayed in abundance in classrooms while dealing with the complexities of philosophers, particularly of the western world, and the ease with which he would transmit their wisdoms to his students at Jnana Deepa Vidyapeeth, Pune. Additionally, he was also adept in translating the contemporary philosophical ideas into stage shows in the city of Pune attracting a sizeable number of youths to join him, thus creating a niche for himself as great philosopher guide. It is certainly a reminder of the Greek thinker Socrates who, much regarded for his role as a philosopher guide in ancient Athens said, "I cannot teach anybody anything I can only make them think." This is exactly what Dr Desbruslais did during his entire academic career. He was never one who would force his ideas and thoughts down the throats of students; rather he always elicited responses from his students and insisting on the free flow of ideas and thoughts. In other words, he was just igniting the mind of those who came to know him in any of his interactions either in classroom or outside.

## 1. His Existentialist Philosophical Moorings

Among all the philosophical systems that he used to deftly handle, existentialism, I think was closer to his mind and heart: mind because his strands of thinking were mostly leaning towards existentialist approaches to life and heart because he was temperamentally inclined to adopt its tenets in his social engagements particularly in the stage shows that he often organized. He used to elaborately dwell on the concept of freedom enunciated by the existentialist philosophers, leading to his quest for liberation of the poor and oppressed. Although he was trained in the western philosophical and theological frame of thought, he gradually discovered the need to move into a thinking pattern that is embedded in the Indian experience of life and faith.

Desbruslais therefore was looking for a philosophical framework that would encapsulate his quest of liberation, particularly of the socially and economically oppressed. In this intellectual search he was greatly influenced by the Peruvian thinker Gustavo Gutierrez who is considered the father of liberation theology who called for a preferential option for the poor and oppressed. According to Gutierrez it is the Christian duty to liberate the poor and oppressed through social and political involvement, and create conditions for the marginalized to voice their concerns and needs.

The liberation theology therefore began from the real experiences of people; its focus was not so much on the dogmatic correctness or orthodoxy, rather it was on the orthopraxis that is to intervene in the day today social, economic and political problems of people. Gutierrez writes "I hope my life tries to give testimony to the message of the Gospel, above all that God loves the world and loves those who are poorest within it."[1] Gutierrez was therefore successful in drawing the attention of the universal Church as well as others to the need for bringing about integral liberation of people which includes not just the spiritual –though very significant – but economic, social and political as well. He emphasized on the structural injustice being perpetuated by the dominant social groups and the Governments in many countries in the world in general and the Latin America in particular.

## 2. The Significance of 'Life World'

The very concept of life world was first introduced by Edmund Husserl in his major work, The Crisis of European Sciences and Transcendental Phenomenology[2]. Although the concept of life world is prominently found in Husserl's work, *Krisis,* it finds mention in his earlier works as well. As for instance, in his work, Idea, II (Appendix) we find Hussserl replacing the concept of natural world with that of life world. J Mohanty puts it well, when he says, "This probably is one of the earliest passages in which the concept of life world is found to replace the earlier 'natural world"[3]

In understanding the concept of life world in Husserls' writings at different times, it is certainly helpful to follow what J.N. Mohanty has said in his enunciation of Husserlian phenomenology. Dealing with Husserls's work, *Krisis,* Mohanty delineates different strands found there: it is the perceived world, the original ground of all theoretical and practical activity, the original source of all verification. It is also the world of known and unknown realities. This life world has a bodily character that means it is the world in which we live with our personal ways of being.[4]

The life world is not an entity; it is a filed, a horizon which is constantly and necessarily pre-given. It is the world for us all, and yet each one of us has his life world meant as the field for all. It is the pre-scientific world in the sense it is the basis on which scientific abstractions are based; it is the objective world which we perceive with our senses and engage with our bodies. It is not a world that is constructed by the science or myths, but it is the concrete world which is the basis for other 'worlds'.

1 John Dear, quoted in *Gustavo Gutierrez and Preferential Option for the Poor*, Nov 8, 2011 published in National Catholic Reporter.

2 Edmund Husserl, *The Crisis of European sciences and Transcendental Phenomenology*, trans. David Carr (Evanston, IL, North Western University Pres, 1973).

3 Edmund Husserl, Ideas, Vol. 2, ed. Marly Biemel, Husserliana 4 (1952) as cited in J.N. Mohanty, "Life-World " and 'a priori' in Husserl's Later Thought," Analecta Husserliana 3, (1974); 52.

4 J.N. Mohanty, "The Life-World" and 'a priori' in Husserl's Later Thought, Analecta Husserliana 3, (1974) : 53-54

## 3. The Life-World in Merleau-Ponty

The concept of life world was further explored by Merleau-Ponty in his own unique manner in his major work: *The Phenomenology of Perception*. In fact Merleau-Ponty gives a new direction to Husserlian concept of life-world. The world that the human beings perceive, according to Merleau-Ponty is not like the 'objective' world; instead it has 'objects' whose properties are not fully determinate but are inherently non-determinate or ambiguous. They are not uniquely situated in a single spatial framework, but differently situated in relation to the human agent's specific field of action. And Merlearu-Pontuy calls this 'the lived-through-world' or the 'lived world'.

What makes Merleau-Ponty's phenomenology existential is because he shows that both empiricism and intellectualism are incapable of offering adequate explanation of the lived world, and he suggests another method which is phenomenological. By employing this method, what is revealed as unprejudiced description is the distinctive characteristic of human existence as 'being-in-the- world'. It is this emphasis on the being in the world that makes his phenomenology existential.

Dr Desbruslais has in his teaching career as well in his foray into the creative world of performing arts explored this life world as the lived through world of his students and associates. This was much more pronounced in his stage plays which touched the very lived through world of the youth who were struggling with their lives in various ways and were looking for some guidance. When it came to the students Dr Cyril was quite candid in drawing their attention to the prevailing social, economic and political structures that were demeaning of human life in the world in general and India in particular. He often used to highlight the unjust social hierarchy in India which has kept millions of fellow Indians away from opportunities to develop themselves fully as human beings. He articulates clearly his vision of life in one of his interviews given to DNC Times, "I suppose it is to help all people become more fully human, more fully alive."[5] And in order to make man fully human and alive he needs to be freed from all shackles that keep him stymied and oppressed. This certainly goes along with his Christian faith and vision of life, for Jesus said, "I have come that you may have life, life to the fullest measure." (Jn. 10:10) Giving 'life' to others particularly those who are deprived of it is therefore the main objective of the Christian witness as Desbruslais sees it. In other words, bringing liberation to those who are victims of all sorts of oppression and deprivation is the chief purpose of the Christian faith and practice.

5 As quoted in Wikipedia on Cyril Desbruslais, 'His Philosophy of Life' downloaded on December 06, 2019.

## 4. The Bodily Dimension of the Lived through World

What Merleau-Ponty added to the Husserlian Phenomenology is his emphasis on the manner in which each man, as an embodied being, interacts with the world. Human interaction with the world around him is not in a disembodied manner, but preeminently in and through the body. It is the body that 'finds its way around' as Merleau-Ponty would say, and this finding its way around is often done in a preconscious mode. Giving an example of a typewriter Merleau-Ponty describes how our body gets itself adjusted to a machine and how certain ease in the interaction between the body and the machine is achieved over a period of time. And Merleau-Ponty calls this as habit. As a matter of fact, the body-subject interacts with the world primarily through habits and not through intellectual powers. It may therefore be claimed as Scot Weiner puts it, the body–subject inhabits the world through his habits; conversely, the body subject acquires habits by inhabiting. In this way of understanding both inhabiting and habits are correlated; anyone aspect cannot be taken in isolation; it will be an 'impoverished' understanding of the complex dynamics involved in the interrelatedness between the body and the space.[6]

This understanding of Merleau-Ponty regarding human interaction with the world around him primarily from a habitual rather than from an intellectual point of view is reflected in Desbruslais' attempt to wean the young men and women from their often harmful habits. Such attempts are more than clear not only in his stage shows but more so in his regular interaction with them on weekends. His stage shows certainly preceded intense interaction with his youth groups, senior citizens, educationists, writers and creative artists in order to delve deep into their life; their life experience, or in the idiom of Merleau-Ponty, lived through world that became template for Desbruslais' plays. His plays covered a range of topics that were contemporary and were meant to enlighten and change mindsets, attitudes and prejudices, as he would claim. His childhood experiences goaded him to work among the youth who faced many problems in life, "he wanted to help other youngsters not to make the mistakes and blunders he did. He wanted to reach out especially to youngsters who normally don't feel drawn to join any youth groups, who seemed to be interested only in "freaking out" and drifting along".[7]

It is these groups of youth who tend to drift along or who are indeterminate in their engagement with the world around them that Desbruslais wanted to transform. In particular he wanted to change their unproductive and at times destructive attitudes, beliefs and behavior patterns that were formed over a period of time not so much from their conscious choices but more so from their

6 K Babu Joseph, *Modalities of the Transcendent and Modes of Human Response*, Intercultural Publications, New Delhi. 2006, p. 46-47.

7 Ibid, 'Searching in Service and Unity' downloaded on December 06, 2019.

pre-conscious experiencing of the world around them. People, particularly the young tend to form harmful and destructive habits over a period of time in association with their peer groups and at times it becomes extremely difficult for them to exit; they get caught up within their own web of habits that eventually do them in.

## 5. Unleash the Liberative Forces within the Life-World

The lifelong efforts of Dr Desbruslais have been to identify those forces and potentials found within the life world and to channelize them to bring about personal transformation and social reformation. As Merleau-Ponty says the body-subject's interaction with the world is primarily through habits. And a habit is understood as a generalized activity that is easily repeatable. Habits are required to live our smoothly or else we require reflective action to organize every discontinuous setting.[8] More often than not a person is led by his habits in life; if the habits are good then they will have a positive and constructive impact on him, on the contrary if they are negative and destructive then they will have an adverse effect on him. The point therefore here is to change the negative habits into positive ones for personal enrichment as well as social enhancement. And this can only be achieved when the habituated person is brought to the conscious level of reflection over his habit and direct him to alternatives that are beneficial to him. Stage shows among others was one of the effective means through which this objective was sought to be realized.

Desbruslais' efforts to bring to consciousness the effects some personal and social habits of people led him to think out of the box; he realized the need to go beyond the usual points of reference and find a more sustainable convergence for people belonging to diverse religious and social background. He therefore emphatically said that no single religion's Holy Scripture or traditions shall suffice to meet the aspirations of people in India; rather we must find ways that lead to the shared understanding of human person. This shared understanding of human person shall serve as an outline for generating a new narrative of liberation in the Indian context.

This new liberation narrative that Desbruslais visualized for Indian context is purported to break down the social, religious and caste barriers and create a new identity that would bring a sense of equality in all realms of life. It is a fact that behind all social, economic, religious and political institutions there remains an ideology (often hidden) that sustains it. Or to put it in Merleau-Ponty's language there is an invisible binding force that connects the visible structures. In our everyday interaction with the world around us as body-subject, there is the subject and object experience, however this apparently dualistic experience is surmounted through a kind of 'circuit' or a 'coiling

8 K Babu Joseph, Ibid, p. 48-49.

over' of the visible upon the invisible. And this intertwining of the visible and the invisible, Merleau-Ponty calls as the 'flesh'. This flesh belongs neither to the subject nor to the world. It is basically a 'primal element' and both the subject and the world are born out of it.[9]

While dealing with the contemporary individual and social issues Desbruslais pays special attention to bring to relief this 'flesh' this 'circuit' or 'coiling over' of institutions and their followers. This is particularly important to expose the unjust nexus between institutions and their followers at the expense of those deliberately kept out of them or are even denied access. Social exclusion based on the caste lines and religious discrimination founded on the majoritarian considerations are all fault lines in the Indian society, and they need some course correction. Desbruslais was on this singular mission of bridging the yawning social gaps and healing the festering religious divide that have long come to characterize our life as citizens of this country.

## Conclusion

Desbruslais relentless fight against all unjust structures (liberative engagement) is not just a footnote to his personality and contributions, but it forms the very core and essence of his life's endeavor. And he firmly believes along with Gutierrez that this liberative message forms the very quintessence of Christian faith and life. What is significant in his case is his unique ability to translate that faith into praxis which encompasses a wider social and religious audience thereby creating a new paradigm for those who wish to engage with multi-religious and cultural societies.

9 *Ibid*, p. 51.

36

# Fully Young! Fully Alive!!!
# The Life and Message of Cyril Desbruslais

**Cedric Prakash SJ**
*Jesuit, Gujarat Province*

**Abstract:** The XV Ordinary General Assembly of the Synod of Bishops (October 2018) issued a path-breaking Final Document on 'Young People, Faith and Vocational Discernment'. The document serves as an important charter of how the Church should be responding to the youth of today. A careful study of this Final Document shows how Cyril Desbruslais, had already epitomised several key dimensions of it, long before it saw the light of day!

Accompanying the youth is a key dimension of this document. Cyril did it! For him, the Eucharist was a powerful means in this process of accompaniment. Cyril always radiated a youthfulness. He highlighted the need for renewal, having an integral approach and above all, to listen.

The document needs to be internalised and mainstreamed by the Church in India. Do we have the courage like Cyril, who stayed *'Fully Young, Fully Alive'*, to dream the impossible dream and above all, to realise it?

**Keywords:** Synod of Bishops, Accompaniment, Youth, Renewal, Listening, Impossible Dream

For someone who first met Fr Cyril Desbruslais almost fifty years ago (late sixties and early seventies), there is one phrase I think which encapsulates this extraordinary human, that is "Fully young! Fully alive!!!" Cyril was a young

Jesuit Scholastic at the time of our first meeting in an AICUF camp; over the years, my admiration for him has grown very particularly in the way he responded to the youth.

The XV Ordinary General Assembly of the Synod of Bishops was held from 3-28 October 2018. At the conclusion of it the Synod issued a path breaking Final Document on 'Young People, Faith and Vocational Discernment'. The document serves as an important charter of how the Church should be responding to the youth of today. A careful study of this Final Document, clearly shows how Cyril Desbruslais, has epitomised several key dimensions of it, long before it saw the light of day.

## 1. Companionship

Cyril always has been a great companion; be it to his Jesuit companions or to the youth 'out there'. He was convinced he had to be there: available, accompanying. As the document says, "*Accompaniment for the sake of valid, stable and well-founded choices, is therefore a service that is widely needed. Being present, supporting and accompanying the journey towards authentic choices is one way for the Church to exercise her maternal function, giving birth to the freedom of the children of God. Service of this kind is simply the continuation of the way in which the God of Jesus Christ acts towards his people: through constant and heartfelt presence, dedicated and loving closeness and tenderness without limits.*"(91). this in a way, was his core competency. He was there for long hours – sipping "chai' in a restaurant in Pune after having cycled the distance from De Nobili College. The youth were never in doubt about their genuine friend.

The Eucharist was a powerful means in this process of accompaniment. Eucharistic Celebrations which were meaningful, participative and which resonated with the youth. 'Breaking the bread 'with them helped the youth over the years to internalise key values of the faith particularly sharing one's life and resources with others. "*As the account of the Emmaus disciples shows us, accompanying requires availability to walk a stretch of road together, establishing a significant relationship. The origin of the term "accompany" points to bread broken and shared (cum pane), with all the symbolic human and sacramental richness to which it refers. It is, therefore, the community as a whole that is the prime subject of accompaniment, precisely because in its heart it develops that drama of relationships that can support the person on his journey and furnish him with points of reference and orientation. Accompaniment in human and Christian growth towards adult life is one of the ways in which the community demonstrates that it is capable of renewal and of renewing the world. The Eucharist is the living memorial of the paschal event, a privileged place of evangelization and transmission of the faith for the sake of mission. In the assembly gathered for the Eucharistic celebration, the experience of being personally touched, instructed and healed by Jesus accompanies each person on his or her journey of personal growth* (92).

For Cyril, accompanying the youth was also ensuring that the youth felt some belonging in an organisation. There was the AICUF, the SSU among others which made this happen. "*This practice continues in the Church today, as the young join groups, movements and associations of various kinds, where they experience a warm and welcoming environment and the intensity of relationships that they desire. Joining organizations of this kind is particularly important once the journey of Christian initiation has been completed because it offers the young an opportunity to bring their Christian vocation to maturity. Pastors should maintain a presence in these environments, so as to guarantee suitable accompaniment*" (96). In these organisations, youth found several opportunities to develop themselves: there were camps, dramas and street plays, get-togethers and outings; serious study and reflection. All of this helped the youth not merely to realise their potential but also grow to complement one another.

Cyril truly radiated what a good accompanier should be: "A good accompanier is a person who is balanced, a listener, a person of faith and prayer, who has the measure of his own weaknesses and frailties. Hence he knows how to be accepting of the young people he accompanies, without moralizing and without false indulgence. When necessary he also knows how to offer a word of fraternal correction". Above all, it was so evident that for him 'accompanying was a mission'; companionship was essential for him to realise his favourite song 'to dream the impossible dream!' Because of his 'spiritual rootedness' he could truly be a great companion, "*The awareness that accompanying is a mission that requires a profound spiritual rootedness will help him to remain free in his dealings with the young people he accompanies: he will respect the outcome of their journey, supporting them with prayer and rejoicing in the fruits that the Spirit produces in those who open their hearts to him, without seeking to impose his own will and his own preferences. Equally, he will be capable of placing himself at their service, not taking centre stage or adopting possessive and manipulative attitudes that create dependence rather than freedom in others. This profound respect will also be the best guarantee against any risk of domination or abuse of any kind*"(102).

## 2. Youthfulness

In Cyril one could see perennial youth! The age-old song "you will never grow old" was so apt for him. He remained young, because he believed that he had to walk always with the young. The Synod document reminds us very emphatically that, "*Passion for seeking truth, amazement at the Lord's beauty, the capacity to share and the joy of proclamation are still alive today in the hearts of many young people who are living members of the Church. This is not about simply doing something "for them", but living in communion "with them", growing together in understanding of the Gospel and in the search for more authentic ways of living it and bearing witness to it. The responsible participation of young people in the life of the Church is not optional, but it is a demand of baptismal life and an essential element for the life of every community. The trials and frailties of young people help us to be better, their questions challenge us, and their doubts cause us to reflect on the quality of our faith. Their criticisms are also necessary for us because often it is through them that we hear the voice of the Lord asking us for the conversion of heart and renewal of structures*" (116)

Cyril reached out to all young; there were young men and women from other faiths (and even non-believers) who were his ardent fans. Among them were drop-outs and also those whom society regarded as 'no-gooders'. Cyril was a friend to all the youth. He lived the Synod document long before it said, "*At the Synod we have always questioned ourselves about young people, by which we mean not only those who belong to the Church and work actively in her, but also all those who have other visions of life, who belong to other religions or who distance themselves from religion altogether. All the young, without exception, are in God's heart and therefore also in the Church's heart. But we recognize frankly that this statement on our lips does not always find real expression in our pastoral actions: often we remain closed in our environments, where their voice does not penetrate, or else we dedicate ourselves to less demanding and more enjoyable activities, suppressing that healthy pastoral restlessness that would urge us to move out from our supposed security. And the Gospel too asks us to be daring and we want to be so without presumption and without proselytizing, testifying to the love of the Lord and stretching out our hands to all the young people in the world.*" (117)

He was also challenged by the youth as they insisted that the adults also 'walk with them'. This he did without any hesitation. He was convinced that the Church – the priests and the religious had to walk with the youth of today. One cannot isolate oneself or be indifferent to their reality. One had to, as Pope Francis says so emphatically, "smell of the sheep". Cyril also believed consistently that youth had to have a more participative and decisive role in the Church. The Synod is aware of this saying, "*The Church as a whole when choosing through this Synod to concern herself with the young, took a very definite option: she considers this mission a pastoral priority of epoch-making significance, in which to invest time, energy and resources. From the start of the journey of preparation, young people have expressed the desire to be involved and appreciated and to feel themselves as having a key role in the life and mission of the Church. In this Synod we have experienced how co-responsibility lived with young Christians is a source of profound joy for bishops too. We recognize in this experience a fruit of the Spirit which continually renews the Church and calls her to practise synodality as a way of being and acting, promoting the participation of all the baptized and of people of good will, each according to his age, state of life and vocation. In this Synod, we have experienced how the collegiality that unites the bishops cum Petro et sub Petro in care for the people of God is called to express itself and enrich itself through the practice of synodality at all levels.*" (119)

## 3. Renewal

Cyril's companionship and youthfulness have also found strong resonance in his desire towards renewal. The teachings of Vatican II; the courage of Pope John XXIII and his profound admiration of his first Superior General Fr Pedro Arrupe have had a tremendous impact on him. Vatican II called for a deep and authentic renewal; Pope John XXIII and Pedro Arrupe in their own inimitable ways made sure that 'renewal' was necessary if one read the signs of the times and needed to respond to them.

For Cyril constant consultation or receiving feedback (even critical comments) was his 'forte'. Since he believed in encouraging youth to be participative in everything – there was this constant urge to move towards the 'Magis'. This was possible only if there a genuine movement towards renewal.

The Final Document emphasizes this saying, "*Synodality is the method by which the Church can address ancient and new challenges, gathering and bringing into dialogue the gifts of all her members, starting with the young. Building on the work of the Synod, the First Part of this Document outlined some areas in which it is urgent to launch or renew the Church's vigour in realizing the mission that Christ assigned her, which we here seek to address in a more concrete manner.*" (144)

## 4. Integral Approach

Cyril has always encompassed an integral approach to all that he did. As a person who is fully young and fully alive, his mission could not be restricted to water-tight compartments. He had problems with those who were exclusive, piece-meal in their approach or for that matter lived in silos. He helped youth to respond to the signs of the times in an integrated and balanced way. He has been doing his best to make them see reality through various prisms

His integral vision is powerfully expressed in the document, "*the contemporary situation is marked by growing complexity of social phenomena and individual experience. In daily life, the changes that are taking place have an impact on one another and cannot be addressed selectively. In real life, everything is interconnected: family life and professional engagement, the use of technologies and the way of experiencing community, defence of the embryo and defence of the migrant. Concreteness presents us with an anthropological vision of the person as a whole and a way of knowing that does not separate but grasps connections, learns from experience, re-reads it in the light of the Word, and draws inspiration from exemplary testimonies rather than from abstract models. This requires a new type of formation which aims to integrate perspectives, makes them capable of grasping the interconnectedness of problems and knows how to unify the various dimensions of the person. This approach is in profound harmony with the Christian vision which contemplates, in the incarnation of the Son, the inseparable encounter between the divine and the human, between earth and heaven".*(157)

## 5. Listening

None of the above would make sense if Cyril was not a listener. Over the years he has been listening with his heart and seeing with empathy. Youth and others have poured out to him their hopes and joys, their griefs and anxieties, their pains and their search for a more fulfilling life. He has had the courage to listen.

Like a true shepherd, he has always believed in the value of listening. "*Listening is an encounter in freedom, which calls for humility, patience, readiness to understand, and an effort to respond in new ways. Listening transforms the hearts of those who do it, especially when it takes place with an inner disposition of harmony and docility to the Spirit. It is not simply a source of information or a strategy for achieving a goal, but the way that God himself relates to his people. God sees the distress of his people and hears their cry; deeply moved, he comes down to deliver them (cf. Ex 3:7-8). The Church, by her listening, enters into the movement of God who, in his Son, draws near to every human being". (*6)

For Cyril the young want to be heard. "The young are constantly called to make decisions that give direction to their lives; they want to be heard, acknowledged and accompanied. Many find that their voice is not considered worthwhile or helpful in social and ecclesial circles. In various situations, little attention is paid to their cry, especially that of the poor and exploited, and there is a lack of adults prepared or willing to listen to them". (7)

He was able to challenge priests, religious and other adults who did not feel the responsibility of being a listening Church. Thankfully the document stresses this dimension in no uncertain way. *"The Church does not lack initiatives and solid programmes that can allow young people to feel accepted and listened to, and to make their voice heard. Yet the Synod acknowledges that the ecclesial community does not always manage to convey the approach taken by Jesus with the disciples on the way to Emmaus, when he asked them, before enlightening them by his word, "What is this conversation which you are holding with each other as you walk?" (Lk 24:17). All too often, there is a tendency to provide pre-packaged answers and ready-made solutions, without allowing young people's real questions to emerge and to face the challenges they pose. Listening makes possible an exchange of gifts in a context of empathy. It allows young people to make their own contribution to the community, helping it to appreciate new sensitivities and to consider new questions. At the same time listening sets the conditions for a preaching of the Gospel that can touch the heart, truly, decisively and fruitfully.*"(8)

Finally, listening to the cries of the people – particularly the youth – has never been an option for Cyril, it is a mandate; a responsibility that has to be shouldered by everyone who is called to exercise a prophetic role today. The Synod Document reminds us, *"Listening is a key element in the ministry of pastors, above all in that of bishops, who, due to their many obligations, struggle to find enough time for this essential service. Many of those who spoke pointed to the shortage of qualified people devoted to accompaniment. Belief in the theological and pastoral importance of listening entails rethinking and renewing the ways that priestly ministry is ordinarily exercised and reviewing its priorities. The Synod also recognizes the need to train consecrated persons and lay people, male and female, to accompany young people. The charism of listening that the Holy Spirit calls forth within the communities might also receive institutional recognition as a form of ecclesial service". (*9)

## Conclusion

In conclusion, as we celebrate the life and times of Cyril Desbruslais on his eightieth birthday , we need to thank God for the gift of him to the World, to the Church and to the Society of Jesus and very specially the thousands of youth and others he has accompanied so faithfully over the years. The Final Document of the Synod on youth reflects so much the many characteristics embodied by Cyril. Above all, his name clearly spells out CYRIL, i.e. **C**ompanionship, **Y**outhfulness, **R**enewal, **I**ntegral, **L**istening: all necessary components for meaningful Christian discipleship today!

Cyril has had many favourite songs/ hymns. One of those is, "The Impossible Dream (The Quest)". It is a popular song composed by Mitch Leigh, with lyrics written by Joe Darion. The song is the most popular song from the 1965 Broadway musical *Man of La Mancha* and is also featured in the 1972 film of the same name starring Peter O'Toole.The complete song is first sung by Don Quixote as he stands vigil over his armor, in response to Aldonza (Dulcinea)'s question about what he means by "*following the quest*". It is reprised partially three more times – the last by prisoners in a dungeon as Miguel de Cervantes and his manservant mount the drawbridge-like prison staircase to face trial by the Spanish Inquisition. Some years ago Cyril also put up a widely acclaimed drama on the same (of course, highly contextualized too). The lyrics of the song are:

*To dream the impossible dream*
*To fight the unbeatable foe*
*To bear with unbearable sorrow*
*To run where the brave dare not go*
*To right the unrightable wrong*
*To love pure and chaste from afar*
*To try when your arms are too weary*
*To reach the unreachable star*
*This is my quest, to follow that star*
*No matter how hopeless, no matter how far*
*To fight for the right*
*Without question or pause*
*To be willing to march*
*Into hell for a heavenly cause*
*And I know if I'll only be true*
*To this glorious quest*
*That my heart will lay peaceful and calm*
*When I'm laid to my rest*
*And the world will be better for this*
*That one man scorned and covered with scars*
*Still strove with his last ounce of courage*
*To fight the unbeatable foe*
*To reach the unreachable star*

Cyril today is the dream made possible: a person who has given so much to many. Above all a human being: "Fully Young!!! Fully Alive!!!"

# Cyril Desbruslais SJ: The Person

Dr Cyril Desbruslais was born on the 21st of December 1940, in Howrah, Calcutta the first child of Cyril and Maisie Desbruslais. The second child, a girl, was born in 1943 and they named her Maisie. A third daughter, Marina, was born some years after but she died 18 months later, of TB. That was a fatal disease at the time and not long after Mummy and Daddy were carried off by it, his father about ten years after my mother. He was nine, Maisie was just seven.

They were cared for by one of his Uncle's brothers, who was a very good man. Desbruslais was schooled at first by the Jesuits at St. Xavier's, Calcutta, then at St. Vincent's Technical School, Asansol, run by the Irish Christian Brothers. His sister began at Loreto House then shifted to Loreto Entally, both in Calcutta, the latter being the former house of St. Mother Teresa.

After school, he went to College – St. Xavier's, for the B. Com – and his sister started working. Later, he too worked at Remington Rand, and we both were submerged into a hectic social life. In the third year of work, I heard a call to uproot himself to serve others with the Lord. His mother's brother was a Jesuit and so he chose the Jesuits. Later on, He had no regrets. He fitted snugly.

He joined the Karnataka Province Novitiate (Calcutta had no novitiate of its own in June 1962). He did a year's Juniorate at Vinaylaya, Bombay, in 1964 - 65: that was the year of the Eucharistic Congress and Pope Paul VI's visit to India.

He followed up that with Philosophic Studies, at DNC, Pune, and was selected for the staff. In 1968-70, He did his MA at Pune University and after a year's stint in St. Xavier's, Calcutta (the first time he had set foot in seven years as an SJ in his native city) was sent a year later back again to Pune, for Theology. After his ordination in Calcutta, he was sent to Paris for my PhD. But he preferred to defend his thesis at DNC, with Frs. Jean de Marneffe and Salvino Azzopardi (of very happy memory) and Fr. Lisbert D'Souza who is still very much with us.

Dr Desbrulais taught philosophy at Jnana-Deepa Vidyapeeth (residing at De Nobili College) from 1978 to 2013 and served two terms as Dean of Philosophy and Superior of the Philosophers at DNC. I now at my retirement serving the parish at St. Xaver's Camp and the SSU, the inter-religious youth group he founded in 1972, and which is still going strong, directing plays he has written for them. In spite of a stroke in 2015 and a speech defect he still has something to say.

Here is the list of the plays Desbruslais has authored/or directed. Sometimes he did a play by another author. But he has directed all of them, except Roses in the Sea, when he was recovering from his stroke. The years of some of the plays are only approximate. He also did repeat performances of my earlier play, with some adaptations, like this year's Two by Two. We did a play from 1972 till last year and still counting.

- The Impossible Dream (1972)
- Pilgrim of the Future (1973)
- Eschaton (1974)
- [He was in France for his doctorate latter part of 1974-1977]
- The Promised Land (1978)
- Boy and Girl (1978)
- Two by Two (1979)
- No. No, Jeremiah (1981)
- The Prince of Whales (1983)
- Dateline Jerusalem (1987)
- Inigo (1990)
- Pedro (1991)
- Even to the Indies (1993)
- Adam and Eve (1994)
- Two by Two (1995)
- Camillo (1997)
- The Ballad of Nestor and Cecy (1997)
- Excelsior (2000)
- 2000 Tom Gaffney
- Oscar Romero (2001)
- Carry on Boy and Girl (2002)
- Boy and Girl Forever (2004)
- It's Great to Be Young (2006)
- Change your Habit (2008)
- Against the Tide (2010)
- The White Rose (2012)
- A.T. (2014)
- Adam and Eve (2015)

- Esperanza (2016)
- Roses in the Sea (2017)
- Giddyap Gideon (2018)
- Roses in the Sea (2019)

## Books by Cyril Desbruslais

- Postmodernity: An Indian Christian Philosophical Appraisal (2019)
- Metaphysics: Philosophy of Be-ing for Today (2019)
- The Philosophy of God: Faith and Traditions (2019)
- Paul F. Röttig im Gespräch mit dem indischen Jesuiten Cyril Desbruslais SJ. Macht Krach! Der Heilige Geist lässt sich nicht einsperren. Eine ignatianische Befreiungspastoral (2019)
- The Philosophy of Liberation: Revisiting Genuine Religious Experiences with Special reference to Christianity (2016)
- Unser Vater: Gespräche mit Gott im Osten und Westen = Daddy Darling (2012)
- The Philosophy of Be-ing: Introduction to a Metaphysics for Today (1997)
- The Philosophy of the Human Person: An Introduction to Philosophical Anthropology (1998)
- Interpretations of Transcendence (1989)
- Relevance of Christianity in India Today (ed) (1984)

## Forthcoming Books in 2020

- History of Ancient and Medieval Philosophy (ed: Valerian Mendonca SJ)
- History of Modern and Contemporary Philosophy (ed: Valerian Mendonca SJ)
- Collection of Desbruslais' Plays (ed. Rajan Barrett)
- Desbruslais' Doctoral Thesis (ed. Sathya Balan SJ)

# Cyril Desbruslais: The Message
## (An Interview to *Asian Journal of Religious Studies*)

**AJRS: Dear Cyril, as you approach 80 years of enriching life, what are the things that you are really grateful for?**

That's easy. I am most grateful for my vocation to the Society of Jesus in the post-Vatican era, of the Church I love. It had come at a time of great openness, at a time when there was never so much excitement and adventure in being a priest and a Jesuit. The church was so much more lovable and humble that I was freer to go to the youngsters, when I was a Theology student, and be with them as a friend. I founded the SSU in 1972, a youth group open to all cultures and religions, not only for the goody-goodies but where students and workers or broken families and youngsters with an unsavoury reputation could find acceptance and encouragement to slowly and gradually improve among people who genuinely loved them and had confidence in them - which is still going strong and active! And there was my being graced to be called to be a formator of young Jesuits and other seminarians. In the spirit of the 31st General Congregation of the Society, I volunteered to teach all faith-and-justice related topics and a sought to bring in that dimension to all the other subjects I taught. I was immeasurably helped by the SSU and my seminarians and the Jesuits whom I taught to make my philosophical and theological more Christic and human!

**AJRS: You have committed yourself to various activities. In most of them, you have succeeded. In some, you failed. Any particular regrets in your life?**

Cyril: Well, there was the occasion when I was returning from a Youth Camp, from Bombay to Pune. I was crossing the overbridge and I saw a nameless villager, with his wife and little children, looking lost and confused while everyone passed them by. I did, too, in spite of having Rs 2000 in my pocket, as a contribution to my projects. I was haunted by the expressions of misery and incomprehension on the faces of the two adults and, almost home to Ramwadi,

I made my rickshaw my turn to go in search of that desperate looking-family, but they were nowhere to be found on the overbridge or anywhere I searched on Pune station. I filed that in my memory and made that experience motivate me to never pass by any forlorn and confused-appearing family on my path. I felt that I had met Christ alone and forgotten and neglected to respond to him!

**AJRS: You have been deeply involved with the youth, learning from them and interacting with them for more than 45 years. How do you evaluate your interactions with them? How has it heped you?**

Cyril: The SSU and I have been teaching each other some things.

I am busy still teaching them respect to each others' religions and cultures.

Youth have more respect for each others' religions and cultures than youth had some 30 or 40 years ago (there are some exceptions, though). And the non-Christians, today in the SSU, are almost as numerous as the Christians (19 and 24 respectively, are dedicated members). But they are slightly better provided. In the beginning, we all used to move around on bicycles; nowadays almost everyone has a motor-bike or scooter. They are on the way to a higher lifestyle than their parents. Of course, not all of them are equally on the same footing. But these ride pillion on their friends' bikes and we all chip in to share in the food and drink. And when they come into their own (with a little help and subsidy from the SSU), they always are there with their contributions to me.

But young people, now, have less time. They have TV, mobile and computers and race around to venues far distant on their mo-bikes. Whereas in the old days, we would all meet almost every day it's rarely we manage to meet each other once a week. Old SSU camps were thronged to about 50-100, but now we can have, if we are lucky, about 20-25 for a maximum of three days, at the most.

Play practices which last daily for about two months require much more commitment and sacrifice than earlier. But the youth are not found wanting.

More come when there are parties or picnics but a considerable number turn out when there are Outreaches (visits to Institutions, Orphanages or such like, where we interact, play games or entertain the inmates).

Inter-religious services, which we have once a month, are well attended. I habitually call God "Daddy Darling", my translation of Jesus' "Abba Father". The Muslims and the Jews (we have a few!) were, on the whole, not prepared to "take such liberties" with God, though most others were warmed by that appellation. And when recently a few Muslim boys and girls ventured to call him by that name, I felt that a life-time goal was realised!

What I have learned from the youngsters? More tolerance: young people will not practice Jesuit obedience, but get to work with a lot of shilly-shallying. And I have become a better counsellor, especially in the context of boy-girl relationships and petty youthful rivalries!

**AJRS: From your experiences, what are the youth looking for in our globalised and fast-changing world? What can the others learn from them?**

Cyril: What are the youth looking for in this fast-changing world? First of all to bring in the bucks as fast as possible. Many of them want to help their parents financially put them through college, for many of the latter are lacking sufficient funds. So they flock to Call Centres, earning much more than their fathers made when they first began working. But their work hours are late evening till early morning, which takes a severe toll on their health, leaving them with precious little time (if any) for exercise and their social life. And when they have made sufficient for their studies, they often become so accustomed to the notes in their pockets that they have problems leaving the affluence to get on with their studies! Some of them drain their health, sacrifice their social life and exercise but they think that the money they bring in is sufficient compensation. They have no training in having to deal with the abundance of money in their pockets and often splurge and go on an alcoholic binge on their days off. I have to wait for them to experience the hopelessness and helplessness of it all before I can be heard!

And there is little active communication and in-depth sharing among them with their Whatsapps and mobiles. How often do we see them in a group, each of them, wrapped in their private selves talking on their mobiles or following events on their Whatsapps? Most young people almost never read books and the average boy or girl exercises less and less when they grow older. Things like treks have to get organised for them, which, at first they see as against the grain, but later they look back with enjoyment!

Bicycles are out. Motor-bikes are in! They want to go faster and to many more distant places and they have very little time to relax with a book or a present friend (they will spend hours talking with a friend on the phone or Whatsapp). They cannot do the simplest piece of mental arithmetic: they call upon the computer for that.

But some of them reflect and make a conversion of their lifestyles and go through a heroic lot of counter-culturing!

**AJRS: You have been teaching philosophy for the last 35 years. What have your learnt from your dealing with young scholastics and seminarians?**

Cyril: After teaching at JDV what have you learnt from Scholastics and Seminarians? In the first place, that they should be treated more like the adults they are, instead of the retarded adolescents they are seen to be. I have seen Rectors treating Scholastics in the fourth or fifth of formation as immature and refusing them permission to indulge in extracurricular activities, which a lay student, at least four years younger than them, have the maturity to handle. A sad commentary on their fancied inadequacy of our Jesuit formation?

I firmly maintain that if you treat scholastics (and seminarians!) like adults they will, in general, behave like adults. And those who persist in behaving like retarded adolescents should be given their walking ticket!

And scholastics (and seminarians!) will have no difficulty in confiding in you as their superior if you come across to them as their friend and give them evidence that you really love them. Then you can work miracles!

Also, train them to relate to the opposite sex in a healthy manner, not as dangerous sources of sin. Celibate youngsters have to be taught carefully to be friends and relax with girls. Then they will become better priests and better men. They will be open and sincere with you as a friend when you don't have a narrowly moralistic and judgemental attitude to them. They will become more mature and be able to help women and girls to be more their authentic selves.

Not every confession of "falling in love" with a girl should be treated as *ipso facto* grounds for dismissal, except when one has ventured to molest another sexually. Good spiritual direction or counselling should result in one enjoying a good relationship with the opposite sex without one or the other taking undue advantage.

**AJRS: You are an ardent admirer of Pope Francis and the former Jesuit General Pedro Arrupe? How does Pope Francis make the Church relevant for today?**

Cyril: I begin with Pope Francis. He wants to reform the Church, bringing it from all its pomposity and making it the servant of the poor. He has declined to live in the Vatican Palace and told Cardinals and bishops to do likewise, not as "princes of the Church" (a living contradiction!), scrapped Monsignori and opened up the people of God, the Church, to be less of a tax-seeking official and more a representative of Daddy Darling (my translation of Jesus invitation to call God, 'Abba Father'). He wants to make married divorcees, in certain cases, eligible for Holy Communion and a whole lot of other things that go against the people who believe in the God of Law more than the God of love, and who reaches out to sinners and overwhelms them with unconditional love, who will not crush the bruised reed and spurn the sorrowing sinner!

People who should have known better were all for turning Vatican II back and nullify its long-awaited reforms. He is all for St. John XXIII and St. Paul VI, the Popes of the Council which was the greatest event of the 20th century.

I equally hail as my maha-guru Pedro Arrupe SJ, the General who spearheaded the Church and the Society of Jesus into the post-Conciliar era and gave others a role model for them to follow. He fathered the General Congregation who opted for faith AND justice, the twin ends of God's Kingdom and he gave us the Jesuit Refugee Service to name only one another of his epoch-making contributions to the world scene. I value I spent with him in De Nobili and treasure his autograph as a future saint!

**AJRS: As you know very well, both the world and India are facing troubled and challenging times. Where lies your hope for the Indian Church of today?**

It is a Church of the young, who feel daring and adventurous. I am aware of the fact that the Church in India dates from ancient times, whether it was St. Thomas who brought it to India in the first century AD or others, it doesn't matter: it was established here more early than the Church in many countries of Europe. But the Church is India is still numerically superior in its young people than the Church in Europe. And whereas, as I see it, the few seminarians in Europe are busily preparing themselves to fill in places in Institutions, a large of Jesuits and other seminarians are "launching out into the depths", preparing themselves for the frontier apostolates, where no one else has gone before, to journey with young people from all religions, for intensive study and dialogue with all types of people, going to all kinds of outlying, far-flung areas where no Christian presence is there and living the life of healing and service that Jesus, their Master, lived. And this includes a myriad of young sisters, besides young priests.

And it was a blessing in disguise for the Church in India that it is a minority religion. That was an occasion for Christians to witness an old and profound culture and religion and ethics, first hand, and avoid simplistic observations that non-Christian religions were inherently deficient, typical of a European-dominated Church. Authentic Hinduism, and its offshoots, Buddhism and Jainism, have a whole history of spirituality, monasticism and religiosity to dialogue with Christianity. with enhancing effects for both parties to the exchange.

In spite of Christianity's heaving taken root in India centuries before it came and established itself in Europe, it had only a relatively a small impact on the Indian psyche, whilst in Europe, there was almost a universal conversion in a relatively short time. This was due to the fact that non-Christian European religions were almost devoid of any serious God-experience and Christianity could fill a vacuum thereby. With India, there was an ancient tradition of meditation, contemplation and monastic life (both male and female) so proselytism was more difficult. Many Indian religions (unlike their counterparts in Europe) and their Holy Books lived on and contain many gems of wisdom for Christian scholars to appreciate. Actually, true Hindutva (and not the superficial form of it marketed today) has a lot to teach the Christian tradition about authentic ecumenism and dialogue. And this is something which the Church in India will contribute to the Church Universal!

**AJRS: How do you visualise the future of the world Church?**

Cyril: "To be religious today is to be inter-religious." I'm not sure who is it that was credited by that saying, but I would not be surprised if it was an Indian. And I hold it to very true in India and all the world!

I visualise Church of the future as a dialoguing Church. It should humbly listen and not merely talk and pontificate. It runs the risk of giving to yesterday's answers to today (and tomorrows!) questions. It must slow down and listen to the people's new experience of today and engage in conversation possibly with new problems and their implications before she rushes into her answers.

I am not denying that she has an authentic revelation, but it does not mean that she straightway understands it exhaustively. Witness the controversies with Galileo and the proponents of the naive literal understanding of the Bible, for example. Our understanding of Scripture is enhanced for all that!

Inter-religious prayer will be more common, but the daily Mass tradition will become everywhere prevalent. There will gradually be no more restriction for the priesthood exclusively to celibate males and the Mass would be celebrated in well-nigh every place. A 500-year-old Church rule would not be allowed to deprive some faithful of their daily eucharist.

As I had said inter-religious celebrations would become more commonplace, motivated by readings of the various Holy Books and prayers addressed to God in a variety of names (like we do the SSU). This would be a marvellous manifestation of our unity and the respect of the people for all religions be furthered.

There will be much more inter-religious apostolates among youth, for example. There will be more pluri-religious outreaches of priests, religious and laypeople. More and more of them would become conversant with other religions and assist young people (and not so young people) to have a genuine God experience which ripens into a dedicated life. Of course, there will be ample opportunities to initiate the Catholics into a solid Christian life, worship and commitment, besides all of these. It will not be priests and nuns who will shoulder the majority of the Christian vocation but the commonly-called "ordinary" Christian. This is the Church of the future I visualise.

**AJRS: Thank you Cyril for your insights. We wish you better health and joy!**

## Our Contributors

**Ananya Dutta** holds a Master's degree in English and worked as a journalist for over six years with *The Hindu* and subsequently *The Times of India*. She trained as a journalist at the Asian College of Journalism. She is currently a Teaching Associate at the Symbiosis School for Liberal Arts, Pune where she teaches courses in Media and Literature. Email: ananya.dutta@ssla.edu.in

**Anil Thomas CM,** a member of the South Indian Province of the Congregation of the Mission (CM), has a Licentiate and Doctorate in missiology from the Pontifical Gregorian University, Rome. He teaches Missiology, Ecumenism and Vatican II documents and is Head of the Department of Systematic Theology at Jnana-Deepa Vidyapeeth, Pune. Email: anilthomascm@gmail.com

**Anuradha Mazumder** is Assistant Professor of English in Prafulla Chandra College, Kolkata. An alumnus of Presidency College and Calcutta University, she completed her M. Phil. in English Literature from Jadavpur University, Kolkata. Her areas of academic interest are Victorian Studies, Indian English writing and literature's interface with cinema and popular culture among other things. She is also the author of Jane Austen's Pride and Prejudice: with an Introduction and Explanatory Notes. Email:mazumder.anu@gmail.com

**Babu Joseph Karakombil SVD** belongs to the Society of the Divine Word (INC) holds a doctorate in Philosophy and has been teaching Philosophy at various Philosophy Institutes across the country. He has published a couple of books and several scholarly articles. He worked as the Spokesperson of the Catholic Bishops' Conference of India (CBCI) for 9 years and also as the Executive Council Member of the Central University of Kerala for six years and for three years as its Court member.Email: bkjoss@gmail.com

**Cedric Prakash SJ** is a Jesuit of the Gujarat Province. He is a human rights and peace activist with a focus on advocacy. He is also a prolific writer on these issues. For three years (2016-18) he worked with the Jesuit Refugee Service (JRS) in the Middle East as the Advocacy and Communications Officer. For his work, Fr. Prakash is a recipient of several national and international awards; these include, the *'Legion of Honour'* from the President of France and the *'Kabir Puraskar'* from the President of India. Email: *cedricprakash@gmail.com*

**Charles Davis** is a postdoctoral Humboldt Research Fellow at the Albert-Ludwigs University of Freiburg. He has a Doctorate in Theology from the Jesuit University of Sankt Georgen Frankfurt. He has been a Professor of Moral Theology and Bioethics at the Pontifical Athenaeum of Philosophy and Theology, Jnana-Deepa Vidyapeeth, Pune. He is a Priest of the Catholic Diocese of Jammu-Srinagar and a Member of the Pontifical Academy for Life in the Vatican City. Email: charlesdavisj76@gmail.com

**Dolichan Kollareth SJ** belongs to the Kerala province of the Society of Jesus. Dr. Kollareth holds Masters Degrees in Psychology and Philosophy and a PhD in Social Psychology from Boston College, USA. He is currently an Assistant Professor of psychology at Jnana-Deepa Vidyapeeth, Pune. He does research in religion, culture, and cognition and has published research articles in international psychology journals. Email: dollychank@gmail.com

**Errol Fernandes SJ** is a Jesuit of the Bombay Province. He is the Vice-Principal (Commerce) of St. Xavier's College and lecturer in Accountancy. He is also a Visiting Lecturer in Scripture at St. Pius X Seminary, Goregaon, Mumbai and JDV, Pune. Besides numerous retreats to the laity, seminarians, priests and religious, he has also conducted four "Net Retreats" for laity and religious from all parts of the world. He has his own blog http://errolsj. blogspot.com/ on which he posts every day and also his own YouTube Channelhttps://www. youtube.com/channel/UCejo1B53RYH9X2a9RtAsYtA?view_as=subscriber on which he uploads reflections on the daily and Sunday readings. Email: errolsj@gmail.com

**Gayatri Mendanha** holds masters' degrees in both Philosophy and English. She is currently an Assistant Professor at the Symbiosis School for Liberal Arts, Pune where she teaches courses in Philosophy and Literature. She is a visiting faculty at Jnana-Deepa Vidyapeeth. She has guest lectured at DePaul University, Chicago. Email: gayatri@ssla.edu.in

**Ginish Cheruparambil Baby** was working with Motilal Oswal Securities as a research economist and currently working in Christ University, Lavasa as an Assistant Professor of Economics. He had been associated with Christ College, Pune and Symbiosis International University. His doctoral thesis is on Amartya Sen. Email: ginishcheruparambil@gmail.com

**Gnana Patrick,** Professor and Head of the Department of Christian Studies, University of Madras, holds a doctorate in Christian Studies. He was awarded a post-doctoral fellowship in 2004 to do a research on Asian religions and Cultures in Hong Kong Chung Che College. In the year 2013, he was awarded the Fulbright – Nehru Visiting Lecturer Fellowship and taught a course on Public Religion: Learning from Indian and American Experiences at the Divinity School, Harvard University. He co-edited a volume with Prof. Elisabeth Schussler Fiorenza under the title Negotiating Border – Theological Explorations in the Global Era (2008). Other publications that he has authored include Religion and Subaltern Agency (2003); Wings of Faith – Public Theologies in India (2013); Oral Traditions and Theology (1996); and Resonances (Tamil), Indian Christianity and Its Public Role (edited, 2019). He has penned 86 research articles, published in various peer reviewed journals. He served as the Chief-editor of Indian Journal of Christian Studies from 2012-2016. He was given the Best Researcher Award by the University of Madras for the year 2017-18. His forthcoming book to be published by the Fortress Press, USA, is Public Theology: Indian Concerns, Perspectives and Themes (2020). Email: gnanapat@gmail.com

**Gnanapragasam Lazar SVD** (b. 1954) is a student of Prof. Stephen Fuchs the eminent Anthropologist of Vienna School. Dr. Lazar has obtained his M.A. in Philosophy, in the University of Poona (1986) and furthered his studies in Anthropology at the University of Lancaster, England where he obtained M.A., M.Phil., and then PhD (1994). Apart from his regular teaching, conducting inter-religious dialogues and research, he has published four books and 38 research papers. He is the Founder Director of SANSKRUTI (Institute of Dravidian Culture and Research). Currently he is the President of Asia- Pacific Mission and Research (ASPAMIR). Email: lazarsvd@gmail.com

**Hector Andrade** has been a Teacher of Philosophy, and Head of Department at the Mahindra United World College of India, Founder of the Van Vihar Biodiversity Park, and Associate Professor of Philosophy at FLAME University, and the Principal of the Mercedes-Benz International School. Presently, he has dedicated his life to the research and conservation of the native medicinal plants for which he has had an undying passion. He continues to teach Theory of Knowledge through online classes and conducts workshops on teacher training, organic farming, sustainable living and Biodiversity. He can be reached at hector.pune@gmail.com

**Isaac Parackal OIC** is a Professor of Philosophy who holds a doctorate in philosophy from the University of St. Thomas Aquinas in Rome. At Present, he is teaching at Jnana-Deepa Vidyapeeth in the faculty of Philosophy, Pune. He has authored a number of books and articles in philosophy and ecology and other secular subjects. He is a visiting faculty in different seminaries and secular institutions. E-mail: isaacparackal13@gmail.com

**James Ponniah** is Assistant professor of the Department of Christian Studies. He was formerly the dean of the Faculty of Philosophy at Jnana Deepa Vidyapeeth, Pontifical Institute of Philosophy and Religion, Pune. He obtained both his M.A. (in Vaishnavism) and doctorate (on Sudalaimadan Cult) from the University of Madras. He was a visiting scholar in the University of California, Berkeley. His areas of teaching and research include Indian religions, folk religions of India, Modern and Contemporary Indian Thinkers, Religion and Globalization, Popular Catholicism and Dalit Christianity. His publications include a monograph *The Dynamics of Folk Religion in Society: Pericentralisation as Deconstruction of Sanskritisation (2011).* He was awarded Collaborative International Research Grant by AAR (American Academy of Religions) in 2015. He won the best researcher's award for the year 2018 in the University of Madras. Email: jamesponniah@gmail.com

**Job Kozhamthadam SJ** is Professor Emeritus of Cosmology, Philosophy of Science and Science-Religion Interfacing at Jnana-Deepa Vidyapeeth, Pune, India. He is the Executive Director of IISR (Indian Institute of Science and Religion), Delhi. He was the President, Jnana-Deepa Vidyapeeth, Pune, India. Email: jobksj@gmail.com

**Joby Tharamangalam OP** is a Dominican friar, and research scholar in philosophy at Jnana-Deepa Vidyapeeth, Pune. He has written numerous academic and research articles. Email: jobytharamangalam@gmail.com

**Joji Valli**: Starting his career in management, he worked in India and abroad. He then turned to teaching and became an associate professor in management. He has a doctorate in Corporate Social Responsibility (CSR) with the topic *"CSR and its Impact on the Society: A Philosophical Study."* Also holds a Master's degree in Personnel Management (MPM) and another in Sociology (MA), from Pune University. He has authored 18 books, number of articles and papers in various journals, books and websites. Now, he is a visiting faculty to some colleges and religious institutions, also conducts motivational workshops and training sessions. Email: jojivalli@gmail.com

**Keith D'Souza SJ** is Rector of St. Xavier's College, Mumbai. He has degrees in Science (Physics), Theology and Philosophy. His Ph.D. in Philosophy is from Marquette University in Wisconsin, USA, with a specialization in philosophical hermeneutics (Hans Georg Gadamer and Paul Ricoeur). He has edited two books and published around forty-five journal articles in the areas of hermeneutical theory, socio-political philosophy and religious studies. He is Vice President of the Bombay Philosophical Society (Dept. of Philosophy, Mumbai University), and is President of the Association of Christian

Philosophers of India (ACPI). He is also on the faculty of a Leadership Programme called Power to Lead. Email: keith@jesuits.net

**Kuruvilla Pandikattu SJ** (born 1957-) is a professor of Physics, Philosophy and Religion at Jnana-Deepa Vidyapeeth, Pune, India. Currently, he is the Dean, Faculty of Philosophy. He has been actively involved in dialogue between science and religion. Author of more than 36 books and 160 articles, Pandikattu is a Jesuit priest belonging to Dumka-Raiganj Province, India. He been involved in organising national and international conferences on science-religion dialogue. Main topics of his research are: anthropology, eschatology, life-management and transhumanism. He may be contacted at kuru@kuru.in (personal) or kuru@jdv.edu.in (professional). Site: www.kuru.in

**Lawrence S. Fernandes SJ** is the Principal of Sacred Heart College, Satya Nilayam, Chennai, a national formation center of Philosophy for Jesuits in South Asia and is the Head of the department of Philosophy, Loyola College, (Autonomous) Chennai. A recognised Ph.D. guide by the University of Madras for philosophy, he is the author of three books (Popular Religiosity: A Quest for Meaning; Shrines and Pilgrimages; Philosophy and Practice; Popular devotions: Philosophy and Practice) and many research articles. Lawrence had his Research program at Dublin and USA. His area of interest includes studies in Popular Religiosity, Philosophy of Religion, Sociology of Religion, Intercultural Studies and Religious Experience. Email: lawrencesj@gmail.com

**Libin Joseph CST** is pursuing his PhD in Philosophy at Pontificia Università della Santa Croce, Rome. He did his MPh in Jnana-Deepa Vidyapeeth (JDV), Pune and MA Philosophy in IGNOU. Email: lkozhikkottu@gmail.com

**M.D. Joseph** (Jose Mannukulangara), is a priest belonging to the Archdiocese of Guwahati Assam. He is an author, writer and researcher at Jnana-Deepa Vidyapeeth, Pune, E-mail: josemannuorama@gmail.com

**M.X. Gnanadhas** is a diocesan priest, belongs to the diocese of Ootagamund, Tamilnadu, South India. He is a staff member of Good Shepherd Inter-diocesan Seminary, Coimbatore. He has Bachelors in Mathematics and in Theology. He has pursued his Master's in Philosophy at JDV and is at present doing his doctorate at Innsbruck University, Austria. His field of interest is on Social Epistemology and Psychology. Email: jmxgnanadhas@gmail.com

**Nishant A. Irudayadason** is a professor of Philosophy and Ethics in Jnana-Deepa Vidyapeeth (JDV), Pune. Besides many papers presented in national and internal conferences, he has published several researched essays in English and French in reputed journals both in India and abroad. He has two doctorates in Philosophy. Email: nishant@jdv.edu.in

**Patricia Santos RJM,** a Religious of Jesus and Mary completed her Doctorate from KU Leuven, Belgium. She holds a Master of Advanced Studies in Theology and Religion from KU Leuven, a Licentiate in Sacred Theology (STL) from Boston College School of Theology and Ministry, and a Master of Arts in Educational Psychology from Pune University. She teaches in the Faculty of Theology, Jnana-Deepa Vidyapeeth, Pune. Her research interests include women and gender studies, psychology, spirituality, and liberation and feminist theologies. Email: patriciarjm@gmail.com

**Paul Thelakkat,** former Spokesperson of Syro-Malabar Church in Kerala, is currently the Editor, Light of Truth, which is published as biweekly from Ernakulam. He pursued his PhD in Literature and philosophy from KU Leuven. Email: thelakatpaul@gmail.com

**Rajan Barrett**, graduated in Mathematics from Wadia College, Pune. He did his post- graduation studies in English from the Department of English, University of Pune. He worked for his M.Phil. with Professor Shridhar Gokhale. His doctorate, the Self and the Sonnet, was with the late Professor Aniket Jaaware. He taught at: Hemchandra North Gujarat University, Patan; Ambedkar College of Commerce & Maharashi Shinde College of Arts, Pune; and Fergusson College, Pune. He currently teaches English in the Department of English, Maharaja Sayajirao University of Baroda. He has put up two plays with the Literary Society he is in charge of. Email: rajanbarrett@gmail.com

**Roy J. J. Pereira SJ** is currently the Provost / Vice-Principal (Academics) and Head of the Department of Chemistry at St. Xavier's College (Autonomous), Mumbai. He has been teaching here since 1993 and began an innovative programme in Neuroscience in 2012. His research covers the effects of cell phones, internet usage and social media on the brain for which he was invited by Google Headquarters, Mountain View, CA in December 2016 to speak to their employees. His research also involves the understanding of the Mind-Body Link, the effect of meditation on health outcomes, the placebo effect, neuro feedback and ways of dealing with stress in our lives. In this connection he was invited by Harvard University in January 2017. He has Masters Degrees in Chemistry, Philosophy and Theology and has done his Ph.D. from Boston College. Email: roy.pereira@xaviers.edu

**Sacaria Joseph SJ** (Shaju Joseph) is Assistant Professor of English at St. Xavier's College, Calcutta, as well as a visiting faculty at the department of Philosophy at Jnana Deepa Vidyapeeth, Pune. His doctorate is in English literature. Email: sjosephsj@gmail.com

**Sathya Balan SJ** is currently pursuing a Master's Degree in Philosophy at Jnana-Deepa Vidyapeeth, Pune. He is a Jesuit belonging to the Madurai Province of the Society of Jesus. Email: balansj@gmail.com

**Stephen Jayard** has a PhD in *Philosophy of Science* (on the theme: Rationality in Science) at the Central University, Hyderabad, 2009. He has Qualified *National Educational Testing* of the University Grants Commission of India, 2002. As a part of the Doctoral Research, visited Prof. Dudley Shapere of the Wake Forest University, Winston-Salem, USA, and the Inter-University Centre for Astronomy and Astrophysics, Pune, India. He has done his postdoctoral research at Boston College, USA and Regis College, Toronto. He has authored many books and articles. Email: sjayard@gmail.com

**Subhash Anand** retired as Professor, Indian Philosophy and Religions, Jnana-Deepa Vidyapeeth, Pune. Now he is working on some of the questions that emerge during inter-religious dialogue. He has authored more than 8 books and edited *Wald-Bulcke Bible-Bhāṣya* (Hindi, 2018), a work involving seventy scholars –women and men – from all over India. His articles have appeared in many reputed journals including *Annals of the Bhandarkar Oriental Research Institute*, *Brahmavidyā: Adyar Library Bulletin*, *Concilium: International Journal of Theology*, *Dialogue*, *Jnanadeep: Pune Journal of Religious Studies*, etc. Email: 43subhash@gmail.com

**Suchetana Banerjee** holds her PhD and MPhil from Jadavpur University with a Gold Medal for the latter for her work on Yoruba Theatre. She was instrumental in ideation and development of Sahapedia, an open online resource on the arts, cultures and heritage of India. Her doctoral research lies at an interdisciplinary juncture of theatre, literature, history and economics. Among her published works in the last few years she has focused on the expansion and consolidation of technical vocabulary of the disciplines of Comparative Literature, Cultural Studies and Theatre Studies. A thespian and a dancer, she has been dealing with performance theory and aesthetics from the ground up for a while now. She is currently an Assistant Professor at the Symbiosis School for Liberal Arts, Pune. Email: suchetana.banerjee@ssla.edu.in

**Thomas Karimundackal SJ** teaches Old Testament at the Faculty of Theology, Jnana-Deepa Vidyapeeth, Pune, and currently serves as the head of the department of Scripture Studies, and coordinator of the Masters Programme in Biblical Studies at JDV. He has presented research papers in many national and international conferences, and published books, and articles in national and international Journals as well as in edited books. He is also a visiting faculty in many seminaries in India and abroad. He can be contacted at: tomksj@gmail.com.

**V. M. Jose SJ** (Vadappuram Mathew Jose), Head, Department of Moral and Pastoral Theology, teaches Liturgy at Jnana-Deepa Vidyapeeth, and the resident staff of Papal Seminary, Pune. He has a doctorate in Theology from the University of Innsbruck, Austria. He has presented research papers in many national and international conferences, and published many articles in national and international Journals as well as in edited books. E-mail: vm.jose@gmail.com.

**V. Y. Dasappan SJ**, formerly a student of philosophy and theology at JDV, Pune, is a Jesuit and Principal of St. Xavier's College, Thumba, Thiruvananthapuram. Apart from several scholarly articles to his credit, he is the editor of the book: *Latin Language and World Cultures* (2013). The latest addition to his scholarly work is his book: *Journey of a Poet: The Agony and the Ecstasy of G. M. Hopkins* (2018). He is an enthusiast in theatre and cultural studies. Email: dasappansj@yahoo.com

**Victor Ferrao** is the priest of Archdiocese of Goa and is teaching Philosophy at Rachol Seminary. He has doctorate in Philosophy from Jnana-Deepa Vidyapeeth, Pune, in philosophy of science with specialization in science and religion dialogue. He is co-founder of Science and Religion Sangam Goa He has published four books and co-edited a volume, Identity, Difference. He has published several research papers in reputed and peer-reviewed journals and edited volumes and has been an active member of the Association of Christian Philosophers of India, He is the Dean of Philosophy at Rachol Seminary and visiting faculty in Jnana-Deepa Vidyapeeth, Pune and St. Pius College in Mumbai. Email: victorferrao@yahoo.co.uk

# Milestones

| | | |
|---|---|---|
| 1940, 21 December | : | Born at Kolkata |
| 1962, 28 June | : | Entered Society of Jesus |
| 1966-68 | : | Philosophy Studies at DNC/JDV Pune |
| 1971 | : | Founded SSU |
| 1971-74 | : | Theology Studies at Pune |
| 1974, April 20 | : | Ordained Priest |
| 1978-2013 | : | Served JDV |
| 1983 | : | Doctorate in Philosophy Sorbonne, Paris and JDV, Pune |
| 1987, June 28 | : | Final Profession in the Society of Jesus |
| 2005, December 21 | : | Official Retirement from JDV |
| 2006-12 | : | Contract with JDV extended |
| 2006-12 | : | Superior of Philosophers, DNC |
| 2016, October 1 | : | Suffered a Stroke |
| 2019, December 21 | : | Entering into 80 Glorious and Creative Years |

Dr. Cyril Desbruslais SJ, is an effective counsellor, committed teacher and a successful playwright.

As a counsellor, he would accompany, both the young and old, and inspire them. He started the group "Searching in Service and Unity" in 1971, when he was beginning his Theology studies at De Nobili College, Pune, India. Based on his personal experience, he wanted to give a home to the youth who are seeking. He wanted to set up an inter-denominational youth group, one made up of young people of different religious and ethnic backgrounds. He wanted to celebrate our differences, not just sweep them under the carpet and so reached out to people of various identities. By these common activities, he helped the youth to develop a deep social sense, a sense of responsibility and concern for the poor, the deprived and all victims of injustice, in our country and all over the world – and do something creative about it

It dawned on him that liberation theology, however fine and noble and biblical an endeavour it may be, was irrelevant to Asia in general and India in particular, precisely because it was a Biblical endeavor. What we need is united action for justice and liberation by all Indians, inspired with a common vision. And this common vision could not be the Holy Book of one religion, but a shared understanding of the human person.

Yet, it seemed to him that we must, through dialogue, establish some sort of common base for this or we'd have no grounds for praise or blame, there'd be no real criterion to challenge white supremacism or the caste system. So, he dialogued with people (common people, youth of all religions and their families, from his youth group, and all over the country and abroad, not forgetting to talk over controversial issues with academics and University professors, too) and eventually formulated an understanding of "common human nature, adequately understood."